"OFF WITH THE CRACK OF A WHIP!"

STAGECOACHING THROUGH YELLOWSTONE,
AND THE ORIGINS OF TOURISM
IN THE INTERIOR OF THE AMERICAN WEST

VOL. 1, 1878-1891.

LEE H. WHITTLESEY

T0244343

RIVERBEND
PUBLISHING

"Off with the Crack of a Whip!": Stagecoaching through Yellowstone, and the Origins of Tourism in the Interior of the American West. Vol. I, 1878-1891.

Copyright 2022 © Lee H. Whittlesey

Published by Riverbend Publishing, Helena, Montana

ISBN: 978-1-60639-137-2

Printed in USA

1 2 3 4 5 6 7 8 MG 26 25 24 23 22

Cover and text design by Sarah Cauble, sarahcauble.com

Riverbend Publishing
P.O. Box 5833
Helena, MT 59604
riverbendpublishing.com

Front cover painting:

Telltale Breeze (1985) by Gary Carter, used with the artist's permission, photographed by Michael H. Francis.

DEDICATION

To my friend Rawhide Johnson—stagecoacher extraordinaire—who hails from the Monida area of the old-days' Montana Trail and from Cody, Wyoming.

ACKNOWLEDGEMENTS

Someone long ago, probably a newspaperman or a scribe with a writing implement, recorded that journalists—ranging from today's persons of the most influential news outlets down to the least influential, often local ones— "write the first drafts of history." Brian Williams of the MSN-BC television network, not the idea's earliest proponent but the one from whom I first heard it, has long echoed that sentiment. In this book, I have indeed used those primary sources—many, many of them—written by the nineteenth-century equivalents of the scribes who wrote those earlier drafts. Thus, much of this book is written from primary sources, and to those newspaper writers and authors of original documents I owe huge debts for writing the original accounts that I quoted and paraphrased.

Nearly one hundred forty years ago, another of those unknown journalists, writing for the Deer Lodge (Montana) *New North-West* newspaper on October 12, 1883, asked what was essentially one very relevant question, just as large-scale stagecoaching was starting to die in Montana Territory:

> Who will speak of the real Knights of the Road who in the past twenty years, by day and by night, through storm and sleet, over icy grades, through swollen streams and blizzards, with a heroism as great and endurance surpassing that it requires to win honors on the battlefield, held the lines over the mountain stage teams and with consummate skill and honorable fidelity safely carried the tens of thousands of passengers entrusted to their care? The stage coaching days of Montana are full of incident and anecdote that if fairly told would be most entertaining. Who will be the historian and the biographer of the stage coach and the stage drivers? ("Turned Out to Grass—The Stage Coach a Thing of the Past," *New North-West*, p. 3.)

Whether these drivers were called "Knights of the Road," "Knights of the Reins," "Knights of the Ribbons," or "Knights of the Silk," a few of us historians have tried to tell some of their stories, and we try again in this volume.

I thank Paul Schullery and Kim Allen Scott, my fellow historians in Bozeman, Montana (Kim is now retired in Arizona), for their reviews and their inspiration to me through many years. I also thank Elizabeth Watry, Curator at Museum of the Mountain Man, Pinedale, Wyoming (now retired), for information, editing, and her creative skills in formulating chapter-titles; Jean Marie Souvigney, Livingston; Alyssa Krekemeier, Bozeman; and Dr. Brad Snow, Livingston, for their research-support as my university interns; Colleen Curry, Anne Foster, Jackie Jerla, Meagan Epperson, Sarah Marino, and Miriam Watson, all on our staff at the Yellowstone Heritage and Research Center, Gardiner, Montana, for general help through a lot of years; Tobin Roop for the final go-ahead for me to write this manuscript; and Paul Shea, Curator at Yellowstone Gateway Museum, Livingston (now retired), for photos and advice. Researcher Tina Schlaile of Fairfield, California made me think about the Lower Geyser Basin's historic hotels in new ways. She figured out what happened to the place-name Shotgun Creek in eastern Idaho's Yellowstone country, and served as a valuable reader for this manuscript, in the process saving me from making several key errors. And Tina has kindly provided me with numerous newspaper-citations, which are individually cited in footnotes.

I thank M.A. Bellingham for support as my long-time volunteer, who provided comments and further materials about this manuscript; Stanley D. Hansen and Stephen A. Hansen of Idaho, descendants of the Bassett Brothers, for writing some of the history of their forebears and then corresponding with me as we sent materials back and forth; Jan Dunbar and her daughter E. Dustin "Dusty" Dunbar, West Yellowstone, Montana, for information on Beaver Canyon, Idaho, and Dwelle's, of Montana; Tamsen Hert, Laramie, Wyoming, and Rawhide Johnson, Cody, Wyoming for information and expertise on stagecoaching through many years; Paul Rubinstein, Charlottesville, Virginia, and Bob Berry, Jay Lyndes, Randy Ingersoll, Michael Francis, and Bob Reynolds for historical photos and photo-expertise, and for permission to use photos from their massive photo-and-artifact collections of Yellowstone and Montana; Cameron Green, University of Wyoming Library, for help with obscure Indian battles; Jane Daniels of

Island Park, Idaho who kindly sent me the results of her newspaper research in eastern Idaho for many years before digital-searching existed; historian and lawyer Steve Mishkin, Olympia, Washington, for his illuminations of obscure, legal points and his meticulous and eagle-eyed editing; Lee Silliman, Missoula, Montana, for many additional YNP materials through the years; and Sally Petersen, Greeley, Colorado for help from afar with research on Idaho counties. Jeffrey Strickler of Big Sky, and E. Dustin Dunbar of West Yellowstone, Montana, found material information on Henry Clay Manley, an important character in West Yellowstone-area history. My thanks also go to two county clerks in Idaho—Pamela W. Eckhardt in Bingham County, Blackfoot, Idaho, and Erika Lehmkuhl in Fremont County, St. Anthony, Idaho—who were kind and efficient in helping me find relevant land-records for those counties so important to the old, stage-coaching Bassett Brothers and George Rea. Finally, I must thank my most long-term hiking friends with whom I have shared many hours, miles, and discussion-points on Yellowstone trails and from whom I have learned immeasurably, including from our walks on many long-gone stagecoach roads: Paul Rubinstein, Mike Stevens, Tom Carter, Rocco Paperiello, Leslie and Ruth Quinn, John and Gail Richardson, and M.A. Bellingham.

During some of the writing of volume one of this book, I was serving as park historian for the National Park Service at Yellowstone, but in this book, I do not represent the National Park Service in my opinions nor does the NPS necessarily endorse this book in any way. All conclusions are my own, and my research utilized no information that was not available to any other writer or historian; my sources are shown in the endnotes. Because I started this volume on government time and then finished it after I retired, all proceeds from it have been donated to the National Park Service.

Volume two, a subsequent book that is being written on my own time following my retirement from the NPS, will follow this one. Hopefully, it will not take too long to produce, for I too am one of the hordes of avid "stage-coachers" who cannot wait to read it. And if you are a fan of the American West, we are hoping that it—like this present volume with any luck—will bring you a wealth of stuff you always wanted to know! It did for me.

CONTENTS

As we bade farewell to our luxurious Pullmans, there was a lively scramble for top seats on the stage coaches, each one eager to obtain the fullest share of the exhilarating pleasure of a mountain ride, and we were off with the crack of a whip…

—LHC, "The Northwest…the Devils Slide and the Threshold of Wonderland," Cleveland (OH) Leader, September 5, 1883, p. 4.

A fully loaded Tally-ho stagecoach pauses in front of the Mammoth Hot Springs Hotel, 1893. These six-horse stagecoaches could carry upwards of twenty passengers and were the largest stagecoaches used in the park. They were so-named because passengers in the high, rear seat, facing backwards, gaily waved "Tally-ho!" as they pulled away from stations and passed other coaches. This coach was operated by the Yellowstone National Park Transportation Company. Other types of coaches are parked next to the hotel. *Francis Historic Collections*

CHAPTER ONE

"Rough and Profane but Men of Undoubted Nerve"

General History of Stagecoaching in the U.S. and the American West

The very mention of [a stagecoach] recalls the huge oval vehicle with its great boot behind, fronted by a lofty driver's seat—swaying, tossing, rocking, lumbering and creaking as it dashes along, impelled by four swift-footed horses, through mud and mire, over hill and dale, in the daily discharge of its appointed office. Anon the rapid toot of the horn, closing with a long refrain, which reverberates from every hillside, winding a different note to the varied motions of the coach, and a rattle of the wheels announces the arrival, and every urchin of the village is on the alert to see its passage to the hotel, and from the hotel to the post office. It was the daily event in the memory of childhood, which no time can obliterate. —Nathaniel P. Langford, *Vigilante Days and Ways* (1890).

That comment by one of the Euro-American "discoverers" of present Yellowstone National Park referred generally to stagecoaching in the American East prior to the building of many railroads, and it included one extra detail, namely the "toot" of the horns present on many coaches, sounds that were and are little known to most twentieth and twenty-first century observers. That there was more to come for stagecoaches in the history of the rest of the nation was affirmed by Mr. Langford in his continuing. "As years wore on," he wrote, "and improvements came, and one by one the old-time inventions gave place to others, the coach began gradually to disappear from the haunts of busy life, and the swift-winged rail-car to usurp its customary duties." The stagecoach shrank away, Langford explained, "and sought a freer life in the vast solitudes of the Great West." "There," he finished, "it had full range without a rival for thousands of miles for a third of a century, and conveyed the van of that grand army of pioneers across the continent."[1]

Indeed, when Yellowstone National Park was established in 1872, the frontier had not yet closed, and the American West was still the site of Indian wars, both immediately and looming. Once the frontier closed—in 1890, according to many historians—stagecoaches remained in Yellowstone for even longer than Langford indicated, more than twenty-five additional years (1890-1916), because the national park remained restricted to stagecoach-only travel, during a period when automobiles were sharing the roads everywhere else in the United States.

But before we reach the American West and stagecoaches relating to Montana, Wyoming, Utah, Idaho, and Yellowstone National Park, let us drop back and learn a bit about the evolution of stagecoaches in America. Stagecoach authority Nick Eggenhofer spent his twentieth-century life learning about stagecoaches. Born in Germany in 1897, he saw the end of the horse-and-buggy era up close. "Our next-door neighbor was a wheelwright and a wagon-builder," he wrote, so Nick spent many happy hours as a child "watching the making of a wagon wheel and its subsequent ironing by the blacksmith." "Down the road a ways," he opined, "there was the shoeing of horses and of oxen, still very much in use even then, and there was the unforgettable smell of the old shops." Eggenhofer emigrated to the U.S. in 1913, where he continued his interest in the old wagons. As late as 1925, he saw a ten-horse freighter in New Mexico and watched mail being delivered by buckboard in outlying places. "I had the chance to listen," he wrote, "to a few old-timers, then well along in their eighties, as they related their experiences talking about Montana in 1862, when Helena and Virginia were the only towns; about crossing the plains with a covered-wagon train, the monotony, the feeling of isolation, the drudgery of it." As he and those old-timers reminisced, he enthused, "somehow it was like fun" to him.[2] So he paid close attention in his childhood to that talk that hailed from days of yore.

Even though they had roots running back to 1687 in the U.S., true stagecoaches, as Langford has pointed out, were latecomers to places west of the Missouri River. But because it "is so long ago" since stagecoaches traversed those dirt trails, today's readers need more explanation about their origins. For example, the word "coaches" is self-explanatory but why were they called "stagecoaches"? The answer is that the driver would chauffeur his coach to travel between stops called "stages" of the trip, at which places during these sections, passengers could get food and drink, and "used up" horses could be exchanged for fresh ones. According to Eggenhofer, the proper term for many of these horse-drawn, passenger-carrying vehicles of the trans-Mississippi West was "stage wagon" or "mud wagon," rather than "stagecoach" proper. Contrasted with that were the best known of all these coaches (and all iterations of the design could also be called simply "stages"), namely the Concord stagecoach, which appeared late in the American West during its final-development form.

Its evolution went like this: Around 1817, a coach appeared that was egg-shaped—rounded in every direction by a sharp undercurve that was met at its ends "by the extremely rounded curve of the roof, and by the outward bulge of the body's size." In other words, it was truly egg-shaped, and this meant that a railing for placing baggage on top of the coach was not possible. The driver's box and a squarish trunk-rack were attached to the "egg," and this design remained in style until around 1827, when Abbot and Downing's classic, Concord coach came into manufacture and fashion. Lewis Downing founded his small, buggy shop in 1813, but it was his teaming with partner J. Stephens Abbot that probably changed the design and really allowed their company to take off.

Originally, many of their coaches were painted red with a yellow undercarriage. By 1860, Abbot & Downing coaches were in use in numerous parts of the world, including by the Butterfield Overland Mail Company (1857-1861, and its modified contract that lasted until July 1, 1864) and by its descendant company, Ben Holladay of Holladay Overland Mail & Express system (1862-1866). One of these Concord stagecoaches arrived at San Francisco in 1850 aboard a clipper ship. Intended for usage in the gold

J. Stephens Abbot, 1804-1871. *New Hampshire Historical Society.*

fields, it presaged many more of that design, which California-transplanted miners would come to love.[3]

Establishment of the overland mail system to California via Denver and Salt Lake City in the early 1850s was the impetus for stagecoach operations all over the American West. After Ben Holladay took over this mail route in late 1861 and named it the "Overland Stage Line," he made many modifications. He purchased Concord coaches and worked to make his line the leading one in America as well as (he vowed) the biggest and best one in the world. The discovery of gold in Montana in 1862-63 has been claimed to have been the factor that saved him financially. His coaches "carried nine passengers inside," said Frank Albert Root (1837-1926) who worked as a messenger-rider, "and one or two [more] could ride on the box alongside the driver." He added:

The first advertisement ever from the Abbot and Downing Company, which appeared in the *New Hampshire Patriot* newspaper, August 3, 1813, courtesy of Lewis Downing (1792-1873). From Root, *Overland Stage to California* (1901).

Some of the 'Concords' were built with an extra seat a little above and in the rear of the driver, so that three additional persons could ride there, making fourteen with the driver. Sometimes it became necessary to crowd an extra man on the box, making as many as fifteen persons who rode on this pattern of coach without much inconvenience. I once made the trip from Denver to Atchison when there were fourteen passengers besides the driver and myself [16], and the coach arrived at its destination on time.[4]

By the early 1880s, Abbot-Downing was "the premier firm in the carriage-making business." Although the partnership split up in 1847, it reunited in 1865 as "Abbot, Downing, and Company," occupying six acres in Concord, New Hampshire, and with its main product becoming informally known as the "Concord coach." The developing West was kind to the company, because settlement "required a sturdy vehicle to transport people and materials over rough or non-existent roads." As with other companies, this one's drivers sometimes became legendary, such as

"One-eyed Charlie" Parkhurst who lost an eye from a horse's kick, but nevertheless continued driving into his old age, one-eyed and filled with rheumatism. Upon his death and before he was buried, it was discovered that he had not only been a woman, but also a mother. The various discoveries of gold in the West increased the demand for tough vehicles that could carry heavy loads. The company eventually built more than forty types of vehicles, but made its reputation on its estimated three thousand Concord coaches, which were built and decorated by skilled craftsmen. "Every coach," explained one historian, "had a unique picture painted on each door by John Burgum and, later, his son Edwin," and other illustrations included scrollwork and portraits of actresses on the footboard or driver's seat," sealed with several coats of varnish. The leather trim, boots, and thoroughbraces required use of at least a dozen oxen hides per coach, and these provided work for the firm's only woman, Mari F. Putnam, who stitched these leathers for thirty years. The Concord's piece-de-resistance came because "although [the company had] pattern books, every vehicle was customized." Historian Elmer Munson Hunt enthused that "there seems to have been no standard coach, and they were built on a no-two-alike basis, an expensive process."[5]

As historian Carlos Schwantes has pointed out, stagecoaches "marked a distinct period" for the northwestern part of the U.S., defined the pace of life for both East and West (obviously a much slower one than today), and "left some of the earliest physical evidence of modern transportation and communication" in the form of buildings and primitive roads.[6] One of the most famous companies was Wells Fargo, later Wells Fargo & Company, still operating today in various forms, but originally established in 1852 by Henry Wells and William Fargo. (Remarkably, this company thirty years later would exhibit one of its connections to faraway Montana Territory in the bestowing of the name Livingston upon a railroad town there for a former Wells Fargo board member, Johnston Livingston.)[7] A reputable history of Wells Fargo published in 2002 gave us a useful explanation of the company's operations and compared those old-days roots with today's equivalent of stage companies. The description explained what stagecoach companies—many of which were also express companies—did in those long-ago times. In addition to carrying passengers:

Imagine a business that combines the communications aspects of letter mail, e-mail, faxes, and the telephone; the transportation of heavier goods by parcel post and express mail, such private carriers as United Parcel Service and Federal Express, and an armored car service; and the plethora of financial arrangements supplied by modern intrastate, interstate, and international full-service banks. That was an express company in the nineteenth century; there is simply no equivalent [for it] today.[8]

In other words, stagecoach companies combined delivering letters with delivering packages, transporting passengers, carrying valuables in a "strong box," and doing all kinds of banking services as well. This was a lot of variable business, and it all depended to a large degree upon a single stage-driver.

In Montana Territory, according to newspapers of the day, the two companies that followed the 1863 mail routes established by Ben Holladay ran between Helena and Virginia City, and were owned (again) by Holladay and Billy Oliver. "So fierce was the rivalry and competition," said the Helena *Daily Independent* in 1890, "that both parties were in a fair way to becoming bankrupt when Holladay sold out to the opposition."[9]

The star of stagecoaching around the West (and the East)—the stage-driver—was of course featured in many accounts of the business. One example appeared in Mark Twain's famous, semi-fictionalized book *Roughing It*, published in 1872, which described his long stagecoach trips across the West "ten or twelve years ago." The actual year was 1861. We have space for only a few of them here, but yes, Twain had horror stories! His party of two paid $150 apiece for their tickets to ride from St. Joseph, Missouri to Carson City, Nevada, which required that they take only twenty-five pounds of baggage apiece, including the weight of the heavy trunks of that time. Inside the coach, they carried two blankets apiece, their pipes and smoking tobacco, a bag of coins for daily expenses like meals at the stage-stops, and a canteen apiece for water. Fortunately for spatial considerations, there was only one other passenger on board. Outside, chauffeuring six horses, two men sat on the "box," the driver on the coach's right side and the "conductor" on the left, an armed man taxed with the task of protecting the coach's "treasure box," the U.S. mail, the express, the baggage, and the passengers themselves. Twain thought him the true "captain" of the ship, but on most stagecoaches, he reported to the driver. Sometimes this man was called a "messenger" or "messenger-rider."

Also famous in Mark Twain's book and in early staging accounts in general was the driver's whip. Everyone mentioned it, probably because it literally trumpeted every stage-driver, the obscure ones as well as the famous ones, and probably because of both its sound "like small-arms fire" and its seemingly legendary and inestimable length. Tourist A.S. Condon exclaimed in Yellowstone in 1887 that "the ring of the driver's whip cleaves the morning air till it would almost reanimate the dead, cold heart of Hank Monk himself." This was a reference to one of the West's most legendary stage-drivers Henry "Hank" Monk (1826-1883), whom Mark Twain celebrated in *Roughing It* as having told Horace Greeley to "Keep your seat, Horace, and I'll get you there on time!"[10]

Another famous stagecoaching element mentioned by Twain was the major, maintenance problem, which often "reared its head" among stage-stops generally located every ten miles to change horses, namely the broken thoroughbrace—that massive combination of belts and springs on which the entire outfit rocked itself and which was a main support for the coach, which was rounded on the bottom (this, said one historian, "transformed the vertical bumps of the road into a fore-and-aft rocking motion of the cradled body," thus allowing the ride to "sway" instead of banging, and also permitted "heavy loads without straining the team"). After a long stop to fix it and the off-loading of numerous bags of mail into the dust for Indians to find, Mark Twain's three passengers climbed up to the seat behind the driver so that the conductor could sleep inside the coach for a time. Awhile later, Twain laid himself down on the bare top of the coach, holding onto the coach's short rail there. "Instinct," said Twain, "will make a sleeping man grip a fast hold of the railing when the stage jolts, but when it only swings and sways, no grip is necessary." He explained that the two men on the box could sit in those spots and sleep thirty or forty minutes at a time on good roads while traveling; "I saw them do it often," and there was no danger in it because "a sleeping man *will* seize the irons in time when the coach jolts." But occasionally, those men needed to go onto the top of the coach and lie down, or get inside the coach when there were few passengers.

At stage-stops, Twain noticed that the driver seemed to pay no attention to the hostlers, barn-dogs, and station-keepers who busily unhitched and changed their horses, instead paying "insufferable dignity" only to his leather gloves. For in the eyes of a stage driver, said Twain, those people "were a sort of good enough low creatures, useful in their place and helping to make up a world, but not the kind of beings which a person of distinction could afford to concern himself with; while on the contrary, in the eyes of the station-keeper and the hostler[,] the stage-driver was a hero—a great and shining dignitary, the world's favorite son, the envy of the people, the observed of nations." When they spoke to him, he was often silent and they took that "meekly, as being the natural and proper conduct of so great a man." When he did talk, it was generally to the hills and the stagecoach, rather than addressing a specific remark to a specific person. And when he saw fit to utter his one jest of the day—"old as the hills, coarse, profane, witless, and inflicted on the same audience, in the same language, every time his coach drove up there—the varlets roared, and slapped their thighs, and swore it was the best thing they'd ever heard in all their lives." Thus, Twain explained the pecking order of the staff at stage-stops. And he noted that both the driver and the other, company employees had the same overwhelming disrespect for passengers.[11]

Stage-drivers and other stage-employees were different from bullwhackers and mule skinners in that they hauled both passengers and freight, as opposed to those other wagon-men who hauled nothing but freight. But drivers of freight wagons were still drivers, and thus many of these freighters also switched back and forth into stagecoaching. When their heavy freight-loads were pulled by oxen (cattle), these drivers were specifically called "bullwhackers," when pulled by mules they were called "mule skinners," and when pulled by horses they were called freighters or teamsters.

Mules, as anyone who had been around them knew, could be difficult, stubborn, obnoxious, and even clannish creatures. One historian has described the U.S. Army mules used by Dr. Ferdinand Hayden on his geological surveys as "cantankerous, full of the devil, unpredictable, quarrelsome, and kicking hell-for-leather toward the sky." Mules had to be broken and trained before they could be trusted in larger groups, called "pack strings." They were generally not put into those strings until they had been thoroughly trained, because such green, unbroken mules were dangerous to the unwary, especially any person located immediately behind them, where a sudden, lash-out kick could cause death, either instantly or after many painful weeks. To guard against this, the Army marked them by shaving their tails down to only a tuft on the mules who were untrained. Thus, they were soon called "shavetails," a term that "with typical frontier humor," wrote Eggenhofer, "was quickly applied to newly commissioned second lieutenants fresh from West Point."[12]

In the 1860s, during the period of high-competition between Ben Holladay and Billy Oliver on the Helena-Virginia City route, unbroken horses were often used because there was little time to train them in the press of business. So, the companies would often place two unbroken horses in the center of a six-horse team (between the two "leaders" and the two "wheelers")." That way when the whole team took off, "there was no alternative for the wild and plunging animals but to move right along with the procession," and in a few trips, "they were thoroughly broken."[13]

Frank Root has discussed how inexperienced stage-passengers were often apprehensive if not downright terrified at leaving their fates to unpredictable animals and questionably qualified drivers, and he did not blame them. "Any sensible person who is obliged to ride behind a spirited team in the hands of an inexperienced or careless driver," he wrote, "must necessarily undergo the same misgivings." "For this reason," he explained, "it was the aim of the stage officials to employ none but careful, experienced men, and, when possible, only such were selected for the responsible duty of 'knight of the reins'."[14]

Stagecoach drivers faced troubles of all kinds from earliest days—bad roads including mud and plank roads, awful weather, runaway teams, dust, uncongenial fellow travelers, unpleasant smells wafting about, and of course holdups that will be specifically treated later. These challenges always made trips by stage into occasions that ranged from being merely interesting to downright dreadful to the stuff of nightmares. Roads were often narrow paths that ran over the tops of stumps of trees, which many coaches could barely clear. Corduroy sometimes improved them when saplings or small trees were laid down across boggy or marshy ground, the rough ends sometimes projecting over drainage ditches dug alongside. These roads shook one's innards at best, and it felt even worse when the coach ran off them. Plank roads, which were common in the nineteenth century, have been largely forgotten, but they were horrible to experience. Workmen laid sawed, wooden planks crosswise on long stringers. The mud below them "squidged" up between the boards as the weight of passing horses and coaches drove them down. When snowstorms occurred, northeastern towns sometimes built sleighs for use during winters, but "out West," where towns were farther apart, these were often not available. Being required to abandon a snow-stalled or mud-stalled coach and walk in the muck to the nearest relay station was sometimes the misfortune of miserable stage passengers during winter or spring months, although when the mud was frozen, conditions were a lot more agreeable than when it was unfrozen, *if* one could stand the cold. Runaway teams provided hazards over and over; they could bolt for almost any reason, from insects to other animals to loud noises to lights to the flapping of laundry. If the driver was unable to stop them, the result could be an overturned coach, broken wheels, sudden sinking in mud or water, or the striking of hard objects, often causing a wrecking that could maim or kill passengers.[15]

The more skillful driver knew what to do in these cases. He could apply the brake with full force, but it had to be done quickly, before the brake-beam broke. Or, if he were really experienced, he could use another trick: Throw his right leg over the reins while bracing his left leg against the footboard. This allowed extra pressure for the reins to exert a sudden, stronger pull on the horses' mouths. It was an often-effective device that worked on many occasions to avoid a terrible wreck.[16]

Complaints about dust and rain were legion in the historical accounts. "Clouds of dust," wrote Eggenhofer, "churned up by the pounding hoofs ahead, sometimes alkali-impregnated, sifted up through the floor boards and billowed in through the windows, enveloping the rocking vehicle fore and aft, choking, irritating noses and throats, reddening sensitive skin, settling inside the clothing." And in a heavy rain, conditions could become almost unbearable:

> The Concords at least let some light come inside through the windows in the coach doors. In a mud wagon, with the side curtains fastened down, the passengers suffered in the dark, unable to see what was going on outside. They could hear and feel the coach bumping, twisting, and lurching along, jouncing and sloshing through chuckholes, perhaps racking and straining over a stretch of corduroy, the whip cracking as the Jehu shouted

profanely, somehow managing to keep the outfit going. If they bogged down in a mudhole, the men might have to climb out and, standing knee deep in muck, *push*, while the ladies stayed inside. It took a real emergency indeed to force the female riders out, to pick their way ahead to firmer ground, gracefully holding up their skirts, careful not to lift them any higher than prudery dictated. After a stretch on the road like that it was good to get a few minutes' respite at even the loneliest way-station while the team was being changed. And rain or no, the chance to stretch, however briefly, seemed a godsend.[17]

Notwithstanding the beautiful illustration of the stagecoach that through time became the symbol of the Wells Fargo Bank, Louis McLane, general manager and later president of Wells Fargo, wrote his wife in 1865, saying, "I thought staging looked very well to the lithographer, but was the devil in reality."[18]

A *New York Times* reporter based in Montana's Miles City journeyed throughout the region for a decade beginning in 1879 and wrote a history of those ten years, paying special attention to the drivers called "bullwhackers." Of these men, many of whom he knew personally, he wrote:

This period was essentially the era of the "Bullwhacker." All the freight conveyed to the several military posts in eastern Montana—there was no other settlement [in that region] besides Miles City—was transported by great trains of ox teams whose conductors and drivers were as hard a class of citizens as ever impressed the gracious savor of their personality upon the outskirts of civilization. By their numbers, their skillful use of the rifle, and their audacious courage they were able to defy the Indians, who prudently permitted the long convoys of prairie schooners to go on their way without molestation. These hardy teamsters were, besides the soldiers and the residents of Miles City, for at least one season, the only white men in eastern Montana. Living constantly in the open air, exposed to every vicissitude of a climate remarkable for its extreme contrasts, roughened by every demoralizing association, and risking their lives at almost every step of their tedious journeyings across the pathless prairies, it was not to be wondered at that their natures became hardened to the verge of brutality. Deprived of every comfort while passing through the solitary wilderness, they sought compensation, on arriving at a settlement, by plunging into every excess which their hard-earned but liberal wages could procure for them, and their brief intervals of rest at Miles City were distinguished by lavish waste and reckless indulgence in every species of debauchery. While their money lasted[,] no procurable luxury was too delicate, no available comfort too expensive.[19]

Some descriptions and characterizations of human nature remained true regardless of the era in which they were written and centered, and this was one of those.

As early as 1881, when it became apparent that advancing railroads would eventually render the stagecoach obsolete, a Salt Lake City traveler on the Utah & Northern Railway to Butte, Montana saw stages being loaded with passengers there and made observations about the "knights of the reins" who chauffeured those vehicles and how much baggage the stages could hold:

Just how much you can get on a coach has never yet been determined…As many as twenty-four persons have been piled on one of these, with eleven trunks, mail, express valises and bedding. It is beginning to look as though the festive stage driver was driven to the wall. His innocent swagger, his immense fob chain will soon be things of the past. He will either degenerate into the proprietor of a job wagon or keep a livery stable, or maybe run a hack. For swearing, the Montana stage driver takes the cake…Once on his seat and started he is business, and as polite as a dancing master, but you must handle him gently. Trusted with human life and immense wealth, he is generally conceded to be strictly reliable…[20]

Salt Lake City, like many places in the American West, constantly saw its share of stage-drivers, so descriptions of these men ("rough and profane, but they are men of undoubted nerve") were inevitable in the newspapers of that city:

> He is the captain of the ship, its complement of officers and crew, and when he gathers up his lines, unwinds his whiplash from its stock and 'pulls out,' he is the 'boss' until he reaches the end of his route. His coach is not run by telegraph; he does not wait at stations for orders to 'go ahead;' he goes fast or slow as he pleases. And the stage driver generally knows his own importance and makes his passengers feel it. If you get on the right side of him[,] he will crowd the journey full of interest and pleasure, but if he conceives a dislike or contempt for you, the sooner you get a seat inside the coach the better it will be for you. A majority of the Western stage drivers are middle-aged men (less than fifty), but they have lived a hundred years if time was only measured by the experience they have had. It is rare to meet one nowadays who did not drive on the old overland route, and many of them served their apprenticeship in the States East of the Missouri River before that route was established. To hear a man whose hair has not yet begun to turn gray tell of his adventures on the plains and in the mountains before there was a Pacific railroad is to me almost like listening to a soldier of the Revolution describe the battle of Bunker Hill...Though not uniformed there are certain peculiarities in the way the stage drivers wear their clothes that though difficult to describe, are unmistakable. But there is more in the manner than in the dress. They sit upon the box as though they were a part of it; they hold the reins in a certain way, and the butt end of the long whip, when not in use, lies loosely between the thumb and forefinger of the right hand, while the top rests across the lines.[21]

Lew Callaway, who wrote a history of Virginia City's vigilantes and added to it his personal reminisces about growing up in Montana during the 1860s and seventies, left us some memories about stagecoaching on the crowded route from Corinne, Utah to Virginia City, important because they were written by someone who was there. In particular, he described stage-drivers generally. He stated that the typical driver on this "Montana Trail" was often "a distinguished individual," or so it appeared to him:

> He wore fine calf-skin boots, in to which, frequently, he tucked his pants. Usually he had on a fine woolen shirt, around his neck an elegant handkerchief or scarf. His head gear was fine hat with a 2 or 2 ½-inch brim. He had doe-skin gloves, except in very cold weather when he put on silk gloves and red woolen mittens. As he drove four or six horses, he had to take his hands from the mittens occasionally to arrange the lines leading to the horses. In winter he used a short overcoat with a great leather band about his body, covering him from the armpits to his middle. Generally[,] he was loquacious, and if so, he spoke in picturesque language, during which he indulged in weird similes to a greater or less extent.[22]

Examples of such good-old-boy "weird similes" were "he couldn't get as far as I could throw a post-hole," "the answer was as plain as the horn on a saddle," and "Skeets was as popular as a wet dog at a parlor social."

Calloway also described for us the interior and trappings of a coach, at least the one that he rode in that year:

> The inside of the stage coach usually had three seats. The back seat was sufficient for three people, who looked forward. The front seat was sufficient for three people also; these passengers sat with their backs to the driver, whom they couldn't see, and they looked backward. The middle seat was between the two, a little forward of the brake blocks. The passengers looked forward, their backs being supported by a leather band stretching from one side of the coach to the other. This leather was 10 to 12 inches wide. The middle seat was occupied when the passenger couldn't find another seat.[23]

Calloway also mentioned other parts of the stagecoach:

This coach had a hind boot in which the trunks and other bags were carried. Usually the mail sacks were carried in the front boot. That most necessary appliance, the brake, was on the right. The driver operated it with his right foot. The vehicle was enclosed, roof and sides, with strong canvas. The openings for entrance and exit, one on either side, were protected by canvas "flaps." The bottom of the vehicle was wood planks, of course.[24]

Lew Calloway's use of the term "boot" reminds us that this referred to the large storage compartment at the rear of a stagecoach and the smaller one at the front, below the driver's feet. Both compartments extended all the way across the coach. Discovering the origins of the term is harder, but "World Wide Words" has helped us. Around 1600 in Europe, the term began to be used for "an uncovered projecting seat outside the doors on each side of a coach in which passengers sat facing sideways to the direction of travel." The term might have come from the French word *boîte*, meaning a *box*, although that was not its function when it was named. By the beginning of the nineteenth century and probably the mid-eighteenth century, the "boots" had been moved to the ends of stagecoaches and were used only for storage. Because the vocabulary of horse-drawn vehicles was the same on both sides of the Atlantic Ocean, it was old enough to have been in the speech of American colonists.[25]

As for what drivers and passengers recommended and wore to avoid cold and bad weather, that was undoubtedly variable, but Nathaniel Langford, who estimated that he traveled some 74,000 miles by stagecoach during his years of working for the government in the West, found that the most comfortable seat for him was outside the coach "on the box" with the driver. For constant travelers, Langford stated that "no dress is more suitable than the one usually worn by express messengers, which consists of warm overalls and fur coat for ordinary winter weather, and a rubber suit for protection against storms."[26]

For our purposes, the "Montana Trail"—which crossed Idaho Territory between Salt Lake City and Virginia City, a distance of around four hundred seventy-five miles—was and is the perfect illustration of an extended territory in the American West where stagecoaches operated across great distances with few or no towns, and did so for a long period of time, namely 1858-

1881. General William E. Strong's party of military men used it in 1875 to reach the new Yellowstone National Park before there was any railroad located even near that remarkable new Wonderland. Disembarking from the Utah & Northern railroad at 11 p.m. in the far southeast corner of Idaho at Franklin, which was as far as that railroad's tracklayers had then built, the general's party found poor lodging with one of the local Mormons. "We have a long journey before us," wrote Strong, "and I fancy we will get tired of it before we reach Fort Ellis." He did not know the half of it, for Fort Ellis was at Bozeman, Montana Territory, 504 miles away by stagecoach, at six to sixteen miles per hour.[27] If they averaged 10.5 miles per hour, the math divides out to forty-eight hours or two full days of travel. Moreover, it is difficult to imagine averaging that fast of a speed on the Montana Trail.

A portrait of General William Emerson Strong of the U.S. Army, who traveled by stagecoach from Corinne, Utah Territory to Yellowstone National Park in 1875. Utilizing the "Montana Trail" four years before the Utah & Northern Railroad arrived in Montana Territory, his trip was one of the earliest stagecoach-trips to the new Yellowstone National Park, which was then only three years old.

On July 22, 1875, at 5:30 a.m., General Strong and his party boarded their coach, which was to be their home for five days. "It is a great, swinging stage," he wrote, "known in this country as a Concord wagon, with immense thorough-braces, and as easy as a cradle on wheels, when well filled with passengers, and properly loaded and balanced."

But affairs quickly got much worse, or so it seemed, as General Strong explained:

The coach had pulled up at the village, and stopped near a whis-
key-shop for the regular driver to take the reins. This dignitary,
who soon appeared, was a slim-built man of five-and-thirty, and
so very drunk that I could hardly believe we were to be conducted over our first run by a person in his condition. He had
most remarkable control over his legs and hands, however, for
he managed to reach the coach and climb to his seat without
aid from anyone. The Secretary [of War W.W. Belknap], [and]
Generals [Randolph] Marcy and James Forsyth were inside. I
had chosen an outside seat, as I wanted to get a good view of the
country." "Are you all ready?" says the driver. "All ready," was
the response. Then gathering the reins carefully in his left and
swinging his whip with the right, the lash cutting sharply across
the flanks of the leaders, "Lee Goddard" (that was his name)
exclaimed, "Git out of here, you pirates," and the next instant
we were off, lead, swing, and wheel horses on the keen jump.
Again and again the whip was applied, and thus we departed
from Franklin at the rate of sixteen miles an hour.[28]

This was a six-horse unit, typically used (according to Eggenhofer) in
Idaho and not as much in Montana. We know there were six horses because
of "lead, swing, and wheel," meaning two lead-horses called "leaders," two
horses in the middle called "swing" horses, and two horses at the wheels and
nearest the driver, often called the "wheelers." General Strong was exhila-
rated and ecstatic, and was starting to think that driver Goddard was not as
drunk as he had initially believed. That was fortunate, because sixteen miles
per hour was *very fast* for a stagecoach, a "furious dashing pace at which we
were whirled over the prairie." When comparing that to the six miles per
hour that eight years later would become the standard rate for traveling
through Yellowstone National Park, one can easily see how terrifying that
speed must have been for many passengers, including Strong's party.

But apparently, Strong himself became used to it. "The intense pleasure
to me of this first morning's ride, in the great swaying Concord wagon,"
he gushed, was "indescribable. We were fairly afloat on the great plains
of Idaho; free from all care and responsibility; no business letters to answer; no telegrams to head us off." Their driver, still described by Strong

as "tipsy," was forced by the terrain to walk his horses for a while, but they reached the first stage stop—at Bear River twelve miles out—in a very fast one hour and ten minutes. After six, bay-colored horses were swapped into place, the coach continued at the same roaring speed. Strong was learning that Lee Goddard's run was sixty miles to Port Neuf Canyon and that this driver would change horses five times on that route. The road was "fearfully dusty" so that they rode in great clouds of it, hour after hour. For many miles the dust hid the lead horses from view, but "still Goddard cracked his whip, and made every horse do his best."[29]

As they entered the canyon, Strong got nervous at a point where "the narrow road was cut out from the mountain's side with frightful precipices below us." The general turned to Lee Goddard and was horrified to see him clearly asleep, reins hanging loosely in his hands, at a point where the stage wheels were barreling along only a foot from a precipice two hundred feet high. If a horse stumbled or a wheel came off, the coach and all occupants would go over the cliff, so Strong grabbed the reins and simultaneously "shook the fellow gently until he awoke" and the general heard him ask,

> "What-ze matter?" and when I told him he had been sleeping, he laughed, saying, "Don't be skeert, ole fellar; them hosses, they knows the road, sure's yer born'd. Never upset a stage in my life. G'long there" [he ordered the steeds], and at the same time he applied the whip to the swing horses, sending us along faster than ever.

"They knows the road!"—a likely story, Strong must have thought. At 5 p.m., they reached the Port Neuf station, covered with dust, and stopped for supper. General Strong learned to his relief that driver Goddard would go no farther, and the party left again at 6:30 p.m.[30]

Now they were driving all night. Their new driver was "a sober, intelligent man," and therefore General Strong decided to ride on the box until midnight. He wrote that he "enjoyed every moment, although, at times, the road was exceedingly dusty, following the Port Neuf River and Cañon for twenty miles; and I have rarely had a lovelier ride."

They reached "Corbet's Station," on Snake River at 5 a.m., in the vicinity of present Blackfoot, Idaho, and had breakfast. On the road at 6:30, they made "Eagle Rock Bridge" (present Idaho Falls) at 11 a.m. and cruised on to "Sand Holes" for supper at 4 p.m., having made 180 miles so far. "From Corbet's to Sand Holes," said Strong, "is a vast, unbroken plain, utterly worthless, except for grazing." He was talking about the "desert of black basalt," ancient lava deposits, huge in size and cracked and broken and vast, and growing nothing but sagebrush on huge upheavals across the great Snake River Plain that stretched for hundreds of square miles. Across these, many future travelers would learn to hate their lives, and future roadbuilders would experience terrible troubles.

Leaving "Sand Holes" at 5 p.m., Strong knew that he was again facing the "all-night shift." About 11 p.m., they "commenced the ascent of the Rocky Mountains," meaning they were ascending northward from where the village of Beaver Canyon would exist less than four years later. There, said Strong, "it turned so cold that I was forced to go inside the coach." At two in the morning they reached Pleasant Valley Stage Station, where "we were all pretty thoroughly used up, having been riding continuously day and night for two hundred and twenty-six miles."[31]

On July 24, they awoke somewhat refreshed and resumed riding in and on the stage. In a few hours they reached "the summit of the Rocky Mountains...where the line dividing Idaho and Montana crosses our track." This was presumably near the spot where the tiny village of Monida, Montana would spring up a few years later, in the late spring or early summer of 1880. Ten miles farther on, they reached Red Rock River and Red Rock Valley (near where Lima, Montana was later established). The descent on the stage road became so difficult that they were forced to get out and walk, while "the driver had his hands full in engineering the coach and horses safely down the fearfully precipitous mountain road" toward what would become the town of Dillon, Montana in five years and two months later.[32]

Continuing for thirty-five miles on the hardest, smoothest stage road that General Strong had ever seen, the party was treated to changes of horses that "were capital, and they were made to do their best," thus exhibiting some of the best conditions that stagecoaching could hope for as a business. "One six-horse team of blooded bays," said Strong, "made fourteen miles within the hour by the watch, enabling us to reach 'Lovell's Station' at 7 o'clock" after following the Beaverhead River downstream for some miles.

It was the night-stop, so the next day they continued down the Beaverhead (for another 35 miles) to Gaffney's (a stage stop located close to the present site of Twin Bridges, Montana, and at that moment about to be renamed "Salisbury" for one of the owners of the Gilmer & Salisbury stage company), up the Ruby River (then called the "Stinkingwater"), and on twenty-eight more miles to Virginia City. The next morning, a new stagecoach, sent over from Bozeman, took them seventy-eight more miles to Bozeman and three more miles to Fort Ellis, in order that they could transfer all their baggage to mules and riding-horses for their trip to Yellowstone.[33]

General Strong's 1875 excursion was typical of most trips before 1879 that traveled to the new Yellowstone National Park on very long stagecoach rides, because the railroad's terminus was still so far away from the new park. But once such a group was inside the park, or even merely near the park, it meant mounting individual horses, because there were as yet no roads there for wagons. Thus, virtually all the park-travel of 1871-1878 utilized horses and mules with the travelers' camping equipment "diamond-hitched" onto the backs of these animals, and often there were no other coaches or wagons in sight. Actual stagecoaching in the National Park could not begin until roads existed (1877-78) and until the first railroad arrived at several small terminuses (1879) located one hundred miles to the west of the park. Yellowstone Superintendent P.W. Norris built the initial wagon-road from Mammoth to Old Faithful in 1878, which connected along the way with a primitive but already-existing (for about a year) road from the west entrance to Madison Junction. Thus in 1878,[34] there might have been some individual stagecoaches or wagons entering the west entrance of Yellowstone driven by regional settlers but, because the U&N Railway was still not yet close enough, commercial stagecoaching in real numbers in the National Park—as opposed to mere individual wagons from sparsely settled southern Montana and eastern Idaho—could not have begun until late 1879 when the rails reached Beaver Canyon. As we shall see, even that travel—at least most of it—waited until the following year (1880) to begin.

Numerous parties from Montana entered the park's west entrance on horse or mule-back before 1879, but not many were using wagons. For example, one of these was the party of Blaine Walker and four others from Helena, probably a horseback party, as most parties had been prior to this date. This party might have been a customer of Virginia City's J.P. Nelson and Company, who began advertising the following in the summer of 1880: "Ho for the Geysers! The most direct route to the National Park is via Virginia City. Teams, horses, and camping outfits furnished. Tents for hire or sale."[35]

That some Montana parties *were* using wagons in the Park in 1879 (rather than riding on horses and pulling pack-strings) was attested to by the Bozeman *Avant Courier*'s editor in speaking favorably about Superintendent Norris's slow and primitive roadwork then being attempted in the Park in fits and starts, that information being announced by travelers returning from Yellowstone. "It seems to us," reported the editor, that "there must be some truth in these statements, or tourists could not make almost the entire tour of the Park in wagons, as they have done and are now doing."[36] This editor was referring largely to local and regional people, mostly Montanans, and not to out-of-state visitors disembarking from trains, because that kind of travel was not yet possible for another year. Additionally, this was an instance in the just-beginning "war" (business competition) between the towns of Bozeman and Virginia City over this burgeoning travel to Yellowstone, and that fact is apparent from the editor's notation that the Bozeman newspaper here was responding to the *Madisonian* of Virginia City. This competition between the two towns would last until late 1883, when the Northern Pacific Railroad reached Cinnabar, Montana, near the Park's north entrance. That allowed proximate stagecoaching to begin on a large scale to and in Yellowstone, in great numbers of coaches, which were suddenly operating alongside the continuing Utah & Northern-based stagecoach-travel from west of the Park. Almost simultaneously with the completion of its branch line to Cinnabar and Yellowstone, which allowed the first train to both arrive and leave there on September 1, 1883, the NPRR also reached Bozeman, Montana.[37]

But before we can understand that, we must first understand how the inaugural railroad came into Idaho and Montana.

CHAPTER TWO

Crossing the "Desert of Black Basalt"

The First Railroad into Idaho and Montana

The whistle shrieks, the bell rings, and a moment later we are whirling away to the south…The old trail by which the pioneers first entered the Territory is seen first on one side of the [rail] road and then the other. It is growing fainter and less easily distinguished every day, for the days of its usefulness have passed. The ox and mule trains that a year ago moved along this road shrouded in clouds of stifling dust are gone, never to return, and the blessed stage coach has gone with them. Occasionally we notice on the trail a covered wagon or two moving along toward Montana. Grim looking women and a small army of children peer out from behind the canvass covering. These are immigrants who are bound for the fertile valleys of the North. F.M.W., "On the Road," *Helena* (MT) *Weekly Herald*, August 5, 1880, p. 3.

The Utah and Northern Railroad crept northward from Brigham City and Ogden, Utah in early 1872,[38] its owners having received their inspiration and impetus from the completion of the nation's Transcontinental Railroad almost three years earlier.[39] The U&N would soon become the first

railroad built into Idaho Territory, and, a few years later, the first one ever
into Montana Territory, eventually extending 412 miles to Butte, Montana. Following the driving of the golden spike on the new transcontinental
railroad at Promontory Point, Utah in May of 1869, the town of Corinne,
just to the east, began to rise as an outfitting point to locations in Idaho and
Montana.

Plenty of people wanted to go to Montana because of the gold rush that
had been in progress there since 1862-63. At Corinne, which the region's
Mormons damned as the "only gentile town in Utah" and which residents
lovingly called "Corinne the fair," disembarking train-travelers boarded
Wells, Fargo, and Company stagecoaches[40] or bargained briskly with often
uncultured men for horses and wagons to take them north through Idaho
Territory, as the Montana goldfields beckoned enticingly to them. These
were rough but exciting years on the far-western frontier. For example, so
crowded were the streets at Corinne that railroad passengers disembarking
there in the spring and summer of 1873 were forced to wait up to three
days to board a packed stagecoach north to Montana. And during the years
1869-1871, Montana explorers were revealing to the world a strange wonderland that would soon become known as Yellowstone National Park, but
virtually no one in Utah or Idaho territories knew that yet. Indeed, as late as
1882, a writer who had toured southern Montana could erroneously report:

> Hitherto[,] the inaccessibility and isolation of the Geyser region
> have deterred all but the venturesome tourist from attempting
> to penetrate this greatest wonderland of the globe. But when
> the railroad shall reach its limit[,] the wonders and delights of
> the Yellowstone Park will be revealed to mankind. Until that
> time, however, this great phenomenon of nature, with its objects of scenic splendor, will remain a 'sealed secret' to the outside world.[41]

The new place of Yellowstone was not a "sealed secret," even though it was
little known. And the new railroad, as will be seen, would be slow at revealing any of it to humankind.

Correspondingly, most if not all histories of travel and tourism to Yellowstone have subscribed to the assumption put forth by J. Philip Gruen and others that the wonders of Yellowstone "remained out of public reach until the completion of the Park Branch Line of the Northern Pacific Railroad in 1883 between Livingston and Cinnabar, Montana."[42] But actually, public travel en masse to the Grand Old Park did technically start at least three years earlier with the Utah & Northern Railway, and that is the subject of this chapter and the following three chapters in this book.

The men who owned the Utah & Northern figured they would soon be riding their iron horse right past those northbound horse-and-wagon travelers on the "Montana Trail." But one year later, the Panic of 1873 shut down all railroad construction in the nation, and U&N's narrow-gauge road was stranded for four years in southeast Idaho at Franklin,[43] while its competitor—the Northern Pacific Railroad—was similarly stymied many miles to the northeast in Bismarck, North Dakota. This quirk of national economics kept these two railroads from reaching Yellowstone National Park early and thus lengthened the era of stagecoach travel by at least five years (the period of the economic depression), as stagecoaches continued to follow the Montana Trail northward from Corinne to Virginia City and Butte.[44]

Meanwhile, naysayers made fun of the little railroad, especially during the years it was stranded at Franklin. "The writer remembers a nine-hour trip over the road from Ogden to Franklin, in the spring of '78,'" wrote one of them six years later, "which was an average of about seven miles per hour, and of 'pushing' up the few light grades between the two points."

> Bull teams traveled parallel with the [rail]road to Corinne, where they loaded for Montana and competed with the railroad, both in price and time. That a railroad would ever be built to Montana seemed a thing so far in the future that no one gave it a serious thought.[45]

Other critics continued to malign the little narrow gauge with its three-foot tracks and small cars, but it persevered, even during the national depression. Doubting wags continued to make fun of it as a "toy railroad" that traveled only seven to fourteen miles per hour, whose passengers were often required to get out and help to physically push its cars up hills or through snowdrifts. Second Lieutenant John Gregory Bourke rode north on the

U&N in 1875, when it was not yet extended north of the Utah-Idaho line. In his diary, he observed, sarcastically:

> The "Utah Northern" is a very funny looking specimen of a Railway; of narrow gauge, 3 feet, it is poorly built and not up to mediocrity in the condition of its rolling stock; the locomotive is of about ten teakettle power. Each train consists of locomotive, tender [coal car], two freight and one passenger cars…The speed attained is on an average about 10 miles an hour; nearing *Corinne*, our engineer nearly took our breath away by making a brief spurt at the soul-destroying velocity of 13 miles [an hour]. I would not write this did I not have corroborative evidence from the other passengers.

Additionally, during its construction, there was always someone who did not like the railroad's route and lobbied to change it, to run it through their town or past their ranch.[46]

For northbound passengers, their trip by stagecoach initially got even harder beyond each temporary rail-terminus. In 1879, geologist Archibald Geikie and his party rode to the terminus at some unnamed spot north of "Eagle Rock" on the Idaho basalt and described the place where they disembarked as "a desert of black basalt and loose sand, with a tornado blowing the hot desert dust in blinding clouds through the air." Calling the further trip "a kind of nightmare," they boarded a stagecoach there and continued north "over the bare, burning, treeless, and roadless desert" for two more days to Virginia City, Montana. But everybody loves a fighter, and the little railroad eventually won out. In July of 1887, U&N workmen—affiliated with the Union Pacific Railroad since 1877, yet retaining the Utah name—changed its tracks to the standard-gauge of four feet, eight inches in width.[47] For years afterward, many observers would find themselves agreeing with Anna Southworth's demeaning assertion. She wrote in 1889 about the Utah & Northern Railway: "The survey was made solely for the convenience of the Mormon settlements, so the road turns and dodges among mountain-spurs, or shoots suddenly across some wide plateau at sharp tangents in bewildering fashion."[48]

Although the economic depression did not lift nationally until the spring of 1879, railroad magnate Jay Gould volunteered some of his personal money to restart the construction.[49] About this, a person who was there remembered that the Gould notice was only a rumor at first:

> Even this announcement caused little attention, for so many attempts had been made [during the depression] to carry forward the enterprise which had come to naught, that no one seemed willing to believe that a proposition so apparently foolish and absurd, as that of doing Montana business with the little plaything of a railroad, would ever be seriously entertained, and bull teams continued to wend their way towards Corinne as of old.[50]

But thanks to Gould, the Utah and Northern was indeed planning to resume its construction and did so in late March and April of 1878,[51] extending the road just beyond Franklin, Idaho. Gould and his Union Pacific Railroad subsequently purchased the U&N on April 3, 1878, and kept its name for nine years but also began operations under the umbrella of Union Pacific management on May 1, 1878.[52] Some businessmen foresaw an electrical age approaching for the nation and postulated that the mines at Butte, Montana might eventually produce much copper that could be needed for wiring. This dream of electricity was at least twenty-five years in the future, but as early as May of 1880, Gould selected Butte as his ultimate destination, likely because he knew that it would provide the largest volume of freight—in ore, machinery, construction materials, and general supplies.[53]

The newly rejuvenated Utah and Northern Railway thus began extending its rails northerly from Franklin in 1878, creating the small Idaho towns or mere train stations (largely gone today) that sprang up as the rail-layers finished—Sand Ridge, Battle Creek, Oxford, Swan Lake, Nine Mile, Oneida (in Marsh Valley a little west of present Arimo), Belle Marsh, Portneuf, and Pocatello.[54] Officials chose the Marsh Creek route instead of Portneuf River because the former was smaller and straighter and thus needed less bridging, but also because Portneuf River was then occupied and being run as a toll road by Henry O. Harkness, as General Strong had noticed three years earlier.[55]

A writer who was there when the announcement came that the railroad would head for what was supposed to be a permanent town named Oneida remembered an important moment in its brief life:

The rails reached Oneida early in July and no grading had been done beyond that point. In a day, Dunnville was abandoned and Oneida was built up—some on foot, some on construction trains, some on passenger trains…Oneida was the model terminus town. Gamblers, loafers, thieves and hard cases generally abounded. Hurdy-gurdies flourished and a "man [killed] for breakfast" was a common thing. Gunning for a man on the street [was] a pleasant pastime and bullet holes through canvas roofs and business places [were] not noticed…Mrs. Kennedy kept a boarding and lodging house, and when on a certain occasion the square front of her establishment blew over into the street, exposing the furniture etc., of the two front rooms, champagne flowed freely for a week afterwards. Wagon freights to points in Montana commanded fabulous figures, which made money plenty and gave an impetus to all classes of trade. Merchants, gamblers, hurdies and everyone made money fast and spent it as freely. This state of affairs lasted until October, when the word was given to move [the railroad terminus] to Black Rock—twenty miles ahead.[56]

The tracklayers were essentially following the Montana Trail (today's Interstate 15), and stagecoaching on that trail changed accordingly, every time that the railhead changed. While many Idaho and Montana newspapers presented only discussions about the constantly changing and much-debated railroad-route, the Bozeman *Avant Courier* reported on September 19 that the terminus would soon be changed to Pocatello, a slow-to-develop spot,[57] and historian Mallory Ferrell has told us the interesting story about it. Pocatello was named for the head of the Shoshoni tribe there, but at that point the simplicity ends. This man was Chief Dono-Oso, meaning "Buffalo Robe," but the white men called him "Pocatello." He was a large, heavy-set Indian, who was "particularly fond of pork and tallow," so the soldiers at Fort Hall called him "Pork 'n Tallow," condensing the phrase to "Pocatello," which might explain why this chief has been hard to find in genuine, historical accounts discussing real Indians. That there was locally an Indian named "Pocatello" was attested to by the *Idaho Semi-Weekly World* on July 16, 1878, which listed several of the (Shoshoni) names of

Indians who lived in the vicinity: "Tin Doy, Capt. Jim, Pocatello…Tygee, and other red men and women till lately unknown to us."[58]

Ferrell's story of how the Utah & Northern got permission from the Shoshonis to cross their land involved Chief Pocatello and remains fascinating today:

> In any event, the Chief stated that he would allow the steam trains to cross the reservation if he would be allowed to ride inside the cars (rather than on top of the cars) in a sleeping wagon (Pullman). The Chief told Assistant Attorney General Joseph K. McCammon that he wanted 'the great white man (president) to put down his hand hard on the paper,' to insure that the Chief could ride as he desired. Chief Pocatello got his wish and the Utah & Northern got its right of way, building the line through the reservation early in 1879. At that time the town of Pocatello had only a box car set out beside the narrow gauge near Pocatello Creek, a short distance from the present city. The box car served both as station and as section house.[59]

Working out a slightly more complicated agreement with the Shoshoni and Bannock Indians at "Ross Fork" station (today's Fort Hall, a name left over from Oregon Trail days), the track-layers moved on to Blackfoot, a stage-station and ferry on the Montana Trail named for Blackfoot River and the Idaho tribe of Blackfoot Indians, which was already evolving into a town in November of 1878, and which became the railroad's winter stopping-point.[60] When construction resumed in March of 1879, track-layers established "Riverside" at the spot where they encountered Snake River. Then they moved on to Idaho Falls (reached in April of 1879),[61] a settlement that had begun in 1878 as "Eagle Rock" or "Taylor's Bridge" (a wooden bridge), and indeed now that the railroad was approaching the spot, company officials ordered a new, metal bridge from the east to be shipped there so that the trains could cross the Snake River.[62]

As exciting as conditions sometimes were for everyone who was following the march of the railroad north, life along the tracks could also be frustrating. In the summer of 1879, the Utah & Northern was trying to lay iron north of present Idaho Falls, across that sagebrush Territory's difficult, basaltic lava-flows, made worse by hot weather, as the company strove to reach the mountain coolness of Beaver Canyon by mid-September. A newspaper-contributor on August 17 used a biblical metaphor, likening terminus towns such as Camas (north of Idaho Falls) to "seeds sown by the wayside." "This life of following up the railroad is awful," fumed that observer known only as "Idaho," "and one is barely able to keep his head above water, the expense of moving every time is so great, and then the climate is so disagreeable."

> [The wind] blows more or less all the time, and most of the time the air would lead one to suppose it was wafted from a red-hot stove. Every day or so we have a little Washoe zephyr. It is but just to say, however, that this place [Camas] is much pleasanter than our last town site [Market Lake or Lava]. The main fault is the water, but that is very much better now, the creek being higher...I am informed we are likely to remain here a month, six weeks and likely two months. That our next place is a little paradise, [with] plenty of green grass and most delightful water [is now known to be true]. Our next terminus is designated as Beaver Canyon, and there we will probably remain for some length of time—a thing devoutly to be wished.[63]

This ending sentiment from Shakespeare's "Hamlet"—namely that remaining in the little paradise was "a consummation devoutly to be wished"— would prove to be true, if one did not include winter in the equation. Winters there would turn out to be much worse than officials and residents anticipated.

And of course, the usual railroad accidents and other prairie incidents occurred "almost daily." All over the nation, these railroad-injuries improved tort-litigation prospects for civil plaintiffs in court, and Idaho's Utah & Northern was no exception. The blasting of rocks during grading was only one cause of injuries:

> There were four men hurt the other day. One had his head hurt severely and will lose one eye, and maybe both; another had his foot mashed and two toes broken; a third had his kneecap

broken. I did not learn the harm done to the fourth. The first two mentioned parties left for Salt Lake on Friday for medical treatment. Report reached us today of a very sad accident befalling Mrs. Freeman of the Ogden *Freeman*, while on her way to Butte, Montana, there to join her husband who is running a daily [newspaper] at that place. It seems she had a loaded shot-gun in the wagon, and from some cause the gun went off, the discharge entering Mrs. F's thigh. The accident occurred at Pleasant Valley, and the party are now enroute for this place on their return to Ogden with the wounded lady.[64]

By summer 1879, Yellowstone National Park—sixty-five air-miles to the northeast but still over two hundred miles away by road—was seven years old and already famous because of hundreds of stories in the newspapers and magazines of the U.S. and Europe. Visited by only about five hundred horse-riding travelers per year during the 1870s, Yellowstone was a place that almost everyone believed would eventually become a tourist-mecca if only the railroads could get there.[65]

Utah & Northern officials were certainly trying to do that, although they were also becoming interested in Butte. Northbound tracklayers had passed Market Lake (today's Roberts, Idaho), Lava, and Camas, and were heading toward Dry Creek (essentially today's Dubois, even though the actual mouth of Dry Creek was and is technically north of High Bridge), High Bridge, China Point, and Beaver Canyon. Beaver's temporary camp, at the south end of the canyon, was established as such in September of 1879, but tracklayers still had to conquer the canyon itself to reach their winter stopping point.[66] Ultimately, the town of Beaver Canyon and its station would be located at the north end of that initial canyon, but south of the larger and more northerly canyon.

A person who lived at Camas for the short time that the terminus was there had this to say about it:

The stay at Camas was short—only sixty days—and the signal was given for another advance—thirty miles to Beaver Canyon, September 16, we commenced tearing down our building and in a few days were settled in the new town. It was again coming

winter, and many, seeing no inducement for hibernating in that
delectable place, retraced their steps toward Ogden. But Beaver
Canyon proved to be more of a town than had generally been
supposed it would, and fully maintained its reputation of our
average stopping places along the line. By December 1, freight
had stopped coming [to Camas], and with no bullwhackers to
prey upon, the gamblers and confidence men had gradually left
for the south, until but few inhabitants were left.[67]

Meanwhile, only 5.3 railroad-miles south of the eventual Beaver Canyon
station was China Point, a name that had been tagged onto the spot sometime in the late 1860s or early 1870s. The exact year is so far missing (the
most likely time for the event seems to have been the winter of 1869-1870),
but it was a site of intense drama.

The story of China Point—about two miles south of present Spencer,
Idaho—is tragic and full of the high adventure for which the "Montana
Trail" became well-known in stagecoaching history. Having heard of
the Montana gold fields, eight or nine Chinese purchased stagecoach
tickets in Utah and completely filled a northbound stagecoach except
for one white man who occupied "the box" with the driver. Headed
north through eastern Idaho by coach, for there was no railroad yet,
the stage-driver hit a snowstorm in Portneuf Canyon and they passed a
fitful night at "Cedar Point" on Snake River. The next day the weather
turned really frightful in the area of Eagle Rock Bridge. The driver on the
box advised the Chinese, all of whom were thinly-clad in only the usual
Celestial pajamas, to purchase cold-weather gear there, but they refused,
saying that they had spent all their money on stage-fare. Proceeding
north, the stagecoach encountered even worse weather at Hole-in-the-
Rock, a stage-station located between the later railroad-stations of Camas
and Dry Creek, where the party ate supper and switched drivers in now-
dark conditions. The new driver, Britt Briggs, "took charge of the ribbons" and whipped the horses on northward. On Beaver Creek, he found
himself in a full-in-the-face blizzard, the wind from which "seemed to
turn the blood of man and horse into ice." Said the best account, rendered by an unknown "P.C.":

> The roads soon became impassable. The leaders [horses] refused
> to face the storm, and despite the oaths and whip used by old
> Briggs, they would "jackknife" and turn their tails to the storm.
> Soon they refused to budge and both the leaders and the wheel-
> ers turned around in a swinging circle and got their tails to the
> storm.[68]

Briggs and his partner on the box were doing okay in the blizzard, but
that was not the case for the Chinese. Poorly dressed in wooden pumps
for footwear and light padded blouses with cotton trousers and with no
gloves or hats, they pleaded with Briggs to let them walk back to Hole-in-
the-Wall. Briggs refused several times but finally turned around and started
driving back southward to the stage-station. Within a few miles, the coach
became impossibly stuck in the snow "in a bottomless drift." At that point,
the Chinese mutinied, and all eight began walking south, back to Hole-in-
the-Wall. Briggs implored them to ride several of the horses, but they would
have none of it, saying they would rather walk. Frustrated, Briggs and his
partner let the two horses they were riding "pick their own trail" through
the snowdrifts back to the station and spent the night there.

When the storm cleared the next day, the stage company's drivers and
stock-tenders started through the snow in a hunt for the Chinese. On a
wind-blown, grass-covered point not over a mile from the stalled stagecoach, they found all of them huddled together and dead, except for one old
fellow who was protected in the center of the bodies. Pouring some brandy
down his throat, the drivers discovered that he revived for a couple of minutes and then fell unconscious again. They put him onto the just-arrived
helper-coach and transported him north to Pleasant Valley station, where
he was doctored for a few days and then sent on to Bannack, Montana.
There he died only a short time later. He was the only one of the Chinese
to survive for a short time. The others were buried on the knoll where they
died, "and which to this day is known as 'China Point'."[69]

By 1890, the spot had become famous as "one of the most obscure and
desolate places on the U.P. railroad." "It is where the wind always blows a
hurricane," explained the *Idaho Register*, "and where at the present writing,
a freight train of thirty-two cars is buried so deep[ly] that the company is
negotiating for well boring machinery to go down to the track and see if the

train is still there."[70] China Point was, and remains today, a frigid, windy, snowbound, and lonely spot, right at the southern entrance to the mountains (it is the high point at the beginning of the canyon and immediately west of today's U.S. I-15).

The route through the canyon to the actual town of Beaver Canyon—the U&N's very next station after China Point—was a "really formidable environment" for the grading crews and tracklayers. Historian Beal has stated:

> The canyon seemed hardly wide enough in many places to accommodate the rushing stream, inappropriately called Dry Creek. Yet in time the stream was so cribbed and circumscribed that a road was wound around the canyon ramparts and creek bed sinuosities. The road approached the Continental Divide on a grade averaging one hundred feet to the mile. For several miles there was no dirt to be had as the canyon floor was covered with broken lava rocks. Consequently, the road bed was very uneven, sometimes on one side, sometimes on the other, and occasionally on both sides for a little way. Even today careful observation will discover evidences of the old road, and attention may be attracted by a sign reading "Paymaster's Tree." That was the spot where paymaster Joslyn once distributed the monthly payroll to the tracklayers.[71]

As early as 1863, when the stage-road called the "Montana Trail" first ran through this place, record cold and snow plagued the spot that sixteen years later would become the town of Beaver Canyon. One horseman from that year foreshadowed what hundreds more travelers would experience as he remembered what was there then:

> At the entrance to Beaver Canyon where we were obliged to stop on account of the cold weather, we cut some brush in a thick grove, where we sheltered our animals as best we could. Nearby there was a toll gate and a large cabin, about 30 feet by 50 feet in dimensions, in which there was an immense fireplace, and here, during those terrible days there were gathered all the travelers, who, like ourselves, were obliged to wait until the storm was

over, and most of them made their rendezvous at the toll gate station, which was well heated and provided with some rough card tables, improvised perhaps for the occasion, and there was ample provision of very poor whiskey at the bar…There was considerable snow on the divide and it again turned very cold, and on the day following our breaking camp at the toll gate, we met a bull train, which, I believe, belonged to King and Gillette, crossing the divide. I witnessed there what I had never dreamed of before, [namely] several cattle in the moving train freeze to death in the yoke and go right down upon the ground.[72]

Thus, Beaver Canyon was known early as a locale where winter was intense. But the U&N had little choice except to build the road through a canyon where the weather could and would blockade its trains during many winters to come.

Once the tracklayers reached Beaver Canyon (four miles north of today's Spencer, Idaho on I-15 at today's exit 184), railroad officials knew that travel by stagecoach to Yellowstone National Park was suddenly possible, even though the park's west boundary was still sixty-five miles away, as the crow flew, and one hundred ten miles away via a rough, mountain-road south of the Continental Divide and east through Idaho (a route that the enterprising Bassett Brothers would adopt within eighteen months to carry stage-passengers to Yellowstone).[73] Although the mines at Butte and Ana-conda, Montana ultimately offered the greatest potential returns to the rail-road, its officials believed that Yellowstone Park could add to their coffers as well. However, Beaver Canyon was higher in elevation (6,020 feet) than China Point, and its winters were similarly cold and snowy. Its station was about 272 rail-miles north of Ogden, but now the railroad remained short of the Continental Divide by eleven miles and short of Butte, Montana by around 140 miles.[74]

The Christmas of 1879 was Beaver Canyon's first, and Charles Julius Bassett was one of the settlers present to see it. He and J.H. McQueeney were roustabouts for the railroad, who both shoveled coal and did all-around labor. "There were probably 150 inhabitants" in the brand-new town, remembered McQueeney, and in good hell-on-wheels style "only a handful of that number were not habitués of the gambling houses and

dance halls." Only five people were employed at the new train-station—the
agent, the telegraph operator, the cashier, and the two roustabouts Bassett
and McQueeney, whom the railroad paid $40 a month each, fabulous wag-
es then. "On Christmas eve," McQueeney recalled, "it was so cold that I
dared not fall asleep in my cabin, a box-car converted into a lodging place,
for fear that I would freeze to death." Within arm's reach was a stove that
he kept at red-hot heat, but even that heat was ineffective against the cold.
"I learned a lesson about covering up that I have never forgotten," he explained. "That was to put as many bedclothes underneath as one put on
top." The next morning, Christmas day, he and Bassett heard a shriek of
surprise and a wail of dismay:

> Looking out, I saw B.F. White, the storekeeper at Beaver Can-
> yon and later governor of Idaho, standing in front of the depot
> thermometer in his shirt sleeves. One glance at the thermom-
> eter was enough for him, judging by his outcry and the way
> he dashed back to his store. The mercury registered exactly 50
> below, but the air was dead still and the day as bright as I have
> ever seen. The cold was for that reason not so noticeable, but
> it would freeze one's ears or nose in just a few minutes. White
> never appeared again that winter with anything less than the
> heaviest clothing he had in the store.[75]

Winter stopping point or not, U&N officials were likely edgy at Beaver
Canyon. Anxious to reach the territorial line and enter Montana Territory,
probably because they knew that it would quickly increase both stage-passenger and freight revenues for their cash-strapped railroad, they counted
the winter days until superintendent Washington Dunn and his assistants
decided to resume construction early—on February 27, 1880. With seventy-five men establishing the first camp at present Humphrey, Idaho, the
tracklayers suddenly faced a March storm that stopped them cold as they
labored north toward Monida Pass, elevation 6,920 feet.[76]

Simultaneously, Helena residents—eager to celebrate the arrival of the
first railroad into their territory—"prepared two eight-ounce silver spikes,
fashioned from the first silver ingot smelted at the Helena Assay Office,"
each carrying the inscription "Welcome ([from] Montana to Idaho) U. &

N.R. 'Ry.'" Territorial and railroad officials were ready for this celebration on March 2, but bad weather delayed it until the storm broke on March 8. (As so often happened in frontier towns during winter storms, the Valley House hotel at Beaver Canyon burned down at 2:30 p.m. on March 5, no doubt another victim of the ubiquitous wood stove.)[77] The celebration began at ten a.m. on Tuesday, March 9, 1880, when a three-car train carrying residents and railroad officials left Beaver Canyon and arrived, a bit later, at a point just north of Monida Pass, on the Montana side of the Continental Divide—close to a spot that would eventually become a station known as "Monida." In what had become standard for this kind of festivity since 1869, officials at the "summit of the Rocky Mountains" hooked telegraph wires to the hammer and "nails" so that people in Montana could "hear" by telegraph the actual driving of the spikes.

In frigid Butte, Helena, and Deer Lodge, assembled crowds waited for word of the spike-driving, with bands and fluttering flags punctuating the wintry atmosphere in those frosty towns. At the summit, a local dentist named William Dodge led the onlookers in some songs, after which Miss Rilla Lingo opened bottles of champagne. Captain E.T. Hulaniski, General Agent for the railroad, spoke on the history of the railroad's construction and, with Superintendent Dunn absent, assistant L.J. Fisk also said a few words. Officials then read the just-received telegrams from Butte and Helena containing the usual freedom-from-isolation sentiments. The terminus agent quickly attached the wires to the spikes and hammer, and Captain Hulaniski drove the first spike, "amid cheers of the people." Throughout Montana, listeners heard the clicking-impulses that represented his blows. Children from Beaver Canyon drove the second spike, and at that moment Territorial towns applauded the railroad's progress "across the border." In the town of Deer Lodge, Foreman Van Gundy and his assistants fired a howitzer and rang the town's fire bell over and over.[78] Subsequently, the U&N construction crew—still fighting another month of winter—began building northward and downhill into Montana. Around the Territory Montanans continued to rejoice, wrote historian Beal, "in the fact that a railroad two hundred and ninety miles long was upon their threshold."[79] At least some city and state officials saw the event as a step toward statehood for their Territory, but statehood would not happen for nine more years.

The U&N Railway would continue for the next twenty-one months to build toward (what became) Dillon[80] and eventually Butte. Before that, a bit more intervened in our story, namely the short-lived, fairly large town of Red Rock (located 38.6 miles north of Monida and 20.3 miles north of "Spring Hill"), which the railroad reached between April 20 and May 10, 1880. It grew fast, having five hundred fifty people by mid-August of that year, and by two years later had dropped to only fifty, if one believes population figures on the 1882 U&N timetable.

That brief population-surge allowed Red Rock to assume short-term importance as both a town and a terminus for Yellowstone stagecoaching, as liveryman George Marshall and travelers Carrie Strahorn and William F. Wheeler would discover in mid-1880. Riding his horse east from Bannack and then spending the night at Shineberger's Ranch, Wheeler—a newspaperman from Deer Lodge hurriedly taking notes with a pencil—saw the railroad's preparations at a point north of Red Rock and heard the local chatter:

> The iron is laid a mile or two below [Shineberger's]. The grading is done nearly through the Beaverhead Cañon and it is said the track will be completed to Watson—Estes'—station by the tenth of September. It did my eyes good to see the steam cars once again. It was more than six years since I had seen them. They give an appearance of life and activity to a town that nothing else can or does. This narrow-gauge is a great success. It can do all the business between Montana and the south [to Idaho and Utah] a[s] well as a wide gauge could…It can carry [freight] cheaper than a broad gauge, because there is not near the capital invested in its construction and is run for about sixty per cent of the cost of running a wide gauge road.[81]

Wheeler was delighted with this part of Montana's sudden commotion and liveliness. "Everything here is bustle and activity," he beamed. "Trains are gliding back and forth discharging their freight and passengers and carrying material for further construction." Watching it all and elated, he rode south up the grading and new iron toward the clamoring terminus at Red Rock:

The terminus is a town on wheels. It must move with the progress of the [rail]road. The houses are built in sections, so as to
be easily taken apart and loaded upon the cars, to be carried to
the next stopping place. In one or two more moves it must become stationary and the active business men must stay in the last
location or scatter to different places to carry on business. The
town has 550 people and is very quiet and orderly. The Railroad
Company will not receive or load freight on Sundays, and, although there is no church here, the day is as still and quiet as a
New England village on Sunday.

Wheeler then proceeded to describe the town in detail, including listing all
businesses and the people who owned and worked for them. It included a
school of fifty-five children and its teacher; the post office, "a rolling insti-
tution," with a postmaster who had continually moved with the railroad
"from Utah through Idaho into Montana," and all the other people who
were listed individually with their enterprises. "The business done here is
very important [and] large," he finished.[82] It was a town that was almost
gone two years later, and which is completely gone today.

The railroad established several other termini before arriving at Butte on
December 15, 1881,[83] but those stories are beyond ours. More important
to us are the facts that the small town of Beaver Canyon, Idaho, and the
spot one mile north of the Continental Divide that would later become the
tiny town of Monida, Montana, were now railroad-accessible and could
thus begin serving as origin-points for the earliest, fleet stagecoach-travel to
Yellowstone National Park.

For all practical purposes, that adventure began in the summer and fall
of 1880, and we shall tell it in chapters five and six. But first, we must
chronicle the story of how the existing Gilmer & Salisbury Stage Line operated from these new railroad terminuses into Montana and Idaho. That
company was already exceedingly successful in its carrying of passengers,
but it would soon struggle in its efforts to carry mail into the mountains of
Yellowstone.

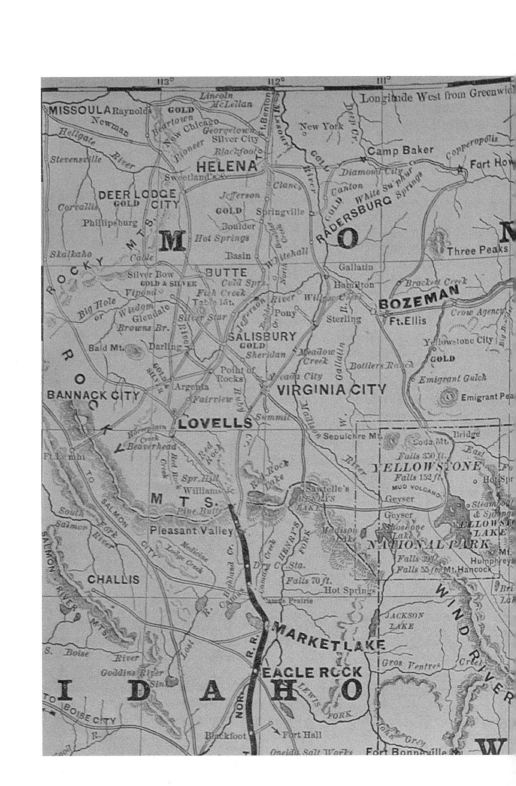

This map, from Robert E. Strahorn's 1879, 1880, and 1881 editions of *To The Rockies and Beyond* (Omaha: New West Publishing, 1879; 1880; and third edition, 1881) is an excellent map for understanding Montana, Idaho, and Wyoming Territories at the time that the Utah & Northern Railroad had just reached Beaver Canyon, Idaho Territory (on September 16, 1879) and Monida, Montana Territory (on March 9, 1880) at the Continental Divide—the boundary between those two Territories. From those two spots, stagecoaching to Yellowstone National Park truly began in the summer of 1880. The maps are essentially the same in all three editions, but in the 1881 one, Strahorn has filled in all the Montana roads in a more complete fashion.

CHAPTER THREE

"Mind-Shattering and Bone-Rattling" Excursions

The Gilmer & Salisbury Stage Line Serves Utah, Idaho, and Montana

"…and then with a whip-crack and a 'Hyah!' they were off."
—Nick Eggenhofer in *Wagons, Mules and Men.*

As it occurred all over the nation, regional stagecoach-operators wasted no time in hooking up to the new Utah & Northern railhead, no matter where its terminus was temporarily located. Gilmer & Salisbury Overland Stage and Express Line (at times called Gilmer, Salisbury, and Company; Gilmer & Salisbury Stage Lines; or most often merely Gilmer & Salisbury) had already been operating all over Montana since 1869, when that company purchased the old Wells, Fargo, and Company stage line, and then (beginning in September, 1879) carried many passengers daily into Montana from the ever-perambulating U&N terminuses at Beaver Canyon, then Spring Hill, and then Red Rock, located 322.4 rail-miles north of Ogden, where Charles Bassett was baggage agent during that summer of 1880.[84] We will hear much more from Mr. Bassett and his brothers, but for now it is important to take a brief detour into the background of Gilmer & Salisbury's legendary stage-line within what would eventually be called the "treasure state."

Wells, Fargo, and Company "pulled out of stagecoaching in Montana in the fall of 1869, ending three years of successful operations on a raw frontier."[85] On September 2, 1869, the newspaper at Corinne, Utah announced that the Company had sold its line of stagecoaches running from Corinne to Helena to another firm known as Salisbury & Gilmer, which soon would be known as Gilmer & Salisbury.[86] By 1880, the year we are discussing, they had become one of the most powerful corporations in the American West, and their lines ran from the Canadian border to southern Utah and from the Great Plains to the Sierra Nevada and Cascade Mountains.[87] Gilmer & Salisbury were poised to stay in Montana in large fashion for the next sixteen years, operating throughout the Territory with reasonable, often stellar service and becoming a dependable employer for hundreds of stage-drivers, shotgun-guards, messenger-riders, sales agents (often called "stagers"), division-agents, stock-buyers, bookkeepers, herders, stock-tenders, hostlers ("barn dogs"), wheelwrights, carpenters, harness-makers, and blacksmiths.[88]

For our story's purposes and prior to the construction of the Utah & Northern Railway, Gilmer & Salisbury operated on the "Montana Trail" from Helena, Montana through Idaho to Corinne, Utah and back. By then, long stagecoach rides had become legendary in the American West for their many horrid qualities that included dust, heat, rain, mud, ice and snow, hold-ups by highwaymen, bad food and abysmal service at stage-stops, a literally painful lack of restrooms for passengers, uncomfortable seats, occasional surly reinsmen, monotony and boredom for overwhelming distances, and the constant rocking and jerkiness of the coaches for days, as chronicled by dozens if not hundreds of travelers. For example, Lt. John Gregory Bourke boarded a northbound stagecoach at the U&N terminal at Franklin, Idaho in 1875, and recorded this:

> The stage line to *Helena* is a poor enough apology for rapid transit; recollections of my recent experience in Utah [on the train—see chapter two] made it seem a luxurious mode of travel. The only passenger besides myself was an old lady traveling from New Hampshire to join her boy in Montana; her case was another illustration of the folly of wisdom where ignorance is bliss; her ideas of the perils and discomforts to be encountered were blissfully vague and indefinite, and I thought it a duty to

keep her in ignorance. Snow and mud clogged up the road to such an extent that we made only 58 miles in 24 hours; several times on the way, the old lady nearly fainted from cold, hunger and exhaustion; luckily, some whiskey was handy and a liberal dosing with it restored her.[89]

Historians of the "Montana Trail" have characterized the ride as at times "mind-shattering" and "bone-rattling." This situation remained the case even after the U&N Railway was completed, as a young bride (known only as "Z.") attested in 1880, traveling from the terminus at Red Rock to Helena, Montana:

> Then followed a terrible night, spent in that instrument of torture, the Gilmer & Salisbury Stage! Sitting in an upright position, we endeavored to close our weary eyes, and sleep; but in vain! We were banged about through the darkness, until we fairly feared for our safety, and alarming thoughts of being overturned, down some mountain-side, suggested themselves to us. How rejoiced we were when a faint flash in the East told us of the coming dawn. Sometime during the afternoon, the second day of our staging, we rolled into Helena, and our hearts fairly leaped with joy, when we realized we had accomplished the dreaded 170 miles from the terminus.[90]

Montanan Lew Callaway described a long, similar sojourn in a stagecoach that he experienced as a young boy in the year 1873:

> The journey from Corrinne, Utah, to Virginia City, Montana, about 400 miles, was not a joyride. The passenger had to remain in his seat or lose it. [There was] No stopping over for a night's sleep. The next stage might be, probably would be, full. Passengers might alight for meals, and for urgent reasons. Otherwise the journey was continuous day and night. You may imagine the difficulty that confronted a mother with two small children.[91]

In other words, relieving bodily urgencies, whether yours or your children's, was not always easy or even guaranteed when one was a passenger.

Sometimes stagecoaching went well, as William Hyde noted when he rode a stagecoach south from Deer Lodge, Montana to Blackfoot, Idaho in late July of 1873. He stated that "a journey over the hills behind Gilmer & Salisbury's six-in-hand with Johnny Davis on the box is delightful." "The air is fragrant," he gushed, "with the perfume of roses, mint and sweetbrier." He mentioned sunflowers, wild flax, "wickiup" blossoms, and hundreds of other blooming plants, along with timothy, red top, and blue joint grasses, which kept the haymakers "busy with their mowers and rakes." It was a rousing experience for Mr. Hyde, who mentioned all the good smells and who, unlike some passengers, apparently did not experience the bad ones, such as the aroma of dead and decaying deer and other animals at roadside, the stench of corrals at stage-stops, the olfactory displeasure of sitting behind six horses that were all passing gas, or the same phenomenon inside the coach when it emanated from one's fellow passengers.[92]

Stage-driver Johnny Davis was also known for his winter acumen. In early January of 1875, he drove the night run at forty-five degrees below zero "on the box" from Helena to Deer Lodge, except for the moments when he walked alongside in the snow to guide that stagecoach while E.M. "Governor" Pollinger did the driving. Meanwhile, his passengers spent much of their time "shoveling snow and getting the team on their feet." Quipped the editor of the Deer Lodge *New North-West* who told the story, "They say Davis is the toughest man in America."[93]

Another early Gilmer & Salisbury employee was Johnny Dunn, whom we know of because of the reminiscences of an unnamed old-timer in the upper Yellowstone country who remembered Dunn. Montana historians know of Dunn's friend "Uncle" Joe Brown who made the earliest gold strike in the upper Yellowstone region at the mouth of Bear Creek in 1865-66, but fewer know that Johnny Dunn was Brown's partner in that strike. Leaving Joe Brown at his claim near present Jardine, Montana, Dunn went to work for Gilmer & Salisbury as a shotgun-guard. The last time this unnamed old-timer saw Dunn, "Johnny had a cut-off double-barreled shotgun, in his capacity as messenger for Gilmer & Salisbury's stage line" in 1877. "He was as brave a guard as ever sat on the box," said this old man, "and if he is yet on [the] surface let us hope that his lines are cast in pleasant places."[94]

W.W. Wylie, a man who would eventually become very famous in
Yellowstone National Park as the owner of the Wylie Camping Company transportation and camps, rode a Gilmer & Salisbury stagecoach from
Oneida, Idaho north to Bozeman, Montana in 1878, and left us a record of
his trip. He boarded the Utah & Northern train north to Cache Valley near
where Logan, Utah is today. Wylie had written ahead to be placed "on the
box" with the Gilmer & Salisbury driver for the 400-plus-mile trip:

> The stage agent at On[e]ida told us to call our first driver Pete.
> While the stage was being loaded, we noticed the driver was
> drunk. We expressed to the agent our concern because of this.
> He assured us that Pete was a better driver drunk, than any of
> the others were sober.[95]

From this, one can get some conception of the looseness in which not only
G&S, but many other western stage companies operated.

Possibly, the agent was merely joking a bit with the passengers because
another driver climbed onto the box to take the first twenty miles of the
trip, while Pete climbed into the coach. The agent explained to Wylie and
the other passengers that Pete "would be sober enough" to take the lines at
the end of the first segment. He instructed Wylie to ride inside for the first
stretch, with nine other passengers including two ladies.

Not totally reassured, Wylie and the others entered the coach and
settled in. At the stop, twenty miles later, Pete insisted that the coach-
wheels be greased, which was not necessary because that had been done at
Oneida. Pete insisted, so the other driver said, "Go ahead, Pete, and grease
her!" After one wheel was completed, the other driver said, "That is all,
Pete!" Wylie stated that Pete was still so unbalanced that he bought the
other driver's story, and so the two of them climbed up onto the box and
resumed the trip.

"About two o'clock that night," Wylie wrote, "the front wheel under me
dropped into a chuck-hole and I thought we were going over." Wylie yelled,
"Whoa!" and all four horses stopped. "Pete had been sleeping," said Wylie.
"I was about to ask him to let me take the lines to let him continue his nap,
when this happened." Wylie explained that he thought the coach was going
to tip over, and Pete exclaimed, "Oh, no, oh, no, we won't upset."

But sure enough, just as Pete got the horses straightened out, over went the coach.

> It took us just four hours to right the coach and reload, and such a load as was on that coach! All of 2500 pounds of freight, mail, and express, besides passengers and their baggage. There [were] even two sacks of coal [bound] for a blacksmith in Montana. Think of carrying blacksmith coal by express [400] miles on a coach. Some of the passengers were incensed at the company for carrying such loads on passenger coaches, and this all with drunken drivers. They bitterly protested against being kept there to reload all this stuff [and] missing their breakfast too, because of the delay. I asked Pete if there was any [other] way but to reload everything. He said it all must be put back on.[96]

Wylie and another man doffed their coats to help reload. They had to cut the binding-ropes, so that they could right the coach away from the load. That made it harder when suddenly they lacked enough rope to rebind the load.

Meanwhile, the two ladies and some of the other passengers had decided to walk. Wylie, Pete, and the other man finished reloading the coach, and Pete looked around puzzled. "Did you see a little keg anywhere," he asked.

Wylie had indeed seen the keg, so he told Pete that one of the other passengers who happened to be Secretary of State for the Territory of Montana took the keg off into the brush to keep Pete from drinking it, or perhaps to drink it himself. All reboarded, and it became apparent to Wylie that Pete was beside himself over that keg. "Pete, I have a flask of brandy," said Wylie suddenly, "in my grip in the front boot of the coach, and if you will let me dole it out to you, I will let you use it." Of course, Pete agreed![97]

Twelve years later (1890), Wylie was Superintendent of Public Instruction for the state of Montana and traveling to a teacher's institute at Boulder, Montana. While changing from a train to a stagecoach at Jefferson City, Wylie noticed that the driver looked familiar to him. At the lunch stop, he sauntered up to the driver's table and overheard the waitress saying, "Pete, what will you have?"

When she left to turn in his order, Wylie ventured:

"Pete, did you drive for Gilmer & Salisbury in Idaho, twelve years ago?" He said, "I sure did."

I said, "Do you remember upsetting a coach in Portneuf Canyon one night with eleven passengers and an awful load of freight?" He did not reply at once, but looked at me and suddenly thrust his hand across the table, exclaiming, "My God, you're the man who gave me the brandy!"[98]

"After dinner" (which was lunch in those days), the two men went out to the barn where they sat and visited. Wylie was anxious to learn whether Pete had been fired because of that affair, "because several of the passengers vowed that they would report him for drunkenness." Pete said that he did not believe they did, "because he had been driving for [Gilmer] and Salisbury ever since."[99] Thus ended Mr. Wylie's adventure with the behavior of a stagecoach driver and his company that lawyers today might describe as incredibly negligent.

Both the Wells, Fargo, and Company and the later Gilmer & Salisbury Stage Lines suffered from so-called road agents. From late 1862 when highwaymen killed stage-driver Charles Guy on his way to Salt Lake City after robbing him of several hundred dollars, through the late 1870s when robberies began slacking off, the highwaymen got more daring and seemingly fearless. Virginia City resident Hugo Hoppe stated that no one left that gold town without being robbed, and if they resisted, they were murdered.[100] Even as late as 1883, there were at least two attempts at stage-robberies, one of them successful. As perilous as these holdups were, by 1900 they were looked back upon as part of the excitement and even the romance of stagecoaching. "The danger, the fear, the thrill of being 'held up' used to be a common experience in Montana," wrote one sentimental rider nostalgically, "up to the time when the railroads came and caused the relegation of Gilmer & Salisbury's palace coaches to the broken down corrals back of the old station-house barns, there to rust and fall to pieces, monuments to pioneer times and civilization's advance."[101]

The Plummer gang-members at Virginia City—notorious stage robbers and murderers—were famously hanged in early 1864, but many other highwaymen worked the Montana Trail farther south, constantly threatening small, operating stage-lines as well as the old Wells Fargo company and the later Gilmer & Salisbury Stage Lines. A well-known spot for highway robberies was Portneuf Canyon south of Pocatello, Idaho. Indeed, Nathaniel Langford effervesced about this place in his 1890 book *Vigilante Days and Ways*: "The ill-starred canyon of the Port-Neuf River, memorable in all its early and recent history, for murder, robbery, and disaster, is about forty miles distant from Fort Hall, Idaho; it was named after an unfortunate Canadian trapper, murdered there by the Indians, and ever since that event a curse seems to have rested upon it." It was there in the Portneuf Canyon, in what was probably the first of these stage-robberies, where outlaw Brocky Jack's Idaho gang likely accompanied by newly-sought murderer Hank Buckner, attacked a south-bound Oliver & Conover stage on August 20, 1864, killing the driver and robbing his passengers of about $24,000 in gold.[102] And it was also there where Virginia City vigilantes caught road agent James Kelley (who might earlier have traveled with Brocky Jack) hiding in a haystack, and hanged him after a very short trial in September of 1864.[103]

During the following year, the robberies in Portneuf Canyon set a record for bloodiness in that location. On July 13, 1865, the south-bound Butterfield Stagecoach left the last station two miles north of the canyon. Seven male passengers occupied the coach, with five of them inside the coach and two—W.L. Mers and former stage driver Frank Williams—riding outside on the box with driver Charles Parks, who was single-handedly guarding a strong-box said to contain at least $60,000 in gold dust. Williams and passenger James B. Brown, both of Boise, appar-ently intended to catch the Boise stage at the Portneuf junction fifty miles south of Fort Hall. As the coach entered the canyon, suddenly a masked man jumped out, aimed his shotgun at the driver, and shouted, "Halt!" Immediately six more bandits emerged from the willows, all armed with shotguns, and began firing. The five occupants inside the coach were all armed and, when A.S. Parker yelled, "Robbers, boys, fire!" all inside im-mediately began firing. On the box, Mr. Mers was killed instantly; next to him, Frank Williams ducked a bit and a bullet missed him and slammed into the coach's lamp. Inside the coach, a massive fusillade fired by at least six bandits perforated the coach and killed A.J. McCausland and David Dinan, and wounded A.S. Parker. The bandits then dragged Parker out of the coach, pulled him by the hair to the side of the road, and dispatched him with another blast of buckshot. Driver Charley Parks was grievously wounded, but Brown and Williams both jumped off the box and escaped into the willow-shrubbery. When McCausland was shot inside the coach, he fell onto Mr. L.F. Carpenter and thus, because both men were covered with blood, Carpenter survived because the bandits thought he was dead. Stage-owner Ben Holladay and his partners posted a $5,585 reward for the murdering highwaymen, published in the *Vedette* newspaper right next to the murder-story. Dinan's body contained more than sixty shots in it, and an inventory of the stagecoach later showed thirty-three shots in its "nigh" side, twenty-one in its "off" side, fourteen in its rear, and seven in its front, for a total of seventy-five shots.[104]

So violent was this affair that it earned a place in Albert Richardson's 1867 classic book *Beyond the Mississippi*. His party entered the Portneuf Canyon from the north, heading from Montana to Salt Lake City, and Richardson used the occasion to describe the robbery that was still on the minds of people with whom he spoke. He portrayed the canyon as thirty miles long (it was and is more like twenty) and mentioned that the mail coach bringing gold dust from Montana had been twice robbed by this time. The journalist chronicled the second trip as being "crowded with passengers, all to the teeth." They were watching for a suspicious horseman, whose face was covered with his slouching hat, who had twice ridden past them. "The canyon is narrow," declared Richardson, "with high walls and shrubbery along the little brook which threads it." Suddenly, in broad daylight when all the passengers were riding with guns and revolvers cocked in their hands:

> seven men with blackened faces abruptly rose up from the dense willows on each side, stopping the horses, and firing into the coach. The passengers returned the fire; but their courage was useless. In these stage robberies, persons are seldom able to defend themselves if they remain in the vehicle. By jumping out and scattering they often succeed in driving away the robbers. On this occasion one of the highwaymen was wounded but escaped; four passengers were killed—one, an old Kansas neighbor of mine, riddled with fifty bullets and buckshot.[105]

The bandits climbed out of the canyon to the nearby sandhill-country, said Richardson, and escaped with sixty thousand dollars in gold dust. None of them was ever caught.

After the 1860s, road agents were a bit less active on the Montana Trail, but the Utah & Northern's northward construction to Dry Creek (essentially today's Dubois, Idaho), High Bridge, China Point, and Beaver Canyon was reminding everyone of the many hiding places that the forested and mountainous Continental Divide offered. For the time being, the stage-station remained at Hole-in-the-Rock, and in early June of 1879, bandits struck again. About 9 p.m., one of four men "concealed behind some rocks" yelled, "Stop the coach—right there!" and fired a shot over the northbound vehicle. Three armed guards inside, sent along because of the great amount of money in the "treasure-box," fired back at them with revolvers. The stage's horses, frightened by the shots, ran faster, as one of the guards cried "Let 'em slide!" and the driver "pushed the team along with whip and ribbons." Amazingly, none of the six people inside the coach was hurt, nor was the coach itself perforated by bullets:

> The passengers, one of them assures us, acted discreetly. They hugged the bottom of the coach with great unanimity, nor could one of them be persuaded to confess that he preferred a cushioned seat to a bare floor until the station was reached. For several miles the stage is said to have made time that would put to shame the ordinary schedule speed of a railway train…It is the first attempt in years to intercept and rob an up-coming coach, and it is presumed it will not be attempted soon again.[106]

Meanwhile, the forebears of expansion for Gilmer & Salisbury were intensifying farther to the northeast, where no railroads yet existed. Montanans needed mail service on the largely unsettled route between Bozeman and Miles City, where Billings, Montana would not exist for eight more years. Miles City was newly established because of nearby Fort Keogh, a U.S. Army post on Yellowstone River set up to protect settlers from Indians following the legendary Custer debacle (Battle of the Little Bighorn) on June 25, 1876. At first, horse-riders filled this mail-niche in the style of the long-dead Pony Express. Then in April of 1877, S.S. Huntley of Helena—

who would later run stages in Yellowstone—won the federal mail contract
to run from Bozeman to Fort Keogh at Miles City. The Deer Lodge *New
North-West* announced the inauguration of service on May 18, 1877, proclaiming that "A.W. Orton, an old Virginia type, left for the Yellowstone
[River] on Tuesday morning, to risk his raven locks on the Bozeman and
Tongue River mail route." Sioux Indians remained fierce on this road.[107] In
November, Huntley announced that his stagecoaches would begin covering
the route instead of the single riders on horseback, which had been serving
from Fort Custer to Miles City, to Bozeman. Along the way, the company established a "stage stop" (eventually it allegedly held a post office so
that mail could be added to the freight-sacks) at the mouth of Big Timber
Creek. This spot, on the north bank of the Yellowstone River where the
stage-route ran, was perhaps the earliest iteration of what became the town
of Big Timber, Montana, and according to information filed today at Crazy
Mountain Museum in that town, this "Big Timber Station" was moved to
the south bank of the river in 1882, thus formally initiating the town.[108]

Mr. Huntley hired C.L. Clark of Bozeman as his manager and began
running this "S.S. Huntley and Company's Stage Line," later called the
Bozeman and Tongue River Stage Line or Yellowstone [River] Stage Line.
His advertisements stated that coaches left Bozeman eastbound on Mon-
days, Wednesdays, and Fridays at 6 a.m., and they also left Miles City
westbound on those same days at the same time, resulting in these coaches
passing each other in transit along the way.[109] In March of 1878, George H.
Platt underbid S.S. Huntley by $4500 and thus suddenly became empow-
ered to take over operation of the Bozeman-to-Miles-City route.[110]

In late November of 1878, O.J. Salisbury of Gilmer & Salisbury Stage
Lines purchased Mr. Platt's entire interest and secured "such increase of service
as will reduce the time between Bozeman and Tongue River to three days."
Salisbury also proposed to extend the route west from Bozeman to "Salisbury
Station," near Twin Bridges, Montana. Finally, Mr. Salisbury hired Huntley's
old manager, C.L. Clark, to be general superintendent of the line.[111]

Gilmer & Salisbury continued to run this stage line until late 1882,
when the Northern Pacific Railroad's track-laying up the Yellowstone valley
made stagecoaching no longer necessary on this route. On November 30,
1882, the Miles City *Yellowstone Journal* announced that "On December
1st, the stage line from this city to Junction City will be discontinued, and

thus another mark of early days passes away." "Owing to the increase of travel on the Yellowstone," continued the newspaper, Gilmer & Salisbury "bought out the original contractor, and increased the route to a daily line from Bozeman to Miles City." The writer finished with this:

> Now we have a railroad that penetrates nearly the whole length of the Yellowstone valley. No more the commercial travel- er, business man and others, sit on top of the jerky coach and are entertained by the jolly driver and the bottle of tarantular juice.[112]

"Tarantular juice" was, of course, a reference to whiskey, carried by many stage drivers, albeit in violation of company policy, and so called from a harsh comparison with the bite of a tarantula-spider.

By the 1870s, the celebratory pageantry of stagecoaches thundering into Montana towns in the evenings was well established as a nightly event for which townspeople turned out. One of the noteworthy stage-drivers in Hel- ena was a man known only as "Pison." We must wonder whether his name represented the usual corruption of the word "poison," and if so, how that name got connected to him. Whatever the explanation, a Helena newspaper recalled him fondly in 1890 by referring to him as "an ideal stage-driver." "To see 'Pison' bring in the overland," gushed this editor, "was one of the principal occupations of the day for the loungers[,] and everybody enjoyed the opportunity when they could." Pison usually drove six, coal-black or dapple-gray horses, and he "handled the ribbons" with aplomb. The Helena post office, then located at the corner of Main and Wall streets, was the usu- al site of this exhibition, as most drivers dropped off the mail-sacks and then unceremoniously took off. But "Pison" made a show of it. After discharg- ing his passengers and the treasure-box, "he drove gaily up Main Street to Bridge and there made as pretty a turn as a man ever saw, returning to the post office to deposit his mail." To this editor, it was clear that "Pison" was mostly interested in showing-off his team and his skill as a driver.[113] In this, he was far from alone in time's march of stagecoach drivers.

In late 1879, as the Utah & Northern Railway was striving to reach Eagle Rock (present Idaho Falls, Idaho), frontier newspaperman Robert Strahorn published a new edition of his western guidebook, this time entitled *To the*

Rockies and Beyond, and he had a lot to say about this railroad and the stage line of Gilmer & Salisbury about distances, costs, and conditions. A portion of it went like this:

> Gilmer, Salisbury, & Co.'s line of daily Concord coaches, carry-
> ing the mails and Union Pacific Express, connects with Utah &
> Northern trains at the terminus for all cities, towns and mining
> camps in Montana and Eastern Idaho. The telegraph also con-
> tinues northward into the Montana settlements. Graders and
> track-layers are busily engaged in pushing the Utah & Northern
> onward in the wake of the pioneering institutions to the Mon-
> tana line, now only 100 miles away. Thus[,] by early autumn
> the Territory will be reached, and that beautiful wonderland,
> Yellowstone Park, will be within less than 15 hours' staging
> distance from the Pullman and parlor coaches of this splendid
> narrow gauge.[114]

Like all stagecoaching lines, the G&S Company was often delayed because of bad weather, and the accompanying crossing of the divide at Malad City, Idaho, where Interstate 15 runs today, was usually one of the worst places. "I know it is an easy matter," explained a stage-traveler from Helena to Corinne, "to sit around a hot stove in Helena and wonder why Gilmer & Salisbury don't make better time with the mails; but when one makes the trip, sees the sick horses, experiences a storm or two, shovels and wades through snow-drifts a mile long at a stretch, gets lost on a prairie in a blinding storm—when one can realize all these things, I wonder that they can get through at all." Indeed, during the difficult winter of 1874-1875 when there was no railroad yet, pedestrian John Kibbler chose to walk the entire three hundred fifty or so miles from Corinne, Utah to Virginia City, Montana, making the tramp in ten days. Not surprisingly to cynical ob-servers, this foot-traveler overtook the Gilmer & Salisbury stage at Pleasant Valley, which had left Corinne on the same day that he did.[115]

Hard winters were routine in Montana and Idaho, as we have already seen in the story of the Chinese at China Point; indeed, another such storm almost killed a Gilmer & Salisbury stage-driver and his two passengers in early December of 1880.

What happened involved a night stagecoach run of eight miles through the usual blowing and brutally deepening Montana snow. The coach left Sheridan, Montana (then "a place of from three to four hundred inhabitants") in the dark on December 1, 1880 around 9 p.m. and struck a blizzard. They successfully faced the storm until just after they crossed Wisconsin Creek, a stream that still flows west to Madison River from the Tobacco Root Range of mountains, when suddenly it became "impossible to keep the road." "The horses became unmanageable, wandering in circles," wrote a reporter, "until the driver, Mr. R.C. Watson, finding he was freezing, stopped the team, unhitched them and climbed into the box of the coach, where there were two passengers, Mr. Thomas Dee of [Sheridan],[116] and a Mr. Dillabaugh." Soon the three of them, wrapped in blankets and robes, discovered that they must move or freeze to death. They left the coach and began walking, leading the horses out into the snow-covered, blizzarding night "in their vain search for some house." They walked all night, trying to stay warm, and late Thursday morning, someone from the Gallahan ranch[117] found them and began leading them to the house "in a half-frozen condition." There they discovered that Mr. Dillabaugh was too chilled and exhausted to continue his journey. Meanwhile Mr. Dee had fallen into a snowdrift during the walk without the other two noticing, and was too tired to get up from his fallen position. He yelled, but his companions did not see or hear him even though they were only about twenty feet away. When they missed him, they began searching and found him in a snowdrift and so nearly covered by the quickly falling snow that he had to be attached to one of the horses to pull him out, with his ears badly frozen. On the next morning, the stage-driver got the coach moving with one of the passengers in it, and arrived at the stage-stop of Salisbury, two miles south of Twin Bridges, about noon on December 2.[118]

As construction of the Utah & Northern Railway pushed northward, Gilmer & Salisbury set up temporary offices and barns near the railroad's stations to transport alighting passengers. For example, John J. Fallon, the G&S agent at Beaver Canyon at the time that railroad terminus was already poised to move north to the next terminus, promptly forwarded six coachloads (eighty-seven passengers) on north into Montana and was praised for his efficiency in early April of 1880.[119]

In July of 1880, businessmen of Virginia City met with officials of

Gilmer & Salisbury to consider the company's proposition "to open a road up the Madison [River] for a line of stages between Virginia City and the Park." The idea was met with general favor, so the merchants embraced it.[120] But this plan would not happen. Instead, George Marshall would take over the company's Park mail-route during that summer and partially use those earnings to operate his Marshall's Hotel, while also operating his own short-lived stage-line from Virginia City to the Park.

For the next four years, Gilmer & Salisbury continued to serve Montana, but the increase in railroads was gradually destroying the company's business, both nationally and regionally. There were rumblings of its demise as early as 1881, but a distinct ending for them came in 1883, when the Utah & Northern Railway agreed with the Northern Pacific Railroad to a joining of the two lines at Garrison, Montana, just west of Butte. That event (again) decreased the amount of stagecoaching necessary in the region.[121]

However, the effective end to stagecoaching for the company in Montana came a bit later. Gilmer & Salisbury had long faced all the usual threats to stagecoach lines across the nation, but none of these had forced them out of business. The ever-present problems included highwaymen who robbed coaches, as we have seen;[122] the Star Route mail-scandals of 1881-82, from which slick lawyers freed stage-companies all over the nation; horse diseases like epizootics, colic, and especially the deadly glanders; and the inevitable lawsuits resulting from an inherently dangerous business involving horses— namely injuries to stage-passengers and the fact that glanders had finally reached Montana. It was the last two of these causes that *combined* to hit the company almost as hard as the two railroads' joining at Garrison—a lawsuit involving passenger Higley in a stage-wreck and the impending threat of the horse-disease *glanders*.

The stagecoach-wreck we mention here badly injured Chester W. Higley of Boulder Valley in late autumn of 1875. On Sunday, November 21, Higley was riding "on the box" with stage driver Doc Earheart near the Three Mile House just outside of Helena when the coach struck a boulder and began to overturn. As the coach fell, Mr. Higley was thrown violently from his high perch down a thirty-foot embankment with such force as to break one of his legs in a compound fracture. Mr. F. McMasters sustained a broken collarbone, while Mrs. Henry of Beavertown suffered only two black eyes. A third passenger, an unnamed black man, jumped onto one of the coach's leader-horses and rode into Helena for help.

Four days later, the *Helena Weekly Herald* reported that although it had been sometime since Gilmer & Salisbury's line had sustained an injury with serious bodily harm, Mr. Higley's injury was now in the forefront of their company's statistics. Friends and relatives of the victim worried that Higley's leg might have to be amputated.[123]

About six months later, Chester Higley sued Gilmer & Salisbury for $30,000 in damages. The case took more than a year to work through Montana courts, but on June 7, 1877, a jury in the trial court awarded $5,000 to plaintiff Higley. Three weeks later, the stagecoach company's motion for a new trial was overruled.[124]

Gilmer & Salisbury appealed and six months later an appeals court not only affirmed the original case but also awarded even more to plaintiff Higley, this time $10,000. The newspaper reported that it was the largest such verdict ever rendered in Montana "in a case of this kind."[125] Once more the stagecoaching company appealed the lawsuit, this time to the Montana Supreme Court. It took two years, but again the judges affirmed the case against the company. Unfortunately, Mr. Higley, age about 47 and a politician who had served two terms in the state legislature, died four months later on May 8.[126] One hopes that he got his money, which would have been at least partly used for his hospital bills through the preceding four and a half years. And of course, one suspects that his premature death was related to his serious injuries in the stage wreck.

A less concrete situation but no doubt one that was becoming more relevant to Gilmer & Salisbury and other stage companies was the appearance of the horse-disease *glanders*. The disease has today been eradicated from the U.S., but it still exists in Africa and other third-world places. It affects horses, mules, and donkeys and remains very dangerous, because it can be transmitted to humans where it is often contagious and fatal. Only isolated cases of the disease had occurred in Montana Territory prior to 1883, but in that year the disease spiked in horses at Deer Lodge and Garrison,[127] only one year after two scientists in Germany isolated the disease's causes from the bacterium *Burkholderia mallei*.[128] Not until 1894, did the first U.S. legal case occur that held a horse-seller civilly liable for the death of a buyer when the horse-seller knew and concealed the fact that the horse had glanders.[129]

The horse-disease glanders represented one more problem for the stage-coaching industry, which was already plagued with numerous other challenges. By 1883, it was clear to nearly everyone in Montana and in most other parts of the nation that stagecoaching was dying nationally from the numerous pressures mentioned earlier, but mostly because of the expansion of railroads. In Montana Territory, as early as spring, newspaper writers were touting the death of stagecoaching. On April 27, Granville Stuart—one of Montana's most important settlers, who had apparently suffered at the hands of authoritarian stage-drivers—was ecstatic about it and gushed:

> No more will the happy denizens of Bozeman and Yellowstone walk o'er the mountains behind Gilmer & Salisbury's "palace jerkies," while the unpleasant driver thereof regards them as did the Roman general of old when looking upon the long procession of prisoners that follow[ed] his victorious chariot...At last, Oh, people of Montana, the hour of your deliverance draws nigh. Job has been handed down [through] the ages as the most patient man, but we all do feel and know that if it had only occurred to Satan to try him with a Montana stage line from the proprietors down to the off-wheeler, he would have sworn.[130]

Among many settlers, clearly including Mr. Stuart, there was no sorrow for the end of stagecoaching, because riding the train was infinitely more comfortable, if nowhere near as romantic.

In Montana and nationwide, it seemed to many observers that the death of stagecoaching kept happening for many years. On June 21, 1883, the *Helena Weekly Herald* reported "The Last Coach" for mail delivery on Gilmer & Salisbury's Bozeman route sweeping into that town at 3 p.m. carrying mail and three passengers. Decorated with evergreens and red, white, and blue bunting and driven by thirty-year reinsman John T. Bingham, the coach was surrounded in the street by well-wishers "with sorrowful hearts and sad recollections" of an earlier time that admittedly "tried men's souls." In September, the same newspaper published "Staging No More," about the last coach between Helena and Deer Lodge. Celebrating twenty years of stagecoaching in the Territory (reaching back to 1863), the paper saluted the stage-drivers, "some of whom are now businessmen, ranchers, and mechanics," and others of whom "are waiting for something," namely a job, "to turn up." "Some of the drivers," proclaimed this effusive editor, "who have gone through untold hardships and endurance on the overland coaches, came west with the Course of Empire and have remained in the business to the present day." Only one route remains, said the paper wistfully, "and that is a line from Helena to Dillon, with branches to Butte and Virginia City." That route too would presumably soon be gone, but for the moment the editor could announce that it was being run by the regionally famous Johnny Davis, "who never found the weather too cold to crack his jokes or his whip."[131]

In October of 1883, the Deer Lodge newspaper published the article "Turned Out to Grass," a reference to the hundreds of Gilmer & Salisbury stage-horses that had been relieved from duty. "The days of stage-coaching are over," lamented the writer, "in this part of Montana, and nearly everywhere."

> We haven't seen a coach and six on the streets for a fortnight, and we miss them not altogether without regret. If there is a prettier street picture of animation than a red Concord coach, with six spirited horses in bright harness and a good reinsman on the box, we have not seen it. But it was not always clean Concords and six prancing horses. There are the jerkeys and mud wagons, with two and four horses, and passengers packed in like sardines, or footing it through the mud at the rate of two miles an hour, in the dark background of memory on which the brighter picture is painted.[132]

Seeing the "writing on the wall," Gilmer & Salisbury reincorporated in 1884 under the name "Utah Live Stock Company," for the purposes of moving into horse-managing, administering their mining interests, and gradually selling their stagecoaching infrastructure.[133] They also continued for a couple more years to operate shorter stagecoaching routes in parts of Montana where there were yet no railroads. On January 1, 1885, the *Herald* reported that the only stage lines G&S was still operating in Montana were Butte to Jefferson City, Boulder to Virginia City, and Sheridan to Dillon.[134] In July, the end of fleet stagecoaching in Montana truly arrived when G&S

"sold their band of horses, over 1,500 head," along with land and buildings worth $4,000, to Jot Travis of Utah and Dan Morris of Los Angeles for $50,000.[135] The Gilmer & Salisbury Company had not gone out with a bang; instead, it went down, little by little through time, with a whimper.

While large-fleet and great-distance stagecoaching was over, in many corners of the West (and even the east in some places) where rural towns were otherwise isolated and not well served by convenient railroads, small stage-lines would survive to as late as 1910, and perhaps a bit later in individual cases. In Montana, for example, numerous such lines remained in business, and we know some of their names. The Montana & Idaho Stage and Forwarding Company, headquartered at Dillon, Montana and Blackfoot, Idaho, operated from Red Rock to Salmon, Idaho from at least 1898 to at least 1908. C.H. Buford and S.R. Buford operated separate liveries during the 1890s in Virginia City, as did the Montana Stage Company (at least 1887 to at least 1908), and the Redrock, Salmon & Gibbonsville Stage Company (at least 1899 to at least 1905). The Anderson Brothers operated the Virginia City Stage Lines (or Twin Bridges and Virginia City Stage Line) during the same period, and another one was the Montana & Idaho. These small, often short-lived companies and many others like them left traces in local and regional newspapers and some museum collections, and at least one private collection contains a few of their paper records.[136] As usual, their names changed often, as they bought out other small companies, added new routes to their schedules, and were themselves bought out.

Surprisingly and uniquely, the existence of Yellowstone National Park with its U.S. Army overseers who took over the park's administration on August 17, 1886, would extend the life of stagecoaches in America—by means of a lucky marriage to *tourism*—for longer than anyone could have anticipated. With regard to lengthy timelines and sizeable coach-fleets, this extension of stagecoaching would happen in large style only in that one special place, and remarkably it would last for another thirty years! We shall tell part of that story in chapters five through twelve. But first, we must explain why Yellowstone would soon become the first, large incentive of tourist-travel to the interior of the American West.

CHAPTER FOUR

Yellowstone

The First Real Incentive of Tourism to the Interior of the American West

"Right from the start, we called it Wonderland."—Paul Schullery in Wrobel and Long's *Seeing and Being Seen: Tourism in the American West*.

With that comment, the inspired western historian Paul Schullery summed up the reason for this chapter in a concise sentence that is monumentally more important than his seemingly off-hand quip. As if to add an explosion or at least an exclamation point to this original sentiment, Schullery ended his Wonderland discussion with these words: "[T]he name stuck most determinedly to Yellowstone, probably because there really was more wonder here."[137] "More wonder" than anywhere else was thus the most significant factor in Yellowstone's place as the first incentive of tourism to the interior of the American West. But several other factors figured in as well.

Of course, U.S. tourism began in the East in the eighteenth century. Even earlier, the word *tour* came from the Latin *tornus*, which in turn came from a Greek word meaning "a tool for describing a circle, a turner's wheel," that expressed the idea of a circular journey. This was basically a trip away from home, traveling from site to site, and then returning to one's home, for the purposes of pleasure. Anthropologist Nelson Graburn defined the noun *tourism* as "a special form of play involving travel."[138] After that, formulating the word *tourist* (1805-1815) was only logical.

Whether they were called travelers, tourists, visitors, health-seekers, or pleasure-seekers (guidebooks used all those terms), tourism in the American West was slow to develop, and the reason was that the distances were too vast and the existing horse-and-wagon travel too slow. Not until May of 1869 with the completion of the Transcontinental Railroad could tourism in the West really begin.[139] The new railroad allowed travelers to go from the east coast to the west coast, at least in 1874, in about seven days for a cost of $139.50. The price appears to have gone up a bit later as people flocked to the railroad, for historian Anne Farrar Hyde noted that the round-trip cost from Boston to San Francisco and return was around $300.[140] But of course, then as now, the price went up and down with the nation's economy.

Historian Lynne Withey, in her *Grand Tours and Cook's Tours*, adroitly summarized its influence on the development of the West for tourism, averring that "perhaps no other event" in American history "made quite such a sudden, dramatic difference in the speed and comfort of travel as did the Transcontinental Railroad, completed in May 1869." Initially first-class hotels were nonexistent and "many of the most interesting sights could be reached only by stagecoach or horseback." "By the end of the 1870s," she continued, "this situation changed dramatically as a host of entrepreneurs began to develop, package, and promote the West." It ended as "a remarkable example of how scenic beauty, popular attitudes, transportation improvements, and clever promotion came together to transform a sparsely settled frontier into a mecca for tourists."[141]

Initially, some visitors were disappointed. Anne Farrar Hyde described the general, initial letdown of many tourists with western scenery; many of them "found the realities of the landscape to be a disappointment." The wonders of the guidebooks "did exist; but only in between long stretches of odd and desolate wastes." Many tourists "appreciated the dramatic scenery of the Far West," wrote Hyde, "but they did not hesitate to point out its grave deficiencies in comparison to Europe."[142] It seemed that Americans' much-vaunted "roots" in Europe were, as had happened earlier in the East, constantly being used to make U.S. travelers feel inferior.

Eventually, they got over that. The West did indeed have stunning mountains, canyons, lakes, and river valleys, but many of those features simply had not yet been found, and most were not available along that initial corridor of tourism, the Transcontinental Railroad. Places like Yellowstone and the Grand Tetons were still several years away from discovery and national consciousness to even a limited number of tourists. As late as 1871, one writer seemed to anticipate this when he wrote: "Of man's works we have less in this country than there is elsewhere, but of Nature's more. Not only more, but of a higher order, and of a unique type. They have only to be known to be appreciated."[143] J. Philip Gruen, whose history of nineteenth-century tourism in the American West was mostly about the cities of Chicago, Denver, Salt Lake City, and San Francisco in his book *Manifest Destinations*, nevertheless admitted that "The majority of the visitors came from urban areas [in the East] and headed West to experience its *natural landscape* and the people and activities commonly associated with it [emphasis added]." According to Gruen, the great historian Frederick Jackson Turner, also agreed with this assessment, Gruen saying that Turner's greatly celebrated "Frontier Thesis," born in 1893, "celebrated the power of the natural landscape," rather than cities. "For Turner," said Gruen, "the openness and ruggedness of the West, not its cities, laid the foundation for the 'dominant individualism' of the American character."[144]

What about other tourist-sites in the American West's interior? While it is true that some small resorts like Manitou Springs, Colorado Springs, Royal Gorge, Glenwood Springs, Pike's Peak (all in Colorado), and Idaho's Shoshone Falls got going in the 1870s, none of those places had the size, the number of wonders, or the massive publicity that Yellowstone obtained early.[145] And most did not have the antiquity of the first national park's establishment (1872).

On the west coast, California had deep settlement, great weather, and even some spectacular scenery (such as Yosemite, which got going in the 1850s and remained only a state park until 1890), but it was not in the West's interior, and until 1881, even it could not be reached by a railroad. And too, "few investors had dared to build the kind of resorts that wealthy visitors demanded." Charles Crocker remedied that problem in 1880 with the Del Monte hotel at Monterey, California, and the Northern Pacific Railroad remedied it in Yellowstone in 1883 with the Mammoth Hot Springs Hotel. The Hotel del Coronado at San Diego was eventually bigger than the Del Monte, but it was not opened until 1888.[146]

Almost none of the great studies of tourism in the American West, including Anne Farrar Hyde's *An American Vision: Far Western Landscape and
National Culture, 1820-1920*, mentions the Utah & Northern Railroad's
role in opening Yellowstone National Park to distant tourism; most speak
only of the Northern Pacific's arrival near its north entrance in 1883. But it
was the Utah & Northern Railway at Beaver Canyon, Idaho, that opened
Yellowstone to those first, eager, stagecoach-riding pilgrims, and that event
occurred in 1879-80.[147] Only Haines and one other author mentioned the
small railroad, which became affiliated with the Union Pacific in 1877.
Haines discussed it only in passing and did not chronicle it, apparently believing that its last-minute deviation to Butte left it out of useful tourism.[148]
But such was not the case. It had already been carrying tourists for eighteen
months when it reached Butte (December, 1881), and it would continue to
do it for many more years.

In addition to arguing for Yellowstone's place as the first incentive for
tourism in the American West's interior, it is here worth examining how
these important, secondary studies looked at Yellowstone. All these studies
mentioned Yellowstone, but none analyzed it thoroughly (Earl Pomeroy
and Anne Hyde arguably did the best jobs). Pomeroy, whose *In Search of
the Golden West* is still considered the classic study, quoted a few travelers
who found Yellowstone "monotonous," and "dreary" or "disappointing."
"It is a mistaken idea that the Yellowstone abounds in grand scenery," wrote
one of them, but of course almost no one in those days took the spectacular route to Cooke City, Montana, which included dramatic views of the
magnificent Absaroka Range, Specimen Ridge, and the Lamar Valley.[149] By
the opening of the twentieth century, tourists like Ray Stannard Baker had
forgotten the original objective of the Park's geysers and instead had started to concentrate on "the natural glory of the wilderness and the outdoor
life." And historian John Jakle correctly indicated that later in the twentieth
century, the Grand Old Park had become merely one more destination.[150]

However, no place was like Yellowstone, especially in early days when
almost no one had seen it or heard about it. Only three years after the
completion of the Transcontinental Railroad, Congress established it as the
first national park in the world, and that came only two years after its Euro-American discovery (1870). N.P. Langford, the Park's first designated
superintendent, was a member of the discovery-party. Schullery pointed

out that during its first years, the Park was called simply "the national park" or "the Yellowstone National Park," because it was the only national park in the world, but once other national parks came to exist, the word *the* was dropped. N.P. Langford was fond of bragging that his initials stood for "national park." As Langford mentioned in his single report as the new park's superintendent, the place could be reached "only by pack train," a most difficult endeavor, and this fact kept the locale from receiving crowds of visitors initially.[151]

Yellowstone did indeed host visitors from earliest days, even if travel to it remained relatively small from 1872 through 1879. Haines has estimated about five hundred visitors per year for most of the years 1872-1876, and then one thousand per year for 1877-1882. This adds up to around 7300 total visitors for its first eleven years, a not insignificant figure for these tourists who were traveling almost exclusively on horseback, and pulling a pack-string through forests, mountains, and prairies, because there were essentially no roads yet in the Park. In 1880, following the completion of the Utah & Northern Railway (in late 1879) to a spot about one hundred miles west of Yellowstone called Beaver Canyon, around one thousand tourists per year began arriving, with the first, larger burst of five thousand of them occurring in 1883.[152]

About this, transportation-historian of the Northwest, Carlos Schwantes, has noted that "travel was not new to the northern West in the 1880s, but tourists from outside the region were still a rarity." Oregon, Washington, Idaho, and Montana "were so geographically remote from Anglo population centers of the East Coast and Europe that they remained well beyond the reach of all but the most venturesome sightseers." "Even after through passenger trains first threaded their way across the northern West on a daily basis in 1883,"[153] wrote Schwantes, "most tourists from the East still preferred to vacation in California or Colorado because of the extra time and money required to travel to the far Northwest—not to mention the lack of good tourist accommodations."[154]

This lack of "good" accommodations was generally true at Yellowstone too, but as we have noted, it did not keep venturesome visitors from traveling to the new park early, even on horseback, because there were two hotels by 1880, and eight by 1886, some of them better than others. The first "grand" hotel opened at Mammoth in 1883, but there also were rustic hotels as well as temporary tent-camps. In addition to Mammoth Hot Springs Hotel, the hotels were McCartney's Hotel built in 1871 at Mammoth and Marshall's Hotel in 1880 at Lower Geyser Basin, followed by Yancey's in 1884, Old Faithful "Shack" Hotel in 1885, Cottage Hotel at Mammoth in late 1885, and small hotels at Canyon and Norris in 1886.

A huge part of the reason that hotels were built so early at Yellowstone was, as Paul Schullery has indicated, because the wonders of the place were larger, more numerous, and more spectacular and unusual than at any other place. Countless newspaper articles, guidebooks, and brochures almost instantly used the term "Wonderland" to refer to the new park, and the Northern Pacific Railroad began using it in 1883 to refer to the entire, huge region from western Montana to the Pacific coast through which their new rails traveled. But as we have mentioned, Schullery made it clear for "Wonderland" that "the name stuck most determinedly to Yellowstone, probably because there really was more wonder here."[155] Word about the "big show" was getting out.

For one thing, no place else in the U.S. had geysers—big, tall ones that explosively shot hot-water 50-400 feet into the air—in an overwhelmingly captivating spectacle!

And for another, Yellowstone had the advantage of ongoing, massive publicity in a world literature: Newspapers and magazines had made it famous in the U.S. and Europe by the late 1870s. A search of only one online archive (for U.S. and Europe) indicates that at least 1,336 newspaper articles, and 209 magazine articles about Yellowstone had been published by 1883. Moreover, more than twenty books written *only* about trips to YNP had been published by 1900. Finally, a more recent check of a second, online newspaper archive (newspapers.com) has shown that at least 1,983 newspaper articles and references to "Yellowstone National Park" were published from 1872 through 1882.[156]

For a third item, Yellowstone held all the same *other* kinds of scenic features—namely the mountains, canyons, rivers, lakes, and waterfalls—that many additional places in the West possessed too!

Finally, there was a fourth argument operating, and it was about unique literature. For and about *no other place* did a railroad publish large, colorful, and ornate guidebooks with the name "Wonderland" emblazoned upon them, containing not only lots of text and photos but also elegant, often romantic, color-illustrations. From 1883 through 1906, twenty-five of these were published (two in 1906) as large pamphlets or full books. That did not include the *Wonderland Junior* editions, published annually, which were often handed out for free on board the trains. Nor did it include other, smaller brochures tapping into the title, and dozens if not scores of newspaper and magazine articles and advertisements that were published independently, all using the term "Wonderland." In some years they carried individual titles like *The Wonderland of the World* (1884), *A Romance of Wonderland* (1889), or *A Journey Through Wonderland* (1890); and in other years they were titled only "Wonderland" combined with the year, such as *Wonderland '97*. All in all, this represented an extensive (and physically beautiful) publicity about an amazing and deserving place![157]

Thus, this conclusion was and is now inescapable: *In the realm of tourism to the interior of the West, there simply was no other location to compete with Yellowstone that was as early or arguably as wondrous*, hence Schullery's comment at the beginning of this chapter. He added: "If the place had not lived up to its unofficial name, 'Wonderland,' and if these people [early visitors] had not carried home such lively stories of its marvels, no amount of commercial promotion could have succeeded in making it the goal of one of American life's foremost pilgrimages. If Yellowstone had not been an authentic global wonder, it would have settled into a regional recreational role, more on the scale of the New York Catskills or the Wisconsin Dells."[158]

We return now to the little Utah & Northern Railway, whose arrival at Beaver Canyon, Idaho in late 1879, was quickly opening the door to the "Marshall and Goff Stage Line," as well as to the Bassett Brothers' Stage Line, which only twenty-one months later would become the first fleet of stagecoaches offering commercial transportation to the new Yellowstone National Park, already known for eight years as "Wonderland."

CHAPTER FIVE

"He Is Prepared to Carry Tourists…."

George Marshall, Yellowstone's Pioneering Stage Line and Hotel Operator

"Marshall is…prepared to carry tourists by carriage or saddle train from his hotel in Lower Geyser Basin, to any part of the Park."—Robert Strahorn, in *The Enchanted Land*, 1881.

To return for a moment to Gilmer & Salisbury's brief connections with Yellowstone National Park in 1879 and 1880, it appears, for whatever reasons (probably the park's terrible, sometimes nearly nonexistent roads with numerous river-fords, especially on its west entrance road), that the Company did not want to carry mail into Yellowstone National Park from the west, even with a lucrative, government contract. So, they subcontracted it in 1879 to a man who was already in the Yellowstone area and about to be firmly connected to the new Park—George W. Marshall, originally from Rock Island, Illinois.[159]

Before we get into George Marshall's Yellowstone Park activities, we must first briefly discuss how he got to Montana Territory. A well-researched (using many primary sources) but unpublished biography of Mr. Marshall written by descendant Charles Marshall Barnes is the best general source we have for George Marshall's activities before 1880, including his own, original biographical statement.[160]

This handwritten statement tells us that he traveled all over the West before 1879. Born in Illinois in 1838, he went to Reno, Nevada in 1868, apparently feeling the draw of mining if not the West in general. He moved to Utah about 1870 to run the Junction House hotel at Ogden for one and a half years, and in 1872, he moved to Elko, Nevada, where he ran stage lines from 1872 to 1876, then "sold out and went to Montana." If his stated years were correct, he arrived in Montana Territory in 1876 or 1877, a period before the Utah & Northern Railroad resumed its march northward after the Panic of 1873. Marshall says he then "put on a fast freight and passenger [stage] line from the Eagle Rock to Butte City, as the terminus of the Utah and Northern Railroad was at [least close to] Eagle Rock."[161] But we know that the railroad did not reach Eagle Rock (Idaho Falls, Idaho) until April 18, 1879, so perhaps he operated freight wagons or stagecoaches in Idaho, conceivably at Blackfoot or Pocatello, before that date, watching and waiting for the tracklayers to reach Eagle Rock.

Regardless, Marshall says he took the mail contract in 1879 in Montana from Virginia City to Mammoth Hot Springs, where he must have (at least initially) operated to the park's north entrance because the west entrance was not yet set up with mail stations, and the roads through the Park to Mammoth were too difficult or nonexistent. Marshall stated that his mail contract ran only that one year until the U.S. government cancelled it. That left him hanging and waiting for another opportunity. Per the U.S. census of 1880, he and his family were then living at "Beaverhead River, Beaverhead County, Montana"[162] a location that was probably either the stage-stop at Beaverhead Rock or more likely a forerunner of present Dillon, Montana, whose earliest town fathers were already in place there and waiting for the railroad. However, Marshall and his partner John Goff were continuing to cast about for passenger and freight opportunities, for the two of them appeared as a partnership in a Butte newspaper in April.[163]

During the summer of 1880, Marshall began enlarging his "cabin" at Lower Geyser Basin. While there, he encountered Secretary of the Interior Carl Schurz traveling with a large party on horseback. Marshall told the story this way:

> While carrying mail (into Yellowstone Park), I saw it would be
> a good location for a hotel. I moved into the Park, built cabin.

Carl Schurz, Secretary of the Interior, was out visiting Park in '80 and had to sleep under trees near my cabin one night when it rained. He told me next morning, 'I would have given twenty dollars to have got into a house last night' and suggested that I should prepare to keep travelers; said that he would see that I got a permit from the Government and when they got their leases fixed, would see that I got a lease. I remained on a permit til last year when the Secretary of the Interior granted me a lease for 10 years. My first year here I did not make anything, second year came out $180 in debt.[164]

After Secretary Schurz left the Park, George Marshall and his partner, apparently by way of simply informing Schurz of their plans, sent the following letter to the Secretary, dated August 10:

Sir[,] we take this mode of addressing a few words of [encouraging?] to you as we are establishing a line of coaches from Virginia C to the N. Park and building a commodious house for the public in the Lower fire hole basin which you saw and which we propose to make a first Class House[.] we wish to ask your permission to open [it] for the benefit of tourist[s] & a small stock of Dry Goods & Groceries with a few Choice [Brands?] of Liquors & Cigars and will—your permission to honor the same—intelligently [?] and in a proper manner these as listed to [be] kept at the Hotel before mentioned In charge of a proper person. Hoping this will receive approbation and immediate attention we remain yours respectfully, Marshall & Goff.[165]

From Yellowstone Park's Lower Geyser Basin, hotel-owner George Marshall began advertising his own stagecoach company in Montana newspapers, for freight on July 13, and for passengers on August 26, 1880. There was as yet no other company to transport Yellowstone tourists from the terminus at Red Rock to his hotel, so he had decided to load passengers onto his already-running mail-coaches.[166] Marshall, who as mentioned had run a hotel at Ogden, Utah, and stage lines in Nevada and Idaho, was physically following the Utah & Northern Railway in its northward construction through Idaho and Montana, and like so many others of that era, was looking for opportunities along the new road. He and his partner John B. Goff were now subcontracting from Gilmer and Salisbury to transport the U.S. mail and other freight from Virginia City to Yellowstone's Riverside mail-station (newly built that summer at a spot four miles inside the park's west entrance) and then through the Park to Mammoth, and they had also been running freight from Butte and Helena. Marshall's subcontract of Gilmer & Salisbury's technical mail-rights to Riverside was thus an entity that operated as close as G&S ever came to running freight and passengers inside Yellowstone National Park.

For a while, the story of the Park's mail became a driving force in both Yellowstone and in George Marshall's life. Mail service from Bozeman going southeast over the mountains to ranches on the upper Yellowstone River and Mammoth Hot Springs had been fraught with difficulty ever since those stations were established in 1874. Those ranch-settlers as well as Yellowstone Superintendent P.W. Norris wanted a better way to get their mail, and they like everyone else were breathlessly watching the northward progress of the Utah & Northern Railway in 1879 and 1880, even though it was located far to the west of them. When the railroad reached Red Rock, Montana, a mail-bidder for Gilmer & Salisbury suggested running the *weekly* mail into the park's west entrance, north to Mammoth via Gibbon Canyon, and then on to Bozeman (instead of going first to Bozeman and then south to Mammoth), and both Superintendent Norris and the postmaster at Bozeman approved that idea as long as it was a summer-only route.

Superintendent Norris was thus very surprised when, in early July of 1880, he encountered Mr. Orange J. Salisbury *in* the Park and learned from him that Gilmer & Salisbury had received the contract for *year-round, daily* mail-service using that approved route. Norris was just as surprised to learn that Mr. Salisbury had come through the Park via its west entrance and was suddenly present at Mammoth to check the route and arrange facilities for his mail-freighters. Although Mr. Norris did not fully approve of the year-round idea because of bad park roads and the known horrors of mountain winters, he accompanied Salisbury back south and west through the Park to select sites for mail stations.[167] Norris was vitally interested in providing better mail-service to the Park, so he acquiesced to the postal officials and Salisbury, all of whom he thought had more influence in the situation than he did.

Using a piece of Mr. Salisbury's stationery marked "Gilmer, Salisbury & Co.," Superintendent Norris dashed off a hasty and somewhat illegible letter to Secretary Schurz. To emphasize what difficult work it was, Norris added a note at the top of the stationery that read "Camp at foot of the Grand Cañon of the Madison [River], July 9, 1880," and then wrote:

> Sir—Mr. O.J. Salisbury & six horses forded the Madison [River] five times & the Gibbon [River] once in this cañon when running as high into snow water as to swim some of the animals and in two days reached our camp at the Mammoth Hot Springs with the mail. As all parties agree that this canyon is the main permanent obstacle to this mail and tourist routes, I at once with one man returned with him and with nearly all the men of both parties spent yesterday in seeking a route down to it, direct from [the] foot of Targhee pass to the forks of the Fire Holes [rivers]. In this we are confident we have succeeded and I again retrace it today. [Heading?] home and also I for the first time this season [obtained? suffered?] a thorough drenching in cold snow water. As Mr. S[alisbury] has to at once report to the P.O. Department as to the practicability of this as a mail route I feel in this [an?] all important[?][task?] and [am] justified in pledging [to] him and to without delay make a road through or around this cañon, proposing to at once bring up my whole force for that purpose even at the constraints of [dropping] for the season some of the rout[e]s previously plan[n]ed—trusting that before your arrival as plan[n]ed (and I most anxiously await) [it][to?] meet your cordial approval. I remain most respectfully, P.W. Norris, Superintendent. P.S.—It is of course understood by you that the proposed route around this cañon is like[ly] without [outside of] the Park Boundary.[168]

Norris and Salisbury personally chose the locations for three mail-stations: one near the site of the present Norris Ranger Museum (to be called "Gibbon Station," on or near "Norris Fork of the Gibbon"), one at Lower Geyser Basin at the mouth of Nez Perce Creek (where George Marshall was even then completing construction of his "Marshall's Hotel"), and a third on Madison River four miles inside the Park's west boundary at "Riverside."[169] They also decided that the agreed-upon, new mail-route through Madison Canyon with its five river-fords and otherwise terrible road was impractical for mail-freighters, and so Superintendent Norris spent the summer of 1880 building a new, high road from Riverside southeast and across the Madison Plateau to Marshall's Hotel.[170] Although the Bozeman newspaper decried the new road as being built "for Gilmer & Salisbury," Norris was arguably building it for G&S's subcontractor George Marshall, whose freighters would actually carry the mail and whose hotel in the Park would soon serve as the mail station. Norris could also claim that he was building the road for Park visitors who wanted to avoid the many, difficult fords of Madison River.

While Mr. Norris labored on this new road, the Red-Rock-to-west-entrance-to-Mammoth mail route was abandoned as impractical; instead, the contractor asked for a further change to service from Red Rock to Virginia City to Mammoth via Bozeman. Once it was operating, this longer route worked difficulties on at least some tourists who had expected to reach the Park by stagecoach directly to the west entrance from the U&N Railway. Even though the mail-route now ran through Bozeman first, the Bozeman newspaper editor criticized Norris, and the people of Bozeman resultingly saw him as somehow siding *against* their town and *for* the U&N and Virginia City.[171] Although these events were arguably unfair and not his fault, Norris would eventually lose his job over this and other perceived slights that were fabricated or made worse by that newspaper and its hostile editor.

Very soon, George Marshall began concentrating on both his mail contract—soon to be if not already a springboard for his stagecoaching operation—and his idea for a hotel at Lower Geyser Basin. Montana pioneer William Wheeler has mentioned that Mr. Marshall began taking the mail on horseback into Yellowstone by July 15 and by wagon on August 9. By August 10, 1880, a visitor to Lower Basin named Omar was stating that George Marshall would begin running a daily stage on August 15. By August 26, Marshall's own advertisement stated that his hotel would be finished by around September 1, so his passenger-coaches—operating in a niche-grant that Gilmer & Salisbury officials were not using—would begin running from Virginia City to his hotel on August 25. He advertised that the distance from there to his hotel was one hundred miles, the time twenty-four hours, and the fare forty dollars.[172]

Marshall's apparent first commercial passenger-trip from the Red Rock terminus to the park got quite a bit of publicity, because at least one newspaper headlined it as "First Stage into the Park." There had been individual wagons carrying campers, of course, and we have chronicled some of them in this book, but this trip, on August 9, 1880, was certainly a candidate to occupy that special niche of first *commercial* stagecoach into Yellowstone from a terminus that was finally close enough to be relevant. At this moment, that terminus should have been Beaver Canyon, Idaho, fifty-one miles to the south. But no one was in place there yet to run stagecoaches, because the Bassett Brothers would not appear for another ten months, and Beaver Canyon was still tiny. However, Red Rock, Montana, which the rails reached on April 20, 1880, had grown almost instantly like a weed. By August, it held five hundred fifty people (two years later it would be only fifty!), *including*, according to a Montana newspaper, "Goff and Marshall, stage line to the National Park, Fare $40 for the round trip." Marshall & Goff, as they would soon be called, had rushed a few horses and wagons into place, so as to be ready for this day. Moreover, the Deer Lodge *New North-West* newspaper seemed to be bursting with desire to trumpet what must have seemed like enormous news to many people in this Idaho-Montana region. Headlined "First Stage into the Park," it and a second article on the same page announced the following:

> To-morrow Messrs. Goff & Marshall [will] leave with light covered wagons to establish a line of stations from here to the National Park. The distance is one hundred miles. The fare going, $20; return, same. On the fifteenth they will also start a similar line from Virginia City. The fare will be the same. As soon as the terminus is moved the line will be abandoned.[173]

At this moment, the Utah & Northern's terminus was at Red Rock, and early Montana resident and newspaperman William F. Wheeler was one of the two occupants of this alleged "first" coach, the other one being the driver, George W. Marshall. "Mr. Marshall has invited me to go with him," wrote Wheeler, apparently an indication that Marshall had no passengers for this opening coach, so he had offered the ride free to Wheeler, possibly in exchange for the publicity or to have physical company, or both. Whether Mr. Goff was also a passenger was not indicated, but probably he was not, as he and Marshall had agreed that he would manage the company's all-night stop at Sawtell House "at Henry's Lake."

Their route was up Red Rock Creek to its source and across Red Rock Pass to Henry's Lake, a course that took the Marshall & Goff stagecoach through Centennial Valley, and this was one of the few times that George Marshall used that route, because the railroad's terminus would soon shift to points north that would include Virginia City. Mr. Wheeler laid out the route, gave extensive background on its context, and then described the vehicle for us. "It is a comfortable, three-seated, platform spring, covered wagon," he explained, and the story also gave us the distance to Henry's Lake from the Red Rock terminus as sixty miles. On the following day, Marshall drove Wheeler across (the old version of) Targhee Pass, entered the park at the place where West Yellowstone would someday stand, ascended Superintendent Norris's new "high road," and dropped into Marshall's still-rising "hotel" at Lower Geyser Basin. Here Wheeler probably mailed another article to the Deer Lodge newspaper, and then apparently spent numerous days touring the park but probably not with George Marshall. Instead, he seems to have struck out on his own, probably riding a horse rented from Mr. Marshall. At Old Faithful, he met Secretary of the Interior Carl Schurz and the many military members of that party, accompanying them around Upper Basin where they saw many of the largest geysers in eruption.[174]

If Marshall and Goff were not already convinced that the park roads were problematic for stagecoaches and their visitors, this trip underscored it for them. Mr. Wheeler used his September 3 article to denounce Superintendent Norris thoroughly for his roadwork in Yellowstone, and he also noted that Secretary of the Interior Schurz along with many of his military attaché were angry about it too (he probably added to their anger by purposely stirring them up). Wheeler and Schurz were particularly upset about Norris's "high road," which was the superintendent's new shortcut between the park's west entrance and Marshall's Hotel. Wheeler no doubt heard George Marshall "venting" about the park's roads while the two of them were riding together, and the newspaperman took that to heart, reporting some of the roadwork that Marshall and Goff had voluntarily funded in order to improve their company's operating problems:

Messrs. Marshall & Goff have spent more money in constructing a first-class wagon road from Henry's Lake toward the Geyser Basins than Col. Norris has yet spent cutting a road over
the mountain. They [Marshall and Goff] have graded all sidling
places and cleared all obstructions from the road for twenty-five
miles and built nine bridges from twenty to sixty feet in length,
all of which should be paid for [reimbursed] from the National
Park improvement fund.

Apparently Superintendent Norris received this message, because the
partners also sent a letter about it to the Virginia City *Madisonian* announcing that Norris "has agreed to pay for the changes of grade which we have
made in the roads through the Park."[175] As we shall see in Chapter Six,
Marshall & Goff would not be the last private, commercial stage-coachers
to take it upon themselves to improve park roads in Yellowstone.

Another of Marshall's trips during 1880 was one where he chauffeured
the later-legendary stage-traveler Carrie Adell Strahorn and her famous
writer-husband Robert Strahorn into the Park at the very end of the season, just as snow was starting to fall. Carrie Strahorn stated that George
Marshall had no passengers of any kind until October 1, but of course we
know that William Wheeler's trip from Red Rock had occurred in August,
and probably George Marshall transported other passengers, perhaps many
of them, unmentioned by newspapers or other, anecdotal sources. (The
railroad would arrive at Dillon between September 16 and October 5, and
that would give Marshall another possible terminus from which to run if
he wanted to travel that far.) Carrie Strahorn asserted that the Marshall and
Goff Stage Company sent its (and *the*—neither of which was true) first public conveyance into Yellowstone National Park on the morning of October
1, 1880, with Marshall himself as driver.[176] Mr. Marshall picked up Carrie
and her husband Robert in Virginia City to drive them through Madison
Valley via Raynolds Pass to Henry's Lake and the park's west-entrance road.
Marshall, who was running his short-lived stage-operation from the primitive hotel he had just built on Firehole River in Lower Geyser Basin, was
newly serving as the second link in the Strahorns' trip from the railhead.[177]

Carrie and Robert Strahorn disembarked from the Utah & Northern
Railway at Red Rock, Montana, and rode a Gilmer and Salisbury stage-

coach one hundred miles to Virginia City, via the slowly emerging town of Dillon and the few ranches that eventually became the towns of Twin Bridges and Alder. Carrie Strahorn was understandably apprehensive about the wildness of the country and the late time of year. "The dear ones at home were in constant fear of our falling into the hands of Indians," she wrote, "or that we would starve or freeze, or a thousand other things that can arise in an anxious parent's heart." George Marshall drove the Stra- horns to Yellowstone's west entrance and on to Marshall's Hotel, where they spent a week touring the Park with him on extremely primitive roads.

While these late-season but nevertheless first-known, Yellowstone stage- coach-tourists were touring the Park, Gilmer & Salisbury continued car- rying its passengers from the new railhead at Dillon—so far Montana's

A Charles M. Russell pen-and-ink drawing of a "runaway stagecoach" having a difficult time on old-style, corduroy road, which appeared in Car- rie Adell Strahorn's classic book *Fifteen Thousand Miles by Stage* (1915).

only railroad—to Virginia City, to Helena and Bozeman, and to numerous other places in Montana. Even as the Strahorns left the Park many days later—retracing their steps back to Virginia City to likely ride a G&S coach back to the terminus—the summer season in Yellowstone was already over and snow was falling in its higher elevations. Thus, the Park's long history of hosting tourists from faraway places *only in the summer* (visitors of that day usually did not come in winter; only local and regional folks did that) had arguably begun that year with the Strahorns. A few months later (in early 1881), Robert Strahorn could write:

> A fast line of first-class Concord Coaches was established late last season by Messrs. Salisbury & Co., and G.W. Marshall, between Dillon, the present terminus of the Utah & Northern Branch of the Union Pacific Railway, and the Lower Geyser Basin via Virginia City, Montana, and the same will be operated tri-weekly during the tourist season of 1881. G.W. Marshall is also prepared to carry tourists by carriage or saddle train from his hotel in Lower Geyser Basin, to any part of the Park, and… furnish entertainment, tents, bedding, etc., to parties making such trips at rates given below.[178]

Because Gilmer & Salisbury's mail-contract, as subcontracted to George Marshall, had suddenly become a year-round and daily one, the winter of 1880-1881 now entered the Yellowstone story as both a horror-story and a convenient transition from the Marshall & Goff Company to the Bassett brothers' major contributions to stagecoaching in Yellowstone, which began in the summer of 1881.

But first came the winter of 1880-1881. Winter in the Yellowstone country is today and was then a time when summer jobs vanished, and winter jobs became few and hard to find. Many residents of Montana, Idaho, and Wyoming simply waited out the winter trying to stay warm, while a few lucky residents worked at the small number of available year-round jobs. And during this particular winter, two men named William Henry Bassett and Ernest Knight Bassett got lucky (if "lucky" was the appropriate word) when they discovered that George Marshall was the subcontractor for Gilmer & Salisbury's mail route into Yellowstone's west entrance, and that he was hiring winter mailmen who were also stage-drivers. At ages twenty-two and nineteen respectively, these two men were young and tough, and they would soon need both of those characteristics and more.[179]

By December 1, 1880, William Henry Bassett and at least one other man were snowed in at Lower Geyser Basin, then called "Fire Hole Basin," and no doubt holed up at Marshall's Hotel, the only real building there, which was also now serving as a mail-station in Yellowstone Park. It took ten or twelve days for the storm to lift, so that he and the other man could take three horses and "snow shoes"[180] and travel west for more than twelve miles across Madison Plateau on Superintendent Norris's new road to the Riverside mail-station. They arrived later that day and spent the night at the station. George Marshall came in the following day from Henry's Lake with two other men and fifteen horses. He told them that he had spent six days on the road to cover only thirty miles. Marshall then ordered William "to start out the following morning on horseback" for Henry's Lake mail-station. "I objected," wrote William, "and told him I thought it impossible for a horse to get through, and asked for a pair of snowshoes." At that, Marshall became angry and said that he would not send William if he could not be sure that William could reach the lake safely.

On the following morning, December 16, William started out with the best horse they had, but he had not traveled ten miles before the animal was unable to carry him farther, due to deep snow. Putting on his skis and leading the horse along the South Fork of Madison River, William reached "some haystacks on the prairie" after dark. Entirely worn out, he took his saddle blankets and crawled into a haystack for warmth and to temporarily rest. Instead, exhausted, he fell asleep and did not awake until morning, discovering then that his feet had been badly frost-bitten. On the following morning he started out again on the horse, "but only succeeded in traveling one mile that day, as the snow was so deep (about three feet on the level) that it was impossible for a horse to travel." Toward sunset, William found himself in a canyon, and so gathered some wood, built a fire, and slept without waking all night. The next morning, he noticed that his feet were frost-bitten and swollen even worse: "I dare[d] not take off my boots to look at my feet, for fear I could not get them on again." Discovering that his horse "was good for nothing," he "started him back to the hay" and continued on skis across Targhee Pass, figuring that he could make Henry's Lake mail-station, still fifteen miles away, by nightfall. Reaching the frozen lake, he started across the snow-covered ice to shorten the distance but broke through the ice when partway across. "I got out," he wrote, "only by hard scrambling, and was then on the ice wet and freezing." The lake had two feet of soft snow on top of its ice, so he again could hardly walk and ski. Spotting the mail station far away on the opposite shore, he attracted the attention of a stock-tender there by swinging his hat before falling down, exhausted and unable to take another step. The stock-tender "carried and pushed me in on snow shoes, and took good care of me."[181]

William Henry Bassett was in dire shape, and he soon would get worse. During three days and two nights, he had been without a single mouthful of food or water, and had eaten snow until his throat was so raw that he was unable to consume a full meal for several days afterward. He treated his feet with arnica, but the other mailmen feared he would lose at least his toes and perhaps his entire foot if he did not reach Virginia City to receive treatment. Receiving word that a company team of horses pulling a southbound sleigh was only eighteen miles away from Henry's Lake, William determined to start for it on skis in company with two other mail carriers. His feet were so raw and sore that he could hardly lift them, but somehow, he made the trip to the next mail station. The following morning, he was unable to walk a single step, so the others carried him to the sleigh. He told the rest of the story as follows:

> That day, on the prairie, a terrific snowstorm came up, the wind being in our faces. We had to make eight miles before dark, and it was then sundown. We knew that unless we did make the station before dark, the chances were that we would never get there. The sleighing was bad on account of there being so many rocks; but I took the whip and then away we went at breakneck speed. We struck a rock and broke one runner in a number of pieces. Fortunately, we happened to have sixty feet of rope with us with which we tied up the runner, and away we went again, and arrived at the station at dark. I froze again on that trip, my hands, feet and chin. My eyes were frozen shut most all the time during our fast driving against the blinding snow. We had a hard time coming the balance of the way, but not so hard as that which I have mentioned. I was in bed in the wagon [for]

the last thirty-five miles. The doctor does not know yet but that I will lose my big toe on the right foot; but pronounces the rest of my fingers and toes safe. The place ["Fire Hole Basin"] where I was [first] on foot is 100 miles from here [Virginia City], and no persons live there except the men at mail stations, which are fifteen miles apart, except at that one place [Riverside to Henry's Lake], and it is a thirty-mile station.[182]

William's brother Ernest Knight Bassett was also working for George Marshall that winter, and he too left a letter about his experiences. He and "Frank Furgenson" departed from what was probably the mail station at Marshall's Hotel one cold, snowy morning in late February of 1881, riding two saddle horses, pulling another horse, and heading north with the mail to Mammoth Hot Springs. With two and a half feet of snow on the ground and the most primitive of roads, they found the going difficult. "By night after a hard struggle," he wrote, "we made Gibbon Station (at present Norris Campground, probably near where Solfatara Creek runs into Gibbon River), a distance of 25 miles." It snowed eighteen more inches after they arrived, and they soon decided that "we could never get the horses out of there in winter." Realizing also that they were low on provisions and could conceivably starve to death if they did not get out of there, they made a crude pair of web snowshoes from pine saplings to add to the single pair that Frank had with him. On the following morning, they left on snowshoes carrying the mail sack and a bag of biscuits (their only food), probably leaving the horses in the mail station's barn. "The snow was so soft," wrote Ernest," that we sank to our knees with our [snow] shoes on." With no station to sleep in between them and Mammoth, they knew they had to make the entire distance of more than twenty miles. "After working all day and nearly killing ourselves," he noted, "we got a distance of 8 miles when we dropped down with fatigue."[183]

Somehow the men made it to Mammoth, where they found beds and warmth. Unfortunately, two pages of Ernest's handwritten letter are missing today, so we do not know the rest of his story as he and Frank traveled north to Bozeman, and then west to Ennis and Virginia City. But we know from the end of his letter, reproduced below, that he suffered badly on the way there. While still a day out from Virginia City he was unable to speak above a whisper; as soon as my feet got warm, they began to pain me, so taking off my boots [I found that] my feet were frozen badly. I suffered terribly that night with them several days and they came back [recovered some circulation] where I suffered a good deal. I have got here [Virginia City] at last and am not well yet. My neck is swelled some on the outside. Rheumatism bothers [me] so that I cannot walk very well sometimes.[184]

Ernest Bassett also stated in this letter that he had been working for George Marshall as a mail carrier for "nearly 8 months," so that tells us that at least he of the six[185] Bassett Brothers did not participate in the family's transportation business at Beaver Canyon during the summer of 1880. And it likely confirms the Bassett descendants' assertion that the Bassett Brothers stage line did not even begin running stagecoach tours to Yellowstone from BC until the summer of 1881.[186]

George Marshall's mail contract was taken away from him by the fall of 1880 as an early casualty of the star route, mail-fraud scandals. He continued to operate his primitive stage line for a while in 1881. As an example of his early 1881 operations, we find the following snippet in the Helena *Independent* newspaper during mid-May of 1881, when patches of snow remained on the ground in this part of southwestern Montana:

Mr. G.W. Marshall, proprietor of the National Park stage line, who was in the city last week, informs us that he is already running stock to Riverside, and next week will be running to Fire Hole Basin. It will be at least one month later before stock can be run to the Mammoth Hot Springs. This will be of interest to those who intend [on] visiting the geysers, and establishes the fact that Virginia City is by [far] the most suitable outfitting point for tourists to the National Park, as the wonders of geyser-land are accessible from this point at least one month earlier in the season than they are from any other.[187]

This paragraph, published originally in the *Madisonian* of Virginia City, made it clear that Virginia City was trying to boost its competitive status against Bozeman as the best outfitting point for Yellowstone National Park. George Marshall abandoned his stage line by 1882, yielding to the greater resources of the Bassett Brothers at Beaver Canyon, Idaho, and concentrating instead on running his Marshall's Hotel within Yellowstone.[188] After all, Marshall was only one man, and the Bassett Brothers numbered six men, who were backed up by their father's money in Salt Lake City.

Meanwhile, one Francis "Frank" Bassett of Salt Lake City had moved to Beaver Canyon in 1880, working first at odd jobs. On October 11, 1880, he was appointed postmaster there. That fortunate opportunity gave him longevity to aid his brothers in the family's suddenly burgeoning plans to run stagecoaches to and into Yellowstone National Park from the west.[189]

The Bassett stagecoaching operation—known first as "Yellowstone National Park Stage Line," which quickly was eclipsed by the informal name Bassett Brothers Stage Line and changed later to the Union Pacific Stage Line—would last for nearly twenty years, providing employment and adventure for the brothers, their wives, their children, and their other relatives. We turn to it in the next chapter.

A Welsh tourist named Thomas Henry Thomas, who traveled to Yellowstone in September and October of 1884, saw at least one of the Bassett Brothers' stagecoaches at Marshall's Hotel. Although not riding with them, Thomas left us this woodcut-drawing of their four-horse coach and its driver with three passengers, and stated: "From the west enters Bassett's stage from Beaver Cañon, about one hundred miles away." Thomas, "Yellowstone Park Illustrated," *The Graphic* (New York).

CHAPTER SIX

Enroute to the "Eden of America" with the Bassett Brothers

Trailblazing Fleet-Stagecoaching to Yellowstone National Park

"These gentlemen are making arrangements for running a line of spring wagons between Beaver Canyon and the National Park."—*Blackfoot* (ID) *Register*, July 16, 1881.

With the Utah & Northern Railway now constructed beyond Dillon, Montana and on its way to Butte, stagecoaching to the national park could begin in earnest, and the Bassett Brothers of Beaver Canyon, Idaho were already becoming the first persons to actually utilize a fleet of vehicles for travel to and in Yellowstone, even though their trips originated from one hundred miles to the west of the already-famous Park.[190] The Bassetts' complex story, involving their "Yellowstone National Park Stage Line," later called simply the "Bassett Brothers, Beaver Canyon," has been little known until now, and telling it requires that we back up a bit.

In the spring of 1881, the new stagecoach travel to Virginia City that began in late 1880 from the recent rail-terminuses at Red Rock and Dillon was continuing. The gold-mining town of Virginia City[191]—where so many Montanans had begun their lives in the Territory eighteen years earlier—suddenly found itself in a two-year period of competing with the Bassett Brothers of Beaver Canyon, Idaho, to attract tourists to Yellowstone National Park from the Park's west side. Both routes had Henry's Lake, Idaho in common. A Helena newspaper took the opportunity to promote Virginia City as "the most suitable outfitting point for tourists to the National Park."[192] Later, Bozeman would become yet another competitor in the contest for trips to Yellowstone, but for now it was VC versus the Bassett Brothers.

Both routes to Yellowstone had advantages and disadvantages. The route from Beaver Canyon east through Idaho to Henry's Lake was shorter in distance than the Virginia City route.[193] The BC route required only about sixty-five or seventy miles of stagecoaching to reach Henry's Lake, and it was also closer to the actual geysers, a selling point that was not lost on BC proponents. In contrast, the Virginia City route required 119 miles of stagecoaching to Henry's Lake, if Dillon was the railhead; if the railhead was Red Rock, the distance increased by twenty-five miles, *unless* the travelers used the primitive Centennial Valley route and did not go to Virginia City. But the VC route was flatter (an asset in bad weather), the roads were better (at least to Henry's Lake), and it had the advantage of passing through a good town (Virginia City) where visitors could obtain supplies and other comforts at cheaper prices. The VC route also had the advantage of flexibility—travelers had the added option of visiting Bozeman, Montana, and then going to Yellowstone's north entrance (instead of the west entrance), if they did not mind the much farther staging distance of about 145 miles beyond Virginia City to the Park at the recently-founded (1880) town of Gardiner, Montana. The competing towns of BC and VC were of course represented on the ground by the stagecoaching Bassett Brothers for Beaver Canyon and by the Gilmer & Salisbury Company and its Yellowstone subcontractor Marshall & Goff Stage Company for Virginia City. Gilmer & Salisbury had headquarters all over Montana, but since 1869, they had operated in the Virginia City area from Pollinger/Gaffney (later called Salisbury), which was then located two miles southeast of today's Twin Bridges, Montana.[194]

One of the earliest moves by the Bassett Brothers was to run the following item in a Salt Lake City newspaper. It resembled a news item but was probably a paid advertisement:

As this is the finest season in the year for visiting Yellowstone National Park, tourists naturally want to know the best, cheapest[,] and most direct route to that famous resort, and *The Tribune* takes pleasure in informing them. Travelers can take the comfortable cars of the Utah & Northern at Ogden for Beaver Canyon, where connection can be made with Bassett Bros' through line to the Yellowstone. This line is composed of covered light spring wagons with the best of teams, and passes over one of the finest roads in the country. This route is 150 miles shorter than by Virginia [City] and the fare is $28 less than by that place. Experienced drivers are furnished and passengers are put through as quick time. Any further information desired will be promptly furnished by addressing Bassett Bros, Beaver Canyon, Idaho.[195]

But for now, the competition between Beaver Canyon and Virginia City was continuing and would continue for a couple more years, as was the competition between Bozeman, Montana, and Virginia City.

An 1882 Trip That Presaged the End of Commercial Competition Between Bozeman and Virginia City.

The commercial competition between Bozeman and Virginia City involving Yellowstone National Park lasted only about four years (from late 1879 to late 1883). A party who sided with Bozeman over Virginia City and who announced it publicly was the 1882 party known as the Helena Delegation of the Omaha Board of Trade. Near Bozeman, the Northern Pacific Railroad began building a tunnel through the high ridge at Bozeman Pass in 1881, in anticipation of their rails reaching it sometime in mid-summer of 1883. In August of 1882, workers on the east side of the Bozeman Tunnel at what would become the tiny settlement of Muir City, Montana, had been working on the tunnel "for over a year" when the party of a Mr. Fitch, editor of Nebraska's *Omaha Bee*, discussed those efforts as he passed the settlement in private wagons. Calling Bozeman "the proper outfitting post for excursionists who visit the Yellowstone Park" even though he spent little time there, Mr. Fitch and his party of eight had traveled to Butte on the Utah & Northern Railway before engaging two drivers and a cook to proceed in wagons to Helena and then Bozeman. From his comment, it was clear whom Fitch was siding with in the ongoing battle between Bozeman and Virginia City.

The party rode eighteen hours in a Gilmer & Salisbury stagecoach from Butte to Helena. After claiming that the trip was "not so bad as one might think," Mr. Fitch admitted that the journey evoked "the dread and fear of overturning the coach and rolling down virtue into the deep chasm below with jolts, jams, and bruises to which a ride over the rocky roads to Dublin would not have furnished a circumstance." That reference to an 1860s Irish song made it appear that Montana roads were scarier than those of Ireland, but Fitch thought the trip worth it because of the "vast expanse" of the country and its beauty: "Objects which appear to be only within 'rifle shot' of you, will continue to appear so for a day's drive." In Bozeman, they met photographer Henry Bird Calfee, who showed them many of his photographs of the new Yellowstone National Park.

But by the time Mr. Fitch's party came to Montana, Bozeman was on its way to winning the battle with Virginia City, and when the Northern Pacific Railroad arrived a year later, Bozeman did win. One factor was that Bozeman sprawled larger than Virginia City. But the main factor was that Bozeman's Northern Pacific Railroad was simply closer to Yellowstone than was the Utah & Northern, which served Virginia City. Like most visitors, Fitch and his party were amazed by the wonders of the Yellowstone, and they spent more than a week there.[196] But the important factor here was that the competition for Yellowstone between Virginia City and Bozeman was over, and Bozeman had won.

An 1881 party from Massachusetts apparently rented supplies from the Bassetts at Beaver Canyon but for some reason chose to ride northward by coach and horse to Virginia City, rather than east to Henry's Lake with the Bassetts. The railroad had reached Dillon, Montana on September 16, 1880, and was just south of Butte when this party arrived, so it is a mystery why they did not continue on the train to Dillon. Perhaps they had been told that supplies were not as available or as good there, or perhaps they feared getting lost. But they got off the train at Beaver Canyon, "where provisions can be bought," they noted, "horses, wagons, and a guide secured, and the park entered in less than three days' ride from the railroad." Probably they rented their "outfit"[197] from the Bassett Brothers at BC, because those pioneers were the only ones doing it there, and it consisted of "a dozen saddle horses and two emigrant wagons packed with tents, luggage and provisions." They also secured a guide but for some reason then rode north rather than east, and were thus forced to choose between a "drag at the snail's pace of an emigrant train, or settle down to the unaccustomed business of making 25 miles a day in the saddle."

They had the capacity to do either, but at least for this first portion of the trip, they selected the slower, emigrant method as safer and not as jarring. "Virginia City has given us its 'freedom' during our stay," said their account, "the editor, doctor, clergymen and leading businessmen dispensing a painstaking hospitality peculiarly hearty and western." Led by the former pioneer of Henry's Lake Gilman Sawtell ("a model frontiersman and westernized Yankee boy from Groton, Mass., now over 50 years old"), the party traveled over Targhee Pass and into the park, complaining fiercely about Superintendent Norris's new, high road and indicting him for it thoroughly. Then they spent weeks in Yellowstone, opining copiously about it and stating that Dame Nature was "beyond civilization now and a freakish gypsy who cuts the maddest pranks and revels in the barbaric glory of unstinted ornamentation." The national park offered to them "a splendor and deli-cacy of coloring that bewilders and intoxicates," which was incredibly "rich in the marvelous."[198]

A large party of citizens going to Yellowstone from Bannack, Montana utilized the Virginia City route in 1882. This party, led by Montana ranch-er Amede Bessette through Dillon and Salisbury, numbered twenty by the time the group reached that latter stage-stop, and Bessette, no doubt the au-thor, titled both his pseudonym and his account as "Geyserland." Traveling leisurely so that they could hunt and fish, the party reached Lower Geyser Basin in eight days. The next morning, they received a report in camp that "Hell's Half Acre" (Excelsior Geyser) was "in full blast, and the grandest scene in the park," so they hastened to the spot and arrived there at ten a.m. "To see it go off," wrote Bessette, "sending pebbles and large stones weigh-ing forty to fifty pounds, with its hot water and steam to a height of at least seventy-five feet, is wonderfully grand." Using a popular misconception, he added that "the eruptions of this geyser are always best in the forenoon, in the afternoon becoming low and feeble." They stayed for four hours, eating lunch there too.[199]

Their wagon broke down on the way to Old Faithful, and, apparently leaving men to fix it, they walked the rest of the way to Upper Geyser Basin, where they saw geysers erupting. With the wagon repaired and brought up to them, they took the park's very primitive trail east to Yellowstone Lake, a rough route that not many travelers would use until it was improved into a road in late 1891. After examining the colorful mud-pots and the Fish-ing Cone hot-spring and spending some time fishing in Yellowstone Lake, they proceeded along the northern lakeshore and down Yellowstone River to Mud Volcano. Then they went to Canyon with the comment that "our wagons were the first to pass over the new road to the Falls," probably a reference to Superintendent Norris's roadwork of that year along the river. Just before reaching Mammoth Hot Springs, Mr. Bessette noted that "we had a narrow escape from being licked up by a prairie fire." This was likely a reference to the 1882 fire in and around the Hoodoos and Golden Gate Canyon. The party left the Park through the north entrance and returned to Bannack via Bozeman, Sheridan, Montana, and Virginia City.[200]

Meanwhile, back at Beaver Canyon, Idaho, the Bassett Brothers had reached the point in their endeavors where they were quickly beginning to occupy a central role in the history of what would much later be called the "Island Park" region. Six months after Carrie and Robert Strahorn went to Yellowstone by stagecoach from Virginia City, the town of Beaver Canyon in the summer of 1881 suddenly went "center stage" by featuring its own trips to the Park, through eastern Idaho rather than through Montana via Virginia City. This happened because of the six Bassetts, at least two of whom—as we encountered earlier—previously worked for George Marshall, and one of them was likely still working for him. Those two Bassetts drove the wagon-mail that winter into the west side of the park for George Marshall's already-dying freight line to the mail stations that extended northwest to Virginia City and northeast through the park. To understand the Bassett Brothers' operations, which lasted at least eighteen years, we must first understand the small town of Beaver Canyon, Idaho.

As a growing town, it was short-lived, because even as the U&N Railway officially established its station there on September 16, 1879, tracklayers were continuing in their efforts to reach today's Lima ("Spring Hill"), Montana 30.3 miles to the north, and then Red Rock, 50.6 miles farther to the north. Beaver Canyon was thus quickly left in the position of being a mere station on the line rather than being the railroad's continuing terminus, and of course that stifled its growth. Red Rock initially became the largest of those three places, because of the relatively long time that the terminus remained there, but today Red Rock has vanished, Lima[201] remains only in a smaller form, and Beaver Canyon, which was moved four miles south in 1897, has disappeared and its descendant, small town is known as Spencer, Idaho.[202]

But the original Beaver Canyon survived as a tiny but tenacious hamlet for more than seventeen years, largely if not completely because of the Bassett Brothers. Regardless of the fact that the tracklayers were already moving northward, two other men seem to have begun setting up a hotel in late 1879, for the *Logan* (UT) *Leader* reported on January 1, 1880 that "a good hotel" called the "Corinne House" was in place or being put into place at Beaver Canyon by proprietor C.L. Bristol and his clerk James Wells.[203] And in August of 1880, in what was probably the earliest description of the more complete town, a correspondent for the *Blackfoot Register*, wrote the following:

> Leaving Red Rock at 1 p.m., on our return [from Montana], a
> ride of two hours brought us to the foot of Beaver Canyon, and

to the station of the same name. The scenery down this canyon, a distance of about ten miles, is grand. The tall pine trees, the huge rocks rising on either side, with first on one side and then on the other, a sparkling stream of water, wending its way down over the rocks and falls, make it picturesque and beautiful.[204]

The article noted that the town's three sawmills were owned by W.T. Van Noy, David Stoddard, and W.N. Thomas, and each of them employed from twenty to twenty-five men who were kept busy cutting timber and sawing. "The agent of the company, Mr. Frank Bassett, has about all he can attend to in looking after the company's interests," continued the article, which did not say whether Bassett worked for one of the sawmills or a shipping company (he would not obtain his job as postmaster until October). However, this year and this article made it clear that Francis Augustus "Frank" Bassett, aged twenty-four, was indeed established at Beaver Canyon in the summer of 1880.

Those early residents were already discovering that winters in Beaver Canyon could and would be very difficult. In early 1880, this hamlet at the junction of Beaver Creek and Stoddard Creek was still trying to get started, and the weather at that high elevation did not make getting through the upcoming winter nor the following one easy. Beginning April 14-15, 1880, deep snow from a late-season storm "blockaded" the tracks, delaying passengers, mail, and a great deal of freight, and of course shutting down construction-progress, as U&N surveyors, graders, and tracklayers were attempting to reach Red Rock. No supplies left Beaver Canyon northward for more than a week. The snowstorm was "the heaviest ever known at this season of the year," wrote settler B.F. White, who later served as governor of Idaho. "Being accompanied by heavy winds, it drifted badly, and the stages have been unable to get through on the old stage road, else the mails and passengers would have been moved in that way." Freight piled up at Beaver Canyon.[205] A storm struck again on the following December 29, and on January 1, 1881, snow once more blockaded the railroad at China Point. The *Blackfoot Register* noted that there were twenty or thirty miles of country "in that vicinity" that for winter weather "is as bad as can be found anywhere."

It is where the wind blows continually and very hard too, and there are several places where the road is obliged to run through cuts from three to five feet deep, which, with half an inch of snow will sometimes drift them full to the top. The snow fall was like sleet, and as it froze, and being mixed with the sand, formed ice that snow plows would have no effect upon. [Officials] Knowing the condition of things, three engines, one with the snow plow attached, and [additional plows] were started out from Beaver Canyon to break the road for the southbound passenger train, but were stalled near China Point.[206]

After a couple of difficult hours, two more engines started for the spot. When they reached High Bridge, the ice was so thick that it suddenly broke the plow, throwing it under the train's wheels and derailing the entire engine, which was instantly demolished. The three trainmen were mixed up in the debris, each certain when he "came to" that he was nearly dead and each assuming that the other two men *were* dead. But somehow all three men survived, bearing bruises, scratches, broken ribs, and head-contusions.

Following these difficult winters, Beaver Canyon began to rollick as a logging camp in the summer of 1881, located mostly on the east side of the tracks. "The sawmills of W.N. Thomas, W.T. Van Noy, and D. Stoddard are running at their full capacity," declared the *Blackfoot Register*, in what was probably a reference to the foundry-owner and later storekeeper for whom Stoddard Creek was named, and whose grisly murder we shall describe later. The account depicted the village at this early time:

The construction of the U&N.R.R. is using immense quantities of timber, ninety percent of which is procured at Beaver Canyon. A number of men are kept constantly employed loading cars, and it is seldom that a freight train passing either way... does not take from two to six cars of lumber...For the week ending July 2, the mill of W.N. Thomas, working ten hours per day, with five hours delay for [a] filing saw, cut 75,000 feet of lumber, the actual working time being fifty-five hours[,] nearly fifteen hundred feet per hour.

"Great quantities of lumber are shipped from here," agreed Charles Savage, a Salt Lake City photographer who would take pictures of Yellowstone three years later.[207] A description of the town's topography from a few years later and a Salt Lake newspaper was and is worth quoting:

> Beaver cañon, just this [south] side of the divide, is well worth seeing; huge, precipitous cliffs overhang the train on either side; giant boulders poised against one wall of the cañon seem to be about to fall. The rock where exposed to the atmosphere for a long time is nearly of the color of the granite used in the construction of the public buildings in Chicago. In some places[,] heaps of small broken rock[s] cover the inclined wall of the cañon, resting one upon another; they look like they were dumped down from behind the hill.[208]

The railroad was still "getting its feet on the ground" and thus was the victim of numerous track-and-rail washouts during the high-water spring of 1881, which temporarily isolated Beaver Canyon from the railroad's southern points. Because of the washouts and people running out of food, explained the *Dillon Tribune* on May 14, "it became necessary for the Beaver Canyon people to come up to Dillon and lay in a supply sufficient to meet their wants until the road is repaired." Around twenty-five people rode a special train north for that purpose.[209] When Mary Richards arrived during the following summer, the town—then consisting of a dozen houses, two saloons, and a water tank—had been supplemented by a village well, the water from which was "clear and cool." "We sent the big tin pail at the rope's end," she wrote, "many times down for coolness and consolation during our days of hard thinking and labor."[210]

By most accounts, Beaver Canyon, Idaho was rough but somewhat paradisiacal. One of the best descriptions of the northbound trip to this town splashed onto the front page of the *Ogden Daily Herald* with colorful fervor that today's northbound travelers on U.S. Interstate 15 can appreciate:

> After passing Market Lake the country is a barren desert upon which nothing but stunted sagebrush grows, between which lava beds rear their black forms in a monotonous sameness. Far away

in the east the Teton Mountains can be seen over the Snake
River settlements and over the rolling hills. These mountains
are very high and have their base in a ten-by-twenty-mile valley
called the Teton Basin. From the summit of these mountains,
which is covered over with snow all the year round, in many
places 100 feet deep, four peaks, pyramid-shaped, rear their
snow-mounted heights to the sky. The highest of these peaks,
which appears nearly perpendicular on the north side, can safely
be estimated to rise 4,000 feet…The valley below is very beautiful in summer clothed as it is with an abundance of grass. It is
inhabited by mountaineers who obtain a living by raising cattle.
I am told by good authority that round about in that region
a large number of refugees from justice, escaped convicts and
runaway soldiers also make their solitary dwelling-place. These
are much dreaded by settlers along the Snake River Valley, from
whom they frequently steal cattle and horses. Having passed
over the dreary lava desert, we arrive in Beaver Canyon, a perfect gem of beauty. The traveler cannot help being refreshed as
he stands upon the platform while the train winds [on] up its
crooked pathway. The end [of the track] is soon reached and
then we are on the summit of the Rocky Mountains…Com-
ing back to Beaver Canyon, we have a prosperous camp, which
employs between three and five hundred men, mostly in the
lumber business.[211]

Meanwhile, the summer of 1882 was the second season in which five of
the six Bassett Brothers of Beaver Canyon were gearing up to make money
by taking tourists to Yellowstone National Park in their growing fleet of
stagecoaches and wagons. (By late July, however the number of brothers
was down to four, when Francis "Frank" Bassett moved to Butte.)[212] Their
available road ran east and then north to Henry's Lake for sixty-five miles
across relatively flat Idaho country that was located south of the Continental Divide's Centennial Mountains. The Bassetts started their plans in
March by partnering with a man named Swift to open the Beaver Canyon Saloon, wherein they immediately sold liquors and cigars and used the
building to set up their offices to plan for summer trips. A website erected

by descendants of the Bassetts has stated that they obtained a contract from the Union Pacific Railroad for this endeavor, but no such contract has been found involving them and either the UPRR or the Utah & Northern Railway.[213] Perhaps the contract came later, sometime after the U&N was sold to the UPRR. Or perhaps not, because no formal contract would have been required for the Bassetts to take people to Yellowstone; all that would have been necessary is that the Railway agree to discharge passengers at Beaver Canyon, which was one of its official stations anyway, to which and from which train-tickets were routinely sold.

The Bassett brothers hailed originally from Salt Lake City, where their father Charles Henry Bassett, Sr. had settled by 1851.[214] He or his son Charles Henry II ran a grocery-and-dry-goods store in 1868, partnering with Bolliver Roberts at the Mormon capital, and his other children appear to have gradually joined the Mormons' ongoing northward movements to colonize Idaho Territory. By the summer of 1881, many of Charles Henry Bassett's male children had followed the Utah & Northern Railway northward into Idaho, such that brothers Charles "Jule" Julius (1851-1918), who would spearhead the Brothers' operation and work it for the longest time; Charles Henry II (1854-1940); Francis Augustus (1857-1919); William Henry (1858-1929), a half-brother; Ernest Knight (1861-1944), a half-brother; and Fred Clayton Bassett (1865-1946) were all living in Beaver Canyon.[215] Not all of them would work every year, and only Charles Julius would stick with the operation all the way through 1898. But they were to a man looking for work and probably adventure, and carrying potential tourists to Yellowstone National Park seemed like it might fill both bills. After all, most if not all of the brothers had not seen Yellowstone either.

Writer William Sturgis wrote humorously of the number of Bassett Brothers in his 1884 book about Yellowstone entitled *New Songs of Seven...A Record of a Journey in Wonderland*. "[Here] We find more Bassett Bros.," wrote Sturgis. "It is said that there are forty-two of them and no end of women and babies."[216] That of course was a joke, poking fun at the Mormons' polygamous marriages and families in Salt Lake City, from whence the Brothers hailed. The Bassetts took Sturgis's party to Yellowstone in 1884, so we will come back to that trip.

The Brothers' plans made the newspapers on July 16, 1881. Most Utah, Idaho, and Montana papers were closely following the northward progress

of the Utah & Northern Railway, and in the boosteristic style of newspapers everywhere, the *Blackfoot* (Idaho) *Register* assured its readers that "Bassett Brothers at the Beaver Canyon saloon are doing a good business." The
editor then announced:

> These gentlemen are making arrangements for running a line of
> spring wagons between Beaver Canyon and the National Park.
> The distance is only 110 miles and ninety miles of the road is as
> good as can be found anywhere in the country. They will make
> the trip in three days. The fare will be twenty-five dollars for the
> round trip to what is known as the Lower Geyser basin. They
> will have their team[s] ready in a short time and be prepared to
> convey any number of passengers.[217]

That number could only grow, the brothers must have thought. But so far,
no actual trip-accounts for the Bassett Brothers have been found for 1881,
although the indications are that coaches ran.

The name of their company varied through time. During much of the
1880s, they called themselves only "Bassett Brothers, Beaver Canyon." By
1888, their official stationery read "Bassett Brothers proprietors of Yellowstone National Park Stage Line," and that name technically lasted through
at least 1890.[218] But it conflicted with the name of George Wakefield's
much larger stage-line headquartered at Mammoth Hot Springs, so around
1890, Charles Julius Bassett changed his company-name to Union Pacific
Stage Line.[219] Until 1883, there had been no chance of any stage-line being
confused with that of the Bassetts. But in January of 1889, YPA and the
Yellowstone National Park Transportation Company were reincorporated
under that name (YNPTC, spelled out), and at least in theory, began painting that name onto their coaches, so that was probably the reason for the
Bassetts' name-change.[220]

The Bassett Brothers believed that most of their customers would arrive on the railroad from the south, so they also began running advertisements in Salt Lake City newspapers during their first summer of existence.
A long-running ad for their trips to "The Eden of America" appeared in the
Salt Lake Daily Tribune on August 20, 1881.[221] That advertisement, which
also ran in Utah and Idaho newspapers in 1882-1883, announced:

YELLOWSTONE NATIONAL PARK.

The Shortest and Best Route from the Railroad to THE EDEN OF AMERICA.

On and after June 1ˢᵗ, 1882, we shall be prepared to carry all parties from Beaver Cañon, U&N.R.R., to National Park. Light spring wagons, good teams, and smooth road. Good hunting and fishing anywhere on the road. Leave Beaver Cañon every day for Fire Hole Basin. Have experienced drivers, well acquainted with the Park.

FARE TO FIRE HOLE AND RETURN, $25. Parties may return when they desire. This route is 150 miles nearer than by Virginia City, and fare $25 less to same point. Parties wishing private conveyances for any period of time will be accommodated by giving timely notice either by letter or telegraph. For further information address: BASSETT BROS., Beaver Cañon, Idaho.[222]

So well circulated was this advertisement during the summer of 1882 that one contemporary journalist (known only as "H.") felt the need to emphasize that this and other published descriptions and advertisements for and of Yellowstone Park's wonders were not exaggerated or "overdrawn." He assured his readers that "Strahorn's simple Wonderland and Bassett Brothers' Eden of America are not purely imaginative."[223]

Returning to that first summer, Salt Lake photographer Charles Savage planned a train-trip to Montana in late summer of 1881. Gushing about the bountiful produce that he saw at Ogden, Utah, he boarded the U&N there and rode northward to the terminus at Silver Bow, Montana, southwest of Butte. On the way, he passed through Beaver Canyon, where he mentioned that "the Bassett Bros. are making arrangements to take passengers to the Yellowstone National Park from this point." Savage described their stage road to the Park as a fine one, "abounding in game, with plenty of fish in the rivers." He reminded readers that the $25 cost was exclusive of provisions and suggested that customers buy provisions before they traveled because the cost of those necessaries was high in the park. "The proper time for visiting," he noted, "is from June 1ˢᵗ to July 10ᵗʰ and from August 15 to October," because "in July the flies are very troublesome."[224] In a world where much travel depended upon horses, Savage's warning about horse-flies was important advice.

As mentioned, little is known today about the Bassetts' 1881 season, other than for the preceding advertisements and plans. But in April of 1882, the *Salt Lake Herald* carried this notice, which looked like a newspaper article but which was actually an advertisement. It was already touting Beaver Canyon's so-called advantages over the Virginia City route (a smaller variation of the Virginia-City-versus-Bozeman competition), as the brothers were apparently anticipating competition from there:

> The Bassett Brothers, on and after the 1ˢᵗ of June, will be prepared to carry parties from Beaver Canyon on the line of the Utah and Northern, to Yellowstone National Park. They have certainly secured the most direct and accessible route, with good smooth roads, and have also chosen that route which affords the greatest inducements to fishers and hunters. They will leave Beaver Canyon every day for Fire Hole Basin, and have secured experienced and trusty drivers. The energetic young gentlemen very reasonably expect that there will be an increased influx into this wonderland of the world, in which the beauty and grandeur of nature are at the same time most marvelously displayed; and have, therefore, made every preparation. The fare from Beaver Canyon to Fire Hole is but $25; while the route is 150 miles less than by Virginia City, and the fare $25 cheaper. They are prepared also to furnish private conveyance, as per their announcement which appears elsewhere.[225]

But even as the Bassett Brothers began to gear up for the summer's trade in 1882, there were challenges to their business. Winter was rough in early 1882, and a fatality occurred on the railroad tracks. Again, it occurred at China Point. In late March, Harry Lovejoy, a pedestrian who apparently did not have money to buy a train-ticket, was walking on the tracks there when a train approached, and "the wind whirled up the snow so densely that the pedestrian was not observed." The snow plow on the front of the train struck him "and caused the death of the unfortunate wayfaring man." Mr. Lovejoy was from Leadville and was apparently headed for Butte, "as he had shipped his blankets ahead to that destination." To no cynic's surprise, a railroad investigation subsequently exonerated all trainmen and the railroad from blame.[226]

More challenges arose when bandits wrecked a U&N train on April 17 and made off with some of its booty. The purposeful wrecking occurred five miles to the north at the nearby Pleasant Valley station, and eight days later, Sheriff Homer of Oneida County arrested seven men at Beaver Canyon and took them south to Blackfoot, where they were charged and tried for robbing the freight cars. "They were hard-looking customers," proclaimed a Butte newspaper, "and evidently tramps." In early June, the Dillon paper reported that two of the alleged robbers escaped from the jail at Blackfoot: "Charles Reed and William Deavers, alias Ohio Monk…were under sentence," said the editor, "for taking part in the train wrecking at Beaver canyon last April and are said to be desperate characters."[227] Thus at least these two robbers had been convicted, but their recapture after the escape, if it happened, has not been found. The Bassett Brothers were likely familiar with this train-wrecking and pillaging near their town, and they must have briefly worried about whether it would affect their business, if potential customers became afraid to travel. That appeared especially true when it became clear that one of the men initially arrested was Thomas Jackson, the section foreman for the railroad at Beaver Canyon. However, charges against him were soon dismissed.

They need not have worried. Travel up the railroad from Utah was extremely high in 1882, notwithstanding numerous, negative incidents of this type all the way to Butte, Montana. An enormous and unprecedented "inflow of pilgrims" began in March of that year, as people from many states, seeking work, hurried to the now-accessible mines at Butte, Montana, many of them "without capital or secured employment." "Every train leaves Ogden full;" rejoiced *the Semi-Weekly Miner* of Butte, "about one-fourth of its human freight is deposited at Dillon, another one-fourth perhaps at Silver Bow Junction, and the remaining half and sometimes more come[s] to Butte."[228] This claim was a bit exaggerated, because a fair number of Yellowstone passengers disembarked at Beaver Canyon to travel east with the Bassetts to Yellowstone, rather than going on to Dillon to travel by stagecoach a longer distance to the Park's north or west entrances.

It was an exciting summer to be in Idaho and Montana, as the heavily loaded Utah & Northern trains picked up and dropped off passengers
and freight at nearly every station along its 400-mile route. There is evidence that the brothers worked to improve the dirt stage-road east to Camas
Meadows to ready it for the summer's travel, and this was logical, because
they would have tried to accomplish it during the period before the snow
completely melted while the meadows were drying up, and before the tourist season began—namely in May and June. The newspaper at Blackfoot
recorded the activity: "Bassett Bros. have finished their stage road to Camas
Creek, but had to quit on account of mud in the meadows."[229]

The Bassetts' stage-route was long but wonderfully scenic, and besides
Yellowstone, it was one of their best-selling points. Their road, bearing east,
left the railroad at the town of Beaver Canyon, near the spot where Miners' Creek, flowing southwesterly, emptied into Beaver Creek. As an 1883
newspaper reporter explained it, "A few miles from the canyon's mouth is
the starting point of Bassett Brothers' stage-line for the Yellowstone Park,
which is a distance of one hundred miles [to the east]." A later traveler explained that past the town "flows a creek that winds down a valley which
the stage-line follows [for] a few miles before turning directly east toward
the park." Indeed, the Bassetts' road ran up Miners' Creek, over Porcupine
Pass (elevation 7,062 feet), and down West Camas Creek. Where that creek
broke into Camas Meadows—south of Antelope Valley and near present
Steel Creek Campground—views of the Grand Tetons far to the east would
enhance the traveler's experience for many miles, at least on clear days. A
few miles farther, the route reached Indian Springs at Camas Meadows
(near present Kilgore, Idaho, at 25 trip-miles), where lunch ("dinner" in
those days) would often be taken. It then continued through "Sheridan
Valley" (including Sheridan Ridge of present maps) and then Shotgun Valley past a later (1893) hotel on Hotel Creek to George Rea's ranch at Glen
Rea (in early years used by the Bassetts as a camping site; later their people
stayed in Rea's cabins), turning north up Henry's Fork of the Snake River
(at 45 miles), and arriving at Henry's Lake, Idaho (at 65 miles). The Bassetts' road then continued east and ascended Targhee Pass, not by the route
of present U.S. 20 up Howard Creek, but rather by the original road, which
ran up the next drainage north, ascending Targhee Creek.[230]

Some specific details of that Idaho route are known. The Bassett Brothers used a stage station, barn, and corral at Indian Springs and later a stage-station just east of Henry's Lake on lower Targhee Creek, after they or Silas McMinn built it and McMinn assumed its ownership in 1890.[231] After that, an even later hotel at Hotel Creek ("located on a slight elevation above the waters of the north fork of Snake River near [its] junction with Shotgun creek") was built in 1893 by area resident Karl E. Hopf, who, according to the newspapers, was the "manager" of the Arangee Land and Cattle Company.[232] Before then, the Bassetts and their patrons camped at George Rea's ranch using tents and an older building that is gone today. Their mileages were listed on the back of the "Bassett Bros." cards that they handed out to visitors.

Stagecoach travelers on the Bassetts' Idaho route were routinely treated to fields of stunningly beautiful wildflowers—a part of what one writer has called the "Colors of the West"—as were later Monida & Yellowstone tourists so treated as they traveled (after 1897) through Centennial Valley, Montana, located across the mountains in the next valley to the north. Yellow balsamroot bloomed early, and by June 25, it was replaced by yellow mules' ears and white mules' ears (*Wyethia*), purplish lupine, blue camas, red Indian paintbrush, pink geraniums and wild roses, yellow cinquefoil, electric-blue penstemon, white death-camas (a poisonous plant), cream-colored buckwheat, purplish mountain irises and daisy-asters, and the striking, yellow-with-a-red-center gaillardia, which was commonly known as "Indian blanket flower" or "fire-wheel."[233] And the Bassetts' tourists usually also saw dozens of mammals and birds, as has been mentioned.

In an era mostly before running water and indoor toilets, there also had to have been outhouses—many of them—to serve the Bassetts' customers all the way to Yellowstone. The brothers probably installed these themselves, spaced at reasonable intervals, and in many places, bare nature itself was probably used instead. The nation's transition to indoor-plumbing was gradual, slow, and quite variable with regard to rural areas.[234] This author remembers my own mother telling me that her father—aged 75 in 1960—had an aversion to abolishing outhouses in his community of Stillwater, Oklahoma, and did not want those facilities moved indoors. This was an activity that began in his family around 1940, and he fought fruitlessly against it long and hard. As late as the 1960s, many rural, American houses still had outhouses located "out back" of the main dwelling.

The Bassett Brothers modified their personnel and fleet in late July of

1882, because a Blackfoot newspaper column then noted that only four Bassetts were running the operation at Beaver Canyon. The newspaper also stated that the brothers had "disposed of their heavy wagons and are putting on first-class light spring wagons that will carry five passengers besides the driver."[235] It is worth noting that the color of the Bassetts' stagecoaches is today unknown (brown is a good guess), but probably their fleet was a motley combination that was unmodified by them, and which arrived on the railroad "as is" from the Studebaker Brothers Manufacturing Company of South Bend, Indiana.

That same issue of the newspaper noted that the brothers were carrying mail as well as passengers. "Messrs. Bassett Brothers' mail line is in fine running condition," said the editor. "Several distinguished visitors from Europe have gone over it to see the wonders of the great Yellowstone Park," he continued, "and expressed themselves greatly pleased with the attentions of the proprietors as well as of the employees."[236] We shall soon see that one of these European visitors—a Baron from Denmark—would experience such hardships on the park's difficult west-entrance road that notable guide G.L. Henderson would use the Baron's experience to denounce road-building efforts in Yellowstone ten years later, while testifying at congressional hearings.

By August, newspapers were reporting an increase in business. "The traffic" for the Bassett Brothers, said Salt Lake City's *Deseret News*, "has increased so rapidly of late that they have been compelled to put four or five additional coaches on the road."[237] The Blackfoot newspaper stated that at Beaver Canyon "a large number of pleasure seekers arrive here daily and leave for the Yellowstone Park by Bassett Brothers stage-line." "The crowd has been so great," wrote this editor, "that during the past two weeks these popular stage men have been obliged to purchase several new teams in order to get them away."[238]

At the same time that the Bassetts were adding new teams and new vehicles, the people of Dillon, Montana were working on their own direct road to Yellowstone, a route on the opposite (north) side of the Continental Divide through their nearby Centennial Valley,[239] which the Monida & Yellowstone Stage Company would begin using sixteen years later for their stagecoach route to the great park. Already mentioned was the commercial competition that arose in late 1879 between the towns of Beaver Canyon and Virginia City. A variation on that competition was this even

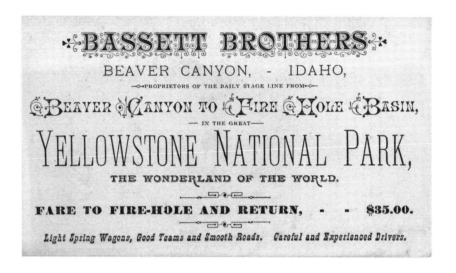

Bassett Brothers advertising card, no date, 1881-1884, office at Beaver Canyon, Idaho. *Jay Lyndes Family Collection, Billings, Montana.*

---

smaller and more short-lived competition that jousted with both the BC proponents and the VC proponents, and it was caused by the new town of Dillon.

Dillon residents had not failed to notice that they, like Beaver Canyon's residents, possessed a shorter, more direct route to Yellowstone's west entrance. That old road (graveled and rough, but passable today) left the U&N railroad at "Spring Hill" (Lima, Montana) or alternatively at Monida, Montana, and traveled east up the Red Rock River on the north side of the Centennial Mountains, passed Red Rock Lakes (today a National Wildlife Refuge), and dropped through Red Rock Pass to Henry's Lake, Idaho—the place where the Bassett Brothers' road also landed, after it came in from the south. Montana pioneer William F. Wheeler, one of the Dillon road's earliest known travelers, left the Red Rock railhead on August 9, 1880, riding with Marshall and Goff on their stage lines. This was apparently one of the few trips M&G ever made using the Centennial Valley route, because fairly quickly the railroad's terminus would change from Red Rock to points farther north, which would change Marshall's route to that of Virginia City, Madison Valley, Raynolds Pass, and Henry's Lake. But on this day, William Wheeler was riding with Marshall through Centennial Valley. Wheeler wrote:

> The road is up Red Rock creek to its very source and has never been worked in the least and never more than half a dozen wagons ever passed over it; yet we made Henry's Lake in a day and three-quarters—distance 60 miles. It is the easiest natural grade to the summit of the Rocky Mountains I ever saw. From where we commenced to ascend the divide over to Henry's Lake the distance to the waters on the other side is but a mile and a half, and the little hill we went over is not more than 600 feet high. The distance to the lake is but four miles…Ourselves and freight weighed 1500 pounds, yet we used but two horses.[240]

From Henry's Lake, Mr. Wheeler went on to Marshall's Hotel in Yellowstone Park, and then apparently on around the park. He stated that its wonders "are too well known to require further description." Wheeler—identified as the General Agent of the *New North-West* newspaper—had promised to recontact the paper later in the trip, and the paper received his article on August 14, not publishing it until August 20. That means that Wheeler must have sent the letter with George Marshall's return-mail as soon as he reached Marshall's Hotel on August 13, in order for the newspaper to have received it on August 14. With six days left before he returned, it appears that Wheeler either toured the park with Mr. Marshall or, more likely, went around it on his own after renting a horse from Marshall or the Brothers.

Wheeler summed up his park trip by saying, "Every visitor will be a missionary to bring others here." That statement remains true today, and this author has seen it in action over and over during his forty-six years of living and working in Yellowstone.[241]

Wheeler's account was very optimistic about the Centennial Valley road itself, but his story contrasted greatly with that of Paul Vandervoort, who used the same route two weeks later. Leaving the Red Rock terminus, the Vandervoort party's stagecoach headed south up the railroad, turning gradually to the left (east) until they struck the old Virginia City stage road that had been recently abandoned because of the progress of the railroad northward. They then turned "up the Red Rock river, which we were told we could follow to its source." Four miles farther, they came to "what their teamster called "a mean place," and Vandervoort agreed that:

> It did look mean. (It is proper to state that there was no road or trail from Red Rock to Henry's Lake, and no teams or wagons had gone over it before ours except those of Salisbury and Marshall, who went over to locate the stage road.) The mountain came abruptly down to the river and so steep were its sides that it seemed impossible for a wagon and mule team to preserve their equilibrium. We all got out without asking. As a rule[,] I cling to my means of transportation but in the present case and several others on this trip I didn't. We started forward with a man upon the wheel lock, and proceeded until it was certain we would be bottom-side up in the river in less than four seconds more, when we stopped and waited for another team that was to accompany us as far as Henry's Lake. Our wagon remained at an angle of forty-five degrees for three hours. I went and hid rather than see the provisions washed and mingled in the waters of the river; but the wagon held its position as if glued to the mountain, and when the other craft hove in sight[,] we felt relieved.[242]

Later iterations of this road through Centennial Valley would keep the route more to the south (as the main road runs today) and away from the Red Rock River, but for now, Vandervoort's party remained hapless. The driver of the second wagon took a long, pine-pole and stuck it through the rear wheels in so-called "dead-x" fashion, and then let the horses slowly drag the coach with its rear wheels immobilized down to level ground. The second driver commented that such places "were nothing" when one got used to them, to which visitor Vandervoort said he thought to himself, "I never want to get used to them." Heading on up the stream, his party was told that this spot was not the meanest place after all, but rather that place was "about six miles ahead." They soon reached a spot where the stream cut steeply between two mountains, and the party again got out to walk. "It seemed impossible," wrote Vandervoort, "for a well-regulated mule to wend his way along the steep sides; and yet our wagons must pass there, for they were marked 'Yellowstone or bust'." The party soon felt busted, when they encountered a yawning ravine, whose bottom could not be seen except with a spy-glass.[243]

All members of the party immediately got out of the coach to walk. What happened next was a fascinating study in stagecoaching choreography, unfamiliar to most of us today:

> First, the wheels were locked from stem to stern; then the team was manacled and hobbled; then the driver gently dropped the horses and covered wagon clear out of sight in that ravine. They did not appear for some time, and I formed the opinion in four minutes, with nine million mosquitoes to assist me, that the ravine was the opening to a subterranean route to the geysers, and that I was left [behind]. But I was not correct. The animals and the wagon were unlocked and scaled the steep side of that ravine, and then came rapidly toward the place where all nature protested against a caravan forcing its passage. The pole was again attached, and the audacious driver moved ahead. How he ever got over I cannot tell, but this I can swear to, that the wagon was run entirely on the front wheels, and that the mules could never have stood up if it had not been for the harness—which was manufactured of course by an Omaha firm. This place was about half a mile long and when we got safely over[,] we found that we were through the canyon and that a level plain stretched away before us for many miles.[244]

At least one trip to the Park via the "Dillon route" through Centennial Valley is known from 1881, and it was the trip taken by H. Banard Leckler and his party of New Yorkers. Because it was a hunting trip during which the party killed many animals and viewed dozens if not hundreds more, Leckler's account—essentially a nineteen-chapter book—has been thoroughly chronicled and analyzed in this author's two-volume book about the history of mammals in the Greater Yellowstone Ecosystem.[245] But we also summarize the Centennial Valley portions of it here.

The Leckler party arrived at Dillon, Montana on the U&N Railway on August 14, 1881, spent a week outfitting there in the new town, and with a total of seven people (which became eight in the park) departed southeast up the Red Rock River on August 21. They spent thirteen days hunting on their way to Yellowstone Park and, like so many parties traveling the "Dillon route" (and its alternate, the Bassett Brothers' "Beaver Canyon route"), saw and killed many animals, including wolf, skunk, antelope (pronghorn), elk, deer, badger, red fox, and far too many fish and birds to enumerate here. In a day when hunting was still legal in Yellowstone Park, they finally entered the Park on September 4, traveling to Marshall's Hotel, the geyser basins, Mary Mountain, Canyon, Mount Washburn, and Mammoth Hot Springs, and exited the Park down the Yellowstone River to the north, via Bozeman and Butte, Montana.[246]

By June 17, 1882, the Dillon newspaper was calling this Montana road "The Direct Route to the National Park" and listing distances from Dillon for both it and the Virginia City route. Another article in late July unhesitatingly called it "The Best Route to the Geysers," and these labels helped press this Dillon route suddenly into competition with Beaver Canyon, although the Dillon route was longer. The article named no commercial stagecoach-operators but stated that the road was "being put in excellent condition" following damage to it by cattle herds in "Blacktail Canyon" (twenty-five miles south of Dillon). In good, competitive style, the Dillon writer then told a commercially fabricated untruth:

> We learn that tourists for the geysers are [now] landed at Beaver Canyon station where they find no mode of conveyance to reach the Park. Parties coming to Dillon to outfit will find no trouble in getting the desired accommodations.[247]

The Bassett Brothers of Beaver Canyon, Idaho, would likely have been quite surprised to learn from this that they were offering no conveyances to Yellowstone. After all, they were just then adding new vehicles to their stagecoaching fleet and had already made numerous trips to the park in both 1881 and 1882.

By August of 1882, the *Dillon Tribune* was proclaiming that "The road from this place to Wonderland is now in order and tourists are traveling over it." The paper mentioned a party of eight who passed east through Centennial Valley and that "Charley Bliven's stables furnished suitable transportation and an experienced guide."[248] Thus, the competition was

on between Dillon and Beaver Canyon, but Dillon was immediately handicapped in not having a commercial stagecoaching service like the Bassetts
were running. If there were commercial stage-coachers at Dillon, Montana
similar to the Bassett Brothers at Beaver Canyon, Idaho, those coachers
seem not to have been in place permanently, so apparently that niche was
only temporarily occupied by a few Dillon ranchers (such as Mr. Bliven)
here and there through time.

Of course, as Paradise Valley did at Yellowstone's north entrance,
Dillon's Centennial Valley route experienced good numbers of parties
who took their own wagons to the national park and camped out along
the way. Like what happened in all fifty states with such travelers to the
already famous place, scores if not hundreds returned home to write their
own accounts of the Yellowstone trip for their local newspapers. Such
a party was that of a woman known only as "A.E.B." who went to the
national park from Dillon in August of 1886. She mentioned Red Rock
Lakes, glistening beautifully in the sunshine, as her party of nine coached
down Red Rock Pass to Henry's Lake. There she commented on the great
numbers of travelers using the Montana Centennial Valley route and others who had arrived via the Madison River road from the north. "On nearly every side of the lake," she observed, "were scattered the white tents and
wagons of the people who were going to and returning from the Park."
Crossing Madison Plateau inside the Park, she noticed the original reason
for the name Firehole River: "We did not wonder how the Fire Hole got
its name, when we saw what fearful fires had been all through the timber." At Lower Geyser Basin, her party delighted in geysers, especially the
"Skull Geyser" (probably today's Fortress Geyser), which she called the
"most remarkable one here." A man they met there "who had been taking
observations," she remarked, "said that it would take two hundred years
to form one of the skulls." This man was probably the park's most noted,
stagecoach-era tour-guide, G.L. Henderson, who had given the name to
the geyser for its skull-shaped, silicon-dioxide formations that did indeed
resemble skulls. Of Park tour guides then, only Henderson is known to
have possessed the kind of imagination and information that our lady
chronicler recorded: "He imagined that one could see all of the different
shaped heads there, from the noble head of a Shakespeare to the deformed
skull of a malefactor, but we failed to see very much difference in them

except that some were large and some were small." Moreover, Mr. Henderson appears to have actually gone with her party to show them further wonders, because their chronicler A.E.B. noted at "Evangeline Geyser" that "one gentleman of poetic mind said you could hear it beat and throb like the heart of Evangeline."[249]

Trips from Dillon as an alternate route to Yellowstone like the ones enumerated here have probably continued almost to the present day, but not that many written accounts of them have been found, even after a search of the *Dillon Tribune* newspaper. Beginning in 1898, this route would be used constantly by the Monida & Yellowstone Stage Company, and that story will be told in volume two of this book.

Returning now to the Bassett Brothers' staging operation, tourists Mary B. Richards and her husband Jesse Richards rode to Yellowstone in one of the brothers' new "light spring wagons" in 1882, and Mary wrote an entire book about it. When she stepped off the train on July 31 of that year at Beaver Canyon, the town consisted of "a dozen log houses, two saloons and a big water tank." "Here are located," she explained approvingly, "some half dozen of the Bassett Brothers, fine enterprising fellows of the true pioneer stamp, who undertake to prepare and carry you in and through the National Park in good form; to bring you out all right by the way you went in, or start you in line for the northern exit by way of Bozeman and the Northern Pacific."[250] This description made it clear that the Bassetts and others were already making arrangements for tourists who wanted to leave the Park via its north entrance toward Bozeman or Billings to be able to accomplish that goal, even though the Northern Pacific Railroad was then completed only to a point just east of present Livingston, a town that did not yet exist. It also indicated that all six of the brothers were in place in 1882, a status that was probably already wrong but regardless would not take long to change. As mentioned, Frank Bassett had moved to Butte and several of the other brothers would go their separate ways within only a few years.

Mary's detailed comments gave us a window into the operations of the Bassett Brothers. She and her husband were allowed from their traveling trunks to take along the following: clothing: a change of boots, a few towels, gloves, and rubber coats; and they stuffed all of it into an English hamper, "scarcely larger than a champagne basket." The traveling-outfit for camping provided by the Bassetts included the following: a wall tent, blankets, buffalo skins, ax, hatchet, nails, ropes, hammer, wheel-grease, flour, sugar, lard, ham, eggs packed in oats, canned meats, fruit and jellies, a long-tailed frying pan, bake kettle, coffee pot, tin plates, cups and spoons, and knives and forks. Their spring-wagon was canvas-covered—large, strong, stiff in the joints and fit for the purpose—and chauffeured by a driver, an accomplished cook, and two balky horses. For all of this, the Bassetts charged eighteen dollars per day in addition to the advertised trip-prices.[251]

Mary Richards revealed that their driver was named Ernest, and it is likely that he was Ernest Knight Bassett, whom we met earlier as George Marshall's winter mailman when Ernest snowshoed north through the park to Mammoth Hot Springs. Ernest told Mary Richards that he was the son of Mormon parents who were polygamists and that he thought he had about twenty-five brothers and sisters from four mothers. Giving us additional maternal information, Ernest explained that "one of these wives is dead, another 'put away,' and the remaining two wives live with their husband," Ernest's father.[252] This thoroughly identified Ernest's family as that of Charles H. Bassett, Sr., about whom more will be said later.

Ernest Bassett drove the party twenty miles east, where they camped at Camas Meadows, near present Kilgore, Idaho. They saw "antelope" (pronghorn), sage grouse, pine-hens (probably blue grouse), and even a mink. Spending the night there, they drove on to Henry's Lake, forty-five miles farther according to her, and maps today agree with that figure. Mary revealed that they forded Henry's Fork of the Snake River twice and encountered the dreaded horseflies, about which Ernest exclaimed for his horses, "Their load is nothing when a fly stings." He meant "when a fly bites," but that misusage did not keep the party from seeing elk, more pronghorn, snipe and geese, fish in the river, and more pine-hens, one of which they ate for dinner. They camped at Henry's Lake.[253]

On August 3, the party arose and traveled on to Yellowstone Park, arriving that evening in the meadow at Marshall's Hotel. They crossed that era's Targhee Pass (one drainage north of present Targhee Pass), which Mary called "Tygee," at an elevation of 7,072 feet and dropped into the meadows along the South Fork of the Madison River, seeing still more antelope, deer, "an elk, badgers, and a large bear's track." An old prospector whom they met in the meadows told them to "Take a big drink before you start out!

There ain't a drop of water between here and the Firehole Basin."[254] He was referring to Superintendent P.W. Norris's high road, completed two years earlier, that steeply ascended the Madison Plateau and then ran gradually downhill and southeasterly to Marshall's Hotel. And sure enough, the party found no water along that route, not even at Consolation Spring, a signboard for which would be noted later that month by traveler Mrs. Foster and her family. From this, it is clear that superintendent Norris's road had

Stagecoaches "Crossing Firehole River, Lower Geyser Basin," no date, probably 1881-1885, in order to reach Marshall's Hotel (renamed Firehole Hotel in 1885). The two stagecoaches shown here were most likely owned by the Bassett Brothers, of Beaver Canyon, Idaho. Probably they were identical, Studebaker coaches, with the one on the left merely sporting a canvas wagon-cover for better protection against the elements. One of the numerous tents in the Marshall's Hotel area used for housing can be seen at rear. "Crossing the Firehole River, Lower Geyser Basin," Vacation Studies No. 460 by F.S. Halsted; Brigham Young University, Harold B. Lee Library, *L. Tom Perry Special Collections, F722.39.A1a, no. 114.*

already become the Bassett Brothers' standard route to their cabins and campsites just south of Marshall's Hotel.

Mary and Jesse Richards then toured the park for eleven days, with Ernest Bassett driving them all the way. They returned by the same route to Beaver Canyon in mid-August.[255]

In other business that summer, the Bassett Brothers took "a party of Salt Lakers" to Yellowstone after those folks arrived at Beaver Canyon on August 17, 1882. "Provided with a good comfortable conveyance and a complete camping outfit," the party reveled in the trip. "A better, easier road cannot be reasonably asked for," wrote one of them known only as "H." "No dust, no mud, and an occasional 'Thank you, ma'am,' when a mountain stream was crossed," said this tourist, "[was] enough to remind one that the road is not macadamized."[256] The exclamation "Thank you, ma'am" appears to have referred to one or more of the Bassetts' drivers' comments (and thus probably to all the Bassett brothers generally) whenever the stagecoaching passengers experienced an audible thump-and-bump at creek-crossings.

As "H." explained, their party took more than the usual two and a half days to reach the Park in order to hunt the "prairie chickens, water fowl and antelope that persistently interfered with our progress." They spent the second evening spearing trout at "Ray's Camp," which was no doubt the early iteration of a ranch owned by George W. Rea, about whom much more will be written in a later chapter. Passing Henry's Lake and crossing that era's Targhee Pass into Montana, they marveled that the streams were suddenly flowing east toward the Atlantic Ocean, and shortly afterward, pitched their tents on Firehole River near Marshall's Hotel. The Bassett Brothers' two cabins for supplies and a camp cook who stayed there for the entire summer would soon follow at this location; but for now, tents sufficed. "Here parties will be outfitted," said the group's scribe, "at reasonable rates with wagons or saddle horses and 'packs,' with guides, or can keep on with the conveyances that brought them over, at about the same expense." This made it clear that tourists could do the park tour with the Bassetts, or they could rent horses and outfits from them (and/or George Marshall, nearby), and make the tour themselves. By this time guides were supposedly no longer needed in the Park "to point out the way," but many parties hired guides and/or drivers to accompany them regardless.[257]

So, it was for these Salt Lake City travelers, and therefore "Joe the driver"—perhaps a hired hand of the Bassett Brothers—became their guide. The next morning, as they traveled south toward Old Faithful and stopped at today's Midway Geyser Basin, they "got lucky" and saw an eruption of the already-famous Excelsior Geyser. This huge spouting-spring was then (and for a short time afterward) known as "Sheridan Geyser," because it erupted just after General Sheridan's visit of 1881, and now it was continuing its major explosions in 1882:

> Its eruptions are irregular, but recently it has been in action three and four times a day. The crater was variously estimated by our party to be between thirty and sixty feet in diameter. Within it is a beautiful, clear body of water, and its depth, I believe, is unknown. Acting upon the suggestion of a lady who had lately visited the geysers, we all stepped up boldly to the yawning abyss, but had scarcely reached the edge before the whole body of water rose with a tremendous roar at least 150 feet into the air, scattering spray and steam and stones over all the spectators without an exception. The ladies had exhausted a large stock of adjectives long before the Basin was reached, and the only response from the audience to the grand exhibition was "Golly!" from Joe, the driver…In the midst of such a sulphurous steam and thundering noise, one could scarcely be much surprised, however much annoyed, to see Satan himself appear and demand tribute for passing over his dominions.[258]

After touring the park for a few more days, they retraced their steps westward to the railroad.

There was one other possible trip made by the Bassett Brothers in 1882, although the reference today is admittedly second hand and was written from memory in 1892, at the time that Congress was holding hearings on whether the Yellowstone National Park Transportation Company would forfeit its transportation rights. Park interpreter and tour-guide G.L. Henderson, formerly in the employ of the Yellowstone Park Association, in testifying about the condition of park roads back in 1882, recalled the following incident that, if it happened, without a doubt involved the Bassett Brothers and an apparently important foreign visitor:

In 1882[,] a baron from the court of Denmark came to the old Marshall Camp [Marshall's Hotel], at the forks of the Firehole [River], after having traveled 110 miles by stage from Beaver Canyon and over 20 miles through a ten-pin alley of stumps. The unfortunate man was so battered up that he could go no further [sic—farther]. After seeing a few eruptions of the Fountain geyser from his tent, at a distance of 3 miles, he went no farther. There were no hotels in those days [except Marshall's at Firehole and McCartney's at Mammoth], and yet the fame of Yellowstone Park had reached the court of Denmark. I doubt if the Baron said much on his return to encourage pilgrimages to Yellowstone Park.

Of course, we do not know how Mr. Henderson got his information and whether or not it was true. Whether Henderson heard a mere story second-hand or actually knew of this traveler's adventure first hand is not known, but if true, it had to have involved the Bassett Brothers' stage lines.[259]

At the end of the 1882 season, a local writer from Beaver Canyon gushed boosteristically about the four brothers and their operation. "Bassett Bros. have a very gratifying success," he wrote, "in their stage-line to the National Park." Even with what he called "their immense facilities" for accommodating and carrying passengers, "they have barely been able to meet the demand." They deserve their good luck, he finished, "as they are a pushing and go-ahead firm, and liked by all here."[260] By December, the brothers had settled into the quieter activity of running their off-season businesses, as they moved their saloon "into the building formerly used by them as a restaurant on the east side of the track" and added a billiard table.[261]

In early 1883, Beaver Canyon was a town of only about twenty families on both sides of the tracks, and as usual the often-severe winters kept affairs there relatively quiet. Longtime area hunter and guide George W. Rea, who came into town that winter from his ranch more than forty miles to the east in Shotgun Valley, announced to the newspaper that the Bassett Brothers would carry a large number of parties to the Yellowstone Park in the summer to come. (Rea, who even at this early time had probably already guided horse-parties to Yellowstone, would eventually find a way to convey wagons full of tourists to the Park for himself, at least for a few years, and we will tell that story in chapter eight.) Julius Bassett bustled around the town and region purchasing a number of new coaches and wagons and several more horses for the upcoming summer. A "Chinaman" named Ah Wah established a Chinese restaurant ("meals served at all seasonable hours"). And of course, in late spring, Beaver Canyon's sawmill-and-lumber businesses began to rehire workers. A newspaperman who passed through from Butte found the town still devoted "to the production of lumber, it having in it and the immediate vicinity eight sawmills, one planing mill and one shingle mill, which altogether employ about 125 men." These mills produced about ten thousand board-feet per day, added the reporter, who continued, "The place has two general merchandise stores, Stoddard and Son and W.T. Van Noy. It also has a fruit and news depot kept by Frank Blanchard; two saloons, one by Poulson [sic—Paulson] & Jackson and the other by C.B. [E.B.] Mount, in both of which is kept the best the market affords."[262]

As the tourist-season of 1883 approached, residents of Beaver Canyon and other regional folks must have known that the Northern Pacific Railroad (NPRR) had nearly completed its spur-line to Yellowstone's north entrance and that by September 1, the Utah & Northern's railroad— west of the park's west entrance—would therefore encounter great competition from the park's north entrance. While everyone knew that the NPRR would soon open the Park to masses of travelers, the Bassett Brothers must have taken some comfort in knowing that they had already been touring the Wonderland for two seasons. Gearing up for the summer, the brothers sold their saloon to Paulson & Jackson and then erected a new office for their stage-line at the end of the railroad's platform. They "purchased a number of new wagons and several horses" to be used this season. Good weather allowed them to take their first tourists to the Park in late May, "the season now being open." And they had begun planning for a different kind of group, a 25-day "Grand First-Class Excursion" to "The Land of the Geysers" to arrive on June 20 from Ogden, Utah. Their new advertisement for this large affair proclaimed that the route would trek "along smooth roads and through beautiful scenery."[263]

It was quickly turning into a busy summer for the Bassetts. Their "Land of Geysers" group would be large. The brothers' advertisement stated that items furnished would include tents, cooking gear, camping outfits (except for blankets), and one cook for each ten persons. Provisions would be hauled free along with fifty pounds of bedding, fishing, and hunting gear per person. The Bassetts would also provide "light spring wagons and teams, or saddle horses beyond Fire-Hole Basin at special figures to the party."[264] Probably preparing for certain people in this group, the Bassetts ordered from the Studebaker Company "two elegant Concord wagons, four-seated and made to order for special service" (these were shipped by June 9). Later that month, a reporter from the *Salt Lake Daily Herald* traveling north on the train elaborated on their fleet, stating that the Bassett Brothers were then operating their business with twenty vehicles and about seventy-five horses.[265]

A writer known only as "C.," who was a member of the Bassetts' "Land of the Geysers" group, wasted no time in writing to the *Salt Lake Herald* on July 14, 1883 about his trip, even before he arrived back at Ogden. "I have just completed a tour" of the National Park, he stated from Beaver Canyon, and then effervesced:

> Everything was favorable. The magnificent Geysers boiled and spouted their wildest and grandest. The Yellowstone Falls rushed, foamed, and dashed in awful fury. The Grand Canyon showed to the best advantage, the clear sunshine bringing out its brightest colors, and all combined to interest and delight the tourist, and to impress him with a sense of the awful majesty of the Creator...

This traveler was also awed that he met, or at least saw, national celebrities in the Park, namely General Philip Sheridan, Chief Justice Morrison Waite, General Grenville Dodge, and Senator George Edmunds. He added: "I must not forget to add that Bassett Brothers' conveyances were comfortable, their horses fine, the Jehu competent, and the cook amiable and proficient." *Jehu* was a commonly used word in those days that meant *stage-driver*, whose origins came from the Bible's charioteers, namely II Kings 9:20: "The driving is like the driving of Jehu, the son of Nimshi, for he driveth furiously."[266]

A newspaper article in the *Salt Lake Tribune* that was really only a long, textual advertisement aided the Bassett Brothers in early June. "From J.C. Bassett of Beaver Canyon, Idaho, who is now in the city," said the paper, "we learn that already many persons have gone to see the wonders of [the] National Park, with its spouting springs, geysers, beautiful lakes, wondrous rivers, and great forests." The story claimed that there was more to interest the tourist in Yellowstone than in any similar-sized area in the world, and that was arguably true. The article shortened the distance to the Park by claiming, "At Beaver Canyon, Idaho, the visitor may alight from the Utah & Northern train within seventy or eighty miles of the most prominent places in the National Park." The real distance was closer to one hundred miles, but apparently most readers were not figuring those distances closely in their excitement to reach the already famous place.[267]

In August 1883, President Chester A. Arthur's horseback-party was approaching the Park on a long trek from the south. The *Salt Lake Tribune* could not understand why General Sheridan had routed the President overland when the Utah & Northern could have gotten him there more quickly and easily. The *Tribune* took the opportunity to bless the Bassetts as well:

> The enterprise and energy displayed by the Bassett Brothers of Beaver Canyon in placing a line of transportation on this [rail]road is commendable. They have built bridges across the streams, and in difficult places have made the road first-class. They are now daily engaged in outfitting parties bound for the Park, and send experienced guides and drivers to carry them to all points of interest in this Wonderland. A trip of five days through the Park is considered long enough to enable parties to visit the Upper, Lower and Middle Geysers, Yellowstone Lake and the Falls and Grand Canyon of the Yellowstone. One of the best outfitted parties now in the Park are [*sic*] Parley Williams and James Little, who are enjoying themselves in the most pleasant manner. Bassett Bros. have had several years' experience, and can give all who apply to them any information desired.[268]

Publicity-wise, the Bassetts also got lucky that summer when a Wyoming newspaper republished a tourist's letter demeaning Yellowstone's new Northern Pacific route from the north and heartily recommending the "southern" (and western) route, which was of course via Beaver Canyon. This tourist entered the park's north entrance from Montana, went south to Old Faithful, and left via the Bassett Brothers and the west entrance. He produced this long description for the Cheyenne, Wyoming *Daily Leader* of what travelers over the Idaho route experienced when they rode west out of the Park back to the railroad, on the stagecoaches of the Bassett Brothers:

> There were four of us at Marshall's Hotel, Fire Hole basin, when Bassett Brothers stage drove up for us, and at 9 o'clock a.m. we seated ourselves in a spring wagon for the journey to Beaver cañon, Idaho, on the Utah & Northern, and 100 miles distant. The road was smooth; the best mountain road I ever traveled over. We drove briskly along, through a beautiful country, fording clear mountain streams, and stopping occasionally to drink from ice cold springs. The first day brings us to [Henry's Fork of] Snake River, where comfortable quarters are taken for the night, and excellent meals are cooked for us by a lady who is skilled in the art of catering to mountain appetites. Good fishing was to be enjoyed near our camp, and several of the party shared scores of trout in the [Henry's Fork of] Snake river by the light of our camp fire. The next day's ride of eight hours carried us through smooth valleys and between high mountains, along the shore of Henry lake, a veritable fairy lake, with floating island and a surface as smooth as glass. The shores are lined with evergreen trees, whose tall shadows reflecting from the surface of the water, add a further feature of beauty to the lake. A few hundred yards from the road we saw a cinnamon bear and two cubs, and we counted twenty-three antelope, two eagles, three elk, and three coyotes as we passed along during the afternoon. I would suggest to our local nimrods that they can obtain heroic hunting here if they care to have it. At 6 p.m. we reached Dillon, and at 11 p.m. the narrow-gauge sleeping car pulls up at the station for us, and off we go to Ogden…Now I have traveled over both routes into the park, and will say that everybody, even if he is a dweller at St. Paul, should go via the Beaver cañon route. All the attractions in the park are in the southern part of it. The northern entrance will never go. No use to try it. The high hills cannot be cut down.[269]

Unfortunately for this observer and the Bassetts, he was factually wrong about a problem that would plague the Brothers for many years. The northern route to the Park was infinitely easier than the Beaver Canyon route because it had many fewer miles of staging—the U&N Railway was too far away from the Park. Secondly, not all the park's attractions—such as Mammoth Hot Springs, Tower Fall, and Norris Geyser Basin—were in its southern part. Thirdly, the high hills were part of the scenery that most flat-land-visitors wanted to see, and the horses did the work of climbing them, not the tourists. Nevertheless, this journalistic recommendation, which was seen and read by a good number of Wyoming residents who could easily ride trains west to Ogden and then north to Beaver Canyon, was a strong endorsement for the Bassett Brothers and likely increased their business for a while, perhaps even for years.

The Wyoming article also showed that by August of 1883, the Bassett Brothers had become amenable to returning their passengers to the U&N via Montana's Centennial Valley route and dropping off some of those outbound travelers at Dillon's railroad-station. After all, that practice made money too. But it could also cost them money, because at Dillon, the brothers were faced with getting their driver and his coach back south to Beaver Canyon, which necessitated either a long "deadhead" drive[270] of nearly seventy-six miles by the stage-driver or (probably more often used) the loading of both the coach and driver onto a southbound U&N train.

This Wyoming journalist's mention of the spot near the crossing of Henry's Fork where "comfortable quarters are taken for the night" with a cook makes it clear that George Rea's "hotel" (ranch) at that spot had begun in service by August of 1883. By May of 1884, the *Dillon Tribune* was touting "Rea's Hotel" near Henry's Fork where George Rea and his brother Thomas kept a good number of horses, camp outfits for tourists, and fishing and hunting supplies. Apparently, Rea's "hotel" was simply the allowed use of some tents and cabins for tourists, and it appears that one of the Bassett wives had been engaged to oversee this "hotel" and cook for the Bassetts' tourists.[271]

Three of the Wyoming residents mentioned above, who had probably read or would read the "journalistic recommendation" in the Cheyenne *Daily Leader*, were W.O. Owen, C.S. Greenbaum, and W.K. Sinclair; they subsequently received credit for completing the first bicycle tour of Yellowstone National Park, which they made in 1883. The men rode trains to Ogden, Utah, and then Beaver Canyon, Idaho, and apparently met the Bassett Brothers there, because their account stated that "Here a team, wagon, complete camp outfit[,] and a good guide, to act also as teamster, were secured, and we set out eastward over an excellent road having a general upgrade and hard as adamant."[272] *Adamant* of course was the legendary stone of impenetrable hardness from ancient literature that was sometimes compared to diamond. For bicyclists of that era, this was the best possible surface for riding the large-wheeled "ordinaries" of the 1880s. The guide who drove their stagecoach was probably one of the Bassett Brothers or an employee, for these bicyclists had to have rented their outfits from the brothers. They spent an ecstatic week or so traveling to and touring the Park and then leaving by the same route.

Another 1883 traveler who arrived on the Utah & Northern Railroad and utilized the Bassett Brothers was a traveler known only as "Charlie," whose trip was reported in the Baltimore *Sun*. Charlie and one other man who served as his "painter," apparently rented their coach and equipment from the Bassetts, for he seems to have driven himself some of the way and did not mention having a Bassetts' driver. They left Beaver Canyon on August 3 and returned via Virginia City, apparently on August 8. Probably there was a second wagon with them, for he mentioned that "I met a party of four men and remained with them all the time." They arrived at "Firehole Basin" on the evening of their third day, "having driven 110 miles." Superintendent Norris's high road ascended "such a steep mountain grade," wrote Charlie, that it "was impossible for the team to pull more than the length of the wagon without stopping to 'blow'." But their drive from Beaver Canyon to Riverside "was charming," he enthused, "about as pleasant as one could wish for, the roads good, [and] the country wild and full of game, particularly mosquitoes, they only in spots." On Monday, August 6, Charlie started, apparently from Marshall's Hotel, on "footback," a little-used word today but which in his day meant that he was on foot (as opposed to horseback) for the section of road to Old Faithful. At Lower Basin's Queen's Laundry (a giant hot spring), Charlie was entranced with the prospect of a hot bath, so "donning my 'Adam's' costume, which I always carry when traveling," he waded into the spring's runoff, it being so terraced that "you can get either warm, hot or cold water within a few feet." He loved the hot-spring experience.[273] His reference to his "Adam's costume" was clearly a joke, and meant that he entered the water naked.

After seeing the huge springs at today's Midway Geyser Basin, Charlie got lucky at Upper Basin, when four of the largest geysers—Giant, Beehive, Splendid, and Grand—all erupted for him "inside of ten hours." In that basin, he was constantly reminded, he said, that he was "standing on the crust of Hades."

Charlie apparently arranged for his companion to drive the coach to Old Faithful to pick him up, for he stated that "we then drove to Yellowstone Lake and spent most of the day fishing." The road between Old Faithful and Lake was not yet in existence, so the route for the two of them had to have taken them back to Lower Basin and across Mary Mountain to the lake, which of course he described vividly.

Then it was on to the canyon, and Charlie considered it "the crowning attraction" of Yellowstone. Like so many other observers both before and after him, he expended many sentences in describing it. "The blended shades of color I never thought could exist as bright as they are," he effervesced. Interestingly, it appears that one of the men they traveled with or perhaps an individual they met enroute was "an old trapper and guide" who had "piloted Prof. Hayden through" the Park in 1871 or 1872, and of course one wonders who he was. Charlie was more definite in stating that "we missed the President; could not wait for Chet," a reference to Chester A. Arthur who was due in the Park some days later. They drove back to Beaver Canyon, visiting Virginia City on the way.[274]

Meanwhile the Bassett Brothers were doing fine. "During the seasons of 1882-3," remembered a later writer, "Messrs. Bassett Brothers fitted up several spring wagons and carried a number of tourists to this wonderful country; last season their business increased so much as to cause a large outlay for wagons and teams, until they are now prepared to carry all who come…"[275] According to this account, business had been good in both of those years and the brothers purchased new teams and new wagons.

By the end of 1883, at least one of the brothers was wintering in Salt Lake City, and it is likely that some or all the others did too, because Beaver Canyon was simply too cold with too much wind and snow in which to spend winters, especially in uninsulated buildings. Charles Julius entrained from the Mormon capital to Beaver Canyon after Christmas to check on his physical plant. Of course, he found everything lightly snowbound and quiet there at a time when the Bassetts' stagecoaches had been inactive for four months, and so far, the winter had been mild.[276]

This would soon change. By mid-February of 1884, trains were stuck in the usual blizzards and snowfields that created ongoing winter-adventures for the Beaver Canyon area; in fact, one train was reported as actually lost between High Bridge and BC. "Beaver Canyon is represented to be full of snow drifts from five to seven feet deep and a thousand feet long," said the newspaper, which also reported that just north of Franklin, Idaho, a northbound train had been forced to turn around at Morrell's Ranch and return south to Battle Creek. This was to become the continuing story of the Utah & Northern Railway every winter on the Utah-Idaho-Montana route. Winter after winter, the newspapers were full of stories of "snow blockades" on this railroad and its successor, the Union Pacific.[277] Additionally, this railroad like all others in the U.S. was plagued by accidents that killed and injured its workers, such as the death of Harry Laird. Laird, 23, who was "coaling an engine" in late June at Beaver Canyon, stepped from the coal bin onto the engine's tank box, fell hard onto the rails between the cars, and died from the fall.[278]

As April of 1884 arrived, the Bassett Brothers began preparing as usual for their summer trips to Yellowstone. One of the first things they did was to buy several new spring wagons "made to order" by the Studebaker Brothers Company, along with several new teams of horses. It appears that they went to Livingston, Montana to do this ordering, and they might have even purchased some of George Wakefield's excess horses. While there, they were told of tour guide G.L. Henderson's ongoing discoveries in Yellowstone, namely a "new fire hole basin" with numerous geysers on the east side of Yellowstone Lake. "Numerous geysers" was stretching it, but the area did have hot springs. The brothers replied that this discovery was not only already known to them but also a mere duplicate of other, more accessible wonders. One wonders whether they truly knew of the new discovery or were merely downplaying it for the sake of competing tourism.[279] No one in the region was experienced with tourism, because Yellowstone was the first iteration of it in the American West's interior, so, at least at its beginning, all players were novices in this equation.

A trip to the Park's Upper Geyser Basin that seems to have been chauffeured by the Bassett Brothers in 1884 was probably accompanied by Butte photographer A.J. Dusseau, for Dusseau took a photo of it. The photo showed what appeared to be a Studebaker wagon with six persons on the ground having lunch and with the person who was probably the driver leaning against a large rock at the far right with Castle Geyser in the background to the northwest. Mr. Dusseau and his wife, the former Amanda Henault, lived in Butte, Montana from about 1873 through at least 1890, where he ran an "artist's" photography shop. The image is one of the only Dusseau stereopticon views known today. It appeared on yellow cardstock with no indicia on the card and is currently owned by the Jay Lyndes Family Collection.[280]

On July 26, 1884, the Brothers wrote to Secretary of the Interior Henry Teller asking for permission to build a cabin at "Fire Hole Basin" as an office "for transaction of our passenger business." Listing good references including Superintendent Patrick Conger and Governor E.H. Murray of Utah, they also requested permission to "cut a few dry logs" with which to build a corral there and to cut five tons of hay for their horses. "We have been running from this point to Fire Hole," continued the letter, "for four years and our business has so increased that the privileges we ask are necessary for the better accommodation of the public."[281] This request was not answered until three years later, on July 27, 1887, when the U.S. Army was in charge of Yellowstone Park. Meanwhile, the Bassetts' would build their own overnight cabins and cook-shack on Firehole River, most likely in the spring of 1885.

The year 1884 was to become their biggest season so far, and this was amazing in a time when the nation was suffering from a mini-depression. Indeed, an Ogden newspaperman known only as "E.H.A." stated that "they have, so far this season, done at least twice as much business as [i]n any previous year," adding that "tourists for the Yellowstone are becoming more numerous each year; nearly every day parties come and go." This writer was a witness to the rampant and destructive souvenir-hunting in the Park, which went on at that time by almost everyone including the Bassetts, and he noted that the brothers "have their office in this place, in which travelers can feast their eyes on specimens of Park wonders."[282]

More good publicity came to the Bassetts five days later, when a writer for the *Salt Lake Tribune* described the park's wonders, encountered the brothers at Marshall's Hotel, and called their operation "very much the better way for Utah people to go" to Yellowstone. "The Bassett Brothers were both here" at Lower Geyser Basin on August 6, announced writer O.J.H. "They bring people from the Utah & Northern at Beaver Canyon," he explained, "about 100 miles, over a high smooth road in two days, lying over in the night, take them the rounds of the Park till they are satisfied, and carry them back for $15." Later in the article, he corrected that price to the proper $25.[283] Nor did bad weather make the Bassetts less than upbeat. A September reporter from the *Salt Lake Herald* proclaimed that even the newly fallen snow of one to six inches on the mountaintops did not deter the brothers from giving good news to "five passengers bound for Wonderland" whom the train dropped at Beaver Canyon. "Bassett Brothers assure them [that] on the morrow it will be more pleasant," wrote this reporter, "and that many warm days will follow yet this fall, and that a better time to visit the Park could not be selected."[284] For most years, this advice had proven and would continue to prove correct.

During that same month, the brothers took C.D. Roys and his party to the park, and Roys authored one of the meatiest of the known accounts about a Bassett trip. Accompanying him were James L. High and a man called only "J.M.," whom the party also called "Studebaker." He was no doubt John Mohler Studebaker (1833-1917), one of the heirs to the Studebaker fortune, for the account later mentioned his "Studebaker mansion."

We know a lot about John Studebaker (originally "Stutenbecker") and his four brothers, who started the Studebaker Brothers Manufacturing Company in 1852 at South Bend, Indiana. John himself went west while the others were running the company, but in 1858 he traveled by boat from San Francisco and returned to Indiana. By 1860, he and his brothers owned a factory worth $10,000. A contract with the Union Army during the Civil War made them rich; their company was worth $250,000 only two years later.[285]

Now John Mohler Studebaker was vacationing in the West and was himself a customer of the Bassett Brothers. Obtaining supplies at Salt Lake City, his party entrained to Beaver Canyon and rode out in a Bassett coach on August 12 with "John" as the driver (apparently only for the supply-wagon) and "Abe" as their cook. James High had waited with great anticipation for eight years to do this trip again, for he had first done it on horseback in 1876, during the Great Sioux War when there was yet no railroad present and when hardly any other "white" person was traveling in the region because of fear of Indians. He had corresponded with the Bassett Brothers "who procured for our use a tent, cooking utensils, a first-class cook and three saddle ponies of the native breed," wrote the party's chronicler Mr. Roys. The party pulled their three riding-horses behind their wagon as they left Beaver Canyon. "In a large covered Studebaker wagon with four horses," explained Roys, "Mr. Bassett drove us out of this infant settlement across silver streams and over natural parks in the very heart of the Rockies."[286] It makes sense that one of the Brothers himself drove the passengers' stagecoach rather than a mere employee, because the Studebakers were selling stagecoaches and wagons to the Bassetts, and with future purchases likely on their minds, the Brothers wanted nothing to go wrong on this trip.

All three of their visiting passengers were excited to the point of near pandemonium. "Ignorant of what we were to meet," proclaimed Mr. Roys, "more anxious to cast a fly than to shoot a gun and in great haste to depart," they left all their ammunition nailed up in its original package, which of course was in the bottom of the coach. Within the first hour, they saw one large gray wolf, one coyote, two badgers, and innumerable sage hens, and before sundown antelope and deer appeared to be everywhere. Roused into "exalted activity" by these animals, "Studebaker" forced a stop to load his Winchester, but he failed to obtain venison for supper so the party went fishing instead.[287]

When they broke camp the next morning, "Studebaker" and Roys "each carried a breech-loader and ammunition enough for an infant battle," and Mr. High, who generally did not hunt, was made custodian of the Winchester with instructions to surrender it when necessary "from the front seat." In less than two hundred yards, they saw a covey of willow grouse. "The noise we made that morning was something fierce," wrote Roys. "For two miles we pursued one covey after another and made the mountainsides reverberate the sound of our artillery," but they killed only nine gamebirds. James High made fun of them, saying, "I never saw better shooting, but the execution was what might be expected from men who shut their eyes before they pull the trigger."[288]

Roys noted that at two p.m. they crossed the Henry's Fork of Snake River "on the same trail over which General Howard followed the Nez Perces" in 1877. The trail was apparently still visible in 1884, and the crossing was probably the one located today about two miles east of George Rea's ranch, which was then located on Shotgun Creek (present Sheridan Creek), today located on the northwest shore of Island Park Reservoir, which lake was not present in 1884. On the river's east bank, Abe, the cook, had their camp and dinner almost ready. The men fished for hours, catching over one hundred trout, packing them in wet grass, and sending them via one of the Bassetts' west-bound wagons back to Beaver Canyon.

They would remain in this camp for this night and three more, because the following morning, area old-timer George Rea came to their camp, and for the next four days he took them hunting. They killed "three elk, four moose, two bears and captured one cub alive," which George Rea "still keeps at his cabin," reported Roys. They also killed deer, antelope, geese, ducks, curlew, plover, willow grouse, snipe, and trout "*ad infinitum.*" They wasted none of it, giving spare game to the occupants of several west-bound Bassett stagecoaches. And their scribe made an important observation about the extent of the Brothers' summer business from Beaver Canyon to Yellowstone Park: "Almost every day during three months of the year [at least] one of Bassett Bros.' teams may be seen taking tourists to and from this greatest wonder of the continent if not of the world, and our surplus [game] was [therefore] always in demand."

On one of the days, they encountered a grizzly bear. The morning began when their driver splashed the coach back across Henry's Fork so that Rea and his three "guidees" could go fishing up "Shotgun Creek," located "about two miles from camp," and which was today's Sheridan Creek.[289] They were not looking for grizzlies, so finding one was a complete accident. Their driver John was the first to spot him, and immediately yelled. It was apparently Studebaker who "seized the rifle and fired."

> None was more surprised than himself when the savage beast sunk apparently dead in his tracks. Abe had previously told us that the only way of knowing that a grizzly is dead is to "cut off his head and let him lie for twenty-four hours, then if he does not show signs of life you may approach him, but with extreme caution." J.M. [Studebaker], in his heroic zeal, had forgotten

this wholesome advice, and, dropping his rifle rushed upon the supposed dead beast, seized him by one hind leg, and holding it partly from the ground shouted in short-lived exultation: "I am the boss bear-hunter, and don't you forget it!" About this time the grizzly began to kick. Returning animation made him furious. And J.M.—afraid to let go and unable to hold on— shouted for help: "Bring a gun, John! He ain't dead." It was time he shouted for help. One more kick and the grizzly was free, and with extended claws and open jaws proposed to resent the insults and injury he had received. The grizzly was in front and the river was behind, but, unconscious of its presence and bent only on protecting himself from the ugly jaws of the advancing and now furious brute, Studebaker backed off kicking but never touching the grizzly as he approached; and when J.M. fell back into the river the grizzly gave one look of surprise and disap- pointment and "lit out" for the timber. Je whiz! How he did go. When this mighty hunter crept dripping to the banks, he was a wiser if not a better man.[290]

Author Roys unreservedly called this excursion "the most satisfactory trip in all my camping experience." He noted that both the Bassett Brothers and George Rea were planning to build cabins "at the great cold springs, which constitute the source of the river," namely today's Big Springs, Ida- ho. Whether they ever did that is not known, but throughout his trip, Mr. C.D. Roys was so taken with the hunting and the Bassett Brothers' service to their customers that he ended his article without ever saying a word about Yellowstone Park. Surely, he traveled on into the Park, but if he wrote about it, we have not found the rest of his account.

1884 was a difficult year in Yellowstone. The nation's economy was weak, because of a minor depression that struck that year. The Mammoth Hotel was open but, so far, unfinished. The YNPI Company's facilities all around the park were primitive and consisted mostly of tent-camps. Marshall's Ho- tel at Lower Geyser Basin was better than most of the YNPIC facilities, but it too was anything but sophisticated. The Wakefield & Hoffman trans- portation company was barely established; it too was primitive and unable to make a profit, but it was probably the best-functioning organism of any of the Yellowstone entities. The park's civilian administration, led by two different superintendents this year, was weak; one man (Patrick Conger) was untrusted and disliked and would be replaced in September; his replacement (Robert Carpenter) would turn out to be downright corrupt. Substantive government roadwork, which had begun the previous year, was barely started by Lt Dan Kingman. Into this difficult scene came about 5,000 tourists anyway, attracted by more than a decade of newspaper and magazine publicity in both the U.S. and Europe.

William Sturgis led one of those parties, a group of seven who appears to have come from Wyoming.[291] At that time in that state, most of the population lived in Cheyenne or Laramie. Hence the easiest route to Yellowstone was to ride west on the Union Pacific Railroad, north on the Utah & Northern Railway almost to Montana, and then east on the Bassett Brothers' stage line.

Sure enough, at Beaver Canyon, William Sturgis found that the Brothers were there, "also our ambulance," a name sometimes used for stagecoaches, but he did not mention whether they hired a driver or merely rented the wagon, but probably they hired a driver. "We bowl along," he stated, composing a poem to sage chickens (probably sage grouse) that he saw along the road.[292] At "Ray Station," probably George Rea's ranch, Sturgis said he found "more Bassett Bros.," and described the place as "two or three hotels under canvas, log cabins, stables, etc." The Rea brothers and/or the Bassetts had set up tents for their passengers, where Sturgis and his folks spent the night.

Passing Henry's Lake, the next morning, they ascended Targhee Creek to Targhee Pass. Interestingly, he stated that there was snow "in every hollow," even though it was only August 13, and they drove on into the Park.[293] Four miles in, they found Riverside Station abandoned, for whatever reason. This was the spot, Sturgis wrote, "where we turn away [from it and everything else through which we have passed] and proceed to climb the mountain that separates us from Firehole Basin and all its wonders." Mistakenly crediting Lt. Kingman for this road instead of Superintendent Norris, Sturgis was one of the few people who felt positively about the arduous and precipitous route, saying "the road though steep is good." Along this route to the famous "forks of the Firehole" at the mouth of Nez Perce Creek, Sturgis noted without elaboration that the party was "confronted by [yet] another Bassett Brother," apparently indicating, with his several other mentions of them, that many members of the Bassetts were employed in the family enterprise this summer. As the road approached Lower Geyser Basin, the steam columns from thermal features beckoned to them, and they appear to have parked the wagon and walked down into the valley to wash their towels and handkerchiefs in the giant, hot spring known as Queen's Laundry, a practice that was then legal.[294]

Sturgis's account did not say much about the hotels, spending much of its space on the park's features. This was August 16, and they watched Fountain Geyser erupt and apparently also saw the new "Cleveland Geyser," named because "it was discovered since the Chicago [Grover Cleveland's] Convention." It was today's Old Surprise Spring in the Kaleidoscope Group of Lower Geyser Basin. He constantly mentioned that one of their number, a woman named "Minnie," was a terrible example of an illegal specimen-collector who had to be remonstrated on numerous occasions. For example, it was at "Specimen Lake where we thought Minnie would camp for a week." At Old Faithful, they met Assistant Superintendent William C. Cannon, who like the other assistants, "volunteers his services as a guide in general," and who took them on horseback to Lone Star Geyser, which they saw erupt on at about 4 p.m." Cannon was then kind enough to let them use his "hot bath," probably a small cabin on Firehole River near one of the hot springs. They then watched Grand Geyser erupt.[295]

The next day, because there was not yet a road to Yellowstone Lake, Sturgis and his party returned north and, after looking at the "Devil's Paintpots" (present Fountain Paintpot), they drove east up Nez Perce Creek, and camped for the night in Hayden Valley.[296]

On the next morning, Sturgis and party started north for Canyon when "suddenly we come upon one of those wretched specimens of tourist semi-civilization—a hotel made of canvas—and we know we are near our goal [of waterfalls]. We dodge the canvas 'abomination of desolation' and pull up" near the brink of Upper Falls of Yellowstone River for which they were headed. They also took in the Lower Falls of the Yellowstone and apparently spent the night camped somewhere nearby.[297]

On the following morning, the party drove south to Yellowstone Lake in a pouring rain. They passed the Mud Volcano, referring to it as a "cave of great despair" and eventually Sturgis enthused: "The great inland sea opened out in front of us, half shrouded in a mist, and we pulled up in a grove beside a forlorn-looking shanty with a hole for a door and another for a chimney, a smoky-looking fire smouldering in the center and a bedraggled-looking party trying to keep warm about it." It was the only building at Yellowstone Lake, a shelter-cabin that was available for any visitor to occupy. They called their overnight spot "Camp Dismal," and thus spent the night in cold and wet conditions.[298]

As thousands of Yellowstone summer travelers have experienced through the years, they awoke to two inches of snow on the ground. Leaving Lake almost immediately, they drove south and then west toward West Thumb, namely "over the hills to Firehole [River]." This was a very difficult route in 1884, because there was essentially no road; the existing track was narrow, sandy or swampy in many places where they inevitably sank, obstructed by timber for most of the way, and abominable in every other way for nearly forty miles. Almost expectedly, they suffered a broken wagon-wheel, but managed to "limp in" to the forks of the Firehole to find a blacksmith (probably George Graham) at Marshall's Hotel. So rough was this trip that they decided almost immediately to drive north to Mammoth rather than returning westerly to Beaver Canyon.[299]

Reaching Mammoth, they encountered, or purposely hired, a guide who turned out to be the well-known G.L. Henderson. "Joined by one of the [assistant] Superintendents, we make a tour of the springs," wrote Sturgis, who also noted that two boys carrying "that forbidden tool, a hatchet" walked with them, and Mr. Henderson wrote a poem denouncing them for specimen-collecting. Sturgis was more interested in listening "to the lucid statements of our guide as to the previous visits of congressional Solons, etc."[300]

After staying at Mammoth Hot Springs Hotel ("the great barn which hopes someday to be a hotel"), they returned south into the park, heading for the Lower Geyser Basin where they apparently hoped to meet up with the Bassett Brothers and adding to the park's trash by leaving their empty bottles behind at a camp just north of Norris Geyser Basin. But first, they scrambled down to a view of Gibbon Falls from its east side, where the road was located then.[301]

Sure enough, at the forks of the Firehole River, they encountered Mr. Bassett, who therein "presents a haunch of blacktail [deer] venison" to their party. Presumably they spent the night here, and on the following morning began climbing the high road to the west entrance.

At "Ray's," which was George Rea's place, Sturgis recorded that "we see a few more Bassetts," and undoubtedly, they spent the night there, after joining other travelers in gathering live grasshoppers for fish-bait.[302]

At Beaver Canyon, the ladies wrote a poem entitled "Farewell Chorus," wherein their three women raised glasses to their recently discovered freedom from skirts and side-saddles. So ended William Sturgis's "New Songs" excursion with the Bassett Brothers.[303]

One of those other Utah people whom the *Salt Lake Tribune*'s previously mentioned advertisement encouraged to use the Bassett Brothers' services was Charles R. Savage (1832-1909), soon to become a well-known Utah photographer. Wanting more time and a more leisurely trip, he looked into renting his own outfit from the brothers in 1884. He called his method "much the cheapest, though more troublesome," so with this rented outfit he left Beaver Canyon in early September. From a comparison of his partner Alfred Lambourne's account with Savage's, it appears that they rented the equipment from the Bassett Brothers and then engaged a Bassett Brothers driver to chauffeur them. "George, Fred Lambourne[,] and I start for the Yellowstone Park today," wrote Savage on August 26, "via the [U] & N." Like C.D. Roys and many other travelers, Savage and his party saw much wildlife. Passing Sheridan Ranch, then located somewhere near Sheridan Ridge on upper Shotgun Creek, he observed "herds of antelope nearly buried up in luxuriant grass and thousands of wild fowl." As usual, Shotgun Creek swarmed with "wild duck, geese, curlew, snipe, and other edible birds." Shortly after that, he reached Henry's Fork of the Snake River (incorrectly called "Snake River" by many early travelers), where he forded the river and followed the road into timber as it ran along the river's south side. "At about eight miles from the first ford," wrote Savage, "we cross the river again, and reach Rea's Ranch, the night station of Bassetts' line." This comment tells us something important, namely that the Bassetts had pressed into service the small but new "hotel" built early this summer by George and Thomas Rea. This arrangement would not last long.

Here Savage remarked on the beauty of the area and noted that George Rea was not always present. Apparently, the Bassetts had an agreement with him, for Charles Savage encouraged his readers to let their horses rest here "and try the repast served up by Mrs. Bassett in the dinner tent." Unfortunately, we do not know for certain *which* Mrs. Bassett was cooking therein, but family lore has it that this was Marette Cook Bassett (wife of William Henry Bassett), who later spent several summers cooking at "Firehole Basin."[304]

After the Reas' "hotel," the road in 1884 passed "over an extensive swamp for several miles," said Savage, and that partially explains today why some twentieth-century Idahoans thought that this was a good place to dam the river and construct today's Island Park Reservoir. One wonders whether the area's birds and animals are as numerous today, having had their wetland habitat so changed, but this reservoir and the Grassy Lake reservoir to the east were built in 1936-1938 as an uneasy compromise to a proposed, larger reservoir *inside Yellowstone Park*. This was fortunately defeated in congress, because it would have flooded the Bechler area of southwestern Yellowstone National Park, destroying at least seventy world-class waterfalls and many of the finest backcountry trails in the Grand Old Park.[305]

After passing Henry's Lake, Savage pointed to what was apparently an overnight "station at South Fork" of the Madison River (probably the house of Henry Clay Manley, known in these early accounts as "Manley's cabin"), making us believe that if the Bassetts ever used the stage-station just east of Henry's Lake (still standing in 2014) it must have been in the 1890s rather than 1884-1889, when they were still using Manley's ranch. Savage then entered the Lower Geyser Basin and enjoyed a multi-day tour of Yellowstone, returning to Beaver Canyon in a "pelting storm," but happy because he had taken at least thirty-nine photographs of Yellowstone Park.[306]

Mention of Henry Clay Manley, who often went by "H. Clay Manley" or "Clay Manley" brings up his small but important role in the history of this part of Montana. Mr. Manley (1865-1932), born in Marion County, West Virginia to parents Harrison and Sarah, somehow found his way to eastern Idaho (initially at Henry's Lake with his wife Alice)[307] and then southwest Montana Territory by the mid-1880s. He ultimately settled near or on Cream Creek and the South Fork of the Madison River in present Gallatin National Forest. His small, remote ranch that happened to be on the route to Yellowstone National Park's west entrance allowed him to make extra money by putting up travelers who elected to come that way when the Utah & Northern Railway made the Park accessible in 1880. His modest homestead eventually resulted in the large mountain on which he settled being called "Manley Peak" or "Manley Mountain" (it is today's Mount Two Top, Idaho).[308] That income was a needed boost to meager earnings that were otherwise limited to hunting and a few cows, which yielded a very fine cream that was responsible for the name of the creek and which was specifically mentioned by some of those early travelers. Eventually Manley found his way to Virginia City, where it appears that he engaged in the sheep business, and he later moved back to his "home" country—to the town of Yellowstone (which eventually became West Yellowstone), Montana. When his children moved in later life to Ennis, Montana, Henry Clay Manley went too, and died there in 1932.[309]

Returning to Charles Savage and his 1884 trip to Yellowstone, we noted that Salt Lake City artist Alfred Lambourne traveled with him. Lambourne unfortunately spent his time composing poetic musings about the scenery instead of recording anything useful about the details of his trip.[310] However, Lambourne did mention "our communicative driver," probably one of the Bassett Brothers in person, who pointed out an erupting geyser that the party saw from the road, while on the plateau above and west of Marshall's Hotel. He identified it as "the Great Fountain [Geyser] in the Lower [Geyser] Basin." The Bassetts were familiar with the geysers and hot springs of this area by virtue of their constant trips to the region. Interpretively, this driver or someone else at the hotel's camping site also told them about the recent eruptions of a new geyser "in sight of the hotel" that had been named "Cleveland Geyser," for Grover Cleveland, who was then running for U.S. president. That geyser was present Old Surprise Spring in the Kaleidoscope Group, and these discussions made it clear that then as now, tour guides—including the Bassett Brothers themselves—were constantly "boning up" on their Yellowstone information.[311]

A Welsh tourist who traveled to the geysers at the same time (September and October of 1884) saw at least one of the Bassett Brothers' vehicles at Marshall's Hotel and recorded it as "from the west enters Bassett's stage from Beaver Cañon, about one hundred miles away." Although he was not riding with them, Thomas Henry Thomas left us a woodcut-drawing of their four-horse coach and its driver with three passengers.[312]

As the spring of 1885 arrived, the Bassett Brothers advertised that "we have better facilities than ever before for taking care of tourist travel" to Yellowstone National Park. And too their trips were getting there faster. The brothers proclaimed in April that they could leave Beaver Canyon each morning at 7 a.m. and lodge for the night at the [Henry's Fork of the]

Snake River station after traveling fifty miles (this was probably an early iteration of John Kooch's "Snake River Crossing Hotel"). On the following morning they would leave there and reach "Fire Hole basin hotel" by 6 p.m. They charged four dollars extra for meals and lodging in route, and the return trip to Beaver Canyon was now made in the same time frame of two days.[313] In early May, Charles Julius "Jules" Bassett, who often worked during the "off season" as an Idaho deputy marshal at Oneida, announced that good spring weather was allowing them to "move their stock to Beaver Canyon at once" and commence running into the Park on June 15.[314] "They use large, four-seated, covered spring wagons," said an 1885 article promoting eastern Idaho, "which makes the tourist feel more like going to a picnic than on a journey."[315]

Articles like "To the National Park" in the *St. Paul Daily Globe* that year did not help the Bassett Brothers. It pointed out that not only was the ticket price higher on the Utah & Northern route versus the Northern Pacific route ($157 versus $138), but the stagecoaching mileage was fifty-seven miles farther by U&N and the time was thus much longer going that way. The Bassetts and the U&N had countered by saying their 99-mile stage ride from Beaver Canyon was in itself "nearly as enjoyable to the tourist as the park is," but the *Globe* article then proceeded to make fun of that claim.[316]

Siding with the Bassett Brothers' route, another long article partially rebutted the distance argument by talking up the wondrous marvels of Henry's Lake, where the salmon-trout were so numerous and easy to catch that "there is some talk of capitalists building a canning factory" on its banks "for the purpose of canning this delightful fish for market."[317] This claim was definitely true, because first settler Gilman Sawtell had sold fish from there by taking them to Virginia City in a wagon during the period 1868 through 1877, and area resident and guide George Rea would later set up his own fishery-ponds at his ranch south of Henry's Lake. But it was also clear that the distance factor causing the much longer stage-ride would ultimately hurt the Bassetts and their Beaver Canyon route.

Meanwhile the Northern Pacific Railroad began advertising that it was "the only all Rail Line to the Yellowstone Park."[318] "All rail" meant no horse-drawn travel necessary, and a lot of people who were exhausted by years of stagecoaching were happy to have that option, even if the route still required sixteen miles of staging from the railhead at Cinnabar, Montana,

Beaver Canyon in 1885. Photo and labels furnished by Stan Hansen, from *Bassett Brothers*.

to Mammoth Hot Springs, Wyoming, and return. Moreover, 1885 was a year when forest fires raged in the region. One account from September of that year stated that "yesterday the fire was within about three miles of Beaver Canyon, but the rain which came just as it was badly needed extinguished it." A regional businessman stated that "more timber has been burned during the past week than all the saw mills of Beaver Canyon have sawed for three years."[319]

These elements may have slightly reduced the Bassetts' business in 1885, but we have no hard evidence for that other than a dearth of accounts by tourists who traveled with them, and that is not an accurate measure. A letter that the Brothers wrote to S.M Knox of Salt Lake City in August stated that they would charge his party of five twenty dollars each to go to the Park and twenty-five dollars each if the party wanted to add Mammoth Hot Springs into the deal. The Bassetts' "comfortable spring wagon" with four horses and driver, said the letter, "seats five persons and driver nicely." Should the party wish to add one more person, the letter noted, the party would have to tolerate placing three people on each seat and the rate would go up to twenty-five dollars per person.[320]

It appears that the Bassetts' biggest event for 1885 was the erection of their two or three log cabins and a corral in the Lower Geyser Basin at a spot that was a short distance southwest of George Marshall's first hotel, and just south of the spot where Superintendent Norris's 1880 road descended from Madison Plateau. This fact is known from W.H. Leffingwell's map of July 30, 1885, which showed the brothers' two cabins and corral at this location. The Bassetts had asked Interior for permission to erect these cabins in the summer of 1884, but as mentioned, it appears that no one answered their letter until 1887.[321] Perhaps they received some kind of verbal approval for the cabins from the Park superintendent, for the cabins were definitely present by late July of 1885 and possibly even in the autumn of 1884.

So far only one actual trip-account for the Bassetts has been found from 1885, and it involved Hoyt Sherman, who was General Agent for the Union Pacific Railroad—shadow owners of Utah & Northern—at their Salt Lake City office. The account stated that sometimes when a big UP party would go to the Park from Beaver Canyon, Sherman would accompany them. In this case he did, traveling east through the usual Idaho wilderness toward Henry's Lake. "Sometimes at night the tourists would camp for a change," said the article, instead of staying at the Bassetts' prearranged cabins, and on this night a bear came into their camp. About midnight, a noise woke Sherman up and he arose, carrying a pistol and his knife. Suddenly a big, black object appeared right in front of him, clearly recognizable in the moonlight as a large bear. At first, he thought he would run, but then decided that action might cause his death:

> The pistol was a small one, but he raised it after his first surprise was over and pulled the trigger. It did not go off. He just remembered that he had neglected to reload the weapon that evening after discharging all the cartridges. When the trigger snapped, the bear looked at the pistol curiously and then at Sherman. The latter took his knife out and slowly backed up until he was protected by a tree. The bear followed and caressingly began to

hug him. Its hot breath was upon his face, and he grew faint. He rallied and drove the knife to the hilt into bruin, who, now fully enraged, rolled Sherman on[to] the ground. Now it was fight or die [for both of them]. Another plunge and the sharp edge of the steel went plowing up the bear, fairly disemboweling him. The struggle soon ended, and although Sherman was the victor, he was not altogether unharmed. The tourists heard the noise, and were in time to witness the end of the battle. For a week after three Englishmen did nothing but curse their ill-luck for not being the man that the bear attacked.[322]

Of course, a reasonable reader suspects that a thread of macho malarkey might be bound up in at least the ending, and perhaps even in the body of this story, but that was the way the newspapers received it from Hoyt Sherman, who in his day was a well-known and reliable personality.

Travel to Yellowstone in 1886 via the park's North Entrance was "the heaviest in its history," reported the *St. Paul Daily Globe* in August, "the number of tourists arriving each day being about 100." The hotel at Mammoth was taxed that summer to its utmost, and some visitors, said the *Globe*, were "returning [home] because every carriage is employed."[323] West of the Park at Beaver Canyon, the Bassett Brothers did not find the crowds so great this summer, but they still had enough for a business. "Tourists intending to visit Yellowstone Park," announced the *Morning Oregonian* later in the summer with good timing about the crowds, "will find ample facilities via the Beaver Canyon route, and will avoid overcrowding, likely to occur via Livingston and Cinnabar."[324] But Beaver Canyon was suffering from a "general sleepiness of the town and its inhabitants," and its lumber business was relatively flat. Regardless, the Bassetts in June were preparing for tourists and planning to open their own hotel in the small town to aid their stage-line.[325]

Among the renowned people that the Bassett Brothers took to Yellowstone in 1886 was one who was internationally famous, namely the Polish actress Mme. Helena Modjeska with her escort, a Count Bozenta.[326] Another well-known person they conveyed that summer was General E.E. Stanley of Cumberland, England, who was then serving as the British Consul at San Francisco. Escorting his own party on July 8, Park tour guide G.L.

Henderson reported this trip, saying that his party encountered Stanley's at Great Fountain Geyser in the Lower Geyser Basin. "These two parties," concluded Henderson, "had entered the Park on the same day from different directions; thus, the Union Pacific and the Northern Pacific railroads were both represented by tourists among the geysers at the same time." As a former assistant Park superintendent who was now running his own transportation and hotel company, Henderson no doubt thought himself far superior as a park interpretive guide to the Bassett Brothers (and probably, he was!). He implied as much when he stated: "We were surprised to see General Stanley, with his so-called park guide, pass by without noticing the great gas-aqueous geysers in Parnassus basin [the present area of Gentian Pool]." Henderson then listed six hot springs and geysers that "were unknown to the guide and were consequently passed unseen."[327] Notwithstanding this put-down by a tour guide of undoubtedly superior ability, the Bassett Brothers continued their trips this summer, although we are so far lacking documentation for them.

But an interesting incident did occur this year. In September, someone tipped off the Virginia City *Madisonian* that game was being illegally killed in the "Madison Basin" for the benefit of tourists arriving at Beaver Canyon. The newspaper stated that its correspondent said the killing "has been done…by one Marshall [probably George Marshall], and the game was mostly bought by Bassett." Whether "Madison Basin" referred to the meadows just west of the Park on the South Fork of the Madison River or to the portion of Madison Valley that was just inside the west boundary of the Park was not stated. But after the newspaper's warning, no further reports of this kind appeared.[328]

Perhaps because of the Park's decreased visitation from the west, the Bassetts used late 1886 to make road improvements. "The route to the Yellowstone National Park," declared the Salt Lake *Daily Tribune* in November, "is to be very much shortened and improved by the time the season again opens."

> Bassett Brothers are making a new road between Camas Meadows and Riverside Station, on Henry's Fork of Snake River, so as to shorten the distance between Beaver Cañon and Riverside Station, thus cutting down the distance between Upper Fire

Hole and Beaver Cañon forty miles, and bringing it down to seventy miles. Most of this work has been done, and the road will be finished in the early spring [of 1887]…The new road will enable them to drive into the Park in one day, and thus shorten the round trip to two days.[329]

While the new road did shorten the round trip to less than two days, it did not allow them to drive into the Park in one day. The article added that the Brothers' headquarters would "hereafter" be in Lower Geyser Basin, indicating use of their cabins there for overnight purposes.

The year 1887 was an important year for the Bassett Brothers, but not altogether a good one for several reasons, as we shall see. The season began harshly on April 21 for the people of Beaver Canyon when a twenty-car, northbound freight-train carrying coal and rail-ties broke loose and wrecked on Beaver Canyon hill, turning thirteen of the cars into a scrap-pile of metal and killing Conductor Isaac M. Lowry by throwing him up the mountainside where he was crushed by many suddenly released, falling railroad-ties.[330]

According to Jule (sometimes he was called "Jules") Bassett, the Brothers' first stagecoach of the season set out for the Park on June 18. A Blackfoot newspaper promoted the Bassetts' hotel at Beaver Canyon as "deservedly popular and well patronized" and noted that it was managed by Mrs. Frank Bassett. And the newspaper stated that "these gentlemen have splendid out-fits and good teams for the drive to the Park, and are opening up with better prospects than at any previous season."[331] The upcoming summer was looking better than it ultimately turned out.

On July 8, 1887, C.J. Bassett and William Henry Bassett of Beaver Canyon applied to the Secretary of Interior for a renewal of their park permit and finished the application-letter with their own stamp that bore the name "National Park Stage Line" and "Fire Hole Basin." Crossed out in the application was the name of C.H. Bassett, making us believe that he was no longer one of the owners of the company or at least no longer a manager/operator. This was probably the official moment when four of the Bassett Brothers no longer worked for the company, although exactly when those separations occurred individually is not known.[332]

The Secretary recommended issuing the permission and forwarded the application to Park acting superintendent Captain Moses Harris at Mammoth Hot Springs. Harris approved the permit, stating that "it is desirable that all possible facilities for access to the National Park be afforded to the public," that it was "just and proper to permit the firm to continue its business as heretofore conducted" and that the firm was "the only line connecting with the Union Pacific system of railroads." On July 27, 1887, the Secretary of Interior also saw fit to answer the Bassetts' three-year-old letter asking permission to build a stable with cabins and to cut hay. He noted that their application was "pending" with Interior and wrote to them asking that they "furnish plans of bldgs., state how much ground & at what points &c."[333] Probably his own letters-file reminded the Secretary or his assistant that the Brothers' 1884 letter had apparently never been answered. All of this was a kindly-if-belated courtesy, but the Bassetts, as mentioned, had already erected their cabins in late 1884 or in the summer of 1885.

One 1887 party, its chronicler known only as "A," came to Beaver Canyon on the "Utah & Northern Branch" of the Union Pacific Railway specifically to compare the Bassett Brothers' route to that of the Northern Pacific Railroad. This party of two from Baltimore arrived from Ogden, Utah at one a.m. on July 24. Already hating that time of day, they were told that the hotel was full, and they would have to wait until 3 a.m. for the southbound train to carry off those guests in order to free-up a room for them. They immediately concluded that "the life of a Union Pacific traveler was not a happy one."[334]

At 9 a.m. that morning, these Baltimoreans began their two-day stage-ride to the Park. The vehicle was a canvas-covered spring-wagon drawn by four horses. It contained besides their party of two "the driver and a German gentleman and his wife from Indiana, the Teutonic element being liberally supplied with bottled beer," which bottles during the trip were often pitched out of their wagon to litter the roadside. Our couple thus learned how the area placename "Bottle Creek" originated.[335] But they were enthralled with acres and acres of "the loveliest and most dainty of wildflowers, representing all the colors and shades of a cultivated flower garden, with the added charm of being nature's unasked production." At 6 p.m. they reached the "little log house" on Henry's Fork of the Snake River "where the stages stop overnight both coming and going."[336] This probably was John Kooch's new "Snake River Crossing Hotel," which had probably begun in 1884 or 1885, and which would eventually be subsumed into the Arangee Ranch and the small town of Arangee that would formally begin in 1890. The party's supper of "mountain trout and venison" makes one wonder whether the nearby Rea brothers might have had a hand in procuring those foods, in some sort of arrangement with Mr. Kooch.

The even wilder country of the Henry's Fork's piney woods and valleys presented itself to the Baltimoreans on the second day with the usual "antelope" and sage hens making appearances. They passed only three houses in the ninety-nine-mile stretch and at the third of these (probably H. Clay Manley's cabin for luncheon), "we had the privilege of paying $1 for a dinner of antelope and canned oyster soup," which they declared "wouldn't pass muster in Maryland." After repairing a broken wagon-bolt and traveling for several more hours, they spied the lights of Firehole Hotel at 9 p.m. Although their long ride was "far from dull and uninteresting," they decided like many other travelers that this route offered too much staging and too long of days. They soon rented a two-horse unit with a separate driver to continue their trip, but without telling us from whom they obtained it. It might have been rented from the Bassetts themselves at Lower Geyser Basin or from the YPA at Firehole Hotel. Regardless, their newly chartered coach allowed them to spend an unlimited amount of time seeing and discussing the geysers of Lower, Midway, and Upper Basins.[337]

This party actually traveled to Yellowstone Lake, in an era when very few tourists did that, because of the alleged lack of lodging there and the terrible roads necessary to reach the lake. They were about to give up on lodging, when they spotted a small flag flying at the edge of the timber and below it a signboard reading "Lake Hotel, 250 yards distant." Upon proceeding a bit farther, "we came upon a few tents," said the author, "presided over by a 'lone fisherman,' who said we were the first people he had seen for eight days." "There was bed and board to be had," this chronicler added, "for the modest sum of $3 per day, and here we passed the night" at the tent hotel. They then visited Canyon, Norris Geyser Basin, and Mammoth, but did not tell us how they left the park.[338]

By August of 1887, newspapers were reporting that travel to Yellowstone was normal in numbers, for the *Butte Semi-Weekly Miner* announced the following: "Many hundreds of tourists are side-tracking at Beaver Canyon awaiting stage transportation from the Utah & Northern to Wonderland over a rough road and returning east over the Northern Pacific."[339] Still, one must wonder why these tourists were "awaiting" stages when the Bassetts presumably had plenty of vehicles, and that strange report makes us also wonder whether the Bassett Brothers had begun operating at a lesser level. Perhaps the lateness of their permit's issuance was a factor.

If the Brothers were indeed suddenly operating at a reduced level, there was another possible reason for it, and they must have had some advance warnings about this upcoming and disturbing, personal event. Suddenly on September 1, 1887, Charles Henry Bassett, Sr.—respected bookkeeper for S.P. Teasdel's store in Salt Lake City, patriarch of the Bassett family, and the father of all six Bassett Brothers of Beaver Canyon—found himself under arrest in Salt Lake City by police for "unlawful cohabitation." It was not quite the same as bigamy, but it was close to it and easier to prove, and he was not the first Mormon in good standing to find himself in such trouble.[340]

Nor was he the first Bassett to be so arrested. For many months during the previous year, one William E. Bassett, also from Salt Lake City and a Mormon bishop besides, had been held for bigamy and was being prosecuted for it. He was accused of having at least one wife beyond his first wife Sarah, and all through 1886, he appeared in story after story in Salt Lake City newspapers. The *Tribune's* accounts dripped with gossipy allegory. William Bassett was not a close relative of Charles Henry Bassett, Sr., although he might have been a distant one. After a grand jury indictment, he was convicted of bigamy on January 6, 1887, and sentenced to five years in prison.[341] Following that, this case went all the way to the U.S. Supreme Court, which three years later (December of 1890) reversed the Territorial Court of Utah and decided that a wife could not be used as a competent witness against her husband in a polygamy case. The U.S. Supreme Court then remanded the case back to Utah Territory to be retried.[342]

Both of these men, and numerous others, were victims of the U.S. government's ongoing war on polygamy against members of Utah Territory's Mormon Church, which was often referred to more broadly as the federal government's "crusade against Mormondom."[343] Having been official church policy since 1852, the practice of polygamy had been somewhat crippled in 1885 with the affirmation by the U.S. Supreme Court of the constitutionality of the Edmunds-Tucker Act (1882), and it would die (if only officially) five years later with the issuance by the LDS Church of its

1890 "manifesto."[344] But for now, polygamy was very much alive, and so were the federal prosecutors of it.

The September 2 headline announced Charles Henry Bassett's arrest. And its subheading stated that he was being "Held in the Usual Bonds on the Usual Charge," and these words suggested either that he had been in trouble for this crime before or else they were the newspaper's general denouncement of what was widely perceived in Utah as "Mormon persecution" by the U.S. government. The fact that the story was buried on page eight of the pro-Mormon *Salt Lake Herald* suggested that Mr. Bassett still held strong influence within the Mormon Church.[345]

Charles Henry Bassett, Sr. was indeed a serial polygamist. He married Permelia Mindwell Dayton in 1845 at Nauvoo, Illinois, and moved with her to Salt Lake City. He married Mary Elizabeth Knight in 1853 with the benefit of Permelia being deceased, and eventually also married Sarah Stageman (Ancestry.com says that she was a "spouse" to him and the *Salt Lake Tribune* called her a "wife"). And finally, he married Millie P. Bassett, his own niece, in 1882.

For a newspaper being published within the City of Saints, the Gentile *Tribune* treated C.H. Bassett extremely harshly, but, as one might expect, the pro-Mormon *Herald*'s statements were kinder and gentler, or at least innocuous. The *Tribune* treated Mary Knight Bassett harshly too, in the unforgivably gossipy and often downright libelous journalism that marked many nineteenth-century newspapers. Second-wife Mary, proclaimed the *Tribune*, was "a broken-down, broken-hearted woman for whose mind there is evidently no peace this side of the grave." Almost crying as she testified, said the newspaper, "not even a glance of reproach did she give the old cadaver of a Saint who sat stolidly in his chair like a clothier's dummy and stroked his patriarchal beard as though this woman's heart was no better than a football, for was she not his slave in the Lord?" The account made it clear that the *Tribune* had no love for the Mormon Church or for Charles Henry Bassett:

> According to the testimony, Mary married the old gospel goat in 1853, when his first wife Amelia [Permelia] was still living, a year in which he also hitched on to his celestial coat tails Sarah, the third wife. Millie (his niece) he took to his polygamous breast in 1872. Witness [Mary] had six children by the old brute, the

oldest being eight years; Millie has had four children by him, the oldest being five years. Two years ago[,] Bassett took it into his head to [finally] marry his niece, which he could do as he had no legal wife alive. So he suddenly ceased living with Mary, fired her out and married his kinswoman, with whom he has since been living. This being within the limit of the Edmunds law, it was a clean cinch, and Brother Moyle, who looked after the temporal welfare of this chaste and beautiful specimen of the priesthood, had nothing to say. Commissioner Norrell held the accused in $1500 bonds, and the witnesses in $200. Bassett's long, gray beard will be in the hands of the Penitentiary whip-makers inside of two months.[346]

It was clear from the final statement here that during that time, this newspaper and many others had no reservations about pronouncing someone guilty, even before a trial could be held.

Meanwhile, the Bassett Brothers in Beaver Canyon, Idaho must have been worried and fearful for their father in Salt Lake City. The fact that Levi Minerly—a bigamist in their own town with six wives and whom they must have personally known—had just been arrested for cohabitation in August could not have given them much peace of mind.[347]

Charles Henry Bassett, Sr. pled guilty to unlawful cohabitation and was sentenced on March 5, 1888, only nine days away from his sixtieth birthday. Considering the harsh sentences meted out to others who had done far less, he got off easy. He was sentenced to pay a fine of only fifty dollars, plus court costs.[348] The publicity for him in Salt Lake City had been devastating, but considering the known viewpoints of many members of the Mormon Church, he was undoubtedly still believed to be a hero in LDS quarters for resisting the ongoing "persecution" of Mormons.

In addition to the polygamy problems that Charles Henry Bassett, Sr. was facing in 1887, there was another, possible reason for the Bassett Brothers' stage-line apparently not functioning that year at its previous level, and it was bound up in the fact that in August, William Henry Bassett—whom we met earlier as a winter mail-carrier—suddenly found himself in trouble in Yellowstone National Park with park authorities, namely U.S. Army acting superintendent Moses Harris. This problem came almost on the heels of Harris's notifying the brothers in a letter of August 3, 1887 that their park-permit had been approved.[349]

Some days later, Captain Harris and his men discovered illicit activities at Lower Geyser Basin's Firehole Hotel. As the tale later unwound, the soldiers found a couple of members of "that unscrupulous class who hang about the borders of the Park to prey upon tourists" to have been drunk and disorderly at the hotel. These men were Charles Armand, a hotel employee, and Thomas Garfield, a less-than-honorable friend of Armand's and a friend of ne'er-do-well William James, who had recently perpetrated the July 4 Park robbery of a YPA stagecoach at "Split Rock," just south of Gardiner. Garfield would eventually be arrested for poaching in the Park and expelled, after which he would be suspiciously caught near a forest fire that Captain Harris believed he had purposely and vengefully set.[350]

But for now, Garfield was merely an acquaintance of Armand, who it developed, had obtained a key to the Firehole Hotel's storeroom. With supplies and especially liquor missing from the storeroom and his key in evidence, suspicion fell instantly onto Armand, and the hotel manager fired him. Discovering that Garfield had possession of some of the incriminating supplies, Captain Harris ordered him out of the Park. Then as now, fired employees were summarily forced to leave the Park because they suddenly had no housing in which to reside, so Garfield moved west, out of the Park to Madison Basin, but not before Harris found a letter in his handwriting addressed to William Henry Bassett—"the member of the [Bassetts'] firm residing in the Park"—which "implicated" Mr. Bassett in the theft. Harris learned from the letter that Bassett had proposed to hire Armand after the theft "and would have done so," wrote Harris, "had I permitted it."[351] Writing to the Secretary of Interior on September 15, 1887 about these events, Harris must have been surprised when the Secretary neglected to answer him, so Harris tried writing again in March of 1888.[352]

Assistant Secretary Muldrow was apparently worried that no parties other than the Bassetts were available in Beaver Canyon to transport tourists through the west entrance into the Park. Perhaps stalling for time or maybe caught failing to answer Captain Harris in a timely manner, Muldrow asked Harris whether the Captain adhered to his earlier opinion of withdrawing the Bassetts' permit, because frankly no one else was offering to fill that business-niche.[353]

Regardless, William Henry Bassett was now in trouble in Yellowstone, and it looked for a while like the incident could spell the end of his role in stage-driving and other in-park duties for the Bassetts' transportation business. But it took nearly a year for all the pieces to come together. Relevantly, William Bassett had managed the Bassetts' office at Lower Geyser Basin and served as the brothers' in-park representative, charged with acquiring permissions of all types including use of the Bassetts' barn at, or a short distance west of, Riverside. Beseeching Captain Harris not to evict him from the Park, William received the Captain's angry reply dated July 25, 1888: "I shall not in any way modify my order directing you to vacate the station at Riverside, nor will I permit Bassett Brothers to occupy any other permit or station, within the park, except at the Lower Basin."[354] This put the Park's final stamp of disapproval upon William Bassett's in-park employment with the brothers' stage line. For the next few years, he seems to have served as the company's bookkeeper at Beaver Canyon while also continuing to operate his general store at Lago, Idaho. But eventually the ever-changing military superintendents either forgot about the incident or forgave him.

While Park authorities were piecing these events together in early 1888, the other Bassetts—apparently assuming that their request for lease of land for buildings had been approved—sent plans to Harris on March 10 and reminded him that the said land was "the same as approved by you last season."[355] But William's bad actions had changed Harris's mind, and the Captain had thus already disapproved their lease for buildings.[356] Harris explained to the Secretary that because of William Bassett's role in the late-summer theft and also for "drinking stolen liquor with the employees of the Park Association," he did not consider Bassett "a proper person to reside in the Park or to transact business therein." These problems, said Harris, were complicated by the fact that the Army had no legal method in the Park for preserving both order and respect for property rights "except through the expulsion of improper characters," and Harris feared that the Bassetts' complex at Lower Geyser Basin was becoming "a rendezvous" for those bad characters. Harris stated that he had heard that the Union Pacific had propositioned George Wakefield to take over this part of the park's transportation but that if this were not the case, he believed the Bassett Brothers' rights in the Park should be restricted to mere transportation from Beaver Canyon to Lower Geyser Basin.[357] That would prove to be the continuing case for more than a decade to come.

Because of the back-and-forth letters required between Harris and Interior and the general slowness of winter mail to the park, William Bassett—still living at Lower Basin if his return address was to be believed—did not receive Harris's order to vacate the "Riverside" barn until "July 22." He wrote to Harris stating that the order to vacate their barn was very surprising to him: "If I had had any idea that you laid any claim whatever to this building," he fumed, "I certainly would not have taken possession of it without your consent." William complained that the barn, which he stated was located two (really four) miles inside the west entrance, had become very dilapidated "since your soldiers have used" it and "this spring was even dangerous and unfit to cover horses." Then William stated that he had even mentioned this fact to Harris in a conversation with him and from that, "I supposed of course that I was at liberty to use it" for our business "as freely as we do other cabins in the Park." William noted that the Bassetts needed this spot "at Riverside" for changing horses "before climbing the big hill." He ended his letter by asking for the brothers to be allowed to keep horses in the barn for a month or six weeks more.[358]

It appears that Harris, perhaps feeling guilty for the slowness of letters and maybe caught forgetting his earlier, personal conversation with William, relented and allowed the brothers to use the barn, at least for the rest of 1888, although no letters confirming this short arrangement have been found.

Returning now to Beaver Canyon and the remainder of the Bassetts' season of 1887, we find that the Bassett Brothers, or more likely one of their employees, chauffeured Edwards Roberts, a tourist from Boston, to Yellowstone late that summer, and except for its ending, this trip was apparently one of the most successful parts of the Bassetts' summer. Roberts wrote two accounts, one that was published as a magazine article and the other, a longer account, for his 1888 book *Shoshone and Other Western Wonders*. Because the two accounts were different, we have used both versions here. "To one loving scenery, and who does not fear the fatigue of a stage ride nearly 100 miles long," wrote tourist Roberts, "the Beaver Canyon route is perhaps the most interesting and attractive." His party left from there headed east on a September morning, not many days after Charles Henry

Bassett, Sr. was arrested in Salt Lake City. "Two teams had been engaged," Roberts noted, "one a wagon drawn by four horses, and the other a lighter vehicle to carry our luggage." The "artist" member of their party rode in this latter wagon by himself so that he could smoke his pipe unfettered, while the others rode in the four-horse wagon with their driver. The artist was W.B. Tyler of San Francisco, who was making sketches for the article that Mr. Roberts planned to write about the trip. Roberts described the serenity of the country as they departed from Beaver Canyon:

> It was very quiet. No sound, other than that made by our horses, could be heard. Nowhere was there a hint of civilization. Not a house could be seen; nothing but bare brown fields and the distant ranges.[359]

In his book, Roberts captured some of the magic of the American West, when he described the way distant views appeared to the observer in that vast country, in ways that were and still are very different from the American East, as well as the very quality of the air itself. "The delicious air," he wrote, "neither hot nor cold, the extended views, the brilliant colorings, the sense of freedom from all prosaic conventionality, were conditions by virtue of which life was given a new meaning; its dull realities were felt no more."[360] This author recalls breathing and feeling the same enchanting, atmospheric phenomenon as a child of twelve while visiting the Yellowstone country from Oklahoma, and nearly fifty years of living in and near the great Park have not dimmed it at all.

Lunching at Camas Meadows twenty-five miles later, they changed horses from a corral and traveled on, soon seeing the "Three Tetons" at a distance to the southeast (a spectacular view that accompanied the Bassetts' stage-travelers for many miles on clear days). They passed consecutively through Antelope Valley, Sheridan Valley, and Shotgun Valley, before splashing across the Henry's Fork of Snake River to find their nighttime cabin. Roberts noted in his book that if a traveler desired, the Bassetts would simply rent the equipment to him and he could camp wherever he liked, rather than using the Brothers' prearranged spots, which sometimes held cabins and prepared meals. His woodcut drawing of the building at "Snake River crossing" and his mention that "just across the stream [on its east side] stood the row of cabins which some adventurous landlord has built for the accommodation of passing travelers" confirms that the owners of what appeared to be a new place—John and Margaret Kooch—were present in 1887 and running this lodging facility, which they called "Snake River Crossing Hotel."[361] Indeed, this was also confirmed for us in 1888 by traveler Albert Zahm. Zahm mentioned what apparently was the same spot after he crossed Henry's Fork and encountered the (same) "row of log huts" that Roberts had called "the row of cabins." Steele mentioned (col. 2) that his party reached "Kooch's hotel" on the river.[362]

Now we return to Mr. Roberts's account. On the following morning, Roberts's horses were missing. His driver's comment when asked where they were was "Blest if I know." That was a clue that this driver was probably employed by the Bassetts, for this was a good Mormon answer as opposed to the usual profanity they might have heard from many other men. Once the driver found his straying horses, the party was off again, this time for Henry's Lake, Targhee Pass, and then H. Clay Manley's cabin, where they were to spend the second night.[363] Later in the *Shoshone* account, Roberts described the driver's pride as he held his own little daughter, indicating that he was probably a Mormon and Bassett-employee living in Shotgun Valley, rather than in Beaver Canyon, and thus making it unlikely that he was one of the Bassett Brothers themselves.[364]

The next day, they entered the Park, crossed Superintendent Norris's high road (walking at times to save wear on the horses on the long, steep hill), and dropped into Lower Geyser Basin, where their plan was to stay at Firehole Hotel. This arrangement indicates for us that the Bassett Brothers were not operating their usual tents and meals at this location, and it makes us believe that the brothers had either ended their season early or possibly were not operating at full strength this summer, perhaps because of the family problems involving their father in Salt Lake City. Regardless, this lack of lodging plus an apparent shortage of supplies for Mr. Roberts's party would soon cause them the trouble with Captain Harris as described above.

The next morning, Roberts's driver took the party to Old Faithful, where they saw lots of geysers. "Guess you're pretty lucky people," remarked the driver later in the day. When they asked why, he answered, "'Cause the 'Giantess' is goin' to go off soon, an' she don't blow more'n once a month."

As Yellowstone tourists, they were indeed lucky, even though the Giantess Geyser's interval was closer to every fourteen days. The party waited by its crater that evening, and when it was nearly dark,

> the entire pool was lifted bodily into the air. Higher it ascended, and still higher, and then, shooting upward from the greater body, rose a solitary column, the top of which we could not see. The roar was deafening; clouds of vapour rolled away toward the forests; streams of boiling water ran headlong to the river close at hand. The scene was one of awful beauty...For some minutes the steaming shaft lifted itself high above us, and then the waters settled, and the basin that had held them was deserted. Earth had reclaimed the flood. Then, with a roar like thunder, the cone [basin] was filled again, and once more the water spurted up into the night and was lost in the darkness. For an hour we watched the eruption, and later, from the hotel, could hear its groans.[365]

The Giantess Geyser was a Yellowstone wonder that all visitors (at least the ones who knew of it) wanted to see erupting, but that few actually saw. Early accounts made it clear that its "solitary column," which shot upward *through* its lower, wider, and more-rounded dome of water, was an unusual characteristic of this geyser, which could then and can still today erupt seventy-five to two hundred feet tall.

After a circuit of the park, the Bassetts' driver ("that knight of the front seat") deposited Mr. Roberts and his party at Mammoth Hot Springs Hotel, and that was the last the party saw of him, for he no doubt then drove south into the park and returned west to Beaver Canyon. The Roberts party, however, found a stage-ride north to Cinnabar, Montana, where they could board the Northern Pacific Railroad to eastern cities.[366]

It was probably events occurring on this trip that only a few days later began to cause trouble for the Bassett Brothers, for on September 15, 1887, Captain Moses Harris, park superintendent, began writing the previously mentioned letters to Assistant Secretary H.L. Muldrow denouncing the Brothers' firm. In October, the Brothers took their horses out of Beaver Canyon and moved them to winter pasture at Gentile Valley, just southwest of Lago, Idaho where both Charles Henry Bassett II and William Henry Bassett owned ranches.[367]

The Bassett Brothers were active in 1888 by June, because one of them went to the Park early "on a trip of inspection" and returned to Beaver Canyon to report to the railroad and a Utah newspaper that "the Excelsior Geyser at Hell's Half Acre," today's Midway Geyser Basin, was "now in eruption, playing every fifty-five minutes." "She throws water," said the account, "from 225 to 250 feet high."[368] That particular Bassett, or one of the brothers' other drivers, reported that the road to the park was "in good condition," so the Bassetts made ready for another season of transporting tourists, and they must have hoped, like everyone else who knew of it, that Excelsior Geyser's activity would increase their business. Apparently, it or other factors did increase the Park's visitation, for historian Haines has estimated a total of 6,000 visitors for this year as opposed to the 5,000 calculated for each of the preceding five years.[369]

We also know that 1888 was a banner year of travel and events for the park's main stage-coacher—George Wakefield and the Yellowstone Park Association Stage Company—which included the visits of two large groups, namely the Dakota and the Iowa Press Associations. The Bassetts' one known trip-account this year was affected by that Iowa press group, because its author mentioned that his party "had been badly fed at lunch" when the IPA "devoured all but the fish, soup and onions." This author—Albert Francis Zahm (1862-1954), who traveled with the Brothers that year and wrote an eleven-chapter account about his trip—became famous in his later life as an aeronautical experimenter, a professor of mathematics and physics, and the Chief of the Aeronautical Division of the Library of Congress. He would testify as an expert witness in the lawsuits between the Wright Brothers and Glenn Curtiss (1910-1914). He would build America's first wind tunnel in 1901. And he would publish the book *Aerial Navigation* in 1911, which described the historical development of experimental aircraft that eventually led to functional airplanes.[370] But in 1888, he was merely a twenty-six-year-old graduate-student who possessed a newly minted master's degree from the University of Notre Dame, the title of "Professor," and an overwhelming curiosity about Yellowstone National Park.

Like Edwards Roberts in 1887, Professor Zahm went first to Idaho's Shoshone Falls on Snake River and then took the train to Beaver Canyon,

where his party was met, not by a raucous, old-days' coachman as he expected, but rather "by a gentleman and a Studebaker's covered carriage." This
was a word-salute to one of the Bassett Brothers himself (probably Julius)
although we do not know for certain which brother served as their driver.[371]
Gamebirds were abundant, Zahm noted as they headed east, along with sage
hens, curlews, sand hill cranes, eagles, buzzards, pheasants, hawks, ducks,
and many waterfowl all visible. Like other travelers, he mentioned the area's great fishing, and he glowingly described the magnificent agriculture
happening in the valley of West Camas Creek, "which Mr. Bassett informs
us, covers an area of one hundred thousand acres." This fact was personally
illustrated to Professor Zahm in the stories of a local ranchman, his wife,
and several children living at the Bassetts' Indian Springs lunch-station and
with whom Zahm's party shared lunch. Those homesteaders within two
years would likely become connected to the new Swiss settlers at Arangee
who were attracted to the valley's magnificent agriculture, and we shall tell
that story shortly.

Professor Zahm then performed a service for future generations by explaining the origin of two of the area's oldest placenames, Shotgun Creek
and Shotgun Valley, which were "named after the lamentations of one of
the early miners" in that region. This miner, said Zahm:

Albert Francis Zahm,
author's collection.

had camped with his comrades at this place, and seeing vast flocks of waterfowl all about him longed to shoot some but had no gun. Then he wished for a shot gun, and said to his friends, if he only had a shot gun. Oh, if he only had a shot gun! And all evening he wished for one, but it came not; and he wished all night till morning, but no shot gun came. "Morn came and went and came and brought no gun." And his friends seeing his great distress, laughed and derided him cruelly, singing: "Oh, for a shot gun, shot gun, shot gun! Oh, for a shot gun, shot gun, oh!" And since that day, the little stream has borne its barbarous name.[372]

This miner, whom Zahm did not name, could certainly have been George Rea.

Zahm's version of the name-origin might be older than two other stories we have, but the other two probably have more credibility because they came directly from the namer himself, the man we have just mentioned, George Rea. Additionally, there were two stories by Zahm and they matched, so our money is on this second version as the correct one. In his earliest days in the region George W. Rea was a miner himself who was in place to have given the name to the stream because he was one of the first settlers in the area. Charlotte Rea, the widow of George Rea who lived for many summers with him on Shotgun Creek, gave this version in 1911, and it was a story that he apparently told her:

> A party of tourists out in the mountains with Mr. Rea as guide became wearied with travel, and one fellow, who had declined to do anything or carry any burden, was handed a shot gun to carry, and he said he wasn't going to accompany the party as a beast of burden. Rea told him he would have to carry that gun into camp or be responsible for its value. The sport stood it against a tree and journeyed, and the creek on which this happened took its name from this incident.[373]

The third story appeared in 1892 and varied only slightly from Mrs. Rea's version, with George Rea claiming—in the story he told to two of his cli-

ents—that it happened in the 1860s, probably in 1865 or 1866. According
to this story as authored by an unknown "Shongo," Rea and a partner were
trapping, and the partner had one of the old-fashioned, smooth-bore rifles
that was "as heavy as a fence rail and Rea says almost as long 'and not worth
a white and black skunk-skin anyway'." "For a thimbleful of beans, I would
chuck it into the creek," said Rea. They did not want to pack it, so his
partner stood the old gun up against a cottonwood tree and the men moved
on. A couple of years later, Rea visited the spot again and saw the rifle still
standing against the tree, and true to his original thought, he "took up the
weapon and cast it into the stream."[374]

The name Shotgun Valley remains on maps today, but Shotgun Creek's
name eventually yielded to (and thus was later officially changed to) Sheridan Creek, as the settlers who occupied Sheridan Ranch witnessed their
own local usage of a placename successfully defeating one of the oldest,
other placenames in the region.

Returning now to Professor Zahm, his party then passed "a number of log
huts embossed at every corner with heads and antlers," a place that sounds to
us today like the settlement of Glen Rea, Idaho, which basically was the ranch
of the Rea brothers. "The driver stopped on business," said Zahm, "and an old
man came out to see us." Described as wearing "two pairs of pants, a slouch
hat, an old woolen shirt, and everlasting boots," this man, who was going to
take them fishing, was most likely George Rea himself, and at this time he
had just turned fifty-six years old. Indeed, Rea was already headed toward
establishing the large fishery-and-hatchery operation that he would operate at
this place until his death in early 1902. Clearly this was the case, for Zahm described fish in the river that came "shooting from every direction, right glad to
see us…by legions from all quarters…Again and again was this performance
repeated, but the fish never took fright, nor lost their eagerness until the old
man came and fed them." Zahm further explained that

> He keeps them here "for everybody's amusement and charges
> nothing. They are not fenced in but have full play of the stream,
> and they gather here because they like me and I treat them like
> pets." Someone asked him if he did not find it lonely here with-
> out neighbors. "No," he said. "I have been living here for thir-
> ty-seven years, and I am the happiest man in the world."[375]

The man's stated time of thirty-seven years for when he settled there, if true, would have dated his occupancy to 1851, long before the known settlement of the region began, so we must believe that this man was indeed George Rea, either adding to his own legend as a long-term guide or else simply misremembering the number of years in his time-statement. As described elsewhere, Rea says he first visited the area in 1865 and located in the region in 1868, just one year after reputed first settler Gilman Sawtell and before Richard W. "Dick" Rock, another early settler of the Island Park area. And of course, we know that Rea spent many years in Montana before returning to Idaho's Shotgun Valley.[376]

Moreover, Zahm's statement that their driver, Mr. Bassett, "stopped on business" here makes sense because the Bassetts had used the Rea brothers' ranch apparently since 1882 to shelter their passengers for the night, so the brothers' discussing business with them in person was always relevant. At some point—perhaps this very year or the preceding one or both—the Bassetts would have been initiating conversations with the Reas about changing their guests' overnight arrangements, for we know that the Brothers were trying to shorten their staging distance to Yellowstone from three days to two days and eventually to one day. There was also the fact that John and Margaret Kooch were operating a new lodging facility on their land a few miles east of George Rea. So perhaps this moment was being used by the Bassetts for one of those meetings. The fact that Zahm's party traveled on after this and "at sunset reached" the Henry's Fork of Snake River, "forded it and halted for the night at the Snake River hotel," suddenly became important to the Bassetts' and the Reas' overarching stories, especially if this was indeed the moment (or one of the moments) when the Brothers quit using the Reas' ranch and moved their guests to the different overnight spot. Clearly Zahm's night-stop occurred at the newer ranch east of the Reas' original place, which was located on the east side of the Henry's Fork at what soon would become the new settlement of Arangee.[377]

The name Arangee requires a detailed explanation, and naturally there is a fascinating story lurking behind the migration of that tiny town's new people to it in this otherwise unsettled area of Shotgun Valley, both of which were so important to the Bassett Brothers who traveled through them to Yellowstone for so long. A reporter for the *Idaho Republican* in 1919, who was searching for a local feature-story, looked back thirty years to find pioneers from the area who remembered the relevant events. No one could recall the exact year, but they did remember what occurred. According to this account, the story involving 130 families was still seldom mentioned locally "because of the discouraging effect it might have on other settlers."

The year was apparently 1890 when a New York capitalist named John Gerber rode the train to Beaver Canyon, boarded a stagecoach belonging to the Bassett Brothers, and rode their coach to Yellowstone Park via "the beautiful Camas meadows in mid-summer when all nature was at its best." Gerber was a Swiss-German immigrant, and he was enthralled with these huge meadows "deep with grass" and also with the "great plain" lying to the east that extended many miles to Shotgun Creek. "If it were only irrigated," he thought, it could be equally as productive as his beloved Switzerland. Gerber's idea was to hire Swiss people from his native country to run cattle and produce Swiss cheese. "He pictured the prosperity of a Swiss colony," explained the reporter, "with their flocks in the mountains in summer and down the valley in winter." After all, was not that the way it was done in Switzerland? Surely it would work in Shotgun Valley, Idaho too.[378]

Traveling to the land office in the then-county-seat of Blackfoot, Mr. Gerber found that the country was open to settlement and obtainable, and he was excited. He returned to Switzerland and with his powers of persuasion convinced 130 families to emigrate to the United States and Idaho's Shotgun Valley. By the following June, the families were occupying their new homes. They purchased hundreds if not thousands of cattle and began laboring to construct "irrigation works to spread the water all over the land."[379]

George Rea lived in Shotgun Valley on his ranch, and in the summer, his wife Charlotte lived there too. On an adjacent ranch lived their friend A.S. Trude,[380] a rich lawyer from Chicago who later would bring wealthy visitors to his dude ranch through time. John Gerber had already told Mr. Rea and Mr. Trude about his plans, and they were surprised but seemed to offer encouragement. Nevertheless, John Gerber did not trust Rea and Trude. Surely Rea wanted the land to make a fortune for himself, thought Gerber. After all, "did he not act as guide to hunting parties and tell them of the riches of all that country round about?" Rea told Gerber about the deep snows of winter, "awfully deep." He spoke of the winters that were long, "terribly long." Like Rea, Mr. Trude was diplomatic and did not discourage

John Gerber. Instead, he asked Gerber whether he had investigated winter temperatures, general climatic conditions, and precipitation records. Gerber saw all these points as sly tricks by Trude and Rea to discourage him to keep the land for themselves. After all, he reasoned, was Trude not the "big king-pin of the Associated Press" and in league with large Chicago stock companies? Surely these two men were plotting against his enterprise. He made up his mind not to be fooled by these diplomatic tricks; "he would not be taken in by these men of cunning," he thought to himself. Instead, "he would turn a deaf ear to all their remarks and suggestions."[381]

"The month [of] June," said the article, "found 130 families in their new homes." The transplanted Swiss settlers were enthusiastic. They worked as laborers for the wealthy Gerber and the other New York and Ohio capitalists who headed the enterprise. They built diversion dams for irrigation and made plans to manufacture great amounts of Swiss cheese from the Arangee Ranch's dairy cows.[382]

Then winter intervened. It came earlier than in Switzerland and "lasted infinitely longer," for this valley was located close to the Continental Divide. Winter was indeed difficult, and the new settlers probably had already heard old-timers like George Rea talking about having four feet of snow on the level for six months of the year. That was a death threat for cows facing a shortage of the grass that should have been put up for winter-hay. Neither Gerber nor any of the new settlers had listened to George Rea, and by December, ominously, the inadequate hay-supply was gone.[383]

The Swiss settlers tried to buy hay. After all, there was plenty of it available for four dollars per ton over at Idaho Falls and down at Blackfoot. But there was no railroad closer than Beaver Canyon, fifty miles away, and the snow was already too deep to transport it from there east to Shotgun Valley. Their other recourse was to drive the cattle south and east to Marysville and St. Anthony, recently founded in 1889 and 1890 respectively. Men and horses broke the trail through the snow, while the cattle followed feebly behind.

> Day after day they were prodded along, and night after night they lay down in the long sleep from which fewer and fewer rose in the morning. Scores of them froze to death standing in the deep snow with their bodies resting on the [snow] pack, and others sank down a little, resting on the snow, and froze their

limbs till they were useless, and gradually the bodies gave up the life. At last the survivors were abandoned in their helplessness, and the locality was given the name of skeleton valley for years afterwards.[384]

Ultimately the drover who was responsible for this cattle drive committed suicide, concluded the article, and thus the "great Swiss Cheese enterprise" ended in failure and death. A check of the cemetery internet-list at St. Anthony shows no burials that could be this drover from this winter, so perhaps he was buried at Blackfoot, which was then in Bingham County. Or he was buried somewhere on the spot, even in the snow temporarily while waiting for the spring thaw and then reburied there in the spring when the ground had thawed.

George Rea and his brother Thomas had been settlers for nearly a decade on the west bank of Henry's Fork at Glen Rea, and indeed they must have felt at least some resentment toward these new interlopers. In that respect, the Reas represented a microcosm of what was happening all over the American West, as newly arrived immigrants invaded neighborhoods and interrupted solitude. The Reas probably disliked the situation, but what could they do? The newcomers had greater numbers as well as the money to hire other locals to be their ranch-hands. According to historian Dean Green, John Gerber had been joined by K.E. Hopf, and perhaps a Mr. "Rutledge."[385] So, the Reas gritted their teeth and decided to unite with the new settlers, because by 1893, George Rea was writing for an area newspaper that referred to him as "our Arangee correspondent." This period represented the early years of the settlement of Arangee, Idaho, which outlived him. George Rea, however, would have had the last laugh if he had known that his name would remain on the tiny "town" of "Rea" through at least 1997,[386] while the "town" of Arangee would be gone in the early twentieth century. Its name would survive only on a nearby mountain, and in a misspelled form ("Arange Peak") at that.[387]

The accounts of Thayer and Zahm as previously chronicled imply that original homesteaders John W. Kooch (1861-1954) and his wife Margaret (1868-1929), who had been in place since 1880, were operating a lodging facility on their own land in 1887 and 1888, and indeed the land-indenture for the property makes it clear that this was the case. Historian Green says

John Gerber and his partners from New York purchased the land from John Kooch in 1889 and named their company the Arangee Land and Cattle Company, but, as will soon become apparent, the land records show that the actual transaction occurred in 1890, and the Blackfoot newspaper backed that up. So, it was indeed John and Margaret Kooch who were operating the "Snake River Crossing Hotel" from 1885 through 1889. Green also says that Gerber's new company hired Swiss people including the Reber brothers.[388]

In the land-deed, John W. Kooch of Bingham County sold to John Gerber of New York City on October 3, 1890 for $1250 all the property known as the "Snake River Crossing Hotel." That land, said the deed, was "situate[d] on [the] Yellowstone National Park Stage Road" in the county of Bingham, Idaho, and the deal included the

> said Hotel, stables[,] and all other buildings of whatever kind pertaining thereto, including fencing and bridge; also household furniture, as follows[:] Kitchen Range and fixtures, 2 tables, and all chairs except 6, 2 horn hat racks, carpets, stoves, etc. as it stands except rocking chair and clock[;] 8 single bedroom[s], and 2 double bed rooms furnished as they stand except 1 bedstead, 1 lounge [chair?] and 1 washstand, all bedding except 4 [pair?] blankets, 4 quilts, 6 pillows, 6 sheets and 6 pillow cases, [and] crockery, glassware and bar room furniture excepted. It is further stipulated that Bassett Brothers have use of stables and pasture so long as their stage line to the Park is run under the present firm name, they, to keep stables in proper repair, the ownership to remain with the grantee [Gerber].[389]

Returning now to Professor Zahm's Yellowstone trip of 1888 with the Bassett Brothers, Zahm began his next chapter with a description of Kooch's hotel, calling it "a row of log huts, one of which serves as a sleeping apartment, another as a dining room, a third as a saloon, [and] a fourth as a museum." This last building was covered with antlers of deer and elk, noted Zahm, "and decked with eagle wings, brilliant feathers and many valuable furs." Moreover, Zahm's long description of the numerous men who were hanging out at this place ("a number of miners, hunters, and trappers"), as the setting sun's rays punctuated the pastoral scene, further made the place sound like it could have been part of Glen Rea. But because the hermit-like Rea brothers probably would not have taken well to enlarging their ranch into a spot with this much activity, and because they are not known to have *ever* expanded their ownings to the east side of the river, it seems more likely that this was the property that John Kooch would sell to John Gerber and his Arangee company two years later. "After supper we went out to the campfire," gushed Professor Zahm, "where the men were sitting on the ground with their dogs, smoking, spinning long yarns, and relating their adventures; the scene was romantic and picturesque." The place "is addicting" to many of these men, volunteered Zahm, "some of whom have become so attached to it as to remain years at a time away from town or railroad."[390] Those men had found the place dreamily idyllic, and so did Professor Zahm.

On the following day, Zahm began listing the region's animals and plants, and this became his paean to the area's prominence as a "masterpiece of nature." The locale's animals included wolves, bears, mountain lions, skunks, badgers, minks, foxes, coyotes, woodchucks (probably marmots), deer, elk, antelope (pronghorn), porcupines, pheasants, sage hens, swans, wild ducks and geese, eagles, hawks, curlews, owls, and sand-hill cranes. He spent almost half a page describing the wildflowers, a firmament "from whose spangled carpet shone buds and bells and blossoms thick as the bright stars of heaven." No other early observer to our knowledge gushed on about wildflowers as Professor Zahm did when he mentioned twenty-two specific bloomers. "Flowers, flowers, [are] everywhere covering the valleys, the hills, the mountains," he enthused, "a host of smiling innocents with sweet cherubic faces."[391]

The party "halted for dinner" (lunch in those days) west of Targhee Pass, two miles east of Henry's Lake and on the original stage-road, which ran up Targhee Creek. It appears that this spot was the Bassetts' new stage-stop and "hotel" just east of the lake, another innovation adopted by the Brothers to shorten their trip to the park to two days instead of three. The origins of this building are, for now, uncertain. Perhaps the Bassetts built it themselves in or about 1888. Regardless, area resident Silas McMinn apparently owned it by 1889 or at least had possession of it. Perhaps the new building became more than the Bassetts could handle, and they sold it to him. "Here they keep venison, spring water trout, and delicious sweet milk," said Zahm, "for them that hunger and thirst." He described this place as a "hotel" with a German "hotel manager," but the party did not stay there.[392] Obtaining spare horses farther on at a spot Zahm called "the relay station on Madison River" (a barn located inside the Park at or near Riverside Soldier Station where the Bassetts housed extra stock), his party "puffed up the mountain" on Superintendent Norris's high road and began descending to Firehole Hotel at 5 p.m.[393]

There they examined the hotel's hot-water bathing-spot at Hygeia Spring, lingered on a wooden footbridge that allowed views of the geyser region's vapor-columns, and took curious pleasure in the great diversity of park visitors who were gathered there for the night:

> Englishmen from Canada and good old Britain; dudes from New York; preachers from Dakota and Michigan; railroad men, professors, whiskey-men from Kentucky; geyser experts from Iceland, and the four corners of the globe; newspaper men innumerable; women and children, mashers and fair young maidens just from school—all roughing it, reckless, and without reserve.[394]

On the following day, Zahm's party saw Fountain Geyser erupt to 150 feet high (one of that geyser's rare, extra-tall eruptions that was twice the height of a regular eruption), listened to two stage-drivers demeaning tourists' general carelessness in the potentially dangerous place that was Yellowstone, and then watched an explosive, and rare, eruption of Excelsior Geyser at Midway Geyser Basin:

> Presently it began to rise at the center, upheaving the bosom of the waters, and thus continued for a moment convulsed as with a spasm and making vigorous but ineffectual efforts to arise, like some great monster in agony; then it would boil and toss and pitch furiously, gaining in strength until, with a tremendous outbreak that tore up the bottom of the lake, it hurled rocks and water with volcanic violence, steaming and sparkling; [and] a mountain of water that arose, stood for a moment and

fell with a crash that shook the earth and then subsided, while upwards, like its departing spirit, soared a great white cloud heavenward. The performance lasted but a few seconds, yet all were well pleased and applauded the wonderful demonstration of power. This geyser is unique in its proportions and manner of operating. The others for the most part rise in high narrow columns, while this one, when at its maximum, has the form of an irregular pyramid one hundred and fifty feet high with the whole lake for a base.[395]

In the next two days, Zahm's party traveled to Old Faithful, Norris Geyser Basin, and Canyon for one night, and apparently Mammoth for the second night.[396] Along the way, they bribed their stage-driver with a chew of tobacco and a "pull" on some Kentucky whiskey, thus "rendering him to become very communicative" with them. As a result, he told them the long story of park superintendent P.W. Norris's shooting of a grizzly bear at Grizzly Lake, complete with "a rich seasoning of 'hics' and profane expletives" and of course a fair amount of good-old-boy malarkey.[397] One has to believe that this driver was not C.J. Bassett, but rather a substitute coachman whom the group probably picked up at Firehole Hotel. At the Canyon, after the usual extended, philosophical gallivanting and some tiresome religiosity,[398] Zahm and his party slept at the "Falls Hotel," and started for Mammoth on the following morning. As a marvelous sunrise greeted them, they left the canyon, visited the "Devil's Graveyard" (the Hoodoos), and then the Mammoth Hot Springs, even bathing in Bath Lake and "borrowing," without attribution, a description of Cleopatra Spring from previous-year visitor Edwards Roberts.[399] And Professor Zahm got so involved with writing two chapters on the theory of geysers and Mammoth Hot Springs that he failed to tell us for certain whether his party spent the night at Mammoth and how they left the park.[400] Thus, Professor Zahm's account became one of the greatest park "guidebooks" of the nineteenth century, but will forever remain incomplete as to whether he returned west to Beaver Canyon or left the park north via Cinnabar and the Northern Pacific Railroad.

Except for Zahm's account, we know little about the Bassetts' stage-coaching operations in 1888. Probably the Brothers were still somewhat hampered by the events of 1887 and William Bassett's ongoing, park correspondence about them in 1888, but one newspaper reported enthusiastically in September that their stage-line was "being run to its utmost capacity this month."[401]

In 1889, the Bassett Brothers (now only William and Jules) began operating early due to a light winter for snow. Park Hotels were attempting to open by May 15, and the Brothers resultingly attempted to begin their trips by June 1.[402] In early June, they wrote to new park superintendent F.A. Boutelle, again asking for use of the barn at "Riverside." One wonders whether the Bassetts, knowing that Captain Harris had been replaced by Captain Boutelle, felt that they might receive approval from the new superintendent when they could not get it from the old superintendent Harris. Apparently, the army was again not using this barn,[403] and so the Bassetts asked to use it in a letter dated June 10. Explaining that "in 1882 we bought a small stable or barn in the park fifteen miles west of Lower Basin and two miles inside of park line situated on the Madison River," they requested permission to again use this building, and that would have been a strange appeal indeed if they had purchased the soldiers' building, so probably it was a different building.[404] Captain Boutelle replied that he could not see a reason for their inquiry nor why they needed a building "in that neighborhood" but that he would submit it to the Secretary of the Interior.[405] In his letter to the Secretary of June 22, Boutelle was puzzled by the Bassetts' request to occupy this "station at Riverside," made because of the "difficulty of procuring water at other points than at Riverside." It was an assertion that made no sense to Boutelle considering the abundance of streams in Yellowstone. Asking for the Secretary's ruling, Boutelle noted that his predecessor, Captain Harris, "has [strongly] objected to their being [issued] any leases in the park and in fact to their doing business in the park" at all.[406] The Secretary agreed with Boutelle, instructing him that "you will inform Bassett Bros. that they will not be permitted to occupy Riverside."[407] However, both the Secretary and Boutelle still had no other applicants to carry Beaver Canyon tourists, so the Brothers' transportation business had to be tolerated. This would remain the case through 1898.

Also operating this year (1889) were the usual tourists on the railroad who were traveling in their own "outfits" to the park. For example, the Union Pacific dispatched a special train to Beaver Canyon from Pocatello (originally Omaha) on August 10, "conveying a large party bound for the park, together with their carriages and camping paraphernalia." Thomas L. Kimball, the General Manager of the UP was one of these people who shipped his own coach on the train, so perhaps the Bassett Brothers were not operating at full strength at this time.[408] The story of this party really appeared in the *Omaha* (Nebraska) *Daily Bee* in two installments that did in fact gave us new information about the hotel at Arangee. The Bassett Brothers probably saw, but apparently did not do business with, this large group of travelers who brought several of their own coaches on the train with their own drivers. The group, discussed in two articles and loosely known as the "Union Pacific excursion," was noteworthy for giving us new information on the Arangee settlement and John Kooch's hotel on the Henry's Fork, but not so noteworthy for the (lack of) information they provided about their trip to Yellowstone. The coaches were two of veteran stage-man Col. James Stephenson's six-horse, Tally-ho coaches, bearing the painted names "James Stephenson" and "Thomas L. Kimball" and operated by the "Western Stage Line," which had solicited fifteen men and their wives for $175 each, with the total number limited to fifty, if they sold that many seats.

The party left Omaha on August 8, supposedly with fifteen persons, expecting to pick up others along the way. As identified, they were: S.A. Orchard, Col. J.A.S Reed (a publicity man for the Union Pacific), Clarence Brown (advertising manager for Union Pacific), the previously mentioned Thomas L. Kimball (a General Manager for Union Pacific), James Stephenson and his two daughters, a Dr. Davis and his wife, Dr. W.D. Smouse, and R.J. Clancey, a reporter for the *Omaha Bee*. The party's plan was to reach Yellowstone on August 12 and return August 29.[409]

At Beaver Canyon, after all dined at the town's hotel where they might have been in the same room with some of the Bassett Brothers, the drivers placed the party-members "on board the gay Concord stages." Attached to each stage "were six prancing steeds that awaited the command of the driver to 'take-her-up'." "All aboard," yelled James Stephenson, and the drivers cracked their whips for Camas Meadows where they spent the night.

The next day, the stages rolled east to the Henry's Fork of Snake River, the halfway point, where they frolicked in the meadows and fished in productive streams that were tributaries to the Fork. At this point, wrote the scribe, "Messrs. Caldwell, Thomas O'Donnell, and John Kooch, a trio of pioneers who remain in charge of the way-station during the summer season, tendered their hospitality, and better and more courteous treatment never was received." The scribe explained that "these gentlemen" made a business of escorting visitors through the forests and mountains of the region. "They have resided on Snake River for nearly a quarter of a century," wrote the journalist, who was sure that they knew every stream and mountain. "They know nothing of the busy world" and "never see a newspaper," but they seemed not to care. This was John Kooch's hotel at Arangee, and if this scribe was telling the truth, Messrs. Kooch, Caldwell, and O'Donnell (and perhaps Huestis below) were very long-term residents of the American West generally, if not of this part of Idaho in particular.

The following day, scribe Clancey was busily writing about their passing through the flat valley of Henry's Lake, crossing the difficult Targhee Pass, and traveling through the horrible deadfall that ushered them to the boundary of Yellowstone National Park, but without naming any of those places. Instead, he claimed that they were on the road cut by General Howard as he chased "Sitting Bull" through these "Little Bighorn Mountains," notwithstanding the fact that the Indians were Chief Joseph and the Nez Perce, and the country was the Madison Range of Montana. He did, however, note correctly that the party reached the Riverside soldier station, where the national park troopers sealed their guns and confiscated their ammunition for the period they were to be in Wonderland.[410]

Unfortunately scribe Clancey was so invested in the Civil War exploits of three men in the party that he failed to tell us anything about their several-days trip through Yellowstone, and instead regaled us with those war exploits. But he did mention that when the party left the park for Beaver Canyon, they stopped at a cabin in the mountains, which must have been Clay Manley's cabin, at that moment occupied for whatever reasons only by a recently arrived lady and her crippled son. The stagecoaches then journeyed on to their night-stop, the aforementioned Kooch's hotel at Arangee. Here the writer added the name of Charley Huestis, as being one of the owners, revealing that he was a former Union soldier who had fought alongside President Benjamin Harrison and who later teamed with former rebel-soldier Thomas O'Donnell and the others to emigrate west and eventually partner with John Kooch there on Henry's Fork.

Scribe Clancey told these Civil War stories but did not mention any-

thing about the party's experiences on this trip to the Yellowstone Park—
not geysers, lakes, canyons, or anything else.[411]

Returning to the Bassett Brothers, an event that probably kept them
from full operation in the latter part of this summer was the horrible death
of their eleven-year-old niece, Ada Crockwell, who died from a terrible,
coal-oil explosion and burning in Salt Lake City on the evening of August
12, 1889. Little Ada was the daughter of J.H. Crockwell who had married
one of the sisters of the Bassett brothers.[412]

The arrival of Anna Husted Southworth's party at Beaver Canyon occurred in late August of 1889.[413] Southworth referred to herself as "Nan,"
a common nickname for Anna, and she even included a photograph of
herself in the article. Her use of alleged conversations in the essay in quotation marks led some readers (including this author) to believe at first that
her writing was fiction, but the story was merely momentarily fictionalized,
because her descriptions of the Bassetts' route and everything she saw in the
Park made it clear that most of her article was factual.

Traveling north on the "twistified" railroad from Utah, Anna (Nan) and
her party arrived at Beaver Canyon at midnight to find that the "excellent hotel" they expected was a "wretched disappointment." On the following morning, they packed up their belongings and their coach pulled
up for loading. They had been promised "comfortable Studebaker wagons,
drawn by four horses," but what horrified them instead was "one antiquat-
ed express-wagon with a very shabby canopy of stained canvas, and the
carriage-rugs of hideously dingy patchwork quilts!" Apparently, the Bassett
Brothers were running a bit light this year. The seats on their coach were
so high that Nan found her feet swinging, and she stated that the seats had
only suggestions of "backs" upon which to lean. "At the first shower," she
wrote, "wind and rain had their own furious way through curtains whose
rents we had not suspected," so they, the horses, and the driver were thoroughly drenched. Their driver was a man named "Andrews," she stated,
whose garments "dated from deluge," apparently a reference to the flood
and Noah's ark of Biblical times, but the driver's appearance improved as
the trip went on.[414]

For lunch, they reached the usual "station" on West Camas Creek (Indian Springs), which was then comprised of "two log-cabins and a corral."
One cabin was occupied by a large ranch family, and the matriarch unlocked

the second cabin—apparently used as a barn, extra bedroom, clothes-closet, and dirty toolshed all combined—in which Nan's party was then invited to picnic. When driver Andrews got the horses "all hitched up," they continued on the narrow, wilderness road through miles of gray-green sagebrush and badger holes. They passed Rea's Ranch ("This cabin belongs to the Ray [*sic*] brothers, whose hunting exploits have made them so famous in both America and England.") to a footbridge over Henry's Fork of the Snake River, across which they walked to their night-cabins that were administered by "a stalwart ranchman, wearing [a] regulation cowboy costume." An "exceedingly fat woman" welcomed them with the words "Walk right inter the' settin'-room, ma'am!" It was a place that was punctuated by coarse sheeting and cheap calico, which Nan described at length as degraded but thoroughly clean.[415] Clearly the Bassetts were no longer using George Rea's ranch on the river's west side, and instead were putting their patrons up at this newer ranch three or four miles to the east, which belonged to John Kooch and would soon be sold to the Arangee Land and Cattle Company.

Nan Southworth effervesced about the freezing temperatures that night, which gave her a reason to announce that the next morning was "August 27," and yet there was "hoar-frost." "The keen crispness of the air was intoxicating," she wrote, as they drove northeast and across Targhee Pass to Manley's cabin for lunch that day. It was a repast, she wrote, that was punctuated with "great goblets of delicious cream to cheer us on our way." Her comment reminds us that H. Clay Manley's presence here during the 1880s was probably the reason for the name Cream Creek being applied to that Montana stream that today flows north from the Continental Divide on Mount Two Top into the South Fork of Madison River.

Suddenly Nan's party was inside the Park climbing Superintendent Norris's steep road, then in its tenth season of existence, with a "long panting pull" that lasted two hours. In the twilight of another long Bassett day, they began dropping into Lower Geyser Basin, their horses slipping and wallowing "in a soil like volcanic ashes," which conveyed many bumps to their poorly lit views of the red-roofed cottages of Firehole Hotel. Like so many other travelers of that time, Nan complained about this hotel, with its "mere sheeting covering thin boards, and such wide cracks that every word of ordinary conversation was audible from room to room." She added that in the dark "you could easily tell how long your neighbors kept their candles burning." It appears that the Bassett Brothers, at least for this trip, were using the Firehole Hotel for their guests instead of their own two log-cabins nearby. Perhaps they could no longer afford to lodge a manager there and pay a cook.[416]

The following morning Andrews drove the party to Fountain Geyser and on to Old Faithful. That he was not one of the Bassett Brothers themselves—who took at least a modicum of pride in their interpretation of park features—was apparent from Nan's report of what he declared about Fountain Geyser in "un-tour-guideish," good-old-boy style: "Ye'd better hurry up! She's gittin' ready ter *shewt!*"

So, they watched Fountain Geyser erupt. Later, at Upper Basin, they thrilled to an eruption of Giant Geyser, punctuated by an army soldier who shouted to no one in particular, "By Jove! There goes the Giant!" and jumped onto his horse, "tearing down the valley to give general notice of the event" to whomever might have been there. Giant Geyser had recently emerged from being dormant for many months and continued to give shows to tourists for the next few weeks.[417]

After spending another night at Firehole Hotel, the party encountered numerous stagecoaches from Mammoth Hot Springs belonging to George Wakefield's reorganized YNPT Company, which Nan called "Northern Pacific stages." Annoyed by the comparison with her own Bassett conveyance, she announced, "The roomy, well-appointed equipages made the contrast with our own shabby 'outfit' very provoking."[418] Apparently, the Bassetts' stagecoaches were by this time not the most up-to-date ones in Yellowstone Park. Or at least the one she occupied was not.

Nan's party spent three more nights in the Park—at Canyon, Mammoth, and Firehole again—before retracing their route westward. The distant Tetons were hidden in clouds during that part of the trip, but Nan reveled in her memories of the Park's "formations," a then constantly used word in Yellowstone and a word that she considered "magical," because it evoked "a vision of alabaster wrought by elfin fingers in dainty patterns of fantastic foliage and fairy flowering." This description of the geyserite formations surrounding the Park's hot springs—even without accompanying mentions of vapor columns and geyser eruptions—made it clear that those silicates were indeed fantastic, and that her trip to goblin-land had been a success![419]

Another patron of the Bassett Brothers in 1889 was an English woman

Two types of stagecoaches are parked in front of the Marshall's/Fire-hole Hotel, circa 1885. The four-horse coach on the left appears to be a six- or seven-passenger, regular touring coach, but its roof has been removed, thus rendering it into a kind of "buckboard." The two-horse coach on the right is an unusual, small coach, perhaps one of the Bassett Brothers' Studebaker coaches, modified a bit for camping because the back seat appears to be filled with bedding and perhaps other supplies. The Bassetts were known for having their customers stay the first night at Marshall's/Firehole Hotel and then camping through the rest of the Park. T.W. Ingersoll, photo #87, in hardbound photo-album that apparently once belonged to him, probably 1884. *Beinecke Library, Yale University, New Haven, Connecticut.*

named Georgina Synge, who arrived in late August. She stated that "near-ly everyone" encouraged her to take the Northern Pacific Railroad to the north entrance, but because she wanted to visit Salt Lake City, she chose the Bassetts' route instead and she did not regret it, even though she had to wait three days at Beaver Canyon for a side-saddle to be shipped to her—an idiosyncrasy of this English lady. "This route leads through a delightfully wild and unfrequented country," she explained, "abounding most of the way with game, and for those who can spare the time it is well worth the extra journey." That was indeed the Bassetts' main selling point.

From the Bassetts, she and her male companion secured for $17 per day "the hire and forage of the horses, a guide, a lad to drive the wagon, a tent, and cooking utensils" plus the wagon itself, which she described as "a vehicle on half springs covered with canvas, something like a grocer's cart." They also took two extra horses, which were to be ridden or else pulled behind the wagon. She stated that they set out on September 1, but this must have been wrong because at the end of the book, she mentioned passing through Gardiner, Montana just in time to see the results of that hamlet's fire (August 31, 1889), which she explained had occurred "the night before, and the belongings of the inhabitants were strewn about all over the road." Her party therefore must have left Beaver Canyon about August 18 to pass through Gardiner on September 1.[420]

With "Jim" as their driver and a cranky guide named "Beesley," who fortunately later resigned, they set out from Beaver Canyon, camping the first evening at Camas Meadows. The next day they drove on past Shotgun Creek and "Bottle Creek" (probably today's Hotel Creek) to stay at a cabin covered with antlers and animal-skins. This was apparently George Rea's cabin, but he was not there. However, the "stage-innkeeper's wife," probably one of the Bassett wives, was present and Georgina called her a "young and handsome woman."

At the bottom of Targhee Pass (which she called "Tygee," a name-form that remains on maps today as Tygee Creek Basin), they encountered a "stage-resting place" (the Bassett stage-stop already mentioned that Professor Zahm had visited in 1888) where they procured corn and milk and picked up their mail, because the locale also tripled as a post office. As they ascended Targhee Pass, they could turn around and see Henry's Lake, back to the west, and shortly after this, they entered the Park where they spent a number of days enjoying it before exiting via the north entrance to the Northern Pacific Railroad.[421]

The writer of another 1889 account involving the Bassetts was the famous Elwood T. "Uncle Billy" Hofer, a resident of Yellowstone Park since 1879, who had long served as the park's official correspondent for *Forest and Stream* magazine. Hofer shared for posterity the story of a Yellowstone stagecoach wreck in September of this year between one of George Wakefield's stage-drivers and a Bassett Brothers stage-driver who entered the park at the west entrance.[422]

"With a pistol-shot crack of the whip," Hofer's YNPT Company driver left Mammoth Hotel heading south and at a very narrow and dangerous spot in Golden Gate Canyon, his party gazed at the stream far below. They heard a carriage rattling-up behind them, and then suddenly a two-horse unit tried to pass their rig at a gallop. "Our driver ripped out a true cowboy oath," declared Hofer, "of the most approved double-headed variety and cracked his long-lashed whip till the canyon echoed." His horses leaped forward and the four-horse coach "nearly stood on end from the sudden lurch," as Hofer's driver somehow stayed ahead of the two-horse coach. Hofer then explained a park rule that was known only to in-park Yellow-stone stage men:

> The driver who came up behind, it seems, had tried to come [with] the sneak act and go by us without asking permission, an offense which is not easily condoned among the stage drivers of these mountain regions, an unwritten law of the western Jehu and woe until him who violates. There seems to be an under-standing among all the drivers of the Park that one vehicle is only to be allowed to pass another upon asking permission and [then only] when the head driver turns out and at a convenient place.[423]

Hofer's driver did not want to be passed in this "unceremonious" way, so he "gunned it" and remained in front. The two-horse carriage was close behind, its driver also whipping his steeds. Hofer's five co-passengers no doubt held tightly to their seats. On one side was the canyon of Glen Creek and on the other were the fallen rocks of a hillside. Suddenly Hofer's driver wheeled his horses over to the mountainside of the road and placed his wheel-hubs against the other coach's hubs. This ran the opposing horses out onto the rocks "where they fell over each other, upsetting the carriage, which fell with a heavy crash to earth," while Hofer's coach bounced on for a bit before the driver reined it to a halt. It all seemed over in moments. "We bounded out," said Hofer, "and went back to the wreck" of the two-horse unit. The horses had torn themselves loose from the carriage and were

struggling among the rocks. The carriage had completely overturned, causing its top to press heavily down onto the occupants. It took a few minutes
for Hofer's companions to reach the overturned passengers and then it was
only by tearing the top off the carriage and carrying it away.

A woman's screams caused them to redouble their efforts. It was the German woman who had so interested them at the Mammoth Hotel's breakfast that morning, alone in the carriage. "Her driver was hurt some," said
Hofer, and thus "slowly extricated himself from the debris." He appeared
as though his desire to run races in the mountains had been pounded out of
him, so he slowly started getting his horses together and picking up pieces
of his rig. Hofer's driver began verbally denouncing the other man, who
did not defend himself. Meanwhile, the woman's signs of being "stunned
and dazed and almost unconscious" made it clear that she had been seriously hurt. "We helped her to get out from the broken carriage," explained
Hofer, "which partly held her like a vice and she could only be removed
with the greatest care and most gentle handling and then suffered great
pain." Luggage was scattered everywhere, and it appeared that the woman
was injured on the left side of her body as well as on the left side of her face.

Fortunately, she was conscious and could talk. The men hailed a northbound coach driven by a Hollander from Europe who was traveling alone,
and he took her back to Mammoth. "We bade farewell," wrote Hofer, "to
the plucky German world-traveler," whose skull would have been crushed
and her neck broken if the canvas roof of her carriage had not been fully
upright at the time of the incident. It developed that her driver was "a
man from the Union Pacific" who had come up with her from the "south"
(west) entrance, who would later be revealed as a driver for the Bassett
Brothers. "No one but an insane person," summarized Hofer, "would
have thought of trying to pass another driver at the place he did, and yet
our driver had no right to cause the calamity by forcing him upon the
rocks in the way he did." In the opinions of all six passengers in Hofer's
coach, both drivers were to blame, although the region's custom augured
against the lady's driver.[424]

Hofer's final opinion was a blanket condemnation of both Yellowstone
stage-drivers and all other stage-drivers. "Nearly all these drivers are a reckless set," he opined, "and seem to delight in showing how rough they can
act and how nearly like a desperado they can carry themselves, when at

heart they are probably as near cowards as can be." It was the unhesitating pronouncement of an educated Elwood Hofer versus two good-old-boy stage-drivers, and Hofer was not shy about writing it. The second part of his lesson was the condition of the injured woman, whom his party later saw at both Norris Geyser Basin and the primitive Canyon Hotel. It was clear, he noted, that she was still suffering intensely from her painful experience, and "there was no medicine or medical attendance to be had" in Yellowstone Park "except a very poor quality of whiskey at fabulous prices." The woman was Margaretha Weppner, a famous author of the day, whose 1876 book *The North Star and the Southern Cross* about her three trips around the world was well known to many travelers of that era.[425]

Of course, from a legal perspective, and notwithstanding any local "rules" for stage-driving in Yellowstone, Miss Weppner had a civil cause of action against both drivers and both stagecoach companies, but it appears that she elected to sue only her own driver and his company. That lawsuit came up for judgment in 1892 in the case of *Margaretha Wepper* [sic] *v. William and Jules Bassett*, and the newspapers quoted the court record as stating that the incident occurred on September 24, 1889. Margaretha Weppner was riding in a Bassett stagecoach when, as she later alleged, "the driver of [her] coach engaged in a race with the driver of another vehicle," overturning her coach and causing her to be injured. In a lawsuit "filed in United States courts," she asked for $18,000 in damages, but according to the newspapers failed to prosecute the case because the judge dismissed it in late August of 1892.[426] It is possible that the statute of limitations ran out on Ms. Weppner's civil suit. The Bassetts were lucky to escape this lawsuit, which clearly was partly their fault.

Another event marred the very end of the Bassett Brothers' season at their office and cabins in "Firehole Basin." The death of their cook, twenty-three-year-old Francella Eastman Wright (wife of their employee J.B. Wright), must have made the Bassetts very sad. She was stricken with an apparent stroke in the park's Lower Geyser Basin on about September 25 in the following freak incident:

> Mr. Wright had charge of Bassett Bro's. stage line at Fire Hole, and was about closing up the business there when Mrs. Wright was taken with a severe pain between the shoulders. A physician belonging to the Military post [nearby] was called who treated

her, but seeming to get worse her husband started for Beaver
[Canyon] with her. She soon entirely lost her power of speech,
and portions of her limbs and body became numb. Although
she retained full consciousness to the last, it was nearly a week
from the time she was first taken. Her remains were brought to
Eagle Rock for burial…She leaves one child, a girl four years
old.[427]

Francella Wright lingered for a short time at Beaver Canyon but died there
on October 1, 1889.

That summer was also the occasion of a tourist's complaint to the
Bassett Brothers for lost luggage, an event that happened dozens if not
hundreds of times to American transportation companies during the
stagecoach era and that still happens today. Such events were often not
recorded, but because this one occurred in Yellowstone, its documentation has survived. In December, acting superintendent F.A. Boutelle
wrote to the Bassett Brothers, who had long been spending winters on
their ranch at Lago, Idaho, insisting that they reimburse Mr. S.W. Scudder of Cambridge, Massachusetts the $3.50 for his lost luggage. "You will
please realize," wrote Captain Boutelle, "that you have only authority for
temporarily doing business in the park and that you are only tolerated in
the belief that you are doing a fair business." Boutelle threatened to take
away their authority if their action of failing to reimburse proved to be "a
fair sample" of the way they did business. During the following summer,
William Henry Bassett responded by sending four dollars to Scudder
while also claiming that the tourist had done the stage-line an injustice
by complaining to Boutelle when Scudder had been riding with George
Wakefield's company rather than the Bassett Brothers. Nevertheless, the
Bassetts sent the money, probably because they wanted no possible threat
to their operating authority from Boutelle.[428] This incident revealed that
the Bassetts had no managing employee in the park at the time of the
affair, which "would not have happened" had one of the brothers been
in the park.[429] It also illustrated a typical moment in the evolution of the
commercial transportation business in America, regardless of whether it
occurred by horse, wagon, stagecoach, boat, bus, truck, train, or airplane.

Newspaper stories that continued to promote Beaver Canyon favored the Bassett Brothers as late as Christmas of 1889. On December 25, the *Salt Lake Herald* ran a long article about the railroad that also described the stage-route from Beaver Canyon to the Park. Calling it the "Utah & Northern Division of the Union Pacific," the article stated that "There is, in the summer, a regular line of stages from Beaver cañon to Firehole Basin in the park," which excursion is "a most exhilarating and delightful experience."[430] Articles like this one were advancing the Bassetts' stagecoaching business even to the few outbound-only parties who had been, since 1883, entering the park on the NPRR from the north and exiting via the U&N Division at the west, as John Trenor's group did that year. "This proved a very interesting part of the trip," wrote Trenor, "the country through which we passed being very picturesque, [with] lots of game to be seen."[431]

January of 1890 began harshly at Beaver Canyon, and it affected people and businesses that the Bassett Brothers knew well, but they might well have not been present in town. Just after New Year's Day, the railroad suffered a "Terrible Smashup" when northbound freight-train number 111, with four engines and heavily loaded, arrived just south of Beaver Canyon at High Bridge but did not side-track as it was directed to do. Southbound freight number 112 almost immediately hove into sight, and its engineer frantically applied the airbrakes, but for some reason they did not engage. Southbound-engine struck northbound-engine, smashing all five engines and derailing nineteen cars on both trains. Fireman O'Neill lost his arm and several other men sustained serious injuries.[432] A few days later, high winds and drifting snow began to plague the U&N Division trains at Beaver Canyon, and that set the pace for yet another dreadful winter, as trains were blockaded for weeks and months. In late February, it turned brutally cold, and yet snow continued to fall. A freight train of thirty cars and its engine got stuck south of BC at High Bridge. Operators cut the engine loose and ran it to Beaver, where three fresh engines with plenty of coal and water, one of them northbound, were sent to rescue them. Instead, the engines were stuck there for nearly three days before workmen could dig them out. "It was about sixty degrees below zero," bemoaned the *Idaho Register*, "and the wind [was] howling and piling the snow back faster than it could be shoveled out."[433]

The winter finally broke, and travel began to look normal for much of the summer. It appears that the Bassetts received some direct competition from the Union Pacific Railroad itself this season, for in July the UP advertised for thirty patrons at $225 apiece to reserve seats on a thirty-day trip from Omaha to Salt Lake City to Shoshone Falls and into Yellowstone National Park. Saying nothing about the Bassetts, the railroad indicated that it would furnish six-horse Concord coaches to run from Beaver Canyon into the park, lodging at park hotels. Whether this heavily advertised trip actually organized and went to the park is not known, but unless the Bassett Brothers rented the coaches to the UP, they must have felt this competing pressure.[434]

By August 8, *The Dillon Tribune* was reporting that the Bassett Brothers' stage line "is doing an enormous business, but it is kept as quiet as possible owing to the opposition to be encountered from the [competing] N.P. railroad." That opposition was to be expected, as usual, but from this it appears that the brothers were doing okay so far this summer.

Also, we have this comment on park visitation in 1890 by a group who traveled in their own wagons via Henry's Lake from Market Lake and Rexburg, Idaho. "While we were there," wrote their reporter from the Park, "the arrivals averaged about one hundred people every day; the hotels were crowded, and stage coaches by the dozen were moving from place to place with excursionists gathered to see these wonders of nature." Indeed, the Park's official visitation for this year at 7,808 would remain the largest until 1897.[435]

The worst news of the 1890 season for the citizens of Beaver Canyon, which no doubt personally impacted the Bassett Brothers because they had to have known him well, was the murder of lumberman and constable David W. Stoddard, who was commonly called "deputy sheriff" in that area. The murder was so gruesome that it made newspapers as far east as Michigan and as far west as San Francisco. On Sunday, August 24, at least thirty-five Italians who worked for the railroad at Beaver Canyon got rip-roaringly drunk and insulted deputy Stoddard, who "told them several times if they did not keep quiet, he would arrest them." One of them then attacked Stoddard, and he struck the man over the head with his revolver. Accompanied by E.B. Collier, the constable then started walking home.

The Italians, called "dagos" by the newspapers in the racist language of that day, decided they wanted revenge. Two of them grabbed Stoddard and "held his arms," wrote a witness, "while the third cut his throat from ear to ear" with a razor. "Stoddard's head was nearly severed from his body," declared the *Idaho Statesman*, "and he died almost immediately." When the other Italians saw what the attackers had done, they ran toward the "outfit car" to get knives and firearms to take over the town but instead got frightened and ran into the boulders and brush behind the town, now defying anyone to capture them. Rail officials wired Blackfoot, Idaho to send its sheriff, and he rode up with twenty-five deputies on a special train and rounded up all the Italians involved except for the one who committed the actual murder. That perpetrator escaped, apparently running or riding south. Constable David Stoddard, age about thirty, left a wife and five children at Beaver Canyon.[436] It was probably this incident that resulted in his name being permanently attached to the nearby creek, if the name were not already in use because of his sawmill.

Other members of the crowd identified the three perpetrators as James Mike, "John Burton," and one "O'Brion," who was the actual murderer. Mike and "Burton" were bound over for trial, but O'Brian remained at large in what the Anaconda newspaper called "the foulest murder in the history of Bingham County." A couple of weeks later while he lurked in the mountains thirty miles west of Camas, Idaho, O'Brian was seen by a rancher named Sullivan and a stage-driver who also reported him, but he eluded the large pursuing posse, which searched fruitlessly for the fleeing man.[437]

Meanwhile, prosecutors at Blackfoot, Idaho arraigned the two accomplices, John Bertoni[438] and James Mike, convicted them of murder in the second degree, and sent them to the Idaho State penitentiary, which could indeed be called that as of July 3, 1890, when Idaho Territory officially became a state. Sentenced to ten years each, the men appealed to the Idaho Supreme Court, and the court affirmed their sentences in 1892, notwithstanding their protestations of innocence.[439]

Joe O'Brian, whose real name might have been Giuseppe Gagliano or Guissipo Glanes, gave his pursuers the slip for more than four years before two newspapers mentioned his capture. On September 21, 1894, a single, Idaho newspaper article splashed this headline across Idaho's capital in its *Idaho Statesman*: "Dago Murderer Caught—Slayer of David Stoddard Nabbed in Portland." On the same day, the *Salt Lake Herald* ran a shorter article, calling him Guissipo Glanes and stating that he had been captured in Portland. According to the *Statesman* article, a rumor about O'Brian "gained wide circulation" that he "had been overhauled and summarily disposed of," but many police officers did not believe it. They "flooded the country with descriptions of Gagliano." In September of 1894, an ex-sheriff of Bingham County named C.S. Smith, who would not give up on finding O'Brian, "got track of the murderer in Oregon." Smith went to Portland, nabbed Gagliano, and extradited him to Idaho.[440]

The trouble with this story of "Joe O'Brian" and his alleged capture was that there seemed to be no confirmation of it anywhere else. Only these two newspaper articles from the *Idaho Statesman* and the *Salt Lake Herald* in 1894 claimed this to be true. No other corroborating newspaper articles seem to exist today to validate it, nor can we find confirming material about the alleged capture from Idaho or Oregon law-enforcement circles or the Idaho prison system. One wonders whether the man caught turned out to be the wrong man who was soon released, for we can find nothing about a trial, a guilty or not-guilty verdict, a sentencing, or a hanging.

In fact, the only other item we can find today about the David Stoddard incident is an oral reminiscence from twenty-six years later. It contained all the usual misinformation and misremembered material—along with a few actually reliable items—which historians have come to expect from any article that was written much later by persons who used only their memories. Published in 1916, this article by an author named "Eagle Rock" claimed that the victim was "John Stoddard" instead of David Stoddard, that the accomplices were sentenced to twenty-five years in prison instead of ten, that Beaver Canyon was "a flourishing lumber camp" (its lumbering was largely gone by 1890) located only "three" miles (rather than four) from Spencer, and that the person who did the actual killing "was never heard of" again. The last statement might well be the only correct one, because, again, no corroborating information about the capture of "Joe O'Brian" has so far been found. This 1916 article offered a theory as to what happened to O'Brian, but even it was tainted with the misinformation that the date of the murder "was late in the fall...the weather up there was somewhat chilly and there was snow upon the ground." The murder actually occurred on August 24, and not "late in the fall," and none of the original articles mentioned snow. The account ended with a theory of what happened to O'Brian, namely that several years later, a herder in the area "found the remains of a man" along Beaver Creek or Stoddard Creek "and roped him and that was the last of the dago."[441] In light of 1890 newspaper articles that spoke of O'Brian having been seen on several occasions by witnesses and chased by posses, these alleged human remains, if they were indeed found, could not have been those of O'Brian. It therefore appears that most of this article by "Eagle Rock" was malarkey and that what happened to O'Brian might never be known. It is a perfect example of why historians *never* rely on undocumented material and use personal memories only when they are carefully labeled and when there is nothing else available.

The Stoddard murder and its lingering, subsequent history probably made C.J. Bassett and his brothers quite sad for years, and it might have even negatively affected travel to Beaver Canyon and thus the Bassett Brothers' operations in 1890.

The season of 1890 was also the summer when increased park visitation caused massive errors by, and complaints about, the Yellowstone Park Association. This resulted in congressional hearings two years later that eventually caused the revocation of YPA's transportation lease and the installing of Huntley and Child's upstart stage-line eventually called the Yellowstone Park Transportation Company.[442] The Bassett Brothers must have at least heard about these events and perhaps even experienced some of the results while discharging and picking up their (Beaver Canyon) passengers at park hotels, but so far nothing can be discerned about possible effects upon them or the brothers' reactions to any of it. And no accounts have thus far surfaced about trips into the park that they took this year. But of course, the newspapers were very busy during 1890-1892 with news about George Wakefield's staging operations, complaints at the national level against the YPA, and eventually congressional hearings about Yellowstone National Park and its main concessioner.

Meanwhile, far to the west at Beaver Canyon, the Bassetts continued their operations, which, if we believe the newspapers, were as busy as ever in this new summer. In June of 1891, the *Dillon Tribune* boosteristically stated that "the stage line from Beaver canyon to the Park, conducted by Bassett Bros., is [operating] under full headway." By the end of July, an Idaho Falls newspaper reported that "the stage line from Beaver Canyon now owned by [C.] J. Bassett" was "doing an immense business."[443] This season of 1891 was the first summer that the new Fountain Hotel was open in Lower Geyser Basin, so that was likely the place where the Bassetts began lodging their guests. Certainly, they were taking them there by the following year.

One would think that with business reportedly good, more actual accounts of their trips to the park would exist from 1891, but those are not easily found today. However, one tourist known from that year was Mary E. Morgan Jones from Camas, Idaho (not far south of Beaver Canyon) who traveled with her husband and another lady. Her notation that she took along "my pony and riding outfit" makes it appear that she loaded her horse into a boxcar on the train-ride from Camas and then rented the rest of their equipment from the Bassett Brothers, because her party seems to have done their own driving. She recorded that the "Beaver Cañon stage route…equaled an eastern road for smoothness," so apparently the Bassetts or someone else had performed a bit of work on the road before the summer opened.[444]

Mary Jones mentioned little else about her route to the Park, but she told us some unusual and important things about Yellowstone. Her description of Riverside soldier station as "an old, dilapidated log hut, looking more as if intended for a barn than a dwelling, and the cracks stuffed with gunny sacks" tells us that the station was in bad shape, but she opined that the friendly soldiers were quartered nearby "in pleasant tents." "A more pleasant, gentlemanly lot of strangers I never met," she stated, adding that "they were perfectly willing to answer all questions, no matter how simple."

And she also told us that the Park's road system continued to fork at "Riverside" (soldier station) and remained difficult, so her party went the other way: "From here we chose the River Road[,] crossing the Madison [River] six times instead of the Hill Road by which we would have had a heavy grade about four miles long." Near Madison Junction, they turned south to Old Faithful, and after that backtracked to Norris, Canyon, and Lake. They spent three days camping at Yellowstone Lake, taking the not-so-busy-yet steamer Zillah on daytrips to go fishing, but not staying at the newly opened Lake Hotel. Oddly, she commented that "skunks were very numerous and came about our camp-fire as a cat would and many a time Mr. J. Had to get up and chase them off to keep them out of the tent, while I trembled 'for fear faith;' I dreaded them more than bears." (Apparently skunks in the park had made something of a rebound in numbers in the eleven years since Park Superintendent Norris killed over four hundred of them at Mammoth.) Passing west down the Devil's Stairway at Mary Lake, they retraced their route to Henry's Lake, where she confirmed other visitors' accounts of a fancy log house "on a small island in the lake" full of mounted animals' heads. "It belongs to a New

York millionaire," she stated, "and the curious part is he only lives there a couple of months and the rest of the year it is left open to care for itself." On the way back to Beaver Canyon, she described their stay at a large ranch in one of the valleys southwest of Henry's Lake. About Yellowstone, she enthused: "One of my pet dreams has been realized and I am more than satisfied," but she mentioned nothing about returning her rented equipment to the Bassett Brothers, if that in fact happened.[445]

In August of 1891, a journalist known only as " H.G.H." entered the Yellowstone country from Beaver Canyon as part of a much longer trip that visited numerous spots around the West. Although he did not mention the Bassett Brothers nor any driver provided by them, he had to have rented equipment from them to go to the Park. Most noteworthy was this visitor's mention of and his lodging at a new establishment some five miles west of present West Yellowstone, Montana, which would soon come to be known as "Dwelle's."

Like so many others who came from the Union Pacific Railroad west of Wonderland, H.G.H. gushed generously about the route. The stage road, he said, traversed a rough mountain region almost uninhabited by humans, "but full of game of all kinds." The first fifty miles was grass or sagebrush, but soon he was greeted with views of the spectacular Grand Tetons, "towering above the surrounding mountains like the horns of a rhinoceros." The road then crossed "range after range of mountains," each seeming to "rise higher than the last, and always descending into parks of loveliest green, the grass standing waist high in the valley, and running up the hillsides and even underneath the timber…Everywhere flowers bloomed in profusion." The party made seventy-five miles the first day, and from that statistic, it is clear that the Bassett Brothers had by then shortened and improved the road so that their visitors could stay the first night at Dwelle's (a "two-story log house on the south fork of the Madison River"), and the second night in the Park at the new Fountain Hotel, twenty-five miles farther on. Mr. Dwelle or one of his hired hands took them fishing the following morning, and entertained them with tales of the animals of the area.[446]

This storyteller, apparently Mr. Dwelle himself, added details of what the increasing settlers had done to modify the region:

> The proprietor told us that last winter he found a drove of seventeen antelope stalled in the snow, and with two other men

to assist him drove them up to the house and into the corral like so many sheep. They soon began to die in captivity and he turned the survivors out in the spring. The settlers in this region all have tame elk, none of them broken to the harness. The elk yards are fenced with very heavy logs, staked and [rendered], 18 to 20 feet high. At Henry['s] Lake there is a 'game ranch.' It is stocked with elk, deer, antelope and other animals. I think there are over thirty head of elk, many of them very tame. Two spans of elk are trained to drive in harness, [and] one moose is also driven in a buggy.[447]

They entered the Park, and after passing the Riverside Soldier Station, they ascended Mr. Norris's precipitous road rather than using the "river route," for H.G.H. stated that they "began a steep climb of three miles over the mountain wall." He expounded for quite a while about the burned forest through the region, which in 1988, nearly one hundred years later, appeared again on the landscape, following the giant fires of that year. Dropping down into the Lower Geyser Basin, the party spotted the Fountain Hotel and its namesake, Fountain Geyser, which H.G.H. mentioned spouted "about every two hours" to heights of twenty to fifty feet. Apparently, the party spent the night there and traveled on to the Upper Geyser Basin the following day, for the writer described geysers there, including Old Faithful.

They moved on to Yellowstone Lake, which was a long way off, said H.G.H., "and the scenery during most of the way is not attractive." But they loved the new hotel there and the big, new one at Canyon, which had opened the previous year. Like everyone else, he effervesced shamelessly about the canyon itself. They moved on to Mammoth and then traipsed back to Yancey's Hotel, out toward Lamar Valley, which was an unusual route for stagecoach days.[448] Whether their party returned west to Beaver Canyon or left the Park by way of the Northern Pacific Railroad and the north entrance, we do not know, because this was apparently the writer's last chapter of his story.

This year of 1891 was unusual in another way in that it recorded the only verified stagecoach robbery ever to occur, or at least to be recorded in the newspapers, on the Bassetts' Beaver Canyon route to the park. Five (or actually six, when we include the one from 1884 added by this book) other stagecoach robberies occurred within the national park, but this previously unnoticed one seems to be the only one that involved the Bassett Brothers' route. On Tuesday morning, August 11, Louis C. Krauthoff (1858-1918)—age 33 and a prominent attorney from Kansas City, Missouri, who was president of the Missouri Bar Association—and his friend John W. Spears, secretary and treasurer of the Kansas City and Martin Distillery Company, left Beaver Canyon for Yellowstone, riding in a stagecoach that was apparently chartered from the Bassett Brothers. Interestingly, Krauthoff was also President of the Western Baseball Association while Spears was President of the Kansas City baseball club, so the *Chicago Tribune* headline called the two men "baseball magnates" in the plural form. No driver or other passengers were mentioned in any of the five known stories about the affair, so the two men probably rented the conveyance and were traveling alone. "About seven o'clock that evening just as the stage had crossed the divide in [Targhee] Pass," explained a reporter for the *Bozeman Chronicle*, "it was halted by two highwaymen, who demanded that the two passengers deliver up their valuables and [to] be quick about it." The road agents were leveling a Winchester rifle and a .45 six-shooter at the coach, and the two men were unarmed and thus in no position to resist.[449]

The most detailed of the stories, this one from the Helena *Daily Independent*, offered this description of what happened:

> The taller of the two robbers seemed very nervous and unused to the business which he very awkwardly accomplished, while his companion kept the passengers' arms above their heads with his rifle. Mr. Spears lost a gold watch, chain and charm, about $58 in money and some minor articles. His companion a gold watch and chain—the searching highwaymen kindly permitting him to retain his Knight Templar charm, which they undoubtedly thought would get them into [even more] trouble; $168 was taken from this gentleman and a pair of field glasses. The robbery occurred in Gallatin county within sight of the Idaho line. The robbers were disguised in blue overalls, quite well worn and patched about the knees. The upper portions of their bodies [were] further covered with gunny sacks, made to serve

as a jacket. Their faces were covered with white hoods, which completely covered their hair and lower parts of their faces. A large opening was left for the eyes. While one of the men kept their victims covered with the rifle the other went through them and left nothing behind.[450]

The *Chicago Tribune* story added that the road agents took $763 from the travelers, a calculation that only became possible after the two men returned home. The victims gave to the police as good of a description of the highwaymen as they could, plus a detailed listing of the items taken. But as far as is known, these road agents were never caught.[451]

The Bassett Brothers were working at normal touring in 1892, for the *Soda Springs* (Idaho) *Advertiser* stated on June 15 that "the stage line running from Beaver Canyon is now in operation" and also stated that C.H. [probably C.J.] Bassett was "now at Beaver cañon." The Edward S. Parkinson party from Trenton, New Jersey traveled with the brothers this year. The Parkinsons arrived on the train in the evening and suffered through the only hotel in Beaver Canyon, whose Danish proprietor had not been told they were coming and thus offered them only bread and cheese sandwiches for their suppers. Traveling east the next day in a coach driven by a Brothers' employee named "Spikes," Mr. Parkinson commented upon the "immense flower-garden" that was in view "as far as the eye could reach" in colors of white, yellow, blue, and occasionally pink or red. The mosquitoes, he noted, were terribly bad, rising in clouds. "We bathed our necks and wrists in menthol," Parkinson said, but it was to no avail. "In the dining room at the dinner station at Camas Meadows," he wrote, "the window panes were black with them, and we were compelled to eat with our veils on, but that did not prevent them from getting into our mouths." And so it went for the next two hours until their stagecoach left and pressed on to Henry's Fork crossing. There they crossed to the east side of the river to stay at Arangee Ranch, which they called "the headquarters of several ranches owned by a company of New York capitalists engaged in stock-raising."[452]

The next morning, surrounded by the usual wildlife, the Parkinsons traveled on, up Targhee Pass to the South Fork of the Madison, where a fancy, new, two-story cabin with apartments—owned by a Mr. Dwelle, a bachelor—was to serve as their overnight spot. "Dwelle's" would later

(1898 and after) become well-known to Yellowstone tourists who traveled in and out of the park with the Monida & Yellowstone Stage Company. On the following day, they rode up Madison River, across the high, steep road to Lower Geyser Basin, and straight on to Old Faithful where they lodged at the wooden "Shack" hotel, serving since 1885. After that, they traveled back north to Norris for a tent-lunch and then east to Canyon Hotel for the night, before returning to Norris and then going to Mammoth to spend a night there. On the next day, they returned south to Norris and Lower Geyser Basin to stay at the Fountain Hotel and watch Fountain Geyser erupt. Finally, on the following morning, they left Yellowstone Park heading west to Beaver Canyon. All in all, this was an unusual itinerary, but because formal Park licenses would not be required for three more years, the Bassett Brothers could still essentially do what they wanted in Yellowstone. On the way back west, Parkinson recorded a dispatch-detail for the Bassetts, when their driver "Spikes" suddenly met several incoming coaches on the Riverside hill. He took over driving one of those inbound coaches and ran those people east into the Park, while a less-experienced driver chauffeured the Parkinson party outbound (west) to Dwelle's, Arangee Ranch, and Beaver Canyon.[453] The Bassetts undoubtedly wanted their most experienced driver-guides to work the Park, a custom for tour-guides that has logically continued to the present day.

The year 1892 was also colored by two complaint letters against the Bassetts for mistreatment of horses, although the allegations in at least the first one were apparently false. In late August, Mrs. Joseph Bartholomew—a member of the Society for the Prevention of Cruelty to Animals (in existence in the U.S. since 1866) and also the wife of a North Dakota Supreme Court justice—complained to acting superintendent George S. Anderson that her stage-driver and the Bassett Brothers in general were treating poorly the horses that were pulling her coach.

Anderson found that her complaint, based at the Canyon Hotel, was "in no case quite borne out by the observed facts," and so he dismissed the entire matter and in fact defended the Bassetts. In that incident, the idea of licenses being issued by the Park to out-of-park transportation companies seems to have been born. Captain Anderson suggested to the Secretary of Interior that the Bassetts be given a "lease" to conduct transportation from Beaver Canyon *to and through* the park, and "that they pay a small sum into the park fund for this privilege." That would not happen formally until 1895, but the license idea was now in the air; meanwhile the Bassetts continued operating from Beaver Canyon even though, according to Anderson, "The route is long, the road bad, and in general it is a most undesirable way of entering the Park."[454]

In late August, park officials received another, similar complaint. Mrs. M.E. Jennings and Miss Mary Stockton, who traveled from Beaver Canyon to the Park, complained to Captain Anderson about the Bassetts' alleged treatment of the horses on their coach. In a rambling, too-long opening sentence, the ladies protested that

> the horses furnished for such trip were small, inferior, and without adequate strength to perform the work required of them, that no change of horses was furnished, that the horses became so worn out and weak that it was not possible for them to travel at any ordinary speed and that to compel them to proceed was so cruel and inhumane that we could not with comfort ride after them and such of us as were able often walked simply to relieve the horses, and in order to get the horses over the road it became necessary to urge and beat them cruelly. We make no charge of cruelty against the drivers, but we do charge that the persons whose duty it was to furnish us with transportation were and are guilty of extreme and wanton cruelty to animals in furnishing horses which they knew had not sufficient strength or endurance for the trip.[455]

If Captain Anderson answered this letter, his reply has not been found. Two letters alleging such treatment of horses would have alerted Anderson to be vigilant about these and all stage-operators, and probably he had begun doing that.

Finally, 1892 was the year that a bit of competition surfaced for the Bassett Brothers for the first real time, even though it was limited in size. Educator David A. Curry of Denver, Colorado began running a small business that year of taking tourists to Yellowstone and lecturing in connection with that business. By 1897, he was living in Salt Lake City, where he was principal of the New West Academy. In 1893, his newspaper advertisement read:

> Your eastern friends will want to visit Yellowstone park this
> summer. Let them know about Curry's camping parties—an
> eighteen-day trip from Beaver canyon. Enquire of David A.
> Curry.[456]

Mr. Curry ran trips to Yellowstone in 1892, possibly in 1893, and 1895-
1898. However, he fell in love with Yosemite National Park in California
in 1895, and moved his business to that place after these Yellowstone trips.
Beginning in 1899, he established Curry Village there, thus starting a park
concession that operated for nearly one hundred years.[457] It appears, however, that his Beaver Canyon business did not offer horses and wagons, so
perhaps Curry rented equipment from the Bassett Brothers and then merely
rode along with the patrons, serving only as his parties' escort and guide.

In 1893, a serious, economic depression struck the nation, beginning in
February. By early summer, it was in full swing, and travel to Yellowstone
dropped precipitously. Known as the "Panic of 1893," it swept across the
U.S. with devastating consequences, lasting until 1897 and affecting park
visitation as follows: from 7,290 visitors in 1892 to 6,154 in 1893; to 3,105
in 1894; to 5,438 in 1895; to 4,659 in 1896.[458] One cannot help wondering whether this national crash of U.S. businesses ultimately helped to drive
the Bassetts out of their local livelihood. Surely at the least, it began their
company's long downward spiral from which there would be no recovery.
On the positive side, the Chicago World's Fair opened this year, and perhaps that extravaganza added briefly to their business, if only in a few individually wealthy parties. However, it could *not* have helped them that an
ironically-named writer—A. Coffin—in the *Nevada State Journal* began his
Yellowstone account by deploring the Bassetts' route. "If you ever go to the
National Park," he wrote, "don't go from any point on the Utah Northern
Railway, Beaver Canyon or other places, for there is too much staging, the
accommodations are poor and the charges out of all reason." Coffin wished
that he had ridden the Northern Pacific Railroad so that he could have departed via Cinnabar and Livingston rather than having suffered "the weary
journey" back west to Beaver Canyon.[459]

Park Superintendent George S. Anderson stated in his report to the Secretary of Interior that 1893's tourist season "was the most peculiar of any
in the history of the park" because of the sudden decrease in visitation.

Anderson confirmed that "Transportation from Beaver Canyon, on the Union Pacific Railroad, is conducted by the Bassett Brothers, but without definite license from the Department." He was pushing for the DOI to require the Park to issue formal licenses of $5 for each wagon, which it approved the following year, to take effect in 1895. Anderson considered that amount "not excessive," explaining that it did "not more than compensate for the expenditure made in cleaning up their abandoned camp grounds and making necessary repairs on the road over which they travel."[460] The year of 1894 was thus the last one that would be free of the government's license-fee for the Brothers and for everyone else as well.

The Bassetts' business indeed began suffering from this depression like that of so many others in the nation. But writer Henry Erskine Smith, known to some of his readers as "Lispenard Rutgers," had the money to go to Yellowstone and did so during the "crispness" of autumn in 1893, apparently outfitted by the Bassett Brothers. Drawn by four horses and chauffeured by "our guide and driver Jim, famous for having been a cowboy in Montana," Henry Smith's stagecoach was "off with a jerk" from Beaver Canyon. They saw the usual numerous animals in Camas, Antelope, and Shotgun valleys, including a herd of two hundred antelope and enough "prairie chickens" to feed the party five times over. At the crossing of Henry's Fork, a "good game dinner" was fed to them and they stayed overnight in a "comfortable clean tent." Punctuated the next day by many coyotes and "an occasional flying fox" (probably either the Northern Flying Squirrel [*Glaucomys sabrinus*], which today is "rarely seen" in Yellowstone country, or else a large bat of some type), the trip offered them the unusual excitement of a "horse thief" being captured by six officers armed with rifles at a cabin on the way to Henry's Lake. Traveler George Wingate, who similarly ran into horse thieves in Madison Valley just west of the park's west entrance in 1885, had slept with his loaded weapons and summed up for us the prevalent attitudes about such bandits by all members of his party:

> We could now appreciate the intense hatred which is felt on the
> frontier for a horse thief. To lose our horses where we then were
> would have placed our party in a terrible plight, and none of
> us felt the slightest compunction at inflicting summary justice
> upon anyone who might attempt to steal them. [In] the West,

whatever leniency may be extended towards homicide, the penalty of horse stealing is death, inflicted by the captors, without
troubling the courts.[461]

Over the next three days, Smith's party traveled to Lower Geyser Basin,
Old Faithful, Canyon, and apparently Norris, Madison, and back to west
entrance, probably staying at the second Canyon Hotel (1890-1910). The
exact route described by Smith is today a bit difficult to discern, because he
skipped discussing that part, instead spending many words in portraying a
forest-and-prairie fire, likely in Madison Valley, that their driver whipped
his horses through "with a strong arm and steady eye…as we thundered on
at terrific speed." But the fire story transformed his account into an exciting
article that "Lispenard Rutgers" published the following year as chapter one
in his book *On and Off the Saddle*. Eventually his party returned west to
Beaver Canyon and the railroad.[462]

Complicating the Bassetts' lives in 1893 was the new town of Dubois, Idaho, which the railroad had founded during the preceding November, and
it was built just north of the former Dry Creek station. Specifically located midway between Beaver Canyon and Camas, it was intended to replace
Beaver Canyon, but the unexpected economic depression stifled its growth
and delayed that plan until Spencer, Idaho could appear instead, four years
later.[463] However, it is likely that the new town of Dubois in conjunction with
the "Panic of 1893" caused a downturn in Beaver Canyon's prosperity, for
traveler W.C. Mabry and his friend found the place more than quiet. Notwithstanding "mosquitoes by the billion," Mabry's party of two planned to
walk (often called "tramping" in those days) from the railhead to and through
the park and back to the railhead. Mabry witnessed Beaver Canyon to be almost dead. It was "once the largest lumber camp in that state," he wrote, "but
[now] only a score of log shacks remained to tell of its bygone prosperity."
Mabry and his colleague were apparently recent college graduates, and it was
clear that the new depression was affecting them too, for they mentioned that
they could afford neither the train-fare to Beaver Canyon nor the stage-fare to
Yellowstone Park and return. So, after "paying" for their train ride by playing
musical instruments for the trainmen, they walked the one hundred miles to
the Park and then back to Beaver Canyon.[464] It was a long way to hike, but
they were young and healthy.

Also in 1893, a party from Wellsboro, Pennsylvania traveled with the Bassett Brothers. Although the party's reporter did not say so, his use of the words "our driver" made it likely that the party was not merely renting the equipment and driving themselves; instead, they had a Bassett-provided driver. The chronicler of this account was identified only as F.S.W. from the *Wellsboro* (Pennsylvania) *Agitator*, who described the route more specifically than did many other tourists. "We filled a coach at Beaver Canyon," he wrote, "and sailed all day over a billowy, sage-green sea...a range of noble, snow-clad mountains to the left and a line of low, sandy buttes at the right." Of course, he was looking at the Centennial Mountains to his left and the Idaho plains to his right, with the Tetons on the horizon in front of him. It was a sunny day and the route as usual was punctuated with wildflowers. The stillness, wrote F.S.W. vigorously, was "broken only by the call of our driver to his leaders and the flourish of his long whip over the heads of the patient wheel-horses, [along with] the occasional flutter of a sage hen or the scream of a timber hawk" as it soared high over their heads "in the crystalline air."[465]

Beginning the climb of Targhee Pass "toward noon of the second day," they reached "at dark" the Fountain Hotel at Lower Geyser Basin, excited to explore "the strangest of wonderlands" on the following morning. Up early the next day, they watched a geyser spouting, only to encounter a tourist "more way wise than we" walk past them remarking, "You are in luck to see the Fountain [Geyser] play in early morning." After breakfast, a morning drive took them to Old Faithful, where they spent time looking at the springs. This is the plateau, laughed F.S.W., "on which the big, bad geysers keep their stronghold and hoot derisively and snicker in their throats at the open-mouthed tourists who profane the place with the ohs! and ahs! of their vulgar curiosity."[466] With this comment, yet another tourist in Yellowstone had demeaned his fellow tourists, a practice that seems timeless, because it remains typical today.

Arriving at the Grand Canyon of the Yellowstone "about an hour before sunset one golden day," author F.S.W. portrayed the canyon, like so many did then, as not really describable but certainly exhibiting "overpowering grandeur" and "inexpressible beauty." During "the long ride back to Beaver Canyon," the party studied guidebooks, and undoubtedly that is where the author obtained some of his inspiration, because his canyon-images of the shapes of "men and women of olden times" sounded a lot like Yellowstone's earlier-traveler Rudyard Kipling in 1889, from whom our author seems to have lifted some text. He did not mention the Bassett Brothers at all, but almost certainly his party traveled with one of the brothers' drivers.[467]

By July of 1894, the Bassett Brothers were in dire straits, like so many other businesses all across the nation. The paralyzing, nationwide depression and its accompanying railroad strike were continuing unabated, and accordingly this was a second lean year for the Brothers. "Jule Bassett was down from Beaver Thursday," noted the *Blackfoot News*. The editor conceded that "the strike is entailing the common loss on his Park stage line as upon everything else."[468]

This difficult summer also provided the occasion when Wyoming courts sent John W. Meldrum to become the first U.S. Commissioner (judge) in Yellowstone National Park. Being a resident of southern Wyoming, Meldrum rode the Union Pacific to Utah, and his story recorded the financial difficulties that C.J. Bassett was experiencing in having to hire at least one young, less-than-qualified driver. Meldrum had "read law" in Wyoming, and now he rode the train to Beaver Canyon, mentioning that it was then called the "Oregon Short Line" only to Pocatello, where it continued northwesterly to Portland, Oregon. North of Pocatello, the line was called the Utah & Northern division of the Union Pacific. Because of the national railroad strike in progress simultaneously with the national depression, the railroad's attorney advised Meldrum to go to Yellowstone overland rather than trying to entrain to Butte, where angry strikers might hold up the train or keep it from running altogether. There was a stage-line at Beaver Canyon, counseled the attorney. Judge Meldrum soon found that it was not much of a stage-line, the national "panic" having apparently come close to crippling the Bassetts' operation. Meldrum revealed:

> The stage line, what they called a stage line, was owned by Bassett Brothers. So I went to the office of Bassett Brothers and made arrangements to come to the park. They had an old pair of horses, old patched-up harness and a spring wagon. We started out. I had a trunk, box of books, typewriter and other stuff and in addition to these there were several trunks belonging to

> people who had preceded me into the park a day or two before. I was the only passenger on the coach. Mrs. Meldrum didn't come up to the park until later, after the house was built. Of all the mosquitoes and flies I ever saw, they accompanied this wagon on that trip.[469]

If Meldrum could have even believed it, the mosquitoes and flies soon would get worse. Meldrum did not mention staying overnight at Henry's Fork, stating only that they lodged at Dwelle's on South Fork. But he did remember that "it was three days getting to the Fountain Hotel," so the Bassetts' line had to have lodged him in at least one other place on one other night.

Now his troubles began in earnest for Meldrum with the Bassetts' driver and wagon. At Dwelle's, the driver told Meldrum that he "would have to have four horses from there on," because the road was getting pretty rough. "I asked him if he had the horses," said Meldrum, "and he said he did, so he went out and found two old horses and harness, and that harness was tied up with strings and ropes." The driver seemed unprepared to Meldrum and not too adept at his job. His whip could not even reach the leader-horses, Meldrum explained, "So I got a pole and walked on the ground and encouraged the leaders going up the hill." On a piece of rough, corduroy road, the rig's king-pin broke, the front wheels followed the horses out from under the outfit, and the rest of the coach collapsed onto the road. Meldrum could scarcely believe his eyes, and he knew from experience that this was going to be an unusually bad, road-moment in stagecoaching:

> I asked the driver what he was going to do. He didn't seem to have the sense of a child. Well, I told him what we would have to do. I showed him how to pry the wagon up. We got it up, [and] put some stones to block up the wagon. I asked him if he had a bolt of any kind in the wagon. He said he believed there was a bolt in the wagon. Well, I told him to find it. We had to unload the whole business. We finally found it…an ordinary half-inch bolt. The original king-bolt was three times as large in diameter. Anyway, we put the bolt in and it was just long enough to barely reach. So we started on. I told him that he

would have to drive carefully or we would have a recurrence of the trouble.[470]

At Lower Geyser Basin, a blacksmith was in place, probably at or near the U.S. Army camp, which oversaw protection of the Park's geysers there. Meldrum's driver stopped to get his wagon fixed, while Meldrum walked on for a mile south to the large and relatively new Fountain Hotel, "so bitten up with mosquitoes and flies I was just in misery." There he got a hot bath and additional clean-up, just in time to be confronted with a stagecoach containing two women whom he knew; it was their baggage that had been riding in his coach from Beaver Canyon.

Making small talk, Meldrum asked the women who the man riding with them was. Amazingly, the dusty man in civilian clothes, wearing "a little old gray hat about as big as a tea-cup," was Captain George S. Anderson, the Park's military superintendent. "I went up to him and introduced myself," explained Meldrum, and "he said right off the bat: 'Good to see you; let's have a drink." Anderson, who knew that Meldrum was coming, was a

Stagecoaches at Fountain Hotel, Yellowstone National Park, no date. *YELL 165777, YNP photo archives.*

red-headed Irishman and a two-fisted drinker, so the two men went into the hotel for drinks, dinner, conversation, and lodging.[471]

The next morning Meldrum reboarded his crippled coach but became quite frustrated with it and the park's continuing mosquitoes by the time he reached "Larry's Lunch Station" at Norris Geyser Basin. There the well-known Larry Mathews oversaw a tent-hotel that served travelers, and Mathews happened to be serving W.H. Humphrey, who was one of the officers of the main Yellowstone National Park Transportation Company. Humphrey "had a good team and a light buggy," explained Meldrum, "and asked me to ride with him; he was going on to Mammoth." So, Meldrum told his driver to meet them at Mammoth—if that driver even needed to drive on to Mammoth—and told us no more about the Bassetts' driver, who, unless he had Beaver Canyon passengers to pick up at Mammoth, probably turned around at Norris to head back to Beaver Canyon. In this manner, Judge John W. Meldrum, who would work as Yellowstone's U.S. Commissioner (judge) for the next forty-one years, came to the Grand Old Park.[472]

In May of the following year, 1895, Acting Superintendent Captain George Anderson wrote to the Bassett Brothers to prepare them for the license fees that would now be required in the Park. He informed them that the Secretary of Interior would grant no permits for transportation through Yellowstone Park "except to reliable parties to connect with the railroad at Beaver Canyon, and others for conducting camping parties only." "As you have conducted the regular transportation business from Beaver Canyon for many years," proclaimed Anderson, "[I] offer you the privilege from that point" at the price of five dollars per wagon employed for the summer. He also stated that they would be required to register each team and wagon upon arrival at Lower Geyser Basin with the soldiers stationed there. The Bassetts remitted fifty dollars for ten wagons that they would use that summer and received their licenses.[473] Additionally, Anderson noted in late August that "for Bassett Brothers I have given a license which permits them to take tourists to the hotels, and they are the only ones who have such a one."[474] In other words, all other transportation companies except Bassett Brothers and the YNPT Company could not pick up or drop passengers at Park hotels; those others were restricted to the Cinnabar railhead.

From this correspondence, it became clear that lingering spring, bad weather had delayed C.J. Bassett's carrying of any passengers east until June

8. Arriving in Beaver Canyon in late May, he answered Superintendent Anderson's letter, enclosing a list of the ten drivers whom he intended to employ during 1895: Henry Sagers, Peter Rasmusen, Conrad Monteith, C.J. Bassett, Jr. (his son), John [A.] Tanner, M.E. Walker, Charles Vogler, Judd Lowes, Richard Burcham, and Paul H. Allred.[475] Unfortunately, no actual trip-accounts for the Bassetts are yet known for 1895. And too, the better evidence for driver John Tanner is that he drove for the Bassetts 1892-1895, and began driving for the Monida-Yellowstone Stage Line in 1896. We will have more to say about him in volume two of this book.

As 1896 began, the town of Beaver Canyon found itself in the fascinating position of being a divorce-mill for Montana, and especially for the city of Butte. A recent change in Montana law required a divorced but "innocent" party to wait two years before remarrying; the "guilty" party had to wait three years.[476] Divorced Butte couples who wished to be married soon found that they could ride the train to Beaver Canyon, Idaho, get married in front of a justice of the peace, stay overnight, and ride the train back to Butte the next day as a newly-married couple. A justice-of-the-peace at Beaver Canyon, reported Montana newspapers, "is said to be getting rich" as a result of this practice. "Four couples" went last month, said these papers, another couple went Saturday, and still another couple "went yesterday, the prospective husband having been granted a divorce only a few weeks ago."[477] Practitioners of this idea would be forced to travel to Spencer, Idaho during the following year for reasons that will be chronicled shortly. During a continuing depression, Beaver Canyon no doubt welcomed the extra money and Montanans reading about it probably welcomed the laughs.

At Yellowstone, as park officials geared up for another summer (1896), Superintendent Anderson again sent his notice to C.J. Bassett regarding the brothers' pending license, as well as some advice on roadwork in the park's Madison Canyon, probably the long-overdue bridging of the river, because the 1896 map showed that there were now only three fords of the Madison instead of the previous five and six.[478] The Acting Secretary of Interior approved Bassett's licenses for ten wagons, to be numbered one through ten. Bassett's letterhead-stationery this year read "Union Pacific Stage Line, C.J. Bassett, Proprietor," and he acknowledged to Anderson that his season got a very late start this year.[479] Meanwhile, Superintendent Anderson faced hassles of his own at Mammoth involving undependable stagecoaching operators such as "Blankenship and Morgan," and resultingly mused that it might be best for the park to restrict licenses for these independent operators to around ten or so, "exclusive of" the one granted to the Bassett Brothers.[480] Although Anderson was, at the moment, a bit annoyed with the Brothers, by this, he apparently meant that the Bassetts' history in the region placed them in a special category, which was seen as somehow more reliable than the independent stagers in Gardiner, Cinnabar, Livingston, and Bozeman. Anderson, like all his predecessors, was continuing to have no far-western stagecoach operators available except for the Bassetts to transport passengers from Beaver Canyon to Yellowstone, so he like his predecessors tended to "cut them some slack."

The practice of bicycling to and through Yellowstone, a custom that had begun in limited form in 1883, increased greatly during the 1890s, especially after a well-publicized 1896 party from Ogden, Utah rode their "wheels" across the entire distance to the park, via Malad, Marsh Valley, Pocatello, Idaho Falls, Rexburg, St. Anthony, Island Park, and Henry's Lake, Idaho; Targhee Pass, Montana; and "Firehole Basin," Wyoming. The following year, the Oregon Short Line issued a pamphlet encouraging bicyclists to simply put their bikes and baggage onto the railroad's cars and ride to Beaver Canyon to start their biking. This publicity undoubtedly added to the railroad's business and probably to the Bassett Brothers' hotel-coffers and freight business. They advertised that even a driver could be used by the bicycle-tourists. "If the trip is made on a wheel," said the article, "and if there are a number in the party, a wagon can be procured in Beaver canyon, and a driver who is also a cook, and all the baggage can be carried in this way."[481]

With the help of these 1896 bicyclists, C.J. Bassett saw an improved year over the preceding ones during the nation's continuing depression. Superintendent S.B.M. Young reported Bassett's passenger numbers for the first time in his annual report. It stated that Bassett carried fifty-nine passengers through August 20 and another twenty-two passengers through November 10, so his total summer-patrons numbered eighty-one.[482] As a result of this increase, one wonders whether Mr. Bassett suddenly had second thoughts about abandoning his business. If so, perhaps they helped extend his son's longevity in the business for a few more years.

The year 1897 was a landmark year of sweeping changes for C.J. Bassett, Yellowstone National Park, and the town of Beaver Canyon, Idaho.

For Bassett, it was a bittersweet time, because of the sudden ending of his beloved town and the ongoing decrease of his business, but it was also the summer of one of his most important trips—the conveying and conducting of the recent U.S. presidential candidate William Jennings Bryan to Yellowstone. For Yellowstone Park, the year marked an increase in visitation by at least 2,700 tourists over any previous year and the arrival of a new superintendent named Samuel Baldwin Marks Young. For all three entities, it marked the end of the nationwide depression that had begun with the "Panic of 1893," and thus this year seemed to be ushering in a more prosperous future. But the biggest change jolted the community of Beaver Canyon cataclysmically, because in the spring, the Union Pacific Railroad moved the entire town four miles south and renamed it Spencer, Idaho.[483] The new location was lower in elevation, so it was not as bitterly cold in winter, and it also did not receive the huge amounts of snow that Beaver Canyon did (most townsfolk had had their fill of many years of snow-blockades for both the railroad and wagon roads). And too, the new spot was physically wider than the canyon at Beaver, so there was suddenly more land available for new businesses.

If we believe the newspapers, the change came quickly, at least officially. By June 11, the *Idaho Register* was reporting that "a switch and sidetrack has been placed at what is now called Spencer, about four miles south of Beaver Canyon." The newspaper went on to state that Eccles, Spencer, and Company had already erected a stone store-building and were "now completing a fine two-story hotel with twelve large sleeping rooms." With the depot-building being transported by flat-cars to this spot shortly thereafter and a post office established by June 24 (and executives appointing Spencer Howard as postmaster), the town's official moving was complete. It is likely that the railroad helped move some of the other buildings using those mentioned flat-cars, and the Brothers too moved their entire operation, including a small hotel, stables, and corrals "well stocked with horses." "The Bassett stage line will start from the new place," explained the *Register*, "saving four miles of the only bad road they have to contend with," which was undoubtedly the initial stretch across Porcupine Pass, "and also making a saving of one full day on their round trip." The article ended by predicting that the Bassetts "will probably take their first load [of tourists] out during the coming week."[484]

The article additionally stated that the plans called for the new place to be "known as Beaver Canyon" (in other words renamed that), because that name had become so well known to tourists and others all over the nation and in Europe too "as the starting point for the National Park."[485] However, it soon became clear that this would not happen and the hastily given station-name remained—Spencer—for Hiram Hupp Spencer, the businessman who was partnering in the town's new general store and who had been in the area since 1880. Mr. Spencer's winter residence was in Ogden, Utah, where he was Mayor, so his migrating back and forth appeared a bit strange to some, but he had long been an area supporter. Hiram Spencer (1851-1934), originally from Ohio and Kentucky, had moved to Ogden in 1874, married Effiebelle Pauline Brown in 1876, and entered the lumber firm of Gibson, Eccles, and Van Noy. When that firm dissolved in 1880, he moved to the recent town of Beaver Canyon, where he and Eccles started a new lumber-and-mercantile firm that W.T. Van Noy also joined. The town of Spencer seemed in 1897 to have a bright future, but it remained small through time and in 2010 had decreased in size to a population of only 37 people.[486]

Meanwhile, back in the Park during early 1897, Captain George Anderson wrote to the Secretary of Interior regarding his troubles with independent transportation operators. He fumed that he had refused a license to Gardiner old-timer Amos Chadbourn in 1896 and that Chadbourn "remains unreliable" this year. Anderson explained that except for the YNPT Company, the Bassett Brothers were "the only parties who have recently had permission to take passengers to the hotels, [but they] fell far short of giving satisfaction last year." Without mentioning what the brothers had done wrong, Anderson stated that he spoke about it to the Union Pacific Railroad and they "promised to give it their attention before another year."[487] As usual Anderson's threat-tactic to keep the Brothers in line would prove not to work, and they would continue operating.

In the late spring of 1897, Captain Anderson reminded C.J. Bassett about the fees being due for his upcoming licenses. "It is discovered," he wrote, "that you are conducting [a] transp. business in park w/o a license, a continuation of which will result in your expulsion from the park." He warned the brothers to make application for a license and it would be considered. As already explained, Bassett had obtained a license in 1896, so perhaps business was better than Anderson thought, but he suspected that Bassett had run some extra, unlicensed wagons into the park during the preceding autumn.[488] For C.J. Bassett the huge event of the summer, which was already being planned, was his personally conveying and escorting the former presidential candidate William Jennings Bryan into Yellowstone. With this in mind, Bassett did not need problems with his license, so he answered Captain Anderson quickly.

Jules Bassett coincidentally addressed his return letter on the very day, June 23, which was slated to be Superintendent Anderson's last day working in Yellowstone. Col. S.B.M. Young was scheduled to replace Captain Anderson on that same day, and Young's approval-letter encouraged the Secretary of Interior to send Bassett the seven permits for his wagons numbered one through seven and to give Bassett the order that he must be "in the park at all times to personally superintend and direct the business thus authorized."[489] This new rule, arguably a bit unreasonable, might well have worked a hardship upon C.J. Bassett, who usually oversaw the business from his office at Beaver Canyon. He likely saw it as taking up his time by requiring him to be a stage-driver or a supervisor-stationed-in-the-park instead of allowing him to perform his usual selling of tickets, renting of teams and equipment, and managing his detraining visitors, all of which activities were now required to be accomplished at the new town of Spencer, Idaho.

1897 was gradually becoming an improved year economically for nearly everyone in the nation. However, Mr. Bassett on June 23 sent thirty-five dollars this year for only seven wagons,[490] which considering his known number of customers this year meant that he badly undershot his needs in the suddenly recovering economy. On the other hand, one can hardly blame Bassett for registering as few wagons as he reasonably thought he needed for a small business being operated during a depression, especially when $5 at that time was the same as about $156.91 in 2021. He could not have anticipated that by the end of 1897, the national depression would completely subside, due in part to the fact that a huge number of Christian Endeavor tourists were journeying from many eastern cities to their national convention in San Francisco and were stopping at Yellowstone on their way back. That raised park visitation to the all-time high of 10,825 and forced the park's main stage-coach line, the YNPT Company, to run out of seats and discontinue selling tickets for more than a week in late July.[491] So the Bassetts' business was already bigger this year than C.J. Bassett anticipated. And indeed, it turned out to be one of only two years that we have actual numbers for his patrons. Mr. Bassett carried 124 total guests this year.[492]

Colonel S.B.M. Young, the Park's new superintendent, was enduring the usual "learning curve" for new employees. Wrestling with both the Bassetts' stagecoaches and David Curry's licenses for his camping parties, Young was forced to communicate twice by telegram and once by letter to his Lieutenant G.O. Cress, who managed the U.S. Army's camp at Lower Geyser Basin. He ordered Cress to gather the names of all tourists traveling with Curry and Bassett; to verify the actual numbers of tourists traveling with both tour-leaders and report them to Young; and to decide whether the Bassetts wagons were adequate for their tourists and whether to permit the Bassetts to continue picking up and dropping passengers at park hotels. Fortunately, the nearby Fountain Hotel had a telegraph and an operator who could send and receive messages quickly.[493]

Now C.J. Bassett's most important summer-event arrived, namely his conducting and escorting of the recently unsuccessful presidential candidate William Jennings Bryan (1860-1925) to Yellowstone from the new town of Spencer, Idaho. Although Mr. Bassett would make limited attempts to run his operation in 1898, the season of 1897 was essentially his last year of doing it, and one wonders whether his contacts and political conversations with W.J. Bryan resulted measurably in Bassett's decision to leave Spencer permanently and go into Idaho politics. We must believe that there was indeed some influence there. Apparently less important was the beginning in July, 1898, of the new lease from nearby Monida, Montana, of F. Jay Haynes's transportation company named the Monida & Yellowstone Stage Company. Much more would soon be heard about it.

Bryan, a conservative Democrat and Nebraskan in a time when the Democrats were conservative and Republicans were more liberal, had lost to incumbent President William McKinley eight months earlier, but Bryan's Idaho supporters and many others in the country still loved him. He had single-handedly invented the nationwide stumping-tour in 1896 by traveling and delivering about five hundred speeches to the nation's common people, and because he was loved by them, he was becoming nationally known as the "Great Commoner." Bryan would run twice more for president (in 1900 and 1908), espousing the popular causes of "free silver" and anti-Darwinism, and would eventually serve as President Woodrow

Wilson's Secretary of State. In 2017, President Donald J. Trump's advisor Steve Bannon would recall his own readings of history by stating that he believed the United States sorely needed another William Jennings Bryan.[494]

C.J. Bassett must have received word from Bryan's staff about their arrangements long before July 16, but it was on that day that Boise's *Idaho Statesman* announced that Mr. Bryan would arrive at Blackfoot on July 23 to speak in that town with U.S. Senator Fred Dubois of Idaho and that C.J. Bassett would have charge of the Yellowstone arrangements.[495] Instead, Bryan arrived on Saturday the 24th, when at least 2,000 people gathered there to hear him speak for two hours, as was the custom of a time when there was yet no radio or television. The article announced that Bryan would proceed to Shoshone Falls and then travel on Sunday with Mr. Bassett to Yellowstone.[496]

The trip did not leave for the park until the following day, Monday, July 26, from Spencer, Idaho, Bryan having been detained by officials from both Idaho and Montana who wished to convince him to lengthen his stay in those states.[497]

As expected with any president or presidential candidate, Bryan's schedule changed constantly, but we have some idea of what happened and when, due to comparisons among the newspapers. He entered the park at west entrance and traveled fast until he reached Fountain Hotel. He went to Old Faithful and either stayed there at the temporary hotel or more likely returned to Fountain Hotel. He then went on to Lake Hotel, apparently arriving on August 1. In route, Bryan's son William, age 8, encountered a black bear with two cubs, which "ran grunting away," but the mother bear then chased the child's horse. She "ran him some distance, William piloting him through the trees." Neither was hurt, said the article, "but the boy was badly scared."[498]

On August 2, they left Lake Hotel at 9 a.m. and stopped to go fishing along the way, where Bryan caught fifty trout, not unusual at that time at Yellowstone Lake. On the night of August 2, they stayed at Grand Canyon Hotel, apparently also staying there on August 3. On August 4, they traveled to Mammoth, where two hundred people stood on the hotel's veranda to greet Bryan when he arrived around 7 p.m. Superintendent S.B.M. Young and Yellowstone Park Transportation Company President S.S. Huntley traveled to Norris to meet him to ride with his staging entourage to Mammoth. Bryan stayed two nights at Mammoth, so he could attend

A stagecoach at Lake Hotel, no date, pre-1903. *YELL 165782, YNP Photo Archives.*

a fancy reception by military and hotel/transportation officials on the evening of August 5. On August 6, he left Mammoth, heading to the west entrance and Spencer, Idaho to spend several days at the ranch of Attorney A.S. Trude of Chicago (southeast of Henry's Lake and later called "Trude Siding" on the Oregon Short Line Railroad).[499]

Then Bryan began his Montana tour. On Thursday morning, August 12, accompanied by Montana Governor R.B. Smith and U.S. Congressman Charles Hartman, the party rode north from Spencer, stopping at Monida, Lima, and Dillon, where 4,000 people heard Bryan give a speech before he moved on to Butte. At tiny Monida, Montana, which would a year later become a new starting point for Yellowstone Park tours from the west by the Monida & Yellowstone Stage Company, the reporter said this:

The town was named like a race horse, receiving part of the name of each state. It is only a small hamlet, but the people were all out and prospectors and ranchmen had come down from the mountains to shake the great man by the hand. Mr. Bryan shook the hands of all of them. "If you start like this," said Charley Hartman, "you will be a pretty tired man before you get out of Montana. You are starting off wrong." "The least I could do to the people of Montana is to shake them by the hand," said Bryan. "I owe them all that." The stop at Monida was but momentary. No speeches were made until Lima was reached.[500]

We know nothing else about C.J. Bassett's role in the tour, but he must have personally chauffeured William Jennings Bryan for much of the way, at times yielding to Silas Huntley's Yellowstone National Park Transportation Company for short tours from the Park's hotels.

A few more sputterings would temporarily emerge to give life to the Bassett Brothers' company, but 1897 essentially marked the end of their operations. In fact, quoting the *Blackfoot News*, another Idaho newspaper announced on September 29, 1897 that "Mr. Bassett has withdrawn his teams from the Park for this season," and this was earlier than normal.[501]

During the following year, apparently still uncertain as to whether he was going to quit the business, C.J. Bassett wrote to the "Acting Superintendent" on June 5, 1898, requesting "the necessary blanks to make formal application." On June 10, 1898, Acting Superintendent James B. Erwin, without mentioning Bassett's letter of five days earlier, reminded C.J. Bassett, as usual, to make application by letter for his license. By June 18, Erwin's first lieutenant was stating that the new transportation lease granted to F. Jay Haynes and W.H. Humphrey was "not being complied with" and that tourists entering from the west were again being brought in by C.J. Bassett's company.[502] If this were true for that moment, it was rebutted later in the summer by Erwin's comment in the park's annual report. That report, dated September 30, stated:

The Monida and Yellowstone Stage Company have seemingly absorbed the business previously conducted by Mr. C.J. Bassett, from Beaver Canyon, Idaho, into the park via the western entrance, as I have no reports of any passengers by his line during the past season, nor has he applied for license to conduct this class of business.[503]

Boise's *Idaho Statesman*, however, believed differently, for it reported in late August that "C.J. Bassett...is proprietor of a stage line running from Beaver Cañon [Spencer] to the Yellowstone Park." The reporter interviewed Bassett, who was visiting in Boise, and Mr. Bassett told him that travel to the park this year was "far below the record of last year," especially with regard to foreigners, but that the Park in general was more popular than ever. Bassett dismissed a rumor that the Park was overrun with cattle and stated that it was splendidly policed and devoid of forest fires this season.[504]

It was apparent from this report that Bassett considered himself to be still operating trips to Yellowstone, or at least he wanted to project that image. Nevertheless, unless we count the report involving Peter Rasmusen, no actual accounts of Bassett's trips from 1898 have been found nor a license from the Park for that year, and, as will be seen Mr. Bassett had already accepted a new job as State Commissioner of Immigration. There was no doubt that he wanted his new employment to happen at Boise, because C.J. "Jule" Bassett had been bitten by the political bug. He was also serving as the "silver Republican leader" from the state's southeast district, and he had been described in February as "prominent in Idaho politics." In August, while he normally would have been running his stage-line, Bassett instead attended the statewide "Silver Republicans convention."[505]

What might have happened with his company was that he simply left it to his son C.J. Bassett, Jr. (1878-1903) to operate it for a few more summers, namely 1898-1901, and there are several pieces of evidence for this proposition. C.J.'s son had been driving stages for him for several years, and in the summer of 1899, C.J., Jr. and friends toured the park on what might have been a pleasure-trip, but what might also have been business.[506]

And too, we have the statement of driver John A. Tanner that he drove for the Bassett Brothers from 1892 through 1900. His newspaper reminiscences, written sixty years later, went so far as to claim that he was in the line of stagecoaches in Yellowstone Park on August 14, 1897 when stage-robbers George Reeb and Gus Smitzer held up seven other coaches on the old road to Norris up Canyon Hill. Tanner stated that he drove for Bassett through the season of 1900, so perhaps C.J. Bassett, Junior, did indeed run the company for several more summers after 1897. If so, he ran it without a park-license (at least in 1899-1900), but in that remote country with the Park's attention focused mainly on the new Monida & Yellowstone Stage Company (located to the north, over in Centennial Valley) and with the Park Superintendent thinking that the Bassett Brothers were out of business, this possibility seems thoroughly believable. However, where driver John Tanner is concerned, it is more likely that he misremembered, and was driving for the Bassetts through only 1897, and then drove for Monida-Yellowstone from 1898 through 1900.[507]

Finally, there is the 1898 letter from Yellowstone tourist S.P. Gibbs to YPT Company employee Axel Johnson, who was stationed that summer at Fountain Hotel and apparently living in the hotel's housing area southeast of the main building. Gibbs complained about their driver, a man named "Peter Rasmus," who was undoubtedly Bassett Brothers' stage-driver Peter Rasmusen, mentioned earlier. "Rasmus" was "what we would call in this part of the country a 'Dead Beat'," wrote Gibbs, who then accused Rasmus of driving through the park stealing and welshing on bills. Gibbs stated that this man "stole about four bushels of oats" at Canyon Hotel. It seemed to Gibbs that people at Canyon and other places should be warned about "Rasmus" in case he should ever "come through the Park again as he states he intends to drive for Bassett next season." Rasmus, it turns out, was C.J. Bassett's brother-in-law. He was apparently still working for the Bassetts even though C.J. Bassett was mostly out of the picture, so, unless Rasmus was driving through the park on his own hook, stealing stuff because he knew the drill, someone, maybe Bassett Jr., was running the Bassetts' company over at Spencer, Idaho.[508]

There is today another bit of evidence that something more was going on with the Bassett Brothers in the form of a last-minute attempt to save their failing business. It is a photo taken at Monida, Montana sometime during this period. The photo (YC-P06641, Jay Lyndes Family Collection) shows an office attached to the small railroad-depot there with one of the offices bearing a sign that says, "Bassett Brothers," an apparent attempt to snag some business from tourists alighting from the train there, probably during the period that the new Monida & Yellowstone Stage Line was beginning (1898-1899). However long the attempt lasted, it ultimately failed. If this attempt made the newspapers during that period, those references have so far not turned up.

Regardless of what would happen to his company during the years 1898-1901, C.J. Bassett had decided by late 1897 that he wanted to go full time into state politics. He continued to visit Boise, and in November of 1898, engaged with others there in wagering money on political candidates. In March of 1899, the governor appointed him Immigration Commissioner for Idaho. And in May, he and his wife Christina Annie Rasmussen Bassett moved from Blackfoot to Boise, Idaho, thus quitting his stagecoaching operation forever.[509]

Nearly a year later, the death of their eighteen-year-old daughter Bertha "Birdie" Bassett from heart disease had to have further cinched Mr. Bassett's resolve to keep busy by staying in politics as a full-time career.[510]After all, who could blame him for suddenly not wanting to drive stagecoaches through the quiet and beautiful Yellowstone country or to continue living in the idyllic, small towns (Blackfoot and Beaver Canyon) where "Birdie" had grown up, as constant reminders of his darling daughter and the happy life that he and his family had known? In the state election of 1900, he ran for Secretary of State of Idaho, was elected, and began a second successful career, this one in Boise. Then after twenty years in Idaho politics, Charles Julius "Jule" Bassett died on November 26, 1918.[511]

If it was the end of one era in Yellowstone stagecoaching, it was the beginning of another. In the summer of 1898, Park photographer F. Jay Haynes and William H. Humphrey founded the Monida & Yellowstone Stage Company and began operating it from Monida, Montana, to Yellowstone National Park through the Centennial Valley of Montana. For the next eighteen years, that company would monopolize the national park stagecoaching business from the west, in that region of Montana and Idaho where the Bassett Brothers had reigned for so long, and where the Union Pacific Railroad, formerly the Utah & Northern, was still king.

We shall tell that story in volume II of *Stagecoaching Through Yellowstone*, but for now, we must return to 1880 to chronicle the story of William Wallace Wylie and how he established his later-famous "Wylie Way" (camping company) in the Park, three years before the larger and more influential Wakefield & Hoffman company came to be.

CHAPTER SEVEN

The Wylie Camping Company

Coaches and Camps

"Special mention may be made of five four-horse coach-teams[,] which we used especially for meeting trains at Gardiner...One four were light colored sorrels with snow-white manes and tails. Another four were jet black. Another snow white; another dark bays; another dapple greys; [and] another dapple bays. These five teams were really the show teams of the park. It is needless to say that their appearance at the Railway station often influenced the undecided arriving tourist in making up his mind as to how he would go."—W.W. Wylie, unpublished autobiography, p. 143.

At the same time that the Bassett Brothers were planning their operations, just before George Rea and Thomas Rea moved to Shotgun Valley from Montana, and at about the time that George Marshall was constructing the first iteration of his "Marshall's Hotel" on the west side of Firehole River, William Wallace Wylie, in Bozeman, Montana, was deciding that he too wanted a piece of the impending Yellowstone touring business. This was in 1880—three years before George Wakefield would begin operating stage-coaches for the Yellowstone National Park Improvement Company.

W.W. Wylie (1848-1930) was born "in the village of New Concord, Muskingum County, Ohio, on June 8, 1848, the son of Moses and Elizabeth (McCartney) Wylie, who had eight children." His parents were both natives of Pennsylvania who relocated to Ohio and then to Iowa in 1855. They raised William in Washington, Iowa, and he eventually graduated from Lenox College in Hopkinton, Iowa in 1873, after which he became a school superintendent at Delhi and then Lyons, Iowa. Wylie has stated that one day "a gentleman accosted me while I was out horseback-riding, saying, 'How would you like to go to teach in the Rocky Mountain country?'" This man was a traveling visitor from Bozeman, Montana who told Wylie that if the position were yet open when he arrived home that he would like to recommend him to the board. This resulted in the board's extending the offer. Wylie thus rode the Union Pacific Railroad west and eventually the Utah & Northern Railroad north to the end of the railroad tracks at Oneida, Idaho, and then took the long, overland trip by stagecoach via the Gilmer & Salisbury Stage Line northward over the Montana Trail to Virginia City and Bozeman.[512]

At Bozeman, he quickly appeared in newspapers as an educator. But he also continued what he had been doing in Iowa, namely that timeless, fallback position of ranching and stock-raising. Two years later, the *Weekly Miner* at Butte announced on June 22, 1880 that Bozeman officials were closing the schools there for the summer. "Prof. Wylie," said the newspaper, "will, no doubt, be retained as principal."[513] Mr. Wylie suddenly faced unemployment for the summer, as generations of teachers, principals, and school employees who came after him would also face. What was he to do?

Having heard of the great Yellowstone wonderland to the south, Wylie decided to make a trip there for pleasure. But he also had the gem of an idea in his head. Could he make extra money by running trips to the strange, new place during his summer breaks? So, with Richard "Dick" Lockey and later a man named Jackson, he rode horses to the park's north entrance and then south and around the park, camping for several days.[514]

Impressed by what he saw, he returned to Bozeman with confidence that he still had time that year to make one more trip. Thus, late in the same summer (1880), Wylie assembled his first tourist-party to Yellowstone composed of two ministers, two young men from Bozeman, one friend of his wife's, and Wylie's own family (including his wife Mary Ann who was

The sheer beauty of the time, place, and subject can be spectacularly seen by enlarging this crystal-clear, Haynes photo of a (later) Wylie Camping Company stagecoach No. 4, carrying Yellowstone Park visitors at Liberty Cap in July of 1897. The party included J. Henry Zeis (standing fourth from left) and Elizabeth Zeis (Nichols, standing second from left), a married couple at the time, as indicated by the two marks of "X" at the top of the picture. The others are unknown. J. Henry Geis committed suicide in Chicago the following year by jumping into Lake Geneva in 1898. *Randy Ingersoll Collection.*

now expecting their daughter Mary Grace), and his other three children: Elizabeth, Fred, and Frank.[515]

The nine party-members in two wagons found the trip to be a challenge at times, because of park superintendent P.W. Norris's primitive roads, which often featured stumps sticking up in their center. Because only some of the routes allowed wagons to "pass without the axle of [the] wagon catching," the party would sometimes hitch another team to the back of their wagon to "draw it back" so that the men could "cut the stump shorter." The party visited Monument Geyser Basin, Norris, Gibbon Canyon, and Upper Geyser Basin, and then returned to Mammoth Hot Springs, and Bozeman. It proved a successful trip and was Wylie's first venture into tourism. Wylie noted: "I have always looked back upon the summer of 1880 with [our] two rather eventful tours of the park, with much interest and pleasure."[516]

In 1881, Wylie decided to spend a summer writing a Yellowstone guidebook (which he would eventually sell in his camps' gift-shops) while also accompanying photographer Henry Bird Calfee around the park. Wylie's information and Calfee's photographs served them both well that autumn when the two of them went on a several-months-long lecture-tour promoting the park in Colorado, Nebraska, Utah, Wyoming, and Minnesota. A Montana newspaper explained that Wylie and Calfee "have gone east to give oxy-calcium exhibitions of the Yellowstone National Park scenery."[517]

Beginning in the summer of 1882, Wylie began offering a "sage brushing" experience to potential tourists by offering to take them through the park in movable tents. That would become his pattern for the next decade. But if the Montana newspapers are any indication, he had few takers for three years. What trips he took in 1882, 1883, and 1884, if any, remain unknown; there is no mention of any such Wylie activities. During these early years, Wylie was getting a slow start in the touring business, writing a guidebook, learning about Yellowstone, and occasionally taking small, camping groups to the park. Yet, he possessed no fleet of wagons or horses; everything was done in small-group fashion. But he was already noticing that his 1882 guidebook was becoming successful and resulting in his receiving requests from Montanans to consider guiding them to Yellowstone.

In 1884, Mary Ann Wylie delivered the family's fifth child—son Clinton Wilson Wylie, born on June 26. Meanwhile W.W. Wylie, apparently looking for additional work to shore up his financial situation, ran unsuccessfully for state legislature.[518]

During summers, Wylie was gradually learning that what he really loved was taking small groups of people to the Park and showing the place to them. Probably his confirmation in Helena in early March as Territorial Superintendent of Public Instruction lessened his financial worries. Whatever the reasons, the Wylies did take at least two parties to Yellowstone in

1885. A party consisting of "Prof. Wylie," Bozeman banker Peter Koch, and a Dr. Waters left for the park in early August.[519] About ten days into their trip, the party was arrested on Firehole River "for leaving a campfire unextinguished." Taken before Justice C.H. Hall at Lower Geyser Basin, they were fined fifty dollars each.[520] This incident resulted mainly in bringing attention to the park's laissez faire system of justice that allowed Wyoming constables to, potentially abusively, pocket a portion of the fines they collected. This event was a lead-up to a more important case known as the "Payson incident," but neither of these cases had any immediate effects on the questionable law-enforcement situation in Yellowstone. Fixing that would become a longer story.

Mr. Wylie also accompanied a "Mr. and Mrs. Bayles," probably the Montana mining family, to Yellowstone this year. Photographer F. Jay Haynes took a photo of them with Wylie at his Upper Geyser Basin movable-camp.[521]

Nor does it appear that the Wylies took any trips to Yellowstone Park in 1886. The death of their infant son Franklin Wylie on February 26 of that year might have figured into this dearth of trips, as the family's situation took priority.[522]

Mr. Wylie took at least one group to Yellowstone in August of 1887. The *River Press* of Fort Benton announced on August 10 that at least twenty teachers had gone to the park with him. This was a three-week trip that included Col. and Mrs. Radford of Bozeman, Prof. and Mrs. Howard of Helena, Prof. Porter of Miles City, numerous female teachers, plus "drivers, cooks, and other attaches." The *Helena Weekly Herald* reported "seventeen ladies and gentlemen, encountered at Canyon, forming an educational group under Prof. Wylie of Bozeman." They were back home by August 25.[523] Like so many tour guides would learn later, the "Professor" was learning that he thrived on showing Yellowstone to visitors and telling them about it.

In 1888, Mr. Wylie took at least one group to the park, and it was again in August. He apparently had some national advertising by this time, perhaps in newspapers, because the *Bozeman Weekly Chronicle* reported that "Prof. Wylie left this week for the National Park with from thirty to forty school marms *from the east*."[524] In the same issue of the newspaper appeared a fascinating column that illuminated the lack of relevant information faced by camping travelers in Yellowstone who did not have a guide. Nine years earlier, Superintendent Norris had erected many signs and guideboards around the park, but most of those were gone by 1888, and this writer known only as "Old Dynamite," probably a prospector who was stating that he was from Red Bluff, Montana, believed that likewise the army-soldiers were of little help:

> Some of the parties returned, who also visited the gysers [*sic—geysers*] in the National Park, saying that there is a very poor show there for visitors coming with their own camping outfits to get any intelligent information in regard to the points of interest there. In fact, unless you engage the services of a guide[,] you are compelled to find out everything as best you can. There are very few people visiting the Park, or have been so far, and you sometimes have to wait hours even at some of the grandest gysers [*sic*] before you see a single human being[;] as soon as anyone else makes his appearance, the parties generally get together hastily, one questioning the other, What place is this? What geyser is this? Will he play? When? and so on. There is even at the biggest geyser of them all, the Excelsior, at Hells Half Acre, not the least sign anywhere in sight to indicate the place you are at or passing. The only sign there displayed is on the old road with the legend "Middle Geyser Basin." You can come upon numerous signs, "Don't get on the formation." In fact, this sign stares you in the face continually. It seems at some former time signs were up, but they have long since tumbled down and are entirely coated over with their beloved formation. Even at the grand geyser, Old Faithful, [there is] not a sign in sight. How easy it would be to put up and keep up a few signs at these places, and probable some blackboards, indicating when and how often the several geysers play. There are other things very aggravating to the visitor, I mean such as came with their own conveyances. For instance, the dense ignorance of the soldiers stationed within the Park. All questions put to them are generally answered with, "I don't know." The professional guides, of course, are not supposed to know anything, unless you pay them for their services, and then most generally, not much either.[525]

Mr. Wylie undoubtedly read this article in a Bozeman newspaper, and it must have given him optimism for the future of his business. He had to have seen the current usefulness of his small transportation, camping, and informational (tour-guiding) services, and thus the potential for a great future—at least in the summertime. After all, the park was so large, wild, and still fairly roadless that using guides remained important to visitors.

Also in 1888, Wylie took a job as President of the Bozeman Academy, which lasted at least through 1891. Whether this was simply hired employment or whether he was a partner in this private academy who shared in its profits is not known, but apparently it improved his financial situation.[526]

The following summer, Wylie told Montana newspapers including the *Helena Weekly Herald* that his first trip to the park this year would be on July 12, 1889, and it would leave Cinnabar on that date.[527] In this way he hoped to pick up at the north entrance anyone else who wanted to pay to go. On July 23rd, Mr. D.D. Smith and wife, Miss Wylie, and Miss Shipman arrived by train in Livingston on their return from a tour through Wonderland.[528] This was the first possible hint that Professor Wylie had thought of teaching at least one of his daughters (Elizabeth, the oldest at age 14) to learn to be a tour guide. She would do more of this later.

According to Elizabeth Watry's master's thesis on this subject, Wylie's earliest known advertising appeared in the *Helena Daily Herald* of May 25, 1889. This was the advertisement:

> Camping Out in Yellowstone National Park. Wylie & Wilson take tourists through the Park in carriages and on horseback. We furnish tents, provisions, cooks, and everything but bedding. Visit all points of interest and give plenty of time, spending 12 days in the Park. Have comfortable carriages, gentle horses, and excellent saddles for both ladies and gentlemen. This is the only satisfactory way to visit the Park. Write the undersigned for particulars and dates of trips. Wylie's illustrated guide and description book mailed for fifty cents. W.W. Wylie, Bozeman, Montana.[529]

By 1890, Wylie was advertising in more of Montana. One item appeared in the *Helena Independent* from March 30 through June 13, and another in the Deer Lodge *New North-West* from April 25 through June 20. The first ad went like this:

> Camping in Yellowstone Park—Those who expect to visit the Park this season would do well to correspond with the undersigned, who takes camping parties, spends twelve days in the Park, furnishes everything but bedding, visits all points that stages do and many more. Plenty of time given at every point to see and enjoy everything, and charges no more than a stage trip of four days will cost. First party will leave Cinnabar about June 26. Write for particulars to W.W. Wylie, Bozeman, Mont.[530]

The second advertisement was entitled "Yellowstone Park Camping Parties," and it explained that "Wylie and Wilson" were in charge of the parties and gave all the same information, but then emphasized that this company spent twelve days instead of four in the park and added that they furnished "everything that can be had in the way of provisions and other comforts" including "campfire entertainments" that were "made a special feature" in the evenings.[531] This was already one of Wylie's successes, and it would continue to be so in the future—offering a cheaper tour of Yellowstone than YPA with its railroad-backers would ever do.

One of Wylie's parties in August included Miss Nellie Kenyon and Miss Nellie Merrill, both of Iowa, who had been visiting friends in Big Timber and decided to accompany them on one of the trips "under the guidance of Prof. W. Wylie for a two week's tour of Wonderland." On August 18, Deer Lodge residents who left to join one of Wylie's trips were the Rev. R.E. Dunlap and wife, and his children Willie and Nellie Mae. The Reverend took "a tourist suit, pencil, book, and field glass" so that he could enjoy "all of the magnificent scenery."[532]

In 1891, Professor Wylie seems to have run no newspaper ads in Montana, but on August 1, he started to the Park with a party of twenty-five persons: seven from Helena, seven from Butte, and the rest from scattered towns. That Wylie took at least two groups to the park this year was attested to by the *Anaconda Standard*, which stated on Sunday, August 23 that "Mrs. Patrick Talent left Monday [August 17] with the second Wylie party for Yellowstone park." Likewise, the same newspaper column stated the following: "Misses Lizzie Busch, Carrie Cox, Miss O'Donnell, and Mrs. Groeneveld, of the Wylie party, returned from the national park Sunday [probably August 16 but could conceivably be August 23], and are very enthusiastic over their trip."[533]

In his 1926 reminiscences, Professor Wylie made a statement that approximately pinpoints the year that he and Mary Ann seriously entered the business of tourism. Regarding his first trips into Yellowstone with paying customers, he remembered that "it was at least ten years after this work began [1880-1881], before Mrs. Wylie and I realized that we were drifting into a tourist business."[534] That would make the approximate year of their realization to have been 1890 or 1891. Considering the sporadic and relatively random nature of Wylie's business discussed so far, his memory was probably correct.

There is more, much more, to the story of the Wylie Company's stage-coaching operation. This chronicles it through 1891, but much of his ultimate story did not begin until 1892. We take up the rest of the story in volume two of this book, where we will discuss Wylie's large, McMaster Camping Cars in 1892; his trip to Washington, DC in 1893 to protest his park-arrest[535] and to ask for permission to establish permanent camps in Yellowstone; and his many larger, more organized trips involving the semi-permanent camps. We shall watch him putting together a formal transportation department with numerous horses, wagons, and camping equipment; obtaining the permits he was seeking; beginning to call his successful system the "Wylie Way;" and finally leaving the business by selling it to other businessmen after winning a much-ballyhooed lawsuit against the railroad. He would eventually move to California, after carving a place for himself in history and ending up fulfilled and contented.

But for now, we must return to 1865, to chronicle the history of George and Thomas Rea and their independent stagecoach company in Shotgun Valley, Idaho—about one hundred miles west of Yellowstone National Park.

CHAPTER EIGHT

One of the Earliest Independent Stagecoach Operators to Yellowstone

---

George Rea—Hunter, Settler, Guide, and Stager in Shotgun Valley, Idaho

"[He] has purchased a number of teams, wagons and carriages and proposes to establish a line of transportation from Beaver Canyon to the Geyser Basin for the accommodation of tourists."—*The Semi-Weekly Miner* (Butte, MT), May 24, 1884.

George W. Rea's connection to Yellowstone stagecoaching was brief, but his nexus to the Camas-Antelope-Sheridan-Shotgun-Island Park valleys of Idaho, to several towns in Montana, and to Yellowstone National Park was early, long, and influential in the region. Rea's Pass, formerly on the Union Pacific Railway between Big Springs, Idaho and West Yellowstone, Montana, is today named for him, and so is Rea's Peak on the Continental Divide west of Sawtelle Peak.[536] Rea (pronounced RAY, as misspellings in newspapers make clear) knew the Bassett Brothers well and housed their traveling customers at his ranch for five or six years, and he maintained a heavy influence upon the Bassetts' route to the Park both before and after the advent of their stage-line. Mining and an interest in wildlife were the initial reasons he came to the area, and his life ended with his being immersed in the area's wildlife by operating Idaho's earliest fish-farm and hatchery. He called his ranch "Glen Rea," which still appears as "Rea" on current maps in a slightly different location, because the original Glen Rea has been completely swallowed by part of the Island Park Reservoir. According to historian Dean Green, George Rea "named his homestead/ranch 'Glen Rea,' using a Scottish custom of titling a valley-abode or haven a glen, and indicating ownership by using the person's last name in the title."[537] Perhaps most important, he ran his own stage-line to Yellowstone for a few years, which is the reason that we tell his story here.

One historian[538] says George Rea was the area's third settler, but conceivably he was second—just after Gilman Sawtell—because he twice stated in his own newspaper accounts that he arrived in the valley in 1868 and in one of them stated that he "settled in the valley" then, and that this was three years before Richard W. Rock, the bison aficionado. On the other hand, it can be argued that Rea did not stay in the area as a permanent settler until later, for we know that he returned to Montana for at least twelve years.[539] Finally, as will be seen, Rea was probably Yellowstone Park's second commercial guide, again following Gilman Sawtell.

Born in Portville, New York,[540] George Walter Rea (1832-1902) appears to have lived there until 1865. From the 1850 census record we know that his parents were Walter Rea (from Scotland) and Mary Rea (from New York), who were sixteen years apart in age, and that he had three sisters and two brothers, one of whom would follow him to Montana and Idaho. His father Walter was a lumberman, and five years after that census, George was following in that occupation. On June 16, 1855, George was living on his own in Portville with two family members—his sister Sarah, aged 23, and a niece named Lilly Minier, aged 14.[541] In 1863, Rea registered for the draft, but whether he served in the Civil War is unknown. In that year, his registration listed him as "married," and his daughter stated later that it was to Martha Rea, but we know little else about this first wife.[542]

We know of George Rea's emigration to Montana primarily because his daughter Mary Rea was fond of telling her life-stories to friends and in fact told them twice to journalists who wrote them down. Despite having only an eighth-grade education (at least until later), Mary H. Rea (1864-1945) married in 1880 the second mayor of Butte—Henry G. Valiton—and eventually ascended to the position of being the first woman president of the Montana Society of Pioneers. Her two accounts explained that her parents—George and his wife Martha—left New York in 1865. According to her, George, like so many others of his time, heard reports of gold in Montana Territory, and when he told Martha about them, she reportedly exclaimed: "Let's go, all of us, you and the baby and I." So, the family entrained to Council Bluffs, Iowa to join a wagon train that George heard was "being outfitted" there. They added their four-horse wagon to the group of around one hundred others and headed for Wyoming and Montana.[543] Their route utilized the original Oregon Trail (apparently the Mormon Trail on the Platte River's north bank), following it through Nebraska and Wyoming. They crossed Green River and stayed on the Trail until somewhere near present Fort Hall, Idaho, where they appear to have taken the Montana Trail (sometimes called the "Corinne Road") northward through Idaho to Virginia City, Montana.

Near Fort Laramie, Indians—probably Sioux—attacked the wagon train while George Rea was out hunting deer. He returned just in time to encounter the marauders and ran through their lines to the wagon train. "He being well armed and an expert marksman," explained his daughter Mary, "father succeeded in killing several of the savages." The skirmishes lasted three days as the Indians left and returned several times, and during those scary moments, Martha Rea put her one-year-old baby Mary into the oven of the cook-stove inside their covered wagon to hide her. Martha then began loading guns for the men, while George fired them over and over at the raiders. "An Indian, seeing her handing out guns," recounted Mary, "made a dash with a spear ready to throw at her when the captain of the train saw the red man's move in time and shot him down." The Indians killed numerous members of the wagon train, but finally a group of soldiers from nearby Fort Laramie showed up to run the raiders off for good.[544]

George Rea lived in the right time to have had numerous adventures with Indians. Twenty-two years later, he recalled another one in a long missive to one of his old friends who lived in Pennsylvania, and even narrowed the location down for us in present New York state:

The 31st day of July, 1865, I had a desperate fight with Indians, between Rock creek and Cooper creek, near the Serine plains…I fought nineteen of the red devils, killing three dead, wounding half dozen more and killed five horses that fell dead

on the field. I used the Henry rifle, a sixteen shooter. That was
the best gun then invented. The Indians were poorly armed at
that time. They now have as good rifles as the white men. I have
had a good many skirmishes with the villains, and I do pray and
hope that I may live to see the race entirely extinct.[545]

Like so many of his day, especially in the West, Mr. Rea despised Indians,
but of course many of them despised him back.

By a fortunate coincidence for the Rea family, 1865 was the year that
two efforts to build a shorter route to the Montana goldfields really got
going, even though the family would not be able to use them. Spurred by
Minnesota and northern Iowa people who wanted a faster route, efforts
exploded this year to build a road north of the Oregon Trail that ran west
up Nebraska's Niobrara River to connect with Wyoming's Bighorn and
Powder river areas and eventually turn north to reach Montana Territory.
The Sioux, Cheyenne, and Arapaho Indians had different ideas however,
and that resulted in the dispatching of the U.S. Army from Fort Laramie on
various campaigns to the north and west. The Bozeman Trail—north-run-
ning from present Casper, Wyoming—was also coming into primitive existence this year. The Rea family ran smack into the coalescing of these two
developments, and that resulted in the Indian attack on their Iowa-based
wagon-train near Fort Laramie. Because of these ongoing advancements,
the Reas probably had more Army protection nearby than might have otherwise been available, and that fact probably saved their lives in a place and
time where other emigrants were being massacred. The Reas' wagon train
was traveling close in time to James A. Sawyers's surveying-party for the
"Niobrara and Virginia City Road," which, like the Reas' party, was attacked by Indians several times (August 24 and following) near the "Black
Hills" (the Laramie Range) and Fort Laramie.[546] The Rea family then traveled on to Soda Springs, Idaho, and turned north on the Montana Trail.

Like many early Montanans, the Reas went first to Virginia City, and
Mary Rea stated that they were carrying "the first quartz mill to be used
in Alder Gulch." The *Montana Post*—at that time the only newspaper in
Montana Territory—confirmed that their wagon train arrived at Virginia City on Monday, October 2, 1865, carrying "a fourteen-stamp mill"
that the Reas "brought over the plains in eighteen ox wagons." (Apparently

some of the other wagons in the train separated from the group along the way.) "On the leading vehicle," said the *Post*, "was rigged a wooden house, in which sat Mrs. Rea, quite comfortable and at home." Confirming Mary's story of the Indians was the newspaper's comment about the family's arrival. While traveling, noted the paper, the Reas narrowly escaped capture by Indians, and "Mr. Rea, as his lady informed us, rubbed out some of them and also erased a few poneys."[547]

George Rea then began prospecting, hoping of course for actual mining, initially in Virginia City's Alder Gulch but also at times leaving Martha and Mary for weeks or months while he struck out for "pay-dirt" elsewhere in the Territory. During one of these trips in the autumn of 1865, if we believe two of his own writings plus something he told the Owen party, he traveled east, probably on a prospecting expedition, into what became Yellowstone Park. He went again in 1866. In an 1882 newspaper, he mentioned the geysers, which he stated were on the headwaters of Madison River. "I hunted and trapped in that country," wrote Rea, "before the public knew there was such a place in existence, as early as the fall of 1869 and was [also] there in 1865."[548] Apparently, in this 1882 article, he misremembered the years, for they were 1865, 1866, and 1868.

In 1883, Rea welcomed the bicycle-party of William Owen to his ranch at Glen Rea at the beginning of his many years of serving park-bound tourists. Mentioning that George Rea was a name familiar to every tourist entering Yellowstone through the Beaver Canyon route, Owen stated of Mr. Rea: "This gentleman claims to be the discoverer of the geysers in the National Park, and says he first saw them in 1865." "Subsequently," continued Owen, "he visited Virginia City, Mont., where his story was told but not believed, [and] the people treating the whole matter with contempt." Well, naturally Rea had returned to Virginia City, because that was where he was living in 1865, even though at intervals he would travel to other parts of the region. William Owen recorded a bit more of what George Rea told him, this time confirming the information that Rea's second visit to Yellowstone was in 1866: "Sometime in the following year, however, Mr. Rea organized a party to explore the then unknown region." This information by Owen thus recorded two visits to Yellowstone by prospector Rea, in 1865 and 1866. Like many prospectors during the period 1863-1869, George Rea entered what was to become Yellowstone National Park, but he did not officially or unofficially make known his discovery. Thus, the Washburn Expedition of 1870 became the credited discoverers of the national park. In his 1882 newspaper article, Rea also claimed a visit to Yellowstone in 1869, but he may have mixed that year up with either the 1866 trip or his trip to the region in 1868 wherein he helped Gilman Sawtell build the road north to Henry's Lake.[549]

Living in Virginia City as they did for their first three or four years in Montana, the Rea family saw first-hand the famous Vigilantes of Montana in action, even though the family arrived after the initial hangings in 1864. "The town was 'wild and wooly'," said Mary, "The slogan was 'A Man for Breakfast Each Morning'," by which she meant a new hanging. "One morning my father, going to his log shed where he kept his oxen," she stated, "found a man hanged from one of the shed rafters with a card pinned on his back saying, 'Hung by the Vigilantes.' My parents never knew from whence he came or what crime he had committed." And she revealed the meaning of the famous "3-7-77" rallying-cry of the enforcers, a phrase that is still honored in the trademark shoulder-patch of today's Montana Highway Patrol:

> Usually…the Vigilantes, the only law and order possible in early day Montana, sent a warning before killing a criminal. The warning read: 3-7-77, which meant "we give you 3 hours, 7 minutes and 77 seconds to leave the country or else you will have a grave, 3 feet wide, 7 feet long and 77 inches deep."[550]

The Reas continued to dwell in Virginia City for several years, while George looked for gold. His peripatetic, prospecting trips during these years 1865-1868 and perhaps again in 1877 were supposedly fodder for a legend that he or others spawned entitled "The Lost Mine of Madison Canyon," which we will discuss at the end of this chapter.

On August 24, 1868, George W. Rea—still living in Virginia City, for the *Montana Post* was announcing it   set out on a prospecting expedition to the Wind River Mountains in northern Wyoming, with four other men: John W. Brown, Tom Haney, Billy Armstrong, and Charles H. Zuther.[551] It was apparently on this trip that Rea met Gilman Sawtell near Henry's Lake and helped him build one of the earliest wagon-roads in the Yellowstone region, for Rea stated in 1882 that "from the mouth of Shotgun Creek to the large park below [south of] Henry's Lake, I cut the timber out of the way and built the road fourteen years ago for hunting and fishing purposes." He reaffirmed this in 1893, writing that "when I cut the road through the timber from Henry Lake bottom in 1868, I stood on the very ground where Mr. Hopf is now building his hotel and saw a band of elk grazing on the opposite side of the river." That spot was just across (east of) the Henry's Fork from where George Rea had already placed his cabin (which he later called his ranch) and named it "Glen Rea." We have no reason to doubt this date because Rea recorded it twice. Gilman Sawtell, credited with being Yellowstone Park's first commercial tour-guide, was, with Rea, one of the builders of that earliest of Yellowstone-area roads, which ran from Shotgun Creek north to Henry's Lake.[552]

At some point, probably in the spring of 1869 after this trip, George Rea and his family moved briefly to the Gallatin Valley near Bozeman. "My father squatted on a piece of land thinking he would develop a farm," said Mary, "but the Indians were so hostile that he was afraid to remain." While the family lived in the Gallatin Valley, whether George was present or not, Mrs. Rea always kept provisions handy in a bag, so that when she saw horsemen, she could take the bag and her baby and hide in a nearby timbered swamp until she was sure the horsemen were whites and not Indians. Every night in the Gallatin Valley, remembered Mary, "my parents never had a light in the cabin, fearing it might guide a band of savages to our abode."[553] Rea has stated that at some point during this year, he made a trip to present Yellowstone National Park, and, if it actually happened and he did not merely confuse it later with his 1865, 1866, or 1868 trips, he was indeed geographically close to the park while living at Bozeman.[554]

While telling her story of living at Virginia City, Mary Rea also remembered that "during her eventful girlhood" she "must have lived at almost every mining camp in Montana." From Gallatin Valley, the Rea family moved to Helena, again remaining only a short time (until sometime in 1869, according to Mary), and then they began a string of brief residencies in various mining camps. Mary says they went to Cedar Creek (six miles from Helena), then to Missoula, then Deer Lodge in 1873, and three years later to Butte.[555]

But there were at least two other mining camps too, and they were both in Madison County. According to the Bozeman *Avant Courier*, George and Thomas Rea discovered and briefly worked the Pole Creek mines (east of present Norris, Montana) in 1870 and sold their interests to A.W. Tanner in 1874.[556] And on May 1, 1872, George Rea and his friends Henry Enselman, M.M. Young, and William Davis discovered silver diggings at Cherry Creek, Montana, which, as was usual with such discoveries, the four men believed would make them rich or at least a living. In fact, George was so excited about it that he offered a fellow miner $10,000 to buy that miner's claim, and the miner turned him down. This location was forty miles from Virginia City and twenty-five miles west of Bozeman, in the lower Madison River Canyon and near the town site of Havana, Montana. By November, Rea and Davis had opened a general store there, and by the following February, twenty-five houses had sprung up at Cherry Creek and George's brother Thomas Rea had joined him in the new town (as mentioned, Thomas Rea came to Montana as early as 1870). Delighted by his luck, George reported his claim—"The George W. Rea"—as having a four-foot vein at a depth of twenty feet, which yielded ore assaying at from $50 to $10,000 per ton.[557]

The new strike lasted for less than two years. Like so many mining ventures, this one played out quickly. George Rea must have been discouraged because he suddenly changed his life radically. In late 1873, he gave up on mining—at least temporarily—to return to hunting and trapping animals, a profession that he knew well. By November, he was at work in this, probably operating initially from Cherry Creek:

> Game.—A good lot of bear, elk and venison came into town on Monday morning last and was readily disposed of. It was for sale at Robinson & Dowell's butcher shop next door to the Courier. George Rea, the famous hunter from Cherry Creek, was the fortunate man that brought down these denizens of the forest.[558]

Then, leaving his newly relocated family at Deer Lodge, he continued this renewed game-enterprise in the winter of 1873-1874, the time of year when animal-furs were at their thickest and most desirable. He headed south toward Yellowstone National Park.

It was a more stable and predictable way of making a living than mining, and he was very familiar with hunting and most of the area's animals, as an 1887 reminiscence would later make clear. In fact, George Rea also recalled there the killing of a bison in the national park near the spot where Marshall's Hotel would later stand and the following day coming back to the spot to find and shoot at four grizzly bears who were feasting on it. Conveniently for George Rea in 1874, Yellowstone-area residents Harry Horr, Jack Baronett, and Frank Grounds were making plans to exhibit "live elk, black tail deer, mountain sheep and other animals" from the park area, apparently in anticipation of the upcoming U.S. centennial celebration in 1876. In Paradise Valley southeast of Bozeman, residents F.D. Pease and the Bottler brothers were already penning up wild animals for their own enjoyment and showing them to others as a kind of zoo, so there was great public interest in the region's wildlife.[559] Whether as an originator or simply a partner, George Rea joined these people whom he already knew fairly well. "Our friend George Rea, known to us for a long time as one of the pioneers of Montana," wrote Bozeman editor Joseph Wright in May, "arrived in this place a short time since with wagons laden with skins and skeletons, the result of his winter's hunt." Wright noted that these animal-products were to be delivered to Professor Ward's Natural Science Academy at Rochester, New York, apparently in an agreement that Rea had negotiated. "Mr. Rea killed about one hundred specimens of the different animals inhabiting the Rocky Mountains," he explained, "and delivered them here for shipment." Rea's summary of his bear-hunting came thirteen years later when he wrote, "There is no doubt but what I have shot more bear than any man in the Rockies in the last twenty years."[560]

Bozeman at this time was becoming southern Montana's key location for the shipping of live animals as well as hides, furs, skins, and robes by commercial hunters to faraway locations such as Salt Lake City and points down the Missouri River. Newspaper editor Wright explained that George Rea was "now on a trip to the Yellowstone country, for the purpose of cap-turing wild animals in their infancy for Major Pease," who wanted to add them to the zoo on his ranch in Paradise Valley. Wright also stated that Mr. Rea was slated to guide the Earl of Dunraven on his splendid hunt in Yel-lowstone later that summer. That would not happen, as Rea got caught up in other activities (perhaps he missed his family), but the Earl did show up in the national park to take full advantage of its then-legal hunting status.[561]

George Rea had made business contracts with the relevant local people who, like him, were interested in animals, whether for domestication purposes (an activity that often failed) or for the very lucrative traffic in hides, furs, skins, and robes. Rea appears to have spent the summer and fall in hunting for animals in the Yellowstone Park region, thus joining many others engaged in what was essentially a slaughter for commercial purposes.[562] During the autumn of 1874, he likely returned to his family in Deer Lodge for a visit, and then struck out for Bozeman to begin the winter hunt. George Rea—called by the *Avant Courier* a man with "warm friends" and someone whom "we cannot help feeling a strong sympathy for"—suddenly found himself in trouble with the law.[563]

As background, let us remember that the American West was continuously a land full of sometimes questionable characters who were often running away from something. Whether it was a Civil War they did not want to fight, wives and children whom they abandoned, relatives who gave them trouble, scrapes with the law, boredom, or precious minerals that sent them looking for adventure, these questionable characters could easily disappear in the vast, sparsely settled West, sinking easily into obscurity in whichever town they chanced upon.

And Montana Territory seemed especially boundless because it was huge and unsettled. Every person that one encountered in the vast Territory was an anonymous stranger—a potential criminal running away from a shady past—and these encounters when coupled with alcohol could produce violence. In this unstable and far-flung setting lived George W. Rea, and on December 2, 1874, he suddenly became one of those questionable characters—at least to some people—when he killed Mr. M. Maguire. While Maguire fit the wandering stereotype better than Rea, it was Rea who served here as the aggressor. Maguire entered a cabin whose occupants, including Rea, were drunk. For whatever reason, Rea refused to give Mr. Maguire a drink and then punched him in the face. Maguire fell against a woodstove, apparently hitting his head, and died a few minutes later.

A "coroner's jury" tentatively concluded that the deceased "came to his death by a blow given feloniously by one George Rea with some heavy blunt instrument." Bozeman officials hauled him to jail on December 4 to await trial. He languished there until March 11, and we do not know whether his wife and daughter visited him during that period. Presumably they attended the trial from their home in Deer Lodge, but we do not know that for certain either.[564]

George Rea's trial at Bozeman for murder began during the week of March 1-5, 1875, and the testimony was conflicting. "Great interest was manifest upon both sides," said the *Bozeman Times*, "and the Court room was crowded during the trial." The uncontroverted facts were that victim Maguire visited the scene of his murder by chance, that the several occupants of the cabin were drunk, and that a quarrel began between the two men, the cause of which was difficult to determine. George Rea testified that they had words, because of Rea's refusal of whiskey to Maguire; that Maguire threatened him with a stick of cordwood; and that in self-defense he struck Maguire with his fist, throwing him back upon the stove, which wounded him and caused his death. The prosecutor countered by claiming that Rea viciously forced a quarrel and then killed Maguire with an ax (presumably the butt of it) that was later found in the room. The witnesses who were present were unable to convincingly testify conclusively about either the quarrel or the blow—probably because they had been drunk—and that did not help Rea. A prosecution witness testified that he "thought some glittering instrument was used." The jury, which the *Times* called "a very capable one" that "manifested great care in arriving at a conclusion," returned a verdict of guilty of murder in the second degree.[565]

On Monday, March 8, 1875, the judge sentenced George Rea to fifteen years in the Territorial prison at Deer Lodge. On Tuesday evening, March 16, Sheriff C.L. Clark of Gallatin County arrived at Deer Lodge with his shackled prisoner to consign Mr. Rea to the Territorial prison. "George Rea has been a citizen of Montana for many years and has warm friends," wrote the editor of the *Avant Courier*, "and we cannot help feeling a strong sympathy for him in his unfortunate condition, and trust his time in prison will be shortened by his good conduct."[566] That comment proved prophetic, for Rea would indeed be released early.

While George Rea languished in prison, affairs in Montana Territory involving Indians got much worse. The Bozeman wagon-road expedition of 1874 had already stirred up trouble among the Sioux, and on June 25, 1876, the Great Sioux War broke out in full when hundreds of Indians killed brevet-General George A. Custer and much of his command. In 1877, the Nez Perce War caused new trouble for settlers in Oregon, Idaho, and Montana, and indeed those Indians passed some 180 miles west of George Rea's prison cell before their eight hundred men, women, and children and around two thousand horses crossed Yellowstone National Park and turned north toward Canada.[567] Rea must have chafed a bit when he heard about the killing of Custer. He also must have chafed this same year, when his wife and daughter moved to Butte, probably because they had no means of support in Deer Lodge with him in prison, but there might have been other reasons for their move. Perhaps it hurt too much to live in the same town in which their husband and father George Rea was imprisoned. Or perhaps they were getting tired of and angry at his being gone so much; after all, his fifteen-year sentence must have, at times, seemed to them like the ultimate abandonment.

Whatever the reason for his family's moving to Butte, Governor Benjamin F. Potts pardoned George Rea on February 9, 1877, after Rea served a little less than two years in prison. The pardon was made "upon the condition that he forever abstain[s] from intoxicating liquors." It was a measure of Rea's ability to make people like him that the pardon was recommended by "Bishop Tuttle, Rev. N. Gilbert, 82 citizens of Olean, N.Y., and 805 citizens of Montana."[568] George Rea, freed from prison during the week of February 12-16, moved to Butte apparently to rejoin his wife and daughter.

This new freedom also meant that George Rea could go prospecting again, perhaps the very pursuit of which his wife and daughter were weary. Regardless of what his family might have thought, Rea, like so many others in the American West, could not resist mining. "Mr. George W. Rea of our town" has recently returned from a prospecting expedition, said the *Butte Miner* in early July, "bringing with him some specimens of a newly-discovered lead that throws into the shade anything that has been seen lately, even in the neighborhood of Butte, for they are literally flaked and studded with free-gold." The paper explained that the location was about twenty-five miles from Butte, and mentioned the "spacious dwelling house," which Rea had recently built for himself "near the Rainbow works."[569] As will be seen, the alleged distance of twenty-five miles was very much understated, probably on purpose by George Rea.

Perhaps the formerly incarcerated Rea was starved for adventure. Or perhaps he wanted a more dependable paycheck than mining could provide, some of which he could send to his wife and daughter. Whatever his motivations were, George Rea by early August was serving as a "citizen volunteer" in the Nez Perce War for General Howard, at least if the Deer Lodge newspaper is to be believed. That meant he was basically a hunter, and the newspaper reported that he was "keeping the camp well supplied with venison, bear etc."[570] From the west, General Howard was pursuing the fleeing Nez Perce who were moving east and north toward Yellowstone Park and Canada, and because of the general's presence that year at Henry's Lake, Howard Creek, which flows west into the far southeast corner of that lake, received its name.

This job did not last long for Mr. Rea, in fact only for twenty days if his later memory could be trusted. Although Chief Joseph and the Nez Perce were defeated at Bear Paw Mountain on October 1, 1877, George Rea was apparently back in Butte by late September working on a mining claim, for a Butte newspaper reported that "Mr. Thomas E. Rea has just come to Butte from Bozeman and will soon go to work to develop a rich gold lead discovered last spring by his brother George W. Rea of our town."[571]

George W. Rea—hunter, settler, early Yellowstone explorer, prospector, guide, and stagecoach-operator, in Shotgun Valley, Idaho. Eventually, he established the small community of Glen Rea, Idaho, and ran a fish-hatchery there during his last years. *YELL 36656, YNP Photo Archives.*

We do not know what George Rea did in 1878. Historian Dean H. Green has stated that he became Shotgun Valley, Idaho's first settler this year,[572] but more is needed to confirm that. Probably he continued his prospecting. Likewise, we do not know what happened to Martha Rea. Apparently, she divorced George.

The evidence for the divorce was two census reports, combined with George's romancing of Charlotte Cronk in 1879. The U.S. Census of June 8, 1880 found George Rea answering the census-taker's inquiries as "divorced" (apparently referring to Martha Rea) and living at Butte while running a sawmill.[573] But on June 21, 1879, George had married Charlotte B. Cronk (1833-1919),[574] and it might have been because of this new marriage that he filled out a second U.S. Census report on June 22, 1880, giving his address as "on Silver Bow Creek and east of Blacktail" and his marital status as "married" to "Charlott" Rea.[575] Why he filled out two reports with two different marriage-scenarios is unknown. Perhaps he merely forgot that he had filled out one already; or perhaps he legitimately wanted to correct the mistakes he had made in the first round; or we can concoct imaginary scenarios wherein he lied to the census-taker because he was engaged in illegal activities, or was having an extra-marital affair, or some such, but those possibilities remain unproven for now.

Regardless, for some reason, George and Thomas Rea began to divest themselves of mining properties at Butte in April of 1880.[576] And George's daughter Mary H. Rea celebrated her nuptials this year on December 1 to Henry G. Valiton, who had recently become the second mayor of Butte. The two of them remained in Butte until 1887, when they moved to Deer Lodge for much of the rest of their lives.[577]

These changes indicate to us that something big was looming for George and Thomas Rea. It took more than a year for it to come together, and except for some dabbling in local politics, we do not know what the Rea brothers did during 1881. Possibly George's relations with his wife, Charlotte, began to deteriorate or were continuing to deteriorate (if so, they recovered later), and the two brothers were gradually shutting down their long-time connections to Montana.

The monumental change was that the Rea brothers were moving to Idaho's Shotgun Valley. George had never gotten that place out of his mind. He probably thought long and hard about the beautiful valley during the years he was in prison, and if he had traveled to Shotgun Valley in 1878, that probably cemented his decision to return, especially if he acquired a homestead there. His daughter was married and gone, but what of his wife

Charlotte? They were temporarily separated by 1885, with her living in Camas and then moving in 1892 to Blackfoot, Idaho, but eventually she would spend summers with George at Glen Rea. Probably armed with some money they made by selling their Montana mining-claims, the brothers George and Thomas left Butte, most likely on the train. By June of 1882, George was at Beaver Canyon, Idaho, posing as an "old-timer" who hailed from that place, which, in a way, he was and did.

The trouble with that claim was that he had spent more than a decade in Montana, and if he had even visited the eastern Idaho country since 1868, we have not learned of it unless it happened once in 1878. What might have occurred is that with his daughter gone and relations with his wife apparently not the best, George decided that a big move and a complete change of lifestyle were necessary. Perhaps he was experiencing a mid-life crisis, or perhaps his "hermit" instincts were kicking in. Running away to the wilderness to escape unpleasantness has appealed to human beings from time immemorial. Undoubtedly George had regaled his brother Thomas with wildlife stories of the bountiful and massive hunting and fishing in Shotgun Valley. Perhaps he also wanted to be near the new excitement of tourists and their stagecoaching travel to Yellowstone, in which his later friends the Bassett Brothers were about to become involved. We know that Frank Bassett moved to Butte by early 1882,[578] so perhaps George and/or Thomas encountered him there by chance and Frank told them of his brothers' plans to run stagecoaches full of tourists to Yellowstone National Park. The center of activity for all of that was at Beaver Canyon, Idaho, where the Park's closest railroad station was located, so that was where George went. Thomas apparently went with him.

Whatever motivated George Rea to move to Idaho, he began settling in, and happened upon a newspaper writer from Blackfoot at Beaver Canyon in July of 1882, a time when the Bassett Brothers were running their stagecoaches to Yellowstone for the second summer in a row. "While there," announced this newspaperman, "we had the pleasure of meeting one of the old timers, Mr. G.W. Rea." "Mr. Rea had been in that part of the country and Yellowstone National Park for the past sixteen years," continued the writer, "and has acted as guide for several parties visiting that section."[579] It was apparent from this that George was acting like he had never left Idaho and was pumping himself up as a local resident, guide, and accomplished old-timer in the region.

A week later he added to this claim by writing an article for the *Salt Lake Tribune* entitled "Yellowstone Park—What a Trapper Says about the Country and the Way to Get There." It summarized some of his earliest history in the area and made it clear from his discussions of Beaver Canyon, Yellowstone Park, and the area's wildlife that he was indeed an expert on the area and could therefore qualify as a guide in the region. By later in the summer of 1882, George was operating at "Ray's camp" (as a Salt Lake tourist misspelled it that year), a location that would soon become his long-term ranch, which he called "Glen Rea." Beginning in December, George Rea spent his first complete winter in many years at his new cabin on Shotgun Creek, traveling at least once to Beaver Canyon, which the newspaper reported in March. Occupying his land as early as 1882, Rea thus had a claim for it in adverse possession if not in homestead rights, but it appears from land records that he did not finish purchasing it or else paying $320 in taxes on it until 1895.[580]

With his home established, George Rea wasted no time hooking up to his new friends the Bassett Brothers and their incipient stagecoaching operation to Yellowstone National Park, and he began partnering with them in the summer of 1883. His homestead at Glen Rea was located a bit short of fifty miles east of Beaver Canyon, just the right stagecoaching distance (on the flat, easily traveled lands of Camas Meadows and Shotgun Valley at least) for him to make some money by putting up the Bassetts' coach-guests at his ranch for the night with a cook who was probably one of the brothers' wives. A Wyoming journalist's allusion to this spot near the crossing of Henry's Fork where "comfortable quarters" could be had for the night indicated to observers that Rea was operating his wayside "hotel" for the first season this year.[581]

And it was at Rea's other cabin, "at the mountain home of George W. Rea" in August, that the fifty-one-year-old Rea entertained the first known party of bicyclists to Yellowstone, namely W.O. Owen's party. Rea told them that he was the "discoverer of the geysers" in Yellowstone and that it occurred in 1865, the first year he arrived in the region. "Discoverer" was close to a true statement. The fur trappers of the 1820s and thirties had been to Yellowstone, but in the history of the prospectors who visited it in the 1860s, only Walter DeLacy, George Huston, and perhaps Jack Baronett were known to have been earlier than George Rea.

The touring bicyclists referred to George Rea as "a name familiar to every tourist entering the Park by the Beaver Canyon route." Although that claim was not completely accurate yet, it was quickly becoming true, as Mr. Rea pressed his "old-timer" status and aided the Bassett Brothers. As numerous travelers would do for the next decade, the party spent the night at Rea's home. In a letter to an old friend a few years later, Rea described his ranch as most effectively reached by the railroad to Beaver Canyon,

> thence by Bassett Brother stage lines to the Park which runs past my door. You will know the place as my house, barn, shop and other outhouses are balustraded with elk horns. Or if hunting parties wish me to meet them at Beaver Canyon and convey them to my place, I will do it free of charge. I am forty-three miles from Beaver Canyon on the Park road.[582]

George and Thomas Rea were determined to make a living by hunting and guiding in Shotgun Valley, and to experiment with and dabble in serving the tourists who were passing their ranch on their way to Yellowstone Park, whether those travelers were interested in hunting, fishing, riding horses, or merely stagecoaching on to Yellowstone. Probably using some of the $3,000 he gained from sale of his land in Montana, George purchased horses, wagons, harnesses, tack, camping gear, and other supplies for his enterprise. In May of 1883, the *Dillon Tribune* featured an article about his business that was more of an advertisement than it was a news item. Headlined "A Guide of Experience," it bragged that he and his brother were "hunters and guides of twenty years' experience" (which apparently incorporated at least two years from George's previous life in New York), and it referred to his place as "Rea's hotel, on Henry's Fork of Snake River" with a post office address of Beaver Canyon, Idaho (because there was as yet no post office closer than that). "The Reas have a large number of trained saddle and pack animals and camp outfits," recorded the writer, "which are held in readiness for the use of tourists and hunting parties." Claiming that George Rea had been the first guide for the Northern Pacific Railroad Company (a claim that we have been unable to confirm), the article boasted that "George Rea is the most experienced guide in the Rocky Mountains." It used the testimony of one of George's 1883 clients, Englishman F.W.

Pattenden, who explained that he rode the Utah & Northern from Market Lake northward to get there. "I have traveled in various countries for the last two years," testified Pattenden, "and I may say that I have found no sport in India or elsewhere to compare with that which George Rea showed us in the Rocky Mountains."[583]

Using such testimonials became part of George and Thomas Rea's stock in trade, and at first, they tended to lean toward the hunting part of the business rather than the traveling-to-Yellowstone part. (After all, that second part was competing with the Bassett Brothers, who had more experience at it and who were better equipped with coaches than were George and Thomas Rea.) But Rea did allow the Bassetts to house their overnight customers at his ranch, initially in tents.

During the winter of 1883-84, George Rea returned to what was probably old employment at the Utah & Northern Railway, guiding its surveyors as the railroad considered building a route east toward Yellowstone Park and Gallatin City, Montana from China Point (the railroad surveyed the line, but never built it). In January of 1884, Rea suddenly purchased from the railroad's "masters of transportation"—two fellow railroad workers named Kooch and Crittenden, who were probably old railroad acquaintances—their entire transportation "outfit and contract." John Kooch—who was also a neighbor of Rea's—would soon build a hotel on the eastern shore of Henry's Fork a few miles east of Glen Rea that his friends the Bassett Brothers would use to lodge their overnight travelers on the way to Yellowstone. Apparently, Rea had been considering for some time the idea of starting an additional business—this one a stagecoaching outfit— with which he could obtain a share of that burgeoning travel to the great new Park. Perhaps George Rea dreamed of obtaining some of the spillover that the Bassett Brothers would no doubt receive in that coming summer, whether by semi-partnering with them in their need for backup coaches and/or offering them overnight-camping facilities for their travelers, or by running the entire operation himself with his brother Thomas. That he was seriously considering dabbling in the public travel to Yellowstone was readily apparent in June of that year, when he and brother Thomas also began building a small "hotel" farther north on Henry's Fork near or at the present site of Mack's Inn, Idaho, an effort about which little is known.[584]

Perhaps George Rea saw this possibility coming in 1883, for it appears from William Owen's description of his bicycle party's eastbound route that Rea had built a second cabin for himself. Nearly fifty miles east from Beaver Canyon, they reached Henry's Fork. They waited for their hired coach to catch up with them to carry them across the river, then began a steep ascent on the river's east side. After several miles, they entered timber, then a gentle descent, then a beautiful, grassy open park, where they once more saw the sky and only a short distance farther crossed the river again, and "after a mile's run arrived at the mountain home of George W. Rea."[585] This describes a different cabin from George's stable location at Glen Rea, so this cabin must have been a smaller one that he built in preparation for the future place near Mack's Inn.

Still leaning hard on his hunting and fishing business, Rea must have worried about "biting off more than he could chew." In May of 1884, the *Ogden Standard* reported that "George Rea, one of the best guides, hunters, and trappers in the West, is making preparations to take tourists on big hunting expeditions, 'roughing it' in nature's solemn solitudes." By 1886, the Reas' business card—"G.W. Rea & Bro., Hunters and Guides of Twenty-Three Years' Experience"— listed numerous important people whom they had guided on hunts, including Professor H.A. Ward of Rochester, New York; George's son-in-law Henry Valiton, the mayor of Butte; W.A. Clark, the minerals magnate from Butte; Samuel Word, a lawyer from Butte, who had represented Rea in his 1875 murder trial; and numerous international travelers from England. The card stated that "we cannot be excelled by any persons as guides in the Rocky Mountains," and noted that in addition to hunting "we have a private trout pond in connection with our business, which we keep thoroughly stocked with the 'speckled beauties,' for the pleasure of our patrons." The Reas seemed to have trouble figuring out whether they preferred hunting or fishing or accompanying tourists on horseback to Yellowstone, but they were not about to miss any bets with any of those activities that might make them money. "We keep fine riding and pack animals," said the card, "that are accustomed to the business."[586]

Most interesting of all was the card's statement about Yellowstone Park: "If desired, we will take parties from our ranch through the mountains to the Park and give them fine shooting, as we would travel with pack animals and traverse a romantic country on horseback, abounding in game." Considering that the U.S. Department of the Interior had outlawed hunting in Yellowstone Park in January of 1883, one wonders how many violations of this edict were encouraged or caused by the Rea Brothers. However, we also know that during the years before the U.S. Army arrived in the Park (August 17, 1886), it was easy to elude the few civilian assistant superintendents who patrolled the place on horseback. And besides, there was plenty of country outside the park that could be *legally* hunted.

But George and Thomas Rea did in fact carry passengers by stagecoach from Glen Rea to the Park and return. In this regard, they were two of the earliest of that long line of independent, stagecoach-and-wagon operators who were headquartered outside the Park but who regularly traveled into the Park. It was a time when nearly everyone in remote areas like this one cobbled together numerous activities in order to make a living. And like everyone else who saw it, George was enamored of the Wonderland. Writing to an old friend of his in 1887, he gushed, "The National Park is a most wonderful place and is becoming a great place of resort; the grand cañon below the Yellowstone Falls is wonderful," too. "The geysers and all things taken into consideration," finished Rea with a superlative, "there is no place in the world that has its equal."[587]

The stagecoaching part of the Rea Brothers' business, as mentioned, had already begun in January 1884, with Rea's purchase of John Kooch's transportation "outfit." When the survey ended, in May of 1884, a correspondent for the Butte *Semi-Weekly Miner* cornered Rea in Dillon, Montana to ask him about it. George Rea, reported this writer,

> has purchased a number of teams, wagons and carriages and proposes to establish a line of transportation from Beaver Canyon to the Geyser Basin for the accommodation of tourists. Everything necessary for convenience and comfort will be provided. He has received notice from a number of parties already who intend visiting the Park to be prepared to convey them the round trip. He expects to be able to accommodate all who apply for transportation in good style.[588]

George Rea probably financed this purchase with money he made from the railroad that winter. Regardless, this news item put him in the transportation business in addition to his hunting and guiding business. But as already mentioned, Rea also began working on "Rea's hotel," or at least a cabin there, in June of 1884.

With three projects competing for his time, he must have been stretched thin. We do not know much about the Reas' stagecoaching, for no accounts written by their patrons have been found, but it seems to have lasted for only two years primarily, but then continued on and off for eight more years as an adjunct business to their hunting and fishing endeavors. Historian Dean Green, who wrote *The History of Island Park* (1990), reproduced the family photographs belonging originally to George Rea's daughter Mary Valiton that showed the Rea brothers' stagecoaches, wagons, and customers through the years as they made ready to travel to the Park or returned to their ranch following trips to the park.[589]

It is likely that Thomas took the reins (literally) of the Rea brothers' tourist-coaches to Yellowstone, at least in 1884, because George is known to have tended to the hunting-and-fishing part of their business that year in the immediate area of Glen Rea. "G.W. Rea, the pioneer scout, hunter, and mountaineer, is out with parties all the time," proclaimed an Ogden newspaperman, "and wonderful stories are told of how he 'corrals' game and lets his tourists shoot it."[590] Two long accounts from this year make it even clearer that Rea spent much of that summer hunting and fishing, rather than stagecoaching, making it likely that Thomas drove the stagecoaches. These accounts included those of the hunting party of C.D. Roys and the fishing-and-photographing party of Charles Savage.

C.D. Roys stated that his party camped on Henry's Fork (where they caught more than one hundred trout), and the next day George Rea, "an old hunter who has tramped the Rockies for twenty years, came to our camp." Rea stayed with them for the next four days while they ecstatically hunted and fished. Including George Rea's contributions, the party killed "three elk, four moose, two bears, and captured one [bear] cub alive, which Ray [*sic*] still keeps at his cabin," wrote Roys. They also shot deer, antelope, geese, ducks, curlew, plover, willow grouse, snipe, and trout, and then had an adventure with a grizzly bear, which was the story we told earlier.[591]

Charles Savage, a Salt Lake City photographer, was traveling to the Park primarily to take photographs, but George Rea treated him to the fishing trip of his life. Upon reaching Rea's ranch, which for the moment still served as the night station of the Bassetts' stage-line, Savage was enthralled. "Of all the lovely spots to invite the tourist to linger," he enthused, "none ever seemed so inviting to me as this one." George Rea had undoubtedly felt the same way since he first saw the spot in 1865. Savage explained that his nearby log hut "was embellished with the skins of grizzlies, elk and other animals." Mr. Rea was not always present there, so he had an arrangement with the Bassett Brothers allowing them to use his cabin to house their overnight visitors. Charles Savage described one of George Rea's specialties for both making money and entertaining tourists:

> One of the attractions here is catching of trout with the spear. A fire of pitch-pine wood is placed on an elevated grating in the bow of a flat boat. The light attracts the fish and the nimble operator spears the finny beauties with barbed spears. The night before I arrived there Mr. Rea caught 1,002 fish in one night. The lot weighed nearly 1,500 pounds. These are shipped to Butte, Pocatello and other points on the Utah Northern, and must prove very remunerative to the parties interested.[592]

That the Rea brothers intended to continue their stagecoaching trips in the summer of 1885 was evident from their letterhead stationery. Along with other information, it announced: "Easy carriages and horses furnished at nearest R.R. points to visit the Yellowstone National Park."[593]

But, as usual, George was also interested in the region's wildlife. In January of 1885, he wrote to the U.S. Secretary of Interior asking for a lease of ten acres within Yellowstone National Park to establish a museum "showing all the different animals inhabiting the Rocky Mountains." "I am going to labor [during] the coming winter," he explained, "capturing the wild beasts." This inquiry represented one of the earliest attempts by anyone to establish such a museum within Yellowstone, but both the Secretary and park officials were probably fearful of promoting hunting within the park with all the trouble they had had with it, for they knew Rea to be a hunter. They did not issue the lease to him.[594]

That was probably a good thing because the Rea brothers were becoming famous as big-game hunters. But amid their burgeoning fame in early

1885, George Rea for some reason sold a large number of his horses and wagons, and why was not apparent. Perhaps he decided that he was not as interested in chauffeuring tourists by wagon to Yellowstone as he thought. After all, that work required a fair number of interpretive and social skills to deal with the customers, and George and Thomas were both reticent and a bit withdrawn in their personalities. Or perhaps he encountered that bane of so many transportation operators, namely that the percentage of return on an expensive investment of horses, coaches, harnesses, tack, barns, feed, repairs, insurance, and overnight costs for drivers required more work than the profits were worth. Or perhaps having to care for all these horses and the duties of the business detracted too severely from the time he wanted to spend hunting and fishing.

Whatever the reason, George sold fourteen horses, one Shuttler wagon, one fish wagon, five harnesses, eleven riding saddles, ten pack-saddles, and a myriad of other equipment. Because a debt of $1832 was involved, this business-venture got recorded in Bingham County records. Interestingly, George sold these trappings to R.D. Cronk of Camas, Idaho, a man who was probably either his wife Charlotte Cronk Rea's father (age about 58) or Charlotte's brother (age about 23).[595] One or both of them had apparently moved to Camas, Idaho to live with Charlotte who seemed to be separating from George Rea at this time, but who, it would develop, would continue to live with George Rea at his ranch during summers only. In the winter-time, Charlotte would move to Camas and ultimately Blackfoot, Idaho, because she had discovered that she wanted no part of remote Glen Rea in the winter with its deep snows and no other neighbors for miles and miles. Talk about isolation! But George and Thomas Rea seemed to thrive in it.

Notwithstanding this sale, the Rea brothers appear to have continued to run occasional wagons and tourists into Yellowstone Park for the next decade or so. Meanwhile, visitor Edwards Roberts added to the Rea brothers' status as hunters in his book, *Shoshone and Other Western Wonders*, which chronicled his trip to the region in 1887. Near Shotgun Creek, wrote Mr. Roberts, "lives a trapper whose log-cabin is decorated on roof and sides with sun-bleached trophies of the hunt." "Huge antlers," he added, "are suspended over the narrow doorway, and skins of animals are tacked to every sunny place." This cabin had to have belonged to one of the Rea brothers, probably George, and after supper, Roberts and his party "adjourned to the dimly lighted kitchen, to talk with the trappers," apparently both Thomas and George, "who had just come in with their load of game." The spokesman, probably George, "was a most voluble individual," said Roberts, who "so fired our enthusiasm for game that we were more than half inclined to abandon our teams and take to the woods," hunting with fervor:

> If there was game in the world, he said, it was here in the forests that surrounded us. Bear? Yes. Elk? In abundance. Deer and antelope? Yes. He had seen a dozen elk in a week, and had that day killed a few. He could not begin to tell us of the sport there was. He had been a hunter in the region for years, and knew every nook and corner in the place.[596]

Not only were the animals abundant in Shotgun Valley, but also, they were plentiful in the area of H. Clay Manley's cabin, to the northeast in Montana, which was east of Targhee Pass. George Rea knew that fact well too, and Roberts soon saw it for himself. "The country round about is overrun with game," he wrote at Manley's. "Once, on gaining the top of a low ridge," he illustrated, "we came upon a band of half-a-dozen antelope." Although the animals quickly ran away, Roberts was echoing what traveler Richard Burton Hassell had seen there in 1879, namely hundreds of pronghorns on the South Fork of Madison River.[597]

The Rea brothers continued working their ranch at Glen Rea, as a base for their stagecoaching trips into the park and their guiding activities for hunting, and they also began to dramatically increase their enterprises that involved fish and fishing. An 1887 newspaper writer known only as "U Know" expounded dramatically upon the improvements at George Rea's ranch, while misspelling Rea's name:

> Twenty-five miles east of Camas Creek is George W. Rae's ranch; he has, I think without doubt, the finest fish pond and the best fishing I ever saw. He is located on Shot Gun Creek, three miles above where it flows into the north fork of Snake River. This section of country about Mr. Rae's is certainly the sportsman paradise. A few days before we passed Mr. Rae shot two elk, one dressed over 800 pounds and the other 450 pounds.

Our party can testify to the fine flavor of the steak. We would advise all parties wanting 'fare sport you know' to give Mr. R. a call, and if he fails to entertain satisfactorily there will be no damage to pay. He showed us moose tracks, fresh ones, as thick as cow tracks on Snake river.[598]

As we have seen, George Rea was beginning to use fish as entertainment and as a portion of his commercial business, aimed at the parties who happened to spend the night at his ranch or merely pass by it. Such a party was the one led by Professor A.F. Zahm in 1888. "As we passed a number of log huts embossed at every corner with heads and antlers," wrote Zahm, "the [our] driver stopped on business and an old man came out to see us." The man wore two pairs of pants, a slouch hat, an old woolen shirt, and everlasting boots, and he was apparently George W. Rea in the flesh. They inquired about fishing, and pointing to Shotgun Creek just above Henry's Fork, Rea replied, "If you want to see the best fishing in the world, just go down there." What happened next was so remarkable that Zahm's account must be quoted:

We obeyed, and on approaching the stream, lo! The fish came shooting from every direction, right glad to see us. They came by legions from all quarters and crowded up to the shore, the big ones looking over the little ones in a vast multitude like the suckers that gather about some great politician. Hurriedly gathering some flies from the bleeding horses[,] we baited, and threw out; but before the flies touched water a hundred heads shot upwards with open mouths, the largest winning—the elevator. With sufficient hooks a large string may be caught at one throw. Again and again was this performance repeated, but the fish never took fright, nor lost their eagerness until the old man came and fed them. He keeps them here "for everybody's amusement, and charges nothing. They are not fenced in but have full play of the stream, and they gather here because they like me and I treat them like pets." Someone asked him if he did not find it lonely here without neighbors. "No," he said. "I have been living here for thirty-seven years, and I am the happiest man in the world."[599]

This claim of "thirty-seven years" of residence is puzzling to us today. Thirty-seven years would have put Mr. Rea's arrival year on Shotgun Creek as 1851, so for some reason he was way off in his remembering of time. Perhaps at his senior age of 56, he was merely misremembering his number of years, or perhaps he was exaggerating his experience as a guide in the region to give himself added credibility. Whatever the reason, this remarkable description made it clear how very assured and confident George Rea was feeling about his ranch, his hunting, his fishing, his stagecoaching, and his life.

It was probably the arrival of the Arangee Land and Cattle Company that cemented George Rea's decision to concentrate on his fishery and hunting businesses and move away from stagecoaching. Certainly, this commercial corporation that came to Glen Rea in 1887 intruded upon and disrupted George Rea's quiet world, but probably their arrival was merely an irritating annoyance, because he and his expanding reputation were heading that way anyway. For example, a year after the Zahm party, tourist Anna Husted Southworth stated when she arrived at Glen Rea with the Bassett Brothers (1889) that "this cabin belongs to the Ray [sic] brothers, whose hunting exploits have made them so famous in both America and England."[600]

The Arangee Company appears to have arrived in 1887, and it likely *was* this company that served as an impetus to send off George Rea into prospecting and mining one more time, where he could again be alone in his beloved wilderness and away from what must have seemed to him like sudden crowds at Glen Rea, with its continuing, stagecoaching-stream of tourist-traffic fed by the Bassett Brothers, all trekking as usual to Yellowstone Park. We tell the story here because the Arangee Company might have been (and this historian believes that it was) the catalyst for a legend about George Rea that endures today in southwestern Montana and northeastern Idaho. Here is the background for the legend, the complete story of which we will tell near the end of this chapter.

By the end of 1889, Rea was apparently ready for a break from the new crowds. So, in January of 1890, he suddenly moved to Lyon, Montana,[601] a spot that has no settlement today and which in Rea's time held only a two-year-old post office and a few families. Today it is located five miles north of Raynolds Pass on Madison River at the place where state highway 87 (Idaho-Montana) dead-ends into U.S. 287. As the crow flew for George Rea, this location was only twenty-five miles north of Glen Rea, Idaho.

Most significantly for him, he had decided to again go mining, and this time it was in the dead of winter.

Headlining his letter "Lyon, Montana," George Rea wrote to the *Idaho Register* on February 24, 1890 with the news that "I am at present running a tunnel into a valuable mine, nine thousand feet above the level of the sea." The place he located was probably in today's Beaverhead National Forest and perhaps even in present Lee Metcalf Wilderness, somewhere just south of Deadman Creek. "I expected when I laid in my supplies for a winter's mining campaign," he enthused, "that we would be obliged to dress in furs to go from the house to the tunnel, [but] "I do not think the thermometer has been lower than 18 this winter, even in so high an altitude." Certainly, the mild weather was helping George Rea's attitude. With total optimism, he effervesced: "If this mine looks as favorable where I will tap it 175 feet deep, in the same proportion as it does on the surface as far down as I went," then, as he put it, the Union Pacific better hurry up and build to the park and down the Madison River "or the Northern Pacific will be in ahead of them for I am satisfied it will be a second Anaconda mine."[602] Of course, this was the optimistic and boosteristic sentiment of nearly every miner in the American West who thought he had struck minerals.

And sure enough, George Rea was prematurely back in Idaho by early September of 1890, although we do not know how long he mined at the Lyon site. Perhaps he was attempting to make-up with his wife Charlotte at this time, but more likely he was merely visiting her when the Blackfoot newspaper editor noted that George Rea, "the great hunter of the Rockies, dropped in to see us Monday [September 8]…Mrs. Rae [*sic*] came down with him from Camas."[603] At the very least, George Rea and his wife remained friends during their long separation, and we know that they remained married. It is clear from land records that they never formally divorced, and a 1919 look back at the time makes it clear that Charlotte Rea lived at Glen Rea during summers only. She owned half of George's land and they sold it together in 1902, just before his death, probably so that she could have a nest-egg for her old age.[604]

This was essentially the end of George Rea's story as a commercial, independent stage-coacher. Although he and his brother Thomas would continue for another few years to take occasional stagecoaches filled with visitors to Yellowstone from his ranch at Glen Rea (which in the 1930s would be inundated by the water of Island Park Reservoir), George Rea more often continued to receive wealthy, paying guests at his ranch whom he took hunting and fishing. This was, after all, his main business and a practice that appears to have continued for nearly another decade, nearly until his death.

One of those stories involving George Rea, which fortunately got recorded in a version longer than most newspaper accounts, appears to have occurred in the fall of 1891, when he took six men and twelve pack-animals on a hunting trip for four weeks from Shotgun Valley, to Split Creek, the head of Warm River, Robinson Creek, Fall River, the west side of the Tetons, and back to Rea's Ranch. The chronicler of the trip, a man known only as "Shongo," published the account in *Forest and Stream* magazine.

"Shongo," along with H.W. Bush (from Neosho, Missouri where he served as treasurer of the Kansas City, Ft. Smith, and Southern Railroad), and Christian Weber (a photographer from Baltimore) met enroute on the train and traveled to Beaver Canyon, Idaho, arriving late on October 4. There they rented a "rig," probably from the Bassett Brothers, which consisted of two-horses and a "light though strong" wagon for $24, or eight dollars apiece. Heading east for George Rea's ranch 45 miles away, the party met a band of about 150 Indians (apparently Shoshones), laden with freshly killed meat and on their way back to their reservation near Blackfoot, Idaho. Their chief, whom Shongo called "Tindo," was no doubt Tendoy (1834-1907), well-known as chief of the Lemhi Shoshones and a nephew of the famous Sacagawea and her brother Cameahwait. Shongo called him "a fine, fat, sleek fellow, apparently about fifty," indicating that Tendoy was well-preserved, for he was nearly sixty at that time.[605]

Arriving at Rea's Ranch, located "on a bluff about two hundred feet from Shotgun" Creek and "twenty-five feet above the water," Shongo and his two partners stared appreciatively at their surroundings. "Bear, deer, antelope, elk, badger, and mountain sheep pelts," he wrote, "were tacked up wherever you gazed, and on the roofs of the building were securely anchored several pairs of elk antlers." Shongo claimed that Rea's ranch consisted of "920 acres," an exaggeration unless he was including the size of the fishing pond, and added that it included a nearby "dead house," in which Rea did his animal-slaughtering, hung his meat, and stored his traps; a general work-shop building, which held a forge, work bench, and artisan's tools; a stable connected to a corral for horses; and a root cellar or "dug-out" in the side of a hill, equipped with a strong door, which one always needed in bear country.[606]

The next morning, Rea introduced his two hired hands to the clients. They were "Bill, the Panama Kid," as packer; and "Frank," a young assistant and general cowboy. George explained and Shongo recorded that a "packer" was a much-revered vocation, which was "a trade, calling or profession distinct from any other in the Rockies," and that such a man's "services are indispensable on a hunt such as we were about to engage in." Bill furnished his own outfit but received eight dollars a day plus food for his services, while Rea furnished Frank's horse plus two dollars a day. Rea then assigned Warrior, his favorite, white hunting-horse to Shongo, a jet-black horse named Wardrobe to Mr. Bush, and Buckskin, a smaller, fractious horse to Mr. Weber.[607] For the first three weeks, the party took nothing but grouse, hares, ducks, squirrels, and fish, with occasional signs of antelope, moose and beaver.[608]

But late in the trip, they shot pine marten, lynx (which got away), and blacktail deer before finally spotting eighteen elk. Trying not to scare them while sneaking closer, the men at a signal began firing and took down fourteen of them—all but four spring calves. During these frantic moments, Shongo recorded this summary of George Rea's physical presence and exuberant sprint:

> "Now come on, we will drive them to the rocks," [exclaimed George], and off goes the giant, sixty years of age and six feet tall, bounding up the steep mountain like an antelope. Were it to save my life I could not have followed him at his pace.[609]

Cutting up and packing up the fourteen elk, including the skull and antlers of one bull elk, took many hours, and the men were forced to give away one pack-load of meat to chance friends who took it to nearby Rexburg, Idaho. After a continuous march of six days, shooting some additional ducks, geese, and a swan, the men reached Rea's Ranch. So ended a thirty-day trip.[610]

During this same period, George Rea also began to move into a business that related directly to the robust fishery in and around Henry's Fork of the Snake River. Eventually, George Rea would expand his single pond to three ponds, build a dam and a fish hatchery, sell fish in large numbers from the ponds along with commercial fishing-trips, and become involved in a water-rights lawsuit with his neighbors. By 1898, his seven-hundred-acre fishpond would be called "the greatest and most complete trout pond probably in Idaho," and he was even appointed postmaster at Arangee, Idaho that year. All of this would earn him a living for another decade, until his death, at age 69, on January 30, 1902.[611]

Ten days before he died, George Rea's friends A.S. and Charles Trude made certain that the *Chicago Tribune* had enough information to run a long story about him entitled "Pioneer Guide is Dying." Because the information came from Rea's friends and customers, the Trude Brothers, it contained a fair amount of correct material. But the article stretched the truth when it claimed that Rea "mapped out" the trails over which Theodore Roosevelt hunted for big game and had been found "dying of starvation and neglect" in his "lonely cabin on the Snake River." Neither of those claims was true. The *Tribune* then asserted that "'Uncle George' Rea has been engaged in Indian warfare [for] so long that it is declared there is scarcely an inch of his body that has been untouched by arrow, bullet or knife." This was only a bit of a stretch, for we have seen some of Rea's adventures with Indians, including the battle in New York, his skirmish on the Oregon Trail, hunting deer for General Howard in 1877, one more skirmish on the head of the Snake River, wherein he lost a finger, and probably others. But thanks to Rea's friend A.S. Trude, who gave much of the story to the *Tribune*, the paper did get correct the story of Rea's "calling out" other guides for falsely claiming that Theodore Roosevelt allegedly shot a bear in a trap.[612]

The *Anaconda Standard* seems to have been the first area newspaper to pick up some of Rea's Roosevelt connection from the *Tribune*, publishing it on Monday, February 3, under the headline "Guide for President—George Rea, Who Acted in that Capacity, Dead—Lived in Isolated Place." The article stated that Rea's daughter, Mrs. H.G. Valiton of Deer Lodge, received word of his death on February 2, after his having been ill for about two months. The article correctly called him "one of the pioneers of the Snake River country and one of the first to explore the Yellowstone park," also claiming that "on different occasions" he had served as guide to President Theodore Roosevelt. "The home of the deceased, Glen-Rea," stated the *Standard*, "is situated about 50 miles east of Spencer, Idaho, and in the winter, it can only be reached by dog team or on snowshoes."[613]

Immediately other regional newspapers jumped on the story, especially the Theodore Roosevelt angle, even though George Rea's nexus to TR was and is more hearsay than documentation. Six days after his death—on February 5—the *Salt Lake Telegram* ran a story still in present-tense, headlined "Roosevelt's Guide is Dying," a testimonial to how long it was taking for the story to reach civilization from the remote Glen Rea. This account repeated some of the *Tribune's* false claims, but the newspaper was probably correct in its assertion that George Rea "is the most widely known guide in the Yellowstone region."[614] The *Anaconda Standard* returned on February 5 with a photograph of George Rea and a much longer story entitled "One of the Earliest of Pathfinders." It noted the arrival of Rea's body at Deer Lodge where it would be buried, added the unconfirmed and apparently bogus claim that he had aided General Sheridan during the Indian wars, and then corrected the *Tribune's* story of dying in a cabin "neglected and starving." At the end, said the *Standard*,

> He was securely housed in a large six-room house, surrounded by watchful friends, who did everything possible to comfort and care for him, and he was attended by a physician who came from Dillon, a distance of 125 miles. His larder was supplied with everything anyone could wish or need, and a sufficient supply to run three men for two years was on hand.[615]

Other Montana newspapers added the information that Mr. Rea had been attended at his death by his niece, Mrs. G.W. Kelley; that he was especially well known to the old-timers of Madison County, Montana; that he died of "catarrh of the stomach"; and that he weighed more than 240 pounds during his life but only one hundred pounds at his death.[616] Considering that he lived in such a remote part of the state, it is amazing that Idaho newspapers picked up his death at all, but a few of them did.[617]

A mythical story—meaning an enduring legend rather than a falsehood—about George Rea lived on after his death, and it lives on today for those who know of it. Writer Frank Conway, who researched and penned the legend in 1903 almost exactly a year after George Rea's passing, titled it

"The Lost Mine of Madison Canyon," but if we believe Conway, the story was entrenched in Montana history and was verbally "making the rounds" long before Rea's death and before Conway wrote it.

As might be expected, Conway's story about George Rea was correct in some points and incorrect in others, but today it remains engaging reading. Conway obtained some of it from local people whom he talked to in Madison County. "As a hunter, scout and guide he [Rea] was known throughout the entire West," said Conway, "and he stumbled on the rich ledge accidentally one day in the early 60's when he was hunting mountain sheep." Conway was wrong about this detail because George Rea did not arrive in Montana until 1865. He stated that Rea took the rock to Virginia City, caused it to be assayed, and discovered that it contained "startling values in copper and gold." (This story hearkens us back to the *Butte Miner*'s story in 1877, about Rea's amazing discovery of a rock-sample some "twenty-five miles from Butte" that was "flaked and studded" with gold and copper.) According to Conway, George Rea "kept the mine secret," vouching only that it was located "in the middle canyon of the Madison." "Some few years" after Rea discovered the ledge, continued Conway, "he found himself in serious trouble—he killed a man—and was in danger of his life." So, he promised lawyer Sam Word an interest in the mine if Mr. Word would defend him.[618] As we have seen, Rea was indeed convicted and sent to prison and then moved to Idaho.

Conway's story continued, now implying that Conway had actually heard the tale from someone else, perhaps more than one person and probably in the middle Madison Valley. "From the day that the rich quartz was brought into Virginia City until a few years ago," he wrote, "the mine has been hunted for summer after summer with but little success." Conway also claimed that hunting for the mine "means death" and that "the old timers of Madison Valley will tell you that it is known that three men have died in their quest for the mine."

The first man who died, Conway declared, was with a party of two in the early 1870s. Laughed at by residents of the valley who did not believe the legend, said Conway, the two men traveled upstream to the canyon to begin their search but were not heard from for months. Finally, one day before Christmas, one of the men showed up in the valley "footsore, ragged and nearly dead from cold and exposure and told rescuers that his companion had died at the pine buttes," just west of the canyon. He reported that the men had made a camp on Beaver Creek and prospected without success all summer. Just before winter set in, the men found enough "color" to keep them there, but then it snowed hard for days. Trapped by deep snow in the mountains and without horses, which they had carelessly allowed to wander away, the men built a raft to float down the river to safety. Launching the boat, the two rode the river, but in approaching the "pine buttes," where they intended to camp for the night, the river-rapids upended their raft. Panicking, one man made it to shore only to spot his companion's body two hundred feet downstream, rolling over and over. Dashing down the bank ahead of the body, he jumped into the river and grabbed his partner's body as it swept by. He dragged him to shore, built a roaring fire, and tried to nurse the man back to health, but to no avail. His friend died right there. He buried the drownee in the snow the following morning, and then started on his hard trek to the settlements, forty miles below. After four days "of the hardest kind of trudging, he walked into the valley and told his story." Immediately men "on strong, well-fed horses" rode up the valley and verified his tale. In the spring, settlers returned to bury the body.[619]

The second man who searched for the Rea mine, according to Conway, was George Graham, who traveled alone to the canyon, his horse threw him, the fall broke his neck, and he clutched the reins so tightly in death that it held his horse there until his comrades found him and carried his remains to "the settlements" for burial. One wonders today whether he was the same George Graham who had earlier worked in Yellowstone Park for Superintendent P.W. Norris.[620]

Notwithstanding weaknesses in the first two stories that today make us skeptical of them, the third story featured Conway as an eyewitness. Conway stated that he was personally present with one other man when they discovered what they believed was the third and last victim of the legend and buried him, and this was probably how the writer came to learn of and research the legend. "Close by the trail which leads into the canyon from the west side," he said, "lies a little pile of boulders, and underneath these stones lies still another victim for the Rea mine." Conway testified that this happened during "the first summer cattle were herded in the valley," and that would have been in the 1870s, probably 1874.[621] Near the skeleton, they found the prospector's outfit—pick, shovel, gold-pan, and a baking-powder tin with a scrap of paper in it. On the paper was scribbled the victim's explanation that he had been hunting for the Rea mine and that he was dying from mountain fever. Conway stated that he and his friend buried the skeleton there.

Fascinating to us today and seeming to confirm some of Conway's story is the fact that the mentioned Beaver Creek empties into the Madison River's middle canyon from the north side, entering the river partway through the canyon, and that Deadman Creek enters the river from the north at present Lyon, Montana. These place names confirm today that someone believed Rea's strike to have occurred here, and therefore it was probably Frank Conway and/or other valley residents who had a role in attaching the name to Deadman Creek. Conway confirmed his belief that this was the proper canyon when he wrote that "some ten years ago, Mr. Rea returned to the Madison valley" and induced two old friends to "put up some money for the development of the long-lost mine."[622]

Conway was apparently referring here to George Rea's trip to Lyon in 1890, and he told us more about Rea's endeavor. "Having two old friends [there in Madison Valley] in the persons of O.B. Varney and William Ennis," wrote Conway, "he induced them to put up some money for the development of the long-lost mine, promising to conduct them to it and to give them an interest." The two men, said Conway, "worked for two years on the claim, spent several thousand dollars and uncovered nothing of value, only a few stringers of rich ore."

Frank Conway's ending to the story included the very wonderings and speculations that we would logically anticipate from reading such a tale. He wondered whether Mr. Rea ever told his friends the correct location of the mine or whether the secret died with him or whether he even made such a strike at all. As Conway ended his story, he noted that numerous men in Madison Valley had given up their lives in the quest—"like many other prospectors in Montana and the West in the never-ending search for the end of the rainbow."[623]

George Rea was not really one of those end of-the-rainbow men. He lived a useful, even a celebrated life, leaving his influence and trail in the big game hunters he guided; in the tourists to Yellowstone Park with whom he traveled on horseback and by stagecoach; in Gilman Sawtell, the earliest eastern-Idaho pioneer with whom he built the first road south of Henry's Lake; in the men

and women with whom he helped settle Montana and Idaho; in the sports-
men with whom he prospected, hunted, and fished; in the settlers to whom
he delivered mail; and in his daughter and son-in-law who, like him, earned
places in the history of the northern Rocky Mountains.

In the history of stagecoaching in and around Yellowstone National
Park, George Rea, George Marshall, and the Bassett Brothers had designed
the earliest "props, sets, and scenery" during the period 1879-1882 for
the lavish stage-production that would soon be performed within the new
Wonderland place. This spectacular pageant would burst forth in full splendor in 1883 in the form of Wakefield and Hoffman's yellow stagecoaches,
headquartered at the north end of Yellowstone. We shall tell that story next.

CHAPTER NINE

The Wings of Wonderland

Wakefield and Hoffman's Yellow Stagecoaches from the North

"It was all wrist motion, not arm. I have seen novices make the popper crack by jerking the whip stock back before the lash has reached its target. But the real driver just gave a sharp flick of his wrist, and the lash would come to a stop when the end was reached, and the popper would bang like a fire cracker."—Roy Fitzgerald, remembering his best friend Herb French and other YPT Co. stage drivers in Gardiner, Montana, 1900-1901, using an older skill.[624]

Having signed a contract with the Department of Interior in September of 1882, the newly established and incorporated Yellowstone National Park Improvement Company wasted no time in starting to erect buildings at Mammoth Hot Springs for what would eventually become an open and notorious plundering of the nation's first national park. National and international newspapers had been singing Yellowstone's praises since its creation in 1872, saying that it was, *inter alia*, "destined to become the grandest natural park in the world." YNPIC's two main officials, Rufus Hatch and Carroll Hobart, sent company sawmills and other machinery to the end of the tracks at Livingston, Montana Territory—where the tracklayers had arrived in the autumn of 1882—and the company's freighters then carried them by wagon through Paradise Valley to Mammoth Hot Springs, which not long earlier had been determined to be just across the boundary line in Wyoming Territory. There the company cut its first timber on December 16, 1882. "The National Park Despoliation Company," fumed the Bozeman *Avant Courier*, "has 150 men at work defacing the scenery of Wonderland and erecting hotel[s] and bath houses to bleed tourists." As one might expect, the first buildings this company put up were shacks, other dwellings, and stables for the shelter of men, horses, mules, and oxen. Although the company's initial task was to erect a large hotel at Mammoth, its men also began building carriage sheds, barns, and corrals for the stagecoach company that everyone knew would soon be organized. Within a year, YNPIC's employees had cut 1.6 million board feet of lumber from the park.[625]

The corporation known as the Yellowstone National Park Improvement Company (YNPIC)—financially backed by the Northern Pacific Railroad, one of the nation's most powerful transportation companies—was busily becoming the central commercial entity in Yellowstone, which itself was then an evolving pleasuring ground for the business of tourism. (Indeed, Yellowstone was the first incentive for tourism to the interior of the American West following the Civil War, as we have argued in Chapter Four.) The emergence of Yellowstone as a Park offered a fertile field for experimentation by corporate executives who were not yet subject to a learning nation's regulations. The story of the company's many abuses in the following three years has been told elsewhere,[626] and so we restrict ourselves here to the story of the company's stagecoach operation. That enterprise would prove to be a story of fewer abuses than those in the rest of the company, probably because YNPIC sublet (to be precise, they verbally contracted) the transportation rights to two stalwart, local Montanans who had previously established themselves with good reputations in the Territory's stagecoaching business.

These men were George Washington Wakefield[627] and Charles Wheeler Hoffman. Hoffman[628] was largely a silent partner, but Wakefield would soon establish himself as head of this powerful transportation dynasty in Yellowstone National Park and rise to become one of the most important men in the region. The descendants of his operation—eventually called the Yellowstone Park Transportation Company—would operate stagecoaches for thirty-three years, would convert to motorized busses in 1917, and would live on in one form or another for one hundred four years and beyond (still operating today). Wakefield's operation was Yellowstone's largest stagecoach company, although three others—the Monida & Yellowstone, Wylie, and Shaw & Powell operations—would eventually be established inside the park along with dozens of independents—such as the already discussed Bassett Brothers, the Rea brothers, and George Marshall—the first two of which were headquartered outside the park.

The YNPIC selected George W. Wakefield (1835-1917) to superintend its transportation operations, but he did not actually work for the company. Instead, as will be detailed, he operated by verbal agreement as a contractor, engaged to run a company that his personal stationery referred to in late 1883 as "Geo. W. Wakefield's Bozeman and National Park Stage Line." Historian Bartlett has described him as "one of those colorful figures of the Old West who knew his men and his horses equally well, and was an excellent judge of both," and that is a good summary. George Wakefield was similar to his contemporary at Mammoth, G.L. Henderson, in that both discovered late in life the place and subject that was their be-all and end-all—namely Yellowstone National Park.

Wakefield was indeed a fascinating character, who had already created many adventures for himself by the time he got the chance to run stagecoaches in Yellowstone. Born in Bangor, Maine so early in the nineteenth century that he was nearly fifty years old when he arrived in the Park, Wakefield went to work in that town at age twelve at the Hotel Stetson. His mother Betsy A. Wakefield presented him to the world as the fortunate son of Whig politician Benjamin Wakefield, and he got his first job at age eleven "as a bell boy in a hotel." His first job that related to horses occurred when he oversaw teams at Lincoln, Maine at the age of thirteen. Because of those early experiences, horses and hotels would serve as his bread and butter for the rest of his life.

Marrying Margaret B. Brittan (1832-1903), a Canadian woman three years his senior in 1855, he took his bride to St. Anthony, Minnesota (a suburb of Minneapolis) and opened a livery. But like so many people of that era, he soon got gold fever and headed across the frontier to Colorado in 1860, where he prospected at Pikes Peak before traveling variously to New Mexico, California, British Columbia, Oregon, and Idaho.[629]

While prospecting in Idaho, Wakefield made a couple of trips across the Bitterroot Range to Virginia City, Montana. His obituary stated that he was in Virginia City in 1862, while two other biographies placed it in 1863. Enthralled by that place like so many early Montanans, he returned to Minnesota in 1864 to pick up his wife. George and Margaret packed everything into a two-horse spring-wagon and headed overland for Virginia City. After "many thrilling encounters with the Indians" (according to an obituary), they arrived there on July 4, 1865, and then they followed the news of another gold strike over to Blackfoot, Montana. When that strike failed, the couple returned to Virginia City to set up both a dairy and a livery. Eventually George and Margaret settled near Dempsey's ranch at Deer Lodge, where they lived for two or three years.[630] Present in 1870 at Virginia City for Montana Territory's first U.S. Census, George and Margaret were parents then to a one-year-old daughter named Mary E. Wakefield, who apparently died in childhood sometime later.[631]

In 1870, Wakefield purchased a ranch at what would become Point of Rocks in unsettled Paradise Valley, north of Yellowstone Park. His presence there was apparently responsible for the place-name Point of Rocks, and Wakefield may have given it to the spot himself, because that place-name appeared in the local newspaper as early as 1871.[632] It was probably there that he fell in love with the upper Yellowstone River country, and from his ranch he likely traveled early into what would become the national park, although so far, we have no record of it. Wanting a better living—and probably a more adventurous one—than he could obtain by farming and ranching, he moved to Bozeman in 1872 to engage in both the hotel and the livery business. "Geo. W. Wakefield, famous as the landlord of the Point of Rocks," proclaimed a Bozeman newspaper at that time, "has removed to Bozeman, and has leased the North[ern] Pacific Hotel, and purchased the Livery Stable" of Leander M. Black at Main and Black streets. Thus, for most of the 1870s, Wakefield ran a stage line between Bozeman and Virginia City and managed at least one hotel. He may have briefly run out of money at one point to operate his own livery, for in April of 1880, he served as mere "agent" for H.F. Galen's Stage and Express Line.[633] At some point, Charles W. Hoffman, whom Wakefield met in Bozeman during the 1870s, joined Wakefield as his partner in the stage-and-freighting business.

George Wakefield and "his excellent lady" became leading citizens of

Bozeman. He managed "Montana's best hotel," helped to found Bozeman National Bank, served as County Commissioner for Gallatin County, and became a leading voice in the local Grange organization. In 1878, a feud with two local brothers resulted in an injury and lifelong disability for Wakefield. Having purchased the Lamme ranch on East Gallatin River, he was driving two mules back to it, when he heard a shot ring out and felt a second shot strike his forearm. A doctor soon amputated his right forearm, which was "badly shattered." Police arrested brothers Thomas and Thornton Street for the shooting and bound them over to District Court.[634] In the banking business, Wakefield met Bozeman notables Peter Koch and Walter Cooper, and in the summer of 1881 the three men tried to interest the Northern Pacific Railroad in building a line up Gallatin Canyon to Yellowstone Park's west entrance. The railroad declined, but Wakefield and his friends had some high adventures there with forest fires, game, and the park's geysers before giving up the quest.[635]

George W. Wakefield, about 1916. *Author's collection.*

But when he returned home to his hotel, George Wakefield spoke to J.V. Bogert, one of Bozeman's writers of humor, whose columns graced the

Avant Courier. To read Bogert, one gets an idea of how Wakefield sounded (or might have sounded) when he talked. Because Bogert wrote for comedy, he might have taken liberties with Wakefield's speech, but regardless of whether he did or not, he "painted" a long picture of his apparently entertaining conversation with George Wakefield. Bogert, who later served as Bozeman's first mayor,[636] wrote under the name "Vesuvius" and titled his article "Wakefield Visits the Park." It described Wakefield's meeting that summer with General Philip Sheridan (then traveling through Yellowstone), Wakefield's impressions of the park's geysers, and the fact that he was a Democrat (the conservatives in those days). Some of it went like this:

> "Yes," said George W., "been to the Park. No. I *didn't go afoot!* I just rode. Met Sheridan—now, he's a gentleman, he is. *He* puts on no airs, he don't—when we bowed to him, he bowed to us; or he bowed to us when we bowed to him…Sheridan—he's a man all over—he's two men, that man. I'll bet *he* likes good grub! Yes, been to the Geysers. I tell you there's a Hell! Must be! See here, Vesuvius, the next time you write anything about the Park, you tell people East there's a Hell—right up in the Park. Most of the Eastern people are on the road to Hell. You just tell them there's one up this way, and to come by way of Bozeman. That's business, you know; and it won't make any difference to them which Hell they go to, you know. And then we'd get the trade. Yes, been to the Geysers—saw them all. Saw ten hundred billion gallons of hot water fired up into the air a mile a minute. Thunder! But it's grand. Wish I could get the Republican party into one of those spouters! Don't wish you any ill-luck Vesuvius, but you fellows have run things long enough. We camped the first night by the Giantess [Geyser]…Well, sir, at midnight there was a sudden thump right under me—then 1000 thumps, and the confoundedest spluttering and hissing you ever heard. And with every chug the ground rose and fell, and things trembled and shook…[637]

Wakefield's speech went on and on, and "John Vesuvius" wrote it all down, noting at conversation's end that Wakefield "kicked over a chair, cut a dou-

A six-horse, Tally-ho stagecoach—number twelve of the YNPT Company—pauses at Mammoth Hot Springs in this pre-1891 photograph. Grass was not established here until 1901, on the sandy, travertine flats where the Fort Yellowstone buildings would eventually stand. That year, geologist Arnold Hague and the U.S. Army's laborers brought soil from the top of a nearby hill to spread over what became the Mammoth Parade Ground. *H-6508, Montana Historical Society.*

ble-shuffle, slammed the door, and retreated." George W. Wakefield must have been an engaging personality.

Like so many Yellowstone Park aficionados who were living in Bozeman, Wakefield could not get Paradise Valley and the Park out of his head, and he knew that the railroad would soon be a big part of it, so in late 1881, he sold his side businesses to concentrate on hauling freight for the approaching railroad. He and Charles Hoffman contracted with the Northern Pacific Railroad—which was then laying track west from Billings, Montana—

to furnish it with one hundred thousand railroad ties from a site on Mill Creek. During those two years, the men established enough of a relationship with Carroll Hobart to obtain a verbal contract to run Hobart's stage lines in the Park for the emerging Yellowstone National Park Improvement Company. Wakefield and Hoffman delivered their last ties to the NPRR's Park Branch on April 21, 1883, while that railroad was building south toward Yellowstone National Park.[638]

As YNPIC was beginning its construction of the Mammoth Hotel in early 1883, President Rufus Hatch already knew that he and Manager Hobart would need stagecoaches and horses, but he left the details to Carroll Hobart, admonishing him that any horses they bought "will eat their heads off before spring" and that would cost the company a lot of money. So, he told Hobart to "hire a good stage outfit." In June, Hobart awarded the transportation rights to Wakefield and Hoffman. Telling the newspaper that he would use Concord coaches in his operation, a claim that was not completely correct, George Wakefield quickly began purchasing teams and equipment for the park's summer season that had already begun.[639]

President Rufus Hatch's laudatory letter to the Department of the Interior about his new coachmen did not tell the entire story. Calling it a "contract" that his company was entering, he mistakenly gave Wakefield's home location as "Helena" (it had long been Bozeman with an office in Livingston), but he correctly referred to them as "old and experienced Montana stage managers" and he made certain to tell the Secretary that all monies from transportation would go to the coachmen and not to YNPIC. What Hatch did not mention to Interior was the fact that the contract was strictly a verbal one, not written down anywhere and existing only as an adjunct to their hotel lease.[640] Although such verbal contracts could and can still be legally enforced when their existence could/can be proven, this one would eventually cause much trouble for liveryman Wakefield.

But for now, all was well, and Wakefield was excited at his new prospects. At Mammoth, he needed a base of operations, and it appears that he moved into YNPIC's elongated carriage-shed that the company completed in February,[641] and which it used initially as a boarding house and offices. (By summer, Hatch and Hobart had relocated their offices and residences to the new Mammoth Hot Springs Hotel, apparently a summer-only arrangement.) This carriage shed was located at the far northeast corner of the Mammoth village, and Wakefield was to live in a cabin near it for five years—until other housing became available in 1888.[642] By locating its buildings there, YNPIC established a base at Mammoth for its transportation operations that would remain in place for eighty-plus years.

In mid-July, the *St. Paul Globe* was announcing that "the stage service by Messrs. Wakefield & Hoffman" would arrive in the Park in only a few days and would "be complete and ample for any emergency during the season." Wakefield was planning to use eighty to one hundred horses on his Concord coaches that would run from Cinnabar to Mammoth. On the Park tour, he was assigning numerous "new two and three-seated spring Concord wagons of Racine manufacture." These were mostly spring wagons, and thus were hardly the luxurious stagecoaches that he would later put into service.[643]

Wakefield's initial agreement with YNPIC engaged him to haul passengers from the Cinnabar railhead to and through the Park at twelve cents per passenger per mile, or $25 per person. On July 8, he moved his "coaches, jerkies, and single and double buckboards, numbering about forty vehicles in all" from Bozeman to Cinnabar and Mammoth to be ready for tourists. He was starting small but would soon get bigger. On July 20, he also began carrying mail to Mammoth. According to press reports, he had eighty to one hundred horses around the park, while the YNPIC had fifty more that it planned to rent to tourists at Mammoth.[644]

Because of the railroad's impending arrival at the park's north entrance, the year 1883 was essentially the grand opening of Yellowstone National Park, and it became a hugely busy season with five thousand estimated visitors, who traveled all summer to the railroad's various termini that were still short of Cinnabar.[645] The Park's roads were anything but ready, even with the season beginning late because the Mammoth Hotel was not finished. Regardless, Wakefield began picking up passengers at the various railheads, then located at times as much as twenty miles north of Gardiner.

Both train and stage travel at that time from Bozeman/Livingston to Gardiner occurred on the west and south sides of Yellowstone River. That wagon road to the Park was (and still is) known as the "Old Yellowstone Trail," and it was a most difficult road in 1883. It was the road that everyone traveled then, which had evolved from a game trail and then an Indian trail into a bridal-path and eventually a wagon-road used by Cooke City goldminers beginning in

1870. It ran from Trail Creek in Paradise Valley up the Yellowstone River on its west and south sides, through Yankee Jim Canyon, over the foothills of Cinnabar Mountain, across Gardner River to Turkey Pen Pass, and east through the new park to the tiny hamlet of Cooke City. Beginning in 1871, an even cruder road ran over Sepulcher Mountain's foothills to Mammoth Hot Springs, and in late 1879 and 1880, the town of Gardiner began to spring up just west of the mouth of that river.

One of the earliest photos of George Wakefield's stagecoaching in YNP at Mammoth Hot Springs Hotel showing a box-type coach with six horses, most likely in 1883, before he purchased his first "Yellow-stone Wagons" in 1885. Looking carefully at the image on the left, we can clearly see that Wakefield was pulling a small freight-wagon behind his stagecoach, so that visitors' heavy trunks---typically carried in those days---could be transported to Mammoth Hot Springs Hotel. *T.W. Ingersoll photo, Bob Berry Collection, ING08.1000.*

F.B. Plimpton of the *Cincinnati Commercial Tribune* regaled his readers with how it felt to ride in one of Wakefield's spring wagons in 1883 from the temporary railhead near Cedar Creek, just south of Yankee Jim Canyon, to Mammoth Hot Springs, a distance of eighteen miles:

The road being over stony hills, narrow valleys, skirting the foot of mountains and fording creeks, was calculated to impress upon the party the great difference between gliding smoothly over such a track as the Northern Pacific with less jar and jolting in its thousand miles than in going half a mile over a Cincinnati street railway, and roughing it over a road which is but little better than a mountain trail. Those of us who had taken to wagons soon wished we had chosen ponies while those on horseback looked longingly at the imaginary comfort of those in the wagons. It was a rough ride and left no bone or muscle of the body unexercised. It was up hill and down dale, over roots, stumps, stones, corduroy bridges into chuck-holes and through marshes[,] the wagons plunging to this side and then that like a ship in chop[ped] seas till one's soul longed for the wings of a dove to fly away and be at rest. A terrific thunder-storm added to the pleasure of the ride but gave some wonderful atmospheric effects to the mountain scenery, which, however, we were not in a condition to enjoy with the delight of an artist.[646]

Indeed, the numerous accounts of journalists who came to the Park for 1883's grand opening described horrendous weather, with torrential rain during July and August that turned this rough road (from the railhead to Mammoth) into nearly impassable muck, and frightened stagecoach passengers terribly.[647]

By August 7, George Wakefield was facing a major financial problem, namely the competition from what he considered illegal in-park coachmen. His letter of that date to Carroll Hobart, which Hobart forwarded to Henry Teller, Secretary of the Interior, complained that park Superintendent Patrick Conger had permitted "all classes of people to establish tents and stables near our own with exceedingly unreliable and inferior equipments and to maintain and operate a regular business the same as has been [supposedly exclusively] granted us under your lease and contract with the Government." Carroll Hobart's accompanying letter tried to expand this complaint to include out-of-park operators like Allen W. Chadbourn and Alonzo Daw, but Wakefield's letter made it clear that he understood directly from Hobart that Interior's regulation did not exclude such out-of-park liverymen.[648]

Perhaps Hobart did not thoroughly understand what the regulation intended and was merely hoping for clarification from Interior. Regardless, by mid-August Assistant Secretary Merritt Joslyn was admonishing Superintendent Conger because Conger had erected signs warning both inside and outside liverymen that they could not operate in the Park. These signs incensed outside-the-park locals, who believed that the regulation, whether truly from Interior or merely being misinterpreted by Conger, was unjust, and they complained loudly about it. In this primitive region where there were only so many jobs, a blow-up was inevitable, and it came during President Chester Arthur's trip two weeks later. A visitor leased a prohibited rig from someone at Mammoth, and Superintendent Conger enforced the ruling by sending an assistant to serve the visitor with a copy of Secretary Teller's previous order against that. Hearing that Senator George Graham Vest was in the Park, the visitor went to him and showed him the order. Senator Vest, who had no use for Hobart's company, exploded to President Arthur: "There, I told you that ___, ___, ___ was in collusion with this Park Improvement Company." President Arthur reportedly laughed and handed back the order, but that action apparently revoked Teller's order.[649] Independent liverymen from outside the park could thereafter carry tourists into the park, but this kind of prohibition and outcry would eventually happen again.

The business of the questionable stagecoaching regulation in the Department of the Interior was probably partly responsible for the eventual dismissal of Superintendent Conger. It reappeared two months later when W. Scott Smith's government report castigated Conger and implicitly defended Wakefield and Hobart, at least in this matter. Unbeknownst to anyone, Secretary Teller sent Mr. Smith to the Park as a government spy that summer with instructions to report on all affairs. On October 15, Smith submitted his report to the Secretary, and the part about this order read as follows:

> I found a great deal of dissatisfaction among visitors to the park over the construction placed upon a sentence embodied in a letter of Acting Secretary Joslyn, bearing date of August 3, 1883, and which Superintendent Conger had caused to be copied and posted up at various points in the park. This sentence reads as

follows: "In order that there may be no opportunity for extortion or unfair dealing toward tourists by unauthorized persons you will be careful to see that no person shall, within the limits of the park, engage in the transportation of visitors, or in providing or furnishing any accommodation or service whatever to them for compensation, or in any other business, without authority in writing, first obtained from this Department." The construction placed upon this was that no person should engage a team outside the park and use it to go through the park, but [was required] to send it back upon entering the park and take such conveyances as the Park Transportation Company were able to provide...I submit that a wrong construction has been placed upon this order, and that the manifest intention was to prevent persons within the limits of the park from engaging in the transportation of visitors without a permit, and not to exclude persons who might engage a team at one of the towns some distance from the park and desired to use it in going through the park.

"If I am right about this," urged Smith in implying that Conger misunderstood the order, "I would recommend that a supplementary letter be sent to the Superintendent so specific that he cannot misunderstand it." Scott stated that Conger, although requested to do so on numerous occasions, declined to notify the Department that the order was causing widespread trouble and ill-feeling.[650] Wakefield and Hobart's actions here, along with those of W. Scott Smith, probably aided in getting Superintendent Conger fired less than a year later. Only a few years later, G.L. Henderson thought this was the case,[651] and the current author agrees.

George Wakefield stated later that he did very little business this summer, "on account of people living outside the Park coming in here with their teams and taking the business away from us."[652] Despite his difficulties, Mr. Wakefield gave satisfactory service during the summer of 1883, and also for at least seven of the eight more summers that he would operate in Yellowstone. Newspaperman L.H.C. of the *Cleveland Leader*—mentioned in the quote at the beginning of this book—rode with him and loved the trip, gushing that "the staid journalists, accustomed to the confinement of the closed cars and close sanctums were so filled with the spirit of the free, wild ride in that invigorating atmosphere, that they could hardly refrain from shouting with delight like a child at a new found pleasure." Of course, some of that excitement could be attributed to the magic of Yellowstone rather than to Wakefield's stages. Another visitor was more specific, proclaiming that he was fortunate to get a seat "behind the spirited team of Mr. Wakefield who had furnished the vehicles and horses for the transportation of the party." This party of journalists was handled personally by George Wakefield, so it is small wonder that the author noted that "at every step, we have experienced the most considerate and generous hospitality."[653]

At the end of the season, Wakefield continued to carry mail from the railhead to Cooke City, and the superintendent gave him permission to cut hay in the park for his thirty or forty horses and to winter his horses in the park. That he did not remain in the park for the winter was attested to by Assistant Superintendent J.H. Dean's request to live in his cabin for the winter. Per Wakefield's letterhead, the official name of his company was "Geo. W. Wakefield's Bozeman and National Park Stage Line."[654]

In December, Carroll Hobart renewed the verbal agreement of Wakefield & Hoffman. The *Enterprise* reported that for the summer of 1884, the men would receive twenty-five dollars per tourist, "instead of $10." The reporter outlined the men's plans:

> They will put on a regular line of coaches from the terminus of the railroad to all points of interest in the Park. Three coaches will arrive at and depart from all stations in the Park at stated times each, and probably several times a day. Passengers will buy their tickets, stop at stations as long as they please, and when they are ready to go, take the next coach and pass on, thus making the tour at their leisure and without limit of time.[655]

But Wakefield would find that allowing such stopovers by tourists was harder to do than he thought. Not until 1890 would YPA make this adjustment, and then, as he predicted, it proved to be a money-loser (the company lost $5,000).[656] However, it did keep some and maybe even many customers happy.

During the winter of 1883-1884, George Wakefield ran his other transportation contracts north of the park (among others, he had a mail contract from Livingston to Mammoth), but he was ready to go with passenger-staging when the summer season of 1884 arrived. The company with whom he had contracted, however, was not. Its Mammoth Hotel and all other park facilities were in receivership, so the season began late. While they waited for YNPIC to get its act together, Wakefield and Hoffman used the delay to erect "buildings to accommodate their stages and stock" and to make another verbal agreement with receiver George B. Hulme. Wakefield decided that regardless of whether YNPIC opened its still-unfinished hotel, he would be ready to run passengers through the Park. The *Enterprise* announced that his coaches, which had so far been "sent out as demanded," would "begin making regular trips through the park next Monday [July 14]."[657]

Assistant Superintendent G.L. Henderson, who had begun writing newspaper columns of park news, reported on June 29, 1884, that George Wakefield was indeed ready to transport passengers:

> Wakefield & Hoffman are at the Springs with their splendid transportation outfit; Concord coaches, elegant spring wagons, buckboards, buggies and a fine assortment of saddle horses. They are selecting the best class of men, men whom they know to be reliable, intelligent, courteous and careful, to insure the comfort and safety of visitors who pass over their line. They will have a well-stocked line by which tourists may go from Cinnabar to the Upper Geyser Basin in one day, or they may stop at way stations and resume their journey at their own convenience.[658]

This last claim, about stopovers, would eventually become a big discussion between Wakefield and YNPIC. As for "well stocked," Henderson seems to have been referring to the high quality of Wakefield's horses rather than to any miscellaneous supplies that the line might have been using or carrying.

The road from Cinnabar to Mammoth remained terrible in 1884. Late in the season, government road-engineer Dan Kingman would reroute it at the town of Gardiner through Gardner Canyon, but that had not happened yet when a traveler from Arkansas, known only as "G.," experienced it with one of Wakefield's drivers:

From Cinnabar there are eight miles of staging to be made over the mountains...The trip is made either in the early morning or in the afternoon. It is one that the tourist cannot well afford to miss. Some of the hardships and dangers of pioneer life and exploration can be fully realized, and some of the grandest views which the Rocky Mountains afford are here presented. A more dangerous stage route cannot be easily imagined. Sometimes you go up a perpendicular hill and then down a rocky and breath-taking-away descent, around ledges of rock just wide enough for the stage to pass with an unfathomable abyss on one side and on the other overhanging mountains streaked with snow...The doors of the hotel are reached suddenly and immediately after [descending] a long and tortuous and breakneck hill.[659]

Meanwhile, it was a disastrous, financial season of 1884 for Carroll Ho-bart and YNPIC, who dropped further into a financial hole due to the low visitation of that summer. This was caused by the economic uncertainty in the country, which some historians have called the Panic of 1884.[660] George Wakefield did better than Hobart, but his season was not without its difficulties.

A bright spot was his rehiring of Adam Deem as an immediate subor-dinate, who in the next three years would prove himself competent and even worthy of praise (Deem, who had formerly worked for the Bozeman Produce Store, seems to have been with Wakefield almost from the begin-ning, for an advertisement in *Livingston Enterprise*, December 31, 1883, p. 3, mentioned him). A dark spot occurred when assistant superinten-dents caught two of Wakefield's drivers "defacing formations and throwing stones into geysers" to entertain their passengers and increase their tips. G.L. Henderson, as mentioned, was still a park assistant superintendent this summer but he was also already making himself into one of the best guides and experts on Yellowstone. He reported a complaint on Wakefield's drivers' tour-guiding abilities for not knowing park geography.[661]

Except for this minor complaint about park interpretation and the more serious one about drivers' vandalism, affairs were so far fairly good for Wakefield, but at some point in 1884, he became concerned that he was operating on only a verbal agreement with YNPIC and formally applied to the Department of the Interior for his own lease. The Secretary refused, saying that DOI had "authority" only to grant leases to hotel-builders and not to transportation-operators. Wakefield would continue to seek a formal lease from each of the succeeding Secretaries of Interior through 1891, but would never get one.[662] He would eventually become a victim of that strange "authority."

Perhaps worrying about his lack of a formal lease and hoping to keep himself in good graces, Wakefield upgraded his fleet in 1884, and he placed a "runner" (advertising man) on the trains from Livingston—an innovation that would continue on those trains for thirty-two more years, through Yellowstone's entire stagecoach-era until motorization in 1917. A journalist known only as "O.J.H." climbed aboard a coach at Cinnabar in August and stated that Wakefield's "wagons are good (as a rule) Concord coaches [with] some vehicles made especially for park use." This traveler recorded that the independent stage-men ("a score of opposition wagons") were also in abundance at Cinnabar, so "no one need fear getting left" behind. He mentioned seeing Wakefield and Hoffman's office inside the Mammoth Hotel and noted that it seemed to be "full every evening of other men seeking employment" with the stage company. O.J.H. recorded Wakefield's charges as twenty-five dollars for the six-day trip and eighteen dollars for the four-day trip, with room and board not included (four dollars per day). Most interestingly, he described the vehicles themselves, stating that "the wagons were invented by the Bassetts [brothers] of Beaver Canyon [Idaho] for the purpose, and made to order." He called his own coach "a sort of cross between the mountain and the Eastern wagon, strong but light, covered with canvas, [with] a brake that would lock both hind wheels, elliptic springs over the axles, and half elliptic [ones] inverted to support the center of the box." "It was an easy riding wagon," he enthused, probably meaning comfortable, "and the drivers are good." His comment that "two seats faced each other" within his coach informs us that Wakefield was still using some of the boxy, old-style prairie stagecoaches this season, and that the more famous "Yellowstone Wagons" (where the seats all faced forward for touring purposes) were not yet present in 1884 and for much of the summer of 1885.[663]

It appears that the chaos of the company's hotel situation and the confusion about independent stage operators from the preceding summer might have opened the door for some price-gouging to have occurred at Mammoth Hotel during the summer of 1884, for a traveler known only as "Occident" encountered a bartering situation there. "Occident" probably rode in Wakefield coaches from Cinnabar, for he referred to them as "Concord coaches," but this is what he says happened before dinner:

> The first thing to do was to see about our transportation, as we would require two covered coaches of four horses each to transport the party. After some dickering we concluded the bargain by agreeing to pay $100 for the teams for two days, being assured that this was the very best that we could do. It really seemed like an expensive luxury and would not have been incurred under other circumstances. But we felt that we were in for it and there was no chance to retreat.[664]

Perhaps "Occident" got taken, for this was a very high rate to pay, but the question was: Who was the stagecoach operator? Was he an independent who had been allowed to hang around the hotel? Or was he (more likely) George Wakefield simply trying to make ends meet during what many accounts attested to as a very slow summer for visitation in Yellowstone? Conditions were so chaotic this summer that this kind of gouging could have occurred. The fact that Wakefield maintained an office in the hotel in 1883 makes it likely that he also maintained one there in 1884, so it seems probable that the operator mentioned by Occident was likely Wakefield himself doing his best to make up for a slow season. Further fuel for this argument came a year later when Wakefield testified before a congressional committee that he lost "over $5,000" in 1884, due not only to opposition from other liverymen but also from a serious loss of horses that season.[665]

More evidence that it was Wakefield bartering in 1884 with "Occident" came from Catherine Bates's account in 1886. This English lady and her party decided to tarry at Mammoth Hotel for several days to bargain for a coach and driver, so they could spend ten days in the park instead of the usual five. "One man had the monopoly of all the stages, wagons, and horses available," she wrote, "and it took us two or three days…to come to anything like terms with him." Determined to charter their own vehicle to be free of the "horrors of public staging," she and her party paid "liberally" for the extra comfort and went into the Park.[666] In light of competition from other stage-men (independents) plus a couple of difficult years, one can hardly blame George Wakefield for engaging in this "extra" way of doing business.

The summer of 1884 was noteworthy for another reason, one that was not surprising considering the nation's difficult economic times. A stage-coach robbery appears to have occurred on September 4, which predated the other five, known Yellowstone hold-ups and which has been overlooked by some historians. One of Wakefield's stages might have been involved, but it is just as likely that the group was traveling in its own personal coach. At least two Michigan newspapers and one California newspaper published the brief story, all three of these articles appearing on the front pages:

> A party of Northern Pacific Railroad tourists from California, a gentleman and two ladies, who arrived here [in Minneapolis] yesterday, report that while driving through the National Yellowstone Park in Montana one day last week they were halted by armed masked robbers five miles from the Upper Geyser [Basin], and their valuables demanded. The party were [*sic*] robbed of all their money, watches and other valuables, but escaped personal injury.[667]

The west coast story added the details that the victims were a Dr. Elliott, his wife, and a daughter from Chico, California, that the affair occurred at "Hell's Half Acre" (Midway Geyser Basin), and that the highwaymen took $48 plus a gold watch from the doctor and small sums and jewelry from the two women. No more is known and no other sources about this event have been found, but we have no reason to disbelieve the story.

With the summer over, Wakefield reverted to his mail contracts and other winter business north of the Park, and his partner Hoffman worked on politics. Hoffman asked Interior for permission to erect more barns and to cut hay within the Park, explaining that the company now had one hundred twenty-five horses. He also asked for some protection from the competition of out-of-park liverymen. It did not hurt that he appended endorsement letters from Montana congressmen Martin McGinnis and successor T.K. Toole, who both argued in favor of granting a license to Wakefield.[668] For whatever reasons, the Secretary did not issue one, but the endorsements kept Wakefield in good favor with both the Park Superintendent and Interior. With their mail contract renewed in July, the two men asked for more permits to cut hay for their horses, and Superintendent David Wear granted them permissions—at Indian Creek, Norris, Lower Geyser Basin, Upper Geyser Basin, Trout Creek, and the Falls.[669]

The 1885 season opened with the park hotels emerging from receivership but still not doing well, as Vice President/General Manager Carroll Hobart attempted to save his failing company in its, and his, last season in the park. Additionally, the Secretary of Interior fired park Superintendent Robert Carpenter in mid-May for being too politically close to the hotel company, and in direct confirmation of that, Hobart immediately hired Carpenter to go to Old Faithful and manage YNPIC's poorly built "Shack" Hotel. George Wakefield probably counted his blessings this season that he was not politically connected to Carpenter or financially allied with Hobart. But he did encounter an official protest of the $2 (instead of one dollar) rate that he had charged for transportation between Cinnabar and Mammoth, a complaint that would come back to haunt him in 1891. Meanwhile, a writer for the *New York Evening Post* reported that the train ticket from St. Paul to Yellowstone and return was priced for tourists at $120, including five days' stage and hotel fare in the park.[670]

That cheaper fare, announced in March and which the railroad kept in place all summer, resulted in an apparent upswing in travel for Yellowstone Park in 1885 and some praise for George Wakefield. Notwithstanding complaints by locals about Wakefield's exclusive transportation rights, newspaper correspondent G.L. Henderson—who would soon begin competing from his Cottage Hotel against Wakefield for stagecoach passengers and against YNPIC for hotel customers—sided for now with Wakefield and the hotel company. He stated that YNPIC "had to contract and deal with...one solid and competent concern and it is difficult to see how they could have made a better selection than Wakefield & Hoffman."[671] Thanks to Jack Ellis Haynes, we know that three of Wakefield's drivers this summer were George Arnholdt, Larry Link, and Billy Haig. Wakefield's "transportation outfit went to the park" from Bozeman/Livingston in mid-June of 1885, stated the local newspaper, with forty vehicles and over one hundred horses. We also know that by the time G.L. Henderson published his newspaper-guidebook in June of 1885, Wakefield's company was called "Wakefield & Hoffman, National Park Transportation Company."[672]

Probably these vehicles were not yet his new ones, but Wakefield would introduce later that season—in 1885—a remarkably simple but theretofore untried innovation in stagecoach travel, which changed not only Yellowstone National Park but also the traveling mode of tourists nationally. It was called the "Yellowstone Wagon." The stagecoach was introduced into America as early as 1687 in Boston (although it was still not in wide usage by 1732, the year that George Washington was born), and ever since that time, these rattling, boxy, horse-drawn vehicles had held seats that faced each other so that passengers could engage in conversation during the slow pace of overland travel on long, boring stretches of dusty road.[673] But in Yellowstone, a coach was needed where all the seats faced forward for the sake of looking one direction—ahead—at the Wonderland scenery. The Abbot and Downing Company of Concord, New Hampshire thus began making these new stagecoaches on special order from George Wakefield. That famous company had been established in 1813 by Lewis Downing (1792-1873) and Joseph Stephens Abbot (1804-1871).[674]

Montana newspapers picked up the story in June of 1885. "Tally-ho coaches are to supersede the more primitive vehicles that were in use last season," stated the *Yellowstone Journal* of Miles City, Montana, "and there seems a strong probability that the tour of the park will be made much more pleasant and expeditious than has heretofore been possible." At Fort Benton, the *River Press* ran the same story. Historian Elizabeth Watry has confirmed the story from information reposited at the New Hampshire Historical Society (NHHS) and the Minnesota Historical Society (MHS). She found the sales-receipts from Abbot-Downing to George Wakefield for three stagecoaches at MHS and the photo of stagecoach #4 (see photo of this coach) at NHHS, a "Yellowstone Wagon" as ordered and received in 1886 by George Wakefield, which most likely meant that stagecoaches one through three were ordered and received by Wakefield in late 1885. Coach number four was a three-seater that held nine passengers on the three seats plus two passengers on the box (eleven passengers), with all seats facing forward rather than facing each other as previous stagecoaches had featured. Meanwhile, "Tally-ho coaches," as described by the *Yellowstone Journal* and the *River Press* in that instance referred only to the eleven-passenger "Yellowstone wagons" with seats facing forward and not to the much larger (six-horse) coaches with a rearward ("tally-ho") seat. But those bigger coaches were also soon to appear in Yellowstone, and in fact it would also happen in 1886. By August 8, 1885, Wakefield was reporting that his investment so far in coaches and horses in the Park was $24,000, due partially no doubt to the new "Yellowstone Wagons."[675] At some point, the new vehicles also became known as "four-in-hand coaches," because they were pulled by four horses, and thus the driver held four reins in his left hand, keeping his right hand free to wield his whip.

Historian Elizabeth Watry found this documentation of George W. Wakefield's purchase of his first Abbot-Downing "Yellowstone Wagons" (stagecoaches) in autumn of 1885 and summer of 1886. *Watry photo in author's collection.*

Wakefield's introduction of the new "Yellowstone Wagons" in late 1885 came only three months after important Park roadwork by the U.S. Engineers, namely Lt. Dan Kingman's completion and opening of a new road through Golden Gate Canyon. "Putting the finishing touches" on it in June (he had started it during the previous season), Kingman effectively eliminated the difficult route over Terrace Mountain, which was exasperating for horses and stagecoaches (it so terrified U.S. Senator Roscoe Conkling after he was scalded in a hot spring that he refused to go farther into the Park, a report that made national news). "All who have seen 'Kingman's Pass' into the park by way of Golden Gate," declared the *Yellowstone Journal*, "and who are competent to form an opinion declare that it is the finest piece of road in the Rocky mountains."[676]

That was an extravagant claim, but almost anything was better than the old, steep ascent of Terrace Mountain via Orange Spring Mound. Engineer Kingman spent more than $14,395 on the government's road, and thereafter, some park stagecoach drivers made jokes about the canyon being named Golden Gate because of its King Midas construction costs, even though the real reason for the name was the gold color of the lichens growing on rocks. In fact, that was a reasonable amount to spend, and G.L. Henderson's technical figure was $14,042.25. The reporter who interviewed Kingman stated that the work would go a great distance toward making the Park "in time a health and pleasure resort unequalled in the whole world."[677]

In park affairs, the famous John Muir of Yosemite Valley (still a California state park) visited Yellowstone in 1885 for his first and only time ever. Muir called the setting aside of Yellowstone "a most noticeable piece of legislation, for which everybody should give thanks." He also stated that it "surpasses in wakeful, exciting interest any other region yet discovered on the face of the globe."[678] Muir probably rode on one of George Wakefield's stages, but we have no definite statement about it. "Setting out, the driver cracks his whip," wrote Muir, "and the four horses go off at half gallop, half trot, in trained, showy style, until out of sight of the hotel." Muir was clearly excited. "The coach is crowded," he continued, "old and young side by side, blooming and fading, full of hope and fun and care."

In one paragraph, he gave us a sense of the rollicking playfulness of it all, saying that some of the passengers "look at the scenery or the horses, and all ask questions, an odd mixed lot of them: Where is the umbrella? What is the name of that blue flower over there? Are you sure the little bag is aboard? Is that hollow yonder a crater? How is your throat this morning? How high did you say the geysers spout? How does the elevation affect your head? Is that a geyser reeking over there in the rocks, or only a hot spring?" All are enthralled!

Most important for history's sake were these memorable lines by Muir, which referred to Yellowstone, and not to Yosemite, which did not become a national park until five years later (1890). "Climb the mountains and get their good tidings," advised Muir. "Nature's peace will flow into you as sunshine flows into trees. The winds will blow their own freshness into you, and the storms their energy, while cares will drop off like autumn leaves."[679]

Now we return to George Wakefield. He faced in the summer of 1885, of all things, a congressional committee, but fortunately for historians the accompanying testimony put much of his operation on record. Congressional arguments over changing the park's northern boundary to accommodate a railroad to Cooke City, the wrestling with YNPIC's possible bankruptcy, expending government monies on the Park's incompetent officials, and its difficult road construction all culminated this summer in special hearings by Congress. Needing also to investigate conditions on nearby Montana Indian reservations and not understanding the geography of the area (let alone the Park's management), Congress sent three House members and their three staff to Yellowstone in early August to look at the country and take testimony in these matters. The members consisted of William S. Holman of Indiana, Joseph G. Cannon of Illinois, and Thomas Ryan of Kansas.[680]

It was highly unusual for a congressional committee to travel to the far west, let alone to a remote place like Yellowstone, and the hearings were a bit difficult for Wakefield. He admitted to this committee that he was charging railroad tourists twice what he charged regular tourists for the stage-ride from Cinnabar to Mammoth, namely $2 and $1, in contravention of the Secretary's regulations. That fact would hurt him in congressional investigations seven years later, but for now the committee had too many other problems to pursue this minor item.[681]

While George Wakefield was dealing with these difficult congressmen, an important traveler whom he would later come to know well, was arriving for his first trip through Yellowstone. Although Charles Gibson called the Park "the most wonderful place on this or perhaps any other continent," he saw much that he did *not* like, and most of it concerned the struggling hotel-operations of the Yellowstone National Park Improvement Company. At this time, no one knew who Gibson was. Writing a letter to the Secretary of the Interior during a gilded-age period when class warfare was forefront in Americans' thinking, this upper-class man hammered first the government's roads and then YNPIC:

I call your special attention to the accommodations. Those who go there are mostly of the higher classes. They not only demand but they need good food and lodging. The price of board in all the hotels and tents is from $4 to $5 a day, yet the walls of [many of] the hotels consist of one plank [probably a sheet of plywood], in some papered over and in others bare. The tents have beds, but stoves for ladies only, and for a few of them only, although it is cold every night in the year in those high regions, and at the Great Falls there is frost every morning. The meats are so tough and mean as to be both unpalatable and indigestible. In most places they have condensed milk and in all rancid butter. In one place they gave me for light a tallow candle stuck in an augur hole bored in[to] a square wooden block. My daughter's candle was put where the cork ought to be in a bottle. In several places the ladies had to sleep all in one room and the gentlemen all in another room. The accommodations were so scanty, compared with the number of visitors (which number constantly increases), that we were glad to get in under any cover at all...[O]ne is fleeced right and left. It is worse than Niagara.[682]

These kinds of complaints were becoming common to this unusual place (Yellowstone) where there would continue to be only a summer hotel-operation (as opposed to a more stable, year-round one) for nearly eighty-seven more years. There were not that many remote, tourist areas like the first national park. And Mr. Gibson would discover later that fixing the hotel company would not be as easy as he thought.

If Gibson noticed George Wakefield's operation while he was in Yellowstone on this initial trip, he did not mention it, and probably that was because even by then Wakefield—unlike the hotel company—was receiving praise from the public. "It is gratifying to learn that Wakefield and Hoffman have this season done extremely well with their stage line through the Park," said the *Bozeman Chronicle*. "Both are hard workers and deserve good fortune, come in whatever shape it may."[683]

As for some of the mechanics of how Wakefield operated during the summer of 1885, we have the testimony of W.H. Dudley, a tourist from Butte, Montana, whose large "Liederkranz expedition" traveled to the Park in August and September. He stated that Wakefield was running two regular (daily) stages from Mammoth to Lower Geyser Basin (Firehole Hotel), two between Firehole Hotel and Lower Falls, and one between Firehole Hotel and Old Faithful. "These stages carry the mails," said Dudley, "and the most of the railroad tourists, of which during the past season there have been quite a large number." Dudley noted that Wakefield and Hoffman had obtained permission to cut hay in the Park and stack it for winter use. "This arrangement allows the company," explained Dudley, "to winter their horses cheaper in the Park than by taking them away."[684] During the summer, Wakefield also completed a few other tasks. He hired Richard "Pretty Dick" Randall (1866-1957) into the Park from the eastern Montana plains. Working first as a night-herder for Wakefield, Randall would later spend ten summers as a stagecoach driver before initiating the nation's first dude ranch (or possibly its second)—the famous OTO Ranch, on Cedar Creek north of Gardiner, Montana.

Toward the end of his life, Dick Randall and his daughter Bess Randall Erskine gave many of his papers to their much-younger friend George Perkins. George Perkins gave those papers to the Yellowstone National Park Library in 2010, when this author was serving as Park Historian. Conducting an interview with Perkins, I asked him whether Dick Randall ever mentioned the ten summers wherein he drove stages in Yellowstone and George stated:

> He said it was one of the hardest things he ever had to do because there were no roads [few roads] in the park. The only vehicle that could stand up was the Concord coach and only because it was leather-hung [thoroughbraces] instead of spring-hung. He said it was a four-horse hitch and a bruising thing to do. He said he was a night herder for George Wakefield and I gathered that what he was saying was that he was such a good night-herder that he got the job as stage driver. He also mentioned the stagecoach being held up at one point [1897].

Dick Randall arrived in Yellowstone in 1885, serving first as a night-herder at Old Faithful, and later as a stage-driver for George Wakefield, variously from 1887-1897.[685]

Returning to George Wakefield, at the end of the summer of 1885, newspaper correspondent G.L. Henderson stated that Wakefield's company "has made some money this year, the first, as they say, that they have ever made in the Park." Henderson praised Wakefield as having "undoubtedly done much to lay the foundation for a continuance of the [increased] travel" in 1885. Although officially we have only an estimate of 5,000 visitors for the park's travel this summer, the lowered train-fares, a more stable hotel company, and numerous newspaper articles like this one all militated in favor of Park travel having increased this year from last. By December all these reports had convinced new Superintendent David Wear that "the travel in the Park this summer has been much greater than ever before."[686]

In late November, probably because of his last-minute desperation for money, Carroll Hobart sued George Wakefield in Minnesota state court. The fact that the lawsuit quickly disappeared was evidence that it had no merit and making that decision to sue was probably one of the last moves Hobart made before his train left Livingston heading east on or about November 14, 1885.[687]

In October of 1885, Wakefield made a management change from previous winters. He decided to take his horses out of the Park to operate his Livingston and Gardiner stage- line for the winter (daily until November 1 and tri-weekly thereafter).[688] Apparently his experiment of leaving them in the park after the seasons of 1883 and 1884 had not worked well.

Even as Wakefield was closing his summer operation, he must have received the news of the coming of a new management-syndicate to Yellowstone. The same issue of the *Livingston Enterprise* that announced Wakefield's exit also announced that St. Louis lawyer and businessman Charles Gibson was purchasing Carroll Hobart's company and arranging to take over the Park's hotels.[689] Gibson would soon be the company's new president, and Wakefield must have felt the same bit of apprehension that we all feel when our new boss comes to town.

Thus, Wakefield made immediate plans to again improve his operation, and part of his plans included more equipment. He traveled to the east coast in February and March of 1886 to purchase new "carriages and stages," visiting both Concord, New Hampshire and South Bend, Indiana.[690] In addition to purchasing four-horse and smaller units, he purchased at least one larger stagecoach—a heavier unit that could hold many more passengers and required the use of six horses instead of four. Called a "tally-ho" stage because of its high, rear seat that allowed passengers to gaily wave both directions at other traffic, this stagecoach entered duty in 1886. That much seems certain, because there is no mention of such a coach until that year, when a traveler known only as W.H.R. referred to one. "Arriving at Cinnabar," wrote this reporter, "our [train] cars were run upon a siding until our return, and we mounted the four and six-horse coaches for an eight-mile ride up a magnificent mountain road to the Mammoth Hot Springs." W.H.R. did not say how many six-horse coaches Wakefield had. It might have been only one that year, but there must have been at least two in 1887, for tourist A.S. Condon proclaimed then that at Mammoth it was "a common thing to see a coach drawn by six beautiful horses dash up to hotel entrances for a load of passengers."[691] It likely would have required two or more of these new stages for this occurrence to have been called a "common thing." That he owned only two of these became clear when Wakefield sold his entire inventory of equipment to YPA in 1889. The detailed list of wagons showed only two that could have been six-horse, Tally-ho stages, those being listed as one "Huntly stagecoach" and one "Bighorn wagon."

George Wakefield's stagecoach #4 of YNPT Company arrived in 1886, and its driver paused here for F. Jay Haynes—then a partner of Wakefield—to take this photo in front of the Mammoth Hot Springs Hotel. *Jay Lyndes Family Collection, YC-P008197, Billings, Montana.*

During this summer of 1886 Wakefield added a total of six new coaches—three from the Abbot-Downing Company and three from the Studebaker Brothers Manufacturing Company.[692]

Wakefield's initial plan was to use the new, big stagecoaches only on the Cinnabar-to-Mammoth stretch of road, because that was where he needed to haul both more visitors and more baggage—namely the large trunks that many travelers carried with them on long train-trips. Also in his mind was the fact that more and more freight for both the hotel company and the government's civilian employees was appearing at Cinnabar on in-bound trains as well as outgoing freight that both the hotel company and the government wanted to ship north. This steadily increasing freight-business would eventually require that he purchase some more large freight wagons, and they too would be six-horse if not eight-horse units.

To appear respectable and responsible to his new boss as well as to relieve himself a bit financially, Wakefield took on the Northern Pacific Railroad's photographer F. Jay Haynes as a business partner (Charles Hoffman sold his interests to Haynes in December of 1885). Wakefield and Haynes planned to put a number of the new coaches onto their stage-line and to run daily from June 16 to October 1 from Mammoth to Old Faithful and to Canyon. Haynes had been in the Park since 1881, taking photographs and selling them, and in the spring of 1885, he built a fancy home and photo-studio immediately across from the Mammoth Hot Springs Hotel that faced it.[693] From there and his other shops, he would sell photographs to tourists in Yellowstone for the rest of his life, eventually passing the business down to his son Jack Ellis Haynes.

We now deviate temporarily from the George Wakefield story to tell the tales of two of his short-term competitors, James A. Clark and G.L. Henderson. Clark was short-lived in the Park. Henderson's stage-line was longer-lived than Clark's, and in many other ways, Henderson was a more major Yellowstone character. Henderson left his government job in 1884 to establish a hotel and a stagecoaching line and had thus recently evolved into a much more influential person in Yellowstone. He would soon press his ideas about stagecoach touring onto the commercial scene and thus exert a direct impact upon George Wakefield and the Yellowstone Park Association, during the years 1884-1889.

CHAPTER TEN

"All Calls Over Hill and Vale"

James A. Clark and G.L. Henderson—Independents Vie in Yellowstone's Transportation Rivalry

> J.A. Clark is preparing to meet all calls for carriages, saddle horses and guides. —G.L. Henderson about his friend James Clark, *Yellowstone Park Manual and Guide*, 1885, p. 1.

> The Cottage Hotel Association's elegant Quincy carriages are waiting at Cinnabar to transport you to Mammoth Hot Springs in care of experienced guides, who after seeing all are safely seated, sing out 'All's right,' and away you go over hill and vale in absolute safety toward Wonderland.—G.L. Henderson, *YP Manual and Guide*, 1888, p. 1.

During the period 1872-1883, when Yellowstone National Park had recently been discovered and established and was gradually being revealed to the world through newspapers, magazines, and guidebooks, various national financial interests were competing to be the ticket-selling agents and operators through which the traveling public could reach the new place—then rapidly coming "on-stage" as the first incentive for tourist travel to the interior of the American West—to tour it and see it. Those entities naturally included railroads and stagecoach companies but also travel-companies, like

Raymond & Whitcomb and the older Thomas Cook tours, and a few hotel chains, most of which failed to compete. As the Utah & Northern Railway laid its rails northward from Utah to Montana, and as the Northern Pacific Railroad worked its way west and south to the same place, stagecoach operators began to lust after the rights to chauffeur the public to Yellowstone over primitive, existing roads or even planning to somehow correct the no-roads-yet-at-all status in the national park. By 1883, when both of these railroads were finished, independent stage operators were angling for a piece of the Yellowstone "pie," such that Montana places like Cinnabar, Gardiner, Livingston, Bozeman, Dillon, Virginia City, and Monida, along with Beaver Canyon, Idaho, were all witnessing independent stage-operators planning to use their own horses and wagons to somehow grab a share, small though it usually was, of the tourist-traffic to Yellowstone National Park. Eventually Cinnabar and Gardiner boasted the lion's share of these independents located outside park boundaries, but most of the other places held onto a few of them until various years after 1900 and before 1917.

Two of these independent stage companies—James A. Clark's National Park Hack and Express (1883-1887) and G.L. Henderson's Cottage Hotel Association (1885-1889)—were located within Yellowstone National Park, at Mammoth. Their brief stories added to the interest and complexity of travel in early days in that new place called Wonderland.

James A. Clark's Short-lived Stagecoach Line at Mammoth Hot Springs, 1883-87—"National Park Hack and Express."

Like nearly everyone else who happened to be living at Mammoth Hot Springs during the period 1883 to 1887, James A. Clark's fortunes were tied up with the private corporation of Yellowstone National Park Improvement Company, its successor the Yellowstone Park Association, three short-lived park superintendents (each a difficult personality in his own way), and the U.S. Army who entered Yellowstone Park in August of 1886 to take over its administration.[694]

J.A. Clark was a mysterious character in his day and, for now, remains that way today. Born in or about 1848 in Nebraska, he spent his early years in and around Fort Collins, Colorado, where he built a hotel on nearby Cameron

Pass in 1881. That is all that is known of him until he showed up in Yellowstone National Park at Mammoth Hot Springs in 1883, just in time to get in on the ground floor of the new park's early development. He tried unsuccessfully to get himself appointed Assistant Superintendent and, when that did not work, accepted the position of U.S. Marshall. A number of buildings at Mammoth that emerged during the period 1883-1885 period were ones associated with Clark's occupancy at the north base of Capitol Hill and at the west-center of what would become the U.S. Army's parade ground.[695]

Fascinatingly, Clark's presence in the park may have occurred because of Carroll T. Hobart, Vice President and General Manager of the Yellowstone National Park Improvement Company. Mr. Clark arrived at Mammoth at the beginning of the season of 1883 and, like so many others, initially lived in a tent. That much is clear, because on August 20, Carroll Hobart recorded that "for the last few months [Clark] has been constantly employed in this vicinity." Hobart himself may have brought Clark into the park to help YNPIC run the Mammoth hotel, because Clark had built and managed a hotel at Cameron Pass, Colorado for a couple of years. Regardless, Hobart was impressed enough with Clark to write him a recommendation letter—perhaps near the end of his seasonal employment—for the position of Assistant Park Superintendent. It no doubt occurred to the crafty Hobart that he and his company could benefit from having a friend on the government's staff. That did not happen, but Hobart's recommendation helped Clark secure the position in November of U.S. Marshall at Mammoth. He and Oscar Swanson were the first two such Marshalls ever hired for Yellowstone. Calling Clark a "worthy, temperate, straight forward man," Hobart gave Clark the endorsement he needed to secure the Marshall's job.[696]

Clark soon found that the position of U.S. Marshall did not afford him an adequate salary. In his day such a person's income depended on the numbers of violators he could apprehend with the fines they would pay, and these were not enough to provide a living. So, Clark moved on to become a park concessioner, secure in having a house to occupy, courtesy of Superintendent Patrick Conger, who was eager for any kind of law enforcement presence in the park.[697] One wonders whether Conger knew of the new Marshall's close relationship with Carroll Hobart, the YNPIC leader whom everyone seemed to despise. And not everyone agreed that Clark was a "worthy" and "temperate" man. Assistant Superintendent G.L. Henderson in August of 1884 told Secretary M.L. Joslyn of the Department of Interior that Clark was a rough man who "has repeatedly threatened to kill his enemies on the spot, drinks and gambles, is running a livery stable under the Supt's permit and is [in] every way unfit to be an arm of the law in any community."[698]

Henderson changed his mind about that later, after Clark prevailed for a few years, probably because the superintendent liked him. Conger "allowed him to build a small cabin exclusively for his own use" in 1883, but it was apparently not the same dwelling erected later on a leasehold immediately southwest of F. Jay Haynes's lease. In the summer of 1884, he began to establish a primitive transportation and freighting business under a verbal permit from Conger.[699]

It was clear to Clark that he needed more dependable income, so he began making plans to enter the transportation (and initially the hotel) business, intending to compete directly with George Wakefield and (un-realistically) YNPIC. In January, 1885 he applied to DOI for a lease of ground at Mammoth, and in February he asked specifically for a hotel lease. The Secretary, aware of such huge needs at Mammoth, issued the lease on February 17 for a site within eight hundred feet of the National Hotel—a mistake by DOI that would soon conflict with photographer F. Jay Haynes's already-existing lease.[700] Road engineer Dan Kingman soon refused to allow Clark use of the government sawmill to erect his buildings, so Clark turned to lumber outside the park.[701] The local newspaper report-ed in March that he had received a lease to build a small hotel at a location "500 feet south of the southeast corner of the National Hotel in the vicinity of McCartney Cave."[702] Clark had both hotel and livery (transportation) experience in his background, and he saw opportunity in both. His lease at Mammoth allowed him to run a primitive hotel of some type during the 1885 and 1886 seasons, but whether he did that in some limited form with a tent or other ramshackle building is not known for sure. Regardless, he was gradually learning that his hotel plans were going to cost more money than he could afford.

James Clark began focusing on his transportation plans while erecting a dwelling. In late April, the newspaper noted that Clark would "soon have a cottage completed for the use of his family." In May, thinking about the summer's looming business and eager to begin work on the new livery-stable,

Clark completed a bath house and outhouse near his cottage.[703] But it was becoming apparent that these three new buildings were on the wrong land at a point just southwest of where photographer F. Jay Haynes's house-and-studio had simultaneously been rising for less than two weeks. The Haynes construction was a painful indicator to James Clark that he had probably erected a building on someone else's lease through no fault of his own.

Clark's new cottage, bath house, and outhouse were located on the south bank of Clematis Creek in the meadow north of today's Harry Child Executive House (of course the creek was not there in Clark's day because it was later physically rerouted to this site, so Clark held a much drier site than the locality of today). His bath house was located a bit north of today's picnic area and just east of a small sinkhole, which is still surrounded by a fence. His cottage was a short distance to the northeast of that (among large trees that still exist today) and on the south side of the much larger sinkhole into which Clematis Creek flows today. These three buildings were shown in F. Jay Haynes photo H-1599 (1885).[704]

With his cottage, bath house, and outhouse now standing on the wrong land, Clark began to encounter the problems that other small businessmen were constantly experiencing in early Yellowstone—problems caused by his being caught among disagreements and misunderstandings of park superintendents, assistant superintendents, secretaries of Interior, and their assistants, plus many well-meaning but meddling advisors. Clark's lease-conflict had been noticed and geologist Arnold Hague, who was advising DOI, was involved.[705] Hague counseled Clark to build his upcoming livery-stable and blacksmith shop at another location, farther to the south at the base of Capitol Hill. Believing that Hague had credibility and needing "more convenient water facilities" anyway, Clark began the task.[706] Superintendent Robert Carpenter confirmed to Interior on May 12 that Clark was "building a blacksmith shop and a large stable."[707] Suddenly confused by Clark's construction at the same time that he himself was fighting a heightening ethics cloud from DOI, Superintendent Carpenter ordered the ceasing of construction at Clark's livery.[708] Clark, who had previously informed Carpenter of this work, was now frustrated at what he saw as a bumbling bureaucracy compounded by too many advisors and great geographical distance.

Clark's plight was relieved by the firing and replacement of Superintendent Carpenter on July 1. That left him unfettered to continue erecting his buildings even though he had no official change of lease. By July, he had completed his blacksmith shop east of the new, large livery stable (30 by 60 feet to hold fifty horses).[709] Both stood on the site occupied today by former Xanterra Operations Director Michael Keller's dwelling. Clark located it mostly on the site of Jack Haynes's later (1920) sales room—it was Mike Keller's house until 2010—but it also covered a bit of Keller's east yard and part of Keller's west yard, to which Frank Haynes's house-and-studio would later be moved. James Clark soon added an elongated carriage shed to the east of his barn, and this extended over the rest of Keller's east yard as well as over a bit of today's 1928 Haynes factory (farther east). F. Jay Haynes took photos of Clark's complex in 1885 and 1886.[710]

The local newspaper announced James Clark's new enterprise in June of 1885. "Clark's Town," stated a Mammoth-based columnist, "is at the foot of Capitol Hill, and contains five houses and a number of tents." The "five houses" included Clark's large barn, elongated carriage shed, blacksmith shop, dwelling, and bath house.[711]

Finally settled, Clark tried to run his business. Like everyone else of the era, he erected tents to accommodate any extra storage or housing that he

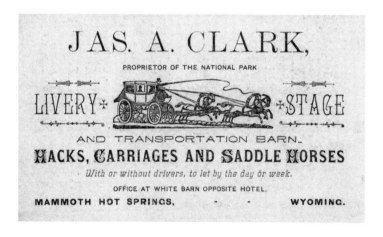

James A. Clark's business card from his stagecoaching days at Mammoth Hot Springs, and its verso, no date (1884-1887). *Jay C. Lyndes Family Collection.*

needed. He advertised his new business by erecting a large colorful sign on the front of his barn that read "J.A. Clark's Transportation and Livery."[712] He promoted his business on stationery that read eloquently as follows: "Office of J.A. Clark, Proprietor of National Park Hack and Express— Hacks, Carriages, and Saddle Horses with or without Drivers [and] Camping Outfits Furnished When Desired." G.L. Henderson touted Clark's "previously established reputation as a careful driver, a most accommodating guide, [and] a tough and tireless mountaineer."[713] Apparently Henderson's opinion of Clark had improved since the previous summer, and soon they became friends.

Clark rented saddle horses to visitors as well as wagon-drawn ones. A customer who patronized him in 1885 noted that to reach the barn he walked "across a patch of sagebrush a quarter of a mile wide to the stable of my newly found acquaintance" to procure a bucking horse. This customer told us something else about Clark's background when he stated that "the proprietor of the stable was from Colorado, where his vocation had been the catching of wild horses, not singly with the lasso, but in droves by 'corralling'."[714]

Sometime in late 1885, pressure climaxed on Clark to move his three earlier buildings to the base of Capitol Hill. Because his dwelling, bath house, and outhouse were on land that conflicted with F. Jay Haynes's lease as griped about by both Arnold Hague and Interior Agent W.H. Phillips, Clark either built new ones (in late 1885) at Capitol Hill or else simply moved the old ones to his new site. In fact, Clark probably built a new dwelling, for it is likely that it became the George Wakefield/Huntley/Nichols house as shown in photo YELL 14316 (1886).[715] We have this information from letters and maps dated April 28-29, November 7, and December 29, 1885, which described and depicted this dwelling and (second) bath house at points farther south. Other small Clark buildings at Capitol Hill that seem to have been short-lived were an ice house, root house, privy, and perhaps greenhouse located just west of his large barn, for these too showed on the maps.[716] Clark "removed his buildings from their original location" on Clematis Creek "to his leased ground" by November 7 for the newspaper reported it then and Superintendent Wear's map confirmed it.[717]

Although he still intended to build a hotel as late as November of 1885,[718] Clark was not able to get the money for it, and "after operating under his lease, in furnishing transportation for tourists during three seasons [1884-1886], he became financially embarrassed." Notwithstanding a "trip to the east" for reasons related to his company,[719] he found himself in too much debt to pay off his loans, so he decided to leave the entire business. He assigned his business to his creditors White, Friant, and Letellier in early 1887, but as late as May, Clark intended to run it himself. Indeed, G.L. Henderson noted on July 23 that "since last season we notice that J.A. Clark has added several fine coaches to his transportation outfit and is prepared to do a large business in that line."[720]

But this was too little too late for Clark. His assignees appear to have tried to run it for a while in 1887 before selling all his holdings to the Yellowstone Park Association and turning the lease and buildings over to stagecoach operator George Wakefield in June, 1888. While Clark's letters made it appear that he went out of business mainly due to his inability to pay his loans, park tour operator G.L. Henderson believed that Clark was a victim of the discriminatory practices of the Yellowstone Park Association and its Wakefield livery company.[721] Henderson went even further in his allegations, blaming Superintendent D.W. Wear personally for driving Clark into bankruptcy while in collusion with YNPIC and the railroad. Said Henderson: "James A. Clark had no capital, and lost nothing in his enterprise. The men who lost by that undertaking were his generous creditors and assignees, White, Friant, and Letellier, of Grand Rapids, Michigan."[722]

Although some documents have stated that park officials removed his barn, carriage shed, and blacksmith shop from beneath Capitol Hill in 1894 or 1895, photos YELL 88808 and 109623 show the barn and carriage shed still there in 1902, when it was removed by its later owners the Yellowstone Park Transportation Company.[723]

James Clark's story was one more instance of vain enterprise in early Yellowstone. Like everyone else in the area, Clark hard-scrabbled about, doing anything he could to make a living. Seeing the end of his business coming, he secured a paying contract to carry the mail between Mammoth and Cooke City beginning July 1, 1886. This put him in touch with the Soda Butte facilities built by former superintendents, so after leaving Mammoth he wrangled permission to settle there in government buildings, such that U.S. Army Captain Moses Harris had to oust him in early 1888.[724]

"J.A. Clark's Transportation and Livery" reads the sign on Clark's livery stable, shown here in 1886 and sporting Clark's recent paint job on both barn and sign. George Wakefield's later house (probably the J.A. Clark dwelling at the time of this photo) can be seen at right. Clark himself is probably sitting on the fourth horse from left. *F. Jay Haynes, H-1692, Montana Historical Society (and YELL 14316).*

Clark's friend Dick Randall left some information about what happened to James Clark for park photographer and researcher Jack Haynes's interview in 1955. Randall stated that Clark went mining at Cooke City from 1889 to 1891 (the newspapers showed him running wagon-transportation from Cooke to Mammoth), sold a prospect-site there for $2,000, divorced his wife in Livingston in 1891, and then moved to St. Paul to marry a woman named "Frankie" who "took his money." "He wore a broad-brimmed hat [and] was a fine specimen of a man," said Randall, "on the order of Buffalo Bill as to his dress...As far as I know Clark never returned to this part of the country."[725]

The Cottage Hotel Association: G.L. Henderson Establishes His Own Stagecoach Company and Makes Park Interpretation into a Significant Entity.

Mentioned earlier as an assistant superintendent and a Park tour guide encountered early by both the Bassett Brothers and George Wakefield, George Legg Henderson—who used the name "G.L." for much of his earlier life and definitely for all of his twenty-year career in Yellowstone—brought his large family of four daughters and one son to Mammoth Hot Springs in 1882, when he obtained the political-appointee job as an assistant Yellowstone superintendent and his daughter Barbara got the job as the park's post-mistress. Almost immediately, he fell in love with Yellowstone and began learning all he could about it, so that he could lead walking and riding tours of it, write newspaper columns about it, and give placenames to it. For his first several years in the park, he concentrated on these interpretive chores but also dabbled in maintenance, law enforcement, and administrative activities for the government, because all those duties fell instantly upon the Park's new assistant superintendents, who would eventually be increased to ten.

By 1884, he had become known in the region as one of the best tour-guides in the area and uniquely knowledgeable about the national park. That reputation would continue to grow. A tourist who encountered him on the walking-tour of Mammoth Hot Springs stated, "Dr. [Frederick] DeDolph and Mr. Henderson, one with his strong German accent and the other with his broad Scotch brogue, are the only persons who can give a true, graphic and glowing description of [Mammoth Springs] while they guide you along the dangerous paths. Mr. Henderson is the assistant superintendent of the park and from him, as well as from Dr. Dedolph who has been a frequent visitor to the springs, I derived much valuable information."[726]

On November 4, 1884, Henderson's political party, the Republicans—the party of the liberals in those days—lost the presidential election to the conservative Democratic party, and Henderson immediately believed that he would lose his political-patronage job sometime within a year. So, he and his family began looking toward making a different living by becoming park concessioners, that is, owning a hotel and a stagecoach company. In

This F. Jay Haynes portrait of G.L. Henderson, was taken on November 22, 1887 when Henderson was aged sixty, and it was later owned by his son Walter Henderson. *Henderson family scrapbook in possession of Susan Henderson Park of Washington state.*

early 1885, Henderson applied to the Department of Interior for a lease of land on which to build the hotel, and Interior granted that lease on March 3, 1885. The Henderson family's action proved prudent, for sure enough, the new Secretary of Interior fired him three months later (in early June), and G.L. Henderson immediately began to look for other work. Initially he helped his daughters Barbara and Jennie at the family's store and post office, sold lodging to park visitors in the family's tents and ramshackle buildings, went on a lecture tour by train where he gave speeches about the park, sold copies of his newspaper-guidebook *Yellowstone Park Manual and Guide*, and probably even worked for his friend, liveryman James A. Clark, as a tour guide or stage driver aboard Clark's stagecoaches.[727] "Professor Henderson is an easy, fluent talker," said a Wisconsin newspaperman, who heard him giving a speech a few years later.[728]

Under their company name of the Cottage Hotel Association, G.L. Henderson and his family began building the Cottage Hotel during the spring and summer of 1885, an activity that would allow Mr. Henderson to stay in the park for seventeen more years and some of his family for a decade beyond that. It would also allow him to run his own interpretive tours of Yellowstone with his own fleet of carriages and staff of tour guides. On August 1, the local newspaper proclaimed that G.L. Henderson "is about to begin the erection of a building." The question naturally arose as to where he obtained the money necessary for this venture, and one newspaper article stated that Henderson's congressman brother David supplied the funds.[729]

The finished hotel was planned to have seventy-five single and double rooms and could accommodate one hundred fifty guests at the rate of $2.50 per day. Initially, however, there were fewer rooms than that. (For example, by early 1886, there were only twenty completed rooms.)[730] The family kept good records of the supplies they used to build and equip the hotel, even drawing up a family (internal) contract for what they called the "Cottage Hotel Association." "The Cottage Hotel," wrote G.L. Henderson, "is intended to supply a long-felt want by parties who desire quiet, homelike and less expensive quarters."[731] The contract included G.L., his son Walter Henderson, and his daughters Helen L. Henderson, Barbara G. Henderson Swanson, and Mary Rosetta Henderson. Although the lease was in his son Walter's and daughter Helen's names, G.L. Henderson arguably played the most important role in the operation of the family's hotel, even being listed as manager on its stationery with his son as assistant manager. That status probably came to him because his brother David Henderson provided the money for the operation.[732]

G.L. Henderson's business card for the Cottage Hotel, no date, probably 1885. *Author's Collection.*

This author has told the full story of the Cottage Hotel in the book *"This Modern Saratoga of the Wilderness!": A History of Mammoth Hot Springs and Mammoth Village in Yellowstone National Park* (in press, 2022) as well as the story of Henderson's role as the "first national-park interpreter" in the book *Storytelling in Yellowstone* (2007), but the chronicle of Henderson's stagecoaching company has not been told until now.

At some point, no earlier than late 1885, G.L. Henderson purchased several stagecoaches, which he referred to as his "fine Quincy carriages." So far, we do not know how many there were because no enumeration is known, but the Hendersons eventually owned at least twelve of these in their fleet and probably at least two smaller wagons. The Quincy carriages were manufactured by E.M. Miller & Company, a stagecoach-maker head-quartered at Quincy, Illinois. If the accompanying (1887) photograph of G.L. Henderson and the McClintock party at Liberty Cap is any indication for us today, his carriages were nine-passenger ones (ten if a passenger was crowded onto the front seat with the driver). These coaches contained two seats and a third seat that (unfortunately) faced backwards, which was at-tached to the front-most seat.[733]

The family's plans to enter the stagecoaching business were apparently no more than a vague plan by the time that the first edition of his *Yellow-stone Park Manual and Guide* was published in June of 1885. In that guide-book-newspaper (p. 2), Henderson did not mention any stagecoaching business of his own and in fact ran an advertisement for J.A. Clark's line, "National Park Hack & Express," and also published his friend Elwood Hofer's advertisement for "Saddle and Pack Horses" to be rented to tourists from a business-site inside the Cottage Hotel. From these advertisements, it can be inferred that Henderson had not yet set up his stage-line. In fact, evidence in the family's handwritten ledger makes it clear that in early Oc-tober, Henderson agreed to work with E.O. Clark and Gardiner business-man C.B. Scott in the stage transportation business. Neither of these men is known to have owned a stage-line, but Henderson's friend James A. Clark did, so perhaps E.O. Clark was related to James Clark.[734]

Regardless, it appears likely that Henderson formally established his own stage-line early in 1886, because by early July he was accompanying a tour-group into the inner park including Lower Geyser Basin (for which he would have required wagon transportation), and he wrote about it. In

October, Henderson implied that he had continued this practice by noting
that he had made his seventeenth and eighteenth trips around the park, apparently tour-guiding for his own stagecoach line, if not (more likely) actually driving the coach as well.[735] Another indicator of his stage-line operating in 1886, occurred when he drove Dr. and Mrs. J.W. Joyce of Cincinnati
and a Miss Lambie of St. Paul to the Norris Geyser Basin, and got one of
his two horses stuck in the soft, hot mud of the Back Basin near Vixen and
Monarch geysers. Henderson would later tell the story in his 1888 guidebook, referring to the dangerous place of hot mud as the "Norris Sinks."[736]

As summer opened for 1887, G.L. Henderson started his stagecoach

The Cottage Hotel at Mammoth Hot Springs, Yellowstone National Park, no date (probably 1886-1890), showing two of what were
probably G.L. Henderson's passenger-wagons and one stagecoach,
called a "Quincy carriage." *YELL 31085, YNP Museum Collection.*

driving and interpretation by late May. He reported that he took "the first
tourist" of that year, English visitor Jabez Gilpin, on a park trip from May
26 to May 31, encountering many snowdrifts that "bore up the carriage."
They saw a cinnamon-colored black-bear at Willow Park, after which Henderson told us no more about the trip. Presumably he took the party across
Hayden Valley to Lower and Upper basins, for he did mention that the

jail on Nez Perce Creek had held no prisoners for all that summer, noting its door stood open all that time and that it bore a humorous sign reading "Rooms to let and boarders wanted."[737]

Also in 1887, G.L. Henderson stated that he had made the "ground rounds" of the Park three times by June 25. He seems again to have served as driver of the coach, rather than merely being a rider/tour-guide, this time chauffeuring a Mr. Millener and his two daughters Jennie and Winnie, and a Mr. and Mrs. Henry Gilbert, all from Michigan. The ladies gushed freely about the beauty of the canyon. In July, Henderson announced that he had purchased and added "a dozen or more leather-topped carriages" to the Cottage Hotel's assemblage of vehicles, no doubt his first venture into large-fleet stagecoaching. He also announced that his family's Cottage Hotel could now hold one hundred guests.[738] Writing about himself in third person, he had this to say concerning the Park in general:

> He still finds new and interesting objects even for him, where six years of careful investigation and indefatigable labor might lead one to suppose that all of Wonderland is discovered, digested and thoroughly understood. He assures us that such is not the case; that those who have visited it a second or third time go away convinced that it is the only field for amusement, recreation and study that can never be exhausted. That it is the cosmopolitan Park of parks, wonder of wonders, a world in itself that surpasses the wildest dreams of poet and philosopher.[739]

Even with these continuing new discoveries, Henderson was gradually learning that the monopoly possessed by the "Yellowstone Park Association Transportation" company—namely George Wakefield's operation of his stagecoaches again, under a verbal contract with YPA and its new owner Charles Gibson—was working against him. It seemed to Henderson that officials of YPA were hostile to him as a competitor and to his friend J.A. Clark who, like Henderson, ran a transportation line in the park.

Henderson, who had busily written columns since 1883 for the *Livingston Enterprise* and the *Bozeman Weekly Chronicle*, decided to omit his own name as writer of the column but otherwise to take on YPA in full, protest form. His long column, "Our Park Letter" in the *Enterprise* issue of July 23,

1887, carried the usual park news, including a commendation of Captain
Moses Harris for sending armed soldier-escorts with YPA's stagecoaches following a July 4 stage-robbery, but it also remonstrated against about YPA's
monopoly. He complained that the "two other lessees in the Park who are
conducting transportation lines," namely he and J.A. Clark, "have scarcely
turned a wheel this season" because of the monopoly. "For one gigantic
company," said Henderson, "to have control of all the business created by
the thousands of tourists who annually visit the Park is a serious and most
unjust state of affairs." He reviewed the history of the old Yellowstone National Park Improvement Company and its successor YPA, protested again
against the "double monopoly" suddenly being operated by the Northern
Pacific Railroad with regard to both hotels and transportation, and called
Yellowstone's situation "no longer a National Park, but instead an annex
to a railroad company." He acknowledged that tourists were now provided
with "cheaper and better facilities than ever before for making a tour of
Wonderland, but to the ruination of all others holding leases or attempting
to do business within." The culprit, said Henderson, was the $120 book-
ticket-with-coupons good for forty days that the railroad was then selling,
compared with a comparable cost of $146.40 that the other lessees were
forced to charge. This was only the beginning of G.L. Henderson's "war"
against the railroad monopolists, and he would continue to fight it for almost two more years. But it was a fight that he could not, and would not,
win, as his complete story in another book has made clear.[740]

We concentrate here only on G.L. Henderson's stagecoaching company,
which he was continuing to operate in conjunction with his family's Cottage Hotel Association. In September of 1887, he drove Dr. J.H. Mummery, "an eminent physician of London, England" who was also a chemist,
around the park for ten days in the interest of studying the science of hot
springs and geysers. As a result, Henderson wrote two articles for the *New
North-West* newspaper of Deer Lodge, Montana. In the first, the two men
categorized the types of travertine terraces as they saw them, and in the
second, Henderson reviewed some of the 1883 pronouncements of German geologist Dr. G.M. Von Rath, with whom Henderson had toured
Mammoth Hot Springs in 1883.[741] As might be expected from the science
of any era, some of it was right and some of it was incredibly wrong, such
as the deposition rates of the travertine terraces, which he and apparently

Mummery thought were the same slow rate as silicon dioxide. Indeed, they mistakenly thought the terraces were made of silica, rather than travertine.

Henderson's sixteenth and last trip through the park in 1887 occurred in late October. After seeing a "splendid elk" on the Yellowstone River at Hayden Valley, Henderson, driving only two passengers—Captain George L. Smith and Mrs. Smith of Nayatt, Rhode Island—took his usual route west on the old, Howard road to Lower Geyser Basin, which passed near his favorite lunch stop in the meadow just south of the small canyon at Glen Africa Basin. They viewed Bombshell Geyser, and then presumably went on to Lower and Upper Geyser Basins, but Henderson unfortunately told us no more about it.[742]

As January, 1888 arrived, G.L. Henderson found himself in debt for both a dozen new carriages and his family's existing financial-note on the Cottage Hotel. Because of these things, he also was continuing to worry about the threatening monopoly now solidly pressing on him by the Northern Pacific Railroad and the Yellowstone Park Association, and how it would manifest itself to his personal detriment when the tourist season opened on (the usual date) June 15. But as ever, reporting on Yellowstone's wonders and events took priority with him, so he put the worries out of his head and wrote about Excelsior Geyser's new eruptions, his memories of guiding former U.S. Senator Roscoe Conkling (1829-1888) around Mammoth in 1883 (Conkling, a national figure from New York, had died on April 18), and his purchase of fourteen new horses from Lawrence Swan of Emigrant to use on his upcoming summer tours.[743] On May 23, Henderson left Mammoth with the "third tourist party this season to visit Hell's Half Acre" (Excelsior Geyser), namely Mr. and Mrs. Wellington Payne of Lexington, Kentucky. The article continued as an advertisement: "Good entertainment is provided at the Cottage Hotel; for transportation, twelve splendid Miller carriages are already stocked with good animals[,] and large tourist parties can be sent out any day."[744]

Eruptions of the Excelsior Geyser were probably responsible this year for a substantial increase in the number of visitors to Yellowstone (from around 5,000 during the preceding two years to 6,000 this year), an increase that G.L. Henderson was already noticing. These eruptions were truly exciting to him and everyone else, because the great spoutings were sometimes three hundred feet tall and three hundred feet wide. Henderson sent an account of the nine eruptions that his party saw on May 25ᵗʰ and 26ᵗʰ to the *Helena Weekly Herald*, which got picked up by at least one other newspaper, the Deer Lodge *New North-West*:

> It threw a column of water 40 feet in diameter at the base to a height of 200 to 300 feet above the level of the earth, continuing a couple of minutes, but the eruption had a duration of 22 to 25 minutes, during which it threw smaller columns and overflowed into Fire Hole River, which raised four inches where it had a width of 100 feet. As the Excelsior eruptions are stated to have only continued [for] sixteen days in 1882, it is not probable it would continue this year much longer than the date at which Mr. Henderson reports.[745]

Fascinated with Excelsior's vast, extruded vapor-clouds and the amount of moisture that it exuded in both rain and humidity, Henderson "went out on some limbs" when he attributed its huge moisture outputs to extinguishing the previous year's forest fires in Yellowstone and estimating its discharge into Firehole River as thirty million gallons.[746] In an era when not as many people were as educated as today, Henderson seemed downright professorial to his tour-groups, and he was ever questing for new facts, as tour guides do today, even when they were merely his postulated stories that "stretched it."

On August 11, 1888, the *Livingston Enterprise* printers issued G.L. Henderson's second edition of his *Yellowstone Park Manual and Guide*. Now more interested in promoting his own stage-line than those of other stage-operators, his newspaper proclaimed on page one: "The Cottage Hotel's elegant Quincy carriages are waiting at Cinnabar to transport you to Mammoth Hot Springs in care of [nine] experienced guides, who after seeing that all are safely seated sing out 'All's right,' and away you go over hill and vale in absolute safety toward Wonderland."[747]

The new publication now comprised four full pages of text, instead of four-with-two-of-them-being-drawings-of-scenery, and reflected several more years of Henderson's personal explorations of park wonders, about which he had published many articles in numerous newspapers. His new publication sold for ten cents, as opposed to twenty-five cents for the 1885 edition, and contained numerous letters of comment and testimonial from visitors to whom he and his family had given satisfactory service at the Cottage Hotel. His second edition was issued much later in the summer than he would have preferred, but his publication and activities were filling a niche that was needed, less expensive for visitors, and dedicated to anti-monopoly sentiments, all completely logical considering that Henderson was well educated and more than a bit erudite. He had arguably already assumed the iconic position of first national-park interpreter[748] and would soon receive other titles of commendation from visitors and newspapers.

For example, visitor Bob Burdette, a national comedic writer of the day, testified: "We had Mrs. Helen Henderson Stuart to guide us over the terraces, and if G.L. Henderson, with his worldwide reputation of Park interpreter, can make them more interesting than Mrs. Stuart he is more wonderful than the grand terraces themselves." The local newspaper had already stated, "We have repeatedly said that Mr. Henderson knows more of the Park than any other man and now repeat it."[749] The editor added:

> If Prof. Hayden is the "Father of the Park" Mr. Henderson is its godfather for he has affixed characteristic and lasting names to every feature of interest in the Park and has done more than any other one person to inform the world of its peculiarly wonderful and beautiful features. He is no mere enthusiast but a firm believer that the Yellowstone Park will become the center of tourist travel in the western world.[750]

While virtually always beating the Yellowstone Park Association Stage Line in adulatory letters and general interpretive knowledge and probably in the commentary of its tour-guides, G.L. Henderson's Cottage Hotel Association had trouble competing for riders against the giant YPA monopoly that was supported by the Northern Pacific Railroad. Henderson fought back in every way that he could conceive: publishing his received, laudatory letters from customers; denouncing the monopoly in his newspaper columns; giving lectures and speeches about Yellowstone in Livingston and Bozeman and in towns east along the railroad all the way to St. Paul; and even personally occupying an office in Livingston for much of the summer of 1888 to meet and solicit arriving train-passengers. Interestingly, one of the men whom the Northern Pacific Railroad forcibly removed in August of this year from its platform at Livingston was Oscar Swanson, who was so-liciting customers for the Cottage Hotel. Swanson had been divorced more than two years earlier from G.L. Henderson's daughter Barbara, but it is clear from this that he had remained friends with the Henderson family, or at least with G.L. Henderson.[751]

Additionally, Henderson routinely took his tour-groups to see park fea-tures that he knew about from his personal explorations, features about which YPA guides had no knowledge. In Lower Geyser Basin, Henderson showed them the Great Fountain Geyser (his "Mammoth Geyser") and Hot Lake (his "Walpurgia Lake").[752] Crossing Hayden Valley, Henderson would show them the Glen Africa Basin with its spectacular Bombshell Geyser, a chance at seeing buffalo, and the strange Flutter-Wheel Spring, which made whirring noises. It appears that because of Henderson's excur-sions across Hayden Valley past Mary Lake 1886-1887, a route that had been abandoned by Wakefield's coaches and notwithstanding that Hender-son charged a bit more for this route, that YPA placed Larry Mathews at the "Trout Creek Lunch Station" to serve lunch to their guests and reinstated the same route for YPA stagecoaches, renamed "Yellowstone National Park Transportation Company," during 1888-1891.[753]

In denouncing the railroad's lack of morality, Henderson printed a letter from J.C. Knauss, a school principal in Pennsylvania, who was himself car-rying an adulatory letter for the Cottage Hotel Association when he arrived at Livingston. The principal told the story like this:

> "Buy your tickets here for Yellowstone Park," said a pallid-faced youth who smoked a cigar with that peculiar twirl that seemed to intimate his importance as a great railroad functionary. "I have a letter to Professor Henderson from Dr. S.G. Wagner of St. John's church, Allentown, Pa., and would like to see him before purchasing." "G.L. Henderson has left the Park," was the official reply, so I bought my ticket and learned later on that you were at the time in Livingston, fighting the battle for a Free Park, and my informant knew it but lied as truthfully and gracefully as he smoked his cigar. I cannot say that my faith in railroad morality was much increased.[754]

Henderson's guidebook told us much more about what happened on his tours and about the Northern Pacific Railroad's attempts to derail him in his attempts to sell his hotel rooms and stagecoach tickets. This was a negative, monopolistic development that seems to have peaked in 1888, as a number of letters that Henderson printed in his guidebook of that year attested. For example, on July 10, his patron George M. Clark of Higganum, Connecticut wrote to Henderson in a testimonial:

> It affords me pleasure to inform you that my trip through Wonderland under your direction was a perfect success. But I warn you that you have to deal with a most unscrupulous and unprincipled corporation who will stop at nothing to effect your ruin as it has done, I am told, with two Park lessees [Henry Klamer and James A. Clark] who attempted to conduct hotel and transportation business in the Park. As soon as the train left Livingston [Burt W.] Harmon, the solicitor on board the train, [mis]represented that the N.P.R.R. held all the privileges in the Park and that the Cottage Hotel Association was not even regarded as a competing line. He persuaded me and others to take passage to their hotel by the monopoly stage, assuring us that theirs were the only carriages running between Cinnabar and Mammoth Hot Springs. On arriving at Cinnabar, I was surprised to see three splendid Cottage Hotel carriages waiting for passengers. I also heard him trying to dissuade those whom you had previously engaged at Livingston from going to your hotel or by your line. This attempt to gobble up the National Park I regard as the most infamous steal that was ever perpetuated on this continent...[755]

Another satisfied patron stated, "I am glad I was persuaded to take your Hayden Valley and Mary's Lake route," which was "well worth the $20 more than the route ordinarily traveled." His party "saw game in East Fork Park," today's Nez Perce Creek, "and the most magnificent landscapes." A third customer, Mrs. T.S.C. Lowe, effervesced over Henderson's stagecoach drivers who were also tour guides:

> I was the first tourist of 1888 that visited Yellowstone Lake and
> but for your most competent and incomparable guide, Wm. C.
> Douglas, that feat, on account of bad roads, would have been
> impossible. Besides being able to converse with me in my moth-
> er tongue (French) he was most courteous, obliging and indefat-
> igable in his efforts to give us a complete revelation of the whole
> Park. I hardly know whether to give the first rank to Douglas
> among the Geysers or to Mrs. [Helen Henderson] Stuart among
> the Terraces…[756]

William Douglas might well have been the Park's first ever foreign-speaking
tour guide, but it seems certain that Henderson's daughter Helen Henderson Stuart was its first ever female stagecoach driver for the entire era 1880-
1916, because no other females are known to have been recorded anywhere
in a vast literature.

Henderson's attempts to elevate park interpretation and information on
the part of his own staff of walking tour-guides and stagecoach drivers were
extended and noteworthy, at a time long before there was genuine recognition of their importance in Yellowstone Park's educational mission (indeed,
the *only* educational mission at that time was Henderson's own attempts).
He mentioned that he had nine tour-guides on his staff, and an attempt
to discern their names has been mostly successful. Two of them—William
Douglas and Helen Henderson Stuart—have already been mentioned, but
there were others, all led by G.L. Henderson himself, along with Charles H.
Stuart (husband of Helen), Sylvester Radan, a Mr. Milligan (first name unknown), Henry Klamer, Walter J. Henderson, and possibly Mary Rosetta
Henderson (the last two being two others of G.L.'s children). It is likely that
most if not all these people served as both stagecoach drivers and walking
guides whenever the necessity arose. We cannot be certain that Mary Henderson was an actual tour guide and/or stage driver because she did not get
so mentioned in G.L.'s 1888 guidebook or in his newspaper columns, but
being a member of the family's Association, she probably was. Klamer was
indeed such a guide because he was mentioned in company advertising. He
had previously been forced to sell his interest in the Lower Geyser Basin's
Firehole Hotel, where G.L. Henderson had worked for a while, and so it
is likely that GLH gave Klamer a job at the Cottage Hotel, where Henry

Klamer's close proximity to Mary Henderson eventually resulted in the two of them being married a few years later.[757]

G.L. Henderson's long editorial in his guidebook explained what the Northern Pacific Railroad was attempting to do to him in (today's) Walmart-style, after one NPRR agent told him what they would do to him to boost the railroad's millions of dollars and "outweigh my gray hairs and our $30,000." Their agent stated:

> The Cottage Hotel Association cannot hope to secure any patronage from the [our] couponed tourists, for they are sent through the Park exactly as they are sent from station to station on its main lines. We shall exclude you from our platforms and

Mary Rosetta Henderson (Klamer) and Helen "Nellie" Lucretia Henderson (Stuart). They were the youngest (b. 1867) and oldest (b. 1854) of G.L. Henderson's children who went with him to Yellowstone. Helen was the only known female stagecoach driver in Yellowstone's history, and Mary might also have served in that capacity. *G.L. Henderson family scrapbook in possession of Susan Henderson Park, Washington state.*

cars so that you cannot reach the uncouponed, and if you cut prices so as to induce them to patronize you, we shall cut still lower, and if you carry your passengers by special routes where much more can be seen than by our routes, we shall follow you on such routes, so that the sword of Damocles hangs over you as sure as that monopolies have neither hearts nor consciences to pity you or protect the public, and when the Cottage Hotel Association has met its doom, as have James A. Clark at the Mammoth Hot Springs and Graham & Klamer at the Lower Geyser Basin, we can then make the public pay us for all we lose in destroying your association in [its] foolish effort to lower the hotel and transportation prices in the National Park. With the Northern Pacific railroad[,] it is a question of dividends; with the public it is one of freedom; and with the Cottage Hotel Association it is one of life or death.[758]

Just after this, when Henderson sold transportation tickets to uncouponed patrons at his office in Livingston's Albemarle Hotel, the owner of the hotel came to him to tell him that the NPRR was pressing him to evict Henderson from the hotel, or else this manager would be subjected to "trouble and loss." So, "I forthwith withdrew," wrote Henderson dispiritedly.

During this ugly competition, Henderson received many complimentary letters that would later aid him by bolstering his reputation as arguably the first, real national-park interpreter. "The past six days in Yellowstone Park," wrote Dr. O.H. Smith of New York City, "were the most delightful ones; your daughter, Mrs. H.H. Stuart, took myself and wife up to the Orange [Spring Mound] geyser in one of your magnificent Quincy carriages; such an accumulation of indescribable wonders with such a guide to point out their beauties, made our first day something like a bewildering dream."[759] Daniel Baker of New Jersey effervesced: "Having just returned from an eight days' tour through the Yellowstone National Park, under the guidance of Chas. H. Stuart of Mr. Henderson's corps of guides, I can most heartily say that I believe no object of interest was left unvisited or unexplained." W.H. Chase of Los Angeles and G.M. Clark of Connecticut declared:

We were taken to new and unfrequented paths by Charles Stuart in a splendid Quincy carriage drawn by a spirited pair of horses. Mr. Stuart took us to Pink Springs, where the famous Bombshell geyser surges within its iron-bound cage like an untamed tiger. Near there we overtook and meandered through a band of 37 elk, who looked upon us without alarm as we did at them with astonished delight...we are informed that G.L. Henderson has been at the baptism of more than three-fourths of the names by which the wonders of terrace, hoodoo, geyser and glen are known...We hope to see the day when the Cottage Hotel association shall have a hotel at every point of interest in the Park, with just such guides as Stuart, Klamer, Douglas, Milligan and others to make [the wonders] comprehensible and fascinating.[760]

Another tourist opined against the stage-drivers of the railroad's company, saying that "our driver, Mr. Sylvester Radan, was kind, attentive and efficient; our tour was one of continued pleasure; by comparison of notes with many tourists escorted by the other company, we found in every case that each day we had visited many important points of interest which they missed by being hurried through by guides whose only study seemed to be the driving of the thundering stages."[761]

Notwithstanding these positive letters from his customers, Henderson sustained a tough summer financially (1888) at the hands of YPA and its railroad sponsors. In January, Henderson stated that he felt like a "miner's tom cat did when its master left it beside a burning fuse that ultimately tore up several tons of gold quartz and sent the cat up into the air, end over end, like a kite caught in a cyclone; the cat lived but never went back into the blasting business." "I lived, too," declared Henderson, "but never thought I would go back into the anti-monopoly business again, to fight for a free Park and fair play all around; but I will." It was his statement of intending to stand his ground at Cottage Hotel. But it was a bit premature—too easy to say and write in winter when the snow was on the ground at Mammoth and no stagecoaches were running.[762]

In early February, Henderson wrote what might have been his parting shot at the NP Railroad and its monopolists and did it in such a way as to make it subtle enough for most readers to think that it referred only to his report on geysers at Norris Geyser Basin. Understandably he sent the letter to the *Helena Weekly Herald*, way "out of town," probably to maximize the chances that no one from YPA would see it:

> There is here a curious analogy between this geyser world and our human [one]. When one becomes feeble from age or has been undermined and one's vitalizing forces drained, another springs up to fill the void. The sublime aphorism of Pascal is typified here: 'That the entire succession of generations must be regarded as one man, always living, incessantly learning, never dying'."[763]

Henderson was referring here to his reporting that Excelsior Geyser had greatly declined, and that Monarch Geyser had quit entirely, probably, he surmised, by having its activity stolen by Steamboat (his "Double Crater") Geyser. But he was no doubt also creating a symbolic reference to allude to himself and his Cottage Hotel Association as having been "undermined" and their "vitalizing forces drained," as well as to himself in a new iteration as springing up "to fill the void" and as "always learning, incessantly living, [and] never dying."

In mid-February, Henderson left Mammoth on a trip to the east to lobby congress, as so many park people did then, pushing for the Cinnabar & Cooke Railroad to be allowed to lay iron through Yellowstone Park to Cooke City. He shook hands there with U.S. Secretary of State James G. Blaine. This was part of the effort in the aid of miners that would continue into the mid-1890s and would fail. The local newspaper also reported that it was rumored that Yellowstone Park Association had made an offer to Henderson to buy out his hotel and transportation franchise.[764]

For the moment, his family's pending sale of their Cottage Hotel Association was only a rumor. But in early May, G.L. Henderson dropped hints in a newspaper column to the "numerous friends whom I have won during the eight years that it has been my privilege to act as guide, and in some degree to act as interpreter," that he and his family might be selling the Cottage Hotel. On May 4, Henderson's son Walter let word of the sale slip from his lips, and a few days later, he, his father, and Henry Klamer took off on a train-trip to the northwest, perhaps using some of the sale-proceeds. In addition to sightsee-ing, Henderson was scheduled to give a Yellowstone lecture in Salem, Oregon, and that might have been the main reason for the trip.[765]

G.L. Henderson made the long announcement of his family's sale of the Cottage Hotel and his own future plans in an article that the *Living-ston Enterprise* published on May 11. Surprisingly, he was joining the very corporate syndicate against whom he had long protested. The reason was simple: That company had made him an offer he could not refuse, namely a chance to become the first paid, national-park interpreter in any park who could also be officially called "interpreter." The company's president, "Mr. Charles Gibson," declared Henderson, "frequently expressed the desire to retain the services of your correspondent and his family," by hiring Mr. Henderson as tour guide and company lobbyist. Henderson explained that his appointment "will enable me to devote more time to the most interest-ing part of what is becoming more and more a necessity in a territory so vast and among marvels so varied as that to be found in Yellowstone Park, [namely] that of interesting the visitor so that he may…comprehend the phenomena that [make] it the acknowledged wonderland of the world."[766]

As for the actual details of the Henderson family's sale of their hotel and stagecoach line for $30,000 to the Yellowstone Park Association, we have the statement of Charles Gibson, Vice President and General Manager of YPA, at the time he testified in front of congress three years later:

> …when the new leases were made by [Secretary of Interior John Noble] in 1889 the Association very shortly afterwards, I think in about a month, bought out the entire outfit and equipment, consisting of horses, stages, carriages[,] harness[es], and all other necessary appurtenances then owned by Mr. G.L Henderson, and with which he carried on the transportation business for a number of years in the park, and which was sufficient for about one-third of the entire [transportation] business of the park. The previous year it carried about one-third of the business during that season…[767]

What Henderson did was to include a clause in his sale-contract, which was agreed to by YPA, that put him on the railroad's payroll—$150 per month plus expenses—as a congressional lobbyist for YPA. He would be working on Yellowstone Park matters during sessions of Congress in Washington, DC. When Congress was not in session, he would return to the Park and "entertain tourists at the Y.P.A. Hotels during the season, thus extending a clearer knowledge of the Park." That quotation from a Henderson letter makes it clear that YPA, the Park's largest concessioner, hired him specifically into an interpretive position, the first such position ever to exist in any national park. At the same time, his son and daughters and their spouses would remain in Yellowstone to run the post office and a curio shop.[768]

Henderson would produce accomplishments in Washington. He would claim to have successfully lobbied "by determined and persistent efforts" through three sessions of Congress to obtain the total sum of $200,000 for roads and bridges in Yellowstone. He would also secure the first "generous" park appropriations of $75,000 for the years 1890 and 1891.[769]

But mostly Henderson could now spend full time in the pursuit of interpreting Yellowstone for YPA, which consisted of the numerous activities around which he continued to center his life. These included writing his newspaper columns and letters, giving speaking-tours of the park for that main company (both walking tours and driving or riding along on coaches), and delivering formal speeches to groups of visitors at Mammoth Hot Springs Hotel and in other regional locations. Interpreting Yellowstone also included the monitoring of geysers and hot springs to talk about them, and as before, he took to that activity with relish. He spent July in this pursuit, and on August 1, the *Helena Weekly Herald* published his article on the subject, carrying a long title as was customary in the nineteenth century: "World of Wonders—The National Park Revisited—Geyser Transformations and Other Changes—Interesting Letter from Prof. Henderson an Accepted Wonderland Authority."[770] On August 5, Henderson submitted one of his usual columns to the *Livingston Enterprise* entitled "Yellowstone Park Paragraphs," in which he discussed the debate between visitors and park officials over the collecting of thermal and other geological specimens, a debate that had to do with actual preservation in Yellowstone.[771] He followed it up with the August 29 publication of a column in the *Helena Weekly Herald* entitled "The National Park—Its Protection Against Vandalism—Capt. Boutelle's Administration Commenced," which also noted the arrival of the park's new

superintendent, F.A. Boutelle. About the U.S. Army's vigilance in protecting the park, one of the visitors whom Henderson interviewed, a doctor at the state university of New Hampshire, stated: "The object [of the
army's preservation-policy] has been to restrain and stamp out game-kill-
ing, [geyser] cone-breaking, [and] forest-burning in which the military
has succeeded most admirably where a too small and utterly inadequate
civil force had failed."[772] Thus, with these and other writings, Henderson
probably influenced Yellowstone's ultimate policy of preservation (which
remains with the Park today) by bringing the elements in that discussion
to the attention of both park officials and the visiting public.

For the next sixteen years, until his death in 1905, G.L Henderson continued to leave a noteworthy trail in history—with his writings, his speeches, and his personally-conducted Yellowstone tours, all in pursuit of his
goal of establishing interpretation in the national park. In what remains his
most important statement of the philosophy of park interpretation—which
he used upon all visitors whom he continued to personally guide and which
he had formerly used upon his staff of stagecoaching-guides in personally
training them—Henderson enthused:

> When I find intelligent and appreciative visitors, I give my whole
> soul to the subject, just as histrionic artists, musicians, or pulpit
> orators do. The proper presentation of the park is a fine art. Many
> will visit it but once in a lifetime. It is expensive to make the visit
> once. How important, then, that there should be men capable of
> so presenting it as to make it the one great event of a life.[773]

In using the word "men" here, G.L. Henderson would probably have been
the first to state that the word was not gender specific and referred to wom-
en, for as mentioned, he hired the first known female interpreter and stagecoach driver in Yellowstone—his daughter Helen Henderson (Mrs. H.H.)
Stuart—at his Cottage Hotel.

And so, he was moving into what was arguably the final stage of his life.
There he began serving as a kind of "professor emeritus" to a good number
of eager and persevering Yellowstone fans, the likes of whom have existed in
every time-era since the Park was established—employees and ever-present
visitors, scientists who continued to correspond with him, avid attendees

at his formal speeches, and the continuing readers and fans of his letters, booklets, and newspaper columns.

It must have been a source of great comfort to G.L. Henderson for the rest of his life (1889 through most of 1905) to know—at the end of his hotel-and-stage-line dreams, and having used YPA to make himself into the first fulltime, paid interpreter in any national park—that he had "played his cards" extremely well.

G.L. Henderson, left, shakes hands with one of his visitors in front of one of his "fine Quincy carriages," as he talks to the group about the park's wonders. This was the William McClintock party of Ohio in 1887. *YELL 693, YNP photo archives.*

CHAPTER ELEVEN

"It was the Rendezvous for All Sorts of Bad Characters."

Charles Gibson and the Yellowstone Park Association, 1886-1890

"When the association entered the park[,] it was the rendezvous for all sorts of bad characters. Its national reputation was bad. No pure woman could dare go there unless well protected. Men had to go armed to protect themselves. Guides were employed at large expenses to tourists. The park is as large as the state of Connecticut, and yet stagecoaches were the only news commu- nications for the Government or individuals."—Charles Gibson to Secretary of Interior John Noble, no date [late 1888 or early 1889], in McRae, "Inquiry," p. 19.

We now return to George W. Wakefield, the Yellowstone Park Associ- ation, and YPA's new owner and on-site manager Charles Gibson. Having purchased the assets of the old Yellowstone National Park Improvement Company for $28,000 in Evanston, Wyoming, Charles Taylor Gibson (1825-1899)[774] burst into Yellowstone Park in a rush, in April of 1886. A lawyer from St. Louis, he was sixty-one years old and suddenly President of the new Yellowstone Park Association, which included six other directors, but he was the real boss. Photos from that time showed him as a thin, gray- haired man with a white beard and a sharp nose, and he was in a hurry to make certain that his new company was doing everything it needed to do to keep its recently-issued lease.[775] Gibson immediately began bragging to the newspapers that he would erect "six new hotels" in the park,[776] but he would soon discover that those projects would take more years and more money than he imagined. Regardless of that bluster, Gibson's presence would soon improve almost everything for liveryman George Wakefield.

Only weeks later (in mid-May), Wakefield left his winter home in Bozeman and arrived in Livingston to begin preparations for the summer season of travel.[777] He wasted no time in heading south to the Park, where he met his new partner F. Jay Haynes. Haynes would not last long as a partner, being stretched thin both temporally and monetarily, and he would sell his portion of the operation back to Wakefield in August.[778] But time would make it clear that Haynes remained interested in Park transportation. Twelve years later he would start his own Monida & Yellowstone Stage Company and twenty-nine years later he would establish the Cody and Sylvan Pass Motor Company. For the moment, however, Haynes and Wakefield were working in tandem for Charles Gibson.

Charles Taylor Gibson (1825-1899), no date. *Author's collection.*

"When I went to the park," Mr. Gibson later told Congress, "I found that nearly all the [transportation] business was done by Wakefield and Haynes, Wakefield's principal man." Park Superintendent David Wear

highly recommended Wakefield to Gibson, so Gibson hired him to continue running stagecoaches—what Wakefield had already been doing for three
years. Gibson was pressed to get that done, because there was a huge party
of tourists booked into the park in the summer of 1886, with predictions of
about eight or nine hundred members of the Grand Army of the Republic,
a fraternal organization of Union Civil War veterans. Two hundred of them
arrived in fifteen train-cars on August 14, and more were coming.[779]

Wakefield and the hotels were overwhelmed, but Gibson told both his
hotel and his stage people to either serve these visitors, or he would find
someone who could. "The association and I wanted a man [whom] I could
hold responsible," explained Gibson in trying to sound like he was fixing
things, "and whom I could order as I pleased." That claim would come
back to haunt both him and Wakefield five years later, because even though
YPA eventually (1889) bought Wakefield and his equipment out (and that
included a controlling interest in Transportation), Gibson kept in place the
very loose arrangements that YNPIC had set up to make George Wakefield
their agent who ran all transportation. Gibson also arranged for YPA to
take a percentage of Wakefield's earnings, namely fifteen percent—a hefty
chunk. Meanwhile Wakefield weathered the G.A.R. storm well, moving
four hundred people through the park in one day, an accomplishment that
was so impressive it made the local newspaper.[780]

Facing his lease's requirement that he build large hotels in a wilderness
area containing primitive roads or no roads, Charles Gibson was discovering that he could not simultaneously run stagecoaches himself. "It was too
much," he stated later, "to supervise the transportation in addition to all
that," which set the stage for his tacit approval of continuing George Wakefield's verbal contract. Gibson did not believe "that service could be well
performed in that way, and for that reason," he later explained, "Wakefield
was not placed under the orders of [E.C.] Waters." Ella C. Waters, the head
of Gibson's hotels in Yellowstone, was an incredibly difficult person who
made people angry everywhere he went, so Wakefield was lucky at this moment to be set free of Waters. Still, both men strove to carry out Gibson's
strict orders to "accommodate each other" and to operate the business "in
as good a way as possible."[781]

It is not known exactly when George Wakefield met his new boss,
Charles Gibson. Gibson was doing nothing new with Wakefield, merely

keeping him in place to run stagecoaches, but regardless, Wakefield quickly encountered Gibson's new rules for the Yellowstone Park Association. The new president ordered that all tickets marked with Wakefield's name be destroyed and YPA tickets substituted for them; he ordered YPA's name painted on Wakefield's coaches ("Yellowstone Park Association Transportation Company" but the tickets, at least in 1887, said "Yellowstone Park Association Stage Line"), a decree that was not always carried out; he gave orders against drunkenness, lewdness, and extortion by stage-drivers; and he directed J.H. Dean, his head of hotels, to require all drivers and other YPA employees to wear YPA badges. Drivers wore the badges on their hats.[782]

Following "a grand dinner and dance" at Mammoth Hot Springs Hotel, Wakefield began running the fourth year of his stagecoach operation on June 16, 1886. Having turned fifty years old the preceding October, he was feeling his age but determined to do this work that he loved in the place that he loved. He was no doubt relieved to see that for the first time in the park's history, tent-hotels for tourists were largely gone and buildings, crude though some of them were, had taken their place. And it must have been a relief to him to see or hear that Gibson's company had begun erecting telephone lines in the park to connect its remote hotels with the Mammoth Hot Springs Hotel.[783]

Park roads were another large consideration for Gibson. When he arrived in Yellowstone in early 1886, he was immediately faced with continuing a road-building project that had been started the preceding autumn by his predecessor, the YNPIC. Concessioners did not usually build roads in the park; that was the government's job. But in this case the (previous) concessioner needed to move building materials from Norris to Canyon to begin work on the required new Canyon hotel, and the government was dragging its feet on building a road, or so it seemed to Gibson. Thus, he embraced that ongoing concessioner road project from the moment he arrived to get the Canyon Hotel, and eventually several of his other hotels, built.

Here's how the project began. In 1885, the Yellowstone National Park Improvement Company was under pressure by means of a threatened revocation of its lease to get a hotel built at the Grand Canyon of the Yellowstone River, but the problem was that there was yet no road between Norris Geyser Basin and Canyon. Instead, freight and equipment wagons had to take the long way around—proceed south of Norris to Lower Geyser Basin's Nez Perce Creek and turn east across Mary Mountain through Hayden Valley and then turn north along Yellowstone River to Cascade Creek, the standard tourist-route prior to 1886. This was fifty miles out of the way for supplies and work-crews who were coming south from Cinnabar, Gardiner, and Mammoth.

This old road was adequate to reach the primitive, first Canyon Hotel from the south, but it was a long way to go from the north, and a shorter route was needed. (Eventually the shorter route would be needed anyway, for the building of the second hotel, 1889-1891, plus a bridge to get travelers back and forth across the Cascade Creek Canyon.) So, Carroll Hobart of YNPIC ordered his workmen in the fall of 1885 to start building the company's own road from Norris to Canyon, a road that through time became known as the Norris/Canyon "cutoff" road, and it went to the spot on the south side of Cascade Creek, where Gibson erected the prefab hotel for $6,000.[784] Government road-engineer Dan Kingman was still working on other projects in 1885, and would not start on this one until 1886.[785] Even then, government fiscal-year rules for allocations guaranteed that Kingman's start on the project would be late in the summer, long after Gibson needed the road in order to prepare his hotel in time for the summer of 1886 (opening on June 15) and thus avoid what he perceived to be a threatened revocation of his lease.[786] Thus Hobart began the road in the fall of 1885, which by the next spring would be called "Gibson's Road." And of course, every road in the park would be used for stagecoaching.

"The park is as large as the state of Connecticut," remembered Gibson three years later from when he first arrived in Yellowstone, "and yet stagecoaches were the only news communications for the Government or individuals." There were no telephones in the park, so Gibson initiated the stretching of telephone lines and installing telephones, as his lease appears to have required. A newspaper reporter called "W.H.R." saw the new lines going in that summer. On October 8, 1886, the Department of Interior asked Gibson whether he had in fact complied with the government's requirements to complete hotels at Norris and Canyon and install "telegraph or telephones by August 1."[787]

According to Gibson, the government refused to settle the company's titles to the land or leases (for Canyon, Mammoth, and Lower Geyser Basin) but the company had to continue spending money to build hotels for the years 1886-1888 anyway.[788] It was the beginning of a longer, more involved story for Gibson that would last for at least seven years.

Meanwhile, George Wakefield was gearing up for operating his stagecoaches during the summer of 1886. At Mammoth, Wakefield's family was settled and happy. His daughter Libbie Wakefield (born 1869) was later remembered by many park people, including renowned cowboy and stagecoach driver "Pretty" Dick Randall (who also lived there), as the "belle of Yellowstone" or at least the "belle of Mammoth," where she passed her teenage-years in the late 1880s. Dick Randall had been just on the threshold of twenty-one years old when he arrived in the Park in 1885, straight from "cowboying" on the prairies of eastern Montana. He worked for George Wakefield first as a night-herder, but graduated to stagecoach driver by 1887, and by which time he was smitten with "Libbie." Conversely, many area women were smitten by Mr. "Pretty" Dick Randall, such as the Ritchie sisters in Gardiner—Edith and Lena Ritchie—too young though they were. Edith reported that Lena or else one of Edith's friends saw Randall in their father's hotel and restaurant in Gardiner and said, "Oh, Edith, come quickly! You've got to see the prettiest man I've ever seen!" No doubt Randall had seen photographer F. Jay Haynes's photo-portrait of Libbie Wakefield and her mother Margaret taken in 1886 when Libbie was seventeen years old, and she later married Dr. S.F. Way, another of Wakefield's stage drivers.[789]

George Wakefield had met his new boss Charles Gibson by early in that summer season, and the first time they met might even have been at this very moment. Wakefield at times could be a bit of a rough customer, but in Montana and the American West, he was not alone in that characterization. According to the *Livingston Enterprise*, he was standing on the railroad platform at Cinnabar one day in July 1886 with H.C. Davis of the NPRR and President Charles Gibson. A tourist from Britain approached them to ask about a murder case then occurring in eastern Montana Territory:

> "And what will they do with the murderer?" inquired the English lord.
>
> "Let him go," answered Mr. Wakefield.
>
> "Is that justice in this country?" asked Johnnie Bull, as his protruding eyes told of his surprise.
>
> "Justice: [it's] the best thing they could do. He only killed one

man. If he had killed two or three or half-a-dozen, they might
have lynched him, but he only killed one. Men are cheap now.
Before the railroad came in and men were scarce, a man would
be strung up for taking another man's life, but now that the
railroad has come in men are only worth $12 apiece or $12.50
and it costs more to hang a man than he is worth."

The Englishman was dumbfounded while Davis got the
lockjaw trying to keep from smiling.[790]

President Gibson must have smiled too. This was no doubt a case of rib-
bing a foreign tourist to terrify him about supposed violence in Montana
and the American West in general, but it also exhibited a bit about George
Wakefield's rough nature.

Another example occurred in September, when Wakefield got into
fisticuffs with a journalist at Livingston. The story was funny, but it
must also have been embarrassing for Wakefield. James E. Harvie was a
newspaperman who had worked as a correspondent "for several eastern"
newspapers, and he was then working as an editorialist at the *Livingston
Enterprise*. From Livingston, he sent a news item to those papers, which
was "not very complimentary" to Wakefield's stage company. Upon
reading it, Wakefield told his fellow train passengers that he was going to
ride the train to Livingston and "lick" Harvie. Then, as now, newspaper
editors were not always held in high esteem, so a number of passengers
got off the train and followed Wakefield to the *Enterprise* office. There
Wakefield, who weighed 180 pounds to Harvie's much lighter and shorter
build, satisfied himself that he was confronting the real James Harvie and
then punched him in the mouth. Harvie fended off some other blows
and landed a right on Wakefield's cheek, which opened a gash. Wakefield
rushed at Harvie, who picked Wakefield up and threw him onto his back.
Wakefield walked away groaning and complaining that he was winded
and injured. Harvie stood ready for more, but the train passengers who
had been watching the fray decided that they had had enough too. All
departed, leaving Harvie on the street by himself.[791]

Wakefield probably got off lucky, because Harvie was athletic and tough,
and he too was bit of a troublemaker. Earlier that summer after working on
the St. Paul *Daily Globe*, James Harvie migrated to Miles City, Montana,

only to be forcibly run out of that town by jealous cowboys who did not like the way he danced with "their" girlfriends. So, he returned to St. Paul, only to soon decide that he wanted to go right back to Montana. He was working on the *Livingston Enterprise* in September, when he and Wakefield got into it. By October, he was trying to start another newspaper in Montana, and may have gotten himself into trouble in whatever town that was, because the following year he was in San Francisco, working there as a newspaperman.[792] George Wakefield must have hoped that his new boss Charles Gibson did not find out about his street fight in Livingston with James Harvie.

In addition to Charles Gibson, there were other new bosses who arrived in Yellowstone in 1886, a troop (about sixty men) of United States Army officers and soldiers, who took over the park's administration on August 17. Initially, Captain Moses Harris, the park's new Superintendent, ignored George Wakefield's operation because he had too much else to do in orienting himself and his men and overseeing Gibson's hotel concessioners. Besides which, the summer was already rolling. Harris eventually became puzzled by Wakefield's seeming lack of a contract with the Department of the Interior, but in 1887, he again let the matter slide until late that year. By that time, Wakefield had proved himself in Harris's eyes so much that the Acting Superintendent wrote the following positive comments:

> He has invested a considerable sum of money in coaches and carriages built especially for Park use always constructed as to enable the visitor to enjoy the scenery of the Park while riding through it with comfort and convenience. His drivers have always been selected with great care and have been kept in an admirable state of discipline. Since I have been in the Park[,] they have always scrupulously observed the regulations of the Park and the orders of the Superintendent. From the many hundreds of visitors who have availed themselves of the transportation facilities provided by Mr. Wakefield, I have heard no complaints, and many words of praise and commendation.[793]

Harris also recommended that Wakefield be given a formal contract and that he should report to the Department of the Interior rather than to the

Yellowstone Park Association.[794] But this contract suggestion would not be implemented until 1892—too late for honorable results.

Both Wakefield and his boss Charles Gibson would come to regret the problems associated with this lack of a formal contract. Having been worried through the years that his verbal contract might prove not to be enough, Wakefield tried on several occasions to obtain a formal contract. In explaining this, President Gibson told the Secretary of Interior the following:

> Mr. Wakefield entered the park when it first opened, under an agreement with the first lessee to do the transportation business, and he has kept it up ever since. No lease was ever made to him directly, but the representatives of the Department always considered that an employment by the lessee, having the right, was a sufficient authority to Wakefield, until the summer before last [1887], when Capt. Harris raised the question as to his right without a lease from the Government, he being also under the impression that Wakefield had no agreement with the association. When I (President Gibson) received his communication I informed him that Wakefield was acting for the association and under its control…Wakefield, however, made application for leases about three years ago, but his application was denied, as I was informed for the reason that the Department had concluded that it had no power under the act of Congress to grant a lease for transportation pure and simple [unless he also erected hotels]…In 1884[,] Mr. Hoffman applied for such a lease, and it was refused by Secretary Teller for the same reason. Wakefield then purchased a lease made to [James A.] Clarke, on which a hotel had already been erected, and applied for the approval of the assignment to him, and that the right of transportation be given him, but he has never been able to obtain any action of the Department thereon. No reason, so far as I know, has been given for not approving the assignment.[795]

Thus, in attempting for years to "do right" by Interior with regard to his "lease," George Wakefield was "damned if he did and damned if he didn't." There was no course of action that did not have a drawback. He tried at least twice to obtain such a lease, but Interior told him they were prohibited by law from granting it, unless he (Wakefield) also built hotels. Obviously, he could not build hotels; he did not have the funds and regardless, would not have been given a lease even if he had the money, because the company already possessed this right of hotels. In turn, he felt that if he did not obtain such a lease, it might come back to haunt him. And too, the company was indicating to him that he did not need to build hotels and that his verbal lease would be adequate. He was truly "between a rock and a hard place." None of this was Wakefield's fault, but he feared, as usual, that he would later be made to suffer for it. Unable to do anything about it, he put it out of his head and ran his stagecoaches.

With the summer of 1886 over, George Wakefield moved his livery operation to Livingston for the winter, running the daily stagecoach to Mammoth Hot Springs and trying to find other ways to finance himself through the winter. Always enterprising, he also opened a shop in Bozeman called the "Bozeman Electric Company" that sold electric-lighting appliances—pretty optimistic for Montana Territory where electricity would not really get a foothold for another twenty-five years. Apparently, it was only a short-term investment, for he sold it in April. He also purchased a barn and several lots there.[796] And there was evidence that Wakefield hired himself out that winter to Surveyor S. Deutch of Livingston to help Mr. Deutch survey the new hotel site at Norris Geyser Basin, which was begun in construction that autumn.[797] Like generations of many later park employees, Wakefield was merely finding ways to get through the winter so that he could enjoy another summer in Yellowstone. According to a newspaper editor who met him a bit later, Wakefield owned two hotels in Bozeman and one or more ranches, plus several stage routes, and, according to one undocumented statement, had "amassed a good fortune" by 1888. So, in these respects, Wakefield was better fixed than most other seasonal park employees.

In late May of 1887, the snow in Yellowstone Park remained three to seven feet deep, such that observers estimated that travel would not be possible "for some weeks." During an era when there was no snow-removal equipment, Wakefield as usual began making serious preparations for the summer in June, rehiring W.M. Maughn as his Livingston agent and hiring John S. Craig as a painter to "touch up the wagons." Wakefield "now has in transit," said the *Livingston Enterprise*, "nearly $5000 worth of buggies, carriages, etc. for use in the National Park the coming season."[798]

His summer was suddenly interrupted, when two highwaymen robbed one of his stagecoaches. The affair was a bit of a fiasco, with one press report describing it as "bungling and amateurish." Late in the evening of July 4, 1887, two masked men stepped out from behind "Split Rock" (in Gardner Canyon, across Gardner River southwest from Eagle Nest Rock, where the road used to bridge the stream), pointed guns at Thea Hamm,[799] who was driving Wakefield's stagecoach "Bighorn" toward Mammoth, and escaped with sixteen dollars, the equivalent of $438.69 in 2021.[800] According to a passenger, one of the highwaymen shouted "Halt and dismount!" while the other one held his gun on the passengers. A Mr. Kirkbride, riding inside, confessed that "the whole performance was such a surprise and so quickly done that time was not given to us to take in the situation and get a correct impression of the parties committing the assault."[801] The robbers forced the passengers—two men and three ladies—out of the stage where they held up their hands and were searched for valuables, and one account claimed that the brigands missed the $800 in the pocket of one of the men.[802] Meanwhile one of the robbers accidentally discharged his gun, scaring the passengers, powder-burning two of them, and causing the other robber to trip over sagebrush and lose his pistol.[803] The following day George Wakefield and driver Thea Hamm rode horses to the site to look for evidence. There they saw William James supposedly fishing but really looking for his lost pistol, and Wakefield asked James if he had heard about the robbery. James said he thought it was all a joke. Meanwhile the two horses were nervous and nickering, and one of them almost stepped on the pistol, so James had to wait until that evening to go back and recover it.[804] But James's big mouth would eventually become a factor that tipped off Wakefield and the authorities.

A distinctive coin carried by stage-passenger John Lacey—soon to become an Iowa congressman—and found later on one of the robbers, also helped to identify the guilty parties. In November, Livingston's Sheriff Templeton arrested Charles Higgenbotham[805] at nearby Horr, Montana for the robbery and noted that park soldiers had already arrested William James. James, who had also been arrested earlier in the park for poaching, fingered himself by shooting off his mouth to two of his friends that "I am the little son-of-a-bitch that held up that stage," and those two men told the authorities. Higgenbotham during the previous year had driven a stage for Wakefield between Cinnabar and Mammoth, while James too was briefly a stage-driver for Wakefield. George Wakefield had fired both men.[806]

Charged with highway robbery and larceny, the two pled guilty and were sentenced to one year in prison and a $1,000-fine apiece.[807] So ended the affair.

Speaking of the stage-driver Charley Higgenbotham, he was also the source of one of Yellowstone's most famous tall-tales told by stage-drivers, the one involving present Chinese Spring, then called "Chinaman Spring." At least two newspapers picked up the story in 1887, one of them attributing it to the *Helena Daily Herald*. Asked by someone in the park as to what the origin was for the name Chinaman Spring, the reporter replied, "I'll tell the tale as it was told to me." It seems that a bank president from Winona, Minnesota approached this reporter at the Canyon Hotel and related this story, "which he had wrung from a reticent driver of one of Wakefield's four-horse coaches."

> "You know," said he, "as a general thing Park drivers are very modest and reluctant in relating travelers' tales to pilgrims, but in this case I was made the confid[a]nt of Charley Higginbottom, one of the most reliable Jehus in the Park (in a horn), who charged me not to give him away, as the Yellowstone National Park Association would be after him with a very sharp stick." "Sit closer," Mr. Wilson, "and draw nigh, for I know you must have something good, as no whip-popper on any of the stages would impose a story on a man of your years that was not strictly reliable." By this time, the bank president, being assured that he had an interested listener, began by saying: "When I left the Upper Geyser Basin this morning, they were still looking for the Chinaman." "What Chinaman?" asked the reporter. "Why the one that was sent up. You see a short time ago [1885] an enterprising Chinaman pre-empted one of the boiling springs and established a wash house over it in the shape of a wall tent, where he was doing a regular land-office business in boiling shirts in nature's cauldron. After some time [,] the Chinaman had ac-

cumulated several tubs full of soap suds which he proceeded to empty on the ground to get them out of the way. The contents, highly impregnated with alkali, found their way into the boiling spring, which, in an inkling, became an active geyser, carrying up with the column of hot water the tent, Chinaman, wash-tubs and all, and the last that was heard of the Celestial as he was spouted up through the air was his cry of 'washee, washee, washee,' and he hasn't come down yet—fact.[808]

Telling tales like this one had become a normal practice for stage-drivers like Charley Higgenbotham and those of the other companies who drove Park roads. Undoubtedly Higgenbotham was one of the original tellers of this story, which tales, as historian Haines has stated, "created a local de-mand for soap all out of proportion to the standard of cleanliness in vogue in the Park at that time."[809] Today, the activity carries a court appearance, a stiff fine, a likely banning from the Park, and sometimes a jail sentence, because the rangers of the National Park Service look upon it as a crime that can be damaging to thermal features, and they are right.

Except for the stage robbery involving Higgenbotham, the summer of 1887 went very well for George Wakefield. He hired Ellery C. Culver of Billings to return to Yellowstone and serve as freight manager for his transportation department. Culver would work for YPA and later YPT for many years, and would spend long years in Gardiner, even serving for a brief time as U.S. Commissioner (judge), prior to John W. Meldrum. Culver's work for Transportation included years on board the Living-ston-Cinnabar trains as a railroad "runner," where he sold the company's ticket-booklets for those who did not already have them. Another note-worthy visitor in 1887 was J.W. Redington, who had last been in the park ten years earlier during the Nez Perce War. He passed through the national reservation this year on Wakefield's coaches and stated that "In this enchanted land you will find the model stage-driver with his splendid stock and big thorough brace." He called Lower Falls "one of the grandest scenes in all of nature."[810]

Most important for Wakefield, James Mills, the editor of the *New North-West* newspaper at Deer Lodge, Montana, reprised his 1872 trip to the park in 1887, and found many pleasant and useful upgrades in the great national reservation. Mills had a lot to say about George Wakefield's stagecoaching, all of it good, and his long account gave us many details about how Wakefield's company operated that summer. Stating that the railroad and Park transportation companies offered the best service for general tourists, Mills wrote:

> What is known as the "five days' trip" ticket, and the one most visitors will desire, costs $40 at Livingston. Persons proposing to purchase these tickets get half fare rates to and from Livingston at all stations on the Northern Pacific. This book-ticket includes all railroad and stage fares from Livingston and return to that place, with five days' board and lodging at the Yellowstone Park Association Hotels and includes visiting the Mammoth Hot Springs, Norris Geyser Basin, Upper and Lower Geyser Basins and Yellowstone Falls and Cañon. In addition to this the Wakefield Stage Company will, if they desire, give parties of 3, 5, 7, or any odd number a private conveyance, with the same vehicle and driver [for] the entire trip, and an additional day's transportation without extra charge, making five days in the Park. The only additional expense is $4 for the extra day's board and lodging and it gives more leisure and better hours of travel. In traveling by the regular conveyances [,] persons can stop over as many days as they desire before Sept. 30th, by paying the hotel charges of $4 per day. Very many take the private conveyances or tarry a day at points of more interest, but the trip can be made from Livingston and return at $40 net cost. There are three-day book tickets issued at $30, but they do not take in the Grand Cañon and are [thus] unsatisfactory. [Here he discussed the hotels.]
>
> With the Wakefield Transportation Company[,] no fault can reasonably be found, nor did we hear but one complaint of the hundreds traveling, and that after the person reached Helena. Geo. W. Wakefield, the well-known Montanian, is proprietor, with Mr. A.A. Deems [sic], a most efficient, thoroughgoing and obliging gentleman as superintendent. They have 175 to 180 horses on the Park run of 135 miles, and can move 150 passengers, comfortably seated, from the Mammoth Springs and keep

that many moving all the time. They run from single buggies to seven passenger hacks, the latter [being] Concord built thorough-braces of the best design and finish, costing $600 each. All have canopy tops with adjustable side curtains in case of storm, and travelers can see everything and ride with comfort. Their transportation charges for the 135 miles are $20, the rules allowing them $25. They have excellent drivers—good reinsmen,

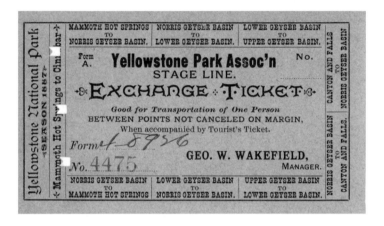

A YPA Stage Line ticket, George W. Wakefield, Manager, for the season of 1887. *Jay C. Lyndes Family Collection, YC-M10026a.*

Northern Pacific Railroad coupon book, $40, coupons from which could be used for meals, transportation, and hotel rooms in Yellowstone National Park, no date, used from the 1890s through 1916. *Jay C. Lyndes Family Collection.*

genteel and obliging without an exception. The transportation service is all that could be desired.[811]

But there was one negative account this summer referring to Wakefield's service that probably should have served as a warning to him and to YPA about the possibility of a looming disaster. It did not, but we see it today with twenty-twenty hindsight as a foreshadowing of events to come. Henry T. Finck, a cranky journalist who wrote for *The Nation*, visited Yellowstone this summer and had bad things to say about much of it. "It is a monarchy," hissed Finck, "and the King's name is Wakefield." Finck went on to claim that Wakefield's single motivation in life was to "make each passenger buy a round-trip stage ticket, no matter how much or how little of the Park he may wish to see."[812] Anyone who resisted, fumed Finck, was purposely subjected to various disadvantages and indignities. Mr. Finck therefore chose riding a horse as his way to avoid the stagecoaches but was told that "there was none to be had for a week or two." So, he went over to a competing livery—that of James A. Clark during the last summer of such availability—and rented a horse there. When he arrived at one of the Park hotels and asked to have his horse fed, he was told it could not be done because it was not a "Wakefield horse." At several hotels, he got around the prohibition by "humbly apologizing for not having a Wakefield horse and by explaining that I tried in vain to get one." But at the Firehole Hotel, even this apology failed and "they absolutely refused to take care of my horse for any price!" The other hotel visitors supported Mr. Finck, all agreeing that it was an outrage. At this point, Mr. Finck editorialized:

> Imagine a company which enjoys special privileges to build hotels in the National Park, where generally there is no other house within ten or twenty miles, then refusing to take care of a horse unless it belongs to one man—Mr. Wakefield—with whom the company has obviously an understanding which, I repeat, deserves the attention of Congress. Not only must this disgraceful monopoly be crushed at once, but Mr. Wakefield and his stage line ought to be abolished altogether.[813]

It was an ominous harbinger for Mr. Wakefield and the YPA of storm clouds to come, especially ironic because it happened at Firehole Hotel, where in 1890 another major "fuse would be lit." We shall tell that story shortly.

With autumn 1887 underway, George Wakefield began his usual activity of casting about for business to get him through the winter. He opened a tri-weekly stage route to Castle, Montana, where the coal business was increasing. He placed Adam Deem in charge of his Livingston operation, stationing him at the Albemarle Hotel, and continued the daily stage to Mammoth as well. He made at least three trips from Bozeman to Mammoth this winter to oversee his stagecoach affairs, even though stages were only running between Livingston and Gardiner. In April, with the summer of 1888 now approaching, Mr. and Mrs. Wakefield and daughter Libby held a smashing, social affair—a dance party—at their residence. All the big names of Bozeman society were present and listed by the newspapers.[814]

In early May 1888, Wakefield headed for Mammoth to get his operations ready for summer. As usual the park was scheduled to open on June 15, so Wakefield began moving his 170 horses from their winter pasture at Cinnabar Basin, noting that he had lost only three equines to the winter. "They lived and grew fat," said the editor of the Bozeman *Avant Courier*, "on the nutritious bunch-grass of the upper Yellowstone."[815] Knowing that the Raymond and Whitcomb touring parties had already booked five large excursions to the park, Wakefield in June purchased the transportation lease and buildings of his competitor J.A. Clark at Mammoth.[816] He was probably elated by the general outlook for tourism this year, which promised "low rates" on the Northern Pacific Railroad (a $110 package to the park from the east coast) and the statement that "The Yellowstone Park is unquestionably attracting more attention at the present time as a tourist resort than any place on the face of the earth."[817] That claim was one more in the many that augured for the continuing likelihood that this place represented the beginnings of tourism in the interior of the American West.

Part of Wakefield's purchase of Clark's livery, and probably the biggest news for Wakefield, was his acquisition of a new house at Mammoth Hot Springs, noteworthy because then as now, housing there was difficult to find. For the preceding five years, Wakefield had lived in a dwelling associated with his and the YNP Improvement Company's elongated transportation sheds at the northeast corner of the Mammoth village.[818] One of the buildings was a house that James Clark had erected at the north foot of

Capitol Hill in late 1884 or early 1885, and Wakefield soon moved into it. A photo from 1888 showed Wakefield and his family sitting on the front porch of their new residence.[819] It still stands today at Mammoth, usually used by the company's Director of Marketing and Sales, and is considered the oldest, continuously occupied building in Yellowstone National Park.

This was a bang-up, crowded summer for George Wakefield and everyone else in the Park, as Excelsior Geyser resumed its 300-foot eruptions every hour;[820] as the Iowa Press Excursion and the Dakota Press Excursion brought their combined 215 people to Yellowstone;[821] and as national comedic personality Bob Burdette came to the park to write and speak about it (he gave two speeches at Livingston and two at Bozeman). The Park's visitation went up by 1,000 visitors to a total of 6,000 for the season. On a vacation-lark, Montana's famous lawman, X. Beidler, spent his third summer of driving stagecoaches in the Park and telling tall tales to visitors.[822]

The two press associations were enthralled by Yellowstone's wonders, one member noting that "at all points the ground was covered with wild flowers of brilliant hues known only to house plants in this region; without exception they were strangers to our [Iowa's] climate and altitude and excited the continued admiration and surprise of all both for their beauty of shape and color." Of George Wakefield's operation, one Iowa writer said that it was "a pleasant ride in comfortable coaches" and that their party fit into twenty coaches of four to eleven passengers each.[823] Another writer, probably Dr. R.M. Davis, wrote for the *Sioux County Herald* that Wakefield's carriages were "for the most part comfortable and the drivers careful, well-posted, and ready to give all needed information to the tourist." A third one wrote that "the wagons were comfortable, the horses fresh, [and] the drivers not afraid of their whips."[824]

With the increase in visitation, horses and coaches ran low during 1888. Military superintendent Moses Harris reported that "during the rush of travel" in August and September, Wakefield was forced to scour the country so that "animals and vehicles of every description were brought into requisition" and many visitors had to ride "in uncomfortable and unsuitable conveyances, or otherwise to forego" the park itself because of crowding. But good fortune prevailed, and the emergency passed.[825]

Up to this time (1888), Wakefield's stagecoaching operation in Yellowstone had been spectacular. Complaints were minimal and Wakefield

A visitor appears to shield her face from the sun on the veranda of Mammoth Hot Springs Hotel in 1888, as a four-horse stagecoach arrives in late afternoon at the hotel. *Stereograph by T.W. Ingersoll, St. Paul, Minnesota, 1888.*

himself was arguably stellar in the way he managed. One autumn tourist, writing an article entitled "The Famous Yellowstone," complimented Wakefield's coaches for punctuality at the front door of Mammoth Hotel at 8 a.m., "waiting to bear us onward into the Park."[826] A visitor named J.E. Williams, who was also the editor of the *Amherst* (Massachusetts) *Record*, gushed enthusiastically in his praise of George Wakefield. Williams, who apparently spent hours interviewing him that summer, also provided us with what was probably the most important personal information about Wakefield up to that time, saying that the liveryman paid good wages and was beloved to "that large class in these mountains" who were professional stage-drivers. Wakefield, said Williams, "employs more than one hundred men of whom seventy-five are drivers and 25 to 50 stable men and herders." Noting that Wakefield held the year-round mail contract from Livingston to Mammoth, Williams additionally reported that Wakefield owned one hundred eighty horses in the park in 1888 as well as a "large number" more on his ranches and stage routes outside the park, and these horses were "large, strong animals and well cared for in accordance with the customs in these mountains."[827]

J.E. Williams was also the source for a great deal of information about Wakefield's horses. "At the Grand Cañon and at other places," wrote Williams, "the horses are put up and fed their grain when they come in, and are turned loose on the plains at night, in charge of a herder who follows that business." "At the close of the summer's work," he continued, "the Park horses are examined and the older ones put to work on other stage routes, while herds of the younger ones are turned out to 'rustle' for a living on the plains in the vicinity of Livingston." Williams spoke to a Wakefield-herder named Tom, who informed him that these horses "winter first rate and come out fat in the spring, the hair of their winter coats being three and four inches long and so thick that the blizzards have no effect on them."[828] Williams was amazed at the way George Wakefield maintained his horses in winter—typical for the American West—compared to the way it was done in the eastern U.S. He enthused:

> [Tom] says when the snow was two and a half and three feet deep on the level, he has seen a score or more of horses standing in a row pawing snow and eating grass with their heads buried to their eyes in snow. This is a common sight, especially after a deep snow, and while it is still soft and moist. This is what they call 'rustling,'—a term common among herders and drivers. The horses *rustle* through the day if the temperature is not too low and the wind [not] too severe, and wander about [un]till they find bare spots in sheltered places in the mountain gulches and cañons, where they stay at night. I am told that a horse that is housed till after cold weather comes on in the fall, will nearly or quite [nearly] starve rather than paw snow for a living; so they turn these herds out as early as possible, and [do] not allow them to become attached to the shelter of a barn, but keep them in total ignorance of any easier way to procure food than to rustle for it. They also want them to prepare their winter coats. Observe the contrast between the life of these herds of old stagers and that of hundreds of our New England pets which are allowed the luxury of woolen blankets, close box-stalls, a fire perhaps,

and straw beds that would make poor people everywhere happy and comfortable. We doubt not that good, young horses in
Amherst would starve and die if treated as the Montana horses
are in the mountains and on the ranches, and possibly the same
would be true of the 'tender-feet' of the East, if they were to
exchange their snug homes for the log cabins and shacks of this
territory.[829]

J.E. Williams also left us information on George Wakefield's fleet of
coaches, noting that a factory at Concord, New Hampshire furnished them
to Yellowstone:

[These] Concord coaches he considers most serviceable and the
best he can procure. Eleven passengers can ride quite comfortably on a coach, nine inside and two on the seat with the driver.
Even the surreys are provided with strong patent brakes, and a
large coach on the steep mountain side is as easily managed with
four or six horses, by an expert Rocky Mountain driver, as a
steam locomotive is with its patent airbrakes, on a dead level.[830]

But 1888, as good as it was, also brought some trouble to George Wakefield. A reporter for the *St. Louis Republic*, who got his information from
two gentleman recently there—one of them a reputable geologist—reported that the two men hated the hotels, food, and service in the park, describing them as "badly prepared food, inefficient service, insolence on the part
of waiters[,] and generally impolite and inconsiderate treatment." Those
things were not George Wakefield's fault, but a bad transportation-agent
at Mammoth Hot Springs Hotel arguably *was*. According to these tourists,
this agent

is a ruffian of the worst kind; his speech is coarse and his manner
is offensive. I heard him say to an old gentleman about 60 years
of age, who had made some complaint, "Oh! Well, I don't care
what you say." This is a sample of the answers he gives everybody who asks him any questions. If you make any complaint
to the hotel people about the behavior of this ruffian[,] they say

that they have nothing to do with it; the transportation agent is not under their control.[831]

One wonders whether this man was Adam Deem, known to have been working at Mammoth that summer, and probably it was. These tourists were correct that the hotel folks had no control over Deem, who was indeed rough at times, because Deem reported only to Wakefield. This tolerance of bad treatment would become a real problem for Wakefield three years later, but for now he and Deem were in absolute charge.

On the other hand, Adam Deem was known for being reasonably and necessarily firm with tourists who were obnoxious. Traveler H.Z. Osborne—owner and editor of the *Los Angeles Evening Express*—on July 15, 1888 found Deem at the helm at Mammoth Hotel in assigning each morning's riders to coaches. Acknowledging that "the excellent system of transportation through the Park is one of its most striking features," Osborne asked Deem how he managed that part of the business, and Deem explained it as follows:

> "Well," he said, "I try to get all the pleasant people together. Then I pick out all the cranks and kickers, and put them all in a carriage by themselves if it is feasible. I have been at this business so long that I can tell a crank as far as I can see him. [Each evening] the minute they go across the floor to register I pick out the cranks and mentally begin to assign them to carriages for the next day. I give the pleasant people the most accommodating drivers, and to the kickers I give some crusty old frost-bitten driver that will fire it right back at them! In that way everything moves as smooth as glass."[832]

In other words, Adam Deem assigned cranks to ride with certain drivers who were also cranks, and the upshot was probably that they ended up deserving each other. Osborne added that "as they are thrown into each other's society constantly for the five days of the trip, it is of no little consequence to the individual that he be parceled off into an agreeable crowd." A postscript easy to understand was that the cranky drivers undoubtedly won most of the encounters with cranky riders. They, after all, were in charge of the stagecoach, the metaphorical "captains of the ship," as park bus drivers would also be (and which some would actually verbally acknowledge to their passengers!)—when their times came—many years away in the future.

One of the most colorful and original visitor-accounts about stagecoaching in 1888 appeared courtesy of a Rhode Island party, whose scribe was identified only as a "Mrs. S." She offered us precious little about the park's hotels but made up for it with details of park wonders and stagecoaching. They arrived in mid-September at Cinnabar and boarded their stage to Mammoth for the night. At 8 a.m. the following morning, their coaches were at the hotel's door. "These are strong mountain wagons," she wrote, "with canvas tops and roomy seats, comfortably upholstered in leather." Her party numbered twenty (separated into various coaches) and the four people in this coach were "ready to be entertained," so they were happy to meet the three assignees to their coach who would provide some of that merriment. Soon given the usual nineteenth-century nicknames (a colorful practice, albeit one that removed their true names from the narrative—a torment for historians), these additional travelers were "the Poetess," "the gentleman of St. Paul," and "The Black Prince" (one wonders whether he was a black man, but we do know that he was British). Mrs. S. gave us a look into the forced camaraderie of stagecoach-riding, which much of the time on such trips was pleasant: "Jokes, repartees, songs, poems, discussions, dissertations, [and] laughter shortened and brightened the long lines of staging." In such surroundings, she observed, it was critical to have agreeable companions.[833]

"Seven persons and a one-eyed driver were allotted to our four-seated vehicle, drawn by four grey steeds," explained Mrs. S., "and another similar led the van, a smaller two-horse carriage bringing up the rear." Such a smaller vehicle was often used by George Wakefield to carry the last of a given party, so that its occupants would not have to be split up from the rest of their group around the park. Assuming that its driver was experienced, this petite coach usually gave these lucky people the good fortune of a more personal tour, because it was often easier to hear this driver spouting his observations. "Delighted exclamations were called forth at each new turn in the road," added the scribe, "whence magnificent views were continually unrolled." The travelers were enthralled. They saw Fountain Geyser, Jet Geyser, and the paint pots, and then approached "Hell's Half Acre," today's

Midway Geyser Basin starring Excelsior Geyser, where the year 1888 was unexpectedly offering that unusual treat:

> The guide warned us not to venture too near the crumbling edge, and to take heed of the time of its irruption, soon at hand; for we were looking into the crater of the largest known geyser in the world, the far famed 'Excelsior.' The pool measures 260 feet in diameter, although but a comparatively small portion is at any one time displayed on account of the dense steam constantly ascending. We waited and watched for the grand display, when its waters should be hurled to the skies…Suddenly, without other warning than that already given, the whole surface of this monster pool was gathered together in a volume seventy feet in diameter and thrown in one solid shaft 250 feet straight into the azure depths above, then it burst and fell in a magnificent shower of boiling water, deluging all the immediate vicinity. And our English friend, the doughty 'Black Prince,' fled, yes ignominiously fled on the wings of the morning…His eyes in frenzy rolled, and, as the woman of old, he looked constantly backward.[834]

Of course, the "woman of old" referred to Lot's wife in the Bible, who was allegedly turned into stone or a pillar of salt, when she made the mistake of glancing back.

After describing the many wonders of the Old Faithful area, they returned to Lower Geyser Basin, spent the night at Firehole Hotel, and the next morning dashed east across Mary Mountain for the Canyon. "All went merry as a marriage bell," enthused Mrs. S., and soon a welcome rain-shower reduced the amount of alkali dust on the road. Accordingly, they lowered the coach's curtains—"the canvas sides of our ark"—which blocked out the sunlight and all park views and immersed them into "a pretty respectable idea of a living tomb." The storm made mud and that created its own problems. "As the wagon wheels would sink into a rut, and our vehicle would swing dizzily to one side," explained their scribe, "the occupants would frantically spring to the other with such dismal groans, and ebullitions of fear as would cause the one good eye of our 'whip' to glare backwards, his steeds being left to their own sweet will." After numerous escapes from danger, the sun came out and they rolled up the curtains. Reaching the meadow just west of Mary Mountain, the driver, deathly afraid of "tipping over," ordered all the men out of the coach, walking to save wear on the horses up this very steep and rocky hill, locally named the "Devil's Stairway." This was the usual practice—allegedly ordered by the bosses, but no one seemed to know whether it was true—for all stagecoaches on this primitive stretch of road, but two years later, the practice would cause great difficulty for liveryman Wakefield. At one point, noted Mrs. S., "our Jehu was the single occupant of his four-seater" when everyone else was forced to walk because "in the place of ruts and logs and stones, huge boulders blocked our way." They passed Mary Lake, wound leisurely down the eastern slope of this divide, and soon were rewarded with views of Hayden Valley.[835]

Beginning this year,[836] Wakefield's tourists ate lunch (then called "dinner" or sometimes "luncheon") at "Larry's Trout Creek Dinner Station," where Irishman Larry Mathews served food and entertained visitors. But because of the rain, the mud, and the Devil's Stairway, this party was late in getting there, and Larry had either already closed the lunch hour or else he was out of supplies. So, the group missed lunch, recorded by our Mrs. S. as "a dinner *only* seven hours behind the breakfast." They drove through the thermal area known as Sulphur Mountain and then ate a "hurried dinner" at Canyon Hotel.[837] Thus ended one of the only known Yellowstone accounts involving tourists from the state of Rhode Island.

With the season of 1888 now over, George Wakefield moved his park horses to winter pasture (probably back to Cinnabar Basin) and began his off-season plans. He arranged to build a warehouse and stable in Livingston to operate his daily routes to Mammoth and Castle, Montana.[838] In October, he extended daily stage service from Gardiner to Livingston, both mail and passengers, because of irregularity of trains.[839] He moved Adam Deem from Mammoth to Livingston to manage his winter operation. With the town of Horr, Montana now growing enough to need its own post office, Wakefield appears to have relinquished his mail contract to that place.[840] And as usual, he looked forward to the summer of 1889.

Also as usual, George Wakefield spent the winter dealing with his outside-park interests to make continuing money in doing work for his other non-Yellowstone operations. Both endeavors were difficult to perform in

summer with the press of Park stagecoaching. So now he went on an extended trip to Helena, Anaconda, and Butte to support both operations, a
Butte newspaper calling him "about the busiest man in this section of the
country these days." He worked on his mining interests at Cooke City, telling two of his co-owners that they needed to pay their share of the associated costs. He convinced his political friends Russell Harrison and Congressman Thomas Carter of Montana to prod the Department of the Interior to
lease a plot of park ground to him on which to erect barns and corrals. He
kept his hand in the Bozeman Distillery of which he was a shareholder (al-
coholic beverages always were and still are a good investment in Montana).
And his company, the YPA, received a new lease on its hotels on March
20, 1889 from Secretary of Interior John Noble.[841] This did not change his
situation any; however, it added a good deal to the hotel-requirements for
the company.

Wakefield's biggest news for the year broke on May 3, when he sold
seventy percent of his park stagecoaching operation to the Yellowstone Park
Association for $50,000, keeping only thirty percent himself. The reorga-
nized "National Park Transportation Company" of St. Paul, Minnesota
was then incorporated by Charles Gibson, T.F. Oakes, E.C. Waters, and
George Wakefield, and they capitalized its stock at $50,000. By November,
according to the local newspaper, the new owners listed its name as the
"Yellowstone Park Transportation Company, apparently the earliest use of
that name, but there would be confusion through the 1890s as to the exact
name of the company because the name on the coaches did not immediately
get repainted, even after YPA dropped the word "association" almost immediately after Wakefield sold out (1889) and then claimed YNPTC during
the 1890s. The name YPT Company (without the "national") would eventually (1898-1901) take over both officially and in general usage, and would
carry the company all the way through the stagecoaching era to 1917, and
way beyond as well.[842]

Wakefield's sale to YPA was at least partially predicated on YPA's anticipation that the Secretary of Interior would soon require the company
to conduct all business, including Wakefield's in its own name, and sure
enough, that order came through in 1890 ("The company thereupon placed
upon all vehicles in the park the name of the association, and required the
agents and teamsters to wear badges indicating the association itself as prin-

cipal.").[843] So it was arguably good for the company that Wakefield had already done his part and sold his ownership to YPA.

The list of trappings that Wakefield sold to YPA was impressive, and it occupied three pages in small print. It included at least 181 horses, about two dozen Concord coaches, thirty-nine wagons of various types including stagecoaches, surreys, carriages, buggies, and work-wagons; thirty-eight saddles of various types; assorted bridles, halters, lap-robes, and tents; one sleigh; one mowing machine; one hay-rake; one safe; one letter-press; and miscellaneous buildings, corrals, water connections, tools, hay, and wagons not yet counted; plus some items Wakefield had ordered for the summer of 1889 but had not yet received. He now employed eighty to eighty-five drivers, a number that would continue to rise as park visitation increased through future years.[844]

At the same time, Wakefield fired or simply did not rehire his assistant Adam Deem, as sometimes happens to seasonal employees today. The record is incomplete on this point, but George Ash—apparently Deem's replacement—was a YPA Stage Line (soon to change to YNPT Company) superintendent by May 4. Deem's friend G.L. Henderson reported that Deem was managing the Capital Hotel in Helena by May 11, so Deem was then gone from the park.[845] What probably happened was that the new owners of Wakefield's company, namely YPA, had simply had enough of Adam Deem's difficult ways. They had, after all, received numerous complaints through the years about him, as the reporter for the *St. Louis Republic* noted in the previously mentioned article. As seventy percent owners of the new company, YPA was within its rights to fire Deem or at least not to rehire him for the summer, and the company's failure to rehire seasonal employees deemed (pun intended) unfit has thus been a part of its operating procedures since at least 1883.

Also at this time, YPA was also purchasing the inventory of one of Wakefield's competitors. He was G.L. Henderson, who with his family held the Cottage Hotel Association, which owned both a hotel and a transportation company in the park. According to Charles Gibson (who bought him out), Henderson operated fully one-third of the park's transportation business involving tourists.[846] We have told the story of Henderson's stagecoaching operation in chapter ten.

As a result of YPA's purchase of Wakefield's equipment and horses along with G.L. Henderson's equipment and horses, George Wakefield was now manager of the reorganized "National Park Transportation Company" (eventually to be called Yellowstone National Park Transportation Company and finally Yellowstone Park Transportation Company). He, like G.L. Henderson, was at least for the present more financially secure than he had ever been, because he had undoubtedly made a profit from selling all his equipment to YPA. As well, YPA retained him as superintendent of transportation and general manager of the "plant" for $3,000 per year, plus the company gave him $15,000 (thirty percent) in stock. Now he could concentrate on merely having fun by running stagecoaches in Yellowstone and not worrying so much about his monies and investments. Within a year, as the company's problems became suddenly huge (1890), he would be at least partially relieved that he had sold out.

A railway conductor who arrived at Mammoth Hot Springs Hotel in 1889 with a number of his fellow railroad-employees described George Wakefield's operation positively:

> G.W. Wakefield, general manager of the National Park transportation line, will also be found at this hotel, ever ready to make it pleasant for his patrons. He can take care of two hundred people a day, and keep them all moving over hill and dale, in his fine coaches, drawn by from four to six splendid, large horses. The company have [sic] 240 horses, and coaches enough to move two hundred people a day very comfortably.[847]

Indeed, new acting park superintendent F.A. Boutelle agreed that the transportation under Wakefield had been increased "and carried nearly to perfection." Gushed Boutelle:

> The coaches are as fine as human ingenuity can invent. In order that there may be perfect safety to passengers only perfectly gentle horses are purchased and used. They are obtained principally in Iowa, and cost about twice as much as the native horse of the country. In the seven years Mr. Wakefield has been engaged in this business no passenger has ever received any injury.[848]

This wonderfully safe and pastoral situation would change after only one more year. But for now, 1889 was becoming merely another idyllic summer in Yellowstone. On July 21, 1889, the president of the Board of Trade at Lima, Ohio, known to us only as "Robb," traveled from Mammoth around the loop and back for four days. He praised one of George Wakefield's stage-drivers:

> We had an excellent driver who knew his business and handled the reins over his four buzzard-headed Cayuses as he called them with the skill of one of the old masters; he pointed out all places worthy of notice, answered all questions, swore at his team and kept ahead of all the other stages during the entire route, although they all 'had it in for us' and tried to get in position at every opportunity to throw dust in our eyes.[849]

Another group found a similar situation, so, when combined with all the good comments from the superintendents through the years, we can probably take these comments as typical for Wakefield. "Our party had a large coach with three wide, roomy seats inside, and space for one passenger with the driver," wrote this traveler, who loved George Wakefield's operation. "The coach," he gushed, "was an exceedingly easy-riding vehicle, the four horses were spirited and the driver careful, courteous and full of information."[850] As often occurs when reading so many of these accounts, we wish that we knew this stage-driver's name.

He could have been Chris Hohenschuh, whom Wakefield hired this year to be a stage-driver; if so, he might have been promoted totally or partially based upon his receiving positive comments like this one. Hohenschuh was probably the same man who got into it with tourist Richard Grant in August during an inter-company squabble with another tour-operator, G.L. Henderson. This complaint would come back to haunt George Wakefield, but in the meantime Hohenschuh was promoted to superintendent of transportation for YNPT Company in late 1890, probably because of the company's sudden troubles and thus immediate need for dependable officers.[851] He worked only in the summers of 1889 and 1890, and not in 1891-92, so he was therefore a relative short-timer who had no time to become a long-term, experienced supervisor.

Also on tap for visitors this year, was the return of a driver who was more of a teller of tall tales than a giver of true park information. This was always a question for park stagecoach managers like George Wakefield and to fellow employees as to whether or not it would actually help make a stagecoach tour better. Montana's famous lawman, John X. Beidler, was heading to Yellowstone for his fourth season of being a Park stagecoach driver, where he would add—entertainingly but arguably negatively—to those drivers' reputations for the telling of tall-tales. (For example, Beidler told a tenderfoot this year that he was in Montana Territory when the telegraph poles along the line of the Northern Pacific Railroad were only a foot high.) Beidler might well have simply been taking a break from the rigors of law enforcement. In his pursuit of stagecoach driving in Yellowstone, he was returning to his roots, because, according to historian George Thompson, he had previously been a "famed shotgun guard for both Wells Fargo and Gilmer & Salisbury."[852]

So busy was 1889 that Wakefield had to purchase extra horses three times. On August 23, he was forced to make his third trip to Livingston to purchase additional stock for his park operation. Perhaps apprehensive about his future in the Park, he also wisely used the summer to sock away extra money from his other activities, notably horse-racing at Livingston, where his "Gray Dave" took a $150, first-place win in trotting.[853]

The summer of 1890 was arguably the most significant one in both George Wakefield's life and YPA's existence, because the summer's dramatic events set the stage for what can be called his nightmares of 1891. The season started out ordinarily enough. In early May, he enlisted the help of his new manager George Ash to bring three carloads of horses to the park by rail (so busy was the summer that he would return to Livingston in late July to purchase another carload).[854] The Wisconsin, Missouri, and Michigan press associations were all making plans to visit the park. So was Carter Harrison, the nationally known mayor of Chicago who would be assassinated only three years later in that city. In Yellowstone, Wakefield knew that the new Lake Hotel was under construction, and he must have reveled in Charles Gibson's decision to open the new and much larger Canyon Hotel (under construction for only about a year) for this season even though it was not finished. Along the way, eruptions of the park's two largest geysers—Steamboat Geyser with a single eruption at Norris, and a brief rejuvenation

John X. Beidler—the already-legendary Montana territorial lawman and former shotgun-guard for both Wells Fargo stage lines and Gilmer & Salisbury—took a vacation from law-enforcement to serve again as a stagecoach-driver for four summers in Yellowstone, 1886-1889. Beidler (far left) is shown here on the porch of one of the Firehole Hotel's cottages in 1886, along with hotel-manager James H. Dean and Mrs. Dean. *H-2685, Montana Historical Society.*

of Excelsior Geyser at "Hell's Half Acre"—would add color, excitement, and even uniqueness to the summer.

These latter geyser-events were yet unknown to George Wakefield, as were the upcoming, calamitous August events involving his stagecoach operation and its parent company the Yellowstone Park Association. Newspaper articles by members of the Wisconsin Press Association complained that not very many of those editors could afford to make the trip, but the WPA nevertheless managed to field fifty-five members.[855] The Missouri Press Association did better but was still plagued by internal politics. One of its reporters succumbed to the constant (and typical) temptation of writing only about the park's bears rather than about its thousands of other features, but another writer paid attention to George Wakefield's operation, saluting the Yellowstone Park Association for having "established magnificent stage lines for the benefit of its patrons." The trip through the park, said this writer, "is made in Concord coaches of the very best pattern, drawn by four horses, each coach carrying seven passengers and the driver."[856] The Michigan Press Association, two hundred fifty strong, showed up in late July, and were simultaneous with two other groups—a Raymond party and a Jewish organization—which altogether made over one thousand visitors. "In order to accommodate this unusual number," said the *Livingston Enterprise*, "Manager Wakefield of the Yellowstone Park Transportation company, came down to Livingston the first of the week and employed a number of outfits and drivers from this city, in addition to the large number of teams and conveyances constantly operated by the company." These other two groups plus the Pelton affair resulted in virtually no coverage of the Michigan group in Yellowstone in the newspapers of the nation. The *Salt Lake Herald* said only that they "were buried in Wonderland five days, feasting their souls on the picturesque."[857]

One 1890 party got the unexpected privilege of going to Canyon for the night, after lunching at Norris, again due to the traveling press-associations and the accompanying, sudden opening of the unfinished Canyon Hotel (its "wood was so new and so fresh and sweet"), instead of the usual practice of going to the Lower Geyser Basin. Lilian Leland loved her Yellowstone experiences, gushing about the camaraderie of the stagecoach ("no place like the box of a stagecoach for the quick growth of friendship") and the prospect of a horseback ride early the next morning. Alas, no horses appeared; the animals had run off during the night, so the party went walking along the canyon and returned to the hotel for breakfast. Once more they waited for their riding horses, which again failed to appear, only to learn that their *coach* horses were also missing. Their wait was forgotten, however, when their coach suddenly arrived and Lilian was smitten by the driver, as evidenced by this description: "Finally, our driver, who is by the way young and handsome, and fair and amiable, and well informed, and has read Bret Harte, and Dickens, and Mark Twain, and is called Charley, heaves in sight with the horses and we climb gladly back into the coach and proceed merrily" over to Norris for lunch.[858] Her infatuation with her driver was one that would be repeated thousands of times by numerous others through many more years of park stagecoaching and park busing. In fact, it still happens in the park today.

One of George Wakefield's bosses this summer was the less-than-upstanding E.C. Waters, the man who had negotiated YPA's purchase of Wakefield's wagons and horses during the preceding year. Despite his other deficiencies, Waters could be a shrewd, if sometimes harsh-bordering-on-dishonest, businessman, and late one afternoon Waters took note of a rare eruption of Yellowstone's, and the world's, tallest geyser—Steamboat Geyser at Norris Basin—and correctly saw it as something that might increase the park's ticket-sales. He telegraphed Northern Pacific Railroad boss Charles S. Fee at St. Paul, and the story made the newspapers.[859]

On Tuesday afternoon July 8, 1890, the already-legendary Steamboat Geyser (sometimes then also called "New Crater") erupted in "major phase" for the only known time this year. Some of the staff of the Norris temporary hotel and a few lucky park visitors saw the "steam phase" if not the water phase, and many newspapers picked up the story on the following day. At 4:15pm, "the new crater geyser at Norris Geyser Basin, which has heretofore been quiescent, was in a violent state of eruption," announced the *Evening Star* of Washington, DC, and it was "throwing up an immense column of steam, stone[s] and water about 200 feet in circumference, which ascended fully 400 feet, shaking the basin in that vicinity and deluging it for at least 400 feet in every direction with an enormous amount of water." The *Los Angeles Herald* reported that the massive spouter "quieted down somewhat during last night," its writer continuing that "at 6:30 this morning there was a solid column of steam forced up constantly to a height of from 150 to

175 feet, and 75 feet in diameter" with the roaring subsiding considerably. Steamboat Geyser here was apparently displaying the type of activity that it still exhibits today, by shooting water up to 400 feet in height for a period of ten to twenty minutes and then settling into a many-hours-long "steam phase" with lots of noise. If there were other eyewitness accounts of this individual eruption written by Wakefield's customers or hotel staff, they have not surfaced.[860]

It was shaping up to be a fascinating summer. In late July, Carter H. Harrison (1825-1893), the mayor of Chicago and a former U.S. Congressman from Illinois, traveled to Yellowstone and was benefited by the sudden opening of the unfinished Canyon Hotel out of the company's necessity. Harrison rode with one of George Wakefield's drivers, and he liked what he saw and heard. "There are associations which control tourist movements in and through the park," he wrote, "one for transportation alone and the other for feeding and housing." Of course, he was speaking of George Wakefield's operation and the hotelier YPA. "The transportation company," he continued, "has some seventy-five vehicles, two-thirds if not three-fourths of them Concord stages and wagonettes carrying six to seven passengers but capable of carrying three or four more by having three on a seat." Noting that these coaches were drawn by four horses, he added that Wakefield's other vehicles were four-passenger surreys drawn by two horses each (he did not mention the company's one or two Tally-hoes). The price of the train ticket from Livingston to Cinnabar, he observed, plus the five-and-a-quarter days' trip around the park and back to Livingston was packaged at forty dollars.[861] It was all good publicity for George Wakefield.

"One thus sees everything in the grand tour," explained Mr. Harrison, "somewhat hurriedly." He recorded for us that Wakefield's bosses at the Yellowstone Park Association had begun the practice of allowing stopovers; in fact, the company started it this very summer. This new system was intended to get rid of the biggest source of complaints for Wakefield and YPA, namely the fact that tourists were "rushed through" the park. Many of them wanted to "stop over" at specific places in the park in order to spend more time looking at geysers or the colorful canyon, and often people in the stagecoaches were "of different minds" as to what they preferred. This innovation was intended to offer the option and, according to William Pearce, the company's general manager, it was accomplished by making a deal with

Wakefield. In return for his not having to pay the annual fifteen percent of his earnings to the company each year, he agreed to run a daily stage that ran the entire park loop road, picking up "stop overs" and dropping them at their next hotel. Wakefield figured out that if his fifteen percent extra was not included, he would end up losing money on this deal, so the company agreed to make up the fifteen percent to him, and with that deal got rid of its biggest source of complaints.[862]

An 1891 party encountered YPA's charged-for "stopover practice," in use for about a year, and described for us how it worked, or, as the writer saw it, did *not* work so well:

> Parties entering the park at Livingston generally purchase round trip tickets of the transportation company, and are hurried on from one hotel to another, stopping a night at each, and leaving each morning at 7 o'clock for the day's whirl and sightseeing. There are no regular stages [having point-to-point times] making the rounds. [Instead] Each party is given a special conveyance for the tour, and if they wish to stop over at any point can do so only by paying an extra charge of $10, $20 or $30 for each additional day's delay: the minimum price being for a party of three in a two-horse surrey and the higher charge for parties of six and eight in wagons and stages of greater capacity, drawn by four and six horses. A solitary tourist is given a seat in one of the large stages, and is thenceforth at the mercy of his ticket, which secures him a five days' trip; or, if he has bargained to visit Yellowstone Lake, six days' transportation. If he leaves his conveyance at any point[,] he must run his chance of finding an empty seat in some subsequent stage. In default of this he can only telegraph back to the mammoth hot springs for a special conveyance, at an expense of $10 per day, beginning at the time the conveyance leaves the spring[s], and ending with its return to that point. These arrangements make the tour through the park *a wild scramble* into and out of the stages and carriages.[863]

In contrast with most other travelers from pre-1892 Yellowstone who denounced the park's hotels and praised the stagecoaches, this writer

("H.G.H.") saw the hotels as "very nearly perfect" and the transportation company as leaving much to be desired. The exhausted tourist would love to stop at one of these comfortable hotels, he whined, "but the terms of his contract with the transportation company forbid this, except at a ruinous penalty, and so he is hurried over the rounds, and at the expiration of the allotted period[,] expelled from the mouth of wonderland as if one of its geysers had exploded behind him."[864]

Returning to Mayor Carter Harrison in 1890, we learn that he left an explanation for the reasons for George Wakefield's practice of keeping the stagecoaches in a line as they traveled around the park, but not too close together: One obvious reason was to keep down the ever-present dust. But also, this practice prevented drivers from driving too fast, as he clarified: "There are at this time, tourists enough to start out each day from Mammoth Hot Springs [in] about five coaches and several surreys, all leaving at a fixed hour and reaching points of interest or other hotels close together, each vehicle maintaining its position in the line throughout the tour; thus racing is prohibited." Mayor Harrison ended his newspaper account by summing up what so many tourists of his time believed, namely that seeing Yellowstone required a trip that was too laborious. "I quit the park glad that I came," he wrote, "but feel that the rush and labor of going through it would hardly repay a second visit, at least for several years." He ended with, "Yet I can recall no excursion of the same length in any part of the world half so full of surprises."[865]

This much larger problem—one of great distances—which was unsolvable in horse-and-buggy days without faster technology, such as electric streetcars, railroad cars, or automobiles, would become fashionable as a discussion-topic in the park for many years. For example, attorney Henry Dodge Estabrook (1854-1917) of New York—who twenty-five years later would run for the Republican nomination for U.S. president—had much to say about stagecoaching. He boiled it down to this:

> The present mode of locomotion through the park is irksome and monotonous. To drive thirty or forty miles each day and spend the few remaining hours of sunlight in climbing around is too much like sawing wood—a pastime for which most of us have an instinctive antipathy. It is too slow one way and too rap-

id another. You are not given enough time at points of interest, most of the time being squandered in getting there. The general scenery does not compensate for this drudgery.

Estabrook thought it admirable that the government was attempting to keep Yellowstone primeval and natural, but he did not think electrically propelled cars would mess it up that badly; in fact, he thought that technology would be "noiseless, rapid, cheap, and entirely practical."[866]

Park hotel owner, former stagecoach operator, and Yellowstone interpreter G.L. Henderson also had noteworthy opinions about this subject, and, like Henry Estabrook, he pushed for "electric carriages" (streetcars) or some other form of rapid, mass transit. After telling the 1882 story of a European traveler who entered the west entrance (likely riding with the Bassett Brothers) and who could go no farther than Lower Geyser Basin because of distance, dust, road-ruts, and standing-stumps—the totality causing overwhelming fatigue—Henderson lobbied as follows:

> As late as 1889, the editor of the *St. Louis Post-Dispatch* rode only 6 miles through the dust and ruts from Cinnabar to the Mammoth Hot Springs Hotel, and said, "Two hours is enough; a whole day would kill me." But could he have had the comfort of an ordinary street car[,] he would have gone on to Norris in an hour or an hour and a half, a distance of 20 miles, where he could have spent three hours instead of thirty minutes and taken an afternoon train to the Fountain Hotel, where he could sit at his window and see the old Fountain 'play'…and feel that the change from car to carriage is rest. With rapid transit[,] building material[s] and hotel supplies could be distributed at one-fourth of the present cost…When we can ride from basin to basin in an hour, and in an elegant coach, and then have hours instead of minutes to see their contents, who could afford to consume a month in doing what can be done in four days?…With improved and rapid transportation…can anyone doubt that [the Park's] visitors will increase to ten, twenty, and thirty thousand annually?[867]

Henderson probably would have been aghast to witness the nearly five million visitors of today's Yellowstone, but he definitely would have been happy to ride the faster transportation.

Returning now to Carter Harrison's trip in 1890, we learn that Harrison was also a fortunate viewer of yet another of Yellowstone's celebrated geysers this summer. He and many other visitors got lucky when the legendary Excelsior Geyser went into a rare, active cycle in 1890. Unlike Steamboat Geyser, which usually erupted in major fashion only once and then was usually quiet for months or years, Excelsior, when it became active, continued to exhibit cyclic eruptions for weeks or months, often on a daily basis. Superintendent F.A. Boutelle telegraphed the Secretary of the Interior to announce the start of the cycle when the geyser began erupting on July 19, and newspapers picked it up. The *Idaho Statesman* of Boise stated excitedly that Excelsior Geyser has been in a state of eruption "since last Saturday, the first time in two years." The *San Francisco Call* averred that the water reached 300 feet in height. Three weeks later, the geyser was apparently still erupting, for the *Idaho Semi-Weekly World* announced on August 12 that "the Excelsior Geyser in Yellowstone Park is throwing hot water 300 feet into the air."[868] Mayor Harrison saw the geyser "go off" sometime just before July 24, and wrote about the unusual phenomenon:

> It erupted just as our party reached it, but not in one of its grand eruptions. A mass of water possibly many feet in diameter was lifted fifty or more feet in the air. It is said that when in full eruption the height of the column is from two to three hundred feet. This I doubt.[869]

But Harrison's doubt was wrong, and his informants were correct; Excelsior could indeed erupt to that height. A party that included Idaho pioneer B.W. Driggs saw it and recorded the following:

> [We] then rode over to the 'Excelsior' just in time to see one of its grandest eruptions. The water in this boiling crater began upheaving, and dense steam hissed forth; then the explosion occurred, sending the water about 250 feet high. This continued for a few minutes, when the river below increased one-half in

size, and was colored like milk by this boiling geyser, the water from which heated the whole river.[870]

Excelsior Geyser was a big deal in stagecoach-era Yellowstone Park, and other tourists from that year continued to make it so. Members of the Missouri Press Association saw it erupt, even though it seemed to them to be losing power:

A little farther on was the Excelsior geyser, one of the largest in the park. It spouts every four hours, and we were fortunate enough to see it in action. Its crater is a huge caldron, 250 feet in diameter, with walls about twenty feet high. On one side the wall is broken down and through this the water flows into the river in channels lined with scarlet, yellow and green. Dense clouds of steam hang over the top of it at all times. The eruption finally came and an immense mass of boiling water shot upward about 75 feet, with a roar undescribable [sic], while we stood on the verge and trembled at the majesty of nature. It continued in action probably two minutes, and changed the Fire Hole river from a modest stream into a turbulent flood of boiling water.[871]

"We visited the Excelsior," announced Maryland tourist Charles Mantz, "which recently erupted for the first time in two years." Mantz enthused that the geyser spouted "200 or 300" feet high and threw out huge rocks. "We saw it spouting," he said, "but could not get near it for it floods the surface for a quarter of a mile and is considered dangerous."[872]

But suddenly events more serious than individual geysers entered the idyllic, Yellowstone picture, and they would radically change everything. Lambert Tree, a circuit-court judge from Chicago, and his party arrived in late July and almost simultaneously, on Thursday, July 24, 1890,[873] an ex-congressman from New York dropped dead while walking up a steep hill. These two incidents would change the course of history in the national park. The dead visitor was Guy Ray Pelton (1824-1890), who had served one term in the U.S. House of Representatives. On that day, along with a party of eight, the 67-year-old tourist was instructed by his stage driver while ascending the Mary Mountain hill known as the Devil's Stairway to do the usual thing, namely disembark from the coach and walk up the steep slope to save wear and tear on the horses. The climb was too much for Mr. Pelton, and he keeled over on the hill. "An examination," said the *St. Paul Globe*, "showed he had ruptured several blood vessels near the heart."[874] The fact that asking visitors to walk up the hill was said by many to be a standard procedure for YPA/YNPTC's stage drivers would prove later to make the company's, and George Wakefield's, political and legal situation much worse.

A national scandal, destined to last for weeks—that starred George Wakefield, the Yellowstone Park Association, and indirectly the dead Congressman—broke on or about August 9, when a Chicago newspaper interviewed a just-returned Yellowstone traveler named Lambert Tree and ran a story about it. Judge Tree had gained fame in that city by presiding over the trial of corrupt officials and had then spent four years as U.S. Minister to Belgium under President Grover Cleveland. The New York *Sun* picked up the story on August 10, and the Philadelphia *Times* and the Washington, DC *Evening Star* on the following day. *The Sun* began by quoting Judge Tree as calling the Park's accommodations "entirely inadequate," the food inedible, the prices charged "extortionate," and the hotel management "outrageous." "He instances a case," said the *Sun*,

> in which a gentleman and his wife were obliged to sleep in one of the hotels in a room with three men and in another instance, at the same hotel, eight persons, consisting of three gentlemen with their wives and two young ladies, were thrust into a small bedroom to pass the night. They could not help themselves, as there was not another house within thirty miles, and no means of conveyance except those supplied by the company, which ran on schedules, and the next stage would not leave till the following day.[875]

That story stretched it a bit, because the Old Faithful hotel was only eight or nine miles away, but this was a moot point because Tree's claim against the stage-drivers was true.

And there was more, a lot more. His allegations against George Wakefield were long and must be quoted:

The transportation facilities are also far from satisfactory. The vehicles and horses are not sufficient in number to insure comfort, and petty tricks are played on travelers in order that the association may save its horses as much as possible. Thus, for example, as each wagon loaded with tourists leaves the Mammoth Springs Hotel, the passengers are told by an official of the transportation company that if they remain in the wagon in ascending Mary's Mountain the company will not be responsible for accidents. This is not because the ascent is dangerous or difficult, but it is because it is rather a hard pull for the horses, which the managers wish to save at the expense of the passengers. The effect upon a number of people of various degrees of nervous sensibility of the announcement of danger at that point may be readily conjectured. Most of them get out when they reach the hill, and, ankle deep in dust, climb it under a hot sun, breathing only the light air of the high altitude, at great risk to their lives. Two or three days before my arrival there[,] Guy R. Pelton, a former member of Congress from New York, dropped dead in endeavoring to make [the] trip on foot in obedience to the transportation company. As it is today, I do not think it is too strong to say that on certain points on the route travelers are treated more like cattle than civilized people.[876]

Guy R. Pelton (1824-1890), formerly a congressman from New York, who dropped dead in Yellowstone on a stagecoach trip. *Author's collection.*

Judge Lambert Tree (1832-1910) of Chicago, whose complaints about Yellowstone in 1890 started a national frenzy. *Author's collection.*

Judge Tree ended by implicitly calling for government action, because "the amount of patronage" that this company received from the U.S. public justified a demand for good accommodations and services in Yellowstone. The *Chicago Herald* agreed, editorializing that "Judge Tree's experience in the Yellowstone Park is worthy of the immediate attention of the government."[877]

The scandal continued for more than six weeks, being revisited numerous times by newspapers. The *Chicago Tribune* ran an updated story on August 15, which included corroborating information from John G.H. Meyers of New York. Meyers had written a complaining letter to Secretary of the Interior John N. Noble dated August 12, which Noble would later submit as an exhibit in congressional hearings. Mr. Meyers, a lawyer, agreed with Judge Tree in their mutual beliefs that ex-congressman Pelton's death had been caused by "trying to climb Mary's Mountain in obedience to the orders of the transportation company when he should have had the privilege of riding." "I met Mr. Pelton just ten days prior to his death," wrote Meyers, "and he appeared then to enjoy most excellent health."[878]

Meyers went on to complain about the YP Association's Firehole Hotel at Lower Geyser Basin:

> We reached the Fire Hole Basin and there were nearly one hundred people to crowd into thirty-seven rooms and a few tents, and the manager, an *impertinent* [italics added, see following paragraph] fellow, assigned my wife and child to a room to be occupied by two other married couples and a young lady, and when I protested against it [I] was informed that was all that could be done, so I occupied the room with them. Here were eight persons, married and single, huddled together in one small room with my child and [my]self sleeping on a mattress on the floor. The toilet accommodations are simply abominable. If you wish to wash, you can go off to the brook and obtain the water, or go without. Eleven miles farther on there is another hotel, and that night only twelve people occupied it, and it could have accommodated sixty. But the drivers of the stages had their instructions to stop at Fire Hole, and would not go farther.

Mr. Meyers had done his homework well in the numbers of people present and in the capacity of and lack of customers at the Old Faithful hotel, and his story with its reference to stage-drivers refusing to drive on to the other hotel added a further black mark to George Wakefield's already-bad problem in the death of Mr. Pelton. To make matters worse for YPA, the *Tribune*, whether purposely or inadvertently, made the lodging appear even more unacceptable by mistakenly substituting the word *impertinent* for *important* in describing the hotel's manager.[879]

Any reader of these stories would likely have been incensed against both YPA and George Wakefield. And the damage to both of them was not yet complete. On August 16, the *St. Paul Globe* highlighted Judge Tree's complaints in an editorial referring to YPA and its transportation company as "an ignoble race of human wolves" and "cormorants who seem to be using" the nation's park to "fill their own pockets merely." On August 21, the *Tribune* ran its longest editorial so far, attributing its information to the *Chicago Evening Post* whose reporters re-interviewed Judge Tree to get more information. Tree stated that he had purchased the standard forty-dollar ticket through the park "for railroad and stagecoach fare, board, and lodging—and misery." Tree praised the park's wonders but called the management of the hotels "atrocious and even brutal." He denounced

YPA's overcrowded Firehole Hotel and castigated the stage-company for refusing to take the people on to Old Faithful. Again stretching the truth with regard to distance, he stated: "There is no other hotel or house of any description within twenty miles and the woods about are alive with bears, lynxes, wolves, and other ferocious animals." (It was probably just as well that Judge Tree did not know about several recent sightings of mountain lions there!) The guests, he said, were obliged to accept the rooms as assigned to them "by a brutal hotel manager or [else] stand out in the road in a country where there is frost every night." More generally, he complained about boat-rental prices, inedible food, the deplorable condition of park roads and bridges, and the attitudes of both hotel managers and transportation managers. He thoroughly indicted the company's monopoly and again called for the federal government to do something about it. The *Tribune* then ran a separate editorial in the same issue condemning the hotel and transportation officials for "outrageous extortion and swindling," reminding its readers that "once tourists have entered the park they are at the mercy of these men." The paper called on Secretary of the Interior John Noble to "abate the evil" because "the monopolists…not only are a hardship to travelers but a disgrace to the Administration so long as it permits them to continue."[880] Whether the *Tribune* meant the administration of Secretary Noble or that of President Benjamin Harrison the writer did not say, but it was clear from this that news of the scandal was now potentially reaching all the way to the President of the United States.

At the Department of Interior, Secretary John Willock Noble (1831-1912) had indeed noticed the fuss, and the *Baltimore Sun* asked him directly for his response to it. "Secretary Noble has been very much annoyed recently," reported the *Sun*, "over the statements by travelers through the Yellowstone Park reflecting seriously upon the management of affairs by the transportation company having the monopoly at the park."[881] Of course, transportation manager George Wakefield had no such monopoly; that was the purview of YPA, but Secretary Noble's having clearly pointed to transportation in his response to the *Sun* made it apparent that he was already looking harder at Wakefield than at Wakefield's bosses at YPA. That was not fair, but little people have always suffered more from powerful governments and corporations than have those with money. This newspaper story should have been, and indeed might have become, a warning to Mr. Wakefield *if* he saw it and read it, which was unlikely. Regardless, it foreshadowed the nasty events to come for the next two years.

George Wakefield certainly could have seen the trouble coming, if he had only read the Deer Lodge (Montana) *New North-West*'s story on August 22 or the *Livingston Enterprise*'s story on August 23. Perhaps he was lulled into a false sense of security by the fact that nowhere in Montana was the story covered with such urgency as in eastern cities. Perhaps he received false security from the *Helena Independent*'s story of September 2, which reported Secretary Noble receiving the letter of a Livingston man who stated that his party in the Park was "given good accommodations and the transportation was all that could be asked."[882] But Wakefield certainly *should* have taken notice of—he admitted later that he did not respond to—the official letter that Secretary Noble personally sent to him before any of those stories was published, dated August 13, 1890. According to Noble, writing later, the letter stated:

> The complaints from travelers over your lines are becoming so frequent that I am bound to believe that you are derelict in your duties, and if you do not reform your treatments to your passengers, I will cancel your contract. You must remember that you are to accommodate the public, and when you fail to do that to the fullest and fairest extent your agreement ends.[883]

In his congressional testimony seven months later, Noble stated that Wakefield did not reply to this letter, and apparently because of that, the Secretary would soon write another one.

There was more recognition of this news coming from Washington, DC, which George Wakefield either inadvertently missed or purposely ignored. A "Special" from Washington, DC to the *Helena Independent* again began with Secretary Noble's pique:

> Secretary Noble has been very much annoyed recently over the publication of stories of travelers through the Yellowstone Park, in which statements have been made reflecting seriously upon the management of affairs by the transportation company having the monopoly at the park...All the trouble seems to have

originated from a desire on the part of Manager Wakefield of the transportation company to save labor for his live stock at the expense of the health and comfort of tourists in the park and who hail from every part of the civilized world. Discussing the subject today Chief Clerk Dawson of the interior department said: "We have been hampered in making an enquiry owing to the fact that no one has come forward and preferred charges either orally or in writing to the department and all that is known to us about the matter is derived from what has appeared in the newspapers; besides Manager Wakefield has no lease from the interior department but is under a contract only to the Yellowstone Park association. It is, however, in the power of the secretary of the interior at any time to abrogate the contract with the association if it is shown that any outrages are perpetrated upon travelers, and in view of recent utterances by well-known public men the time seems to have arrived for such complaints to be filed. There is no occasion for travelers being compelled to foot it upon Maris [sic—Mary] mountain, nearly nine thousand feet above the sea level and yet this is made obligatory by an agent of the transportation company."[884]

Unfortunately, this article's subheading, alleging that Interior would formally investigate tourists' complaints, did not get confirmed in the article's text, but if Wakefield had read it, the article would probably have scared him a bit.

Secretary Noble had one more chance to warn Wakefield. In October, 1890, Noble wrote to George Wakefield again, this time saying the following:

The Department is informed that in conducting the business of transporting passengers in the Yellowstone National Park, you are not acting for or under the authority of the Yellowstone National Park Association; and you do not appear from the records to have any authority in the premises from this Department. If you are acting for or under the Yellowstone National Park Association, you are directed to transmit to this Department the evidence of such fact without delay. If you are not, and you

desire to continue in your present occupation, you will make
application to this Department for permission to do so under
such rules, regulations, and restrictions as it may be deemed ad-
visable to impose. If you do this at the earliest day possible, the
Department will give it consideration.

As mentioned, Wakefield stated in his congressional testimony two years
later that he received but did not answer the first letter.[885] Regarding this
second letter, Wakefield, assuming he received it, could easily have inter-
preted it as merely a (likely welcome) request or invitation for him to make
application for the actual contract that he had long wanted, and if so, he
likely did not see anything too threatening or even urgent in the matter.
He did not yet see the congressional investigations coming, let alone anything worse.

But increasingly troublesome times stemming from this difficult summer
of 1890 were looming for George Wakefield. He would formally learn of
them in early 1892, and they would dramatically change his life.

CHAPTER TWELVE

Wakefield

An Unfortunate Victim, 1891-1892

"He [Wakefield] states that the reported sale of his stock to Huntley & Clark of Helena…is wholly without foundation." Wakefield in "Local Layout," *Livingston Enterprise*, April 9, 1892, p. 3.

George Wakefield did not seem to be worried. At the end of the summer season of 1890, and during the succeeding winter, it appears that he did nothing differently from usual and instead made preparations for the summer of 1891 in Yellowstone National Park, just the same as he had been doing for the previous eight years. But first, as he always did in the autumn, Wakefield continued to expand his other money-making schemes beyond Yellowstone Park, and as usual, that plan turned out to be prudent. In late August of 1890, he had made plans to join with four partners to incorporate the Livingston Land and Improvement Company, organized for the purpose of building flumes and digging ditches for water-power and sites for the same; and for purchasing and developing real estate. This activity was not the only other one that Wakefield was using to support himself during the coming winter season. He also would soon lease the Bozeman Hotel in a business venture calculated to add to his winter-season income. In early

December, he traveled to Washington, DC to lobby congress in the inter-
ests of Cooke City miners for permitting a railroad through Yellowstone
Park. Wakefield, after all, owned a one-third interest in the "Baby Mine" in
Cooke City, along with two other men.

Just before Christmas, he spoke to the press and showed his usual optimism for managing the Yellowstone transportation company's summer
operations. The *Anaconda Standard* reported it as follows, the "he" being
George Wakefield:

> "The season covers only about four months of the year," he re-
> marked last night, "and during that time we handle from 2,500
> to 3,000 people. To do this requires about three hundred horses
> and one hundred vehicles, the latter accommodating from three
> to eight persons as may be desired…The crowds are increasing,
> rather than diminishing, yearly, and if the season was longer my
> business would be very profitable."[886]

For the moment, Wakefield was making preparations to again run
YNPT's affairs in the Park. In January, the Yellowstone National Park
Transportation Company filed articles of incorporation with the Mon-
tana secretary of state, and George Wakefield joined with T.B. Casey and
W.G. Johnson of the Yellowstone Park Association to become one of the
three incorporators of this now-official company. The Yellowstone Park
Association no doubt intended this incorporation to lend legitimacy to
George W. Wakefield's role in the Yellowstone National Park Transportation Company, for theretofore Wakefield had held no written contract
of his own. The documents placed the headquarters of this company at
St. Paul, Minnesota, and capitalized its stock at $250,000.[887] Importantly,
this action marked the moment when the new name, Yellowstone National Park Transportation Company, was placed into officiality and attempted general usage. However, it would take a long time for the old name,
"Yellowstone Park Association Stage Line/Transportation Company,"
to disappear from the company's fleet of stagecoaches. Repainting them
would cost money and take a while to accomplish. Some coaches were
apparently never repainted, the company—whether owned by Wakefield,
YPA, or (later) Huntley—not worrying about whether the coach pro-

claimed "Yellowstone Park Association Transportation" or "Yellowstone National Park Transportation Company."

Apparently in connection with this new incorporation and because he was trying, as he had a number of times before, to secure a lease in his name, Wakefield traveled to Washington "early in February" (1891)[888] to meet with the Secretary of Interior, for he mentioned it in his congressional testimony in 1892. While there, Wakefield encountered Charles Gibson and Thomas Casey of YPA. The three of them went to Noble's office together, where Noble told Wakefield that "there had been a good many complaints, but that was not what bothered him." Said Wakefield:

> He says to me, "Let them [the complaints] pass; you have been doing business in the park without any authority;" and I stated then and there that I had been doing business under the lease of the association with Mr. Gibson and Mr. Casey…and Gen. Noble said that was unbeknown[st] to him…that I had been the agent of the association.

At this point, President Charles Gibson defended Mr. Wakefield and stated that he knew of and could present to Noble all kinds of proof of Wakefield's having been an agent for YPA. According to Wakefield, Secretary Noble seemed pleased to hear about the new [Fountain] hotel, and he added, "After we were very nearly ready to go (they were all standing up), Gen. Noble said…, '[T]here should not be a thing done to interfere with you in any way,' meaning the association." "So then," resumed the 1892 congressional questioner, "you parted under the impression that the complaint about the transportation would all be adjusted if the association assumed the responsibility for it." Wakefield answered, "Yes, sir; as I understood it."[889]

With this assurance and understanding by Secretary Noble given to the trifecta of Gibson, Casey, and Wakefield, *it was no wonder that both YPA and Wakefield were suddenly not worried about any threats to their transportation company.* Right up to the last minute, Secretary Noble continued to assert that he "was well satisfied with the association, and would under no circumstances do anything that would injure it."[890] But in November, 1891, and again in May, 1892, Secretary Noble would unexpectedly renew the threat against Wakefield.

Just after the company's new incorporation in January of 1891, George Wakefield announced that he and a partner, John Callaghan, had leased the Bozeman Hotel for $650 per month with the intention of operating it for profit, its grand opening to be held no later than March 1.[891] We do not know what George Wakefield was thinking here. Perhaps in leasing this hotel to run, he was only doing what he had done before, namely finding new ways of supplementing his income within the constraints of his mainly summer-seasonal business (stagecoaching). Or we can today argue that in the twenty-twenty hindsight of history, George Wakefield had become uneasy, because he had seen the possibility that he would somehow lose his permission to operate Yellowstone's main stage-line. So perhaps he leased the Bozeman Hotel with that in mind, as he made plans to run the hotel.

Whichever it was, Wakefield and his partner missed predicting the hotel's actual opening-date by only one day; he and his partner held the gala celebration on March 2 rather than March 1. Numerous Montana newspapers covered the event, with the *Butte Weekly Miner* referring to it as "A Handsome Monument," the *Helena Independent* calling it "The Pride of Bozeman," and the *Anaconda Standard* emblazoning its article "A Pride to All Montana."[892]

It became apparent to Wakefield, perhaps as early as March of 1891, that he might have to travel again to Washington, DC, this time to testify in front of the U.S. House of Representatives Committee on Public Lands, which would eventually investigate problems that had surfaced during the summer of 1890 at Yellowstone, including the death of ex-congressman Pelton. The actual congressional hearings would not begin until April 25, 1892, more than a year later and nearly two years after the nationalized events of 1890. Wakefield's boss, Charles Gibson, confided at that time that Secretary John Noble issued the new lease to S.S. Huntley on March 30, 1891, and just after that, on April 3, announced Wakefield's forfeiture. Wakefield later stated that he learned about it by reading a newspaper article.[893] The fact that Secretary Noble issued the lease to Huntley *before* he (Noble) notified Wakefield and YPA of their forfeiture did not make the Secretary look good, especially after the positive impressions that he had given them in February. Instead, this new affair looked clumsy, poorly planned, preconceived, predetermined, and inconsiderate to the parties involved.

More than a year later, Chairman McCrae's comments made it clear that the entire affair stunk to him and that he thought Noble handled it horribly:

> …on April 3, 1891, he [Noble] declared a forfeiture of the right of transportation of the association without notice, without trial, or any statement of any complaints for nonuser or misuser of the right, and at the same time provided that the forfeiture should not take effect until the 1st of November thereafter; thus in effect requiring the association to do the business for 1891 at the same time that he forfeited the right because of the manner in which it had or had not been done for the previous years. Not only was no sufficient notice given, but the testimony shows that Secretary Noble personally, in the conference with Messrs. Wakefield and Casey in December, declared that all that he asked was to have a responsible party to do the business; that he repeated that declaration in his conference with Messrs. Gibson, Casey, and Wakefield on the 17th of February, 1891, and in addition declared that he was well satisfied with the association and would not injure it under any circumstances.[894]

The announcement of forfeiture no doubt shocked Wakefield, Gibson, and probably most other people within the Yellowstone Park Association, in the Park itself, and in the region. They immediately made plans to contest it, and it is likely that Chairman McCrae's announcement or other indications soon after—that he would hold congressional hearings—gave the Yellowstone people the encouragement that they might have a chance to "head off" or at least contest both some elements in the upcoming proceedings and the forfeiture itself.

As Wakefield was proceeding with his intentions to run Yellowstone's stagecoaching operation in summer, he was forced in late April and early May, to suddenly travel to the east to purchase additional horses. Back by May 11, Wakefield accompanied at least seventy-five head of horses. Whether it was three or four train-carloads (the accounts conflict), it was not enough. He was back in Livingston on July 1 looking for more horses.[895]

The tourist season was late this year. The *Livingston Enterprise* called it "nearly a month later than usual," owing to stormy weather that prevailed over Yellowstone. In late July, Wakefield and his bosses welcomed one hundred forty-six members of the Wisconsin Editorial Association, a group that had visited Yellowstone during 1890 in smaller numbers. Now in 1891, these journalists were back in much larger numbers. Member Charles W. Bowron wrote a gushing, six-part article about the trip for the Oshkosh *Daily Northwestern* newspaper, and it was clear that the WEA, or at least Bowron himself, approved heartily of the Yellowstone Park Association, including George Wakefield. After praising the park's hotels, Bowron noted that "Similar hotels are maintained at every point of interest in the park and nearly 500 horses are employed in conveying tourists from one to the other on the regular tours of sightseeing."[896] That comment implied praise for YPA's transportation department, and sure enough, after five more installments of this article, Charles Bowron openly praised George Wakefield and YPA:

> The coaching is far easier and more enjoyable than one would expect. The transportation facilities in the park are ample and admirable. The stages are very comfortable. The drivers are accommodating and full of information. They are expert with the [ribbons] and handle four well-trained horses with perfect safety to passengers in the most ticklish places. The manager and attaches of the association that have exclusive charge of the park are courteous and attentive to all wants and inquiries of their guests. The party felt under great obligations to Mr. Wakefield, the manager of the stage lines, to Mr. Johnson, manager of the hotels, and to Mr. Culver, the superintendent of transportation, for their incessant efforts to make the trip pleasant and profitable. They accompanied the editorial party through the whole trip and extended much valuable information.[897]

Bowron also mentioned something about which almost everyone seemed interested—that the train ticket from St. Paul to the Park cost $110 and that the in-park ticket for meals and transportation added $40 more to the cost of the trip.

Another journalistic organization that came to Yellowstone at nearly the same time was the National Editorial Association, which had just finished its huge convention in St. Paul. The *St. Paul Globe* made the extravagant claim that this gathering was "the largest aggregation of editors in the world's history," and indeed there were six hundred journalists present, July 14-17, 1891. The convention broke up late on July 17, and at least one hundred fifty-four attendees left St. Paul on July 18, riding a Northern Pacific train bound for Yellowstone Park.[898]

At the Park, several of the reporters sang George Wakefield's praises. One of them, who was probably James Mitchell of the *Arkansas Democrat*, called George Wakefield "a veteran in his business and a gentleman who has justly earned the praise of the thousands of tourists who every year make the circuit of the park":

> Mr. Wakefield has in his employ a large force of men, which with sixty-five coaches and carriages and 400 horses and mules are required in the transportation of tourists. Everything connected with this transportation line is of the best quality. The stages are large and comfortable and the drivers careful, polite[,] and attentive. It is a great tribute to the successful management of this company and its manager to point to the fact that since the opening of the line in [1883] to the present time there has not been a single accident to any one of the many thousands of visitors who have made the tour of the Park.[899]

"Making the circuit of the park" was what they did, traveling to Norris Geyser Basin, the Canyon, Hayden Valley, Mary Mountain, Fountain Paint Pot, Old Faithful, Gibbon River, Golden Gate Canyon, and back to Mammoth. Mr. Mitchell quoted the Northern Pacific's ticket price as a mere "$110," and he thought it well worth the money.

Another member of James Mitchell's party was E.B. Alrich of the Cawker, Kansas *Public Opinion* newspaper. At the end of the trip when back at Mammoth Hot Springs, he remembered the beginning of the trip and summarized Wakefield's transportation operation by saying, "Here all the available vehicles were in line to transport the largest party that has ever been in the National Park...The system of transportation is a grand one, careful, methodical and prompt." Although Mr. Mitchell did not mention it, Alrich's comments about the party's crossing of Mary Mountain confirmed

that only one year after Congressman Pelton keeled over and died on the
Devil's Stairway, his death and that event were already legendary in the
stories told by Park stagecoach drivers. Of the Mary Lake area, wrote Alrich:

> The driver said: "[F]olks often died up there and it was the
> rule for all passengers to walk down the Devil's Stairway but
> he would make an exception" [for us]. Being the most careful
> driver of all[,] the descent was made [as] comfortably as possible
> [for our party] down Mary's Mountain...[900]

So, people did not "often die" on Mary Mountain; they had died there only
once, but now the legend was ensconced, at least in the lore of one (E.B.
Alrich's) stagecoach driver.

The debate over the "walk up the hill" orders was illuminated, strangely,
by a piece of Yellowstone fiction, which dated the instructions to at least
the summer of 1889, because it was published in May of 1890, and that
was prior to the death of the congressman and prior to the park's opening
in 1890. Like everywhere else geographical, Yellowstone was used by fic-
tion-writers as a location for their made-up stories. In this case, writer Ida
M. Lane used it in her work of fiction entitled "Miss Morrison's Stage-driver" as something her stage-driver made them do, namely exit the coach and
walk up the Devil's Stairway to save wear on the horses. Lane's clearly fabricated direct-quotations along with her placement of geographical locations
that were impossible to reach in the time allowed made it clear that her
magazine article—which additionally starred a less-than-believable, coun-
trified-hick stagecoach-driver—was complete fiction.

At the end of their trip, this large group of journalists came together at
Mammoth and heartily commended George Wakefield and others in the
company for a grandly executed trip. They "recognized a commendable spirit
of zeal and enterprise" by "George Wakefield, Superintendent; E.C. Culver,
Superintendent of Freight Transportation;" and YPA for its "stage service far
superior to our anticipations, and one which we do not think is excelled anywhere, more especially in view of the numerous difficulties and obstacles that
are to be encountered and overcome, the park stages being especially adapted
to the business, [and] the employees careful, courteous and attentive."[901]

By early August of 1891, it seemed clear that there was "a marked falling off" of large excursion parties, and it thus appeared that the season would end early. But the indicators were wrong; there were two large parties left to arrive. On September 6, the International Congress of Geologists arrived in Livingston, headed for Cinnabar. Because there were only eighty of them and they were being managed by the hired Raymond & Whitcomb tour company,[902] they were badly overshadowed by YPA's preparations for the ticket agents' association, which was slated to arrive a few days later.

The geologists were so blunderingly eclipsed in the press by the ticket agents that anyone reading only the newspapers could easily have been persuaded that they did not even visit the park. Fortunately, at least one diary has survived from the trip. Thomas McKenny Hughes and his wife (Mary) Caroline Hughes traveled from Cambridge, England to attend the affair and left the diary under both their names, although probably it was Caroline who wrote it. They traveled through the park in the company of Arnold Hague, Joseph Paxton Iddings, and Walter Weed, three of the era's most famous geologists, especially where studies of Yellowstone National Park were concerned.

Detraining at Cinnabar, the Hughes described their drivers as apparently all dressed to stand out for a special party, namely in "big hats and blue linen coats" that were probably dusters (ordinarily the drivers wore smaller hats and white dusters). At Mammoth Hotel, black waiters fed them a good lunch, while a band was playing, and probably they went on the usual walking tour of the springs and then spent the night. On the following morning, the procession headed south. Strangely, "Pretty Dick" Randall, who had not been mentioned as driving park stages for two years, was suddenly serving as driver for Thomas and Caroline Hughes, for they described him as their driver. Perhaps George Wakefield had made a special arrangement for him to drive this party.[903]

The party apparently stayed at Old Faithful, but without confirmation or elaboration. The Hughes remarked that the party saw Giant Geyser erupt on September 9. They then turned back north and ascended Nez Perce Creek, at the head of which they climbed the "Devil's Stairway." "Someone gave it the name of the Devil's Staircase," stated the Hughes, "and wrote it up on a big label, but Mr. Hague had it suppressed at once." Their friend Arnold Hague (one of the most important givers of place names in early Yellowstone) did not like "Devil" names, but his attempt to censor failed,

and the older, satanic name survived anyway. Reaching Larry Mathews's
lunch station on upper Alum Creek (officially but wrongly called "Trout
Creek" by the park people of that era), they were treated to one of Larry's
sterling lunches and had an entertaining conversation with him.[904]

At Yellowstone River, the stagecoaches turned south. They passed Mud
Volcano, describing it, and drove on to the Lake Hotel, which was now
open for its first summer. "Women waiters" served them dinner, and they
spent the night. Heading north again, this time for Canyon Hotel, the
Hughes noted as they crossed Alum Creek that it "was named by Hague to
keep the fishermen away," an apparent misunderstanding by these writers,
for the name had been used by prospectors and appeared on an 1869 map
from the stream's sour taste. At Canyon Hotel, open for only its second
season this year, the Hughes called the lunch "nasty" and stated that the
entire place reeked of garlic. They spent the night there anyway, apparently
handing their "soup tickets" (letters of introduction) to the hotel manager,
remarking on that strange American colloquialism.[905] Strangely, the diary
gave us little information on the party's geologic discoveries or conclusions.

Wakefield's much larger party arrived six days after the geologists. On
September 12, YPA's transportation company welcomed members of the
International Railroad Ticket Agents association to Yellowstone, and at
least one newspaper called it the largest party ever to visit the Park to that
time, at 270 or so persons.[906] George Wakefield personally took charge of
the arrangements by appearing at Cinnabar, reported the *St. Paul Globe*,
"bright and early this morning with adequate transportation for all the 270
people who will go into the park." In another fine compliment to him, the
Globe stated:

> Today there are over 500 people moving about in the park.
> There is probably no other wheel[ed] transportation compa-
> ny in this country that could move 270 people from this place
> through the park and at the same time take care of the fifty
> regular tourists each day.[907]

The agents' own chronicler praised Wakefield too, saying that "Supt.
Wakefield of the transportation department in the Yellowstone Park, has
been often complimented on his large and well-appointed outfit, but on

this occasion[,] he has surprised even old Park travelers by the extent of his resources."[908] The party left the park on the morning of September 18.

However, it was the railroad agents and other employees themselves, in their organizational account of the trip for their magazine *The Station Agent*, who said the most about George Wakefield's operation, which they correctly called "the transportation department of the Yellowstone Park Association":

> Fifty vehicles and 200 horses were required to take the party through the Park, and so perfect were all the details that there was not the slightest hitch or delay, and everyone was more than satisfied. The majority of the coaches were of the Concord make and particularly well adapted for the purpose. The drivers were all familiar with the roads and the country, and were a never-ending source of information to the tourists…Under the direction of Manager Wakefield of the Yellowstone Park Association, the party was handled throughout with the utmost expedition and skill, and there was nothing but praise for the magnificent management shown by the officials who planned the trip and had it in charge.[909]

It is clear from these and many other such quotes that Wakefield gave good service to his patrons right up to the time—and even for months afterward—that he was first denied the renewal of his license. And the numerous quotations of praise prior to 1890, as given in this book, have made the same points earlier.

In late September, rather than early or mid-October per most years, Wakefield made arrangements for closing his transportation operations for the season of 1891.[910]

It was the last time he would do it. He did not know it yet, for he still believed that the hearings would exonerate him, but in a very real way, he was closing his very soul. Ten days later in Livingston, he superintended the transferring of the horses and mules to winter quarters, again for the last time.

Then, in mid-November, Wakefield and his family spent several days trying to relax at Hunter's Hot Springs—a place that then served in the same recreational manner that Chico Hot Springs does today for residents of this part of Montana. Mr. Wakefield probably did this to help him forget the impending threat whose foreboding had begun descending over his spirit.[911]

It must have been a depressing winter for George Wakefield. In early March of 1892, again as if he had a continuing premonition of disasters to come, Wakefield sold his long-leased (to others) Northern Hotel in Bozeman to his old partner Charles Hoffman, "who it is rumored will erect a fine block," said the *Helena Independent*. "The locality is the best in town," continued the newspaper, "and the figure paid was $10,000."[912] Wakefield made the sale but also made a deal for his daughter Libbie Wakefield to use the hotel to throw a party for her friends, in accordance with her typical-twenties desire to socialize. Libbie, whose twenty-third birthday was coming up on May 29, invited some sixty people to her coming-out party, most of whom accepted, including her father George himself.[913] The sale of his Northern Hotel turned out to be another prudent move for Mr. Wakefield, because bad luck appeared to be coming his way and he would need money.

Meanwhile, an important story in Helena and Anaconda newspapers on March 14 brought mixed news to Montana. Wakefield probably saw it, and if he did, it must have worried him. It reiterated the extensive background of affairs in Washington five weeks before any congressional hearings began. The story, which attributed much of the already-happening, behind-the-scenes chicanery to Russell Harrison, the son of President Benjamin Harrison (in office at the time of the hearings), whom YPA's Charles Gibson believed was the hidden power influencing the Secretary of Interior. The story essentially announced what would be the secretary's ultimate decision, but gave Wakefield and YPA some last-minute hope by emphasizing that both sides were having to wait for the decision of Representative Thomas McCrae's upcoming congressional committee. The article elaborated:

> In 1891, Secretary Noble decided that the association had forfeited the part of [Wakefield's] charter relating to transportation, from non-use, alleging that Wakefield was not an agent, but that, in fact, he was the independent owner of the line, and that therefore there was no responsible head to this branch of the service. This part of the lease was consequently abolished, as

far as the association was concerned, and it was re-let to Huntley and Childs [*sic*—Child], two residents of Helena. When this matter was up, charges of incompetency were alleged against Wakefield, and many serious criticisms were passed on the service he had furnished, as well as on the general management of the park's [the association's] affairs. Of course, there may have been reason for some of this criticism, yet it is unquestionable that much of it was without foundation…At present neither of the companies [Noble and YPA] is taking any steps in relation to next summer's business, as far as the coach lines are concerned. Both are waiting [for] the action of the congressional committee, to which the whole subject has been referred…Gibson charges the secretary of interior with industriously serving the interests of Mr. Russell B. Harrison, who, he asserts, is behind the new lease granted to Huntley and Childs [*sic*—Child].[914]

Wakefield had known for nearly a year of Secretary of Interior John Noble's attempt to make his company forfeit its transportation-permit and of Noble's attempted awarding of the rights to Silas Huntley (in late March and early April of 1891). His hope was that the controversy surrounding Secretary Noble's actions (it seemed to him that everywhere he turned, Montana people were yelling about those actions and siding with him and with YPA) would result in a reversal by Chairman McRae's congressional committee. "Hope springs eternal," wrote the English poet Alexander Pope, and indeed it seemed to Wakefield and numerous others that there was still a chance that he would not have to forfeit his operations for the company and essentially his life in the national park.

It turns out that Secretary of Interior John W. Noble was sneaky, underhanded, and backbiting about his dealings with George Wakefield and Charles Gibson, and Chairman McRae would later "tell off" on him in the congressman's long summary of what had transpired in several years' worth of the history of the affair. Those aforementioned adjectives applied well to Noble, who was both a lawyer and a brevet-brigadier general in the Civil War, and known to some for his arrogance and vindictiveness. A graduate of Miami University of Ohio (where he had been a member of Beta Theta Pi fraternity), Yale University, and finally Cincinnati Law School, Noble was a college friend of President Benjamin Harrison, which explained his appointment to this office. A National Park Service historian, writing about the Department of Interior in 2001, called Noble "one of the most irrepressibly insubordinate figures in American political history."[915]

On February 19,1892, Noble "submitted to his assistant attorney general, Mr. Shields, not the question of whether he could make the lease to Huntley, as Messrs. Gibson and Casey [and Wakefield] understood him, but whether he could force a forfeit of the association's right of transportation without forfeiting its rights to hotels and everything else." On March 17, 1892, Noble telegraphed Charles Gibson at St. Louis that "the transportation matter would be disposed of soon, and he would consider anything that was presented on the subject during that week." He did not bother to contact Wakefield, apparently leaving that to Gibson. "That was all the notice ever given to the association," fumed the peeved Chairman McCrae, "of any intention to forfeit its right of transportation, or of any dissatisfaction with it on the part of the Secretary of Interior."[916]

Wakefield must have received some kind of personal notice of those upcoming hearings, because on Sunday, April 24, 1892, he boarded a train heading east for Chicago and Washington, DC. Probably Gibson or other YPA officers gave him the notice to attend, and it was likely that the company even paid for his trip. Regardless, the hearings would last from April 25 through May 13, and McRae's committee would accept additional, written testimony as late as July 18.

George Wakefield was gone from Bozeman for twenty-one days. Because his testimony was not needed for all the time occupied by the hearings, he made it back to Montana on May 14. Unfortunately, the Montana newspaper-story announcing his return also carried the ominous note: "It is said Huntley secured the lease."[917] That information—devastating to Wakefield if it were true—had leaked twice in early April, at least locally, but those very reporting newspapers simultaneously denied it.[918] So Wakefield continued to make normal plans for the summer's transportation and lived in hope that Congressman McRae's committee's decision would somehow help him, perhaps by "ruling" for his side, if McRae even had the power to do that, which was doubtful. Additionally, he was also hoping a recently introduced congressional bill would somehow negate Secretary Noble's likely ruling.[919]

Although he too had to technically wait for the congressional hearings, Secretary Noble—deceitfully and cowardly—had already made plans to carry out his original decision of forfeiture. While it was true that each of the existing leases made by Noble to YPA gave the government the right of forfeiture for any nonperformance or misuse of any stipulations on the part of the lessee (after sixty days' notice), there arguably in this case was *neither* misuse of stipulations *nor* nonperformance by George Wakefield.[920] The alleged reason that Noble eventually gave for the revocation—non-use— was merely a legal technicality, for he and anyone else who had studied the situation knew quite well that YPA *had indeed constantly used its rights* to the transportation "lease" and did it by employing a verbal contract with George Wakefield. (In this, there was no secrecy or concealment of any kind by YPA or George Wakefield, and there never had been; their arrangement was out in the open for all to see, and many people had said so, in both documents and testimony.) Noble also had to have known that within the leases, there was no prohibition on the use of verbal contracts to yoke an agent to a principal. Even a verbal contract was and is today enforceable in court whenever the holder could prove that the contract existed, and in this case, it seemed to all reasonable parties (except for Secretary Noble) that the proof of their innocence was, and always had been, clear. It was yet another reason that Wakefield and YPA officials remained optimistic through early 1892.

To those congressional hearings, George Wakefield traveled in April and May of 1892. The U.S. House of Representatives passed the resolution on April 8, 1892 to investigate *both* YPA's 1889 leases and Secretary Noble's rescinding the simultaneous grant to YPA for transportation, awarding it instead to Silas S. Huntley of Helena.[921] Other attendees included Thomas Chipman McRae of Arkansas (the Chairman) and the other ten members of the House Committee on the Public Lands; YPA's Charles Gibson; park military superintendent (Captain) George S. Anderson; park interpreter G.L. Henderson, now working for YPA; Secretary of Interior John W. Noble; and many others from YPA, the U.S. Government in Washington, and Yellowstone National Park generally. Numerous people from the Park had an interest in the outcome and/or had been summoned by the House of Representatives as witnesses for the proceedings.

The report they produced—entitled "Inquiry into the Management and Control of the Yellowstone National Park"—was three hundred ten pages long, and was loaded with appended letters, maps, and documents, along with the transcribed testimony of many relevant people.[922] Reading it to-

U.S. Representative Thomas C. McRae of Arkansas (1885-1903) who oversaw the 1892 congressional hearings about Yellowstone National Park's main concessioner. *Author's collection.*

day is a history lesson about Yellowstone and its main concessioner for the period 1882 through early 1892, with all of its surrounding governmental oversight in both the Park and Washington, DC.

Highlighting the hearings was a portion of Charles Gibson's official statement to Congress about George Wakefield's operation. It is worthy of quoting here, because of its relevance to the hearing and Gibson's seeming, complete support for liveryman Wakefield, whom Gibson had first met in 1886:

> In regard to the transportation, it was always carried on in the same way, as far as I know; not differently in 1889 from any other year, and not differently in 1891 from what it was in 1889 or the previous year. The outfit was improved. As the drivers established good characters they were retained, and in that way[,] there was a gradual betterment in the business, but there was no change in it. There was no secrecy whatever in the transaction of the business by the stage company, nor by Wakefield, nor

in the relations between the association and the transportation company. There was no concealment of any kind from the Secretary of the Interior of anything relating to the management of the park, either in regard to the transportation, the hotels, or anything else. On the contrary, it was notorious throughout the park exactly how the business was done. It was known to all [Park] superintendents who were there, and most of them reported officially to the Department.[923]

A look today at the various Park superintendents' reports up through 1891 reveals that every one of them who commented on Wakefield's operation found it top-notch and anything but deficient.

In April and May of 1892, these hearings—which received only fair notice from the national press—must have astounded the many participants and witnesses as to the alleged depth of YNPIC's "depravity," the difficulties faced by and strides accomplished by its successor YPA, and the untruths foisted upon George Wakefield and his transportation-operation because of politics. Unfortunately, and immediately apparent to anyone watching, there was a tendency for both the press and Secretary Noble's office to simply lump Wakefield's operation in with all the easier-to-prove hotel-abuses of YPA, but Wakefield was certainly not responsible for any of those problems.

It is clear today from Secretary John Noble's testimony in the hearings,[924] which was printed first in the transcript, that he was riveted like steel—focused like a telescope—upon Wakefield rather than upon YPA, and that the complaints from Judge Tree and others were what motivated him to ultimately, and probably irrationally, blame Wakefield and let YPA off the hook. The testimony made it clear that Noble knew that YPA controlled Wakefield's unwritten contract, but he ignored that as only an apparent, technical and momentary prick of conscience. Noble's overwhelming tendency—unfair for numerous reasons in the opinion of this author—was to blame only Wakefield, apparently painting him as a rogue-operator of some kind who was acting without the permission of YPA. But that had never been the case, as various YPA officials and park superintendents confirmed and as numerous documents attested.[925]

Regardless, Noble was clearly looking for a scapegoat, partly because he was still smarting from all the complaints and bad publicity of 1890, which had made him look so bad to his boss, President Benjamin Harrison, who might have even dressed Noble down at some point. It is still a rule today in corporations and government that when affairs go badly and solutions are needed, the person at the top (in this case Wakefield) is the one who gets fired, while the entity retains all the lower-level people, because it needs them to continue running the operation during the time the new CEO learns the job. In this case, the obvious and most efficient solution for Noble would have been to fire both Wakefield and one or more heads of the Yellowstone Park Association. But YPA also held the hotels in the national park, and that presented the separate problem for Noble that in addition to the significant investment in buildings that this company had made, he needed for the public—Park visitors—to continue receiving good service in lodging from the company that must have appeared to him to be "the only reasonable game in town" and therefore his "only" choice. This was especially true because the new summer season was slated to begin in about six weeks. Thus, the easiest solution for Noble was to fire George Wakefield by giving a new lease to someone else—a man named Silas S. Huntley who had already applied for the job—and to leave YPA in place, even though *it* had been responsible for most of the complaints that ultimately burned Wakefield.

It was also clear that in ejecting Wakefield from the Park, Noble completely changed Interior's existing rules for leasing. In the fall of 1890, G.L. Henderson, then working in Washington for YPA, heard rumors that S.S. Huntley had applied for the new contract, so he went to Noble's office to inquire. There he encountered S.S. Huntley in person, and Huntley told Henderson that "he would have nothing to do with the transportation unless he could secure the whole thing," including, presumably, hotels. According to Henderson, he immediately expressed to Huntley "very strong doubt about his procuring such a lease unless it was coupled with the construction of hotels, for that had been the prevailing policy of the Department [of Interior] heretofore."[926] But Noble was about to unilaterally change that long-standing policy.

Apparently, Wakefield's first hint that his park-permission would not be renewed came very late (it occurred more than a year after he learned of Noble's first announcement of the forfeiture), namely sometime after May 3, 1892, and probably on May 5. We know this because Wakefield told a congressional subcommittee on May 3 that he had encountered S.S. Huntley "in Helena about three weeks ago" and, when he asked Huntley "are you going to take [over] this line of transportation," Huntley "kind of laughed, and he says 'I do not know'." Huntley was clearly lying, as Chairman Mc-Crae made clear in the congressional report, but poor Wakefield had not yet received final notice of the forfeiture-and-transfer by this meeting-date, which would have occurred on or about April 12, 1892. Nor did Wakefield yet know the outcome at the moment he was telling this Huntley-story to congress on May 3.[927]

The "sword of Damocles" did indeed fall on May 5, 1892 in New York, and it was truly a last-minute revelation—and thus yet another low and sneaky abandonment of notice—for George Wakefield. On that date, Silas Huntley and Harry W. Child purchased from the Yellowstone Park Association all of the assets of its transportation operation, once owned by George Wakefield, and on May 6, Silas H. Huntley officially took possession of those assets.[928] At the same time, or slightly before, five men in Helena signed the papers to incorporate, under the laws of Montana, a company known as Yellowstone National Park Transportation Company. They were S.S. Huntley, H.W. Child, E.W. Bach, L.H. Hershfield, and Aaron Hershfield, which named S.S. Huntley the general manager of the company and capitalized its stock at $250,000. The newspaper article that reported this event also stated that the new contract given to Mr. Huntley and the other men was to last for ten seasons, beginning November 1, 1891. Their action effectively made true, or at least backdated, the rumors of a takeover that had been circulating in Montana since that date. The newspaper also announced the new company's intentions and plant holdings, stating: "The season opens June 1 and to start it the company has 500 horses, from seventy-five to 100 vehicles, and will employ about 100 drivers in addition to the stock tenders."[929]

There was no indication from this article as to exactly when or how Secretary of the Interior John Noble had informed either George Wakefield or Huntley, Child, and company of exactly when and how this transfer was to occur and to be made to happen. One suspects that Noble informed Huntley and Child before he told George Wakefield. If so, it was not Noble's finest hour, but his actions in that vein had been the case for more than a year. On May 10, Mr. Huntley was in Yellowstone National Park formally taking physical possession of transportation, as a telegram from Army Lieutenant George H. Sands to Secretary Noble announced.[930]

In congressional testimony, it became apparent that Secretary John Noble, and no one else, had made the decision for Wakefield to forfeit his park-permission, notwithstanding a great deal of evidence presented in the hearings in favor of Wakefield by Charles Gibson, several Park superintendents, and numerous other relevant witnesses and documents. One glaring piece of bad luck for Wakefield appears to have happened because Charles Gibson was sick in St. Louis in March and April of 1891, and was thus forced to send his son Charles Eldon Gibson in his stead to Washington to speak with Secretary Noble. The son, like his father a lawyer, was nevertheless not as well versed as his father for making the best possible case in favor of YPA and George Wakefield. Immediately suspicious was the fact that the telegram Noble sent to the elder Gibson about this upcoming meeting was dated "3/19" with no year included, so that the son, in testifying, was forced to state to the congressional committee, "The year does not show here."[931]

Perhaps that was mere oversight by Noble or his trying to save characters and thus money on a pricey telegram. But it was suspicious, because it could possibly indicate that Noble was trying to cover up the fact that he had awarded a new contract to S.S. Huntley *before* notifying the holders of the old contract—a move that was against normal business practices and impolite at best, or arguably and realistically, downright contemptible! After all, the younger Gibson stated that while he was sitting in the Secretary's outer office, he had overheard one of the government's attorneys saying to someone he did not recognize, "Mr. Huntley, I will see the Secretary about that this afternoon."[932]

From other testimony by the younger Gibson, it seems likely that Noble had received some heat from his boss, the President of the United States Benjamin Harrison, about the 1890 complaints and that the president's son Russell Harrison had very recently reminded Noble of that. Moreover, the younger Gibson testified that he had overheard Russell Harrison speaking to a government attorney about "a harbor in Texas," and the suspicious words that "he [Russell] would like to benefit St. Louis," which was perhaps not coincidentally the city in which both the older and the younger Gibson resided.[933]

From all this testimony by the younger Gibson, it is apparent that a whiff of questionable politics was in the air and that those machinations *improperly influenced the Yellowstone forfeiture!* And none of these important men was ever called to task for it. That Congressman McCrae and his committee also thought that Secretary Noble, Russell Harrison, and Silas Huntley were guilty was apparent from McCrae's words: "Mr. Wakefield is a Democrat; Mr. Huntley is a Republican and a personal and political friend of Mr. Russell B. Harrison, son of the President."[934]

With regard to his schedule in Washington, the younger Gibson (Charles Eldon Gibson) stated that he at first had trouble getting in to see Secretary Noble, but finally received the meeting on March 23, 1891.[935] He began by acknowledging to Noble that he understood YPA's transportation would possibly be forfeited for "nonuser," but that "we had not been guilty of nonuser" [because] "we had performed our duties under the lease through an authorized agent." Young Gibson thereafter called Noble's attention to a provision in the lease, which he read to Noble, and then stated to Noble

> that that provision of the lease did not require the association to perform the [transportation] business directly, and that it [also] did not forbid them from performing it through an agent, and I began to talk on that theory, when he cut me short. I may say I had not said hardly five words to him before I saw that he was very much out of humor, and he said, in reference to my position, that the work could be done through an agent, "The lease contains no such provision [it did not have to]; that is all nonsense." He seemed to be in an extremely inflamed state of mind, and began quite a tirade against Mr. Wakefield and [against] the manner in which he conducted this business, and referred to complaints, which were on file in his office.[936]

Chairman McCrae's statement about all of this, after he had heard all the evidence in the hearings, clearly sided *against* Noble: "The evidence produced before this committee does not support the forfeiture on that ground [of "nonuser"]. Even more damning was McCrae's summary of Noble's actions, which he called a "gross abuse of power."[937] It thus appeared to numerous people, especially McCrae, that Secretary John Noble was not so noble.

The Noble affair involving George Wakefield was thus a disgraceful, shameful affair based mainly on politics. Noble was a vindictive type of person, and his annoyance at bad national publicity and his political con-

nections reaching to President Harrison's son Russell Harrison resulted in
his handling the affair badly. It arguably devastated a good human being,
George Wakefield, who fortunately survived and did fairly well, but who
was arguably emotionally harmed for the rest of his life. However, it ended
well for the Park in that it brought two competent, even noteworthy people, Harry Child and Silas Huntley, into Yellowstone.

Wakefield lost his lease through little or no fault of his own: He was
the unlucky victim of a bad regulation that would not award him his own
contract for many years; of YPA's bad hotel-service and negative, national
publicity in 1890 that was not in his control; and most of all, of Noble's
wrath about these 1890 problems. Furthermore, there likely were other political machinations that reached to Russell Harrison.[938]

When he learned of his forfeiture, George Wakefield was devastated, and
it can be argued that he spent the succeeding eleven if not twenty-five years
of his life trying to get over it, and to get back to Yellowstone.

Absolute proof for this statement is lacking, but the indicators lean unde-
niably toward that proposition. Stagecoaching in and through Yellowstone
was a job that George Wakefield truly loved in a place that he adored. To
be simply thrown out, when he had done nothing to deserve it, had to have
inflicted a long-lasting wound. Initially, he did what anyone would have
done, and that was to take time off with his family to "lick his wounds" on
a vacation. He and Margaret moved into the cottage they owned on Black
Street in Bozeman, and then in August, he took family members camping
in Gallatin Canyon on Squaw Creek, which then as now was being used as
a public campground.[939]

As early as 1893, George Wakefield was applying for the rights of the
Bassett Brothers over on the Utah & Northern Division of the Union Pacific Railroad or to compete with them, "provided the increase of travel...
warrants it." But the park superintendents continued to maintain Julius
Bassett, as prior holder, in that position. Nevertheless, the Great Falls *Weekly Tribune* reported that Wakefield was indeed granted a "lease" to pick up
Beaver Canyon passengers disembarking from the Union Pacific Railroad,
so perhaps he competed with Julius Bassett that year.[940] If he did, the records of it from the Park seem to be lacking. Nor have newspaper articles
about it turned up.

In late 1894, Wakefield purchased a Livingston livery business, apparently with an eye toward taking visitors to Yellowstone and moved his family from Bozeman to Livingston. The Anaconda newspaper reported the following summer that he and another man had been granted the rights to operate separate, small, private stage-transportation businesses in Yellowstone Park this season.[941]

Notwithstanding attempts at working in other places at other jobs, Wakefield could not get over Yellowstone. He tried. His newspaper obituary states that sometime during the period 1896-1899, he served as manager of the Albemarle Hotel, and indeed a Billings newspaper stated in early 1897 that he leased the hotel for five years, while a Butte newspaper reported him still at the Albemarle in 1899.[942] Probably with an eye toward returning to the Park, he obtained a ranch in late 1897 at what would later be called Chadbourn, Montana by trading his Bozeman Hotel (or perhaps merely its lease) for the Paul Zuber ranch of eight hundred acres in Shields Valley.[943] It appears that his continuing desire to transport horse-drawn visitors around Yellowstone, like Banquo's ghost, "would not down," and he then traded his Shields Valley ranch for Amos Chadbourn's ranch at Cinnabar. Per two local historians, he did this in 1901, to again carry "the dude with the knickerbockers and checkered suits"[944] around the Yellowstone loop. The newspaper noted that Wakefield will engage in "transportation of tourists again," stating that he had already contracted to take a party of one hundred forty persons through the park on May 22.[945] After two years of this, said his obituary, Wakefield "sold his coaches and horses and returned to Livingston," that action occurring upon the death of his wife in June of 1903. She died at their home at Cinnabar, and he then moved back to Livingston to bury her and to reside with his daughter Libbie Wakefield Way and her husband Dr. S.F. Way at 416 North Third Street. It was a two-story, and today green-shingled, house near the end of the block on the east side of the street and almost up against the hillside. Wakefield died there on June 3, 1917.[946] One almost instinctively wonders whether he knew at this early summer date that motorized buses would succeed the old stagecoaches *during this very summer*, and if so whether it shortened his life, even at an advanced age.

George Wakefield's life in Yellowstone and his years after that seem today to impart a message that generations of subsequent Wonderland dwellers have come to embrace or at least to recognize: Once forced to leave

Yellowstone, many of those people spent—and today *spend*—years trying to get back there or at least regretting *that they ever left. This author has seen that message embraced and repeated over and over* in Yellowstone National Park during the forty-six years that he lived and worked there.

As for the management of YNPT Company's stagecoaches beginning in the summer of 1892, George Wakefield was now out of the picture, and Silas Huntley and Harry Child were in, and eventually they, or maybe just Harry, would rename it YPT Company. For twenty-four more years, Yellowstone tourists would again climb aboard stagecoaches and be "off with the crack" of their driver's whip.

YPT's long story, and the rest of W.W. Wylie's story, along with the chronicles of two later stage lines—the Shaw & Powell Camping Company and the Monida & Yellowstone Stage Company—will all be told, or continue to be told, in volume two of this book.

ENDNOTES

1. Nathaniel P. Langford, *Vigilante Days and Ways* (Missoula, MT: University Press, 1890, 1957), p. 429.

2. Nick Eggenhofer, *Wagons, Mules and Men: How the Frontier Moved West* (New York: Hastings House, 1961), pp. 7-8.

3. Eggenhofer, *Wagons, Mules and Men*, pp. 146-151, 154; and Frank A. Root and William Elsey Connelley, *The Overland Stage to California* (Topeka, KS: Crane and Company, 1901), p. 10. For Butterfield, see generally, Roscoe P. and Margaret B. Conkling, *The Butterfield Overland Mail, 1857-1869: Its Organization and Operation Over the Southern Route to 1861; Subsequently Over the Central Route to 1866; and Under Wells, Fargo and Company in 1869*, three volumes (Glendale: Arthur H. Clark, 1947). For a fascinating description from an 1850 issue of the *Missouri Commonwealth* about the painted and water-tight stagecoaches that served in the first stage line across the plains carrying mail from Independence, Missouri, to Santa Fe beginning in 1849, and the way each one was guarded (with eight men capable of discharging 136 shots without reloading), see Root, *Overland Stage to California*, p. 4.

4. Root, *Overland Stage to California*, pp. 47-49. For more, see the inventory of the Frank A. Root papers, Kansas Historical Society, at https://www.kshs.org/index.php?url=archives/40489. Additionally, the Wikipedia site for "Butterfield Overland Mail Company" offers an evolving but accurate overview of that company and the subcontractors who operated it through 1864. They included Edwin R. Purple who transferred many of the Butterfield stagecoaches from the Southern Overland Route to the Central Overland Route in 1861, when the Civil War broke out. In May, 1861, Mr. Purple left Los Angeles with thirty men, wagons, and horses, and on June 16, 1861, he arrived in Salt Lake City with eighteen stagecoaches and 130 horses, which became the center of the company's operations north on the Montana Trail and on points west to California. Ben Holladay coalesced the Overland Mail Company, the Pioneer Stage Company, and Wells Fargo in early 1866, and later that year Wells Fargo bought all three of them. For a primary source on Mr. Purple, see "Exciting and Terrifying Occurrences," *Deseret News* (Salt Lake City, UT), January 22, 1862, p. 5, which mentioned "Mr. Purple, the agent of the Overland Mail Company in this city."

5. Sherry Wilding-White, "The Abbot-Downing Company and the Concord Coach," *Journal of the Society for Industrial Archeology*, vol. 20, numbers 1 and 2, 1994, pp. 80-90; and E.M. Hunt in Wilding-White, as cited, pp. 87, 89, 90n16.

6. The literature on stagecoaching in the American West is voluminous, but it is not so with regard to Yellowstone stagecoaching, which, with regard to overarching examinations, has been only sparingly treated, if at all. The Abbot-Downing Company is treated in Harry N. Scheiber, *Abbot-Downing and the Concord Coach* ([Concord, NH]: New Hampshire Historical Society, 1965, 1979, 1989); and Wilding-White, "The Abbot-Downing Company," as cited. And see generally, Carlos A. Schwantes, *Long Day's Journey: The Steamboat and Stagecoach Era in the Northern West* (Seattle: University of Washington Press, 1999); and Schwantes, "The Steamboat and Stagecoach Era in Montana and the Northern West," *Montana the Magazine of Western History* 49(4), Winter, 1999, pp. 2-15; Ralph

Moody, *Stagecoach West* (Lincoln and London: University of Nebraska Press, 1967, 1998); Edwin G. Burgum, *The Concord Coach* (Concord, NH: Concord Coach Society, 1990); John A. Sells, *Stagecoaches Across the American West, 1850-1920* (Surrey, BC: Hancock House, 2008); Eggenhofer, *Wagons, Mules and Men*, as cited; W. Turrentine Jackson, "Wells Fargo Stagecoaching in Montana," four parts, *Montana the Magazine of Western History* 29# 1-4, Winter, Spring, Summer, and Autumn, 1979; Phillip A. Fradkin, *Stagecoach: Wells Fargo and the American West* (New York: Simon and Schuster/Free Press, 2002); Betty M. Madsen and Brigham D. Madsen, *North to Montana: Jehus, Bullwhackers, and Mule Skinners on the Montana Trail* (Logan: Utah State University Press, 1998), p. 290; Madsen and Madsen, "The Diamond R Rolls Out," *Montana Magazine of Western History* 21#2, Spring, 1971, pp. 2-17; Frank Root, *Overland Stage to California*, as cited, and in GOOGLE BOOKS at https://books.google.com/books?id=sBUWAAAAYAAJ&printsec=frontcover&-source=gbs_ge_summary_r&cad=0#v=onepage&q&f=false; Christine Houze, "Coaching in Yellowstone National Park," *Points West*, Fall, 1997, available at https://centerofthewest.org/2016/08/06/points-west-coaching-yellowstone/; James H. Nottage, *Stagecoach! The Romantic Western Vehicle*, Museum Studies, vol. 1 #1 and pamphlet, 1990, in YNP Library, Vertical Files; and Alvin F. Harlow, *Old Waybills: The Romance of the Express Companies* (New York and London: D. Appleton-Century Company, Inc., 1934. According to some sources, stagecoaches were also called "jerkies," but others say they were not the same, so that term has been confusing through time to many observers.

7. The name Livingston was given to the town in 1882-1883 for Johnston Livingston by his nephew Crawford Livingston, the townsite owner there. By that time, Johnston Livingston was working for the Northern Pacific Railroad, which arrived in Livingston in 1882. Lee H. Whittlesey, *Gateway to Yellowstone: The Raucous Town of Cinnabar on the Montana Frontier* (Helena, MT: Two Dot Books; Guilford, CT: Rowman and Littlefield, 2015), p. 58; and Fradkin, *Stagecoach*, p. 10.

8. Fradkin, *Stagecoach*, p. 1.

9. "Montana Stage Coach—The Overland and Other Lines that Formerly Centered in Helena—The Elegant Six-in-Hand that Carried the Mails in Early Days," Helena (MT) *Daily Independent*, April 27, 1890, Morning, p. 6.

10. A.S. Condon, "The Yellowstone Park—A Fresh Description of the Glories Seen There," *Salt Lake Tribune*, September 8, 1887, p. 6; and Mark Twain, *Roughing It* (Hartford, CT: American Publishing Company, 1872), pp. 151-152. Anne Farrar Hyde gave Twain's year of trip as 1861, in her *An American Vision: Far Western Landscape and National Culture, 1820-1920* (New York and London: New York University Press, 1990), p. 113.

11. Twain, *Roughing It*, pp. 22-40; and Willing-White, "Abbot-Downing Company," as cited, p. 81.

12. Richard A. Bartlett, *Great Surveys of the American West* (Norman: University of Oklahoma Press, 1962, 1966), p. 19; and Eggenhofer, *Wagons, Mules, and Men*, p. 17.

13. "Montana Stage Coach…," Helena (MT) *Daily Independent*, April 27, 1890, Morning, p. 6.

14. Root, *Overland Stage to California*, p. 66.

15. Eggenhofer, *Wagons, Mules and Men*, pp. 172-174.

16. *Ibid.*

17. Eggenhofer, *Wagons, Mules and Men*, p. 174.

18. Louis McLane in the McLane letters at Wells Fargo and Company headquarters, San Francisco, quoted in Carlos A. Schwantes, "No Aid and No Comfort: Early Transportation and the Origins of Tourism in the Northern West," in David M. Wrobel and Patrick T. Long, *Seeing and Being Seen: Tourism in the American West* (Lawrence: University Press of Kansas, 2001), p. 128.

19. Unsigned article, "The Progress of Montana—How the Civilizing Process Has Advanced—The

Eras of Savage Warfare, the Stage Coach, the Railroad, the Ranch, and Now Agriculture," *New York Times*, August 11, 1889, p. 6. Also, see generally, Henry Pickering Walker, *The Wagonmasters: High Plains Freighting from the Earliest Days of the Santa Fe Trail to 1880* (Norman: University of Oklahoma Press, 1966), especially chapter ten, "Montana Gold."

20. C.R. Savage, "The North Country—From the Basin Metropolis to Butte—What a Salt Laker Saw and Heard on a Trip to that Place," *Salt Lake Daily Herald* (Salt Lake City, UT), September 29, 1881, p. 5. At this time, the U&N Railroad was not quite finished to Butte.

21. "The Western Stage Driver," from the *Salt Lake Tribune* as published in *The Buffalo* (NY) *Commercial*, August 28, 1880, p. 4.

22. Llewellyn L. Callaway, "To Virginia City from Corinne, Utah, by Stage, 1873," in his *Montana's Righteous Hangmen: The Vigilantes in Action* (Norman: University of Oklahoma Press, 1982), p. 219.

23. Callaway, "To Virginia City," in *Montana's Righteous Hangmen*, pp. 219-220.

24. Callaway, "To Virginia City," in *Montana's Righteous Hangmen*, p. 220.

25. "World Wide Words," at http://www.worldwidewords.org/qa/qa-boo5.htm.

26. Langford, *Vigilante Days and Ways*, p. 431.

27. General W.A. Strong (Richard A. Bartlett, Ed.), *A Trip to the Yellowstone National Park in July, August, and September, 1875* (Norman: University of Oklahoma Press, 1968), pp. 14-15. For the distances from point to point, see Mallory Hope Ferrell, "Utah & Northern: The Narrow Gauge that Opened a Frontier," *Colorado Rail Annual No. 15: A Journal of Railroad History in the Rocky Mountain West* (Golden, CO: Colorado Railroad Museum, 1981), pp. 36-39, 61-62.

28. *Ibid.*

29. Strong, *Trip to the Yellowstone*, pp. 16-17.

30. Strong, *Trip to the Yellowstone*, pp. 17-18. We note parenthetically that General Strong was not the only known stagecoach passenger to encounter a drunken driver. It must have happened dozens if not hundreds of times in the history of the American West. William Wallace Wylie has stated that his Gilmer & Salisbury driver, who chauffeured him in 1878 from the Union Pacific Railroad north into Idaho toward Bozeman, Montana, was drunk when Wylie boarded the stage (as we have told in Chapter Seven).

31. Strong, *Trip to the Yellowstone*, pp. 18-19.

32. Strong, *Trip to the Yellowstone*, pp. 19-20; and see generally, Stanley R. Davison and Rex C. Myers, "Terminus Town: The Founding of Dillon, 1880," *Montana the Magazine of Western History* 30#4, Autumn, 1980.

33. Strong, *Trip to the Yellowstone*, pp. 21-22. He reported that Virginia City then had a population of seven or eight hundred, including around three hundred to four hundred miners.

34. Aubrey L. Haines, *The Yellowstone Story* (Boulder: Colorado Associated University Press, 1977, 1996), I, p. 242. For now, this 1878 stagecoach travel to Yellowstone is only theoretical, because we have no actual accounts from any such traveler, but the Utah & Northern Railway reached present Idaho Falls, Idaho on April 18; Camas on July 20; and Beaver Canyon on September 16, 1879. From these and a few more Idaho places south of them, stage and wagon traffic to Yellowstone's west entrance could have happened in isolated, individual instances in 1878 and 1879, even though it was still a long wagon-distance to the park. But continuous, fleet-stagecoaching to Yellowstone did not begin until 1880, from Beaver Canyon as this book will soon show. Likewise, primitive wagons probably began in use sometime 1875-1877 on the rough road that existed between Cooke

City, Montana and the park's north entrance, but most of that was composed of local and south-ern-Montana traffic, rather than traffic by tourists from farther away.

35. "To the Geysers," *Helena* (MT) *Weekly Herald*, August 14, 1879, p. 7; and J.P. Nelson & Co., advertisement in *The Madisonian* (Virginia City, MT), August 7, 1880, p. 2.

36. "Is Supt. Norris Properly Improving the Park?" Bozeman (MT) *Avant Courier*, September 4, 1879, p. 3. Norris himself mentioned an instance of this early competition in his 1879 *Report* (along with how scanty the travel was) when he wrote: "Through [Targhee Pass] I alone passed to the summer military post at the head of Henry's Lake and Hickman's camp of Virginia City tourists in the Red Rock Pass." Philetus W. Norris, *Report upon the Yellowstone National Park to the Secretary of the Interior, for the Year 1879* (Washington: GPO, 1880), p. 5.

37. Sources cited in Whittlesey, *Gateway to Yellowstone*, pp. 12-13, and endnotes 16 and 18.

38. Incorporated on August 23, 1871, the Utah & Northern Railway saw its first spike driven at Brigham City on March 25, 1872, a fact that co-owner John W. Young of Salt Lake City told his father, the famous Brigham Young. Young in Robert G. Athearn, "Railroad to a Far-Off Country: The Utah and Northern," *Montana the Magazine of Western History* 18#4, Winter, 1968, pp. 2-23 (these dates appeared on page 4). See also Robert L. Wrigley, Jr., "Utah and Northern Railway Company: A Brief History," *Oregon Historical Quarterly* 48#3 (September, 1947), pp. 245-253; and Mallory Hope Ferrell, "Utah & Northern: The Narrow Gauge that Opened a Frontier," *Colorado Rail Annual*, as cited, pp. 2-81. Athearn noted (p. 3) that as early as 1869, the Mormon lead-ers contemplated an extension of their local, Salt-Lake-to-Ogden rail-line "northward to the rich mining regions of Idaho and Montana." The "desert of black basalt" quotation is from Archibald Geikie, "The Geysers of the Yellowstone," *Good Literature* 2, November 19, 1881, p. 354.

39. Literature on the building and influence of the Transcontinental Railroad is voluminous, and it has more recently included Stephen Ambrose, *Nothing Like it in the World: The Men who Built the Transcontinental Railroad, 1863-1869* (New York: Simon and Schuster, 2000); and Richard White, *Railroaded: The Transcontinentals and the Making of Modern America* (New York: W.W. Norton, 2011).

40. See generally, W. Turrentine Jackson, "Wells Fargo Stagecoaching in Montana—Final Months," *Montana the Magazine of Western History* 29#4, Autumn, 1979, pp. 63-65; and Brigham D. Mad-sen, *Corinne: The Gentile Capital of Utah* (Salt Lake City: Utah State Historical Society, 1980). Like Montana far to the north, Idaho was so small in population that Blackfoot, laid out in 1878 in anticipation of the railroad, was considered a major population-center, per Merrill D. Beal, *A History of Southeastern Idaho* (Caldwell, Caxton Printers, Ltd., 1942, p. 221). The newspaper there explained in 1883 that "Idaho was created a Territory by an Act of Congress of March 3, 1863... The name is taken from an Indian word *E-da-hoe*, signifying 'The Gem of the Mountains'." "Idaho Territory—*The Gem of the Mountains*—Its Area, Soil, Climate, Productions," *Blackfoot Register* (Blackfoot, ID), February 3, 1883, p. 1. But the word "Idaho" was not really Indian in origin; it was a word invented by Idaho settlers, largely white men, as explained in Carlos A. Schwantes, *In Mountain Shadows: A History of Idaho* (Lincoln: University of Nebraska Press, 1996), p. 59.

41. "Its Climate, Soil and Resources—Staging and Its Incidents—The Yellowstone National Park," *Cincinnati* (OH) *Commercial Tribune*, October 7, 1882, p. 1.

42. J. Philip Gruen, *Manifest Destinations: Cities and Tourists in the Nineteenth-Century American West* (Norman: University of Oklahoma Press, copyright 2014), pp. 34, 44.

43. Mormon tracklayers reached Ogden, Utah from the south on February 5, 1874, and Franklin, Idaho on May 2, 1874. Athearn, "Far Off Country," p. 4. Meanwhile, the Gilmer and Salisbury Overland Stage and Express Line was operating stagecoaches north into Montana on the "Montana Trail." See Athearn, "Far Off Country," p. 8n21; and Madsen, *Corinne*, p. 48, with his map of the "Montana Trail," p. 64.

44. See generally Madsen, *Corinne*, as cited; Merrill D. Beal, *The Utah and Northern Railroad: Narrow Gauge* (Pocatello: Idaho State University Press, 1980); Athearn, "Far Off Country," as cited; Carlos Schwantes, "The Steamboat and Stagecoach Era in Montana and the Northern West," *Montana the Magazine of Western History* 49#4, Winter, 1999, pp. 2-15; and Madsen and Madsen, *North to Montana*, as cited. A 1917 history of the U&N by one of its employees is L.O. Leonard, "The First Railroad Entering Montana," *Anaconda* (MT) *Standard*, March 25, 1917, part two, p. 10. A fascinating primary-source on Corinne is "The City of the Gentiles—Corinne, Its Rise, Fall, and Revival," *New-York Tribune*, July 10, 1878, p. 2.

45. "Historical Resume—Building of the Utah and Northern Railway—The Terminus Towns Along the Line," *Dillon* (MT) *Tribune, Holiday Supplement*, January 1, 1886, p. 2 of supplement.

46. For a discussion of the criticisms, see Madsen, *Corinne*, p. 306, and for a rebuttal, see "The U. & N. Railroad," *Blackfoot* (ID) *Register*, August 28, 1880, p. 2. The Bourke diary was quoted in Ferrell, "Utah & Northern," pp. 24-25.

47. Geikie's trip was published in his "The Geysers of the Yellowstone," *Good Literature* 2, November 19, 1881, p. 354. For a discussion of the switch to broad (standard) gauge, see Byrd Trego (who worked on this railroad) in Beal, *Utah and Northern*, p. 57; and "A Great Day's Work," *Butte* (MT) *Semi-Weekly Miner*, July 27, 1887, p. 1.

48. Anna Husted Southworth, "Nan in Goblin Land," *Frank Leslie's Popular Monthly* 29 (January, 1890): 70. My thanks go to fellow historian Lee Silliman of Missoula, Montana for bringing this article to my attention.

49. In January 1877, the U&N was reorganized using Jay Gould's money and influence, and its new directors included Gould, Sidney Dillon, Royal M. Bassett of Connecticut, and Monroe Salisbury. Royal Bassett may have been distantly related to the Idaho Bassett Brothers who will soon become part of our story, and Monroe Salisbury and his brother Orange J. Salisbury were two of the guiding lights behind the Gilmer & Salisbury Stage Line, which was already becoming important in Montana history. Sidney Dillon took over as the railroad's new president. The company was incorporated under the laws of Utah Territory on April 30, 1878, capitalized for $960,000, and registered as a railroad corporation in the territories of Utah, Idaho, and Montana. These connections made it a subsidiary of the Union Pacific. An Act of Congress approved June 20, 1878 (20 Stat. 241) gave the railroad permission to build northward through Marsh Valley toward Snake River. Beal, *Utah and Northern*, pp. 13-14. Mineral strikes made in Montana 1875-1877 resulted in the founding of Anaconda and Butte, and by 1877, rich copper deposits had been discovered at Butte. Accordingly, the U&N headed toward Butte, changing its original route (Soda Springs-Gray's Lake-Lowe Creek-Eagle Rock) to Marsh Valley and Portneuf Canyon, a route discovered by Dr. F.V. Hayden's 1872 survey of the area and a route that offered lesser grades, fewer bridges, and a shorter distance to an intersection with the wagon-road to Montana (at Oneida). Beal, *Utah and Northern*, p. 17; and Madsen, *Corinne*, p. 301. Gould changed the name "U&N Railroad" to U&N Railway, in 1878. Ferrell, *U&N*, p. 31.

50. "Historical Resume—Building of the Utah and Northern Railway—The Terminus Towns Along the Line," *Dillon* (MT) *Tribune, Holiday Supplement*, January 1, 1886, p. 2 of supplement.

51. Beal, *Utah and Northern*, p. 17 says "work was resumed beyond Bear River" to Dunnville, Idaho, twenty miles north of Franklin, in April and May of 1878. Athearn, "Far Off Country," p. 15, says that "during the spring months" construction superintendent Washington Dunn pushed the road some forty miles beyond Franklin. This corresponds with newspaper references that say the road was "seven miles beyond Dunnville" and would be "completed to Watson's ranch (later called Oneida) in Marsh Valley by June 20 or July 1. "City Jottings," *Salt Lake Tribune*, May 18, 1878, p. 3; and Dick, "Northern Utah—A Trip along the Extension," *Salt Lake Tribune*, June 1, 1878, p. 1. The name Oneida was later changed to Arimo, for a local Indian (probably a Shoshoni) chief, per Ferrell, "Utah & Northern," p. 32.

52. Beal, *Utah and Northern*, p. 45; Athearn, "Far Off Country," p. 15; and Jay Gould, "Progress of the Utah Northern Railroad," *Helena* (MT) *Weekly Herald*, February 21, 1878, p. 7. Of U&N's demise, Wrigley, "Utah and Northern Railway," p. 253 says: "The life of the Utah and Northern as an independent corporation ended on July 27, 1889 when the company was consolidated with the Oregon Short Line to form the Oregon Short Line and Utah and Northern Railway Company." The Oregon Short Line was already part of the Union Pacific Railroad. That the name Union Pacific Railroad was in use in the minds of Yellowstone Park officials by the summer of 1887 is apparent from Captain Moses Harris's statement to Assistant Secretary of Interior H.L. Muldrow in approving the Bassett Brothers' permit to operate in the Park that the Brothers' transportation company "is the only [stage] line connecting with the Union Pacific system of railroads." See Harris to Muldrow, July 10, 1887, in Army Era Records, Series I: Pre-1909 Correspondence Files, box 23 (ledger-volume II, March 17, 1887 through August 18, 1889), p. 46, YNP Archives.

53. Stanley R. Davison and Rex C. Myers, "Terminus Town: The Founding of Dillon, 1880," *Montana the Magazine of Western History* 30#4, Autumn, 1980, p. 22.

54. These stations, some of them towns, were listed in Utah & Northern Timetable (with distances) in *Dillon* (MT) *Tribune*, May 14, 1881, p. 1. Historian Beal, a Mormon himself, stated that both Wells, Fargo, and Company offices and the Gilmer and Salisbury stage-operations moved with the U&N as it was built northward. The U.S. Post Office, he said, also "perambulated with the terminus," along with the usual "saloons, dance halls, gambling holes, and wild women." Beal, *Utah and Northern*, pp. 17n10, 18. Beal has maintained that in contrast with the usual, raucous railroad-workers in most places ("Swedes, Irish, and Chinese, heavily fortified by whisky, tea, and opium"), the U&N was built by "mild Utah farmers [Mormons] who eschewed all of these, and coffee as well." Mormons, like everyone else, were not perfect, but Beal was probably largely correct in this assessment, although we have included in the main text some exceptions to that rule.

55. Beal, *Utah and Northern*, p. 19; Madsen and Madsen, *North to Montana*, p. 229; and Strong, *Trip to the Yellowstone*, p. 18. Port Neuf, originally called "Black Rock Camp," was located two miles below (west of) present Inkom, Idaho in Portneuf Canyon. "Inkom" came from *eggakahni*, a Shoshoni word meaning "red house," originally a red barn erected on the Fort Hall (Shoshoni-Bannock) Reservation, which was established in 1869 as a home for those two tribes. Wrigley, "Utah and Northern Railway," p. 249.

56. "Historical Resume—Building of the Utah and Northern Railway—The Terminus Towns Along the Line," *Dillon* (MT) *Tribune, Holiday Supplement*, January 1, 1886, pp. 2-3 of supplement.

57. "News of the Week," Bozeman *Avant Courier*, September 19, 1878, p. 2. Because Pocatello was so slow to develop, the U&N timetable did not even mention the spot until the *Weekly Miner* (Butte, MT), July 13, 1880, p. 1 published the mileage and times that showed Pocatello located at the 156.3 mile-marker.

58. New York Sun (author), "One of the Few Discoverable Uses of Indian Wars," *Idaho Semi-Weekly World* (Idaho City, ID), July 16, 1878, p. 3. According to Ferrell, the word *Pocatello* was not and is not of Indian origin.

59. Ferrell, "Utah & Northern," p. 36.

60. "Black Rock City—The Utah Northern and the Great Snake River Valley," *Idaho Statesman* (Boise, ID), December 14, 1878, p. 2. When the railroad reached Blackfoot, Gilmer & Salisbury began advertising in Montana: "Stage time reduced to 48 hours from Helena, Virginia City, Deer Lodge, and Butte." For another example, see the U&N advertisement in *The New North-West* (Deer Lodge, MT), February 21, 1879, p. 3. As for land-rights through the Fort Hall Reservation, Wrigley says the Indians were ignored, while both Beal and Ferrell say that a complicated agreement was negotiated. For Blackfoot's early history, see "Blackfoot—A Review of this Live Western Town,"

Blackfoot (ID) *Register*, January 1, 1881, p. 4; and "Blackfoot—What It has been and Is Going to be," *Blackfoot Register*, March 5, 1881, p. 2.

61. Beal, *Utah and Northern*, p. 21; and "The Utah Northern Railroad," *Idaho Statesman* (Boise, ID), April 26, 1879, p. 2.

62. Winnamuck, "On the Wing—Viewing a Town [Eagle Rock] which Travels with the Railroad—The Utah and Northern and its Objective Point," *Salt Lake Tribune* (Salt Lake City, UT), May 3, 1879, p. 3; "Utah and Northern," *Deseret News* (Salt Lake City), July 17, 1879; and Beal, *Utah and Northern*, p. 22. For a long and fascinating primary-source on Eagle Rock (today's Idaho Falls), see "Seeing Montana by Rail—Glimpses of the Development of the Territory," *New York Times*, March 27, 1881, pp. 1-2.

63. Idaho, "Terminus Utah & Northern—Business—Beaver Canyon—Chapter of Accidents—Yankee Fork District," *Salt Lake Tribune*, August 23, 1879, p. 1.

64. Idaho, "Terminus Utah & Northern," as cited. Pleasant Valley and Pleasant Valley Creek were and are located four miles north of where the town of Beaver Canyon would soon spring up and three miles south of present Humphrey, Idaho. N.P. Langford's use of the name "Pleasant Valley Divide" in his stories of 1863 Virginia City makes it likely that the name dates from that period on the Montana Trail (Langford, *Vigilante Days and Ways*, p. 199). "Tort litigation" refers to civil lawsuits that historically could be filed against those defendants who intentionally or negligently caused injuries (torts) to others. The legal field of tort-litigation increased greatly during the nineteenth century, as railroads, with their many inherently dangerous practices and aspects, began to increase all over the United States.

65. Omaha Bee, "An 'Old-Timer' Interviewed—Montana, the National Park, Railroad Matters, etc.," *Helena Weekly Herald*, August 15, 1878, p. 3; Eagle Eye, "Snake River—The Route from Salt Lake to Eagle Rock," *Salt Lake Tribune*, May 31, 1879, p. 6; "The Utah & Northern R.R.—The Rapid Progress," *Helena Weekly Herald*, June 5, 1879, p. 2; and "Utah and Northern," *Deseret News* (Salt Lake City), July 17, 1879. For Yellowstone's quick fame in the 1870s because of newspapers and magazines, see Lee H. Whittlesey "Yellowstone: From Last Place Discovered to International Fame," *Site Lines* (University of Virginia, Foundation for Landscape Studies) 5 (Fall, 2009): 8-10, available at: www.foundationforlandscapestudies.org/pdf/sitelines_fall09.pdf. For Yellowstone National Park visitation on a year by year basis, see Haines, *Yellowstone Story*, II, p. 478.

66. Stanley D. and Stephen A. Hansen, *Bassett Brothers, Proprietors of Yellowstone National Park Stage Line* (No place: privately printed by Blurb.com, second edition, March, 2011), p. 16, reproduced in full at http://www.ourgenerationsancestors.org/histories/Bassett%20Brothers%20Stage%20 Line_Pages_Std_Landscape_Reduced%20filed%20size_Final.pdf. "Harsh winters," these authors have said, "and the development of better situated settlements led to the move of the town of Beaver Canyon in 1897 six [actually four] miles south [downhill] to the new town of Spencer named for area businessman Hyrum [*sic*—Hiram] H. Spencer. At that time Beaver [Canyon] became 'Old Beaver,' and today's maps show it as such. Only a historical marker on the Old Beaver town site survives today." Beaver Canyon and Dubois, Idaho are today located in Clark County but in 1879 were located in Bingham County. About Roberts, Idaho, descendant Stan Hansen has stated to this author that the Bassetts "owned 1200 acres near Roberts at one time and it was called Bassett Station," but I have not attempted to confirm it. Stan Hansen to Lee Whittlesey, author's Bassett Brothers file, September 5, 2008.

67. [Anonymous], "How the Utah & Northern, the First and Only Railroad to Penetrate Montana from the South, Made Its Way from Salt Lake, Through Idaho and on to the Terminus at Dillon…" [1886], *Dillon* (MT) *Tribune*, December 18, 1925, p. 25.

68. P.C., "Tragedy of China Point," *Anaconda* (MT) *Standard*, May 3, 1903, section two, p. 3; and

"With the Dillon Pipe-Dreamers—How China Point Got Its Name," *Dillon* (MT) *Examiner*, July 8, 1903, p. 2. This latter account gave the number of Chinese involved as nine.

69. The two articles cited above are the best of the known accounts, but see also "The Park Branch," cited earlier, and F.M.W., "On the Road—A Delightful Ride Over the Utah & Northern—The Scenery in Beaver Canyon—The 'Paymaster's Tree'—The Dives—China Point," *Helena Weekly Herald*, August 5, 1880, p. 3; and "Terrible Plight of Butte People...An Historic Spot," *Anaconda* (MT) *Standard*, January 7, 1910, p. 9, which inconsistently from the first 1903 account above gave the number of dead Chinese as seven and the year of the event as sometime in the early 1870s.

70. "The Park Branch—It Will Be Built this Season and from China Point," *Idaho Register* (Idaho Falls, ID), March 1, 1890, p. 2. The survey happened, but the building of that spur-line never did.

71. Beal, *Utah and Northern*, p. 24; and F.M.W., "On the Road...'The Paymaster's Tree'...China Point," as cited. This latter article makes it clear that Beaver Canyon's original name was "The Dives," apparently from its difficult geography, but more specifics we have been unable to ascertain.

72. "The Mining Metropolis [Butte] in the Days of its Infancy," *Anaconda Standard*, August 24, 1919, section II, pp. 1-2. The quote is at p. 2, columns 6-7.

73. Robert E. Strahorn, "The Utah & Northern Railway—Some Interesting Facts on the Empire it Develops," *New West Illustrated* (Omaha, NE), vol. II, no. 1, January, 1880, p. 3; Strahorn, "Good News and True—The Railway now within Sixty-Five Miles of Yellowstone Park—Concord Coaches to the Geysers in the Summer of 1880," *New West Illustrated*, same issue, p. 5; "The Utah & Northern Railroad and its Prospects" [Terminus now at Beaver Canyon and grading completed to Red Rock; YNP accessible next season.], *The Madisonian* (Virginia City, MT), January 31, 1880, p. 2; and "Railway Notes" [Gould hopes to turn railroad travelers toward Yellowstone], *Winona* (MN) *Daily Republican*, August 5, 1880, p. 2. In a peripheral note, the railroad listed "all of its rolling stock" in 1880, in "The Utah and Northern," Bozeman *Avant Courier*, April 15, 1880, p. 3.

74. Utah and Northern Timetable with exact railroad distances, in *Dillon* (MT) *Tribune*, May 14, 1881, p. 1; and "The Utah & Northern R.R.," *Helena Weekly Herald*, February 5, 1880, p. 2. For elevations, I have used Benchmark Maps, *Idaho Road and Recreation Atlas* (Santa Barbara, CA: Benchmark Maps, 2015), and in this case p. 57.

75. J.H. McQueeney, "My First Christmas in Montana Told by Some Old Timers and Some Who are Not Old—He Shoveled Coal on Utah Northern," *Anaconda Standard*, December 22, 1921, part III, p. 1.

76. Beal, *Utah and Northern*, pp. 24-25; and "Helena [private advices today say 75 men have begun laying track]," *The Benton Weekly Record* (Fort Benton, MT), February 27, 1880, p. 3. See also "The Utah & Northern...Letter from Sidney Dillon, President of the U.P.R.R.," *Helena Weekly Herald*, February 12, 1880, p. 2; and E.H. Beckler, "Railroad Building in Montana," *Butte* (MT) *Daily Miner* (*The Holiday Miner*), January 1, 1889, pp. 70-71. There is a mystery as to the person for whom the town of Humphrey, Idaho, founded in 1901, was named. It might well have been for one of the two owners of the Monida-Yellowstone Stage Company, namely William H. Humphrey, who prior to his stint with M-Y, was a manager of Silas Huntley's Yellowstone National Park Transportation Company. Or it could have been named for George Humphrey (or Humphery), an area resident who died in an avalanche in the winter of 1894-1895 while cross-country skiing in nearby Centennial Valley. See "Humphrey's Death Signal," *The Madisonian* (Virginia City, MT), October 5, 1895, p. 1; and "Centennial—Still Searching for George Humphery," *The Madisonian* (Virginia City, MT), January 19, 1895, p. 1. However, the most likely possibility, in the opinion of this author, is the early settler George Humphrey who probably also served as postmaster, and who was mentioned with his residence shown in Jacob V. Brower, *The Missouri River and Its Utmost Source* (St. Paul: The Pioneer Press, 1897), p. 99 (this George Humphrey might also have been the

father of the avalanche victim). Today Humphrey is essentially a ghost town, consisting only of the large, abandoned school-house on the west side of Interstate 15 and one residence on the east side of the highway.

77. "Burned," *Helena* (MT) *Weekly Herald*, March 11, 1880, p. 8.

78. "Across the Border—The First Rail Laid and the First Spike Driven in Montana," *Helena Weekly Herald*, March 11, 1880, p. 7; "The Railroad—The Driving of the First Spike on Montana Soil," *The Weekly Miner* (Butte, MT), March 16, 1880, p. 5; and "Across the Border—Driving the Silver Spikes in the Utah & Northern Railway," *New North-West* (Deer Lodge, MT), March 12, 1880, p. 3. See also Davison and Myers, "Terminus Town: The Founding of Dillon, 1880," as cited, pp. 16-29, especially p. 21. For a fascinating primary-source history of Montana Territory before 1880 written by those who were there, see "Pilgrim and Pioneer—A Colloquy," *Helena Weekly Herald*, January 1, 1880, p. 16; and for Montana's climate and geography during the mid-1880s, see "Montana Territory," *Livingston Enterprise*, November 20, 1886, p. 4.

79. Beal, *Utah and Northern*, p. 25. For the efficiency of the narrow gauge, see "The U&N Railroad," *Blackfoot* (ID) *Register*, August 28, 1880, p. 2. The 1880 U&N Timetable with distances showed the length of the route (tracks) from Ogden, Utah to Monida station as 283.8 miles. The extension to Red Rock would soon make that figure 322.4 miles and at Dillon the figure became 347.6 miles. See the distance-table and timetable in *Dillon Tribune*, May 14, 1881, p. 1.

80. A report of the founding of Dillon reached New York on September 18, 1880, and appeared as "Founding a New Town," *The Sun* (New York, NY), September 18, 1880, p. 3. By October 10, 1880, Dillon had a population of three hundred inhabitants, and its first regular passenger train arrived there in mid-October. Beal, *Utah and Northern*, p. 28; Davison and Myers, "Terminus Town: Founding Dillon, 1880," p. 24; and Madsen and Madsen, *North to Montana*, p. 240. For an overview of the route beyond Dillon, reprinted from the *New York Times* of March 27, 1881, see "Seeing Montana by Rail," *Blackfoot Register*, April 9, 1881, p. 1.

81. W.F. Wheeler, "Our 'Artist' Aboard—Graphic Pencil Sketches of Montana—Terminus [Red Rock] of the Utah and Northern Railroad—All about It and Its Business People," *New North-West* (Deer Lodge, MT), August 20, 1880, p. 3, col. 4.

82. Wheeler, "Our 'Artist' Aboard—Graphic Pencil Sketches of Montana…," *New North-West*, August 20, 1880, as cited. Here is a summary of U&N's lead-up to the town of Red Rock. About 8.8 miles north of Monida, Montana, the railroad established the station of Williams (Junction), and 9.5 miles beyond that erected a station first known as "Allerdice," then "Spring Hill," and eventually and still today known as Lima, Montana. Reaching the area of Big Sheep Creek, the railroad established Red Rock (reached April 20, 1880, per the "Progress" article cited above and reached May 10, 1880, per Madsen, *Montana Trail*, p. 240) at a point 20.3 miles north of Spring Hill. For more on Red Rock, see F.M.W., "Red Rock, the Present Terminus of the Utah & Northern," *Helena Weekly Herald*, August 26, 1880, p. 3; "Our New Route East," *Helena Weekly Herald*, May 6, 1880, p. 8; and Z., "On the Plains [of Montana]—A Pleasant Account of a Young Bride's Trip," *The Buffalo Commercial* (Buffalo, NY), November 24, 1880, p. 4. After that, the railroad placed Grayling at 8.7 miles north of Spring Hill, and recognized Dillon at 16.5 miles north of Grayling. There were two stations at Red Rock. The original one was located where Dell now stands, and the second one was fifteen miles farther to the north, per Beal, *Utah and Northern*, p. 28n18. A stagecoach passenger from Helena south to Red Rock in June of 1880 stated that the time required for that jolting ride was thirty-three hours, including an overnight stop at Whitehall. By that time, dozens of people were taking daily stagecoaches in the opposite direction, from Red Rock north into Montana, and the "rustling, thriving, portable town of Red Rock" possessed three hotels and about thirty saloons, many of which were gone later that summer. See Viator, "Overland to the States," *Helena Weekly Herald*, June 3, 1880, p. 2; "Passengers from the Terminus," same issue, same page;

and "Utah & Northern—Opening Up of a Great Country by the Little Narrow Gauge," *Salt Lake Tribune*, July 24, 1880, p. 1.

83. Butte's first real train arrived December 21, 1881, per Beal, *Utah and Northern*, p. 29 and the list below. For the complete list of the dates on which the many termini were completed and physically moved to those points, see "The U&N Railway, A Few Facts Concerning its Progress," *The Daily Miner* (*The Holiday Miner*, Butte, MT), January 1, 1882, p. 1. Here is the short list of those arrivals: Dunnville, Idaho, April, 1878; Oneida, July 20; Black Rock, November 1; Blackfoot, January 1, 1879; Eagle Rock, April 18; Camas, July 20; Beaver Canyon, September 16, 1879; Red Rock, Montana, April 20, 1880; Dillon, September 16; Melrose, July 1, 1881; Silver Bow, November 1; and Butte, Montana, December 21, 1881.

84. "Red Rock Terminus—Extracts from a Letter to S.L. Tribune, July 19, 1880," *New North-West*, July 30, 1880, p. 4. In this article, the author gave a detailed breakdown on Red Rock, population 555, and the businessmen who were living and working there. Discussing the railroad, he stated: "The railway business is managed by the following persons: E.T. Hulaniski, general agent for this place; John H. McQueeney, cashier; David Newton and A.B. Hilliker, telegraphic operators; Sam Ayers and James Holt, bill clerks[;] and Charles Bassett, baggage agent." This last man was probably Charles Julius Bassett, the eldest brother, but it could have been Charles Henry Bassett II, the second oldest.

As for stagecoach passengers, so far as known, they were not carried from the stations of Pleasant Valley (immediately north of Beaver Canyon, at 271.8 miles), Monida (until 1898), Williams (north of Monida, at 292.6 miles), or Grayling (north of Red Rock, at 331.1 miles), although they were carried for a brief time from "Pine Buttes," probably present Pinetop Hill, sixteen miles north of Beaver Canyon (see "The Terminus [Is] Still at Beaver Canyon," *Helena Weekly Herald*, March 25, 1880, p. 7).

For Gilmer and Salisbury Stage Lines in Montana, there is so far no exhaustive history of the company, but see generally Madsen and Madsen, *North to Montana*; Jackson, "Wells Fargo Stagecoaching in Montana—Final Months," p. 64; and George A. Thompson, *Throw Down the Box! Treasure Tales from Gilmer & Salisbury the Western Stagecoach King* (Salt Lake City: Dream Garden Press, 1989), a book that would be fairly exhaustive if the author had cited his sources. For actual names of passengers, see "Passengers from the Terminus," in many issues of *Helena Weekly Herald* (such as September 2, 1880, p. 7), Deer Lodge *New North-West*, and other Montana newspapers, which carried the names of these daily stagecoaching passengers who were traveling from the railhead, wherever it temporarily terminated, north into Montana. One of the conditions that has made Gilmer & Salisbury difficult to chronicle is the company's habit of purchasing good numbers of local stagecoaching companies and then running them under their own, already established names rather than immediately changing their names to G&S.

85. Jackson, "Wells Fargo Stagecoaching in Montana," p. 53.

86. *Utah Daily Reporter*, quoted in Jackson, "Wells Fargo Stagecoaching in Montana—Final Months," p. 64. See also Madsen and Madsen, *North to Montana*, p. 174; the G&S classified advertisement in *Idaho Statesman* (Boise, ID), September 9, 1869, p. 1; "Montana Stage Coach—The Overland and Other Lines that Formerly Centered in Helena—The Elegant Six-in-Hand that Carried the Mails in Early Days," *Helena Independent*, April 27, 1890, morning edition, p. 6; and H.S. Howell, "Before Railroads Came," *Anaconda Standard*, October 6, 1895, p. 9. Jack Gilmer had been a manager for Wells Fargo, while Monroe Salisbury had been one of the principal contractors for the Union Pacific Railroad. For an example of the type of advertising that Gilmer & Salisbury ran in Montana newspapers in the 1870s, see Helena (MT) *Independent-Record*, July 10, 1877, p. 1, which announced: "Gilmer, Salisbury & Co., Carriers of U.S. Mail, and of Wells, Fargo and Co.'s Express Run a line of Daily Passenger Coaches to Franklin Terminus, Virginia City, Deer Lodge, and Tri-Weekly to Missoula."

87. The senior partner, John T. "Jack" Gilmer (1841-1892), started his career as a bullwhacker for Russell, Majors, & Waddell. Later he served as a stage-driver for Ben Holliday and as the agent on Holliday's Bitter Creek Division. After making a fortune in the express business, Gilmer lost it in mining. The ghost town of Gilmore, Idaho, was named for him, and the Post Office misspelled his name there. In 1869, proprietors Gilmer and Salisbury purchased the surplus of Wells Fargo's Utah assets and the Idaho and Montana branches of the Wells, Fargo & Company line. They also bought out the Cheyenne and Black Hills Stage, Mail, and Express Line in 1876. See Thompson, *Throw Down the Box!*, pp. 1-3, 15, 33-38, 82-87; and "Cheyenne Deadwood Stage," at: http://www. wyomingtalesandtrails.com/deadwood.html. Thompson's book, although amateurishly written in a few places, is nevertheless a pretty good narrative, but it falls down from the author's greater interest in finding lost treasure than in presenting dependable facts about stagecoaching, and even more so from its lack of cited sources. An example is the stagecoach picture on p. 132, which is labeled "one of the first stagecoaches into Yellowstone Park," when in fact the photo was taken in 1922 at the park's fiftieth-anniversary commemoration, six years after stagecoaching had ended in the park. See also "The Great Mail Steal," *Dillon Tribune*, April 30, 1881, p. 1, which importantly summarizes owner J.T. Gilmer in this sentence: "He was a very ignorant man and could scarcely write his own name, but he had a shrewd eye for business."

88. Pay rates for these employees by Gilmer & Salisbury have not been found, but they were probably comparable to, or slightly more than, the amounts paid to Ben Holladay's employees on the overland trail to California (Atchison, Kansas to Denver to Salt Lake to Placerville, California, a distance of 1,913 miles by stagecoach) during the Civil War, about which Frank Root has elaborated as follows: "Drivers in the employ of the stage company received from $40 to $75 a month, and board; stock tenders, from $40 to $50; carpenters, $75; harness-makers and blacksmiths, $100 to $125; and division agents, $100 to $125." In the late sixties, when Indian problems were becoming so intense, drivers' pay was increased to $200 "for first-class men, and even then[,] they were hard to get." Finally, Root added that the messenger-riders in charge of the express were the poorest paid employees: "They received $62.50 a month, and meals free on the road, but they were idle—that is, had a lay-over—nine days out of every three weeks; so that their real working time was somewhat reduced and their days of exposure that much lessened." Root, *Overland Stage to California*, pp. 72-73.

89. Bourke quoted in Ferrell, "Utah and Northern," p. 25.

90. Z., "On the Plains [of Montana]—A Pleasant Account of a Young Bride's Trip," *The Buffalo Commercial* (Buffalo, NY), November 24, 1880, p. 4.

91. Callaway, "To Virginia City from Corinne, Utah, by Stage, 1873," in his *Montana's Righteous Hangmen*, as cited, p. 220.

92. "Blackfoot Items," *New North-West* (Deer Lodge, MT), August 2, 1873, p. 3.

93. "Personal" [drivers Davis and Pollinger], *New North-West* (Deer Lodge, MT), January 15, 1875, p. 3.

94. "Yellowstone Pioneers—Being Brief Reminiscences by the Old Man" [about Johnny Dunn and others], *Livingston Enterprise, The Holiday Enterprise*, December 25, 1889, p. 6. For Joe Brown, see the preceding article and also Bill and Doris Whithorn, *Sixty Miles of Photo History, Upper Yellowstone Valley* (Livingston: Park County News, [1965]), p. 35.

95. William Wallace Wylie, unpublished autobiography, no date [1926], his original mimeographed copy with "W.W. Wylie" and his mailing address stamped on its front page, in locked file-cabinet of Rare Book Room, YNP Library, pp. 2-3.

96. Wylie, unpublished autobiography, pp. 2-3.

97. Wylie, unpublished autobiography, pp. 3-4.

98. Wylie, unpublished autobiography, p. 4.

99. Wylie, unpublished autobiography, p. 4.

100. Madsen and Madsen, *North to Montana*, p. 43; and Hoppe in Ida McPherren, *Imprints on Pioneer Trails* (Boston: Christopher Publishing House, 1950), p. 118. For Hoppe's life story, see generally, Whittlesey, *Gateway to Yellowstone*.

101. "Knights of the Road!—Attempt to Waylay the Eastward Bound Coach from Deer Lodge," *Helena Weekly Herald*, June 28, 1883, p. 2; and "Waylaid—The Butte Coach Held up by Road Agents on the Prickly Pear Divide—The Passengers Made to Disgorge and the Treasure Box Rifled," *Helena Weekly Herald*, June 28, 1883, p. 4. For the reminiscence quoted, see "A Highway Robbery in Montana," *The Daily Intermountain* (Butte, MT), December 21, 1900, Christmas number, p. 5.

102. Langford, *Vigilante Days and Ways*, p. 431; "Robbery of Passengers," *Daily Union Vedette* (Camp Douglas, UT), August 24, 1864, p. 2; and Ronald H. Limbaugh, "'Escaped Up Certain Trees,': Fugitive Hank Buckner and the Fight for Law and Order in Idaho and Montana Territories, 1864-1866," *Montana the Magazine of Western History* 69(3), Autumn, 2019, p. 34. In a conflict with his (earlier) statement about the river's name, Langford added (p. 432) that he believed that the canyon's eroded coverts and gateways of rock were responsible for the name of the river, "the word Port-Neuf in compound form signifying 'ninth gate'." A later *Vedette* article ("Highway Robbery and Murder!" July 17, 1865, p. 2) agreed with this ("ninth gate") origin for the name, stating it had been given "by old French adventurers."

103. Madsen and Madsen, *North to Montana*, p. 129; "The Road Agents," *Daily Union Vedette* (Camp Douglas, UT), September 10, 1864, p. 2; "The Search after the Robbers," *Daily Union Vedette*, September 15, 1864, p. 2; "The Scoundrel Kelly," *Montana Post* (Virginia City, MT), September 17, 1864, p. 2; and "In Transitu," *Montana Post*, September 17, 1864, p. 3. These last two newspaper articles implied that "Kelly" was lynched without a trial, which was also the conclusion of Callaway, in *Montana's Righteous Hangmen*, p. 115. See also "Seeing Montana by Rail—Glimpses of the Development of the Territory," *New York Times*, March 27, 1881, p. 1; and "The Mining Metropolis [Butte] in the Days of its Infancy," *Anaconda Standard*, August 24, 1919, section II, pp. 1-2.

104. "Highway Robbery and Murder!", *Daily Union Vedette* (Camp Douglas, UT), July 17, 1865, p. 2; "More of the Port Neuf Murders," *Daily Union Vedette*, July 21, 1865, p. 2; "Massacre and Robbery," *Deseret News* (Salt Lake City, UT), July 19, 1865, p. 5; and "Overland Stage Attacked by Robbers—Four Men Killed and Three Badly Wounded—$60,000 in Gold Taken by the Villains," *Montana Post* (Virginia City, MT), July 22, 1865, p. 2. See also Limbaugh, "Escaped Up Certain Trees," as cited, pp. 43-44.

105. Albert D. Richardson, *Beyond the Mississippi: From the Great River to the Great Ocean* (Hartford, CT: American Publishing Company, 1867), pp. 493-494.

106. "Road Agents—An Attempt to Waylay the Overland Coach," *Helena Weekly Herald*, June 12, 1879, p. 8, from the *Daily Herald* of June 5. A shorter version of this story, with the same headline, appeared in Bozeman *Avant Courier*, June 12, 1879, p. 2.

107. "Territorial" [A.W. Orton], *New North-West* (Deer Lodge, MT), May 18, 1877, p. 3; and "Washington Items" [S.S. Huntley], *New North-West*, April 27, 1877, p. 2. Huntley's winning bid was $34,000 for the statewide contract and $17,700 for the stretch from Bozeman to Miles City, "via Crow Agency, Fort Pease, Big Horn, etc., to Tongue River 340 miles semi-weekly." "General News," *Rocky Mountain Husbandman* (Diamond City, M.T.), June 28, 1877, p. 7.

108. "Brevities," *Helena Weekly Herald*, November 8, 1877, p. 8; "Territorial," *New North-West*, November 9, 1877, p. 2; and information collected by the author at Crazy Mountain Museum, Big Timber, Montana, September 18, 2018. See also Nan Sigrist and Ruth Quinn, "Harry's Grand

Tour: Building Yellowstone's Legacy of Service" (book-manuscript about Harry Child and Silas Huntley, in review, 2021), pp. 6, 9-12.

109. "S.S. Huntley & Co's Stage Line," advertisement, Bozeman *Avant Courier*, February 7, 1878, p. 3. This advertisement was still running on May 9 in the same newspaper. Also in February, officials announced that the U.S. postmaster general had officially changed the name and site of the post office at Tongue River to Fort Keogh and appointed John H. Aylesworth of Chico (Gallatin, later Park, County) to be postmaster there to replace John Coner, resigned.

110. "Bids on Tongue River Mail Routes," *Helena Weekly Herald*, March 28, 1878, p. 8.

111. "New Arrangements for the Tongue River Route," Bozeman *Avant Courier*, November 28, 1878, p. 3; "Dissolution Notice," in same issue, same page; and "Dissolution Notice," *Avant Courier*, December 5, 1878, p. 3. That this was a three-day trip in 1878 and into 1879 was affirmed by "Eastern Montana Mail Service," *Helena Weekly Herald*, December 5, 1878, p. 7. But see also "Brevities," *Helena Weekly Herald*, January 9, 1879, p. 8, which says that "Gilmer & Salisbury's coaches now ply between Bozeman and Miles City in four days, instead of six, as heretofore."

112. "Marks of Early Days," *Yellowstone Journal* (Miles City, MT), November 30, 1882, p. 4. Junction City, Montana was then located between Virginia City and Alder, MT at the junction of Granite Creek with Alder Creek.

113. "Montana Stage Coach—The Overland and Other Lines that Formerly Centered in Helena—The Elegant Six-in-Hand that Carried the Mails in Early Days," Helena (MT) *Daily Independent*, April 27, 1890, Morning, p. 6. This editor did us a favor by listing the names of some memorable Montana stage-drivers, even if he did not tell us much about them. They were: Chris Vassube, Ira Mott, E.M. "Governor" Pollinger, H.N. Galen, P.B. Clark, John Rohrbaugh, James H. Mc-Farland, John Zeigler, and of course S.S. Huntley who figures into this book later and even more so in Volume Two.

114. Strahorn, *To the Rockies and Beyond*, as quoted in Ferrell, "Utah and Northern," p. 39.

115. "Gilmer & Salisbury's Stage Line," *Helena Weekly Herald*, March 27, 1873, p. 8; Madsen and Madsen, *North to Montana*, p. 185; and Thompson, *Throw Down the Box!*, pp. 39-45.

116. This town was Sheridan, Montana, where the short-lived newspaper entitled the *Sheridan Messenger* was founded in 1879, per [M.A. Leeson], *History of Montana, 1739-1885: A History of its Discovery and Settlement, Social and Commercial Progress* (Chicago: Warner, Beers and Company, 1885), p. 335. For the quote about the size of Sheridan, Montana, see A., "Montana—The Great Territory as Seen by an Iowan," *Burlington Hawk-Eye* (Burlington, IA), June 3, 1880, p. 1.

117. Gallahan ranch or the settlement of "Gallahan" apparently consisted of the ranch of George W. Gallahan (1843-1917), who was briefly postmaster at Cataract, Montana (in northern Jefferson County just west of the town of Boulder) in early 1880. See "New Post Offices," *Helena Weekly Herald*, February 26, 1880, p. 7; and "The Cataract Mining District," *The Weekly Miner* (Butte, MT), August 3, 1880, p. 5. Also living at Gallahan at about this time were W.J. and Isabella Gallahan, per "Died" [at Gallahan, Lizzie, infant daughter of W.J. and Isabella Gallahan], *Helena Weekly Herald*, September 8, 1881, p. 7.

118. "Nearly Perished" [from the December 7 edition of the *Sheridan Messenger*], *Helena Weekly Herald*, December 16, 1880, p. 8.

119. "Heavy Travel and Immigration," *Helena Weekly Herald*, April 8, 1880, p. 8.

120. "Brevities" [from the Virginia City *Madisonian*], *Helena Weekly Herald*, July 22, 1880, p. 7.

121. "Chips," *Salt Lake Daily Herald*, September 2, 1883, p. 12. The *Herald* stated: "The Utah & Northern connected with the Northern Pacific at Little Blackfoot last week." The small town

of Little Blackfoot was later renamed Garrison. For the 1881 rumblings about the end of stage-coaching, see "Railroad Notes—As They are Picked up Promiscuously," *New North-West* (Deer Lodge, MT), November 4, 1881, p. 3; and for the entire story, see Athearn, "Railroad to a Far-Off Country," as cited.

122. Madsen and Madsen, *North to Montana*, pp. 183-184.

123. "Accident on the Overland Stage Line—The Coach Upsets and Seriously Injures Two Passengers," *Helena Daily Herald* of November 22, as reprinted in *Helena Weekly Herald*, Nov 25, 1875, p. 7; "Serious Casualty," Bozeman *Avant Courier*, November 26, 1875, p. 2; and "Local Brevities" [stage wreck], *New North-West* (Deer Lodge, MT), November 26, 1875, p. 3.

124. "Territorial Items" [lawsuit asks for $30,000], *New North-West* (Deer Lodge, MT), May 12, 1876, p. 3; "C.W. Higley vs. Gilmer & Salisbury" [$5,000 awarded to plaintiff], *Helena Weekly Herald*, June 7, 1877, p. 7; and "Court Proceedings" [motion for new trial is overruled], *Helena Weekly Herald*, June 28, 1877, p. 4.

125. "Supreme Court," *Helena Weekly Herald*, January 31, 1878, p. 6, ending at "A Large Verdict," *Helena Weekly Herald*, December 26, 1878, p. 7. The case and its first appeal appeared officially at *Higley v. Gilmer*, 140 Mont. 252, and 3 Mont. 90 (1878).

126. "Supreme Court" [Montana Supreme Court affirms case], *The Weekly Miner* (Butte, MT), January 13, 1880, p. 7; and "Death of C.W. Higley," *Helena Weekly Herald*, May 13, 1880, p. 8.

127. George Fleming, "Glanders" [from *Nineteenth Century* magazine], *Benton Weekly Record* (Fort Benton, MT), April 27, 1882, p. 6; "The Deer Lodge Horse Disease," *Helena Weekly Herald*, November 29, 1883, p. 4; "The Horse Disease," *New North-West* (Deer Lodge, MT), November 23, 1883, p. 3; and "Glanders in Horses," *Helena Weekly Herald*, December 13, 1883, p. 6. Glanders reached Livingston and Billings in 1885, per "Local Layout," *Livingston Enterprise*, June 13, 1885, p. 3; and "Glandered Montana Horses," *Livingston Enterprise*, October 17, 1885, p. 1. Naturally, denial prevailed among numerous stockmen in the Territory who were financially threatened by the disease, and who thus did not want to admit that the disease was present. For example, see "Glanders," *Livingston Enterprise*, October 28, 1885, p. 2.

128. https://en.wikipedia.org/wiki/Burkholderia_mallei and https://en.wikipedia.org/wiki/Glanders. That this horse-disease eventually became a massively important issue in the U.S. is clear in that from 1890 through 1910, at least twenty-three states and territories had horse-glanders cases occur in their state supreme courts and/or appellate courts, along with one U.S. Supreme Court case and a couple of other federal cases. We have cited many of them here:

138 Ill. 48 (1891); 67 Miss. 405 (1890); 65 N.Y.S. 376 (1900); 152 Mass. 540 (1891); 60 S.W. 334 (Texas Appellate, 1900); 16 N.D. 248 (1907); 100 Mich. 190 (1894); 120 Wis. 151 (1904); 45 Ct. Cl. 1 (US Court of Claims, 1900); 91 Ark. 69 (1909); 106 S.W. 42 (Texas Court of Civil Appeals, 1897); 77 Neb. 436 (1906); 19 N.D. 317 (1909); 206 Mass. 223 (1910); 109 Minn. 64 (1909); 29 Neb. 301 (1890); 103 Cal. 50 (1894); 20 R.I. 233 (1897); 6 Kan. App. 136 (Court of Appeals of Kansas, 1897); 72 A. 220 (Supreme Court of Rhode Island, 1909); 30 Tex. Civ. App. 19 (Texas Court of Civil Appeals, 1902); 79 Md. 514 (Court of Appeals of Maryland, 1894)[*State v. Fox*, seller liable for death of human when he conceals that a horse is afflicted with glanders]; 14 Haw. 533 (1902); 51 Wash. 664 (1909); and U.S. Supreme Court at 211 U.S. 306 (1908). My thanks go to my friend and fellow historian and lawyer Steve Mishkin of Olympia, Washington for finding these cases and discussing them with me.

129. *State v. Fox*, 79 Md. 514 (Court of Appeals of Maryland, 1894).

130. Granville Stuart in *Weekly Missoulian*, April 27, 1883, as quoted in Schwantes, "The Steamboat and Stagecoach Era…," as cited, p. 3. Stuart was the author of the classic Montana books *Montana As It Is* (1865) and *Forty Years on the Frontier* (1925).

131. "The Last Coach," *Helena Weekly Herald*, June 21, 1883, p. 8; and "Staging No More," *Helena Weekly Herald*, September 6, 1883, p. 7.

132. "Turned Out to Grass—The Stage Coach a Thing of the Past," *New North-West* (Deer Lodge, MT), October 12, 1883, p. 3.

133. "Montana News" [Utah Live Stock Company], *Livingston Enterprise*, February 15, 1884, p. 1. See also "Gilmer & Salisbury—The Proprietors and Managers of the Largest Stage Line in the West" [a requiem], *Salt Lake Tribune*, January 3, 1884, p. 6; and "Notes of the Day," *New North-West*, February 22, 1884, p. 2, which quotes the *Salt Lake Chronicle* as saying that the new G&S corporation will be known as "Gilmer, Salisbury, and Company." Clearly this last was in conflict with the news about the name "Utah Live Stock Company."

134. "Gilmer and Salisbury," *Helena Weekly Herald*, January 1, 1885, p. 2.

135. "Herald Roundup" [Gilmer & Salisbury sell out], *Helena Weekly Herald*, July 16, 1885, p. 7.

136. For example, organization of the M&ISFC appeared in "Bayhorse Gleanings," *The Silver Messenger* (Challis, ID), January 11, 1898, p. 1. The RS&GS Company appeared in *The Silver Messenger*, January 3, 1899, p. 1, sporadically through at least January 7, 1902, p. 1. For the Anderson Brothers, see "The City in Brief" [Dan Callahan and Anderson Brothers], *The Madisonian* (Virginia City, MT), April 25, 1896, p. 1. The Jay C. Lyndes Family Collection contains many original items from these and other stagecoach companies.

137. Paul Schullery, "Privations and Inconveniences: Early Tourism in Yellowstone National Park," in David M. Wrobel and Patrick T. Long, *Seeing and Being Seen: Tourism in the American West* (Lawrence: University Press of Kansas, copyright 2001), p. 227.

The origin of the term "Wonderland," as applied to the upper Yellowstone River country, which eventually became present Yellowstone National Park, has been discussed some but not exhaustively, so we take up that discussion here. See Shaffer, *See America First*, pp. 49-52; and Whittlesey, *Yellowstone Place Names*, 2006, p. 265. The term came naturally from Lewis Carroll's (Charles Dodgson's) books *Alice's Adventures in Wonderland* (1865) and *Through the Looking Glass* (1871), but when applied to Yellowstone, the story quickly got more complicated. Historian Aubrey Haines has attributed its first use to the personal diary of prospector A. Bart Henderson for July 24, 1871 (Haines, *Yellowstone National Park: Its Exploration and Establishment* [Washington, DC: Govt. Printing Office, 1974], pp. 104, 178n241 [citing "The Yellowstone Expedition," *New York Times*, September 18, 1871], 179n242 citing [Henry W.] Elliott, "The New Wonder Land," *New York Times*, October 23, 1871, and A. Bart Henderson's diary, July 24, 1871]; and Haines, *Yellowstone Story*, I, p. 188 [citing Henderson's diary]). Paul Schullery in "Privations" cited Haines and the Henderson diary, but as his footnote 1 (p. 244) explained, it is possible that Henderson added that entry later. Regardless, it seems most likely that the term "Wonderland" as applied to Yellowstone originated in 1871, if not from A. Bart Henderson, then possibly from Calvin C. Clawson, a Montana newspaper editor and guide for the first known, commercial tourist-party into present Yellowstone National Park that same year. Clawson wrote a series of articles entitled "Notes on the Way to Wonderland" for the *New North-West* (Deer Lodge, MT), beginning September 9, 1871, p. 2. The third candidate is Henry W. Elliott, one of the artists for the 1871 Hayden Survey, who authored the above-mentioned article for the *New York Times*, October 23, 1871, p. 4. This article also appeared in several other places: Henry W. Elliott, "The New Wonder Land. The Upper Yellowstone Country," *Evening Star* (Washington, DC), October 14, 1871, p. 1; H.W. Elliott, "The New Wonderland. The Upper Yellowstone Country," *The Superior Times* (Superior, WI), November 11, 1871, p. 3; and H.W. Elliott, "The New Wonderland. The Upper Yellowstone Country," *The Donaldsonville* (LA) *Chief*, November 25, 1871, p. 1. Thanks to Montana historian Lee Silliman, the Clawson accounts have been published as a book: Calvin C. Clawson (Lee Silliman, ed.), *A Ride to the Infernal Regions: Yellowstone's First Tourists* (Helena: Riverbend Publishing, copyright 2003).

138. Marguerite S. Shaffer, "Seeing America First: The Search for Identity in the Tourist Landscape," in Wrobel and Long, *Seeing and Being Seen*, as cited, pp. 168, 177; and Shaffer, *See America First: Tourism and National Identity, 1880-1940* (Washington, D.C.: Smithsonian Books, copyright 2001), pp. 11-15, 158-159.

139 . J. Philip Gruen, *Manifest Destinations: Cities and Tourists in the Nineteenth-Century American West* (Norman: University of Oklahoma Press, copyright 2014), pp. 11, 26.

140. Gruen, *Manifest Destinations*, p. 26, quoting John Codman, *The Mormon Country: A Summer with the "Latter-Day Saints"* (New York: United States Publishing, 1874), p. 211; and Anne Far-rar Hyde, *An American Vision: Far Western Landscape and National Culture, 1820-1920* (New York and London: New York University Press, 1990), p. 108. Hot Springs Reservation, Arkansas became a federal reservation in 1832 to preserve those hot springs for commercial bathing purposes and recreation, and a national park in 1921, but was handicapped early for tourism by the Union's Army's sacking of it in 1864, and fires (1878, 1905, 1913), which destroyed 150 buildings in 1878, and many blocks of city on two later occasions. https://en.wikipedia.org/wiki/Hot_Springs_National_Park

141. Lynne Withey, *Grand Tours and Cook's Tours: A History of Leisure Travel, 1750 to 1915* (New York: William Morrow and Company, 1997), p. 299.

142. Hyde, *An American Vision*, as cited p. 144.

143. John H. Tice, *Over the Plains and on the Mountains...* (St. Louis, 1872), as quoted in Hyde, *An American Vision*, p. 145.

144. Gruen, *Manifest Destinations*, pp. 29, 32, partially quoting Turner, "The Significance of the Frontier in American History," in Turner's *The Significance of the Frontier in American History* (New York: Henry Holt, 1921), Chapter One, pp. 22-23,

145. The earlier, eastern equivalents were Saratoga Springs, New York; and the seaside resorts of Cape May, New Jersey; and Long Branch, New Jersey. Hyde, *An American Vision*, pp. 109, 125, 147-149, 154, 174-190. For Shoshone Falls, see generally Edwards Roberts, *Shoshone and Other Western Wonders* (New York: Harper and Brothers, 1888). Pike's Peak is in Earl Pomeroy, *In Search of the Golden West: The Tourist in Western America* (Lincoln: University of Nebraska, second edition, 1957, 1990, 2010), pp. xxxii-xxxiii, 33, 60, 62.

146. Hyde, *An American Vision*, pp. 164, 184-185; and Pomeroy, *In Search of the Golden West*, pp. 27-28. Except for falling for the incorrect "Colter's Hell" legend (p. 193—and in fact, "Colter's Hell" was near present Cody, Wyoming, not Yellowstone) and her erroneous claim that Yellowstone "offered no accommodations for tourists" in "its first decades" (p. 245—The "McCartney's Hotel" [1871] and the "Marshall's Hotel" [1880] were both in operation, primitive though they were.), Hyde's account of the evolution of Yellowstone National Park was accurate, even fairly exhaustive. But she, like everyone else except Haines and Cindy S. Aron in *Working at Play: A History of Vacations in the United States* (Oxford and New York: Oxford University Press, 1999, 2001), did not mention the Utah & Northern Railway, which arrived at Beaver Canyon, Idaho in late 1879, as chronicled in this book. Cindy Aron got the year of opening for the Mammoth Hotel wrong (p. 296n47—it was 1883, not 1884), but found the 1882 Mary Richards account and read it well enough to note their arrival on the U&N and the amount of equipment and its cost that they needed to tour Yellowstone (p.169). She did not index the railroad, but scored a coup in also finding the Webner trip through Yellowstone at the University of Virginia.

147. See generally, Pomeroy, *In Search of the Golden West*, as cited; Gruen, *Manifest Destinations*, as cited; Wrobel and Long, *Seeing and Being Seen*, as cited; Hyde, *An American Vision*, as cited; Shaffer, *See America First*, as cited; Cindy S. Aron, *Working at Play*, as cited; Withey, *Grand Tours and Cook's Tours*, as cited; and John A. Jakle, *The Tourist: Travel in Twentieth-Century North America* (Lincoln and London, University of Nebraska Press, 1985).

148. Haines, *Yellowstone Story*, I, pp. 194, 255-256; 262; II, pp. 31, 102, 185, 259. Haines might also have omitted the U&N because he had enough to do to write the massive history of Yellowstone National Park itself. Lynne Withey in her *Grand Tours and Cook's Tours*, as cited, mentioned (p. 313) that the Union Pacific acquired the Utah & Northern in the late 1870s but did not chronicle the little railroad, adding only that UP eventually completed a branch line to the park's west entrance in 1907-08.

149. Pomeroy, *In Search of the Golden West*, pp. 53-54, 240, Yellowstone as "monotonous."

150. Pomeroy, *In Search of the Golden West*, p. 152; and Jakle, *The Tourist*, p. 148.

151. Schullery, "Privations and Inconveniences," as cited, p. 228.

152. These travel estimates are in Haines, *Yellowstone Story*, II, p. 478. The larger portion of 1883 visitors arrived that year by the new Northern Pacific Railroad at the park's north entrance, which was completed to Cinnabar, Montana, in late August. But another portion of visitors continued to arrive for many years via the little-known Utah & Northern Railway at Beaver Canyon. It later affiliated with the Union Pacific Railroad.

153. Schwantes referred here to the Northern Pacific Railroad, but did mention the Utah & Northern Railway briefly. Only Haines seems to have spent much time and space with it, and he, too, mentioned it only briefly and in connection with Superintendent Norris's attempts to reroute the mails into the Park. For the complete story, see Chapters Two and Three in this book, and cursory mentions in Haines, *Yellowstone Story*, I, pp. 194, 255-256, 262; II, pp. 31, 102, 185, 259.

154. Carlos A. Schwantes, "No Aid and No Comfort: Early Transportation and the Origins of Tourism in the Northern West," in Wrobel and Long, *Seeing and Being Seen*, as cited, p. 125; and Schwantes, *Long Day's Journey: The Steamboat & Stagecoach Era in the Northern West* (Seattle and London: University of Washington Press, 1999), p. 286. For 1883 in Yellowstone, see Whittlesey, "'Oh, Mammoth Structure!': Rufus Hatch, the National Hotel, and the Grand Opening of Yellowstone in 1883," as cited, pp. 2-20; Haines, *Yellowstone Story*, I, pp. 279-290; and Bartlett, *Wilderness Besieged*, pp. 45-49, 51-52.

155. Schullery, "Privations and Inconveniences," as cited, p. 227.

156. Lee H. Whittlesey, "Yellowstone: From Last Place Discovered to International Fame," *Site Lines* 5(Fall, 2009): 8-10, quotation on p. 9, University of Virginia, Foundation for Landscape Studies. Available at: www.foundationforlandscapestudies.org/pdf/sitelines_fall09.pdf; and newspapers. com, accessed November 12, 2020. This inquiry was made with the name "Yellowstone National Park" in quotation marks, so as to eliminate all references to "national," "park," and "Yellowstone," which could turn up many singular, non-references to the park.

157. Olin D. Wheeler, the NPRR's historian and publicity manager, was the author of many of these books. Beginning in 1906 (when both a *Wonderland 1906* and a *Land of Geysers* were published), the booklets were issued under the title *Land of Geysers*, smaller and less ornate but lasting until at least 1917. The complete set is cited individually in Whittlesey, *Yellowstone Place Names*, 2006, pp. 284-285.

158. Schullery, "Privations and Inconveniences," as cited, p. 240.

159. George Marshall stated this himself in his handwritten biographical statement [1885], Bancroft Library, Berkeley, California; copy in manuscript file, Yellowstone National Park Research Library, and partially reproduced in Whittlesey, "Marshall's Hotel in the National Park," as cited: "In 79 [I] took mail contract," wrote Marshall, "to carry mail from Vir[ginia] City to Mammoth Hot Springs, run that one year when the Government discontinued [it], at a great loss to me." See also "The Pioneer Resident of the National Park," *Livingston Enterprise*, January 1, 1900, p. 15. Gilmer & Salisbury leased their transportation rights in the Park to Marshall in July of 1880, per "Minor Items," *The Weekly Miner* (Butte, MT), July 20, 1880, p. 7. Notwithstanding Thompson,

Throw Down the Box!, p. 133, I can find no evidence that Gilmer & Salisbury ever ran coaches inside of Yellowstone Park; instead, they subcontracted their mail-route(s) to George Marshall. The title-quote for this chapter is from Robert E. Strahorn, *The Enchanted Land, or An October Ramble among the Geysers, Hot Springs, Lakes, Falls, and Cañons of Yellowstone National Park* (Omaha: New West Publishing Company, 1881), p. 45.

160. Charles Marshall Barnes, "The Life of George Washington Marshall, 1838-1917," unpublished manuscript in possession of author from Barnes, who has also posted a version of it at https://www.wikitree.com/wiki/Marshall-8457 with illustrations. Mr. Barnes is the son of Antrim E. "Pat" Barnes, who formerly lived at West Yellowstone, Montana, and whom this author interviewed back in 1979-80 in preparation for the first journal-article I ever produced, namely Lee H. Whittlesey, "Marshall's Hotel in the National Park," *Montana Magazine of Western History* 30, Fall, 1980, pp. 42-54.

161. George Marshall, handwritten biographical statement, no date [1885], Bancroft Library, Berkeley, California, with photostat-copy at YNP Research Library, Gardiner, Montana. Much of this original statement is quoted in Charles Barnes's manuscript.

162. U.S. Census of 1880, Beaverhead, Montana, as quoted in Barnes, "Life of George Washington Marshall," p. [2].

163. Davison and Myers, "Terminus Town: The Founding of Dillon, 1880," as cited, pp. 23-26; and "List of Letters," *Butte* (MT) *Weekly Miner*, April 13, 1880, p. 8. My thanks go to researcher Tina Schlaile of Fairfield, California for bringing my attention to this latter article.

164. Marshall, handwritten biographical statement, quoted in Barnes, "Life of George Washington Marshall," p. [3].

165. Marshall and Goff to Hon. Carl Schurz, August 10, 1880, in NA, RG 48, microfilm no. 62, roll 1, hardcopy at YNP Library.

166. "Marshall & Goff's Passenger and Fast Freight Line," advertisement in *The Weekly Miner* (Butte, MT), July 13, 1880, p. 4; and Viator, "The National Park—Stage Line to Wonderland," *Helena Weekly Herald*, August 26, 1880, p. 7. See also, William F. Wheeler, "The National Park—The Wonderland of the World Opened Up," *New North-West* (Deer Lodge, MT), August 20, 1880, p. 2; and "Utah & Northern—Opening up of a Great Country by the Little Narrow Gauge," *Salt Lake Tribune*, July 24, 1880, p. 1. The latter article says Marshall & Goff have secured a contract to carry the mail between Red Rock (railroad terminus) and Mammoth Hot Springs.

167. Haines, *Yellowstone Story*, I, p. 256; and "Star Route Exposures" [Norris learns from Gilmer &Salisbury's "dummy" bidder about its new contract and mail route], Helena (MT) *Daily Independent*, May 24, 1881, p. 2.

168. P.W. Norris to Hon. Carl Schurz, Sec. of Interior, July 9, 1880, in NA, RG 48, microfilm no. 62, roll 1, hardcopy at YNP Library.

169. Riverside (mail station) was a cabin and barn, erected by O.J. Salisbury's men at this time (summer, 1880), which in 1882 would become an office for the park's assistant superintendents and in 1886, a U.S. army station. See P.W. Norris, *Annual Report of the Superintendent of the Yellowstone National Park, to the Secretary of the Interior, for the Year 1880* (Washington: GPO, 1881), pp. 37, 48. Salisbury and his men spent "a couple of weeks" in late summer of 1880 searching for a reasonable wagon-route between Red Rock and Mammoth Hot Springs, but failed in that endeavor and stated that the better route remains via VC and up the Madison to Henry's Lake. "The mail is now being carried on horseback," said Salisbury, who also reported "there are about 100 people in the Park." See "Messrs. O.J. Salisbury and H.S. Howell," *The Madisonian* (Virginia City, MT), August 7, 1880, p. 2.

170. Norris, *Annual Report…1880*, p. 4. This 1880 road appeared on the 1961 park topographic map as "Old Fountain Pack Trail."

171. Haines, *Yellowstone Story*, I, p. 256; "Yellowstone Park Matters" [P.W. Norris is portrayed as building the road west of park toward railroad], Bozeman *Avant Courier*, August 5, 1880, p. 3; "A Fraud on Tourists to the Park" [implies that the scheme was perpetuated by railroad or P.W. Norris or both], Bozeman *Avant Courier*, August 12, 1880, p. 3; A Tourist, "A Newsy and Interesting Letter from the Yellowstone National Park" [condemns Mr. Norris for spending money building road allegedly for U&N mail, even though this money was intended to be used on road-building], Bozeman *Avant Courier*, August 19, 1880, p. 2; and "Rakings" [sarcastically denounces Mr. Norris's new, high-elevation road as a route unnecessarily close to the snow-line, where "mercury can freeze" and which is accessible only "by balloon"], *The Benton Weekly Record* (Fort Benton, MT), October 1, 1880, p. 3. As we shall see, once Mr. Norris's road was finished, officials would change the mail-route back to the Red-Rock-through-the-park-to-Mammoth for at least the winter of 1880-1881.

172. Wm. F. Wheeler, "The National Park—The Wonderland of the World Opened Up—The Terminus Route to be Abandoned for One from Virginia [City]," *New North-West* (Deer Lodge, MT), August 20, 1880, p. 2; W.F. Wheeler, "Our 'Artist' Aboard—Graphic Pencil Sketches of Montana—Terminus of the Utah and Northern Railroad—All About it and its Business People," *New North-West*, August 20, 1880, p. 3, col. 4; Omar, "To and Through the Park—A Rugged Wagon Route," *Helena Weekly Herald*, August 19, 1880, p. 3; and Viator, "The National Park—Stage Line to Wonderland," *Helena Weekly Herald*, August 26, 1880, p. 7. See also Norris, *Annual Report…1880*, pp. 37, 48; and Perham, "Letter from Old Madison" [Marshall & Goff want a bridge built on Madison River north of Raynolds Pass], *Helena Weekly Herald*, September 23, 1880, p. 3. Other chapters in this series appeared in the August 13, August 27, September 3, and September 10 editions. My thanks go to researcher Tina Schlaile of Fairfield, California for bringing my attention to these articles by William F. Wheeler.

173. Wm. F. Wheeler, "First Stage into the Park—Reaches Henry Lake August 10th," *New North-West* (Deer Lodge, MT), August 20, 1880, p. 3, col. 6; and Wheeler, "Our 'Artist' Aboard—Graphic Pencil Sketches of Montana," *New North-West*, August 20, 1880, as cited.

174. Wheeler, "First Stage into the Park—Reaches Henry Lake August 10th," *New North-West*, August 20, 1880, as cited; Wheeler, "The National Park—The Wonderland of the World Opened Up," *New North-West*, August 20, 1880, p. 2, as cited; Wheeler, "Our 'Artist' Aboard—Graphic Pencil Sketches of Montana," *New North-West*, August 20, 1880, as cited; and Wm. F. Wheeler, "Our 'Artist' Aboard—Graphic Pencil Sketches of the National Park—Correspondence of the New North-West," *New North-West*, September 3, 1880, p. 2, cols. 3-4.

175. Wheeler, "Our 'Artist' Aboard—Graphic Pencil Sketches of the National Park—Correspondence of the New North-West," *New North-West*, September 3, 1880, as cited; and Marshall & Goff, "A Card to the Editor of the Madisonian," *The Madisonian* (Virginia City, MT), October 16, 1880, p. 2. My thanks go to researcher Tina Schlaile for bringing these articles to my attention.

176. Carrie Adell Strahorn, *Fifteen Thousand Miles by Stage* (New York and London: G.P; Putnam's Sons, 1915), pp. 254-255. Four days later, on October 5, the Utah & Northern officially moved its terminus from Red Rock to Dillon, Montana. Davison and Myers, "Terminus Town: The Founding of Dillon, 1880," p. 24. See also "Correspondence Dillon the Future Terminus," *Blackfoot* (ID) *Register*, October 2, 1880, p. 4.

177. Whittlesey, "Marshall's Hotel in the National Park," as cited, especially p. 44. For a more fulsome history of George Marshall and the Marshall's Hotel aided by thirty years of additional research and experience, see Lee H. Whittlesey, "Hotels on the Firehole River (Yellowstone, 1880-1891) and the Origins of Concessioner Policy in National Parks," *Yellowstone History Journal* 3#1, 2020, pp. 4-27, and notes pp. 59-66.

178. Robert E. Strahorn, *The Enchanted Land*, p. 45. Strahorn stated that George Marshall's rates in the Park were as follows: "Three-seated carriage and driver, $8 per day; single-seated rig and driver, $6 per day; saddle horses, $2.50 per day for 3 days or more, or $3 for single day; pack animals, $2 per day; attendant who will act as guide, packer and cook, and furnish his own animal, $4 per day."

179. William Henry Bassett (1858-1929) was born in Salt Lake City to a large, Mormon family, and married Marette Cook of Cedar Valley, Utah. Ernest Knight Bassett (1861-1944) was also born in Salt Lake City, and he married Lucy Goodwin. Both of the men had the same father, Charles Henry Bassett, Sr. (1828-1907), but William's mother was Permelia Mindwell Dayton, while Ernest's mother was Mary Elizabeth Knight. See Ancestry.com, under those two names, plus their father Charles Henry Bassett.

180. At this time in the Northern Rockies, cross-country skis were often referred to as "Norwegian snow shoes." William Bassett's comments that "he...pushed me in on snow shoes" and "broke one runner" later in this letter make it clear that he was mounted on cross-country skis, rather than on web-snowshoes.

181. Letter from William Henry Bassett to his father [Charles Henry Bassett], labeled Virginia City, Montana, dated January 22, 1881, and later published as "Thrilling Experiences—Alone on a Montana Prairie Three Days and Two Nights...The Life of a Mail Carrier in a Houseless Country," *Salt Lake Daily Herald*, January 27, 1881, p. 3. Mistakenly attributed to the "Salt Lake Tribune," this letter was also reproduced, somewhat roughly, in Hansen and Hansen, *Bassett Brothers Proprietors of Yellowstone National Park Stage Line*," pp. 12-14. The mileage at that time between Marshall's Hotel ("Forks of the Firehole") and Riverside mail station was given as 12.23 miles by Superintendent P.W. Norris (*Fifth Annual Report*, 1881, p. 65).

182. "Thrilling Experiences—Alone on a Montana Prairie," as cited.

183. Ernest Knight Bassett to his father [Charles Henry Bassett], labeled Virginia City, Montana, and dated February 22, 1881, reproduced in Hansen and Hansen, *Bassett Brothers Proprietors of Yellowstone National Park Stage Line*," pp. 14-15.

184. Ernest Knight Bassett to his father, February 22, 1881, as cited.

185. "G.J. Bassett of Beaver Canyon," who was either a seventh Bassett brother or who more likely was simply C.J. with his initials wrongly rendered by the newspaper, was mentioned in "Hotel Arrivals," *Salt Lake Herald*, March 21, 1883, p. 8.

186. Hansen and Hansen, *Bassett Brothers*, as cited, p. 18, which says: "The stage line appears to have begun operation in 1881." This author concurs, because no newspapers or other sources have been found indicating Bassett operations in 1880.

187. "Brief Items," Helena *Independent*, May 17, 1881, p. 4, col. 2.

188. Haines, *Yellowstone Story*, I, pp. 245, 254; Whittlesey, "Marshall's Hotel in the National Park," *Montana the Magazine of Western History* 30#4, Autumn, 1980, pp. 42-51, especially p. 44; and Whittlesey, "Hotels on the Firehole River (Yellowstone, 1880-1891) and the Origins of Concessioner Policy in National Parks," *Yellowstone History Journal* 3#1, 2020, pp. 4-7, 12n50.

189. Hansen and Hansen, "Bassett Bros. Stage Line, 1880-1898," website: http://www.ourgenerationsancestors.org/histories/BASSETT_Basset%20Brothers%20Stage%20Line_REV20090625.pdf, p. 13. For the official names of the stage line, see the original documents reproduced in Hansen and Hansen, *Bassett Brothers*, pp. 20, 22, and 45.

190. George Marshall appears to have owned only two or three wagons, and certainly had no large fleet of 25-plus coaches, as the Bassetts would soon possess. For Yellowstone's ever-increasing fame in the 1870s because of newspapers and magazines, see Lee H. Whittlesey "Yellowstone: From Last Place Discovered to International Fame," *Site Lines* (University of Virginia, Foundation for Landscape Studies) 5 (Fall, 2009): 8-10.

191. Because it involves mining, Virginia City's history is complex. Except for Fort Benton, it was the earliest sizeable center of settlement in Montana Territory. See generally, Thomas J. Dimsdale, *The Vigilantes of Montana, or Popular Justice in the Rocky Mountains* (Virginia City, MT: D.W. Tilton and Company, 1866); Nathaniel Pitt Langford, *Vigilante Days and Ways* (Boston: J.G. Cupples Company, 1890, two volumes); Larry Barsness, *Gold Camp: Alder Gulch and Virginia City, Montana* (New York: Hastings House, c1962); Llewellyn L. Callaway, *Montana's Righteous Hangmen: The Vigilantes in Action* (Norman: University of Oklahoma Press, 1982); Ken and Ellen Sievert, *Virginia City and Alder Gulch* (Helena: American and World Geographic, Publishing Company, 1993); Frederick Allen, *A Decent Orderly Lynching: The Montana Vigilantes* (Norman: University of Oklahoma Press, c2004); Evalyn Batten Johnson, *Images of America Virginia City* (Charleston, SC: Arcadia Publishing, c2011); and John D. Ellingsen, *Witness to History: The Remarkable Untold Stories of Virginia City and Nevada City, Montana* (Helena: Sweetgrass Books, 2011). For an eyewitness description of Virginia City in May of 1880, see A., "Montana—The Great Territory as Seen by an Iowan," *Burlington Hawk-Eye* (Burlington, IA), June 3, 1880, p. 1. A useful history of mining in the Territory giving important background for Virginia City and many other Montana locations is Kent A. Curtis, *Gambling on Ore: The Nature of Metal Mining in the United States 1860-1910* (Boulder: University Press of Colorado, copyright 2013), chapter one.

192. "Brief Items," Helena (MT) *Independent*, May 17, 1881, p. 3.

193. The Virginia City stagecoaching route went from Dillon, Montana, to Twin Bridges to Salisbury to Virginia City to Ennis to Raynolds Pass to Henry's Lake, Idaho. See map in Madsen and Madsen, *North to Montana*, p. i. Twin Bridges, Montana had a post office as early as 1869, per Roberta Carkeek Cheney, *Names on the Face of Montana: The Story of Montana's Place Names* (Missoula: Mountain Press Publishing Company, 1984), p. 27c1; and see generally, Rich Aarstad et al., *Montana Place Names: From Alzada to Zortman* (Helena: Montana Historical Society, 2009).

194. Cheney, *Names on the Face of Montana*, p. 238. The stage-stop of Gaffney (formerly Pollinger), located two miles southeast of Twin Bridges, was renamed Salisbury in 1875. The town came to an end in June of 1883, when its post office was closed, per "Post Office Discontinued," *Helena Weekly Herald*, June 28, 1883, p. 7. My thanks go to historian Ellen Baumler of the Montana Historical Society for helping me sort out this obscure history involving the stage-stop of Salisbury and its relationship to the Gilmer & Salisbury Company.

195. "Yellowstone National Park," Salt Lake *Daily Tribune*, August 23, 1881, p. 4.

196. See F[itch], "Out of the World—An Omaha Outfit on its Way to Yellowstone Park," Omaha (NE) *Daily Bee*, August 28, 1882, p. 2, col. 3; and F[itch], "In Montana—Visit of the Board of Trade to Helena—What a Canyon Is—What Sluice Mining Looks Like," Omaha *Daily Bee*, August 29, 1882, p. 8, col. 2-3. Other chapters in this series appeared in the issues of August 30, August 31, and September 1, 8, 15, 1882.

197. "That word [*outfit*] covers everything in Montana," explained this writer (cited in the following note), "from a bride's trousseau to a traveler's luggage."

198. "Yellowstone National Park—From Virginia City to Wonderland—Nature Run Mad," *Springfield* (MA) *Republican*, September 28, 1881, p. 4. A search of this and other Massachusetts newspapers in late 1881 and all of 1882 on several digital, newspaper-sites failed to find further chapters of this article.

199. Geyserland [Amede Bessette], "Geyserland—The 'Sheridan Party's' Raid on Geyserland—Scenes in the Lower and Upper Basins," *Dillon Tribune*, October 14, 1882, p. 1. Likely identification of the author is in "Personal" [Mr. and Mrs. Amede Bessette], *Dillon Tribune*, September 30, 1882, p. 4; and in "Personal," *Dillon Tribune*, August 26, 1882, p. 4. A photo of Bessette, who was a noteworthy early Montanan, appeared in Allen, *A Decent Orderly Lynching*, p. 306.

200. [Amede Bessette], "Geyserland," as cited.

201. Regarding Lima, Montana, a prominent cattleman, originally from the Ohio city of the same name, suggested the name for the Montana town, which before that was known as "Allerdice" and later "Spring Hill." The name in Montana is pronounced *LYE muh*. The "accepted version of the [origin for the] Ohio city says that an early settler here had at one time visited Peru, and was so favorably impressed…that he prevailed upon residents here to give its name. It is said that after the name was chosen, the man spent the rest of his life trying to persuade the townspeople to pronounce it Lee'ma; but without success." Armond and Winifred Moyer, *The Origins of Unusual Place Names* (Keystone Publishing Associates, 1958), p. 75.

202. Utah & Northern Timetable No. 12, with exact distances, published in *Dillon Tribune*, May 14, 1881, p. 1. No town occupies the original site of Beaver Canyon, and today there is only an interpretive sign at that site, which is at exit 184 along Interstate 15 and marked "Old Beaver" on current maps.

203. "A Good Hotel," *Logan* (UT) *Leader*, January 1, 1880, as reported in "Utah & Northern Railway (1878-1889)" and its "Timeline," internet history site at http://utahrails.net/utahrails/utah-and-northern-ry-1878-1889.php. By September 16, 1880, this establishment had either moved to Dillon, Montana, or else had had its name usurped by a hotel at that location. See "Railroad Dignitaries," *Helena Weekly Herald*, September 16, 1880, p 7. That the mentioned C.L. Bristol did indeed move to Dillon to run the "Montana Hotel" was so indicated in "Dillon," *Helena Weekly Herald*, November 18, 1880, p. 4.

204. "Up the Road—A Trip to the Terminus; Beaver Canyon, Camas, Etc.," *Blackfoot* (ID) *Register*, August 14, 1880, p. 4. This was also reproduced as Idaho State Historical Society, "Beaver Canyon," Reference Series No. 908, 1988.

205. B.F. White, "From the Terminus," *Helena Weekly Herald*, April 22, 1880, p. 7.

206. "Accident on the U&N—Narrow Escape of [three trainmen]," *Blackfoot* (ID) *Register*, January 1, 1881, p. 4.

207. "Beaver Canyon," *Blackfoot Register*, July 16, 1881, p. 3; and C.R. Savage, "The North Country… What a Salt Laker Saw and Heard on a Trip to that Place," *Salt Lake* (UT) *Daily Herald*, September 29, 1881, p. 5. One of the best Beaver Canyon columns is "Beaver Canyon—A Pen Picture of its Prosperity and Prospects," *Ogden Standard* (Ogden, UT), June 3, 1882, p. 3, mentioning the Bassetts' saloon and noting that Julius Bassett was now "Justice of the Peace." But by October of 1882, several of the lumber mills had already shut down, "business was getting dull," and it thus appeared that the brief boom for the town was over. See M., "Beaver Canyon," *Blackfoot Register*, October 14, 1882, p. 2. For more on logging at Beaver Canyon, see "Where to Enter the Park—A Citizen of Omaha Says that the Best Route is from the South," Cheyenne (WY) *Daily Leader*, August 25, 1883, p. 3.

208. The Flying Dutchman, "Lively Letter on Montana…The Railroad Route," *Salt Lake Tribune*, August 5, 1890, p. 2.

209. *Dillon Tribune* for May 14, quoted in "From Dillon," *Helena Weekly Herald*, May 19, 1881, p. 7.

210. Mary Bradshaw Richards (William W. Slaughter, ed.), *Camping Out in the Yellowstone, 1882* (Salt Lake City: University of Utah Press, c1994), p. 12.

211. E.H.A., "Northern Notes—The Teton Mountains—Rich Ranchers—Busy Beaver Canyon," *Ogden* (UT) *Daily Herald*, August 16, 1884, p. 1. From this vantage point today, the Grand Tetons appear to be four prominent peaks, even though the fur-traders who named them around 1810 from this (west) side saw them as only three main summits. The most northerly summit is the shortest and arguably the most innocuous, so probably the southern three were the original "Three Tetons," namely today's Grand, Middle, and South Tetons.

212. "Beaver Canyon" [Frank Bassett], *Blackfoot Register*, July 29, 1882, p. 3.

213. The Bassett Brothers websites by Stanley D. and Stephen A. Hansen are at http://www.bassettbranches.org/stories/BassettBrosStageLine.pdf and http://www.ourgenerationsancestors.org/histories/BASSETT_Basset%20Brothers%20Stage%20Line_REV20090625.pdf. The Bassetts' advertisement in the *Blackfoot Register*, March 19, 1881, p. 1, stated: "Beaver Canyon Saloon: Swift and Bassett invite all their friends when passing over the road or visiting Beaver Canyon to call and see them. The best brands of liquors and cigars are sold at the bar. Give us a call. Beaver Canyon, Idaho."

214. The Bassetts were Mormons. Their father, Charles Henry Bassett, Sr. (1828-1907), married Permelia Mindwell Dayton on March 18, 1845 at Nauvoo, Illinois, just before the Mormons' historic, mass-migration left there and traveled to Wasatch Valley, Utah in 1846. On November 3, 1851, the couple's first son—Charles Julius Bassett—was born at Kanesville, Iowa. See Ancestry.com under Charles Henry Bassett and Charles Julius Bassett. For more on Permelia M. (Dayton) Bassett, see "In the Probate Court," *Salt Lake Herald*, July 10, 1889, p. 6.

215. Hansen and Hansen, *Bassett Brothers*, with photos of the six brothers, as cited, p. 17, including their individual biographies. For C.H. Bassett's store in Salt Lake City, see the advertisement for Bassett & Roberts on East Temple Street in *Salt Lake Daily Telegraph*, March 14, 1868, p. 1. Family lore has it that Fred Clayton Bassett drove the brothers' first stage to the Park. He was the youngest, being sixteen years old in 1881. See the Hansens' website at http://www.bassettbranches.org/stories/BassettBrosStageLine.pdf, accessed on April 20, 2017. According to a later reminiscence by his friend Charlie Armey, Charles Julius "Jule" Bassett, immigrated to Idaho in 1877, where he hung around the advancing Utah & Northern Railway until it reached Beaver Canyon. Charlie Armey, "Reminiscences of Well-Known Idaho Pioneers," *Idaho Statesman* (Boise, ID), January 26, 1919, p. 5.

There were other Bassetts in Idaho Territory, Montana Territory, and near the Park. In early August of that year, the *Hailey Miner* mentioned that "The Bassett brothers, of Virginia City [Montana], have two good prospects, which they are working." See "Wood River Notes," quoting the *Hailey Miner* for July 29, in *Salt Lake Tribune*, August 6, 1881, p. 1. Thus, this separate group of Bassetts, sometimes similarly referred to as the "Bassett Brothers," was mining in Virginia City and would soon move to Idaho's Wood River country near Hailey, Idaho, where they continued as miners and appeared many times in *Wood River Times* and other proximate newspapers. There also were Bassetts in Montana who appeared in Fort Benton, Helena, and Butte newspapers; and there were W.H. Bassett and his son Phillip Bassett, who lived just north of Yellowstone Park at present Corwin Springs and who left their name there on Bassett Creek (Lee H. Whittlesey, *Death in Yellowstone: Accidents and Foolhardiness in the First National Park*, Boulder: Roberts Rinehart, 2014, p.250; and Whithorn, *History of Park County 1984*, p. 97). Whether any of these Bassetts were related to our Bassett Brothers of Beaver Canyon is unknown, but in light of the known polygamy of Charles Henry Bassett (who stood trial for it in 1887) and the 1882 comment by Ernest Bassett that he thought he had two dozen or so brothers and sisters, it is possible and even likely.

216. [William Sturgis], *New Songs of Seven (Not by J.I.): A Record of a Journey in Wonderland. Printed, Not Published, by the Performers, For Their Own Amusement* (Cheyenne, Wyo.: Bristol and Knabe, Gas Power Printers and Bookbinders, 1884), p. [10], copy at Buffalo Bill Historical Center Library, Cody, Wyoming.

217. "Beaver Canyon," *Blackfoot Register*, July 16, 1881, p. 3.

218. Archive Documents 651-652 (1889); 653-654 (1888); and 655-656 (1890), YNP Archives.

219. Archive Documents 2081 (1896); and 2085 (1895), YNP Archives.

220. "Two New Concerns" [incorporating YNPT Company] *St. Paul* (MN) *Globe*, January 21, 1891,

p. 2; and "Local Layout" [incorporating YNPT Company], *Livingston Enterprise*, January 24, 1891, p. 3. While the Bassetts' name "Yellowstone National Park Stage Line" was not precisely the same as YPA's "Yellowstone National Park Transportation Company," it was probably close enough to cause worry for the Bassett Brothers. For an example of the new paint-jobs placed on YNPTC coaches 1889-1891, see coach #12 in F. Jay Haynes photograph H-6508, Montana Historical Society.

221. Advertisement for "The Eden of America" in *Salt Lake Daily Tribune*, August 20, 1881, p. 1; and October 16, 1881, p. 4. This advertisement stated "We are prepared to carry all parties," but the ads in 1882 said, "On and after June 1st 1882, we shall…"

222. Advertisement for "The Eden of America," *Salt Lake Daily Tribune*, April 23, 1882, as reproduced in Hansen and Hansen, *Bassett Brothers*, p. 18. Among many other places, it also appeared in *Blackfoot* (ID) *Register*, July 1, 1882, p. 1.

223. H., "National Park—Pleasant Trip of a Party of Salt Lakers to the Yellowstone Who Tell of the Wonderful Sights in that Region," *Salt Lake Tribune*, September 23, 1882, p. 3.

224. C.R. Savage, "The North Country—From the Basin Metropolis to Butte—What a Salt Laker Saw and Heard on a Trip to that Place," *Salt Lake Daily Herald* (Salt Lake City, UT), September 29, 1881, p. 5. See also "Yellowstone National Park," text advertisement for the Bassetts, in *Salt Lake Daily Herald*, April 19, 1882, p. 8.

225. "Yellowstone National Park," *Salt Lake Daily Herald*, April 19, 1882, p. 8.

226. "W.N." at Beaver Canyon, "From the North—A Man Killed on the Track—Wind and Weather," *Ogden* (UT) *Standard*, March 28, 1882, p. 3.

227. "Justice Court," *Blackfoot Register*, April 22, 1882, p. 3; "Pickings from the [Ogden] Pilot's Railway Intelligence" in *The Semi-Weekly Miner* (Butte, MT), April 26, 1882, p. 1; and "Gleanings from the Rockies," *Dillon Tribune*, June 17, 1882, p. 1. An extensive search of these men's names and events in the newspapers of Idaho, Montana, Wyoming, and Utah has so far failed to turn up any more about this case, even in the Blackfoot newspaper.

228. "Traffic—In Freight and Pilgrims—Latest Railway Intelligence," *The Semi-Weekly Miner* (Butte, MT), April 8, 1882, p. 4.

229. "Beaver Canyon Items," *Blackfoot Register*, June 3, 1882, p. 3. Camas Meadows is one of the oldest place names in Idaho, having appeared on S. Augustus Mitchell, Jr.'s 1863 map of "Oregon, Washington, and Part of Idaho" (Washington State Library, Rare Maps Collection) and Johnson's 1865 map as "Camas Prairie," which was changed later to Camas Meadows, probably to prevent confusion with a more northerly Camas Prairie at Cottonwood, Idaho. On the 1863 map, "Camas Prairie" (today's Camas Meadows) appears at the head of Henry's Fork, and on the 1865 map, "Camas Prairie" appears just south of the Idaho-Montana boundary on the uppermost, unnamed fork of Snake River, between "Henry's Fork" and "Lewis Fork." See Johnson and Ward, map, "Johnson's Nebraska, Dakota, Idaho and Montana," New York, 1865. This same map also shows "Three Tetons" and "Jackson's Lake," both of them then incorrectly shown within Idaho Territory, as does the 1863 map.

230. "Butte—Its Attractions and Surroundings—A Trip from Here [to] There Graphically Described," *Salt Lake Herald*, June 29, 1883, p. 5; Edwards Roberts, *Shoshone and Other Western Wonders* (New York: Harper and Brothers, 1888), p. 180; and Hansen and Hansen, *Bassett Brothers*, p. 23. A post office was established at Kilgore in 1884, a "town" that likely had its origins in 1882, when George Rea built the first cabin there "(in this book, p. 451, endnote 580). The distances used here are those of the Bassett Brothers' distance-card.

231. Bassett Brothers, "Distances" [card printed and distributed by them], no date but probably

1882-1884, included with Bassett Brothers to H.M. Teller, Sect. Interior, July 26, 1884, in National Archives, RG 48, microfilm 62, roll 2, folder 3 of 4 (hardcopy at YNP Library). Essentially the same distance-card is also reproduced at "Bassett Bros. Stage Line," p. 8, located at http://www.ourgenerationsancestors.org/histories/BASSETT_Basset%20Brothers%20Stage%20 Line_REV20090625.pdf, accessed April 11, 2017, which also pictures the facilities at Indian Springs as still standing in 2008. The Bassett Brothers listed their own, cumulative distances from Beaver Canyon (as opposed to the earlier listing by the *Dillon Tribune*) as follows: To Indian Springs 25 miles; to Sheridan [Ranch] 33 miles; to [Henry's Fork of] Snake River 50 miles; to Henry Lake 65 miles; to South Fork 75 miles; to Riverside 85 miles; and to Fire Hole Basin 100 miles. A later card adjusted the distance "to Snake River" as 45 miles. Like many internet websites, this one suffers from unproven assumptions and inadequate documentation, but it contains important information from the Bassett family and excellent photographs, even though more documentation is arguably needed about the repositories where those historic photos reside today. For Silas McMinn's assumed ownership of the "Targhee Creek Stage Station" in 1890, see Way Farer, "Henry's Lake, Idaho," *The Dillon Tribune*, August 8, 1890, p. 1, col. 2, datelined July 6: "The Widow Chase was married to Mr. McMinn, by Judge Fergerson, two weeks ago. Mr. McMinn has a large house underway." That house was near Howard Creek, east of Henry's Lake.

232. G.W. Rea, "Our Arangee Correspondent," *Idaho Falls Times* (Idaho Falls, ID), June 29, 1893, p. 5. This hotel was either the same as or a forerunner of the Bellevue Hotel, which was built by the three partners of the Arangee Land and Cattle Company, who historian Dean Green has stated were Hopf, Gerber, and Rutledge. (Hopf, however, seems to have been only the manager of the place and not one of the owners.) A photo and discussion of it are in Dean H. Green, *History of Island Park: A Pictorial and Written History from before 1890 to Idaho's Centennial Year 1990* (Ashton, ID: Gateway Publishing Company, 1990), pp. 46-47. The hotel was built on land homesteaded by John W. Kooch in 1880, which he sold in 1890 to Gerber and the partners, and which was the property (Arangee Ranch) that historian Green says they sold to A.S. Trude in 1891. It passed to Trude's descendants, and the hotel was torn down before the land was partially flooded by today's Island Park Reservoir. Researcher Tina Schlaile of Fairfield, California owns an actual hotel key (to room 10) for this hotel, and its name on the key is spelled *Bellevue*.

233. The author saw all of these flowers blooming on a trip through both valleys on June 24, 2017. Jacob V. Brower, on his 1895 trip to Centennial Valley, noted that Mrs. Lillian Culver, for whom he named Lillian Lake in the valley, was a botanist who had collected many species of wildflowers there, and he listed them. Brower, *The Missouri River*, p. 116. See also Molly Hashimoto, *Colors of the West: An Artist's Guide to Nature's Palette* (Seattle: Skipstone, copyright 2017).

234. "Plumbing in America," *Plumbing and Mechanical Magazine*, July, 1987, posted at http://theplumber.com/plumbing-in-america/ with no author listed.

235. "Beaver Canyon," *Blackfoot Register*, July 29, 1882, p. 3. It is not known which two Bassetts left the operation, but a reasonable guess is the two, former mail-carriers, William Henry Bassett and Ernest Knight Bassett. However, William Bassett returned through at least 1893, and C.H. Bassett departed by July 8, 1887, the date when the Bassetts requested their formal license. No formal, Yellowstone Park licenses for these and other stagecoach-operators have been found until the year 1894.

236. Subscriber, "Beaver Canyon Letter," *Blackfoot Register*, July 29, 1882, p. 3.

237. "Beaver Cañon," *Deseret News* (Salt Lake City, UT), August 16, 1882, p. 12; bound volume p. 476.

238. "Beaver Canyon Items," *Blackfoot Register*, August 26, 1882, p. 1; also in bound volume, p. 476.

239. Centennial Valley was named in 1876 (in honor of the nation's centennial and its centennial year) by ranchmen Philip Poindexter and William Orr who arrived in the valley that year, and for which fact they gave the name. They were the first settlers in the valley, driving their cattle south from the headwaters of Ruby River. Callaway, *Montana's Righteous Hangmen*, p. 177; and [Leeson], *History of Montana*, pp. 994-995.

240. William F. Wheeler, "The National Park—The Wonderland of the World Opened Up," *New North-West* (Deer Lodge, MT), August 20, 1880, p. 2. At Red Rock Pass, elevation 7,120 feet, was and is located Mount Jefferson (10,216 feet or 3114 meters) and its Hell Roaring Creek, initially discharging west and eventually northeast toward Red Rock Lakes and the Jefferson and Missouri rivers. Just across the pass east were and are the waters of Henry's Lake and Henry's Fork of the Snake River, which discharged initially south and eventually west toward the Snake and Columbia rivers. During the 1890s, it became fashionable to talk of the Red Rock Lakes as being the ultimate source of the Missouri River, when the Jefferson River was realized to be its longest branch. The premier book on the subject, produced at that time, was Jacob V. Brower's *The Missouri River and Its Utmost Source*, as cited. Brower's Spring, at the head of Hell Roaring Creek on the south side of Mount Jefferson (some 4,200 river-miles from the Atlantic Ocean), was named for the writer of this 1897 book. See also "Up in the Rockies—Locating the Fountain Head of the Great Missouri River in Centennial Valley...Queer Little Post Offices," *St. Paul* (MN) *Daily Globe*, September 29, 1898, p. 13; Brower's map in "Headwaters of the Missouri," same newspaper, May 10, 1896, pp. 9, 12; and Ben Pierce, "Mount Jefferson Access Rises to Forefront of Forest Bill Controversy," *Bozeman* (MT) *Chronicle*, December 30, 2009. One wonders whether Brower, whose research-trip to the area occurred in 1895, named Nemesis Mountain (just northwest of Mount Jefferson) because of the difficulty it caused him in reaching the upper stretch of Hell Roaring Creek and Hell Roaring Canyon (which he called "Culver's Canyon" for the earliest resident there, W.N. Culver), but he easily could have. Brower also noted that the area immediately west of Red Rock Pass had been named Alaska Basin by resident S.B. Burnside for its deep snow in winter time or perhaps for some of Burnside's relatives in Alaska. And Brower recorded that he personally named Blair Lake and Blair Creek for resident James Blair, and also named Lillian Lake for resident Lillian Culver. Brower, *Missouri River*, map opposite the book's title page, and pp. 95, 114, 116.

241. Wheeler, "The National Park," *New North-West*, as cited; Wm. F. Wheeler, "First Stage into the Park—Reaches Henry Lake August 10th," *New North-West*, August 20, 1880, p. 3, col. 6; and W.F. Wheeler, "Our 'Artist' Aboard—Graphic Pencil Sketches of Montana—Terminus of the Utah and Northern Railroad—All About it and its Business People," *New North-West*, August 20, 1880, p. 3, col. 4. Wheeler was identified as "General Agent for the *New North-West*" in "Local Brevities," *New North-West*, August 20, 1880, p. 3.

242. Paul Vandervoort, "Yellowstone Park—The Journey Thither," from the *Omaha Republican*, as published in *Nebraska Advertiser* (Brownville, NE), September 2, 1880, p. 1.

243. Vandervoort, "The Journey Thither," as cited.

244. Vandervoort, "The Journey Thither," as cited.

245. Lee H. Whittlesey and Sarah Bone, *The History of Mammals in the Greater Yellowstone Ecosystem, 1796-1881: A Multi-Disciplinary Analysis of Thousands of Historical Observations* (Seattle and San Bernardino: Kindle Direct Publishing, 2020), two volumes (1,305 pages), and accompanying computer database (in custody of National Park Service at Yellowstone National Park), Vol. I, pp. 733-771. Leckler's account, as we therein state, "is one of the premier sporting memoirs of early Yellowstone National Park" and "in his account alone with its many comments about hunting, there is fulsome evidence that the park had been and was continuing to be a reservoir of mammal-presence and abundance, even as late as 1881." Readers of the present book will no doubt find

the many animals seen on the trips chronicled here (through the Antelope, Sheridan, Shotgun, and Centennial valleys and the Henry's Lake area) to be supportive of that assertion. All of these areas today are geographically within the Greater Yellowstone Ecosystem.

246. H.B. Leckler, "A Camping Trip to the Yellowstone National Park," *American Field* 2: 41-42, 71-72, 93-94, 117, 141-142, 166, 190-191, 214, 236-237, 261-262, 286, 310-311, 335, 359-360, 382-383, 407-408, 430-431, 455-456, in the issues of January 12, 19, 26; February 2, 9, 16, 23; March 1, 8, 15, 22, 29; April 5, 12, 19, 26; and May 3, 10, 1884.

247. "The Best Route to the Geysers," *Dillon* (MT) *Tribune*, July 29, 1882, p. 4; and "The Direct Route to the National Park," *Dillon Tribune*, June 17, 1882, p. 4. See also "Fixing the Direct Road to the Park," *Dillon Tribune*, July 15, 1882, p. 4. In the June 17th article, the newspaper gave the distances between points at that moment, for both routes. For the Centennial Valley (Dillon) route, the figures were as follows: Dillon to Poindexter & Orr's [Ranch] 10 miles; to Old Dairy Ranch 10 miles; to Blacktail Canyon 5 miles; to Centennial Valley Ranch 15 miles; to Red Rock Lake 20 miles; to Henry's Lake 34 miles; and to the National Park 45 miles, for a total of 139 miles. For the Virginia City route, the figures were: Dillon to Virginia City 60 miles; to Ennis 13 miles; to Wolf Creek 23 miles; to Henry's Lake 23 miles; and to the National Park 45 miles, for a total of 164 miles.

248. "The Direct Route to the Park," *Dillon Tribune*, August 12, 1882, p. 4.

249. A.E.B., "A Day at Henry's Lake—Some Interesting Items from a Visitor's Diary," *Dillon Tribune*, October 1, 1886, p. 8; and A.E.B., "Our Trip to the National Park," *Dillon Tribune*, November 12, 1886, p. 8. For identification of this writer as a woman, see A.E.B., "Voice for Prohibition," *Dillon Tribune*, July 24, 1886, p. 4. For G.L. Henderson's "discoveries" and namings of the geysers in this area, see his bylined article, "Lower Geyser Basin—A Glance at the Unfrequented Wonders of that Region," *Livingston* (MT) *Enterprise*, July 18, 1885, p. 1; Henderson in "More Wonders—Fresh Discoveries in the Yellowstone Park," *Salt Lake Herald*, May 31, 1885, p. 8; Henderson in "Yellowstone Park—New Wonders in the National Park Described," *Reno* (NV) *Evening Gazette*, May 25, 1885, p. 1; and "Yellowstone Geysers—Ex-Supt Henderson tells of a Visit to the National Park," *Daily Tribune* (Bismarck, ND), March 21, 1890, p. 2. Henderson's "Evangeline Geyser" was the same feature as present Thud Geyser in the Lower Geyser Basin.

250. Mary Bradshaw Richards, *Camping Out in the Yellowstone, 1882* (Salt Lake City: University of Utah Press, 1992), William W. Slaughter, ed., p. 11. Richards's account appeared originally in the *Salem* (MA) *Observer* and was first published as a book in 1910.

251. Richards, *Camping Out*, p. 12.

252. Ernest to Mary Richards, in *Camping Out*, p. 14.

253. Ernest to Mary Richards, *Camping Out*, p. 18 and following. One wonders whether their evening, "pioneer" guest was George Rea, and probably it was, because this spot was close to his ranch at "Glen Rea" (later just Rea, and, still later for a time, Arangee), Idaho. The town-site of Rea was later moved to a different spot farther north but which nevertheless continued to honor his presence in the area.

254. For the old prospector's quote, see Richards, *Camping Out*, pp. 26-27. For the road over Madison Plateau, see Robert E. Strahorn, *The Enchanted Land*, p. 7. For Consolation Spring, see Lee H. Whittlesey "Wonderland Nomenclature. A History of the Place Names of Yellowstone National Park," that entry in 1988 manuscript, Montana Historical Society; and Mrs. ___ Foster, "From Foster Ranch to Wonderland and Return, August 17, 1882," typescript of handwritten letter, YNP Library, p. 31. The old spelling of "Tygee" survives in Tygee Creek, running west into Idaho, and in Tygee Creek Basin, located on both sides of the Montana-Idaho divide at its summit. As for Consolation Spring, in this high but arid country, any water-source, however small, was

important, which was undoubtedly how and why that spring was deemed important enough to receive a name. It was probably the same as "Forest Spring," mentioned by Superintendent Norris as being on the plateau three miles west of Marshall's Hotel. P.W. Norris, *Fifth Annual Report of the Superintendent of the Yellowstone National Park*, December 1, 1881 (Washington: GPO, 1881), p. 65.

255. Richards, *Camping Out*, p. 45 and following.

256. H., "National Park—Pleasant Trip of a Party of Salt Lakers to the Yellowstone," *Salt Lake Tribune*, September 23, 1882, p. 3. "Not macadamized" meant "not graveled or [in later times] paved."

257. H., "National Park," as cited; and Lee H. Whittlesey, *Storytelling in Yellowstone: Horse and Buggy Tour Guides* (Albuquerque: University of New Mexico Press, 2007), p. 200. The Bassetts' use of tents rather than cabins at Lower Geyser Basin from 1882 through at least August of 1884 was documented by O.J.H., "The Yellowstone—The Improvement Company and Mammoth Hot Springs Hotel—[?] of the Norris and Firehole Geyser Basins—Where to Go, How to Go, and What it Costs—A Flying Trip Through Uncle Sam's Great Inferno," *Daily Tribune* (Salt Lake City, Utah), August 17, 1884, p. 6. A partially defective edition of this article appeared in *Salt Lake Weekly Tribune*, August 21, 1884, p. 5.

258. H., "National Park," as cited.

259. G.L. Henderson to congressional hearing, April, 1892, in Thomas McRae, "Inquiry into the Management and Control of the Yellowstone National Park," 52d Cong., 1st Sess., House Report 1956, SN-3051, July 20, 1892, p. 289.

260. M., "Beaver Canyon," *Blackfoot* (ID) *Register*, October 14, 1882, p. 2.

261. "Up the Road—Beaver Canyon and Eagle Rock Items," *Blackfoot Register*, December 30, 1882, p. 3.

262. "Beaver Canyon Notes," *Blackfoot Register*, February 17, 1883, p. 3; "Town and Vicinity," *Blackfoot Register*, March 10, 1883, p. 3 (in this article, Rea was mistakenly referred to as "E.W. Rea."); and "Town and Vicinity," *Blackfoot Register*, May 12, 1883, p. 3. Ah Wah appeared in "Beaver Canyon Notes," *Blackfoot Register*, May 19, 1883, p. 3, and in an advertisement on the same page. The newspaperman's observations appeared in P., "Our Traveling Correspondent—Healthy Prosperity at Dillon—Points of Interest on the Railroad—Spring Hill, Beaver Canyon, Eagle Rock, Pocatello," *The Semi-Weekly Miner* (Butte, MT), June 9, 1883, p. 2.

263. "Town and Vicinity" [new wagons and horses], *Blackfoot Register*, May 12, 1883, p. 3; "Beaver Canyon Notes" [saloon and office], *Blackfoot Register*, May 19, 1883, p. 3; and "Town and Vicinity" [Bassetts' season now open], *Blackfoot Register*, June 2, 1883, p. 3.

264. Advertisement for "Land of the Geysers!" *Salt Lake Daily Herald*, June 3, 1883, p. 9. See also "Land of the Geyser" [sic], *Salt Lake Daily Herald*, June 22, 1883, p. 4.

265. "Town and Vicinity," *Blackfoot Register*, June 16, 1883, p. 3; "Serviceable Wagons," *Salt Lake Herald*, June 9, 1883, p. 8; and A.B.T., "Butte—Its Attractions and Surroundings," *Salt Lake Daily Herald*, June 29, 1883, p. 5.

266. C., "Yellowstone Park—Beaver Canyon," *Salt Lake Daily Herald*, July 18, 1883, p. 8; and Haines, *Yellowstone Story*, II, p. 108.

267. "Yellowstone Park—How to Get There," *Salt Lake Tribune*, June 6, 1883. His "J.C. Bassett" was no doubt C.J. Bassett.

268. "Yellowstone Park—The Presidential Party and Their Long Road—Convenience of Wonderland to Salt Lake," *Daily Tribune* (Salt Lake City, UT), August 24, 1883, p. 4. The reason for President Arthur's party taking the long route on horseback was that General Sheridan wanted the

President to meet with Wyoming Indian tribes to the south of Yellowstone Park. For that story, see generally, Frank H. Goodyear III, *A President in Yellowstone: The F. Jay Haynes Photographic Album of Chester Arthur's 1883 Expedition* (Norman: University of Oklahoma Press, 2013); and Robert E. Hartley, *Saving Yellowstone: The President Arthur Expedition of 1883* (Westminster, CO: Sniktau Publications, 2007).

269. "Where to Enter the Park—A Citizen of Omaha Says that the Best Route is from the South," Cheyenne (WY) *Daily Leader*, August 25, 1883, p. 3, wherein this traveler wrongly reversed the facilities on Henry's Fork and Henry's Lake. Notwithstanding the advantages of the NPRR's northern route over Utah & Northern's western route, Salt Lake City newspapers continued to trumpet the western route, which probably was indeed better, or at least more convenient, for that city's travelers. Eleven days later, the *Tribune* again claimed that the Beaver Canyon route was superior to the NPRR's northern route, even though the staging was "ninety-nine miles" to "Marshall's in Fire Hole Basin," and falsely asserted that the northern route was over bad roads and less beautiful country. The western route did *seem* closer to the geysers, even though it was not, and thus the BC proponents would continue for years to make that point. See "Yellowstone Park—Beaver Canyon Route the Most Direct," *Daily Tribune* (Salt Lake City, UT), September 5, 1883, p. 4.

270. A "deadhead" was a drive made without passengers or freight. Such a drive was not lucrative for the company, but it was often a necessity for getting drivers and wagons to other places for further assignments. The term is still used today in commercial busing and trucking.

271. "Where to Enter the Park," as cited; and "A Guide of Experience" [George Rea], *Dillon Tribune*, May 24, 1884, p. 4. A photo of George and Thomas Rea is in Green, *History of Island Park*, p. 37.

272. W.O. Owen, "The First Bicycle Tour of the Yellowstone National Park," originally published in *Outing Magazine* for June of 1891, reproduced in Paul Schullery, *Old Yellowstone Days* (Albuquerque: University of New Mexico Press, 2010), pp. 33-44.

273. Charlie, "Among the Geysers—Some of the Wonders of the Famous Yellowstone Region," Baltimore (MD) *Sun*, August 20, 1883, p. [4].

274. Charlie, "Among the Geysers," as cited.

275. "Eastern Idaho and a Sketch of the Counties Comprising It—Bingham County," *Idaho Register* (Idaho Falls, ID), vol. 1, no. 1, April 4, 1885, p. 11.

276. "Beaver Canyon," *Salt Lake Herald*, January 3, 1884, p. 5.

277. "Heavy Snow," *Salt Lake Herald*, February 17, 1884, p. 12. For two examples of later hard winters on this railroad, see "The Trains" and "Tough Railroading," both in *Helena Weekly Herald*, January 19, 1888, p. 4, column 5.

278. "Gleanings from the Rockies," *Dillon Tribune*, June 28, 1884, p. 1; and "Montana News," *Daily Enterprise* (Livingston, MT), June 24, 1884, p. 1.

279. "Yellowstone Excursions," Livingston (MT) *Daily Enterprise*, April 18, 1884, p. 1.

280. "Personal" [A.J. Dusseau wed to Amanda Henault at Butte], *New North-West* (Deer Lodge, MT), November 4, 1881, p. 3.

281. Letter from Bassett Brothers, Yellowstone National Park Stage Line, Beaver Canyon, Idaho, July 26, 1884 to Hon. H.M. Teller, Sect. Interior, Washington, DC, in National Archives, RG 48, Microfilm 62, roll 2, folder 3 of 4 (hardcopy at YNP Library). This letter included the Bassett Brothers' business card, advertising "From Beaver Canyon to Yellowstone Park, the Wonderland of the World," giving the fare as $35.00, offering "special rates to parties of ten or more," and noting that the "tents and camp outfit [are] free." A second, included card showed cumulative

"Distances from Beaver Canyon" as follows: to Indian Springs 25 miles, to Sheridan [Ranch] 33 miles, to [Henry's Fork of] Snake River 50 miles, to Henry['s] Lake 65 miles, to South Fork [of Madison River], 75 miles, to Riverside 85 miles, and to Fire Hole Basin 100 miles, as well as giving distances around the park.

282. E.H.A., "Northern Notes—The Teton Mountains—Rich Ranchers—Busy Beaver Canyon," *Ogden* (UT) *Daily Herald*, August 16, 1884, p. 1. The mini-depression known to some historians as the "Panic of 1884" has been treated in Lee H. Whittlesey, "'Oh, Mammoth Structure!': Rufus Hatch, the National Hotel, and the Grand Opening of Yellowstone in 1883," *Annals of Wyoming* 83 (Spring, 2011): 18, 20. Because 1884 was such a busy summer for the Bassetts at the same time that George Rea, their neighbor to the east in Shotgun Valley, entered the business of transporting tourists to Yellowstone, researcher Tina Schlaile and I have wondered whether the Bassetts dropped off some of their eastbound customers at Mr. Rea's "Glen Rea" ranch for him to transport on to the park, with the brothers returning to Beaver Canyon to pick up more passengers. We discuss this in chapter eight, but so far proof of it is lacking.

283. O.J.H., "The Yellowstone—The Improvement Company and Mammoth Hot Springs Hotel—[?] of the Norris and Firehole Geyser Basins—Where to Go, How to Go, and What it Costs—A Flying Trip Through Uncle Sam's Great Inferno," *Daily Tribune* (Salt Lake City, Utah), August 17, 1884, p. 6. A partially defective edition of this article appeared in *Salt Lake Weekly Tribune*, August 21, 1884, p. 5.

284. "On the Wing—Notes of a Trip from Salt Lake City to Garrison," *Salt Lake Herald*, September 18, 1884, p. 3.

285. Jeffrey D. Wert, *Civil War Barons: The Tycoons, Entrepreneurs, Investors, and Visionaries who Forged a Victory and Shaped a Nation* (New York: DaCapo Press, 2018), pp. 131-135.

286. C.D. Roys, "A Camp in the Rockies," *The American Angler: A Weekly Journal of Fish and Fishing*, Vol. 6#15, October 11, 1884, pp. 225-226, reproduced by Google Books at: https://books.google.com/books?id=Tl0vAAAAYAAJ&pg=PA225&dq=%22the+american+angler%22+%22a+-camp+in+the+rockies%22+%22bassett%22&hl=en&sa=X&ved=0ahUKEwj_uqOZ8JvTAhX-oz4MKHdTiB7kQ6AEIJDAA#v=onepage&q=%22the%20american%20angler%22%20%22a%20camp%20in%20the%20rockies%22%20%22bassett%22&f=false. My thanks go to Randy Ingersoll of Gardiner, Montana, who, in his usual sleuthlike fashion, discovered this little-known written account of travelers on their way to Yellowstone. Unfortunately, neither he nor I can find any hint of a Part II or Part III by Mr. Roys.

287. Roys, "A Camp in the Rockies," p. 225.

288. Roys, "A Camp in the Rockies," p. 226.

289. We can surmise this because of the following snippet, which appeared thirteen years later in W.J. Miller, "Going After Game," *Anaconda* (MT) *Standard*, April 18, 1897, p. 18: "Shotgun valley is one of the natural homes of the sage hen…Shotgun creek empties into the [Henry's Fork of the] Snake River at Avangee [*sic*—Arangee], where there is a fine hotel with good accommodations, and if you are fortunate enough to meet Nel Hudson on the river, he will take pleasure in either directing or piloting you to…good fishing grounds." The hotel was located near Hotel Creek that flowed into Henry's Fork from the north, and on the east side of Henry's Fork.

290. Roys, "A Camp in the Rockies," p. 226.

291. [William Sturgis], *New Songs of Seven (Not by J.I.): A Record of a Journey in Wonderland. Printed, Not Published, by the Performers for Their Own Amusement* (Cheyenne, Wyoming: Bristol and Knabe, Gas Power Printers and Bookbinders, 1884), p. (2). Copy at Buffalo Bill Historical Center, Cody, Wyoming.

292. [Sturgis], *New Songs*, pp. (6), (9).

293. [Sturgis], *New Songs*, p. (10).

294. [Sturgis], New Songs, p. (12).

295. [Sturgis], *New Songs*, pp. (14), (19).

296. [Sturgis], *New Songs*, p. (25).

297. [Sturgis], *New Songs*, pp. (25), (28).

298. [Sturgis], *New Songs*, pp. (29)-(32).

299. [Sturgis], *New Songs*, p. (33). For George Graham, see Whittlesey, *Storytelling in Yellowstone*, indexed references.

300. [Sturgis], *New Songs*, pp. (35)-(36). The poems were entitled "Washingtonian Episode" and "Episode After Camp Hours."

301. [Sturgis], *New Songs*, pp. (35), (42)-(43).

302. [Sturgis], *New Songs*, pp. (42)-(43), (45)-(46).

303. [Sturgis], *New Songs*, p. (49).

304. C.R. Savage, "A Strange Country, Geyserland—Incidents of Travel to the Great Falls of the Yellowstone and Geyser Basin," *Deseret Evening News* (Salt Lake City, UT), September 17, 1884, p. 4; and Charles R. Savage, personal diary of August 26-September 5, 1884, as reproduced in Bradley W. Richards, *The Savage View: Charles Savage, Pioneer Mormon Photographer* (Nevada City, California: Carl Mautz Publishing, 1995), p. 168. The Bassett Brothers' "family lore" has appeared in Hansen and Hansen, *Bassett Brothers*, and on their website, cited earlier. Very little is currently known about the Rea Brothers' "hotel," but for a mention of its construction, see "Messrs. G.W. and Thomas Rea" ["hotel"], *The Madisonian* (Virginia City, MT), June 28, 1884, p. 2, col. 3.

305. These events are chronicled in Hugh T. Lovin, "Fighting over the Cascade Corner of Yellowstone National Park, 1917-1935," *Annals of Wyoming* 72 (Spring, 2000): 14-29, especially p. 28; and Michael J. Yochim, "Beauty and the Beet: The Dam Battles of Yellowstone National Park," *Montana the Magazine of Western History* 53 (Spring, 2003): 14-27. See also "Bids Called…Contract for Island Park Reservoir to be Let at Ashton August 5," Idaho Falls (ID) *Post-Register*, July 5, 1935, p. 1; "Reservoir to Supply Water for Valley Land," *Post-Register*, December 6, 1936, p. 6; and "Water Storage Shows Increase" [completed "last fall"], *Post-Register*, March 29, 1939, p. 10. The actual waterfalls are in Paul Rubinstein, Lee Whittlesey, and Mike Stevens, *The Guide to Yellowstone Waterfalls and Their Discovery* (Englewood, CO: Westcliffe Publishers, 2000), pp. 68-135.

306. Savage, "A Strange Country," and his personal diary, as previously cited.

307. The Manleys at Henry's Lake were mentioned in "Captured—The Madison Boys Take in the Horse Thieves—One of the Robbers Gets His Quietus—And Goes Where Horses are not Needed," *The Madisonian* (Virginia City, MT), June 21, 1884, p. 3. My thanks go to researcher Tina Schlaile of Fairview, California for this article. Ancestry.com shows Manley's wife as Alice Lamay Riblett Manley. Accessed January 19, 2021, per Henry Clay Manley, 1865-1932.

308. Although the mountain's summit is technically in Idaho, its north, east, and northeast slopes, where the Manleys settled, are today located in Montana.

309. Ancestry.com for Henry Clay Manley (1863-1932), accessed November, 2019; "Funeral is Held for Ennis Man," *Montana Standard* (Butte, MT), February 21, 1932, p. 13; "Clay Manley, Well

Known Madison Co. Trapper, Drops Dead," *Independent-Record* (Helena, MT), February 23, 1932, p. 10; and "Virginia City News…Diseased Sheep are Being Treated," *Anaconda* (MT) *Standard*, May 21, 1897, p. 6. See also map, block 5 of Second and Madison streets, in Sam and Ed Eagle, *West Yellowstone's 70th Anniversary, 1908 to 1978* (West Yellowstone, MT: Eagle Company, Inc., copyright 1978), pp. 3-8, and the included 1910 tax list. The two obituaries cited here both gave Manley's birthday as having occurred in October of 1863, as opposed to the Ancestry site, which lists the year as 1865. The information on "Manley Peak" appears in the Jan Dunbar papers, West Yellowstone Historical Museum Archives, West Yellowstone, Montana. My thanks to Jan Dunbar for our useful conversations about area history.

310. Alfred Lambourne, "Striking Pictures—Impression Sketches of the Yellowstone," *Salt Lake Herald*, October 19, 1884, p. 9. This account, slightly abridged, also appeared as "Art Sketches of the Yellowstone," in *The Contributor* 10 (November, 1888): 22-27, which was a Mormon Church publication.

311. Alfred Lambourne, "The Geysers—The Grand, the Beautiful and Wonderful—Nature's Startling Freaks," *Salt Lake Herald*, April 12, 1885, p. 5. This article was partially reproduced without his byline as "The Geysers—A Great Natural Curiosity," in *Indiana Weekly Progress* (Indiana, PA), July 16, 1885, p. 1. See also Lambourne, "In Wonderland—A Pen Picture by a Utah Artist," *Salt Lake Herald*, December 25, 1887, p. 14. For Old Surprise Spring and its history, see that entry in Whittlesey, "Wonderland Nomenclature." As for "Cleveland Geyser," today's Old Surprise Spring, tour guide G.L. Henderson noted in his *Yellowstone Park Manual and Guide* (1888, p. 2, col 1) that the name Cleveland was suggested in September 1884, before the national election, by Hank Beaman, who had been deputy sheriff of Gardiner and after that of Livingston, Montana.

312. Thomas Henry Thomas "Yellowstone Park Illustrated," *The Graphic* (New York), August 11, 1888, pp. 190, 192. Haines, *Yellowstone Story*, I, p. 362n38, gave the month and year of Thomas's visit. Thomas's account has been reproduced with notes and with his many previously-unknown watercolor paintings in Janet Chapple, ed., *Through Early Yellowstone: Adventuring by Bicycle, Covered Wagon, Foot, Horseback, and Skis* (Lake Forest Park, Washington: Granite Peak Publications, 2016), pp. 102-160.

313. "To Yellowstone Park," *Salt Lake Herald*, April 24, 1885, p. 8. See also advertisement "The Most Direct Route from the East to the Great Yellowstone National Park," in *Idaho Register* (Idaho Falls, ID), April 4, 1885, p. 11. George Marshall sold his Marshall's Hotel during that spring, and thus his building had already been renamed Firehole Hotel.

314. "Territorial Talk" [Deputy C.J. Bassett], *Idaho Register* (Idaho Falls, ID), May 2, 1885, p. 1; and "Charles W. Nibley" [Bassett arrests him while serving as Idaho deputy marshal], *Deseret News* (Salt Lake City, UT), November 18, 1885 (vol. 34, number 44, p. 700).

315. "Eastern Idaho and a Sketch of the Counties Comprising It—Bingham County," *Idaho Register* (Idaho Falls, ID), vol. 1, no. 1, April 4, 1885, p. 11.

316. "To the National Park—The Difference between Two Transcontinental Lines," *St. Paul* (MN) *Daily Globe*, April 28, 1885, p. 4 has these discussions.

317. "The Great Park—Additional Wonders to be Seen in the Yellowstone Reservation," *Sunday Gazette* (Fort Wayne, IN), May 3, 1885, p. 2.

318. Advertisement headlined "Northern Pacific Railroad," in *Bismarck* (ND) *Daily Tribune*, October 20, 1885, p. 2. For Gilman Sawtell's delivery of fish to Virginia City in 1868, some of his earliest, see "The Manager Was the Recipient," *Montana Post*, November 20, 1868, p. 6, col. 2. Sawtell was the first settler in the region. That he was present in Virginia City in 1866, or at least expected to arrive there shortly, is evidenced by an unclaimed letter addressed to him at the VC post office ("Letter List," *Montana Post*, September 8, 1866, p. 8, col. 3). The notice in the Deer Lodge

newspaper (from the Virginia City *Montanian* of June 4) on June 13, 1874 that Gilman Sawtell's wife and family would soon join him at Henry's Lake and that he "has not seen his folks in eight years" makes it likely that he left them and emigrated to Montana in the summer of 1866, apparently arriving sometime after the "Letter List" notice of September 8. See "Virginia City Items," *New North-West*, June 13, 1874, p. 3; and "Local Brevities" [confirming Sawtell's 1866 arrival], *New North-West*, August 15, 1874, p. 3. When Frank Bradley of the Hayden survey arrived at Henry's Lake in 1872, he stated: "Messrs. Sawtelle [*sic*] and [Levi] Wurtz here conduct a large trade in fresh fish, caught in the lake and its outlet, which they pack in ice and haul fifty miles to Virginia City." Bradley in F.V. Hayden, *Sixth Annual Report of the United States Geological Survey of the Territories...Being a Report of Progress of the Explorations for the Year of 1872* (Washington: GPO, 1873), p. 226.

319. "Prairie Fires," *Idaho Register* (Idaho Falls, ID), September 26, 1885, p. 5.

320. Bassett Brothers, Yellowstone National Park Stage Line, to S.M. Knox, Salt Lake [City], August 18, 1885, copy in YNP Library, Vertical Files, under "Concessions (Bassett Brothers)"; original in library's Manuscript File, Rare Book Room.

321. W.H. Leffingwell, Map: "Forks of Firehole River[,] Yellowstone National Park, July 30, 1885, Arnold Hague, Geologist in Charge," in YNP Archives Maps. This map showed two buildings marked "log cabins" and a third structure on it marked "corral." By 1891, surveyor Hollingsworth's hand-drawn sketch of the area showed three small buildings marked "Shacks Bassetts," located a distance to the south of two buildings that undoubtedly represented George Marshall's first hotel. See C.F. Hollingsworth, 1891 survey notebook, book 2, pp. 107-109, in Army Era Records, (formerly box K-44), YNP Archives. By 1929, one of those cabins had apparently been removed, for only two were shown on "Sketch of Map of Lower Portion of Lower Geyser Basin Showing Hotel Sites 1885," in National Park Service, *Ranger Naturalists' Manual* (Mammoth: NPS mimeographed, 1929), p. 196.

322. "Clasped by a Bear—Exciting Midnight Adventure Related by a Railroad Man," time-lined "three years ago," and attributed to *San Francisco Examiner*, appearing in *Idaho County Free Press* (Grangeville, ID), April 20, 1888, p. 2. There was no indication as to whether this was a black bear or a grizzly bear.

323. "Yellowstone Park," *St. Paul Daily Globe*, August 18, 1886, p. 4.

324. "Yellowstone Park," *Morning Oregonian* (Portland, OR), August 18, 1886, p. 3.

325. J.M., "Beaver Canyon Notes," *Idaho Register* (Idaho Falls, ID), June 5, 1886, p. 5. See also "Personal" [H.H. Spencer], *Idaho Register*, June 26, 1886, p. 5. "Town and Territory," *Helena Weekly Herald*, May 20, 1886, p. 7 stated that the Union Pacific Railroad was also building a hotel there.

326. "Local Briefs" [by a *Herald* correspondent], *Salt Lake Herald*, June 3, 1886, p. 8. See also, "Etiquette of the London Pit," *Salt Lake Herald*, July 18, 1886, p. 9. Modjeska's biography appeared in Mabel Collins, *The Story of Helena Modjeska* (London: W.H. Allen & Company, 1885); and in Beth Holmgren, *Starring Madame Modjeska: On Tour in Poland and America* (Bloomington: Indiana University Press, 2012), neither of which mentioned her Yellowstone trip.

327. G.L. Henderson, "At the National Park—Incidents Connected with the Opening of the Tourist Season—Some of the Most Beautiful Places to Visit—The Scenery, Etc., Etc.," *Livingston Enterprise*, July 10, 1886, p 4

328. "Violating Game Laws" [from the *Madisonian*], *Livingston Enterprise*, September 4, 1886, p. 3.

329. "Road into Yellowstone Park," *Daily Tribune* (Salt Lake City, UT), November 14, 1886, p. 4. The new road's exact route is not known today, but it likely shortened the distance by deviating to the northeast.

330. "Train Wrecked—Thirteen Freight Cars Tumbled into a Scrap Pile in Beaver Canyon," *Idaho Register* (Idaho Falls, ID), April 23, 1887, p. 3; and "Accident on the U&N," *Helena Weekly Herald*, April 28, 1887, p. 8.

331. *Idaho News* (Blackfoot, ID), June 18, 1887; and "Part of Beaver Cañon," *Idaho News* (Blackfoot, ID), July 2, 1887. Mrs. Frank Bassett was Ruth E. Sagers Bassett (1860-1911). Like brother Jule, the Frank Bassetts by this time lived in Blackfoot during the off-season. See "Instruction in Music," *Idaho News*, October 1, 1887.

332. Bassett Brothers, "To the Hon. Secretary of the Interior Department, Washington, D.C.," July 8, 1887, in National Archives, RG 48, microfilm 62, roll 2, folder 3 of 4 (hardcopy at YNP Library).

333. Secretary of Interior's summary note dated July 10, 1887 on reverse of letter from Bassetts, stating "Application (forwarded through Act'g Supt of the Yellowstone Park with his favorable recommendation) for permission to continue transportation business through the Park"; and Moses Harris to Department of the Interior, July 10, 1887, "Approved…it is desirable…"; H.L. Muldrow to Captain Moses Harris, U.S.A[rmy]., July 27, 1887 [authorizing Harris to issue permit]; and "Letter to Bassett Bros" from Secretary of Interior, all four in National Archives, RG 48, microfilm 62, roll 2, folder 3 of 4 (hardcopies at YNP Library). Another copy of this is H.L. Muldrow to Moses Harris, July 27, 1887, Archive Document 24, YNP Archives. Harris's original, handwritten version of his July 10 letter to Muldrow is in Army Era Records, Series I: Pre-1909 Correspondence Files, box 23 (ledger-volume II, March 17, 1887 through August 18, 1889), YNP Archives, p. 46. The Hansen and Hansen book, *Bassett Brothers*, pp. 32-33 shows photos of two or three of the cabins. A map of buildings in the Marshall's Hotel area in 1885 in National Park Service, *Ranger Naturalists' Manual* (Mammoth: NPS mimeographed, 1929), p. 196 shows two buildings, apparently those of the Bassett Brothers, at a spot just south of the first Marshall's Hotel marked "log cabins" and a "corral" close by that were indicated by the publication's date to have been still standing in the late 1920s.

334. A., "Yellowstone Park—A Baltimorean's Visit—Beautiful Scenery and Plenty of Mosquitoes," *The Sun* (Baltimore, MD), August 8, 1887, p. 1 of supplement.

335. Edward Roberts's stage-driver told him in 1887 that the name Bottle Creek originated when "Generals Sherman and Sheridan happened to meet and make camp on its banks." He claimed that when they departed, "the number of bottles left behind gave the creek its name." Author Roberts stated that "this story of our driver may not be true, but locally it is thought to be." If the incident happened, it probably occurred in 1877, during the Nez Perce War when both generals were present in the region. Bottle Creek has since been renamed, and it was probably today's Hotel Creek. Roberts, *Shoshone and Other Western Wonders*, p. 185.

336. A., "Yellowstone Park—A Baltimorean's Visit," as cited.

337. A., "Yellowstone Park—A Baltimorean's Visit," as cited.

338. A., "Yellowstone Park—The Lake and Great Falls—Grand Canyon of the Yellowstone," *The Sun* (Baltimore, MD), August 15, 1887, p. 4.

339. "A New Line Headed for Butte," *Butte Semi-Weekly Miner*, August 6, 1887, p. 3.

340. "Mr. C.H. Bassett Arrested—Held in the Usual Bonds on the Usual Charge," *Salt Lake Herald*, September 2, 1887, p. 8; and calendar published in "Chronological—The Record of the Year 1887," *Salt Lake Herald*, December 25, 1887, p. 18, showing an arrest-date of September 1.

341. "Bishop Bassett Arrested," *Salt Lake Herald*, October 16, 1886, p. 8; "The Bassett Case—Held on the Charge of Polygamy," *Salt Lake Herald*, October 19, 1886, p. 8; "Mrs. Bassett Sues for Divorce—Her Polygamous Brute of a Husband Shown Up in an Odious Light—His Treachery," *Salt Lake Tribune*, April 7, 1887, p. 4; "Chronological—Record of the Year 1887," *Salt Lake*

Herald, December 25, 1887, p. 18; and "The Bad Bassett Case," *Salt Lake Tribune*, December 22, 1887, p. 3.

342. "Polygamous Wives," *Helena Independent*, December 23, 1890, morning edition, p. 1. See also "The Bassett Case," *Salt Lake Herald*, December 23, 1890, p. 1; and especially "A Most Important Case on Appeal," *Deseret Evening News* (Salt Lake City, UT), December 11, 1890, p. 2, which discussed the case before it was decided and correctly predicted that it would be reversed by the U.S. Supreme Court. Lawyer and historian Steve Mishkin of Olympia, Washington has searched legal sources unsuccessfully for any evidence that Utah Territory continued to pursue this case after the remand, and my thanks go to him. Mishkin e-mail to Lee Whittlesey, August 28, 2017.

343. Stephen Cresswell, *Mormons and Cowboys, Moonshiners and Klansmen: Federal Law Enforcement in the South and West, 1870-1893* (Tuscaloosa and London: University of Alabama Press, copyright 1991), chapter three, especially p. 99 and note 52.

344. Cresswell, *Mormons and Cowboys*, pp. 95, 98-99, 101, 106; and Richards, *The Savage View: Charles Savage, Pioneer Mormon Photographer*, pp. 77-82, discussing in detail the effects of the law and polygamy in general upon Charles Savage and his family. The updated Edmunds-Tucker Act of March 1, 1887 appeared at 48 USC 1461, 24 Stat. 635, and among other items it disincorporated the LDS Church, required anti-polygamy oaths, required civil marriage licenses to help fight polygamy, and replaced local judges with federally appointed judges. Cresswell, *Mormons and Cowboys*, pp. 102-103. The item that disincorporated the Mormon Church was clearly unconstitutional as a violation of the First Amendment's freedom-of-religion clause.

345. "Mr. C.H. Bassett Arrested," *Salt Lake Herald*, September 2, 1887, p. 8. The case of *U.S. v. Charles H. Bassett* was mentioned in "Third District Court," *Salt Lake Herald*, October 9, 1887, p. 6.

346. "Charles H. Bassett Pulled—He is Held by the Commissioner for his Sins—Witnesses Also Bound Over," *Salt Lake Tribune*, September 8, 1887, p. 3. The names, numbers, and relationships among the people of this family are befuddling to us today, but here is what Ancestry.com says about them, as of March 22, 2017. The children of Permelia Mindwell Dayton Bassett (all Bassetts) were: Helen Maria, Flora Elizabeth, Charles Julius, Charles Henry, Francis Augustus, William Henry, and Annie Matilda. The children of Mary Elizabeth Knight Bassett (again, all Bassetts) were: Mary Ellen, Melvie Amanda, William Hewig, James Lester, Ernest Knight, Fred Clayton, Lutie C., Ruby Rosaltha, Roscoe Knight, and Lois Knight. Children of Millie P. Bassett in 1900 (all Bassetts) were Freeman, Allen, and Cora. If there were children by Sarah Stageman, we have not found them. For all of this, see Ancestry.com, Charles Henry Bassett (Sr.) (1828-1907).

347. "One Levi Minerly," *Butte Semi-Weekly Miner*, August 31, 1887, p. 3. This article stated that one of Minerly's wives was "called" after she had been "sealed," probably slang-terms for her having been subpoenaed and given immunity to testify against him.

348. "Other Business" [Charles H. Bassett, Sr.], *Salt Lake Herald*, March 6, 1888, p. 5, col. 3.

349. Moses Harris to Bassett Brothers, August 3, 1887, in Army Era Records, Series I: Pre-1909 Correspondence Files, box 23 (ledger-volume II, March 17, 1887 through August 18, 1889), YNP Archives, p. 64.

350. These activities by Garfield and James have been chronicled in Haines, *Yellowstone Story*, II, pp. 12-14, 23-26.

351. Moses Harris letters to Secretary of Interior, March 8, 1888; and March 25, 1888, both in Army Era Records, Series I: Pre-1909 Correspondence Files, box 23 (ledger-volume II, March 17, 1887 through August 18, 1889), YNP Archives, pp. 223, 228.

352. Moses Harris to H.L. Muldrow, September 15, 1887 [accusing William Bassett of theft]; and Moses Harris to Secretary of Interior [reiterating that permit should be revoked], March 25, 1888, both in National Archives, RG 48, microfilm 62, roll 2, folder 3 of 4 (hardcopies at YNP Library).

353. H.L. Muldrow to Moses Harris, March 14, 1888, Archive Document 25, YNP Archives.

354. Moses Harris to William Henry Bassett, July 25, 1888, in box 23, ledger-volume II, p. 308, YNP Archives.

355. Bassett Brothers to Captain Moses Harris, March 10, 1888, Archive Document 653, YNP Archives.

356. Moses Harris to Secretary of Interior, March 20, 1888 [disapproving Bassetts' application for a lease of land], in box 23, ledger-volume II, p. 225, YNP Archives. In this letter, Harris mentioned the Bassetts' letter to him dated March 10, 1888, enclosing their proposed survey of the land.

357. Moses Harris to Secretary of Interior, March 8, 1888, in box 23, ledger-volume II, p. 223, YNP Archives. At this time, Wakefield had been managing YNPIC's/YPA's main stagecoach company, headquartered at Mammoth Hot Springs, for nearly five years.

358. W.H. Bassett, Lower Geyser Basin, to Captain Moses Harris, July 23, 1888, Archive Document 654, YNP Archives. Apparently, this incident at Lower Basin involving William Bassett, as bad as it was, did not keep him from living there for at least five more summers, because in 1893, William recommended his friend, Rube Scott, for the position of civilian scout for the U.S. Army to military superintendent George S. Anderson and used the return address of "Lower Basin." See W.H. Bassett, Lower Basin, to Captain Anderson, Superintendent, July 24, 1893, Archive Document 660, YNP Archives.

359. Edwards Roberts, "The American Wonderland," part one, Art Journal 40 (July, 1888):193-198. The newspaper that identified artist Tyler revealed that he was W.B. Tyler. See "W.B. Tyler," Helena Weekly Herald, September 22, 1887, p. 7.

360. Edwards Roberts, Shoshone and Other Western Wonders (New York: Harper and Brothers, 1888), p. 183. On page 192, while ascending Targhee Pass, he again emphasized this: "The air was like a tonic, and our blood flowed free and fast."

361. Roberts, Shoshone, p. 186 and woodcut drawing of "Snake River Crossing." This actually was Henry's Fork of the Snake River. These people were John William Kooch and Margaret McAlpine Woodward Kooch. Information from Tina Schlaile, in contact with historian at Island Park who is working on an updated history of the Island Park area.

362. A.F.Z., "Approaching the Yellowstone Park—the Paradise of Hunters," Notre Dame Scholastic 22#13, November 17, 1888, p. [201]; and Walter L. Steele, "A Visit to the National Park," Raleigh (NC) Christian Advocate, September 25, 1889, p. 1, cols. 1-4 (my thanks go to researcher Tina Schlaile for this account). In 1887, bicyclist George Thayer, after crossing Henry's Fork, referred to this spot as "a log hut with rows of tents," still fairly early in the beginnings of the new hotel. Thayer (pp. 193-194) further confirmed this by noting that he rode fifty-five miles east from Beaver Canyon where he reached "the Half-Way Hotel sometime before sundown." He described it as "a log hut, with rows of tents on the sides, for sleeping-rooms, and [it] is situated close to Snake River [Henry's Fork], a splendid trouting stream…About dark nearly a dozen passengers arrived in the stages bound for the Yellowstone, and the sleeping apartments were taxed to their utmost; so when the bar-tender offered me a bed with him, on the ground, in his tent or bar-room rather, I was glad to accept it. Drinks were twenty-five cents here…The second day I came to Snake River Crossing…" This place must have been the new settlement of Arangee because of the longer distance (fifty-five miles instead of fifty-one to this spot); and because the "log hut with rows of tents" was a spot apparently bigger than Rea's ranch, as it sported a bartender and sleeping apartments. If this was indeed the case, then Thayer's later mention of coming to "Snake River" on "the second day" probably referred to either to another (upstream) crossing of Henry's Fork, or perhaps Buffalo Fork of the Snake. See George B. Thayer, Pedal and Path across the Continent Awheel and Afoot (Hartford, CT: Evening Post Association, 1887), pp. 191-201. The

YNP Library (vertical files) contains chapter twenty-one only, but Thayer's full book is available on Google Books. Thayer stated that the route from Beaver Canyon to Firehole Hotel was one hundred five miles long and of that "ninety miles is as fine riding as any wheelman could desire."

363. Roberts, "American Wonderland," part one, p. 196. In *Shoshone*, p. 195, Roberts described their staying with H. Clay Manley at his cabin, where he "told us of his life," which was "very uneventful" and in winter "most dreary." "For a living," said Roberts, "Manley supplies the park hotels with meat, eggs, and milk." His "life was a struggle, and the income was discouragingly small."

364. Roberts, *Shoshone*, p. 201. On page 232, Roberts described his suspicion that their driver engaged in illegal soaping of park geysers to aid in the party's viewing of them.

365. Edwards Roberts, "The American Wonderland," part two, *Art Journal* 40 (November, 1888): 325-328.

366. Edwards Roberts, "American Wonderland," part two, p. 328; and Roberts, *Shoshone*, p. 256.

367. "Town and Country" [horses to Gentile Valley], *Idaho News* (Blackfoot, ID), October 22, 1887; and Hansen and Hansen, *Bassett Brothers*, pp. 42-43.

368. "In Railway Circles" [Excelsior Geyser active], *Salt Lake Herald*, June 9, 1888, p. 8. See also "Home and Neighborhood" [Bassetts will begin running on June 1], *Idaho News* (Blackfoot, ID), May 5, 1888.

369. Park visitation statistics are in Haines, *Yellowstone Story*, II, p. 478.

370. There is a Wikipedia biography of Albert Zahm at https://en.wikipedia.org/wiki/Albert_Francis_Zahm and further documentation in its citations.

371. A[lbert] F[rancis] Z[ahm], "A Ride to Shoshone Falls," *Notre Dame Scholastic* 22#5, September 22, 1888, pp. 75-79; and A.F.Z., "A Drive through the Camas Meadows (Enroute to the Yellowstone Park)," *Notre Dame Scholastic* 22#7, October 6, 1888, pp. 108-111. Zahm's mention of the "little yellow flower" of the camas—a plant that was and is inescapably *blue* with an edible bulb—might have been a reference to the plant's yellow-tipped stamens.

372. A.F.Z., "A Drive through the Camas Meadows," as cited, p. 111.

373. "Back from Island Park [Mrs. Charlotte Rea Tells How the Creek Received Its Name]," *The Idaho Republican* (Blackfoot, ID), October 27, 1911, p. 1. Shotgun Creek was thus one of the oldest place names in the region, appearing on all the following maps: the 1879 General Land Office map of Idaho by C. Roser; the Samuel Augustus map of 1880; the 1883 GLO map drawn by G.P. Strum; the George F. Cram map of 1883; and the 1895 Rand McNally & Company map. Shotgun Valley, of course, took its name from Shotgun Creek. These maps all showed the stream flowing generally east, as does today's Sheridan Creek.

374. Shongo, "A Hunt in the Rockies, in Three Parts, Part I," *Forest and Stream* 39, August 11, 1892, p. 115.

375. A.F.Z., "A Drive through the Camas Meadows," as cited, p. 111. For George Rea's story, see Chapter Eight in this book, and Ancestry.com (George Walter Rea, 1832-1902). An 1887 description of Rea's Ranch gave its location: "Twenty-five miles east of Camas Creek is George W. Rae's [*sic*] ranch; he has, I think without doubt, the finest fish pond and the best fishing I ever saw. He is located on Shot Gun creek, three miles above where it flows into the north fork [Henry's Fork] of Snake River." See U Know, "The National Park—An Interesting Communication from Our Special Correspondent," *Idaho News* (Blackfoot, ID), August 13, 1887, p. 1. An interesting inconsistency appeared in 1893 in a column by "Dick" entitled "Our Northern Neighbors" and locationally headlined "Arangee, Idaho" (*Idaho Falls Times*, January 19, 1893, p. 5), wherein this writer, whoever he was, discussed G.W. Rea and stated that his ranch was located "at the junction

of Moose Springs with Sheridan Creek." At first, we chalked this up to being a simple mistake by that writer (because all other information placed Rea's ranch at Glen Rea, Idaho, today partially covered by the waters of Island Park Reservoir), but the discovery that the name Sheridan Creek replaced the old "Shotgun Creek" gives new meaning to this writing by "Dick." It likely indicates that the name *Sheridan Creek* was in the process of eclipsing the name *Shotgun Creek* by early 1893, and sure enough the name Shotgun Creek failed to appear on the Fremont County map in the 1912 Rand McNally & Company Atlas, the creek itself being shown unlabeled. For a photo of Rea's ranch, out on the treeless mud-flats of Shotgun Valley, see Green, *History of Island Park*, p. 53. After A.S. Trude purchased it in 1891 (Green, p. 47), part of it became known as the "Algenia Ranch," for Trude's wife Algenia Trude.

376. Historian Green has stated that George Rea scouted for General O.O. Howard through this area in 1877 and was Shotgun Valley's first resident in 1878 (Green, *History of Island Park*, pp. 36-37), but as we have made clear above and in Chapter Eight, Rea by his own statement first arrived in Montana in 1865 and visited the present Island Park area in the fall of that same year. See G.W. Rea, "Yellowstone Park—What a Trapper Says About the Country and the Way to Get There," *Salt Lake Tribune* (Salt Lake City, UT), August 5, 1882, p. 3.

377. A.F.Z., "A Drive through the Camas Meadows," as cited, p. 111.

378. "An Echo of the Long Ago—Big Colony in Snake River Valley Comes to Grief—A Valley Named," *Idaho Republican* (Blackfoot, ID), December 9, 1919, p. 1. Per the real-estate record at St. Anthony, Idaho (see endnote 389), the land-deed, wherein Gerber purchased the land from Kooch, was dated October 3, 1890. So, if this newspaper article had it correct that Gerber's new Swiss settlers arrived in June, that arrival, when coupled with Gerber's acquisition of the land in late 1890, must have occurred in June of 1891. This calculation also requires the winter wherein their cattle starved to have been the succeeding winter of 1891-92. The newspaper article, which assumed that the reminiscencers who spoke to the newspaper (probably Chris and John Reber) had their facts right, stated that the new settlers tried to drive their cattle during a difficult winter to Marysville and St. Anthony (not founded until 1889 and 1890 respectively), so this calculated scenario for that cattle drive must also have occurred in the winter of 1891-1892.

379. "An Echo of the Long Ago (continued)," *Idaho Republican*, December 9, 1919, p. 6.

380. Green, *History of Island Park*, p. 47.

381. Green, *History of Island Park*, pp. 45, 47; and "An Echo of the Long Ago (continued)," as cited, p. 6.

382. "An Echo of the Long Ago (continued)," as cited, p. 6.

383. "An Echo of the Long Ago—Failure and Suicide Follow an Unhappy Venture—A Famous Resort—Chapter II," *Idaho Republican*, December 12, 1919, p. 1.

384. "An Echo of the Long Ago, [Chapter II] (continued)," *Idaho Republican*, December 12, 1919, p. 6. For a more general account of these Swiss settlers, which is a secondary source (as opposed to "An Echo of Long Ago," which is arguably a primary source), see Dean H. Green, "The Swiss Colony of Island Park," *Snake River Echoes* (Idaho), vol. 11#2, 1982, pp. 78-79, bound volumes at Idaho Falls (ID) Public Library. Green stated here that shortly after the Arangee settlement was established, the Bassett Brothers changed their route and began running through Centennial Valley, Montana to Yellowstone Park, but I have been unable to confirm that. The best evidence is that the Bassetts continued running through Shotgun Valley and never operated through Centennial Valley. Additionally, the facts that the town of Beaver Canyon moved four miles south to Spencer in 1897 and that according to local newspapers the Bassetts operated from there are further arguments for the proposition that the Bassetts never used the Centennial Valley route, which would have required a complete move north to Monida, Montana.

385. Both Hopf and Gerber appeared in land records and newspapers of that era, but so far there is no trace of Rutledge. However, the last names of four other men have turned up in newspaper accounts who appear to have teamed with Gerber to start Arangee, and they were Heard, Burns, Meyer, and Meyer. According to Dean Green the word "Arangee" was coined by the men as some sort of acronym made from parts of their names. We can envision the "R" for "Rutledge," the "G" for Gerber, perhaps two E's from the Meyers, and even a possible "N" from Burns, but the origin of the "A" remains a mystery. Perhaps it came from a first name of one of the men, because we know only the last names of seven of them. Green, *History of Island Park*, pp. 46-47. Said the *Idaho News*: "Messrs. Meyer, Gerber, and Heard, of New York, and Burns and Meyer of Ohio, capitalists, spent Friday in Blackfoot on business with the land office." See "All Around Home," *Idaho News*, Saturday, October 4, 1890, p. 1.

386. The old town site of "Rea" remains today on close-up Google Maps, even though the name of the "town" was moved northward from Rea's original ranch after the flooding of Island Park Reservoir in 1937. "Rea" does not appear in today's atlas (Benchmark Maps, *Idaho Road and Recreation Atlas*, Santa Barbara, CA, Benchmark Maps, 2015, p. 59), but it appeared on the 1997 map in the *Montana Atlas*, as cited below. For more on the Arangee Land and Cattle Company, see Green, *History of Island Park*, as cited, pp. 42, 45-46. For an example of George Rea's newspaper column, see G.W. Rea, "Our Arangee Correspondent," *Idaho Falls Times* (Idaho Falls, ID), June 29, 1893, p. 5. For the region's recent geography, see Benchmark Maps, *Idaho Road and Recreation Atlas*, 2015, as cited; *Montana Road and Recreation Atlas* (Santa Barbara, CA: Benchmark Maps, 2015), pp. 120-121; and No author, *Montana Atlas and Gazetteer* (Yarmouth, Maine: DeLorme, 1997), p. 22. This area today is in Fremont (formerly Bingham) County, Idaho. In early days, Blackfoot was the county seat of Bingham County, but in 1893, Fremont County was carved from Bingham. St. Anthony, Idaho, founded in 1890 by C.H. Moon, eventually became the county seat of Fremont County and was named after St. Anthony Falls, Minnesota, per "C.H. Moon Founded St. Anthony in '90," *Fremont County* (ID) *Chronicle-News*, August 8, 1963, p. 8. There were probably some ranches there for a couple of years before that.

387. "Arange Peak," located at the head of Yale Creek just east of Rea's Peak and south of Mount Jefferson, remains on maps today in that misspelled form, which seems to have come from mistakes in county land-records. That the Arangee Land and Cattle Company was still hiring colonists for transplanting to their ranch in 1892 became evident when one of them died, as mentioned in "Sharps and Flats in Home Music" [colonist Muhleman dies], *Blackfoot News*, April 16, 1892, p. 1. A post office formally opened at Arangee in 1891, per "State News," *Idaho Falls Times*, September 3, 1891, p. 8, with Karl Hopf as postmaster. For Hopf and Arangee in 1892, see "Upper Country—Future Great Resources of Bingham—New Towns, New Farms, New People," *Idaho Falls Times*, September 22, 1892, p. 5, which stated: "A day's travel north [of St. Anthony] brought us to the celebrated 'Island Park'." This article stated that Arangee Ranch was located on Shotgun Creek four miles from [east of] George Rea, and the long winters required feeding cattle for six months. Voting in 1904 showed that at least 38 people were then living at Arangee. See "Official Vote of Fremont County," *Teton Peak Chronicle* (St. Anthony, ID), December 15, 1904, p. 1.

388. Green, *History of Island Park*, p. 45. The Reber brothers, John and Chris, were still living at Kilgore, Idaho in 1919 at the time of the *Idaho Republican*'s "An Echo of the Long Ago," if not also later, during Dean Green's research. Regarding John Gerber, the *Idaho News* of Blackfoot recorded his presence in the land office on Friday, October 3, 1890: "Messrs. Meyer, Gerber, and Heard, of New York, and Burns and Meyer of Ohio, capitalists, spent Friday in Blackfoot on business with the land office" ("All Around Home," *Idaho News*, Saturday, October 4, 1890, p. 1). That the original owner, John Kooch, was dissolving his business partnership (Kooch & Caldwell) at Beaver Canyon with D.D. Caldwell during the summer of 1889 is evident from "Dissolution Notice," *Idaho Register* (Idaho Falls, ID), August 10, 1889, p. 3, which notice also

ran in the editions of August 14, 24, and 31. The advertisement referred to him as both "John M. Kooch" and "John W. Kooch." Interestingly, John and Margaret might have divorced by October 3, 1891, because the witnessing information for the Indenture referred to "J.W. Kooch unmarried." Regardless, John W. Kooch and Margaret Kooch were eventually interred in the Riverview Cemetery at St. Anthony, Idaho.

389. This Indenture (warranty deed) as recorded at Blackfoot, Bingham County, Idaho (and today held at St. Anthony, Fremont County) mistakenly reversed the grantor (Kooch) and the grantee (Gerber), so that the entire document had to be rewritten to show these corrections. Both documents appeared in Deed Record, Book D. Page 193 holds the incorrect document, and page 312 contains the corrected, operative document showing Kooch as grantor and Gerber as grantee. This corrected, operative document was recorded on June 13, 1891.

390. A.F.Z., "Approaching the Yellowstone Park—the Paradise of Hunters," *Notre Dame Scholastic* 22#13, November 17, 1888, p. [201]. With this statement, Zahm indicated that these men had had some time to become hangers-on in this remote region, a scenario that adds further to the likelihood that this was the "Snake River Crossing Hotel" as still owned by John and Margaret Kooch. From Zahm's account, this settlement that became the town of Arangee was already beginning to grow a little in 1888.

391. A.F.Z., "Approaching the Yellowstone Park," as cited, pp. 202-203, including an uncaptioned woodcut-drawing of the footbridge at "Snake River hotel" on p. 203.

392. Because 1888 was apparently the first year to carry mentions of this stage-stop on Targhee Creek about two miles west of Henry's Lake, the Bassetts, or someone else, must have built it in that very year or late in 1887. As previously indicated, area resident McMinn apparently came into its ownership or perhaps built it himself in 1889, per the Steele account, and then the following year made the place larger at the time he married "the widow Chase," per Way Farer, "Henry's Lake, Idaho," *The Dillon Tribune*, August 8, 1890, p. 1, col. 2, datelined July 6; and Walter L. Steele, as cited, col. 2. History-researcher Randy Ingersoll of Gardiner, Montana mapped and located the site in 2013 using Google Earth maps, and the main building was still standing that year with two outbuildings that might also be original ones. A photo taken of the spot with horses and wagons indicates that the Monida & Yellowstone Stage Company began using it (after the Bassetts went out of business) possibly in M-Y's first year of operation, 1898. The road to the site—which is the original road up Targhee Pass—leaves U.S. 287 about 1.5 miles north of where 287 dead-ends into U.S. 20. See Randy Ingersoll to Lee Whittlesey, "Found the Targhee Stage Building—Still Stands," e-mail in author's files under "Bassett Brothers," November 15, 2013 with maps and photos; and Facebook page for Caldera National Monument Idaho Advocacy at https://www.facebook.com/photo.php?fbid=333640750114331&set=a.249038218574585.1073741826.249000091911731&type=1&theater showing a photo of the building with horses and wagons, probably taken in the 1890s. The building was removed in or about 2017.

393. A.F.Z., "Approaching the Yellowstone Park," as cited, pp. 203-204. At the relay station, they encountered an Irish stableman who cussed out one of the Bassetts' horses and raised a stick at the animal. The equine was saved from a serious beating by the presence of Zahm's driver, a "Mr. Bassett."

394. A.F.Z., "Approaching the Yellowstone Park," as cited, pp. 204-205.

395. A.F.Z., "Along the Firehole River," *Notre Dame Scholastic* 22#14, November 24, 1888, pp. 227-228. For the dangers of Yellowstone, see generally Whittlesey, *Death in Yellowstone*, 2014, as cited.

396. A.F.Z., "The Upper Geyser Basin," *Notre Dame Scholastic* 22#16, December 8, 1888, pp. 260-264. See also A.F.Z., "The Yellowstone Park. III. From the Firehole Valley to the Norris Geyser Basin," *Notre Dame Scholastic* 22#17, December 15, 1888, pp. [273]-277.

397. A.F.Z., "The Yellowstone Park. III," and "IV. Norris to Yellowstone," *Notre Dame Scholastic* 22#18, December 22, 1888, p. 291. The full account, both of these parts, appeared on pp. [289]-293. Norris's grizzly story has also been recounted in Lee H. Whittlesey, *Yellowstone Place Names* (Gardiner, Montana: Wonderland Publishing Company, 2006), p. 123.

398. A.F.Z., "The Yellowstone Park—V. Grand Cañon and Falls," *Notre Dame Scholastic* 22#19, January 12, 1889, pp. 311-315.

399. Prof. A.F. Zahm, "The Yellowstone Park—VI. Mammoth Hot Springs," *Notre Dame Scholastic* 22#20, January 19, 1889, pp. 329-332. See also Prof. A.F. Zahm, "The Yellowstone Park. VI. (Concluded.) Mammoth Hot Springs," *Notre Dame Scholastic* 22#21, January 26, 1889, pp. 344-346.

400. Prof. A.F. Zahm, "The Yellowstone Park. (Conclusion.) VII. General Features," *Notre Dame Scholastic* 22#22, February 2, 1889, pp. 360-363. There are eleven total chapters to this article, and many are confusingly numbered and titled but all are faithfully delineated here.

401. "Home and Neighborhood," *Idaho News* (Blackfoot, ID), September 1, 1888.

402. "Gossipy News" [Bassetts in operation], *Idaho News* (Blackfoot, ID), June 1, 1889.

403. George Chandler, Acting Secretary, to F.A. Boutelle, August 10, 1889, Archive Document 218, YNP Archives. This letter referred to Boutelle's letter of June 23, 1889 enclosing the Bassetts' request to "establish and occupy a stage station at Riverside in the park."

404. Bassett Brothers to Superintendent, June 10, 1889, Archive Document 652, YNP Archives. Assuming that their description was correct, this barn would have been located two miles inside the park's west boundary and thus could not have been the same as the Riverside soldier-and-mail station, which was four miles inside the boundary.

405. F.A. Boutelle to Bassett Brothers, June 10, 1889, in Army Era Records, Series I: Pre-1909 Correspondence Files, box 23 (vol. II, March 17, 1887 through August 18, 1889), YNP Archives, p. 444; and Boutelle to Secretary of Interior, June 22, 1889, in same volume, p. 454. See also Bassett Brothers to F.A. Boutelle, July 11, 1889, Archive Document 651, YNP Archives, asking permission for use of the "station" at Riverside and stating that the park did not answer their similar letter of June 10.

406. F.A. Boutelle to Secretary of Interior, June 22, 1889, in box 23, vol. II, YNP Archives, p. 454. See also Boutelle to Bassett Brothers, July 18, 1889, in box 23, vol. II, saying Bassetts' assertions in their letter of June 20 were not "borne out by the facts" so he was forwarding their letter to Secretary of the Interior.

407. George Chandler, Acting Secretary, to F.A. Boutelle, August 10, 1889, Archive Document 218, YNP Archives.

408. "Local News Notes" [Kimball and other campers], *Idaho Register* (Idaho Falls, ID), August 17, 1889, p. 3.

409. R.J. Clancey, "The Merry Men in Coaches—Penetrating the Fastnesses of the Wild and Wooly West—Rumbling Among Mountains—Colonel Stephenson's Vehicles and the Union Pacific Provide Fun and Fresh Air for a Very Jolly Party—Chasing the Setting Sun," *Omaha* (NE) *Daily Bee*, August 25, 1889, part II, p. 11. Members of the party and its itinerary were identified in "To Yellowstone Park—The Tally Ho and Pullman Outing in the West," *Omaha Daily Bee*, Aug 2, 1889, p. 8; and "Going to Yellowstone," *Omaha Daily Bee*, August 9, 1889, p. 8.

410. Clancey, "The Merry Men in Coaches," as cited.

411. "Two Soldiers of Fortune—A Queer Partnership Growing Out of the Late War—How Ben Harrison Fought—He Was a Little Nervous Before the Shooting Began but Warmed Up When Once

the Battle Was On—Two Odd Mountaineers," *Omaha Daily Bee*, September 8, 1889, p. 6. The "mountaineers" were Charley Huestis and Thomas O'Donnell. The party presumably traveled on to Shoshone Falls, but no other chapters of this story have been found.

412. "A Horrible Death—A Little Daughter of J.H. Crockwell Burned to Death," *Salt Lake Herald*, August 18, 1889, p. 5.

413. Although there is no year indicated for her visit, the article's publication in January of 1890 and its description of Giant Geyser's erupting for them in August both point to 1889 as Anna "Nan" Southworth's trip-year. Giant Geyser did not erupt at all in 1886 until September, or much if any in 1888, but it erupted at least four times in 1887, including an eruption on August 26, *just three days too early* for Southworth's observations of it to have occurred that year. Giant is known to have rejuvenated from months-long dormancy in 1889, and by September 14, it was being reported in newspapers as having regular eruptions as of old. See "Local Layout" [Giant Geyser], *Livingston* (MT) *Enterprise*, September 14, 1889, p. 3; and Whittlesey, "Wonderland Nomenclature," entry for Giant Geyser. It thus appears that the eruption they saw occurred on August 29, 1889.

414. Anna Husted Southworth, "Nan in Goblin Land," *Frank Leslie's Popular Monthly* 29, January, 1890, pp. 70-71. My thanks go to fellow historian Lee Silliman of Missoula, Montana, for alerting me to this account.

415. Southworth, "Nan in Goblin Land," as cited, p. 71.

416. Southworth, "Nan in Goblin Land," as cited, pp. 71-74; and Whittlesey, "Hotels on the Firehole River," as cited, p. 22.

417. Southworth, "Nan in Goblin Land," as cited, pp. 74-75. For this history of Giant Geyser in 1889, see Whittlesey, "Wonderland Nomenclature," as cited, entry for Giant Geyser, 1889.

418. Southworth, "Nan in Goblin Land," as cited, p. 76.

419. Southworth, "Nan in Goblin Land," as cited, pp. 77-79. The last quote is from p. 74.

420. Georgina M. Synge, *A Ride Through Wonderland* (London: Sampson Low, Marston and Company, 1892), pp. 4-8, 131-132. For Gardiner's 1889 fire, see the three newspaper citations in Lee H. Whittlesey, "A History of Park Street that Faces Yellowstone National Park in Gardiner, Montana," unpublished manuscript completed for National Park Service, YNP Research Library, 2013, p. 8 and footnote 23.

421. Synge, *Ride Through Wonderland*, pp. 10, 12, 15, 19, 27.

422. Although Hofer did not identify either stage company involved, a number of factors make it clear who the two companies were. Hofer's coach was a four-horse coach carrying six men (including Hofer, who lived at the park's north entrance) plus the driver, and it was "chartered for the round trip" from Mammoth Hotel and thus could not take the injured woman back to the hotel. These factors make it clear that it had to have been a Yellowstone Park Association Stage Line coach. The other driver chauffeured a two-horse unit "from the Union Pacific" (obviously a Bassett Brothers stage) who had come up with his single passenger "from the south entrance." (He had to have referred to the west entrance. Because the Bassetts operated from a great distance southwest of the park but entered through the west entrance, their routing was sometimes confused with the park's genuine south entrance.) Hofer stated that this driver "was not one of the regular Park Association drivers or perhaps the accident would not have happened."

423. E. Hofer, "Tales from a Journey to the Pacific—IX," *McGregor* (IA) *News*, November 20, 1889, p. 1, copy in the George Ash Collection, YNP Archives. Hofer gave the date of the incident as "September 27." Dr. Scott Herring of the University of California-Davis has finished a full biography of Elwood T. Hofer, and it has been published by Riverbend Publishing, Helena, Montana.

424. Hofer, "Tales from a Journey to the Pacific," as cited.

425. Hofer, "Tales from a Journey to the Pacific," as cited; "New Books," *Philadelphia Inquirer* (Philadelphia, PA), December 18, 1876, p. 7; and "A Traveled Woman [Margaretha Weppner]," *The Inter Ocean* (Chicago, IL), April 23, 1886, p. 7, from the *Philadelphia Press*.

426. "News of the Courts—A Suit for Heavy Damages Dismissed," *Idaho Statesman* (Boise, ID), August 16, 1892, p. 8; and "Dismised [*sic*] at Plaintiffs' Costs," *Idaho Register* (Idaho Falls, ID), August 19, 1892, p. 4. Both of these articles stated that this case ended up in the "United States circuit court," which was and is a court of appeals above the U.S. District (trial) Court. From this, it is apparent that one side or the other lost in the district court and then appealed it to the circuit court, where Ms. Weppner ultimately lost the case.

427. "Death" [of Francella Eastman Wright], *Idaho Register* (Idaho Falls, ID), October 5, 1889, p. 3. See also "In Our Trapper's Trap" [Mrs. Wright dies], *Idaho News* (Blackfoot, ID), October 5, 1889.

428. F.A. Boutelle to Bassett Brothers, Lago, Idaho, December 18, 1889, in box 24, vol. III, p. 72; and Bassett Brothers to S.H.[W.] Scudder, July 1, 1890, Archive Document 656, both in YNP Archives. This latter letter was reproduced in Hansen and Hansen, *Bassett Brothers*, p. 20, wherein the Hansens identified William Henry Bassett as its writer. Per pp. 42-43, Charles Henry II and William Henry both built homes in Lago, and lived there for many years. These descendants have stated that William Henry built his first store at Lago in 1880 and a larger store there in 1900. See also Sam W. Scudder to F.A. Boutelle, July 5, 1890, Archive Document 440, YNP Archives.

429. Bassett Brothers to F.A. Boutelle, January 27, 1890, Archive Document 655 [apologizes for Scudder affair and says it would not have happened had one of them been in the park at the time], YNP Archives.

430. "The Pioneer Route—The Original and Only Overland Route…The Union Pacific," *Salt Lake Herald*, December 25, 1889, p. 27.

431. John J.D. Trenor, "Our Remotest Territory—A Trip to the Far West—Alaska and the Yellowstone Park," *Irish American Weekly* (New York, NY), December 21, 1889, p. 2.

432. "Terrible Smashup—Two Freight Trains Dispute the Right of Way," *Dillon Tribune*, January 3, 1890, p. 1.

433. "Condensed News" [high winds and drifting snow], *Idaho Recorder* (Salmon City, ID), January 8, 1890, p. 3; and "Local News Notes" [trains blockaded by snowstorm with low temperatures], *Idaho Register* (Idaho Falls, ID), March 1, 1890, p. 3.

434. "Grand Excursion to Yellowstone National Park and Other Western Resorts," *Idaho County Free Press* (Grangeville, ID), July 11, 1890, p. 3. This advertisement also appeared in *Lewiston* (ID) *Teller*, July 17, 1890, p. 7; and *Idaho Register* (Idaho Falls, ID), August 8, 1890, p. 4, published too late to help recruitment.

435. For the Bassett Brothers, see Way Farer, "Henry's Lake, Idaho," *The Dillon Tribune*, August 8, 1890, p. 1, col. 2. For visitation this summer including at Henry's Lake, see D., "The Yellowstone Park," *The Deseret Weekly* 41#9, August 23, 1890, pp. 298-299, available on internet at http://books.google.com/books?id=lmHUAAAAMAAJ&dq=%22yellowstone%22%20%22hot%22&pg=PA273#v=onepage&q=%22yellowstone%22%20%22hot%22&f=false. For complete, yearly park visitation statistics, see Haines, *Yellowstone Story*, II, p. 478,

436. Nero, "Our Correspondence—Lima—The True Particulars [on Stoddard]," *Dillon* (MT) *Tribune*, August 29, 1890, p. 1, col. 4; "Knifed by the Dagoes—A Beaver Canyon Constable Murdered in Cold Blood," *Salt Lake* (UT) *Tribune*, August 26, 1890, p. 2; "Murderous Dagoes," *Idaho Daily Statesman* (Boise, ID), August 26, 1890, p. 1; "A Constable's Death," *Sacramento* (CA) *Daily Record-Union*, August 26, 1890, p. 1; "Officer Beheaded—Shocking Tragedy at Bea-

ver Canyon, Idaho," *The Morning Call* (Sacramento, CA), August 26, 1890, p. 8; "Murderous Italians," *Idaho Register* (Idaho Falls, ID), August 29, 1890, p. 3; "Blackfoot Items" [Thirty-three "Dagos" placed in jail and two put on trial at Blackfoot], *Idaho Register* (Idaho Falls, ID), August 29, 1890, p. 3; "Cut to Pieces by 'Dagoes'," *The Times* (Owosso, MI), August 29, 1890, p. 7; "Killed by Dagos—Constable D. Stoddard of Beaver Canyon Foully Murdered," *Idaho News* (Blackfoot, ID), August 30, 1890, p. 1; Eagle Rock Register, "Severed His Head—Two Dagos Hold a Constable While a Third Cuts His Throat," *Caldwell* (ID) *Tribune*, September 6, 1890, p 2; "Murdered by Rowdies," *Helena* (MT) *Independent*, August 26, 1890, p 1; Ogden Standard, "Foul Murder," *Deseret News* (Salt Lake City, UT), August 27, 1890, p. 3; and "[Accomplices] Want a New Trial," *Idaho Statesman* (Boise, ID), January 15, 1892, p. 1.

437. "They Cut His Throat—Dastardly Murder of an Idaho Officer by Drunken Dagos," *Anaconda* (MT) *Standard*, August 26, 1890, p. 1; and "Hot Chase after the Beaver Canyon Murderer," *Salt Lake Tribune*, September 12, 1890, p. 2.

438. Newspapers variously spelled Bertoni's name as "Burton," "Bertone," "Bretone," and "Bectoni" before the announcement of the accomplices wanting a new trial settled on "Bertoni."

439. "[Accomplices] Want a New Trial," *Idaho Statesman* (Boise, ID), January 15, 1892, p. 1; "Idaho Supreme Court," *Salt Lake Herald*, February 16, 1892, p. 1; and "Many Decisions—Important Supreme Court Decisions," *Idaho Statesman* (Boise, ID), February 16, 1892, p. 5. James Mike was pardoned and released in early 1896 because of his poor physical condition, and he then entrained to Kansas City. See "Local Brevities," *Idaho Register* (Idaho Falls, ID), January 17, 1896, p. 1.

440. "Dago Murderer Caught—Slayer of David Stoddard Nabbed in Portland—History of the Awful Deed," *Idaho Statesman* (Boise, ID), September 21, 1894, p. 3; and "After Many Days—Murderer of Constable Stoddard Arrested," *Salt Lake* (UT) *Herald*, September 21, 1894, p. 1. This article, datelined September 20, referred to the alleged murderer as "Guissipo Glanes" and stated that he was arrested in Portland, Oregon. Newspaper searches for "Guissipo" and "Glanes" in Oregon, Washington, Idaho, Montana, and Utah have turned up nothing else, nor have newspaper-searches in all fifty states in 1894 for references to David Stoddard. Also searched was the *Blackfoot News*, 1890-1894, to no avail.

441. Eagle Rock, "Early Days in Idaho," *Idaho Falls Times* (Idaho Falls, ID), March 16, 1916, p. 4.

442. Yearly park visitation statistics appeared in Haines, *Yellowstone Story*, II, p. 478. Background for these events appeared in McRae, "Inquiry," p. 78; and more recently in Whittlesey, "Hotels on the Firehole River," as cited, pp. 22-25.

443. "Henry's Lake," *Dillon Tribune*, June 19, 1891, p. 8; and "Local News," *Idaho Register* (Idaho Falls, ID), July 31, 1891, p. 1. The "E.J. Bassett" mentioned in this last article was probably a misprint for C.J. Bassett. The only "E" Bassett brother was Ernest Knight Bassett. Not only do the initials here not match, but also Ernest had neither the seniority nor the longevity in the operation that CJB had. The best guess is that Ernest was gone from the operation by 1891. In general, Bassetts' descendant Stan Hansen agrees with this assessment. In a letter to the author, he stated: "It appears the other brothers got out of the business at the end of the eighties but CJ kept the business going until the end of the nineties...His customer numbers were low during the nineties...After a few months studying them I have come to believe they were opportunists and not very good business men." Stan Hansen to Lee Whittlesey, e-mail dated October 2, 2008, in author's hard-file of materials marked "Bassett Brothers."

444. Mary E. Morgan Jones, "A Trip to the Yellowstone National Park," *Mower County Transcript* (Lansing, MN), October 14, 1891, p. 5.

445. Mary E. Morgan Jones, "A Trip to the Yellowstone," as previously cited. For skunks in the Park, see Whittlesey and Bone, *The History of Mammals in the Greater Yellowstone Ecosystem*, II, pp.

1106-1110. The "New York millionaire" that she mentioned was probably Phillip Liebinger of NYC who purchased the summer residence of H.A. Pierson on the "floating island" of Henry's Lake in 1890. See Way Farer, "Henry's Lake, Idaho," *The Dillon* (MT) *Tribune*, August 8, 1890, p. 1. My thanks go to researcher Tina Schlaile for bringing this article to my attention.

446. H.G.H., "A Land of Marvels—The Yellowstone National Park and Its Wonderful Scenery—Works of Nature that are Strange, Fantastic and Majestically Beautiful—Rivers of Boiling Water—The Paint Pots and the Great Geysers—Letters from a Naturalist—VI," *Detroit* (MI) *Free Press*, August 30, 1891, p. 8.

447. H.G.H., "A Land of Marvels…Letters from a Naturalist, VI," as cited.

448. H.G.H., "Wonders of Nature—In Yellowstone Park They are Found in Magnificent Profusion—Mud Volcano into which the Beholder Cannot Gaze without Horror—Great Game Roaming About, Half Tame, Amid Beautiful Scenery—Letters from a Naturalist—VII," *Detroit Free Press*, September 27, 1891, p. 13.

449. "Held Up in the Park—Prominent Missourians Robbed by Highwaymen" [from the *Bozeman Chronicle*], *Daily Independent* (Helena, MT), August 20, 1891, p. 4; "Highwaymen in Montana—Two Travelers Held Up Near Yellowstone National Park," *Salt Lake Tribune*, August 20, 1891, p. 1; "Highway Robbery—A Party of Yellowstone Tourists Held Up," *Salt Lake Herald*, August 20, 1891, p. 1; and "'Hands Up!'—Two Travelers Robbed Near the National Park by Highwaymen," *Fergus County* (MT) *Argus*, August 27, 1891, p. 2. For mention of the baseball organization, see "Baseball Magnates Had to Disgorge—Held Up in the Yellowstone Park Region and Relieved of $763," *Chicago Tribune*, August 18, 1891, p. 5.

450. "Held Up in the Park," *Daily Independent* (Helena, MT), August 20, 1891, p. 4.

451. Two more possible stage robberies involving the Bassett Brothers have come to light, but they cannot so far be confirmed. One of them on the Bassetts' route is alleged to have occurred in 1888 or 1889, but a thorough search of Montana, Idaho, and Washington newspapers for the years 1887-1890 has failed to turn it up. Two notorious bad-men brothers from Virginia City—John H. Johnson and Edward "Pinhead" Johnson—were believed to be the likely perpetrators of this hold-up and were fingered as such when the newspapers reported the "end of two bad men" in 1894. One brother was shot by police in the area of Spokane, Washington, and the other one received a life sentence to prison in South Dakota. See "End of Two Bad Men—One Was Killed and the Other Is Locked Up for Life," *Anaconda Standard*, April 13, 1894, p. 8. The same story appeared in the *Philipsburg* (MT) *Mail*, April 26, 1894, p. 4. So, did it happen? We do not know. A second alleged stage robbery supposedly involving a Bassett Brothers stage at Henry's Lake was reported by the *Dillon* (MT) *Tribune* as having occurred on August 13, 1891, but no other references to it have been found either. The report stated that the bandits took $200 and two gold watches from the passengers and sixteen dollars from the stage-driver. See Truthful James, "Henry's Lake, Idaho," *Dillon Tribune*, August 28, 1891, p. 8. We await further information, as no more is so far known about these two alleged hold-ups.

452. "State News" [Bassett Brothers], *Soda Springs* (ID) *Advertiser*, June 15, 1892, p. 5; and Edward S. Parkinson, *Wonderland; or Twelve Weeks in and out of the United States* (Trenton, NJ: MacCrellish & Quigley, 1894), pp. 225-230.

453. Parkinson, *Wonderland*, pp. 231-257.

454. George S. Anderson, Acting Superintendent, to Secretary of Interior, August 31, 1892, in box 25, Item 216 (ledger-volume IV, June 25, 1892 through March 17, 1894), pp. 64-68, YNP Archives. A letter from Anderson the following year again suggested the license idea, wherein the superintendent recommended that the Bassett Brothers "be required to pay the same license fee," namely five dollars per wagon, as Mr. Dixon, an independent stage-operator at Gardiner. George

S. Anderson to Secretary of Interior, June 26, 1894, in box 26, Item 217 (ledger-volume V, March 17, 1894 through July 23, 1896), pp. 76-78, YNP Archives.

455. Mrs. M.E. Jennings and Miss Mary Stockton [to George S. Anderson], August 28, 1892, Archive Document 1068, in "first ten thousand documents," YNP Archives.

456. "Random References" [David Curry advertisement], *Ogden* (UT) *Standard*, May 7, 1893, p. 8.

457. Lee H. Whittlesey, *Storytelling in Yellowstone*, p. 66. Superintendent Young issued a license to David A. Curry in 1897 for his "camping parties" from the Union Pacific Railroad at Beaver Canyon and called it the "only license issued for this class" of transportation operators. See Col. S.B.M. Young to Secretary of Interior, July 24, 1897, in Item 218, Box 27 (ledger-volume VI), p. 329, YNP Archives.

458. Haines, *Yellowstone Story*, II, p. 478. On June 26, 1894, Superintendent Anderson confirmed that "travel is very light this summer" and he would reiterate that to the newspapers in December. See George S. Anderson to Secretary of Interior, June 26, 1894, in ledger-volume V, Box 26, Item 217, pp. 76-78, YNP Archives.

459. A. Coffin, "Wonders of the Yellowstone—Impressions of a Veteran Traveler," *Daily Nevada State Journal* (Reno, NV), October 22, 1893, p. 2.

460. George S. Anderson, *Report of the Acting Superintendent of the Yellowstone National Park to the Secretary of the Interior, 1894* (Washington: GPO, 1894), p. 7. Anderson dated this report August 13, 1894, making it clear that it referred to the fiscal year of 1893 (July 1, 1893 through June 30, 1894).

461. George W. Wingate (Gordon B. Dodds, ed.), *Through the Yellowstone Park on Horseback* (Moscow, ID: University of Idaho Press, 1999), p. 149; and Lispenard Rutgers [Henry Erskine Smith], *On and Off the Saddle: Characteristic Sights and Scenes from the Great Northwest to the Antilles* (New York: G.P. Putnam's Sons, the Knickerbocker Press, 1894), pp. 1-19.

462. Rutgers, *On and Off the Saddle*, pp. 1-19. This Rutgers/Smith account was also reproduced in Whittlesey and Watry, *Ho! For Wonderland*, as cited, pp. 156-166.

463. "A Very Healthy Village Named After Our Popular Senior U.S. Senator," *Idaho Register* (Idaho Falls, ID), December 16, 1892, p. 1. The town of Dubois was located about 14.5 rail-miles south of Beaver Canyon and the same distance north of Camas at 257.3, which technically placed it between Dry Creek just to its south and High Bridge to its north. Dubois remains in existence today as a small town, which in 2010 had a population of 647.

464. W.C. Mabry, "A Tramp Trip to the Yellowstone Park," *Iowa Postal Card* (Fayette, IA), November 24, 1893, p. 4. The newspapers.com website states that this newspaper was the *Fayette* (IA) *County Leader* for this same date and page number, but the newspaper's printed heading on page one of this issue clearly calls it the *Iowa Postal Card*, so perhaps the story appeared in both newspapers. Author Mabry's use of the notation "'92" after his name and the fact that this article was previously published in *The Collegian* indicates that his college-class graduation-year was 1892. Their viewing of Splendid Geyser on July 6 makes it clear that their year of travel was 1893, because Splendid Geyser was dormant for much of 1892. Whittlesey, "Wonderland Nomenclature," entry for Splendid Geyser, 1893 summary.

465. [F.S.W.], "Shore and Plain…On the Way to the Yellowstone Park—Written for the Agitator," *Wellsboro* (PA) *Agitator*, September 27, 1893, p. 2.

466. [F.S.W.], "In the Yellowstone Park—Nature's Grandest Fountains—Where Mother Earth Blows Off Steam—Written for the Agitator," *Wellsboro* (PA) *Agitator*, October 4, 1893, p. 2.

467. F.S.W., "The Yellowstone Canyon—Beauty and Sublimity of the Great Gorge—The Park as a Whole…Written for the Agitator," *Wellsboro* (PA) *Agitator*, October 11, 1893, p. 2.

468. "Purely Personal Paragraphs" [Jule Bassett], *Blackfoot* (ID) *News*, July 21, 1894, p. 1.

469. Joseph Joffe, ed., "John W. Meldrum, the Grand Old Man of Yellowstone Park," *Annals of Wyoming* 13#2 (April, 1941), pp. 105-140, and especially p. 108. This installment was Part II, and Part I was published in the preceding issue of January, 1941. Readers should compare it to the unpublished version at YNP Research Library, which is Joseph Joffe, "The Grand Old Man of Yellowstone National Park—John W. Meldrum," unpublished typescript (131 pp.), hard-bound in 1940 by the Yellowstone Library and Museum Association. There are differences between these two versions, but probably the published version represented Joffe's final thoughts about the trip.

470. Joffe, ed., "John W. Meldrum," as cited, p. 109; and Joffe, "Grand Old Man," typescript, p. 77.

471. Joffe, ed., "John W. Meldrum," as cited, p. 109. For the story of Fountain Hotel, see Lee H. Whittlesey, "Music, Song, and Laughter: Yellowstone National Park's Fountain Hotel, 1891-1916," *Montana the Magazine of Western History* 53 (Winter, 2003): 22-35, a version sporting many illustrations; and a much longer text, which is Whittlesey, "'Music, Song, and Laughter': Paradise at Yellowstone's Fountain Hotel, 1891-1916," *GOSA Transactions: Journal of the Geyser Observation and Study Association* 10 (2008): 149-168.

472. Joffe, ed., "John W. Meldrum," as cited, p. 110. For Larry Mathews, see Lee H. Whittlesey, "'I Haven't Time to Kiss Everybody!': Larry Mathews Entertains in Yellowstone, 1887-1904," *Montana the Magazine of Western History* 57 (Summer, 2007): 58-73, a version sporting many illustrations; and the much longer text, which is Whittlesey, "'You Only Count One Here!': Larry Mathews and Democracy in Yellowstone, 1887-1904," *Yellowstone History Journal*, Vol. 1#1 (2018): 3-27.

473. George S. Anderson to Bassett Brothers, Beaver Canyon, Idaho, May 9, 1895, in box 26, Item 217 (ledger-volume V, March 17, 1894 through July 23, 1896), p. 237, YNP Archives; Anderson to Secretary of Interior, June 13, 1895, in same ledger, p. 255; Acting Secretary [William H. Lewis?] to Captain George S. Anderson, June 24, 1895, Archive Document 1916 [approving license for ten wagons]; and C.J. Bassett to George S. Anderson, June 8, 1895, Archive Document 2085 [sending fifty dollars and regretting no passengers until today], all in YNP Archives.

474. George S. Anderson, *Report of the Acting Superintendent of the Yellowstone National Park to the Secretary of the Interior, 1896* (Washington: GPO, 1896), p. 6. This report was dated August 11, 1896, making it refer to FY-95.

475. C.J. Bassett to George S. Anderson, May 25, 1895, Archive Document 2089 [Bassett will try to open by June 1 and will apply for license then]; and C.J. Bassett to George S. Anderson, June 1, 1895, Archive Document 2086 [makes application and encloses no money but includes list of ten drivers], YNP Archives. We have knowledge of one more driver for Bassett Brothers, namely W.O. Dockstader who wrote in 1902 that he had driven for the Bassetts for ten years and "now asks for own permit" (license). See W.O. Dockstader, St. Anthony, Idaho to Acting Superintendent, YNP, June 10, 1902, Archive Document 3758, YNP Archives.

476. In those days, parties wanting a divorce had to show "fault" to obtain it. California became the first U.S. state to move to "no-fault" divorce in 1969. Herma Hill Kay, "Equality and Difference: A Perspective on No-Fault Divorce and Its Aftermath," *University of Cincinnati Law Review* 56(1), 1987, as cited at https://en.wikipedia.org/wiki/No-fault_divorce, note 7.

477. "Wine and Whoops…Butte's Handy Gretna Green," *The Columbian* (Columbia Falls, MT), January 30, 1896, p. 1, reprinted from the *Anaconda Standard*. For an actual instance of this practice, see "Married in Idaho—Pete Sorenson and Miss Taggart Have an Experience," *Anaconda Standard*, September 26, 1896, p. 3.

478. George S. Anderson to Bassett Brothers, Beaver Canyon, May 25, 1896, Archive Document 400 [offering permits to Bassetts as usual], YNP Archives. The bad hill at Riverside soldier station was still in place in 1896, per E.A.S[mith], "From Ogden to the Yellowstone," *Ogden Standard*

Examiner (Ogden, UT), August 4, 1896. But the 1896 topographic map showed the high-road as merely a trail, indicating that its use as a road had declined if not ceased.

479. C.J. Bassett to George S. Anderson, June 1, 1896, Archive Document 2082 [acknowledging Anderson's advice on roads but not sending money yet]; George S. Anderson to C.J. Bassett, June 6, 1896, Archive Document 420 [accepts C.J. Bassett's $50 for ten wagons]; C.J. Bassett to George S. Anderson, July 14, 1896, Archive Document 2081 [enclosing fifty dollars for ten wagons; says late start to season; letterhead-stationery]; George S. Anderson to Secretary of Interior, July 14, 1896, Archive Document 482 [enclosing Bassett's $50]; and Acting Secretary [William H. Lewis?] to George S. Anderson, July 31, 1896, Archive Document 1959 [approving ten licenses], YNP Archives. The itinerary for C.J. Bassett's "Union Pacific Stage Line" this year was as follows: Leave Beaver Canyon 8am; arrive Camas Meadows 22 miles at 1pm for lunch; arrive Arangee 23 miles at 6pm for night; leave Arangee at 7am; arrive Dwelle's 25 miles at 1pm for lunch; arrive Fire Hole Basin 25 miles at 7pm; leave Fire Hole Basin 8am (here the park tour went on for several days, staying again at Fire Hole Basin, Canyon, Mammoth, Fire Hole, Arangee, and Beaver Canyon, for an eight-day and seven-night tour). See "Yellowstone Excursion—The Union Pacific Itinerary for This Year," *Salt Lake Herald*, February 1, 1896, p. 3. For woodcut-drawings of wagon styles, including the "Ludlow Spring Wagon" that was in use at Arangee, Idaho by K.E. Hopf, and the "Old Style Spring-Wagon," which was used everywhere, see "As a Farmer's Market," *Ogden Standard* (Ogden, UT), April 9, 1893, p. 7.

480. George S. Anderson to Secretary of Interior, June 14, 1896, Archive Document 428 [suggests restricting the number of independent transportation-operators], YNP Archives.

481. E.A.S[mith], "From Ogden to the Yellowstone," *Ogden Standard Examiner* (Ogden, UT), August 4, 1896; and "A New Leaflet—Just Issued by the Oregon Short Line Company," *Salt Lake Herald*, June 29, 1897, p. 5. See also "Through Yellowstone Park on a Bicycle—A Trip Worth Taking," advertisement in the *Broad Ax* (Salt Lake City, UT), August 1, 1896, p. 3. For a second and longer version of the E.A. Smith trip in three parts, see Fritz, "A Letter from 'Fritz'—His Trip from Ogden, Utah to the Yellowstone National Park, Awheel," *New Oxford* (PA) *Item*, August 21, 1896, p. 4, and succeeding parts in the August 28 and September 4 editions.

482. S.B.M. Young, *Report of the Acting Superintendent of the Yellowstone National Park to the Secretary of the Interior, 1897* (Washington: GPO, 1897), report for FY-96 dated August 31, 1897, pp. 2, 4; and Young, *Supplement* for FY-96, dated November 10, 1897, p. 22.

483. Or perhaps Hiram Spencer, because he intended to move his buildings south, named the town for himself and the railroad merely went along with his proposal. The sources conflict on this distinction, but the latter interpretation is that of Bassetts' descendant Stan Hansen. In further information, Hansen spoke to a "direct descendant of the man who established Spencer," who still lived in Spencer in 2008, and that descendant told him that rather than moving quickly to Spencer, the town of Beaver Canyon "moved slowly over years." While certainly possible, that is not what the newspapers of the time lead us to believe. Stan Hansen to Lee Whittlesey, emails September 5, 2008, and September 4, 2008, in personal hard-file "Bassett Brothers."

484. "New Beaver Canyon," *Idaho Register* (Idaho Falls, ID), June 11, 1897, p. 1. For the new post office, see "Idaho at Washington," *Idaho Daily Statesman* (Boise, ID), June 24, 1897, p. 3. See also "Spencer, the New Station—It Bids to be a Lively Place—Its Good Start," *Salt Lake Tribune*, September 27, 1897, p. 7.

485. "New Beaver Canyon," as cited.

486. "Hiram H. Spencer," in "Utah Constitutional Convention" [Utah biographies], *Salt Lake Tribune*, March 4, 1895, p. 11; Ancestry.com, Hiram Hupp Spencer (1851-1934); "Spencer, Idaho" and "Hiram H. Spencer" at http://spenceridaho.weebly.com/history.html.

487. George S. Anderson to Secretary of Interior, February 6, 1897, Item 218 in Box 27 (ledger-volume VI, July 24, 1896 through October 1, 1897), pp. 154-156, YNP Archives.

488. George S. Anderson to Bassett Brothers, Beaver Canyon, June 19, 1897, Item 218 in Box 27 (ledger-volume VI), p. 252, YNP Archives.

489. S.B.M. Young to Secretary of Interior, June 25, 1897, Item 218 in Box 27 (ledger-volume VI), p. 259 [enclosing $35 check from Bassett]; and Secretary of Interior [illegible—C.N. Bliss] to S.B.M. Young, July 12, 1897, Archive Document 3396 [approves Bassetts' license for seven wagons], YNP Archives. In the June 25 letter, Young added: "He [Bassett] can take people to hotels and his number of wagons has never been limited." By "wagons," Young must have meant "trips," because the actual number of wagons in use by a given licensee were indeed limited and required the $5 payment for each numbered wagon that was being used in a season.

490. C.J. Bassett to George S. Anderson, June 23, 1897, Archive Document 2076 [sending money], YNP Archives.

491. "Wending Their Way West" [Christian Endeavor tourists], *Salt Lake Tribune*, June 30, 1897, p. 2; and Haines, *Yellowstone Story*, II, p. 478. Equivalency calculations for money as used here appear at https://www.officialdata.org/us/inflation/1897?amount=5.

492. S.B.M. Young, *Report of the Acting Superintendent of the Yellowstone National Park to the Secretary of the Interior, 1897* (Washington: GPO, 1897) including *Supplement* for FY-96 and much of 1897, dated November 10, 1897, p. 22, listing "aggregate" for Bassett of 124 passengers in 1897. This report and its supplement together covered the seasons of 1896 and 1897, in order that the annual report for 1898 could return to the calendar year and thus get away from the awkward and cumbersome fiscal-year reports.

493. S.B.M. Young to Lt. Cress, Lower Geyser Basin, July 20, 1897, p. 314; S.B.M. Young to Secretary of Interior, July 24, 1897, p. 329; Superintendent [S.B.M. Young] to Lt. Cress, Lower Geyser Basin, August 18, 1897, p. 410; and Superintendent S.B.M. Young to Lt. Cress, Lower Geyser Basin, August 31, 1897, p. 441, all in Item 218 in Box 27 (ledger-volume VI), YNP Archives.

494. Michael Wolff, *Fire and Fury: Inside the Trump White House* (New York: Henry Holt and Company, 2018), p. 45. Whatever Bannon meant by this comment, Donald J. Trump was apparently not what he was talking about, at least in most observers' recognitions.

495. "Blackfoot to Celebrate in Honor of Bryan—Silver Leader Will Spend a Day There on his Way to the National Park," *Idaho Statesman* (Boise, ID), July 16, 1897, p. 1.

496. "Bryan at Blackfoot—Silver Champion Most Cordially Received," *Salt Lake Tribune*, July 24, 1897, p. 3. He spoke again at Blackfoot on Friday, July 30, per "Bryan at Blackfoot," *Idaho Register* (Idaho Falls, ID), July 30, 1897, p. 1.

497. "Off to the Yellowstone," *Idaho Statesman* (Boise, ID), July 27, 1897, p. 1; "Bryan to Tour Montana—He is to Make his First Speech at Dillon," *Dillon* (MT) *Tribune*, July 30, 1897, p. 1; and "Bryan in Yellowstone," *Dalles-Times Mountaineer* (Dalles, OR), August 7, 1897, p. 1.

498. "Bryan Badly Scared—The Son of the Orator Chased by a Bear," *Deseret Evening News* (Salt Lake City, UT), August 3, 1897, p. 3.

499. The best account of Bryan's park trip is "Bryan Enjoys His Trip—Impressed by the Wonders of the Yellowstone—At Inspiration Point…Given a Cordial Reception at Mammoth Hot Springs—His Itinerary for Montana," *Salt Lake Herald*, August 9, 1897, p. 5. But see also "Bryan as an Angler—He Whips Yellowstone Park Streams—His Boy Chased by a Bear," *Idaho Statesman* (Boise, ID), August 3, 1897, p. 1; "Bryan Catches Fifty Trout—His Son William Chased by a Bear," *Salt Lake Herald*, August 3, 1897, p. 8; "Bryan's Park Tour," *Idaho Statesman* (Boise, ID), August 5, 1897, p. 1; and "The Same Bryan," *Salt Lake Herald*, August 7, 1897, p. 7.

500. "Welcomed in Royal Style—Bryan's Triumphal Journey…" [six articles], *Anaconda* (MT) *Standard*, August 13, 1897, p. 1. See also "Bryan Off for Montana," *Idaho Statesman* (Boise, ID), August 7, 1897, p. 1. The A.S. Trude ranch where Bryan stayed was likely Trude's ranch at Arangee, Idaho. See "Jacob Kern is Back…Shot All Kinds of Game," *Daily Inter Ocean* (Chicago, IL), September 8, 1895, p. 5; and "Discovers Mr. Trude—Adventures of Hon. W.E. Mason in the Yellowstone Country," *Daily Inter Ocean* (Chicago, IL), August 24, 1895, part II, p. 16.

501. "Local News," *Montpelier Examiner* (Montpelier, ID), September 29, 1897, p. 4.

502. C.J. Bassett to "Acting Superintendent," June 5, 1898, Archive Document 2074; Acting Superintendent [Erwin] to C.J. Bassett, Beaver Canyon [Spencer, Idaho], June 10, 1898, Box 28, Item 219 in ledger-volume VII (October 1, 1897 through November 9, 1898), p. 244; and 1st Lt. [G.O. Cress] Acting Superintendent to Secretary of Interior, June 18, 1898 in ledger-volume VII, p. 265; all in YNP Archives.

503. James B. Erwin, *Report of the Acting Superintendent of the Yellowstone National Park to the Secretary of the Interior, 1898* (Washington: GPO, 1898), p. 8.

504. "Talks with Visitors [at Boise]—C.J. Bassett," *Idaho Statesman* (Boise, ID), August 24, 1898, p. 4.

505. "Personal Mention" [Bassett proprietor of stage line], *Salt Lake Tribune*, August 5, 1897, p. 5; "Dubois is for Union" [Bassett prominent in Idaho politics], *Salt Lake Tribune*, February 3, 1898, p. 5; "Silver Republicans," *Idaho Statesman* (Boise, ID), March 4, 1898, p. 8; and "Silver Republicans…Elect Eight Delegates" [including Bassett], *Idaho Falls Times* (Idaho Falls, ID), August 18, 1898, p. 8.

506. "Local Brevities" [C.J. Bassett, Jr.], *Idaho Statesman* (Boise, ID), July 29, 1899, p. 6; and "Local Brevities" [C.J. Bassett, Jr.], *Idaho Statesman*, August 15, 1899, p. 4.

507. Rose Cordon [*News* Correspondent], "Stagecoach Driver in 1890 Era Recalls Yellowstone Park Tours," undated [about 1960] clipping from unknown newspaper, and labeled "Grace, Idaho" on Hansen and Hansen website at http://www.ourgenerationsancestors.org/histories/BASSETT_Basset%20Brothers%20Stage%20Line_REV20090625.pdf, p. 14. Tanner stated that he was driving a rich lady named Madame von Fickenstein Mounteford when the robbery occurred. There were seven other vehicles including an army wagon in the hold-up, so perhaps he was not noticed in the confusion of coaches or perhaps outside-the-park companies like his were not enumerated. Haynes, *Yellowstone Stage Holdups*, p. 10. For John Tanner, see Catherine M. Tanner, Bothell, Washington, to Lee H. Whittlesey, September 3, 1983, enclosing John A. Tanner's unpublished manuscript ("family story") entitled "Stories of Old Timers," May, 1954, 8pp., including his days driving stagecoaches with Bassett Brothers and Monida & Yellowstone (personal file "Transportation").

508. S.P. Gibbs, Menominee, Wisconsin to Axel Johnson, Yellowstone Park, Wy., October 28, 1898, Archive Document 4831, YNP Archives. This Peter Rasmusen (note different spelling for some reason, including in Ancestry.com) was C.J. Bassett's brother-in-law, and C.J.'s wife Christina Rasmussen was Peter's brother, who was apparently a less-than-upstanding stage-driver, at least on that 1898 trip into the park. When C.J. "Jule" Bassett and Christina R. Bassett moved to Boise, Idaho in 1899, Peter Rasmusen went with them and continued to live in their house. See Ancestry.com, Christina Rasmussen Bassett (1854-1927), including Peter Rasmusen (b. 1846) in the U.S. Census of 1900, Boise, Idaho.

509. "Some Large Bets" [made by Bassett], *Idaho Statesman* (Boise, ID), November 6, 1898, p. 4; "C.J. Bassett Made Immigration Commissioner—Confirmed by the Senate," *Idaho Statesman*, March 5, 1899, p. 5; and "Local Brevities" [Bassetts move to Boise], *Idaho Statesman*, May 8, 1899, p. 2. See also "Local Brevities," same newspaper for May 10, saying they have arrived in Boise.

510. "Local Brevities" [Death of Bertha Bassett], *Idaho Statesman*, April 11, 1900, p. 6.

511. "Election Returns," *Idaho Falls Times* (Idaho Falls, ID), August 2, 1900, p. 2; "The Fusion Pie," *Idaho Register* (Idaho Falls, ID), November 16, 1900, p. 1; and "Prominent Man Suddenly Called—C.J. Bassett, Widely Known Throughout Idaho, Passes Away at Boise Home," *Idaho Statesman*, November 27, 1918, p. 6. One wonders if he succumbed to the massive flu-outbreak of that year.

512. Amos Bowen & Company, *Progressive Men of the State of Montana* (No Place: A.W. Bowen & Company, 1902), pp. 974-975; William Wallace Wylie, unpublished autobiography, no date [1926], his original mimeographed copy with "W.W. Wylie" stamped on its front page, in locked file-cabinet of Rare Book Room, YNP Library, pp. 2, 4, 6; and Jane Galloway Demaray, *Yellowstone Summers: Touring with the Wylie Camping Company in America's First National Park* (Pullman, Washington: Washington State University Press, 2014), pp. 13-15.

513. "The Territory," *Weekly Miner* (Butte, MT), June 22, 1880, p. 3, quoting the *Bozeman Courier* of June 19; and "W.W. Wylie, Park Pioneer, Dead," [National] Park Service Bulletin, April, 1930, vertical files, employees, YNP Research Library.

514. Demaray, *Yellowstone Summers*, pp. 13-15; Wylie, unpublished autobiography, p. 8; and see generally, Elizabeth A. Watry, "More than Mere Camps and Coaches: The Wylie Camping Company and the Development of a Middle-Class Leisure Ethic in Yellowstone National Park, 1883-1916," Master's Thesis, Montana State University, Bozeman, Montana, 2010.

515. "Prof. Wylie," Bozeman *Avant Courier*, August 12, 1880, p. 3; and Demaray, *Yellowstone Summers*, p. 23. Mary Grace was born in 1881, and son Clinton would follow in 1884. *Bozeman Weekly Chronicle*, July 2, 1884, p. 3.

516. Wylie, unpublished autobiography, pp. 14-15; and Demaray, *Yellowstone Summers*, pp. 24-25.

517. "Territorial Items," *New North-West* (Deer Lodge, MT), October 21, 1881, p. 3; and Whittlesey, *Storytelling in Yellowstone*, pp. 43, 62. The Wylie-Calfee lecture-tour was mentioned often in the *Bozeman* (MT) *Avant Courier* from April 7, 1881 to March 2, 1882. Wylie's guidebook was entitled *Yellowstone National Park, or The Great American Wonderland* (Kansas City: Ramsey, Millett, and Hudson, 1882).

518. "County Election Returns," *Livingston Enterprise*, November 6, 1884, p. 1; November 8, 1884, p. 3; "Born," *Bozeman Weekly Chronicle*, July 2, 1884, p. 3; and Demaray, *Yellowstone Summers*, p. 60.

519. "By Wire from Helena—W.W. Wylie Confirmed for Superintendent of Public Instruction," *Butte Miner*, March 13, 1885, p. 4; and "Personal Points," *Bozeman Weekly Chronicle*, August 5, 1885, p. 3.

520. "Rounding Up Offenders, *Livingston Enterprise*, August 15, 1885, p. 1; "Local Layout," *Livingston Enterprise*, August 15, 1885, p. 3; "Going for Tourists—Violators of the Law in the National Park Treated to Their Deserts," *Helena Weekly Herald*, August 20, 1885, p. 7; "From an Eye Witness," *Bozeman Weekly Chronicle*, August 26, 1885, p. 2; and "Avant Courier," *Helena Weekly Herald*, August 27, 1885, p. 8. The article "Arrests in the Park," *Helena Weekly Herald*, September 3, 1885, p. 7, added the Payson case to the policing situation in the park, for which see also Haines, *Yellowstone Story*, II, pp. 38-39, 392n21.

521. Reproduced in Demaray, *Yellowstone Summers*, p. 50.

522. "City News," *Bozeman Weekly Chronicle*, March 3, 1886, p. 3.

523. "The Pat Donan of Montana," *The River Press* (Ft. Benton, MT), August 10, 1887, p. 5; "Camping on the Trail," *Helena Weekly Herald*, August 18, 1887, p. 7; and "In the Park—A Few Days Spent in Wonderland…The Touring Season at its Height," *Helena Weekly Herald*, August 18, 1887, p. 5.

524. "Personal Points," *Bozeman Weekly Chronicle*, August 8, 1888, p. 3, emphasis added.

525. "Old Dynamite Sends Us Some Interesting Items Regarding the Park, etc.," *Bozeman Weekly Chronicle*, August 8, 1888, p. 2. Red Bluff, Montana is an essentially non-existent town today, located in Madison County just east of present Norris, Montana, and in the canyon on State Highway 84.

526. Advertisement in *Anaconda Standard*, March 16, 1891, p. 12; and Demaray, *Yellowstone Summers*, p. 75.

527. "Town and Territory," *Helena Weekly Herald*, July 4, 1889, p. 8.

528. "Personal Points," *Livingston Enterprise*, July 27, 1889, p. 3.

529. "Camping Out in Yellowstone National Park," *Helena Daily Herald*, May 25, 1889, p. 5; and Watry, "More than Mere Camps and Coaches," as cited, master's thesis, Montana State University, 2010, p. 32.

530. "Camping in the Yellowstone Park," Wylie's advertisements in *Helena Independent*, March 30, 1890, p. 10; April 6, p. 7; April 13, p. 10; April 20, p. 3; April 27, p. 7; May 4, p. 3; May 11, p. 7; May 25, p. 11; May 28, p. 5; June 1, p. 10; and June 13, p. 2.

531. "Yellowstone Park Camping Parties," Wylie's advertisements in *New North-West* (Deer Lodge, MT), April 25, 1890, p. 3; May 16, p. 2; May 23, p. 4; May 30, p. 3; June 6, p. 3; June 13, p. 4; and June 20, p. 4.

532. "Personal Points," *Livingston Enterprise*, August 9, 1890, p. 3; and "Local Brevities," *New North-West*, August 22, 1890, p. 3.

533. "General News of the State—Bozeman," *Helena Independent*, August 4, 1891, Morning, p. 6; and "The Social World," *Anaconda Standard*, August 23, 1891, p. 6, two stories.

534. Wylie, unpublished autobiography, 1926, p. 19.

535. See for example, "Ordered from the Park," *Helena* (MT) *Independent*, August 1, 1892, Morning, p. 5.

536. Sawtelle Peak—it is misspelled, because Gilman Sawtell's signature shows that he did not use the final "E"—is "so named in honor of him who has born it company of late years." C.C. Clawson, "Notes on the Way to Wonderland," *New North-West* (Deer Lodge, MT), November 4, 1871, p. 3. See also Haines, *Yellowstone Story*, I, p. 339n44.

537. Green, *History of Island Park*, p. 37; and (No author), *Montana Atlas*, 1997, as cited. The site on today's maps marked "Rea" is not the same as the historic ranch-site. The current interactive maps on the internet from the "Roadside Thoughts" series show a "town" named Rea, Idaho. For example, go to http://roadsidethoughts.com/id/arangee-xx-bingham-map.htm and manipulate (move) the map eastward until you see Island Park Reservoir, Idaho. Then, using the "plus" sign, keep magnifying the map from the spot where "Kilgore-Yale Road" meets U.S. Highway 20, while focusing your attention on the spot to the west where the Kilgore-Yale Road turns into the A-2 Clark County Road. When you see the Shotgun Bar and Grill appear (near "Island Park Services"), look east to road "375" (running north from the Kilgore-Yale Road) and you will see the letters "Rea" at today's (the second) town site. Again, it is not the site of the original Glen Rea, which was in section 33.

538. Green, *History of Island Park*, 1990, p. 36.

539. For Richard W. Rock, see Green, *History of Island Park*, 1990, pp. 30, 33-36; and Whittlesey, *Death in Yellowstone*, 2014, pp. 39-41. For Rea's claim to have "settled in the valley twenty-five years ago [1868] with no neighbors closer than one hundred miles," see G.W. Rea, "Our Arangee

Correspondent," *Idaho Falls Times* (Idaho Falls, ID), June 29, 1893, p. 5. As for Gilman Sawtell, the "Letter List" cited earlier shows that he was probably in Virginia City as early as 1866, and he appears to have told the *Montanian* (Virginia City) in 1872 that he settled at Henry's Lake in 1867. This was reproduced in "Territorial Items," *Helena Weekly Herald*, December 19, 1872, p. 7.

540. Both the U.S. Census of 1850 and the New York State Census of 1855, cited below, gave George Rea's birth-year as 1833 (census records routinely get information wrong, especially where inter-viewees have a reason to fib), and the former showed him as aged 17 in 1850, consistent with a birth-year of 1833 and his birthday having passed. However, the U.S. Civil War Draft Registra-tion Records, 1863-1865, New York, 31st congressional district (accessed via Ancestry.com), listed George Rea's age on July 1, 1863 as 31, which points to 1832 as his birth-year if his birthday had passed. (He likely would have known how old he was at this time and probably told it to the draft-registrar.) His actual birthday most likely was in July, because he appears to have told the June 7, 1900 U.S. census-taker at Rea, Idaho that his birthday was in July and that he was 67 years old at that time (consistent with a birth-year of 1832 and his birthday *not* having passed). Addi-tionally, George Rea's gravestone at Deer Lodge, Montana proclaimed (and today still proclaims) 1832. In this historian's opinion, there is almost always a rebuttable presumption in favor of the year on a grave-marker, because relatives and friends in charge of emplacing the grave-marker generally knew the deceased and made every effort to get the year correctly inscribed. Thus, in the face of all this described and varying evidence, this author sides with 1832 as the most likely year for George Rea's birth. See also U.S. Census, June 7, 1900, at Rea, Fremont County, Idaho, sheet 2A (accessed via Ancestry.com, George Walter Rea).

541. The U.S. Census of 1850 listed other members in Walter Rea's household as Sarah A. Rea, aged 15; Amelia Rea, aged 10; Florence Rea, aged 7; and Edwin T. Rea, aged 4. George's brother Thomas (aged about 3 then) was apparently inadvertently omitted. The parents were listed as Walter Rea (birthplace Scotland), age 58, occupation lumberman; and Mary Rea, age 42 (birth-place New York). Seven other persons were listed as living in the household and who were thus considered part of the family, including a Martha Graham, aged 22, and thus five years older than George. One cannot help wondering whether she became George Rea's first wife, who traveled with him to Montana, but we have been unable to confirm this from genealogical or newspaper records. See U.S. Census, Portville, New York, October 12, 1850, p. 122, accessed July 24-25, 2017 via Ancestry.com. The New York State Census of 1855 listed much of the same information but added George's brother Thomas Rea to the household, stating that he was aged 8 (thus born in or about 1847) in that year, and changing Sarah Rea's age to 23 in 1855. See New York State Census, June 16, 1855, sheet 136, line 21, accessed July 24-25, 2017 via Ancestry.com (George Walter Rea).

542. U.S., Civil War Draft Registrations Records, 1863-1865, Portville, New York, June, 1863, p. 371 listed his age on July 1, 1863 as 31 and his congressional district as 31 (accessed at Ancestry.com [George Walter Rea, b. 1832]).

543. Mary H. Rea's accounts are George H. Beebe, "Mrs. Mary Valiton, in Montana 70 Years, Tells of Wagon Train's Battle with Sioux in 1865—Mother Put Her in Stove Oven to Escape Rain of In-dians' Arrows," *Billings* (MT) *Gazette*, May 27, 1934, second section, p. 1; and Glendolin Damon Wagner, "Mrs. Mary Valiton, 74 Years in Montana, Looks Back Upon Days of Fear, Hardships and Fun," *Flathead Courier* (Polson, MT), August 17, 1939, p. 3. Mary Rea also mentioned that she owned her parents' carefully kept diary of the trip from which she took information, and she also utilized their stories told to her through the years. As of 2017, George and Martha Rea's diary had not been donated to the Montana Historical Society at Helena, and thus it may still be in possession of the Valiton family or other descendants. George Rea's daughter's full name was Mary H. "Mamie" Rea Valiton, and as it is for so many other people, there are inconsistencies for

her year of birth. Her tombstone stated (and still states) 1864, while the U.S. Census of June 29, 1900 at Deer Lodge, MT, p. 10 (via Ancestry.com), listed "March, 1863" and "age 36," which do not equate to each other. Hence, this author sides with 1864 as her year of birth, with the 1900 Census's misinformation perhaps attributable to Mary's knowing that she had turned 36 but misstating her birth-year to the census-taker as "1863."

544. Beebe, "Mrs. Mary Valiton, in Montana 70 Years"; and Wagner, "Mrs. Mary Valiton, 74 Years in Montana." Attempts by this author and Special Collections Library Aide Cameron Green at the University of Wyoming to find this skirmish in existing records have been unsuccessful. Green searched George Michno, *Encyclopedia of Indian Wars* (Missoula: Mountain Press Publishing Company, 2003) and Peter Cozzens, ed., *Eyewitnesses to the Indian War 1865-1890* (Mechanicsburg, PA: 2001-2005), four volumes, vol. 4, part one, section two, pp. 13-42, without success. What happened was that George Rea, his wife, and daughter encountered the beginnings of an Indian war against the Overland Trail and the Bozeman Trail that the Lakota, the Cheyennes, and the Arapaho started in 1865, following events in Colorado. Gold had been discovered there in 1858, high up on the South Platte River, within the limits of present Denver. Within one year, at least 100,000 white prospectors were storming into the area, in numbers greater than any Indian-tribe on the plains. They founded Denver, and their prospecting and killing of buffalo effectively ousted the Cheyennes and Arapahos from their homeland to the northeast, between the North Fork and South Fork of the Platte. Having no choice, many Cheyennes and Arapahos removed to the northwest, getting permission from their Sioux allies to settle in the Lakota's newly-acquired homelands in the Bighorn Basin of Wyoming and on the head of Powder River, land through which the new Bozeman Trail would soon run. For the next few years, all three tribes more or less united here to oppose white invasions of their land on the new Bozeman Trail (1863) and west on the existing Overland Trail, as well as what the Indians saw as continued killing of their game and ignoring of existing treaties. When a large village of Cheyennes who remained in Colorado was attacked, tortured, and massacred by white prospectors in 1864 at Sand Creek, all three Indian tribes declared total war along both trails in their usual strike-and-retreat manner. It was this anger and skirmishing that George Rea, his wife Martha, and baby Mary encountered as they traveled in 1865 on the Overland Trail. Details are in Kingsley M. Bray, *Crazy Horse: A Lakota Life* (Norman: University of Oklahoma Press, 2006), pp. 74, 76, 78.

545. G.W. Rea, "An Interesting Letter from Beaver Canyon, Idaho," *Potter Enterprise* (Coudersport, PA), November 9, 1887, p. 3. My thanks go to researcher Tina Schlaile, for bringing this item to my attention.

546. B.F. Rockafellow, "Diary of Capt. B.F. Rockafellow, Sixth Michigan Cavalry," in LeRoy R. and Ann W. Hafen, eds., *Powder River Campaigns and Sawyers Expedition of 1865* (Glendale, CA: Arthur H. Clark Company, 1961), p. 185; and 219-223. For two dramatic Indian fights involving emigrant-trains at nearly the same place and perhaps involving some of the same soldiers on August 2-3, along with a denunciation of eastern commissioners and citizens who were soft on Indians, see "We Have Been Kindly Permitted to Read...," *Nebraska Advertiser* (Brownville, NE), August 24, 1865, p. 2, column 2.

547. "The First Quartz Mill from the States" [The Rea family arrives in Virginia City], *Montana Post*, October 7, 1865, p. 3, col. 1.

548. G.W. Rea, "Yellowstone Park—What a Trapper Says About the Country and the Way to Get There," *Salt Lake Tribune*, August 5, 1882, p. 3; and G.W. Rea, "Our Arangee Correspondent," *Idaho Falls Times* (Idaho Falls, ID), June 29, 1893, p. 5.

549. W.O. Owen in Paul Schullery, ed., *Old Yellowstone Days* (Boulder: Colorado Associated University Press, 2010), p. 36. In not making public his "discovery" of what became Yellowstone National Park, George Rea joined numerous prospectors from the 1860s (George Huston was another

one) who traveled through the area but did not receive credit for the discovery. For yet another example, see the article by "F." entitled "The National Park—A Veteran Montanan Claims to Have Been the First Man to Suggest Its Creation," *Helena Weekly Herald*, April 29, 1880, p. 7.

On another subject, George Rea's name appeared in the local newspaper for having unclaimed letters at the local post office, specifically in his case at Virginia City and in 1867. One wonders whether he ever picked them up and if not, whether these letters were the ones informing him about the death of Mary's grandfather, which the family did not learn about for many years after they reached Montana. "Letter List," *Montana Post*, June 29, 1867, p. 8; July 27, 1867, p. 8; Oct 12, 1867, p. 8; and Oct 19, 1867, p. 4.

550. Wagner, "Mrs. Mary Valiton, 74 Years in Montana," as cited. These hangings in 1864 have been chronicled in Allen, *A Decent Orderly Lynching*, pp. 327-328.

551. "Virginia Items" [George Rea and four other men departing], *Montana Post*, August 28, 1868, p. 6, col. 1.

552. Rea, "Yellowstone Park—What a Trapper Says…," *Salt Lake Tribune*, August 5, 1882, p. 3; Green, *History of Island Park*, 1990, pp. 29, 32-33; and G.W. Rea, "Our Arangee Correspondent," *Idaho Falls Times* (Idaho Falls, ID), June 29, 1893, p. 5. For Gilman Sawtell as first commercial tour-guide to Yellowstone, see Calvin C. Clawson (Eugene Lee Silliman, ed.), *A Ride to the Infernal Regions: Yellowstone's First Tourists* (Helena: Riverbend Publishing, 2003), pp. 12-14, 37, 50n37-38, 54; Dean Green, "Island Park's First Settler Gilman Sawtell," *Snake River Echoes* 10#3, 1981, pp. 51-52; and Ancestry.com (Gilman Sawtell, born 1836). For Sawtell's superintendence of the 1873 road-building that was sponsored by citizens of Virginia City and built into the present west entrance of Yellowstone Park, see "Autumn Trip to Wonderland," *Helena Weekly Herald*, October 30, 1873, p. 2; and Haines, *Yellowstone Story*, I, p. 195.

553. Beebe, "Mrs. Mary Valiton, in Montana 70 Years," as cited. For an example of Indian activities in the Bozeman area of Montana in 1869, see "Opening of the Spring Campaign—Great Indian Fight," *Montana Post*, April 16, 1869, p. 2.

554. G.W. Rea, "Yellowstone Park—What a Trapper Says…," *Salt Lake Tribune*, August 5, 1882, p. 3; and G.W. Rea, "Our Arangee Correspondent," *Idaho Falls Times* (Idaho Falls, ID), June 29, 1893, p. 5.

555. Wagner, "Mrs. Mary Valiton, 74 Years in Montana," as cited; and Beebe, "Mrs. Mary Valiton, in Montana 70 Years," as cited.

556. "The Pole Creek Mines," Bozeman *Avant Courier*, March 31, 1876, p. 3. Pole Creek flows into Cherry Creek from the south, and shortly after that, Cherry Creek flows into Madison River at a spot about 1.5 miles northeast of the present bridge across Madison River, east of Norris, Montana on State Highway 84.

557. "Cheery [*sic*—Cherry] Creek," Bozeman (MT) *Avant Courier*, February 28, 1873, p. 2; "Cherry Creek Mines," Bozeman *Avant Courier*, October 17, 1872, p. 2; and "Zig-Zag Notes by the Judge," *Helena Daily Herald*, November 13, 1872, p. 1. See also R. [probably one of the Rea brothers], "Letter from Cherry Creek," Bozeman *Avant Courier*, April 18, 1873, p. 2. For George Rea's $10,000 offer, see "Territorial Items," *Helena Daily Herald*, December 9, 1872, p. 3. For the location of these mines, see "Zig-Zag Notes," *Helena Weekly Herald*, November 14, 1872, p. 6; and "Pencil Points," *Helena Weekly Herald*, July 17, 1873, p. 2. See also "Items from the Montanian" [Thomas Rea on Cherry Creek], *Helena Weekly Herald*, February 27, 1873, p. 8; and "Vibrating Around" [Thomas and George Rea on Cherry Creek], *New North-West*, March 8, 1873, p. 2. Havana, Montana had a post office in 1873-1874 with John Thomas as postmaster, per Cheney, *Names on the Face of Montana*, p. 131.

558. "Game," Bozeman *Avant Courier*, November 21, 1873, p. 3.

559. Whittlesey, *Storytelling in Yellowstone*, p. 92; and "National Park in the Centennial," Bozeman *Avant Courier*, July 31, 1874, p. 3. For his earlier memories of hunting including these bison and bears within present Yellowstone Park, see Rea, "An Interesting Letter from Beaver Canyon," as cited.

560. "Returned to the Mountains," Bozeman *Avant Courier*, May 29, 1874, p. 3; and Rea, "An Interesting Letter from Beaver Canyon," as cited. This complex trafficking in and hunting (and slaughter) of animals in northern Wyoming, southern Montana, and eastern Idaho has been detailed in Whittlesey and Bone, *The History of Mammals in the Greater Yellowstone Ecosystem*, II, Appendix Three; and Lee H. Whittlesey, "Abundance, Slaughter, and Resilience of the Greater Yellowstone Ecosystem's Mammal Population: A View of the Historical Record, 1871-1885," *Montana the Magazine of Western History* 70#1, Spring, 2020, pp. 3-26.

561. "Returned to the Mountains," Bozeman *Avant Courier*, May 29, 1874, p. 3. Throwing light on a side issue, we see that editor George Wright stated here: "The Earl will visit what Rea calls the wonders of the world—Geyserland," thus crediting Rea with the origination of this long-used nickname for Yellowstone Park, and certainly he was in the area early enough (1865-1869) to have been the first to use that term. For the Earl of Dunraven, see generally Wyndham Thomas Wyndham-Quinn, *The Great Divide: Travels in the Upper Yellowstone in the Summer of 1874* (New York: Scribner, Welford, and Armstrong, 1876); and his hunts are analyzed in Whittlesey and Bone, *The History of Mammals in the Greater Yellowstone Ecosystem*, I, pp. 321-350; II, 892, 906.

562. The Montana and regional commercial slaughter of animals is detailed in Whittlesey and Bone, *The History of Mammals in the Greater Yellowstone Ecosystem*, II, Appendix Three, but see also Paul Schullery, "Yellowstone's Ecological Holocaust," *Montana the Magazine of Western History* 47(3), Autumn, 1997, pp. 16-33; and Whittlesey, "Abundance, Slaughter, and Resilience of the Greater Yellowstone," as cited.

563. "Sentenced—Geo. W. Rea," Bozeman *Avant Courier*, March 12, 1875, p. 3. This same story appeared as "George W. Ray," *New North-West* (Deer Lodge, MT), March 19, 1875, p. 2.

564. "Fatal Affray—M. Maguire Killed by George W. Rea" [coroner's jury], *New North-West* (Deer Lodge, MT), December 11, 1874, p. 2; and "Eastern Montana Items—From the *Courier* Dec. 4th—Geo. W. Rea" [remanded to jail], *New North-West*, December 18, 1874, p. 2. "Items," *Helena Weekly Herald*, December 10, 1874, p. 3 says that the George W. Rea who killed Maguire in a drunken quarrel "is the well-known hunter, trapper, and guide, and one of the discoverers of the Cherry Creek silver mines." A list of letters being held at the Helena post office on March 3 included one for "Miss M.M. Rea," probably George Rea's daughter with her middle initial misread or misprinted, perhaps indicating that Mary and her mother were attending the trial. "List of Letters," *Helena Daily Herald*, March 3, 1875, p. 3.

565. "Sentenced—George W. Rea," Bozeman *Avant Courier*, March 12, 1875, p. 3; Bozeman Times (author), "Trial of Geo. W. Rea," *Independent-Record* (Helena, MT), March 13, 1875, p. 3; and "Trial, Conviction and Sentence of Geo. Rea" [from the *Bozeman Times*], *Helena Weekly Herald*, March 18, 1875, p. 4. See also "Trial of George Rea," *Bozeman Times*, March 9, 1875, p. 2; and "Trial of Rea," in same newspaper, same issue, p. 3.

566. "Sentenced—George W. Rea," Bozeman *Avant Courier*, March 12, 1875, p. 3; and "Personal" [George Rea arrives at Montana territorial prison], *New North-West*, March 19, 1875, p. 3.

567. One of the best accounts of the Great Sioux War is John S. Gray, *Centennial Campaign: The Sioux War of 1876* (Norman and London: University of Oklahoma Press, 1988). Literature on the Nez Perce War is voluminous, but two recent treatments are Elliott West, *The Last Indian War: The Nez Perce Story* (New York: Oxford University Press, 2009); and Daniel J. Sharfstein, *Thunder in the Mountains: Chief Joseph, Oliver Otis Howard, and the Nez Perce War* (New York: W.W. Norton and Company, 2016).

568. "Local Brevities" [George Rea Pardoned], *New North-West*, February 16, 1877, p. 3; and "Montana Legislature—Council—Twenty-Second Day, Afternoon Session" [Rea pardoned from prison], *Helena Weekly Herald*, February 6, 1879, p. 2.

569. "Mr. George W. Rea," *Butte Miner*, July 10, 1877, p. 2.

570. "Scouts in from Big Hole," *New North-West*, August 10, 1877, p. 3.

571. "Personal" [Thomas E. Rea and George W. Rea], *Montana Standard* (Butte, MT), September 25, 1877, p. 3; and Mark H. Brown, *The Flight of the Nez Perce* (Lincoln: University of Nebraska Press, 1967), p. 400. For his time with the Nez Perce, see Rea, "An Interesting Letter from Beaver Canyon," as cited. A bit more information on the Rea brothers' claim at Butte was available in October, when another newspaper identified the two men as "owners of the bed-rock flume in the South Fork of Silver Bow Creek." See "Wood Flume," *Weekly Miner* (Butte, MT), October 14, 1879, p. 5.

572. Green, *History of Island Park*, p. 37. Shotgun Valley is today located in Fremont County, Idaho, but in George Rea's day it was in Bingham County.

573. U.S. Census of 1880, taken at Butte, Deer Lodge County, Montana, June 8, 1880, p. 28, accessed via Ancestry.com (George Walter Rea, b. 1832). Here George appears to have told his census-taker that his daughter's age was 18 (this was wrong; she was 16), and that his own age was "43" (also wrong, because he was 48). He referred to his daughter here by her nickname "Mamie."

574. Like those of many other people, Charlotte's existing, genealogical record so far is complex and inconsistent. Ancestry.com (George Walter Rea, b. 1832) states that "Montana County Marriages 1865-1950" shows George W. Rae [*sic*] married Charlotte B. Cronk at Deer Lodge, Montana on June 21, 1879, per FHL film number 1906088. The Deer Lodge newspaper placed the ceremony at Butte, reporting at "Marriages," *New North-West*, July 4, 1879, p. 3 that the "REA-CONK [*sic*—Cronk] marriage [occurred] in Butte on June 22, 1879 at Centennial Hotel," and also stated that the marriage was Mr. George W. Rea of Butte to Mrs. Charlotte B. Conk [*sic*—Cronk] of Killburn [*sic*—Kilbourn] City, Wisconsin. A Helena newspaper reported in "Married," *Helena Weekly Herald*, June 26, 1879, p. 7 that George W. Rea of Butte has married Mrs. Charlotte B. Conk [*sic*—Cronk] of Killborn [*sic*—Kilbourn] City, Wisconsin. A search of ancestry.com (Charlotte B. Cronk, b. 1833) turned up her grave-marker at Deer Lodge, Montana, which today lists her as "Charlotte B. Rea" with her dates as "1833-1919," and Ancestry's accompanying information gives her birth-date as May, 1833, and her death-date as November 22, 1919, at Powell, Montana. The U.S. Census of 1860 (ancestry.com, Charlotte B. Cronk, b. 1833, accessed August 15, 2017) taken on June 21, 1860 at Newport, Columbia County, Wisconsin (post office at Kilbourn City, WI) showed that Charlotte gave her age as "25" at the time of that census; that her father was Runa Cronk, aged 38, born in New York, with occupation listed as *surveyor*; that Charlotte was born in Pennsylvania; and that she had one sister, Helen, aged four. No mother was listed, and a known younger brother named R.D. Cronk was not yet born. According to a newspaper death-notice, she made her home in Blackfoot, Idaho "for over thirty years" (which would put her removal to that city in 1888 or 1889 from Camas, Idaho, but that cannot be correct because the *Blackfoot News* recorded her move to there in May of 1892). She served as city treasurer of Blackfoot, Idaho for eight years, continued to live there through 1918, and removed to Deer Lodge in early 1919 in ill health to live with her step-daughter Mary Valiton, whom we earlier chronicled. See "Deer Lodge News" [Mrs. Charlotte B. Rea dies], *Anaconda* (MT) *Standard*, November 23, 1919, p. 15; and "Our Bouquet of Spring News" ["Mrs. George Rae (*sic*), late of Camas, has moved to Blackfoot"], *Blackfoot News*, May 23, 1892, p. 1, col. 4.

575. U.S. Census of 1880, taken at Butte, Deer Lodge County, Montana, June 22, 1880, p. 4, accessed via Ancestry.com (George Walter Rea, b. 1832). In this Census, George told the census-taker that his age was 48, listed his occupation as "work in mill," and listed his wife as "Charlott" and her oc-

cupation as "keep house." He also listed his brother Thomas, age 33, as occupying their residence with them and gave Thomas's occupation as "work in mill." Finally, he listed R.D. Cronk as his stepson, aged 18, and stated that he too lived with them in the residence.

576. "Real Estate Transfers" [Rea selling his mining properties], *Weekly Miner* (Butte, MT), April 27, 1880, p. 5. "Transfers of Property," *New North-West*, April 16, 1880, p. 2 indicated that both Thomas E. Rea and George W. Rea were trying to sell their claims. According to this article, George sold one of his properties located in the "unorganized district" in Deer Lodge County to J.A. Talbott for $3,000.

577. "Montana County Marriages 1865-1950," via ancestry.com (Mary H. Rea, b. 1864); and "The Butte Municipal Election" [H.G. Valiton elected], *Helena Weekly Herald*, May 13, 1880, p. 8. See also Wagner, "Mrs. Mary Valiton, 74 Years in Montana," as cited; and Beebe, "Mrs. Mary Valiton, in Montana 70 Years," as cited. Mary Valiton died on October 20, 1945, per "Rites for Montana Pioneer," *Havre* (MT) *Daily News*, October 22, 1945, p. 1. She lived in Billings for the preceding ten years. Her daughter was Mrs. Ernest T. Eaton, wife of the Lt. Governor of Montana. While Mary was sick in March of 1945, the *Standard* of Butte referred to her as "one of the three [living] covered-wagon babies of Montana." See "Mrs. Mary Valiton Seriously Ill," *Butte* (MT) *Standard*, March 25, 1945, p. 12.

578. In his article "Beaver Canyon" (*Blackfoot* (ID) *Register*, July 29, 1882, p. 3), the writer stated while visiting there: "We found our old friend W.S. Lyle formerly of Blackfoot installed as agent in place of Frank Bassett, who is now in Butte."

579. "Beaver Canyon," *Blackfoot* (ID) *Register*, July 29, 1882, p. 3. Sixteen years would have placed Rea's arrival in the area at 1866, which is close to his actual arrival year of 1865 in Virginia City, Montana and, by his own statement, in Shotgun Valley, Idaho as well.

580. G.W. Rea, "Yellowstone Park—What a Trapper Says about the Country and the Way to Get There," *Salt Lake Tribune*, August 5, 1882, p. 3; and H., "National Park—Pleasant Trip of a Party of Salt Lakers to the Yellowstone," *Salt Lake Tribune*, September 23, 1882, p. 3. For Rea's winter of 1882-1883, see "Town and Vicinity," *Blackfoot* (ID) *Register*, March 10, 1883, p. 3. The relevant land-record for George Rea is a "Receiver's Final Receipt," dated December 2, 1895, at St. Anthony, Fremont County, Idaho, which stated that on this date he paid $320 for 320 acres (he had already paid the other twenty-five cents per acre) for land described as: E2 of NE4 and the SE4 of S32; and the SW4 of the NW4 and the NW4 of the SW4 of S33, T13N, R42E, which record appeared in Deed Record, Book C, p. 313. Rea's 1896 deed for this land, dated April 30, 1896 and recorded September 30, 1896, is at Patent Record, Book A, p. 470. Sections 32 and 33 are today almost completely covered by the west side of the Island Park Reservoir. But that covering did not happen until 1937, and meanwhile George Rea would occupy this land.

There is evidence from a 1904 oral-history piece written by a resident of St. Anthony, Idaho that George Rea erected the first building at present Kilgore, Idaho in Camas Meadows. If true, his activity started that small town and he built that cabin before he built his long-term ranch at Glen Rea. A newspaper article from *The Teton Peak* newspaper that year presented its readers with some of the early history of the area, including this note: "Geo. Ray [*sic*] built the first house on Camas Meadows, now Kilgore." The writer listed no date for that occurrence, but if it happened, 1882, when he and Thomas first arrived in the area, is the most likely year. See [Nellie Smith], "First Prize Composition—At Closing Exercises of Our Public School Composed by Miss Nellie Smith," *The Teton Peak* (St. Anthony, ID), May 26, 1904, pp. 2, 5.

581. "Where to Enter the Park—A Citizen of Omaha Says that the Best Route is from the South," Cheyenne (WY) *Daily Leader*, August 25, 1883, p. 3.

582. W.O. Owen in Schullery, *Old Yellowstone Days*, 2010, p. 36; and Rea, "An Interesting Letter from Beaver Canyon," as cited.

583. "A Guide of Experience," *Dillon* (MT) *Tribune*, May 24, 1884, p. 4.

584. "Generalities and Personals" [Rea, Kooch, and Crittenden] *The Madisonian* (Virginia City, MT), January 26, 1884, p. 2; "Utah Northern Extension" [attributed to *Madisonian*, February 2, 1884], *Lewiston* (ID) *Daily Teller*, February 21, 1884, p. 5; and "Messrs. G.W. and Thomas Rea" ["hotel"], *The Madisonian*, June 28, 1884, p. 2, col. 3. My thanks go to researcher Tina Schlaile for bringing this article to my attention. We know that George Rea spent part of 1884, trying to build what the newspapers called "Rea's hotel" (in progress by June), about a mile above present Mack's Inn. But there the record becomes incomplete for now.

My interpretation is that Rea initially established his homestead at Glen Rea in 1882 or 1883, and then saw a money-making possibility near present Mack's Inn to "put up" travelers, but which was *not* his homestead (because it did not appear under his name in land records). I think he abandoned it when he kept seeing all those Bassett travelers passing by and decided to go into stagecoaching back at Glen Rea instead. Or maybe he ran out of money to finish his hotel, a common problem of these early settlers, as they tried their best to cash in on the rapidly-increasing traffic to Yellowstone. At the same time, I believe that ultimately George Rea could not stay away from the almost magical fish-ponds at Glen Rea and all that wildlife, because those things were guaranteed money-makers!

But thanks to researcher Tina Schlaile and an unnamed researcher in the Island Park area, the possibility exists that George Rea only camped in the (his later) Glen Rea area in 1882-83, and did not move formally to Glen Rea until 1885, because we know that he spent the summer of 1884 building his "Rea's hotel." Tina believes that because there is no ironclad mention of George Rea's cabin at Glen Rea until 1885 (only mentions of his "camp" there), Rea did not establish his homestead at Glen Rea until later, instead settling near Mack's first, probably in 1884, and then moving to Glen Rea in 1885. Thus, we do not yet know the order of these scenarios.

585. Owen, "First Bicycle Tour," in Schullery, *Old Yellowstone Days*, as cited, pp. 35-36.

586. "Beaver Canyon" [George Rea, big game hunter], *Ogden* (UT) *Standard*, May 26, 1884, p. 3; and business card: "G.W. Rea & Bro., Hunters and Guides," no date [probably 1886, from its years-of-experience notation], Don Valiton collection, reproduced in Green, *History of Island Park*, p. 38.

587. Rea, "An Interesting Letter from Beaver Canyon," as cited.

588. "The Geyser Basin Road—The Line Surveyed from China Point to Wonderland," *The Semi-Weekly Miner* (Butte, MT), May 24, 1884, p. 1. For more on Rea's work with these railroad surveyors, see "Montana Matters," *Daily Independent* (Helena, MT), March 12, 1884, p. 7.

589. Green, *History of Island Park*, p. 40, reproduced several photos, such as "George Rea's wagons and guests getting ready for sight-seeing trip to Yellowstone Park, circa 1890"; and "George Rea carriage and guests at his ranch house, circa 1890s."

590. E.H.A., "Northern Notes—The Teton Mountains—Rich Ranchers—Busy Beaver Canyon," *Ogden* (UT) *Daily Herald*, August 16, 1884, p. 1.

591. C.D. Roys, "A Camp in the Rockies," *American Angler: A Weekly Journal of Fish and Fishing* 6#15, October 11, 1884, pp. 225-226.

592. C.R. Savage, "A Strange Country, Geyserland—Incidents of Travel to the Great Falls of the Yellowstone and Geyser Basin," *Deseret Evening News* (Salt Lake City, UT), September 17, 1884, p. 4. This also appeared in *Deseret News*, September 24, 1884, p. 4 (bound volume, p. 564).

593. The text of the entire letterhead read as follows: "G.W. Rea & Bro. Hunters & guides of 21 years' experience in all parts of the Rocky Mountains. Tents, stoves, trained riding and pack horses furnished [to] hunting and fishing parties, easy carriages and horses furnished at nearest R.R.

points to visit the Yellowstone National Park. Orders received for fresh trout Game Dried Elk Moose Venison etc. [at] Beaver Cañon, Idaho." This was contained in G.W. Rea to Secretary of Interior, January 3, 1885, in National Archives, Record Group 48, microfilm 62, roll 3, folder 1 of 4 (hard-copy at YNP Library).

594. G.W. Rea to Secretary of Interior, January 3, 1885, as cited; and Whittlesey, *Storytelling in Yellowstone*, pp. 92-93.

595. G.W. Rea to R.D. Cronk, bill of sale and promise to pay $1832 by October 28, 1886, dated April 28, 1885, in Deed Book D, pp. 101-104, Bingham County Clerk's Office, Blackfoot, Idaho. Interestingly, p. 104 has a note that this instrument was "recorded by mistake in book of deeds." The recording probably should have been made in the books for Contracts, Mortgages, or Liens (Lis Pendens). Each of Rea's horses was described here by physical appearance, brands it carried, and the actual horse's name, to wit: Bounce, Jay, Pacer, Chaff, Lot, Lightfoot, Jip, Browney, China, Billey, Charley, Baldy, Sullivan, and Col.

596. Roberts, *Shoshone and Other Western Wonders*, pp. 187-188.

597. Roberts, *Shoshone and Other Western Wonders*, p. 197; and Richard Hassell in Whittlesey and Bone, *The History of Mammals in the Greater Yellowstone Ecosystem*, I, pp. 607-609, as cited.

598. U Know, "The National Park—An Interesting Communication from Our Special Correspondent," *Idaho News* (Blackfoot, ID), August 13, 1887, p. 1.

599. A.F. Zahm, "A Drive through the Camas Meadows," *The Notre Dame Scholastic* 22#7, October 6, 1888, p. 111.

600. Anna Husted Southworth, "Nan in Goblin Land," *Frank Leslie's Popular Monthly* 29, January, 1890, p. 71.

601. A website for Lyon, Montana, accessed August 16, 2017, states: "Never home to more than just a handful of families, Lyon did have a school, and a post office was established here in 1887 (June 10) with George Barnard as postmaster. The post office was named for a local family (probably that of George H. Lyon) and lasted until 1935 (October 31)." See also Cheney, *Names on the Face of Montana*, as cited, p. 174. George Lyon was mentioned in "Things Territorial," *Bozeman* (MT) *Chronicle*, September 21, 1887, p. 3, col. 5.

602. G.W. Rea, "A Second Anaconda," *Idaho Register* (Idaho Falls, ID), March 22, 1890, p. 3. Also in this letter, George Rea noted the occurrence of several earthquakes, fascinating because his locale was so close to where the 1959 Hebgen Lake quake of magnitude 7.5 formed a new lake on Madison River, which is known today as Earthquake Lake. Said Rea: "On the night of the 13th inst[ant] we had four shocks of an earthquake. The heaviest one shook the house about dusk, then about 8 o'clock [there were] three in succession. They shook the house and everything in it. There might be a big blow out up in the National Park—something new for the tourists to look at."

603. "All around Home," *Idaho News* (Blackfoot, ID), September 10, 1890.

604. Charlotte Rea's practice of living with George Rea only in summers is mentioned in "An Echo of the Long Ago, [Chapter II] (continued)," *Idaho Republican* (Blackfoot, ID), December 12, 1919, p. 6. A land record (An "Indenture," also known as a "Deed") completed at Fremont County, Idaho, Office of County Clerk, shows that on January 13, 1902, seventeen days before George's death, George W. Rea and Charlotte B. Rea personally appeared, and conveyed to Genevieve W. Kelley for $190 their land described as follows: E2 of NE4 and the SE4 of S32 (on Moose Springs Creek where their fish-pond was located); and the SW4 of the NW4 and the NW4 of the SW4 of S33, T13N, R42E (where Rea's house was located), totaling 320 acres with all water rights and privileges. Deed Record, Book E, p. 547, St. Anthony, Idaho. Virtually all of sections 32 and 33 today are under the waters of Island Park Reservoir. This site at that time was about three miles

west of Henry's Fork, close to "Shotgun Creek," today's Sheridan Creek. Charlotte Rea died on November 22, 1919, per "Death of One of Blackfoot's Pioneers," *Idaho Republican*, November 25, 1919, p. 5. I have looked at virtually every historic map of this region, from the 1860s through the 1970s, and the best one I have found is the 1912 U.S. Geological Survey map, a piece of which is included in the Island Park Historical Society's pamphlet, *The Trude Legacy in Shotgun Valley—A Family's First One Hundred Years in Island Park* (Island Park: no publisher, no date, Island Park Historical Society). This map shows Sheridan Creek flowing southeast and northeast into Shotgun Creek, and Moose Springs Creek flowing southwest into Shotgun Creek. Shotgun Creek then flows generally east into Henry's Fork. The "townsite" of Rea (formerly Glen Rea) is shown in Section 33 on the north bank of Shotgun Creek at the mouth of Moose Springs Creek, and across Shotgun Creek from the mouth of Sheridan Creek. Using these designations, it is clear that this section of Shotgun Creek ceased to exist when the waters of Island Park Reservoir covered it, and the place-name Sheridan Creek then became the prevailing name for the east-flowing stream.

605. Shongo, "A Hunt in the Rockies, in Three Parts—Part I," *Forest and Stream* 39, August 11, 1892, p. 115.

606. Shongo, "Hunt in the Rockies," Part I, p. 115-116.

607. Shongo, "Hunt in the Rockies," Part I, p. 116.

608. Shongo, "A Hunt in the Rockies, in Three Parts—Part II," *Forest and Stream* 39, August 18, 1892, pp. 137-138.

609. Shongo, "A Hunt in the Rockies, in Three Parts—Part III," *Forest and Stream* 39, August 25, 1892, p. 159.

610. Shongo, "A Hunt in the Rockies, in Three Parts—Part III," *Forest and Stream* 39, August 25, 1892, p. 160.

611. "Something Fresh and Newsy" [Rea's delightful summer home has wealthy guests], *Blackfoot News*, July 30, 1892, p. 1; "Local and Other News" [greatest fishponds in Idaho], *Idaho Falls Times*, July 7, 1892, p. 5; "Our Bouquet of Summer News" [Rea's wealthy paying guests], *Blackfoot News*, July 30, 1892, p. 1, col 3; "In Legal Circles—Fremont County Water Case," *Idaho Statesman* (Boise, ID), March 30, 1893, p. 2; K.E. Hopf, "From Island Park—Interesting Description of Snowshoeing in the Park—Arangee, Idaho," *Idaho Falls Times* (Idaho Falls, ID), February 23, 1893, p. 5; Dick, "Our Northern Neighbors—Stock-Raising, Fishing and Hunting in Northern Bingham—Arangee, Idaho," *Idaho Falls Times*, January 19, 1893, p. 5; "A Land Office for Rawlins" [George Rea appointed postmaster at Arangee], *Salt Lake Herald*, February 24, 1898, p. 1; and "Over the State—A Big Fish Hatchery," *Idaho Register* (Idaho Falls, ID), March 11, 1898, p. 6.

612. "Pioneer Guide is Dying—Roosevelt's Favorite Found in Lonely Cabin," *Chicago* (IL) *Tribune*, January 20, 1902, p. 9. See also "Veteran Guide Is Believed to be Dead," *Chicago Tribune*, January 24, 1902, p. 4; "'Uncle George' Rea is Dead—Attorney Trude Hears News of Aged Frontiersman Who Defended President's Reputation as Sportsman," *Chicago Tribune*, February 4, 1902, p. 6; and Indian adventures in Rea, "An Interesting Letter from Beaver Canyon," as cited; and his daughter's newspaper reminiscences, as cited.

613. "Guide for President—George Rea, who Acted in that Capacity, Dead—Lived in Isolated Place—Engaged by Roosevelt to Escort Him on Hunting Trips—Died at Glen-Rea, Idaho—Father of Mrs. H.S.[*sic*] Valiton," *Anaconda* (MT) *Standard*, February 3, 1902, p. 3. The documentation about Rea's connection with Theodore Roosevelt is not perfect, but apparently George Rea talked about it at some length with his friend A.S. Trude, who passed it all on to the *Chicago Tribune* for the articles herein cited. In Louis J. Clements, *A Collection of Upper Snake River Valley History* (Rexburg: Eastern Idaho Publishing, 1968), p. 48, Clements quoted Theodore Roosevelt (from

TR's book *Hunting Grizzly*) that Roosevelt went hunting "in the Island Park country of Idaho," which was described by Roosevelt as "just south of the Montana boundary line, and some twenty-five miles west of the line of Wyoming" in 1889 for some of the few remaining bison in the nation. TR was accompanied by an "old hunter" who tracked the bison, and the area appears to have indeed been located along Henry's Fork in Shotgun Valley. Dean Green (*History of Island Park*, p. 38) has stated that his research into the Rea/Valiton family history collection convinced him "that the 'old hunter' was most assuredly George Rea." This historian too finds the likelihood to have been high that the old hunter was Rea. Only Gilman Sawtell and possibly Dick Rock predated George Rea in the area. Sawtell was not a hunter and Dick Rock was not that much of a tracker. Rea was both.

614. Attributed to *Chicago Tribune*, "Roosevelt's Guide is Dying—The Trapper Who Defended President's Reputation as Sportsman," *Salt Lake* (UT) *Telegram*, February 5, 1902, p. 7.

615. "One of the Earliest of Pathfinders," *Anaconda Standard*, February 5, 1902, p. 1.

616. "Old Timer Gone—Will be Buried in Cemetery at Deer Lodge," *Kalispell* (MT) *Bee*, February 5, 1902, p. 1; "He was a Pioneer—George Rea, The Old Time Scout and Guide, Is Dead," *Butte* (MT) *Inter Mountain*, February 5, 1902, p. 9; "Daniel Boone of the West—A Pioneer Explorer and Trapper of Two States Passes Away," *Dillon* (MT) *Tribune*, February 7, 1902, p. 1; and "George Rea is Dead—Famous Trapper Passes to the Great Beyond," *Fergus County Argus* (Lewistown, MT), February 12, 1902, p. 1.

617. "Death of George Ray" [*sic*], *Idaho Register* (Idaho Falls, ID), February 7, 1902, p. 8; "World's News Briefly Told" [Rea death], *Camas Prairie Chronicle* (Cottonwood, ID), January 31, 1902, p. 2; and same story in *Coeur d'Alene* (ID) *Press*, February 1, 1902, p. 1.

618. Frank Conway, "The Lost Mine of Madison Canyon," *Anaconda Standard*, February 1, 1903, section two, p. 3. There are three canyons on Madison River: The lower canyon east of present Norris, Montana; the middle canyon containing present Earthquake Lake with its western boundary located near present Lyon, Montana; and the upper canyon in Yellowstone National Park extending from present Seven Mile Bridge east to Madison Junction. When one considers the long-established tendencies of most miners to keep secret the locations of their discoveries, George Rea's claim for the "middle canyon" might be an outright prevarication. It can be argued that his work in the lower (Cherry Creek) canyon seems more likely to have been the point of his discovery, but in the final analysis, no one knows for sure.

619. Conway, "Lost Mine of Madison Canyon," as cited.

620. For Norris's friend George Graham, see the various indexed references to him in Whittlesey, *Storytelling in Yellowstone*.

621. "Territorial News," *Daily Independent* (Helena, MT), July 28, 1874, p. 3, which mentioned that on July 21, "524 head under charge of Mr. William Ennis were started up the Madison Valley, and by way of Henry's Lake will make a junction with the main band under charge of Mr. Allen himself on Snake River, at or near Market Lake…"

622. Conway, "Lost Mine of Madison Canyon," as cited. As a final, confounding note, one wonders whether Lost Mine Canyon, located just south of nearby Cliff Lake, also figured somehow into this scenario.

623. Conway, "Lost Mine of Madison Canyon," as cited. George Rea left us one more item to wonder about with regard to his mine. In his aforementioned letter of February 24, 1890 from Lyon, Montana, he stated: "It is twenty miles to the nearest post office and [I] have to go on snow shoes for mail." Rea had to have known that there was a post office right there at Lyon, Montana, so one wonders whether he was using this comment to help disguise the location of his mine from newspaper readers. G.W. Rea, "A Second Anaconda," *Idaho Register*, March 22, 1890, p. 3.

624. Roy M. Fitzgerald, "The Roving Fitzgeralds," unpublished manuscript about the Fitzgeralds of Gardiner, Montana, no date [received 2017], YNP Library, p. 67.

625. Rufus Hatch, President, to Hon. H.M. Teller, December 1, 1883, in [U.S. Senate], "Letter from the Secretary of the Interior," 48th Cong., 1st Sess., Sen. Ex. Doc. No. 47, SN-2162, January 10, 1884, pp. 25-27; "The Yellowstone Hotel," *Helena* (MT) *Independent*, December 7, 1882, p. 3; "The Yellowstone Scheme," *New York* (NY) *Times*, December 31, 1882, p. 1; "National Capital Topics—The Proposed Lease of the Yellowstone Park," *New York Times*, January 6, 1883, p. 2; and snippet from the editor in Bozeman (MT) *Avant Courier*, January 5, 1883, p. 3. The "grandest" quote is from "Montana, The Queen of the Territories," *Cincinnati* (OH) *Commercial Tribune*, February 9, 1884, p. 2. See also "Western Empire—Foreign Travelers Advised to Visit the Grandeur and Beauty of Montana," Helena (MT) *Independent*, August 22, 1883, p. 1. For Yellowstone's promotion by newspapers and magazines and resulting fame during the period 1872-1882, see Lee H. Whittlesey, "Yellowstone: From Last Place Discovered to International Fame," *Site Lines* 5 (Fall, 2009): 8-10, University of Virginia, Foundation for Landscape Studies, posted at www.foundationforlandscapestudies.org/pdf/sitelines_fall09.pdf on the internet.

626. For general information on the creation of YNPIC, see Aubrey L. Haines, *The Yellowstone Story* (Boulder: Colorado Associated University Press, 1977, 1996), II, pp. 31-54; Richard A. Bartlett, "The Concessionaires of Yellowstone National Park: Genesis of a Policy," *Pacific Northwest Quarterly* 74 (January, 1983): 2-10; Bartlett, *Yellowstone: A Wilderness Besieged* (Tucson: University of Arizona Press, 1985), pp. 125-129; Lee H. Whittlesey, "'Oh, Mammoth Structure!': Rufus Hatch, the National Hotel, and the Grand Opening of Yellowstone in 1883," *Annals of Wyoming* 83 (Spring, 2011): 2-20; and Whittlesey, *"This Modern Saratoga of the Wilderness!": A History of Mammoth Hot Springs and the Village of Mammoth in Yellowstone National Park, Wyoming-Montana-Idaho* (National Park Service and Colorado State University, in press, 2022).

627. At congressional hearings nine years later (in 1892), George Wakefield stated: "I have been in the park since 1882." In stating this date, he must have been taking license from his time in carrying rail-ties that year and/or helping build the first buildings, for he lived outside the park until 1883. Wakefield in McRae, "Inquiry," pp. III, 141.

628. Except for financial backing and office labor, Charles Wheeler Hoffman seems to have been relatively silent in the Yellowstone venture. Born on September 2, 1846, he was in Bozeman as early as 1870, per the U.S. Census for that year and per the *Montana Pick and Plow* (Bozeman, MT), July 29, 1870, p. 4, in a groceries and notions advertisement. Helen F. Sanders's biography of him (*A History of Montana*, Chicago and New York: Lewis Publishing Company, 1913, vol. II, pp. 1010-1011) says he was born at Niles, Michigan, and was the son of George W. and Esther Louise (Wheeler) Hoffman. After a good education at Detroit, Michigan, and Burlington, Vermont, he was appointed post sutler in 1866 at Fort Randall, Dakota Territory, on the Missouri River. Marrying Elizabeth B. Penfield of Buffalo, New York on April 27, 1869, he appears to have become post sutler at Bozeman's Fort Ellis. Mrs. Marion Eltonhead has stated that Hoffman was also post trader at Crow Agency in 1871 (Eltonhead, "Montana Memories," unpublished manuscript, 1919, YNP Library, p. 15), which squares with what Bozeman resident Peter Koch wrote about Hoffman's dealings with Indians (Peter Koch, *Splendid on a Large Scale*, Kim Allen Scott, ed., Helena, Bedrock Editions, 2010, pp. 277, 295; see also Crystal Alegria and Marsha Fulton, "Fraud at Fort Parker: How Corruption and Contracting Built Early Bozeman," *Montana the Magazine of Western History* 66(3), Autumn, 2016, pp 58-59, which includes a photo of Hoffman.). In the late 1880s, C.W. Hoffman went to Helena for a while, where he served as quartermaster-general on the staffs of several Montana governors and where he was often mentioned in newspapers. Returning to Bozeman, he served two terms as a state senator until 1904 and as president of Bozeman National Bank until 1905. A bit of biography for him from the time when he was a Montana state legislator is in *Livingston* (MT) *Enterprise*, supplement, January 19, 1889,

p. 4. See also "Serious Accident Last Saturday" [to C.W. Hoffman], in Bozeman *Avant Courier*, August 12, 1880, p. 3.

629. Bartlett, *Yellowstone: A Wilderness Besieged*, as cited, p. 157. Biographical information on George Wakefield can be found in Albert L. Babcock, *An Illustrated History of the Yellowstone Valley* (Spokane: Western Historical Publishing Company, [1907?]), pp. 393-394; and Sanders, *History of Montana*, vol. II, p. 978. As for Mrs. Wakefield, one of the 1900 census sheets stated that Margaret Brittan Wakefield was then age 68, with her birthday having passed, and the other agreed that she was born in April of 1832. However, her gravestone in Livingston today says that she was born April 14, 1831 and died June 8, 1903. The couple gave their number of years of marriage to the census taker as 45, and if that was true, the likely year of their wedding was 1855, but George's bios gave it as 1853 and 1854. See the following footnote for these citations.

630. "George W. Wakefield, Pioneer of Montana Dead—Operated First Stage Line in Park," *Livingston* (MT) *Enterprise*, June 5, 1917, p. 3 (this also appeared in *Big Timber* (MT) *Pioneer*, June 7, 1917, p. 1); "Daughter of an Old Timer," Gardiner (MT) *Wonderland*, November 16, 1902, p. 1; "Testimony of George W. Wakefield" in Thomas McRae, "Inquiry into the Management and Control of the Yellowstone National Park," 52d Cong., 1st Sess., House Report 1956, SN-3051, July 20, 1892, pp. 132-150; U.S. Census, Bozeman, Montana, June 2, 1880, p. 9; and U.S. Census, Livingston, Montana, June 9, 11, 1900, p. 11, the last two via Ancestry.com (George Wakefield). If we believe his own testimony to congress and the 1880 census at Bozeman, he was born on October 15, 1835. But the two biographies listed above plus his gravestone gave his year of birth as "1833." The 1900 U.S. Census agrees with the 1880 census in indicating his year of birth to be 1835, by stating that he was then age 65 with his birthday approaching, and both of these sources square with his testimony in front of Representative Thomas McRae's congressional committee in May of 1892. Therefore, this historian declares that Wakefield's congressional testimony and these two censuses make the birth-year of 1835 to be more convincing than the biographies. In his testimony to Congress, Wakefield confirmed: "I was 56 years old the 15th day of last October" [1891].

In 1900, the Wakefields were living in Livingston, and the census listed George's occupation as "landlord (hotel)," where he had twelve boarders who lived and worked at his hotel. Their adopted daughter Libbie, born May 29, 1869 if we believe her gravestone (her birth-year was 1870 per the census), was unmarried and still living with them at age 30. A few years later, she would marry Dr. Samuel F. Way (1862-1946), a Livingston dentist who had also been a stage-driver in Yellowstone Park. A mystery is why, in his congressional testimony in 1891, George Wakefield was referred to by numerous others on several occasions as "General Wakefield," because his long obituary mentioned no service in the Civil War (even though there was a George Wakefield from Maine, born 1835 and probably not the same person, who enlisted on December 3, 1863 as a corporal, per Ancestry.com). The *Enterprise* obituary's chronology showed Wakefield's activities during 1861-1865 as being constantly traveling in the far West, with no apparent time for Civil War service. So perhaps the name "General" was merely a term of respect or affection, as often happened in the nineteenth century. For the importance of both George W. Wakefield and Dr. Samuel F. Way in the history of the training of Yellowstone National Park tour-guides, see Whittlesey, *Storytelling in Yellowstone*, p. 348n155.

631. U.S. Census, Virginia City, MT, no month and day, 1870, p. 36; U.S. Census, Bozeman, MT, June 2, 1880, p. 9; and U.S. Census, Livingston, MT, June 9, 11, 1900, all via Ancestry.com (George Wakefield).

632. An unknown writer known only as "Buckskin" stated on November 2, 1871 in the Bozeman *Avant Courier*: "Bart Henderson has been working with his [labor] force on the Point of Rocks. And… he now has his wagon road completed up to the [Yankee Jim] canyon where his camp is located." Buckskin, "Mammoth Hot Springs—Graphic Description of the Wonders of Our Mountains," Bozeman *Avant Courier*, November 2, 1871, p. 1.

633. "Geo. W. Wakefield," Bozeman *Avant Courier*, November 14, 1872, p. 3, col. 2; "George W. Wakefield, Pioneer of Montana Dead," as cited; advertisement for "North[ern] Pacific Hotel" in Bozeman *Avant Courier*, May 9, 1873, p. 3; advertisement for H.F. Galen, Bozeman *Avant Courier*, April 29, 1880, p. 3; and [Leeson], *History of Montana, 1739-1885*, pp. 616, 620. Wakefield's and his daughter's later home (for many years) in Livingston was located at 416 North Third Street, a residence that still stands today (2022).

634. "New Officers" [county commissioner], Bozeman *Avant Courier*, December 5, 1873, p. 3; "G.W. Wakefield," Bozeman *Avant Courier*, February 21, 1878, p. 3; "A Shooting Scrape," *Bozeman Times*, February 21, 1878, p. 3. See also "Yellowstone Correspondence" [Wakefield's women], *Bozeman Times*, May 30, 1878, p. 3; and August 1, 1878, p. 3. Wakefield was additionally mentioned in Bozeman *Avant Courier*, March 31, 1882, p. 3.

635. Phyllis Smith, *Bozeman and the Gallatin Valley: A History* (Helena: Two Dot/Falcon Publishing, 1996), pp. 141, 225; "Direct and Feasible Route to the Park—Importance of the Discovery," Bozeman *Avant Courier*, September 1, 1881, p. 3; and Haines, *Yellowstone Story*, I, p. 259. The route up Gallatin River had been explored earlier (1872) by Thomas Gray, as chronicled in his "The Road to Wonderland," Bozeman *Avant Courier*, August 22, 1872, p. 2.

636. Phyllis Smith, *Bozeman and the Gallatin Valley*, as cited, p. 145.

637. John Vesuvius [J.V. Bogert], "Wakefield Visits the Park," Bozeman *Avant Courier*, September 8, 1881, p. 1. On page three of this issue, the editor revealed that "John Vesuvius" was really J.V. Bogert. It is fascinating that Wakefield would be so unabashedly partisan as to call out the Republicans at the very time that Republican president James A. Garfield was dying a pitifully slow death from his gunshot wounds. Garfield died on September 19, 1881, only eleven days after this article was published.

638. Snippet on tie contract in Bozeman *Avant Courier*, October 19, 1882, p. 3; and "The Northern Pacific" [Wakefield and Hoffman deliver last ties in their tie-contract], *Grand Forks* (ND) *Herald*, April 22, 1883, p. 1.

639. R. Hatch to CTH, May 29 [1883], in Carroll Hobart papers, box 2, folder 3, Yale University Beinecke Library; "Local Layout" [Wakefield given YNP contract and says he will use Concord coaches], *Livingston Enterprise*, June 30, 1883, p. 3; and "Montana," *Winona* (MN) *Daily Republican*, July 18, 1883, p. 2. That YNPIC would gladly have let the government perform the stagecoach chores had it been willing was stated in "The Yellowstone Park," *Salt Lake* (UT) *Herald*, January 9, 1883, p. 2.

640. Rufus Hatch to Secretary of Interior, July 16, 1883, in McRae, "Inquiry," p. 207. For Wakefield's Livingston connection, see "At the Gateway—Entering the Wonderland through Livingston…," St. Paul (MN) *Daily Globe*, September 1, 1883, p. 2.

641. Item in Bozeman *Avant Courier*, February 15, 1883, p. 3, col. 2; and Inhotwater, "Park Items," *Avant Courier*, February 15, 1883, p. 3, col. 5.

642. Wakefield's cabin was mentioned by Assistant Superintendent J.H. Dean when he asked for official use of it in late 1883, as described in Haines, *Yellowstone Story*, I, p. 301. Photos of Wakefield's carriage-shed complex are Carleton Watkins, D-229 and F.J. Haynes H-1287, both reproduced in Whittlesey, *"This Modern Saratoga of the Wilderness!": A History of Mammoth Hot Springs and the Village of Mammoth in Yellowstone National Park* (NPS and Colorado State University, 2022, in press), pp. 117-118. The 1885 Leffingwell map showed the location of Wakefield's complex at Mammoth.

643. "Rail and River—The Yellowstone," *St. Paul* (MN) *Globe*, July 18, 1883, p. 2. The *Livingston Enterprise* for December 31, 1883 ("Local Layout," p. 3) confirmed that Wakefield used mostly spring wagons in 1883, stating that for 1884 "the coaches will be much more comfortable than the spring wagons that were used last year." Wakefield apparently also had a few "old Concord coach-

es," per the account of reporter F.B. Plimpton, in F.B.P., "The Yellowstone—Western Associated Press Excursion," *Cincinnati* (OH) *Commercial Tribune*, August 19, 1883, p. 3.

644. Haines, *Yellowstone Story*, I, p. 277; "Neighborhood News" [coaches and jerkies], *New North-West* (Deer Lodge, MT), July 11, 1884, p. 3; "The Yellowstone" [facilities for 1883], St. Paul *Daily Globe*, July 18, 1883, p. 2; and G.L. Henderson, "[To] J.R. Monroe," *Monroe's Iron-Clad Age* (Indianapolis, Indiana), July 12, 1884, p. 1. Rates for horses at Mammoth were $1 for the first hour, and fifty cents for each additional hour up to the day-cutoff at $3.50 per day. Pack horses were $2.50 per day. A double-team wagon with driver was $10 per day, while a single horse and buggy was $6 per day. See "Yellowstone Park," *Blackfoot* (ID) *Register*, July 28, 1883, p. 1.

645. Lee H. Whittlesey, "'Oh, Mammoth Structure!': Rufus Hatch, the National Hotel, and the Grand Opening of Yellowstone in 1883," *Annals of Wyoming* 83 (Spring, 2011): 2-20. Yearly park-visitation statistics are in Haines, *Yellowstone Story*, II, p. 478.

646. F.B.P[limpton], "The Yellowstone—Western Associated Press Excursion," *Cincinnati* (OH) *Commercial Tribune*, August 19, 1883, p. 3.

647. For another example, see Haines, *Yellowstone Story*, I, pp. 277-278.

648. Wakefield and Hoffman to Secretary of Interior, August 7, 1883; and Carroll Hobart to Secretary of Interior, August 8, 1883, both in McRae, "Inquiry," pp. 208-209. Wakefield stated: "You [Hobart and YNPIC] assured us that we should have the carrying trade within the park, but could not expect to interfere with those who engaged passengers from outside the park to go through the same." Assistant Superintendent G.L. Henderson named names, as to who the violators were that ran illegal in-park liveries: "J.A. Clark, Mike Earley, Tony Earley, Thomas Earley, George Metcalf, Charles Shoreman, George Ruder, C. Nord, S. Nake, and many others." Henderson in McRae, "Inquiry," p. 209. James A. Clark was a friend of Superintendent Conger's and eventually obtained a verbal permit from him, so park officials looked out for him much better than the others. Whittlesey, *This Modern Saratoga*," unabridged edition, p. 172. For Alonzo Daw in 1885, see William C. Gray, *Camp-Fire Musings: Life and Good Times in the Woods* (New York: A.D.F. Randolph & Company, and Chicago: The Interior Company, 1894), pp. [33]-38. For Allen Chadbourn, see footnote 216 in Whittlesey, *This Modern Saratoga*," unabridged edition.

649. Haines, *Yellowstone Story*, I, p. 279, quoting "Local Layout," *Livingston Enterprise*, August 17, 1883, p. 3. Both Merritt A. Joslyn and Edward Dawson in the Secretary's office were early supporters of YNPIC, at times working against their own employer's (the government's) interests. Bartlett, *Wilderness Besieged*, pp. 159, 243, 322n9.

650. W. Scott Smith, quoted in McRae, "Inquiry," p. 208.

651. "Testimony of G.L. Henderson," in McRae, "Inquiry," pp. 201-202.

652. G.W. Wakefield in William S. Holman and S.W. Peel, "Report to Provide for the Appointment of a Commission to Inspect and Report on the Condition of Indians, Indian Affairs, and for Other Purposes," 49th Congress, 1st Session, House Report No. 1076, SN-2438, March 16, 1886, pp. 259-260, hereafter cited as "Indians and Yellowstone Park."

653. L.H.C., "The Northwest…the Devils Slide and the Threshold of Wonderland," *Cleveland* (OH) *Leader*, September 5, 1883, p. 4; and [Paul] S[elby], "Notes of Summer Travel—A Post Excursion Letter" [Part Two], *Daily Illinois State Journal* (Springfield), September 10, 1883 p. 2. Part one of this article by Paul Selby appeared as "Notes of Summer Travel," in the edition of August 18, 1883, p. 2.

654. Haines, *Yellowstone Story*, I, p. 277; and Wakefield and Hoffman to Secretary of Interior, December 16, 1883, in National Archives, RG 48, no. 62, roll 1 (folder 3 of 3), hardcopies in YNP Library. This letter also stated that Wakefield had built a mail station at Lamar, and he asked permission to build two more.

655. "Local Layout," *Livingston Enterprise*, December 31, 1883, p. 3.

656. Charles Gibson in McRae, "Inquiry," p. 79; and Pearce in McRae, p. 108.

657. "Local Layout" [Wakefield and Hoffman begin], *Livingston Enterprise*, July 10, 1884, p. 3. For the mail contract, see advertisement in *Livingston Enterprise*, February 27, 1884, p. 3. For Wakefield's erection of buildings, see snippet in Helena (MT) *Independent*, June 12, 1884, p. 7.

658. G.L.H[enderson], "Park Notes," Livingston *Daily Enterprise*, June 30, 1884, p. 1.

659. G., "Summer Saunterings—Life Among the Rockies as Viewed by a Little Rock Tourist—A Beautiful Picture of Scenery in [Yellowstone]," *Arkansas Gazette* (Little Rock, AR), August 31, 1884, p. 6.

660. Haines, *Yellowstone Story*, I, pp. 309-311 has details of YNPIC's story. Whittlesey, "Oh, Mammoth Structure," as cited, pp. 19-20, discusses the Panic of 1884. Although the park's visitation-estimate for 1884 per Haines (*Yellowstone Story*, II, p. 478) was 5,000, newspaper articles made it clear that people were still trying to save money, and the NPRR was running light in passengers. See for example "Yellowstone Park Travel," *Oregonian* (Portland, OR), September 5, 1884, p. 2. A snippet in *Duluth* (MN) *Weekly Tribune*, August 22, 1884, p. 2, stated that "the Yellowstone Park season has not been a good one thus far." Another article stated that "the present tourist season which is now almost ended, has not been a profitable one to the hotel managers, the number of visitors as compared with that of last year being less than one-half." B., "Letter from Butte," *Salt Lake* (UT) *Tribune*, September 25, 1884, p. 5. Finally see new Superintendent Robert Carpenter's comments on possible reasons for the low visitation in 1884, in "The Yellowstone Park," *New York Herald*, January 2, 1885, p. 5.

661. G.L. Henderson, "Notes on a Visit to Mammoth Hot Springs" [Adam Deem], *Livingston Enterprise*, August 6, 1884, p. 1; J.W. Weimer to P.H. Conger, August 10, 1884, Archive Document 1586 [two drivers guilty], YNP Archives; and L.C. [G.L. Henderson], "Park Notes" [Wakefield's guides do not know "Lemonade Lake"], *Livingston Enterprise*, August 4, 1884, p. 1. For G.L. Henderson's biography, see Whittlesey, *Storytelling in Yellowstone*, chapter nine; and Whittlesey, "G.L. Henderson: From New York Free-Thinker to Yellowstone Gentleman of Science," *Annals of Wyoming* 88#3, Summer, 2016, pp. 2-16.

662. Charles Gibson's testimony, in McRae, "Inquiry," pp. 78-81.

663. O.J.H., "The Yellowstone—The Improvement Company and Mammoth Hot Springs Hotel—[?] of the Norris and Firehole Geyser Basins—Where to Go, How to Go, and What it Costs—A Flying Trip Through Uncle Sam's Great Inferno," *Daily Tribune* (Salt Lake City, Utah), August 17, 1884, p. 6. A partially defective edition of this article appeared in *Salt Lake Weekly Tribune*, August 21, 1884, p. 5, with its left edge smeared.

664. Occident, "A Trip to the Park," *Forest and Stream* 27 (October 28, 1886): 262. Although published two years later, this account stated that the trip occurred in August of 1884.

665. G.W. Wakefield, August 8, 1885, in Holman and Peel, "Indians and Yellowstone Park," SN-2438, pp. 259-260. Wakefield stated that he agreed to give YNPIC's receiver Hulme fifteen percent of his earnings for 1884, but that Hulme later forgave the debt because of Wakefield's failure to make money that summer.

666. E. Catherine Bates, *A Year in the Great Republic* (London. Ward and Downey, 1887, in two volumes), II, pp. 170-171.

667. "Masked Robbers in Yellowstone Park," *Kalamazoo* (MI) *Gazette*, September 10, 1884, p. 1; same headline, *Muskegon* (MI) *Chronicle*, September 10, 1884, p. 1; and "A Californian Robbed in Yellowstone Park," *Sacramento* (CA) *Daily Record-Union*, September 6, 1884, p. 1. The location of this hold-up, if correctly reported, occurred in the Wyoming portion of Yellowstone National Park.

668. Superintendent R.E. Carpenter to Secretary of Interior, March 26, 1885, endorsement letter carried by Charles Hoffman; C.W. Hoffman to Secretary of Interior, April 3, 1885; Endorsement by Martin McGinnis, April 3, 1885; and T.K. Toole to Secretary of Interior, no date [April 3, 1885], all in RG 48, microfilm no. 62, roll 3, folder 2 of 4, YNP Library.

669. George W. Wakefield to D.W. Wear [hay at Soda Butte], July 6, 1885; Wakefield & Hoffman to D.W. Wear [request to cut hay at several locations], July 6, 1885; Endorsement [for hay] of D.W. Wear to Secretary of Interior, received July 14, 1885; and George W. Wakefield to D.W. Wear [re: Sowash station], August 21, 1885, all in RG 48, microfilm 62, roll 3, folder 2 of 4, hardcopies at YNP Library.

670. D.W. Wear to [Secretary] L.Q.C. Lamar [re: rates from Cinnabar], August 22, 1885, in RG 48, microfilm 62, roll 3, folder 2 of 4, hardcopy at YNP Library; "In the Yellowstone Park—Correspondence of the N.Y. Evening Post," *Worcester* (MA) *Daily Spy*, July 11, 1885, p. 3; and "Yellowstone Park" [NPRR's ticket and description], *St. Paul Daily Globe*, July 4, 1885, p. 2.

671. [G.L. Henderson], "Noticed in the Park—What the Year has Brought Forth in the Nation's Wonderland," *Livingston Enterprise*, September 19, 1885, p. 1; and "Railroad Notes" [lowered fares], *Livingston Enterprise*, March 21, 1885, p. 1.

672. "The Yellowstone Park," *Livingston Enterprise*, June 20, 1885, p. 3. The cheaper fare was exemplified this year by the Northern Pacific's offering of a coupon book that covered every expense from St. Paul to and through the Park and return. This coupon book would continue for years to be a source of both savings and complaints. See A.L.O., "In Yellowstone Park—The Travel to the Great National Park," St. Paul (MN) *Daily Globe*, September 26, 1885, p. 4. For the name of Wakefield's company, see Henderson, *Yellowstone Park Manual and Guide*, 1885, p. 4, col. 5; and "Personals" [George Wakefield], St. Paul *Sunday Globe*, June 7, 1885, p. 8, col. 2. For Wakefield's drivers this year, see Jack Ellis Haynes, "Facts from J.N. (Pretty Dick) Randall," Jack Haynes Papers, Box 112, Folder 20, January 22, 1950, Montana State University Library Special Collections. Larry Link later became a store owner in Gardiner. George Arnholdt lived in the area all his life, his son Walt Arnholdt growing up in Gardiner, such that as an old man, Walt could meet park bus-driver Lee Whittlesey at Mammoth in 1976 to tell him his story of encountering President Theodore Roosevelt in 1903 at Gardiner and of living in the Capitol Hill blockhouse as a child.

673. Seymour Dunbar, *A History of Travel in America* (New York: Greenwood Press, 1968), pp. 46-48. For Senator Conkling, see Whittlesey, *"This Modern Saratoga of the Wilderness,"* in press, NPS, 2022, pp. 113-115; and [Lt.] Dan [C.] Kingman in "Yellowstone Park—Its Curiosities," *Wisconsin State Journal* (Madison, WI), February 4, 1887, p. 6.

674. Scheiber, *Abbot-Downing and the Concord Coach*, 1989, pp. 1-4.

675. "At the Park," *Daily Yellowstone Journal* (Miles City, MT), June 7, 1885, p. 3; and "At the Park," *River Press* (Ft. Benton, MT), June 17, 1885, p. 7. Wakefield mentioned his total investment in congressional testimony that occurred on August 8, 1885, as recorded in Holman and Peel, "Indians and Yellowstone Park," SN-2438, pp. 259-260. Watry has stated that this sales receipt states that these coaches had 4 seats for 3 people per seat, which means three seats in the main compartment, plus driver and one passenger "on the box" (the fourth seat), so eleven total passengers. Watry adds, "I think it will be less confusing to stick to calling them three-seaters, meaning three bench seats in the main compartment." Historian Whittlesey's research (in 2012) on the history of Mammoth Village, including photo YELL 128013 showing several of James Clark's buildings erected before August of 1885 and also present in the Hallam Webber album (catalog number 127995) of Yellowstone Wagons, but *without* Clark's main dwelling, bath house, and ice house at the base of Capitol Hill, indicates that album 127995 has to date from after August of that year, which also dates the arrival of the Yellowstone Wagons shown in that album as after

August, 1885. Author's conversations with Watry, various, 2010-2020; and Elizabeth Watry, "Compilation of Research Notes about YNP Stagecoaches/Vehicles," 2019, p. 1, showing three 11-passenger coaches, ordered July 3, 1886 @$375 each, from Abbot-Downing Company, Concord, N.H., serial numbers 12249, 12250, and 12283—apparently coaches 4, 5, and 6. Thus, coaches 1, 2, and 3 were likely ordered in the summer of 1885, and received in late summer or fall.

676. "National Park Notes" [Kingman's Pass], *Daily Yellowstone Journal* (Miles City, MT), June 17, 1885, p. 1. For Conkling, see "How Mr. Conkling Was Scalded," *New York Times*, August 23, 1883, p. 3; "Why Conkling Cursed," *Wheeling* (WVA) *Register*, August 13, 1883, p. [1]; "A Correspondent of the Detroit Free Press," *Cincinnati* (OH) *Commercial Tribune*, August 25, 1883, p. 4; and Dan Kingman in "Yellowstone Park—Its Curiosities," *Wisconsin State Journal* (Madison, WI), February 4, 1887, p. 6, which stated, "This is the same hill which Roscoe Conkling saw on his trip and turned back, deeming it too dangerous to travel." A textual advertisement for 1888 encouraged tourists to "try one of Wakefield's 'seven passenger' chariots for a delightful trip." See *New North-West* (Deer Lodge, MT), July 13, 1888, p. 3, column one. For Kingman's opening of Golden Gate, see L.C. [G.L. Henderson] "Doings in Wonderland," *Livingston Enterprise*, June 13, 1885, p. 1; and "The Yellowstone Park—Items of Interest from the Wonderland of the World," *Livingston Enterprise*, June 20, 1885, p. 3.

677. "The Park and the Indian—Extract from the Yellowstone [Road] Report," *Omaha* (NE) *Daily Bee*, December 15, 1885, p. 8; "Yellowstone National Park" [Kingman interviewed], *Omaha Daily Bee*, October 28, 1885, p. 8; and Henderson, *Yellowstone Park Manual and Guide*, 1888, p. 2. Origins of the place-names Golden Gate Canyon and Kingman Pass are in Whittlesey, *Yellowstone Place Names*, as cited, pp. 118-119, 144, with the following additions. Of Golden Gate Canyon, G.L. Henderson wrote: "We were standing under the cliffs that rose in columnar pillars 300 feet overhead and were admiring the yellow mosses that ornamented the walls on both sides of the Cañon, and which suggested the name of <u>Golden Gate</u> to this mountain pass from the lower to the upper park." G.L. Henderson, "Wonderland Caves and Terraces—Excavation, Formation, Erosion: A Gale at the Golden Gate," handwritten manuscript, no date [March or April, 1888], p. 25, YNP Library manuscript file. Of Kingman Pass, Henderson wrote: "All who have seen 'Kingman's Pass' into the Park by way of the Golden Gates *[sic]* and who are competent to form an opinion declare that it is the finest piece of road in the Rocky [M]ountains." [G.L. Henderson], "National Park Notes," *Daily Yellowstone Journal* (Miles City, MT), June 17, 1885, p. 1. See also "Noticed in the Park—What the Year Has Brought Forth in the Nation's Wonderland," *Livingston Enterprise*, September 19, 1885, p. 1.

678. John Muir, "The Yellowstone Park—A Trip to the Great National Reservation in the Northwest," *Daily Nebraska State Journal* (Lincoln, NE), November 28, 1885, p. 6; John Muir, "The Yellowstone—John Muir's Letter to the San Francisco Bulletin," *Wisconsin State Register* (Portage, WI), December 12, 1885, p. 1; and also in *Evening Bulletin* (San Francisco), October 27, 1885.

679. John Muir, "The Yellowstone National Park," *Atlantic Monthly* 81 (April, 1898), pp. 514, 516.

680. G.W. Wakefield statement, August 8, 1885, in Holman and Peel, "Indians and Yellowstone Park," SN-2438, pp. 259-260; and "Congressional Committee Coming," *Morning Oregonian* (Portland, OR), August 14, 1885, p. 3. This congressional investigation was spurred by W. Scott Smith's negative report on Park affairs in 1883. Congress would get even more upset in October of 1885 when a second park investigator, William Hallett Phillips, submitted his own negative report.

681. Wakefield, August 8, 1885, in Holman and Peel, "Indians and Yellowstone Park," SN-2438, pp. 259-260. In this same report, Superintendent David Wear listed (p. 256) the government's stated transportation rates from point to point through the Park.

682. Charles Gibson, letter to Secretary of Interior, August 24, 1885, included in "Testimony of Edward M. Dawson," in McRae, "Inquiry," pp. 241-242.

683. "City News," *Bozeman Weekly Chronicle*, September 9, 1885, p. 3.

684. W.H. Dudley, *The National Park from the Hurricane Deck of a Cayuse, or, the Liederkranz Expe-dition to Geyserland* (Butte City, Montana: Free Press Publishing Company, 1886), pp. 98-99. Dudley also stated that he met a Mr. Smith on the Mary Mountain road "who has been cutting hay for the company for two seasons; he informed me that they commence cutting hay in June or July and continue till snow comes."

685. "[OTO] Dude Ranch Memoirs Go to Yellowstone Park Archives," *Missoulian* (Missoula, MT), August 3, 2010, p. B5; Lee Whittlesey, "Lee Whittlesey's Interview with George William Perkins, Age 84, Regarding His Friends 'Pretty' Dick Randall, Dora Randall, and Bess Randall Erskine on July 28, 2010," p. [2], YNP Library; and Jack Ellis Haynes, "Facts from J.N. (Pretty Dick) Randall," Jack Haynes Papers, Box 112, Folder 20, January 22, 1950, Montana State University Library Special Collections. Haynes's "Facts" says that Randall first came to YNP in 1884, could not get a job, and so returned to Billings; then returned in 1885 as a night-herder at Old Faith-ful, returned to near Billings for 1886, and finally came back to YNP in 1887 to serve again as a night-herder.

686. [G.L. Henderson], "Noticed in the Park—What the Year has Brought Forth in the Nation's Wonderland," *Livingston Enterprise*, September 19, 1885, p. 1; "Railroad Notes" [lowered fares], *Livingston Enterprise*, March 21, 1885, p. 1; and "Yellowstone National Park—Superintendent Wear's Report to the Secretary of the Interior," *Livingston Enterprise*, December 19, 1885, p. 4. See also, A.L.O., "In Yellowstone Park—The Travel to the Great National Resort—A Great Improvement Over Last Year," *St. Paul Daily Globe*, September 26, 1885, p. 4. Estimated visita-tion-statistics are in Haines, *Yellowstone Story*, II, p. 478.

687. Mention of the court case, *C.T. Hobart v. George Wakefield, et al.*, appeared in "The Special Term Calendar," St. Paul (MN) *Sunday Globe*, Nov 22, 1885, p. 3. Hobart's train-departure eastward from Livingston was noted in "Personal Points," *Livingston Enterprise*, November 14, 1885, p. 3.

688. "Local Layout" [Wakefield removes horses from park], *Livingston Enterprise*, October 17, 1885, p. 3.

689. "New Park Syndicate" [Charles Gibson], *Livingston Enterprise*, October 17, 1885, p. 3. See also "Yellowstone Park Hotels—A New Syndicate," *Washington* (DC) *Critic-Record*, October 28, 1885, p. 1; and "Park Affairs—Outline of the Plans of the New Park Company," *Livingston Enterprise*, October 31, 1885, p. 1.

690. "Local Items" [Wakefield goes east], *Daily Yellowstone Journal* (Miles City, MT), March 31, 1886, p. 3; and "George Wakefield," *St. Paul Daily Globe*, March 29, 1886, p. 5. Concord was the home of Abbott and Downing stages and South Bend was the home of Studebaker. Both manufactured stagecoaches and other wagons.

691. A.S. Condon, "The Yellowstone Park—A Fresh Description of the Glories Seen There," *Salt Lake Tribune*, September 8, 1887, p. 6; and W.H.R., "A Yellowstone Trip—Interesting Account of the Marvels of the Great American Park," *Philadelphia* (PA) *Inquirer*, August 4, 1886, p. 7.

692. "Inventory of George W. Wakefield's Stock and Transportation Company…February 6, 1889," in McRae, "Inquiry," p. 135. Wakefield's new coaches were: two wide, six-passenger, canopy surreys, blue in color at $350 each; and one six-passenger, Depot Wagon, sea-blue in color, at $460, dated June 25 and July 10, 1886 respectively (Studebaker); and three Passenger-Wagons, four-seats each, at $1,188 total, dated July 3, 1886 (Abbot-Downing). My thanks go to historian Elizabeth Watry, who found these receipts in Box 136, D.12.2F, Ledger Book, Vol. 12, Northern Pacific Railroad Company Records, Minnesota Historical Society, St. Paul, MN.

693. "Local Layout" [Haynes joins Wakefield as partner], *Livingston Enterprise*, January 29, 1886, p. 3; "Preparations" [what Wakefield and Haynes will do], *River Press* (Fort Benton, MT), March 24,

1886, p. 5; and "Local Layout" [Haynes and Wakefield partnership dissolved and Wakefield carries on], *Livingston Enterprise*, August 7, 1886, p. 3. Charles W. Hoffman's selling out to Wakefield was dated December 7, 1885, and may be found today in a handwritten note in the Aubrey Haines Papers, Montana State University, Special Collections, filed under "Hoffman, Charles," which assigned all right, title, and interest in the stagecoach company to George Wakefield. For Haynes's building of his home and studio and more of his history, see Lee H. Whittlesey, *"This Modern Saratoga,"* unabridged version, 2021, pp. 163-168.

694. The background for all of this appears in the author's long study of Mammoth Hot Springs village, written for the National Park Service. It is Lee H. Whittlesey, *"This Modern Saratoga of the Wilderness": A History of the Mammoth Hot Springs Village in Yellowstone National Park* (Yellowstone National Park: National Park Service and Colorado State University, 2022, in press). The original, unabridged version is 541 pages in length with much longer footnotes, while the published version is considerably shorter.

695. Clark's original lease for the site of his several buildings was dated February 17, 1885, and the site conflicted with that of photographer F. Jay Haynes, so Clark went ahead with his construction while attempting to have the location changed. Clark's modification was dated March 24, 1886. J.A. Clark to Secretary of Interior, November 7, 1885; and L.Q.C. Lamar to James A. Clark, March 24, 1886, both in RG 48, roll 3, no. 62, folder 1 of 4 (there are many J.A. Clark letters in this folder), YNP Library. See also J.C. [A.] Clark to D.C. Kingman, March 15, 1885; and Dan C. Kingman to Secretary of Interior, March 25, 1885, both in Marcy Culpin Files, YNP Historian's Office. My thanks go to researcher Bob Flather of Yellowstone National Park for this additional information. James A. Clark appeared in the census of 1880 for Fort Collins, Colorado as being aged 32, and Ansel Watrous's *History of Larimer County, Colorado* (Ft. Collins: Courier Printing, 1911), p. 268, stated that Clark built a hotel on Cameron Pass in 1881. The 1880 U.S. Census has stated that his wife then was Mary B. Clark from Indiana and that he had two male sons named Harry T. Clark and Lee R. Clark, ages 4 and 2 respectively.

696. Carroll Hobart to Secretary of Interior, August 20, 1883 in RG 48, no. 62, microfilm reel marked "assistant superintendents, YNP Archives; and J.A. Clark to Secretary of Interior, May 12, 1885, in RG 48, no. 62, roll 3, folder 1 of 4, YNP Library. Clark's appointment as U.S. Marshall was announced in "Local Layout," *Livingston* (MT) *Enterprise*, November 20, 1883, p. 3. Hobart stated that Clark had lived in Ft. Collins, Colorado for "the past seventeen years." My thanks go to historian and lawyer Steve Mishkin of Olympia, Washington for bringing this information to my attention. Mishkin is almost finished writing a book about the law in early Yellowstone.

697. Hobart to Secretary of Interior, August 20, 1883, cited above; and author's conversation with Steve Mishkin, historian and lawyer, Olympia, Washington, July 27, 2009.

698. G.L. Henderson to M.L. Joslyn marked "Personal," August 1, 1884, in "Records of the Office of the Secretary of the Interior Relating to Yellowstone National Park, 1872-1886," Roll 2 (1883-1884), microfilm at University of Washington. My thanks go to Steve Mishkin for this letter.

699. Patrick Conger to Secretary of Interior, January 31, 1884, in "Letter from the Secretary of the Interior," 48th Cong., 1st Sess., Sen. Ex. Doc. 207 (July 5, 1884), SN-2168, p. 6; and C.L. Davis to SOI, January 22, 1885, included in J.A. Clark to SOI, January 19, 1885, in RG 48, microfilm 62, roll 3, folder 1 of 4, YNP Library.

700. J.A. Clark to Secretary of Interior, January 19, 1885; Clark to SOI, February 6, 1885; and SOI to James A. Clark, February 17, 1885, all in RG 48, microfilm 62, roll 3, folder 1 of 4, YNP Library. These files show that Clark enclosed many local letters and signatures endorsing his petition.

701. James A. Clark to Dan Kingman, March 19, 1885; and Kingman to SOI, March 25, 1885, both in RG 48, microfilm 62, roll 3, folder 2 of 4, YNP Library.

702. "Another Hotel at Mammoth Hot Springs," *Livingston Enterprise*, March 14, 1885, p. 3; and "Local Layout," *Livingston Enterprise*, May 9, 1885, p. 3. McCartney Cave is a cave-like, extinct spring-hole in the army parade ground a few hundred feet west of today's Mammoth Visitor Center. Whittlesey, *Yellowstone Place Names*, as cited, 2006, p. 168.

703. L[iberty] C[ap][G.L. Henderson], "Park Notes," *Livingston Enterprise*, April 25, 1885, p. 3. See also R.E. Carpenter to Secretary of Interior, May 12, 1885; and Clark to SOI, May 12, 1885, both in RG 48, no. 62, roll 3, folder 1 of 4, YNP Library. Superintendent Carpenter stated on May 4 that J.A. Clark "has just finished" his dwelling. R.E. Carpenter to W.N. Muldrow, May 4, 1885, in RG 48, roll 3, no. 62, folder 2 of 4, YNP Library.

704. Other relevant photos are H-1599, 1885, and H-4191, Montana Historical Society. See also photos YELL 36433 (probably 1885) and YELL 30285a (1900). The 1900 photo shows the scar on Capitol Hill and the large trees above Michael Keller's house (Jack Haynes's sales room) that together allow us to accurately locate Clark's old buildings.

705. T.O. Towles and Ferris Finch to House of Representatives (copied to SOI), April 15, 1885, in RG 48, no. 62, roll 3, folder 1 of 4, YNP Library.

706. Hague to Clark, April 6, 1885; Clark to Secretary of Interior, enclosing map, April 29, 1885; and Hague to Secretary of Interior enclosing map, April 30, 1885, all in RG 48, no. 62, roll 3, folder 1 of 4, YNP Library. See also History Card File, "James A. Clark," YNP Library; and H.L. Muldrow to Moses Harris, February 10, 1888, Archive Document 58, YNP Archives. Arnold Hague, Walter Weed, and Superintendent Carpenter all approved of Clark's lease, per Hague to D.W. Wear, September 3, 1885; Weed [to Hague?], August 30, 1885, and Carpenter to Secretary of Interior, May 12, 1885, all in RG 48, no. 62, roll 3, folder 1 of 4, YNP Library.

707. "Local Layout," *Livingston Enterprise*, May 9, 1885, p. 3, reporting Clark's construction of "a large feed and livery stable"; and R.E. Carpenter to Secretary of Interior, May 12, 1885 in RG 48, roll 3, no. 62, folder 1 of 4, YNP Library. See also "Another Hotel at Mammoth Hot Springs," *Livingston Enterprise*, March 14, 1885, p. 3.

708. R.E. Carpenter to Secretary of Interior, May 12, 1885; and James A. Clark to SOI, November 7, 1885, both in RG 48, no. 62, roll 3, folder 1 of 4, YNP Library.

709. W.H. Leffingwell, Map of "Hotel Terrace, Mammoth Hot Springs, Yellowstone National Park," July, 1885, YNP Archives, showing "Blacksmith Shop, J.A.C." and "James A. Clark's Stable."

710. Photo YELL 14316 (H-1692). See also Photos YELL 30285a (1900) and YELL 36433 (probably 1885). The 1900 photo shows today's scar on Capitol Hill and the large trees above Keller's former house that allow us today to accurately locate Clark's old buildings.

711. L.C. [G.L. Henderson], "Doings in Wonderland," *Livingston* (MT) *Enterprise*, June 13, 1885, p. 1.

712. Both the 1891 map and the 1901 Chittenden map show a barn and corral on the site of Jack Haynes's later "sales room." On the 1901 map, an additional elongated east-west building (probably a carriage shed) is shown on part of the site of today's Haynes (1928) photo factory. The arrangement is well shown in the photograph above, YELL 36433.

713. L[iberty].C[ap]. [G.L. Henderson], "Doings in Wonderland, *Livingston Enterprise*, June 13, 1885, p. 1; and Clark to SOI, May 12, 1885, as previously cited.

714. [Horace White], "In the Yellowstone Park. A Horseback Ride to the Great Geysers," newspaper clipping attributed to [Chicago] *Evening Post*, no date [trip in June, 1885], included in NA, RG 48, no. 62, roll 3 (hardcopy at YNP Library).

715. Photo H-4984 (late 1885 or early 1886), Montana Historical Society; "Notes from Mammoth

Hot Springs," *Livingston Enterprise*, November 7, 1885, p. 3; Arnold Hague to Secretary of Interior with map, April 30, 1885, on microfilm M62, roll 2, YNP Archives; and W.H. Phillips, "Letter from the Acting Secretary…Transmitting…report of…W.H. Phillips," September 12, 1885, in SN-2333, 49th Cong., 1st Sess., Sen. Ex. Doc. No. 51, p. 11.

716. James Stevenson to James A. Clark, enclosing map, April 28, 1885; James A. Clark to Secretary of Interior, enclosing map, April 29, 1885; and J.A. Clark to Secretary of Interior, November 7, 1885, all in RG 48, no. 62, roll 3, folder 1 of 4, YNP Library. See also W.H. Weed map and note, August 30, 1885, in same file.

717. "Notes from Mammoth Hot Springs," *Livingston Enterprise*, November 7, 1885, p. 3; and D. Wear to SOI, with map, December 29, 1885 in RG 48, microfilm 62, roll 3, file 1 of 4, YNP Library. The Secretary finally issued Clark's new lease in March, 1886, per L.Q.C. Lamar to Clark, March 24, 1886, both in RG 48, microfilm 62, roll 3, folder 1 of 4, YNP Library.

718. "Personal Points," *Livingston Enterprise*, November 14, 1885, p. 3.

719. "Local Layout" [J.A. Clark returns from a two-weeks' trip to the east], *Livingston Enterprise*, July 30, 1887, p. 3.

720. [G.L. Henderson], "Our Park Visit," *Livingston Enterprise*, July 23, 1887, p. 3.

721. Charles Gibson discussed the sale to his company, YPA, in his congressional testimony (Gibson in McCrae, "Inquiry," p. 195). The quote is from H.L. Muldrow to Moses Harris, February 10, 1888, Archive Document 58, YNP Archives. See also J.A. Clark to Secretary of Interior, January 3, 1887, in RG 48, roll 3, no. 62, file 1 of 4, YNP Library; "Park Transportation," *Livingston Enterprise*, April 16, 1887, p. 3, and May 7, 1887, p. 3; the two letters from Moses Harris to Interior regarding Mr. Clark in Letters Sent, vol. II, pp. 55, 76, YNP Archives; and G.L. Henderson, *Yellowstone Park Manual and Guide*, 1888 edition, p. 3, column 3, with several references to Clark on p. 4. Henderson wrote: "if the Yellowstone Park association succeeds in crushing the Cottage Hotel the way it has [James] Clark and [Henry] Klamer, there will be no show of anyone being well treated…in the Park…" Archive Documents 59 through 64 have more on the assignment of Clark's lease to creditors. See also White, Friant, and Letellier to Moses Harris, June 14, 1888, Archive Documents 1119-1120, YNP Archives; and "Local Layout," *Livingston Enterprise*, June 16, 1888, p. 3, which announced that Clark turned his lease and his buildings over to George Wakefield.

722. Henderson in McCrae, as cited, p. 287, and see also pp. 268-269, for more about Clark, including two long letters that Henderson wrote in the names of Clark and G.L.'s son Walter Henderson. Clark and G.L. Henderson were friends even though they were in competition for stage-passengers. Henderson stated that Superintendent Wear "compelled Jas. A. Clark to suspend improvements on his lease and harras[s]ed him into bankruptcy, [Clark] having been compelled to go to Washington at great expense to present his case before the Department [of Interior]." Archive Document 1024-A, G.L. Henderson to Capt. M. Harris, February 2, 1888, pp. 4-5, YNP Archives.

723. History Card File, "James A. Clark," YNP Library, says 1894. Photo H-5117 [no date, 1895-1902] shows Clark's Livery present along with the Henderson/Ash Store of 1895. See also J.C. [A.] Clark to D.C. Kingman, March 15, 1885; and Dan C. Kingman to Secretary of Interior, March 25, 1885, both in Marcy Culpin Files, YNP Historian's Office.

724. Department of Interior to Moses Harris, December 16, 1887, in Letters Sent, vol. II, p. 179; and Harris to Clark, March 24, 1888, in Letters Sent, vol. II, p. 226, YNP Archives. See also Letters Sent, vol. II, p. 237 (March 27, 1888) for Clark's vacating at Soda Butte; J.A. Clark to Moses Harris, December 5, 1887, Archive Document 739; Clark to Harris, March 26, 1888, Archive Document 738; and White, Friant, and Letellier to Moses Harris, June 14, 1888, Archive Docu-

ments 1119-1120, YNP Archives. My thanks go to Bob Flather for providing the date of Clark's mail contract.

725. Dick Randall to Jack E. Haynes, February 17, 1955, about "James A. Clark," in JEH Papers, Montana State University, Bozeman, Montana. My thanks go to researcher Bob Flather for alerting me to this information. For mention of Clark's transportation-operation, see "Local Layout," *Livingston Enterprise*, May 25, 1889, p. 5.

726. G., "Summer Saunterings," *Arkansas Gazette* (Little Rock, AR), as cited. Except for his stagecoaching operation, this author has chronicled G.L. Henderson's complete biography in these four places: Lee H. Whittlesey, "The First National Park Interpreter: G.L. Henderson in Yellowstone," *Montana the Magazine of Western History* 46 (Spring, 1996): 26-41; in Whittlesey, *Storytelling in Yellowstone*, chapter nine, pp. 119-166; in Whittlesey, *"This Modern Saratoga of the Wilderness": A History of Mammoth Hot Springs and the Village of Mammoth in Yellowstone National Park* (Mammoth Hot Springs: National Park Service and Colorado State University, in press, 2022), chapter six, p. 181; and in Whittlesey, "G.L. Henderson: From New York Free-Thinker to Yellowstone Gentleman of Science," *Annals of Wyoming* 88 (Summer 2016), 2-16.

727. Whittlesey, *Storytelling in Yellowstone*, pp. 140-143, 145, 201, 318n70; and Haines, *Yellowstone Story*, I, p. 318. Henderson wrote a gracious letter to the Secretary dated June 2, 1885, acknowledging that he would not occupy his position after June 15. *Storytelling*, p. 143 and note 68. For his winter lecture-tour, see "Local Layout" [GLH to go on lecture-tour], *Livingston Enterprise*, January 17, 1885, p. 3; "Lectures on Yellowstone National Park," *Livingston Enterprise*, January 17, 1885, p. 3; and "Personal Points, *Livingston Enterprise*, March 28, 1885, p. 3.

728. Clipping attributed to *Wisconsin State Journal* (Madison, WI), December 30, 1889, in Ash Collection, YNP Archives, quoted completely in Whittlesey, *Storytelling in Yellowstone*, p. 157.

729. Whittlesey, *Storytelling in Yellowstone*, p. 145; "Local Layout" ["Earnest" Henderson has timber on the ground for his building], *Livingston Enterprise*, May 9, 1885, p. 3; "Local Layout" [The Hendersons begin hotel-construction], *Livingston Enterprise*, August 1, 1885, p. 3; [G.L. Henderson], "Park Matters" [Lease of land], *Livingston Enterprise*, March 28 1885, p. 3; and "Yellowstone Park Notes—The Failure of the Appropriations," *Pioneer Press* (St. Paul, Minnesota), August 15, 1886, copy in George Ash Collection, YNP Archives.

730. G.L. Henderson, "Yellowstone Park—The Great Winter Sanitarium for the American Continent," *Livingston Enterprise*, January 30, 1886, p. 4.

731. In this, Henderson appears to have been first to advocate for two classes of hotels in Yellowstone, a position that probably influenced the U.S. Army to keep the existing Wylie and Shaw/Powell operations, and later influenced Horace Albright of the National Park Service to allow and promote the system of lodges to operate along with hotels in the Park. This kind of economic democracy has gradually disappeared from the YNP of today. For these origins, see Henderson in McRae, as cited, pp. 287-289.

732. Supplies for the hotel and the family's contract were listed in Ledger 6290, George Ash Collection, pp. 127-139, YNP Archives. The quote is from Henderson, *Yellowstone Park Manual and Guide*, 1885, p. 1, feature #22, and the hotel rate is from p. 4, col. 3. See also Whittlesey, *Storytelling in Yellowstone*, p. 145. Cottage Hotel letterhead stationery can be found in the George Ash Collection, YNP Archives. Henderson's daughter Jennie Henderson was not included in the contract, probably because she had married John Dewing by this time and was preparing to resume her previous position at Mammoth as postmistress. For Jennie's marriage, see "That Elopment" [*sic*], *Bozeman Weekly Chronicle*, December 8, 1886, p. 3. Meanwhile, Jennie's sister, Barbara G.H. Swanson, had received a divorce from Oscar S. Swanson at Evanston, Wyoming in late April of 1886, per "Local Layout," *Livingston Enterprise*, May 1, 1886, p. 3; and then G.L. Henderson's

oldest child, Helen L. Henderson, married Charles H. Stuart on November 15, 1887, per "Local Layout," *Livingston Enterprise*, November 19, 1887, p. 3. Jennie divorced John Dewing and took her time marrying again, finally tying the knot with George Ash in June of 1893, per "Local Layout," *Livingston Enterprise*, July 1, 1893, p. 5.

733. In accordance with his interest in politics, G.L. Henderson served that day as an election judge at the precinct of Mammoth Hot Springs, where, on election day, 47 men and 11 women voted for local justices of the peace and constables, and of course for president of the United States—a race between Grover Cleveland and James G. Blaine. See L[iberty] C[ap][G.L. Henderson], "National Park Elections," *Livingston* (MT) *Enterprise*, November 8, 1884, p. 3. The opening of Henderson's Cottage Hotel is told in Whittlesey, *"This Modern Saratoga,"* chapter six, but see also G.L. Henderson, "A Garden of Eden" [at Cottage Hotel on Christmas day], *Bozeman Weekly Chronicle*, January 4, 1888, p. 2. The McClintock photo can also be seen in Whittlesey, *Storytelling in Yellowstone*, p. 150. The stagecoach company at Quincy, Illinois was the E.M. Miller & Company (1857-1930), which once hired up to three hundred men. It can be seen at http://www.coachbuilt.com/bui/m/miller_em/miller_em.htm and was owned by Emerson M. Miller (b. 1836). See also Jack Hilbing, "Buggies to Hearses: The E.M. Miller Company" at http://hsqac.org/buggies-hearses-e-m-miller-company-jack-hilbing/.

734. Henderson family ledger, Army Records, Bound Volume 141, entry for October 4, 1885, YNP Archives.

735. G.L. Henderson, "At the National Park—Incidents Connected with the Opening of the Tourist Season—Some of the Most Beautiful Places to Visit—The Scenery, Etc., Etc.," *Livingston Enterprise*, July 10, 1886, p. 4; and G.L. Henderson, "Park Notes," *Livingston Enterprise*, October 2, 1886, p. 3.

736. G.L.H[enderson]., "Interesting Description of New Wonders in the National Park," *Livingston Enterprise*, July 16, 1887, p. 4; and Henderson, *Yellowstone Park Manual and Guide*, 1888, p. 2, feature #16, "Norris Sinks." In his "Interesting Description," Henderson identified the original event as having occurred in 1886.

737. Henderson, "Park Notes," *Bozeman Weekly Chronicle*, November 16, 1887, p. 1.

738. X. [G.L. Henderson], "Park Notes," *Livingston Enterprise*, June 25, 1887, p. 1; and [G.L. Henderson], "Our Park Visit," *Livingston Enterprise*, July 23, 1887, p. 3.

739. X [G.L. Henderson]., "Park Notes," *Livingston Enterprise*, June 25, 1887, p. 1.

740. [G.L. Henderson], "Our Park Visit," *Livingston Enterprise*, July 23, 1887, p. 3. For more on Henderson's battle against the railroad-monopoly, see Whittlesey, *Storytelling in Yellowstone*, pp. 146-150, 153-155. Henderson's first YNP writings were sent to the St. Paul *Pioneer Press*, and they began appearing in the *Livingston Enterprise*, or at least the first column about him appeared, on July 16, 1883, as "Park Notes," p. 1.

741. G.L. Henderson, [Part I] "Wonderland—Facts That Seem Impossible—The Mammoth Springs—The Grand Terraces—Origin, Antiquity, Growth and Modes of Action," *The New North-West* (Deer Lodge, MT), November 18, 1887, p. 2; and G.L. Henderson, [Part II] "Wonderland—Facts That Seem Impossible—The Mammoth Springs—The Grand Terraces—Origin, Antiquity, Growth and Modes of Action," *The New North-West*, November 25, 1887, p. 2.

742. G.L. Henderson, "Park Notes," *Bozeman Weekly Chronicle*, November 16, 1887, p. 1. See also "The National Park," in the same issue, p. 2.

743. Henderson's purchase of horses is in Conceited Simpleton, "Upper Yellowstone Notes," *Livingston Enterprise*, May 26, 1888, p. 1. Excelsior Geyser is in G.L. Henderson, "Excelsior Geyser in Active Eruption," *Livingston Enterprise*, May 12, 1888, p. 1; Henderson, "First in the Park—

Hammond at Hell's Half Acre—The Great Excelsior Geyser in Action—A Sermon at Mammoth Hot Springs," *Helena Weekly Herald*, May 24, 1888, p. 7; and other articles cited in Whittlesey, "Wonderland Nomenclature," 1988, entry for Excelsior Geyser. G.L. Henderson's seven-part series of articles about guiding (former U.S. Senator) Roscoe Conkling in 1883 were published in *Helena Weekly Herald* in April 26, May 3 (two articles), May 10, May 17, May 31, and June 7, 1888. Conkling's death was treated in "Roscoe Conkling Dead," *New-York Tribune*, April 18, 1888, pp 1-2; and "Roscoe Conkling is Dead," *The Sun* (New York, NY), April 18, 1888, p. 1.

744. "Geyser" and G.L.H., "Excelsior Geyser in Active Eruption," *Livingston Enterprise*, May 12, 1888, p. 1; [G.L. Henderson], "The Park—The Opening of the Wonderland Season—Tourist Parties Going to See the Excelsior," *Helena Weekly Herald*, May 31, 1888, p. 8; and G.L.H., "Park Notes," *Livingston Enterprise*, June 2, 1888, p. 1.

745. "Mr. G.L. Henderson of Mammoth Hot Springs," *The New North-West* (Deer Lodge, MT), June 8, 1888, p. 2. Annual park visitation has been reported in Haines, *Yellowstone Story*, II, p. 478.

746. G.L.H., "Park Notes," *Livingston Enterprise*, June 2, 1888, p. 1; G.L. Henderson, "Excelsior Geyser," *Livingston Enterprise*, June 9, 1888, p. 1; G.L. Henderson, "Cork It Up" [Excelsior], *Livingston Enterprise*, June 23, 1888, p. 3; and G.L. Henderson, "Rev. E.P. Hammond Enquires About Excelsior," *Livingston Enterprise*, July 28, 1888, p. 4.

747. G.L. Henderson, *Yellowstone Park Manual and Guide*, second edition [Livingston, MT: Livingston Enterprise printing, 1888], a guidebook published as a newspaper. There is a copy of this rare newspaper in National Archives, RG 57, Arnold Hague Papers, Reference File Reports of Superintendent of Yellowstone National Park, 1887-1903, folder 117, and also a copy at YNP Library. The *Enterprise* reported the guidebook's actual date of publication a week later in "Local Layout," *Livingston Enterprise*, August 18, 1888, p. 3, adding that "the demand for them has been quite active since their issue."

748. The arguments for this status have been made in Whittlesey, *Storytelling in Yellowstone*, pp. 153, 165-166.

749. H.W. Chase and G.M. Clark quoting Bob Burdette, "California and Connecticut Meet," *Livingston Enterprise*, July 14, 1888, p. 4; and "Yellowstone Park Manual and Guide," *Livingston Enterprise*, June 27, 1885, p. 3.

750. "The Yellowstone Park—Items of Interest from the Wonderland of the World," *Livingston Enterprise*, June 20, 1885, p. 3.

751. "Local Layout" [NPRR removes Swanson for soliciting], *Livingston Enterprise*, August 25, 1888, p. 3.

752. G.L. Henderson, "Lower Geyser Basin—A Glance at the Unfrequented Wonders of That Region," *Livingston Enterprise*, July 18, 1885, p. 1; L[iberty] C[ap][G.L.Henderson], "Park Notes," *Livingston Enterprise*, April 25, 1885, p. 3; Henderson, "Yellowstone Park—New Wonders in the National Park Described," *Reno* (NV) *Weekly Gazette*, May 28, 1885, p. 6 (this last article also appeared in *Daily Morning Astorian* [Astoria, OR], October 23, 1885, p. 1); and see generally G.L. Henderson, *Yellowstone Park: Past, Present, and Future* (Washington, DC: Gibson Brothers Printers and Bookbinders, 1891), pp. 7-9.

753. For Henderson and Glen Africa Basin, see his *Yellowstone Park Manual and Guide*, 1888, p. 2, feature #8. For Larry Mathews at Trout Creek Lunch Station, see Whittlesey, "'You Only Count One Here!': Larry Mathews and Democracy in Yellowstone, 1887-1904," *Yellowstone History Journal* 1#1 (2018): 3-27; and Whittlesey, "'I Haven't Time to Kiss Everybody!': Larry Mathews Entertains in Yellowstone, 1887-1904," *Montana the Magazine of Western History* 57 (Summer, 2007): 58-73.

754. "Railroad Morality," in Henderson, *Yellowstone Park Manual and Guide*, 1888, p. 3.

755. George M. Clark, in "Friendly Letters," July 10, 1888, in Henderson, *Yellowstone Park Manual and Guide*, 1888, p. 4.

756. Mrs. T.S.C. Lowe in "Friendly Letters," July 5, 1888, in Henderson, *Yellowstone Park Manual and Guide*, 1888, p. 4.

757. Henry Klamer as a guide for Henderson was mentioned in "Yellowstone Park—California and Connecticut Meet," *Livingston Enterprise*, July 14, 1888 p. 4. The forced sale of the Firehole Hotel of Klamer and George Graham was mentioned in "Senators Farwell, Cameron, and Vest Interviewed at the Firehole Hotel by Citizens of Illinois," *Yellowstone Park Manual and Guide*, 1888, p. 4. As for Walter J. Henderson who served as Assistant Manager of the Cottage Hotel Association, an article by G.L. Henderson entitled "Park Paragraphs" (*Livingston Enterprise*, March 31, 1888, p. 1) stated that Walter served as a walking guide on the terraces on March 18 for tourist Horace F. Brown. Thus, Walter was a tour guide at least once for the family and probably a lot more. Walter Henderson married Eva S. Fitzgerald on January 3, 1889, per "Local Layout," *Livingston Enterprise*, January 5, 1889, p. 3, thus powerfully allying the Henderson family with Gardiner's huge and successful Fitzgerald family.

758. Henderson, paraphrasing what an NPRR official told him, in *Yellowstone Park Manual and Guide*, 1888, p. 4.

759. Smith in Henderson, *Yellowstone Park Manual and Guide*, 1888, p. 4.

760. H.W. Chase and G.M. Clark, "California and Connecticut Meet," *Livingston Enterprise*, July 14, 1888, p. 4.

761. George A. West, in "Friendly Letters," in Henderson, *Yellowstone Park Manual and Guide*, 1888, p. 4.

762. G.L. Henderson, "Park Notes," *Livingston Enterprise*, January 26, 1889, p. 2.

763. G.L. Henderson, "The National Park—A Mild Winter—Gathering a Late Crop of Ice—Subsidence of the Excelsior Geyser—The Monarch Quiets Down and Another Spouter Takes Its Place," *Helena Weekly Herald*, February 7, 1889, p. 7.

764. "Local Layout" [G.L. Henderson left for Washington; and Mr. Henderson has received an offer for his hotel], *Livingston Enterprise*, February 16, 1889, p. 3; and "Blaine Received Them," *Helena Weekly Herald*, March 7, 1889, p. 7. See also G.L. Henderson, "Helena Letter," *Livingston Enterprise*, May 11, 1889, p. 6.

765. G.L. Henderson, "The Park Hotels—The Two Associations to be Consolidated—The Reasons Therefor," *Helena Weekly Herald*, May 2, 1889, p. 7; "Personal Points" [W.J. Henderson], *Livingston Enterprise*, May 4, 1889, p. 3; "Park Visitors," *Helena Weekly Herald*, May 9, 1889, p. 5; and "Local Layout" [GLH lectures in Oregon], *Livingston Enterprise*, May 25, 1889, p. 3.

766. G.L. Henderson, "Park Hotel Management," *Livingston Enterprise*, May 11, 1889, *Enterprise Supplement*, p. 5.

767. Charles Gibson in Thomas McRae, "Inquiry into the Management and Control of the Yellowstone National Park," 52d Cong., 1st Sess., House Report 1956, SN-3051, July 20, 1892, p. 82-83, 88, and 288.

768. Henderson to C.S. Mellen, February 20, 1900; and E.C. Waters to Henderson, May 21, 1889, both in Ash Collection, YNP Archives. For more on this complex story, see Whittlesey, *Storytelling in Yellowstone*, pp. 151-156.

769. Henderson, "The Two Wonderlands," *Livingston Enterprise*, December 3, 1898, p. 1; Henderson,

Yellowstone Park: Past, Present, and Future, pp. 1, 4; Henderson, "Here's Henderson," *Helena Daily Herald*, September 24, 1890, pp. 2, 6; Henderson to Mellen, February 20, 1900, as cited; and Archive Document 1004, YNP Archives.

770. G.L. Henderson, "World of Wonders—The National Park Revisited—Geyser Transformations and Other Changes—Interesting Letter from Prof. Henderson an Accepted Wonderland Authority," *Helena Weekly Herald*, August 1, 1889, p. 2. For speeches given by Henderson, see "Park Lectures—Appreciative Audiences Attend the Evening Lectures of Professor Henderson at Mammoth Hot Springs," *Helena Weekly Herald*, September 12, 1889, p. 8.

771. G.L Henderson, "Yellowstone Park Paragraphs," *Livingston Enterprise*, August 10, 1889, p. 2.

772. G.L. Henderson, "The National Park—Its Protection Against Vandalism—Capt. Boutelle's Administration Commenced," *Helena Weekly Herald*, August 29, 1889, p. 6. See also William A. Imes, "An Open Letter" [to G.L. Henderson], *Livingston Enterprise*, August 31, 1889, p. 1. The new U.S. Army superintendent was Captain Frazier A. Boutelle, who would serve from June 1, 1889 to February 16, 1891. Haines, *Yellowstone Story*, II, pp. 453-454; and Whittlesey, *Yellowstone Place Names*, as cited, 2006, p. 288.

773. Henderson, "Naming a Geyser," *Norristown* (PA) *Weekly Herald*, January 19, 1889, preserved in Ash Scrapbook, pp. 10-11, G.L.H. Ash collection, YNP Archives.

774. Charles Taylor Gibson, born February 16, 1825, married Virginia C. Gamble (1830-1907) on May 29, 1851, and they had seven children by 1870, who were Louisa, Victor, Archie, Preston, Charles Eldon, Lizzie, and Gerolt. Charles T. Gibson died October 27, 1899. Missouri Death Records; St. Louis, Missouri Marriage Records; U.S. Census of 1870, St. Louis, June 27, 1870, p. 105; and U.S. Census of 1880, St. Louis, November 8, 1880, pp. 10-11, all accessed via Ancestry. com on April 3, 2014.

775. "Testimony of Charles Gibson," in McRae, "Inquiry," p. 184; and "Yellowstone Park Syndicate," *Livingston Enterprise*, April 3, 1886, p. 3. This article stated that the leases were issued in Washington to Gibson in March, and Gibson himself gave the date as March 20. The leases were issued for ten years at a lease-rate for YPA of $500 per year. "Personal—Secretary Lamar has Leased," *Anglo-American Times* (London, England), April 30, 1886, p. 14. Gibson's purchase of YNPIC assets was reported at Evanston, Wyoming in "Local Layout," *Livingston Enterprise*, May 17, 1886, p. 3, and confirmed by Gibson himself in McRae, "Inquiry," pp. 18-19, 233, 236-238, 253. Gibson's lease of December 20, 1885 is at pp. 246-250. See also "The Yellowstone Park" [formation of YPA], *St. Paul Daily Globe*, April 24, 1886, p. 6.

If we believe H.C. Davis, Assistant Passenger Agent of the Northern Pacific Railroad whose hand was in Yellowstone in the form of loans to the new company, Davis himself was the person who got Charles Gibson and friends interested in purchasing the assets of the old YNPIC. Because the old company "was bankrupt with two receivers fighting for possession," stated Davis, "it was deemed…impossible to reorganize it on any sound financial basis, and so I set about to…interest…a party of well-known capitalists" including Charles Gibson. See *Chicago Tribune* interviewing H.C. Davis in "The Yellowstone Park—Six New Hotels to be Built," *Omaha* (NE) *Daily Bee*, April 29, 1886, p. 5; and "Tourists in the National Park" [arrangements for the season of 1886], *St. Paul Daily Globe*, March 10, 1886, p. 4. Gibson and the Clerk of Interior, Edward Dawson, both told their versions of how Gibson obtained YPA and the leases in McRae, "Inquiry," pp. 75-106, 184-185, and 240-277, especially pp. 243-253.

776. "Montana Mention" [Gibson in early 1886], *Yellowstone Journal* (Miles City, MT), January 29, 1886, p. 1, col. 6.

777. "Local Layout" [Wakefield leaves for park], *Livingston Enterprise*, May 17, 1886, p. 3.

778. "Local Layout" [Haynes sells out to Wakefield], *Livingston Enterprise*, August 7, 1886, p. 3; and

"Notice of Dissolution of Partnership," same issue, p. 1.

779. "The G.A.R. Boys," *St. Paul Daily Globe*, August 15, 1886, p. 5; and Gibson in McRae, "Inquiry," pp. 18-19.

780. W.G. Pearce, "Testimony of W.G. Pearce," in McRae, "Inquiry," pp. 118-119; and Gibson, "Testimony," pp. 184, 260. Wakefield's moving of four hundred people is in "Local Layout," *Livingston Enterprise*, August 28, 1886, p. 3. See also "Local Layout," *Livingston Enterprise*, August 21, 1886, p. 3, wherein Wakefield moved 270 people; and "Yellowstone Park—A Large Influx of Tourists—A Brush Fire on the Mountains," *St. Paul Daily Globe*, August 22, 1886, p. 5, which says Wakefield moved 400 people.

781. Gibson, "Testimony," in McRae, "Inquiry," p. 184; and "Montana Mention" [Gibson calls for elaborate improvements in Park], *Daily Yellowstone Journal* (Miles City, MT), January 29, 1886, p. 1, last column. For a recent look at E.C. Waters, see generally Mike Stark, *Wrecked in Yellowstone: Greed, Obsession, and the Untold Story of Yellowstone's Most Infamous Shipwreck* (Helena: Riverbend Publishing, 2016).

782. Gibson, no date, "Reply to Secretary Noble's Protest," in McRae, "Inquiry," p. 78; "Testimony of George Wakefield," p. 139; Gibson, "Statement," p. 187; and J.H. Dean in Archive Document 590 [ordering YPA employees to wear badges], 1886, YNP Archives. George Wakefield stated in his 1892 testimony to congress that his drivers continued to wear badges, at this point "on their hats," after the company received its new lease in 1889. Wakefield in McRae, "Inquiry," p. 139. That Gibson was indeed "President" of YPA from 1886 to 1892 was attested to by YPA's financial officer Pearce in "Affidavit of W.G. Pearce," April 27, 1892, in McRae, p. 108.

783. "Yellowstone Park," *Chicago Daily Tribune*, June 17, 1886, p. 3; and "Opening of Hotel Accommodations in the Park," *Livingston Enterprise*, June 19, 1886, p. 3, which confirmed that the hotel opened on June 15. Telephone linemen at work were mentioned by a journalist known only as W.H.R. in "A Yellowstone Trip," *Philadelphia* (PA) *Inquirer*, August 4, 1886, p. 7. In congressional testimony, Gibson and Wakefield each gave his own reasons for why telephones were so fervently needed in the park. Gibson and Wakefield in McCrae, "Inquiry," pp. 19, 24, 138-139, 260.

784. Gibson stated (in McRae, "Inquiry," p. 20) that his company in late 1885 spent $1,600 to build a road to reach the spot south of Cascade Creek for which he understood that his company had a lease to erect the first Canyon Hotel, a prefabricated building located at the present Brink of Upper Falls parking area, a bit west of the present restroom and just east of the meadow where the rental-cabins would stand in the 1950s. The prefab building was permitted on May 27, 1886 in the park's *Annual Report of the Superintendent*, jointly written by David W. Wear and Captain Moses Harris, to wit, as quoted by historian Aubrey Haines: "Permission was granted Mr. Gibson to erect a temporary building to be used for hotel purposes at the Grand Cañon…with the understanding that it should be removed on or before the 1st day of August, 1886. It was not removed and continued in service until 1891…" Haines, *Yellowstone Story*, II, p. 402n60.

785. At the end of his 1885 road report, Lt. Dan requested $10,000 extra for 1886, in order: "To construct a new road from Norris Geyser Basin to the Yellowstone Falls (12 miles)." Kingman, handwritten [Report to] "The Chief of Engineers, U.S. Army, Washington, D.C.," November 23, 1885, in NA, RG 48, microfilm 62, roll 3, folder 4 of 4 (hardcopy at YNP Library), pp. 28-29.

786. Gibson said three years later that he was never able to get Col. Muldrow to issue the assignment to him of YNPIC's old lease, but he apparently proceeded for three years with confidence that he could eventually get that lease. One wonders whether Carroll Hobart had found some way to legally hold up the lease, in hoping to stall for time to help his old company (then in arrears) and his ex-partner Rufus Hatch. If so, that ploy did not work, and Charles Gibson and his partners purchased YPA. Gibson in McRae, *Inquiry*, pp. 19-20.

787. Haines, *Yellowstone Story*, II, pp. 133, 215, 255; Charles Gibson to Secretary of Interior John Noble, no date [late 1888 or early 1889], in McRae, "Inquiry," pp. 19, 24, 260; and W.H.R., "A Yellowstone Trip—Interesting Account of the Marvels of the Great American Park," *Philadelphia* (PA) *Inquirer*, August 4, 1886, p. 7.

788. Gibson in McRae, "Inquiry," p. 23.

789. Edith Ritchie, oral interview of her by Aubrey L. Haines, November 7, 1961, tape 61-3, side 2, YNP Archives; and James Norris "Dick" Randall (George Perkins, ed.), "The Writings of Dick Randall," unpublished manuscript, no date [about 1954], donated to YNP Library, 2004, p. 61. Besides this manuscript, Randall's life story has been told in several books, including L.W. "Gay" Randall, *Footprints Along the Yellowstone* (San Antonio: The Naylor Company, 1961); and Roberta C. Cheney and Clyde Erskine, *Music, Saddles, and Flapjacks: Dudes at the OTO Ranch* (Missoula: Mountain Press, [1978]).

790. "Justice in this Country," *Livingston Enterprise*, July 24, 1886, p. 4.

791. "Wanted to Lick the Editor," *Great Falls* (MT) *Tribune*, September 18, 1886, p. 3. This story attributed its source to the "Independent," presumably the Helena *Independent*, but a search of that newspaper has failed to turn up the story.

792. "Midst the Madding Throng" [a ruckus in Miles City], St. Paul *Daily Globe*, June 22, 1886, p. 4; "Howard Hetrick" [Hetrick forms Montana partnership with James Harvie], St. Paul *Daily Globe*, October 17, 1886, p. 10; and "The Legislature—Press Representatives [Harvie]," *Sacramento* (CA) *Daily Record-Union*, January 3, 1887, p. 3.

793. Captain Moses Harris to Secretary of Interior, December 27, 1887, in Letters Sent, Vol. II, YNP Archives.

794. The Secretary of the Interior could not yet do this legally, as Gibson discussed in McCrae, "Inquiry," pp. 78-79.

795. Gibson to Secretary John Noble, no date [1889], in McCrae, "Inquiry," p. VII.

796. "Wakefield Stage Line" [Livingston to Mammoth], advertisement in *Livingston Enterprise*, January 8, 1887, p. 3; "The Bozeman Electric Company" advertisement in *Bozeman* (MT) *Weekly Chronicle*, March 2, 1887, p. 4; "City News" [sells electric business], *Bozeman* (MT) *Weekly Chronicle*, April 6, 1887, p. 3; and "City News" [purchases real estate], *Bozeman Weekly Chronicle*, March 23, 1887, p. 30.

797. "Local Layout" [Wakefield and Deutch], *Livingston Enterprise*, December 4, 1886, p. 3.

798. "Neighborhood News" [Deep snow still in park], *New North-West* (Deer Lodge, MT), May 20, 1887, p. 5; "George W. Wakefield" [hires painter; has new buggies], Bozeman *Avant Courier*, May 19, 1887, p. 3; "Personal Points" [Wakefield prepares], *Bozeman Weekly Chronicle*, June 15, 1887, p. 3; and "Local Layout" [Maughn is Wakefield's agent in Livingston], *Livingston Enterprise*, June 18, 1887, p. 3.

799. Hamm seems like the most likely driver, as noted by both Aubrey Haines and Jack Haynes, but G.L. Henderson says the driver was Charles Kern and Haynes has noted that the driver, if not Hamm, was "possibly named Hunter." See X. [G.L. Henderson], "Park Notes," *Livingston Enterprise*, July 9, 1887, p. 1; Haines, *Yellowstone Story*, II, p. 12; and Jack Ellis Haynes, *Yellowstone Stage Holdups* (Bozeman: Haynes Studios, Inc., "enlarged edition," 1959), p. 8.

800. A money-conversion calculator is available at http://www.in2013dollars.com/1887-dollars-in-2015, which can be adjusted there to the current year.

801. J.B. Kirkbride quoted in Haines, *Yellowstone Story*, I, pp. 12, 389n15. There seems to be no basis for the claim that this robbery was a parodied hold-up, rather than a real one. G.L. Henderson

started this interpretation from the seemingly bungled nature of the affair ("Park Notes," *Livingston Enterprise*, July 9, 1887, p. 1), treating the episode very lightly and calling it "an attempt to parody Dick Turpin." Turpin was an eighteenth-century English highwayman. For other subscribers to that notion, see Bill and Doris Whithorn, *Pics and Quotes of Yellowstone* (Livingston: Park County News [1972]), p. 37.

802. "Stage Held Up—National Park Tourists Get a Taste of 'Rowdy West' Life," *Great Falls Tribune*, July 9, 1887, p. 1; "Yellowstone Park Stage Robbers," *Chicago Daily Tribune*, November 20, 1887, p. 18. See also "Highway Robbery," *Bozeman Weekly Chronicle*, July 13, 1887, p. 2; and "City News—Mr. George Wakefield," *Bozeman Weekly Chronicle*, July 13, 1887, p. 3.

803. Haines, *Yellowstone Story*, II, p. 13; and "That Park Episode," *Livingston Enterprise*, July 9, 1887, p. 3.

804. Haines, *Yellowstone Story*, II, p. 14; and Haynes, *Yellowstone Stage Holdups*, pp. 7-9.

805. Higgenbotham's name was variously spelled by the newspapers. My spelling is from Haines and Haynes, who are arguably the most reliable sources about him.

806. "City News" [the stage robbers], *Bozeman Weekly Chronicle*, November 9, 1887, p. 3; Haines, *Yellowstone Story*, II, p. 13; and Haynes, *Yellowstone Stage Holdups*, p. 9.

807. "Local Layout" [arrest], *Livingston Enterprise*, November 5, 1887, p. 3; and "Local Layout" [guilty plea], *Livingston Enterprise*, December 3, 1887, p. 3.

808. "A High Celestial," *Daily Yellowstone Journal* (Miles City, MT), August 20, 1887, p. 1, attributed to "Herald."

809. Haines, *Yellowstone Story*, II, pp. 17, 390n28.

810. J.W.R[edington], "On the Yellowstone—Past and Present Wanderings in the Great Wonderland—Capt. J.W. Redington Revisits the Scenes of the Nez Perce War," Portland (OR) *Oregonian*, September 25, 1887, p. 2; "Local Layout" [E.C. Culver goes to Mammoth to accept a position with transportation department], *Livingston Enterprise*, July 9, 1887, p. 3; "Local Layout" [Mrs. Culver dies; husband is manager of freight transportation], *Livingston Enterprise*, March 9, 1889, p. 3; and Haines, *Yellowstone Story*, II, pp. 23, 65, 185.

811. [James Mills], "Re-Visited—The Yellowstone Park in 1872 and 1887," *New North-West* (Deer Lodge, MT), September 9, 1887, p. 3. This last paragraph also appeared in "Things Territorial," *Bozeman Weekly Chronicle*, September 14, 1887, p. 3. For another excellent endorsement of Wakefield's service this summer, see Luther L. Holden in "A Route for Tourists—An Experienced Man Talks about the Northern Pacific," Portland (OR) *Oregonian*, August 9, 1887, p. 8: "I never saw a better outfit of stage horses, and the passenger wagons are excellent. The drivers are the most obliging and courteous men of their vocation that I have ever met anywhere, and the fact that there has not been an accident in the park for several years speaks volumes in itself."

812. Finck was not wrong in proffering this allegation, and Wakefield's advertisement the following summer continued the practice. See "Excursion Rates to National Park," [Wakefield's rates], *New North-West* (Deer Lodge, MT), July 13, 1888, p. 3.

813. H.T. Finck, "A Week in Yellowstone Park," *The Nation*, vol. 45, September 1, 1887, p. 169. This article also appeared in *American Settler* (London, England), September 24 and October 1, 1887.

814. "Tri-weekly Stage from Livingston to Castle Mountain," *Livingston Enterprise*, October 1, 1887, p. 3; advertisement for "Livingston and Castle Stage Line," *Livingston Enterprise*, October 22, 1887, p. 4; and "Local Layout" [Adam Deem and Castle], *Livingston Enterprise*, December 3, 1887, p 3. For Wakefield's winter trips to Mammoth, see *Livingston Enterprise*, January 28, 1888, p. 3; February 4, 1888, p. 3; and *New North-West* (Deer Lodge, MT), March 30, 1888, p. 2. For the dance-party, see "A Recherché Affair," *Bozeman Weekly Chronicle*, April 11, 1888, p. 3.

815. "Personal Points" [Wakefield goes to park], *Bozeman Weekly Chronicle*, May 2, 1888, p. 3; and "Local Layout" [Cinnabar Basin per *Courier*], *Livingston Enterprise*, May 12, 1888, p. 3.

816. "Personal Points" [Wakefield ready for Whitcomb parties], *Bozeman Weekly Chronicle*, May 30, 1888, p. 3; and "Local Layout" [buys out J.A. Clark], *Livingston Enterprise*, June 16, 1888, p. 3.

817. Low Rates," *St. Paul Daily Globe*, August 16, 1888, p. 2, column 4; and NPRR, "Yellowstone National Park, Pacific Coast, and Alaska," *Springfield* (OH) *Daily Republic*, June 23, 1888, p. 4.

818. "Local Layout" [Clark "disposes of his lease and buildings to George Wakefield"], *Livingston Enterprise*, June 16, 1888, p. 3.

819. Lee H. Whittlesey, *"This Modern Saratoga of the Wilderness!": A History of Mammoth Hot Springs and the Village of Mammoth in Yellowstone National Park* (NPS and Colorado State University, 2022, in press), pp. 160-162; and Wakefield in McRae, "Inquiry," pp. 131-132.

820. For the history of Excelsior Geyser generally, see Whittlesey "Wonderland Nomenclature," that entry in 1988 manuscript, Montana Historical Society; and Lee H. Whittlesey, "Monarch of All These Mighty Wonders—Tourists and Yellowstone's Excelsior Geyser, 1881-1890," *Montana the Magazine of Western History* 40#2 (Spring, 1990), cover and pp. 2-15. For specific 1888 material on it, see "Excelsior Geyser Again Playing," *The Sun* (New York, NY), May 19, 1888, p. 4; "Geyser" (author), "Excelsior Geyser in Active Eruption," *Livingston Enterprise*, May 12, 1888, p. 1; G.L. Henderson, "Hell's Half Acre," same issue and page; G.L.H., "Park Notes," *Livingston Enterprise*, June 2, 1888, p. 1; G.L. Henderson, "Excelsior Geyser," *Livingston Enterprise*, June 9, 1888, p. 1; G.L. Henderson, "Rev. E.P. Hammond Enquires about the Excelsior," *Livingston Enterprise*, July 28, 1888, p. 4; G.L. Henderson, "First in the Park—Hammond at Hell's Half Acre," *Helena* (MT) *Weekly Herald*, May 24, 1888, p. 7; and G.L.H., "Hell's Half Acre—The Marvelous Eruptions," *Helena* (MT) *Weekly Herald*, June 7, 1888, p. 2.

821. "The Iowa Press Excursionists," *Butte* (MT) *Semi-weekly Miner*, July 21, 1888, p. 2; and "The Press Excursion," *Livingston Enterprise*, September 8, 1888, p. 2.

822. "In the National Park, Bob Burdette," *Livingston Enterprise*, July 28, 1888, p. 3; a longer version of the same story in *Brooklyn* (NY) *Eagle*, July 15, 1888, p. 8; "Dissipated Geysers, Bob Burdette on the Deleterious Effects," *Helena Weekly Herald*, August 2, 1888, p. 4; and "Robert Burdette," *Bozeman Weekly Chronicle*, July 4, 1888, p. 3. See also, "Local News" [Burdette's two lectures], *Bozeman Weekly Chronicle*, June 6, 1888, p. 3; "Local Layout" [Burdette's Livingston lectures], *Livingston Enterprise*, June 23, 1888, p. 3; "Personal Points" [X. Beidler goes to park for summer], *Livingston Enterprise*, July 7, 1888, p. 3; and "Local News" [X. Beidler is park attraction], *Bozeman Weekly Chronicle*, September 26, 1888, p. 3. For park visitation, see Haines, *Yellowstone Story*, II, p. 478.

823. "Winding Up the Story—The Visit of the Editors to Yellowstone Park," *The Upper Des Moines* (Algona, Iowa), August 22, 1888, p. 1; and P., "The Wonders of the Yellowstone Park," *Iowa State Reporter* (Waterloo, IA), August 2, 1888, p. 4. The author of the first piece listed here was probably Harvey Ingham of Algona, and the author of the second one was likely Matt Parrott of Waterloo. The complete list of these Iowa editors appeared in "Moulders of Opinion," *St. Paul Daily Globe*, July 25, 1888, p. 2.

824. R.M.D., "Wonderland," *Sioux County Herald* (Orange City, IA), August 23, 1888, p. 5; and [Harvey Ingham], "Winding up the Story—The Visit of the Editors to Yellowstone Park—Reaching Their Journey's End," *The Upper Des Moines* (Algona, IA), August 22, 1888, p. 1.

825. Moses Harris and F.A. Boutelle, *Report of the Superintendent of the Yellowstone National Park to the Secretary of the Interior, 1889* (Washington: GPO, 1889), p. 6, dated June 1, 1889 and discussing season of 1888.

826. [Mrs. S.], "Wonders of Wonderland—The Famous Yellowstone—Five Days among Its Geysers, Its Peaks, Its Passes," *Newport* (RI) *Mercury*, October 6, 1888, p. 1. The author, a "Mrs. S.," was identified at the end of Part II (October 13) of this account.

827. J.E. Williams, *Vacation Notes, Summer of 1888, Copied from the Amherst Record* (Amherst, Massachusetts: no publisher [Amherst Record], no date [1889?]), pp. 12-13.

828. Williams, *Vacation Notes*, p. 13.

829. Williams, *Vacation Notes*, pp. 13-14.

830. Williams, *Vacation Notes*, p. 14.

831. "Yellowstone Park—Attractive Natural Features and Bad Hotel Accommodations," *St. Louis* (MO) *Republic*, August 26, 1888, p. 21.

832. H.Z. Osborne, *A Midsummer Ramble, Being a Descriptive Sketch of the Yellowstone National Park* (No place [Los Angeles]: Los Angeles Evening Express, no date [probably 1889]), pp. 5-6. This account has also been reproduced in Lee H. Whittlesey and Elizabeth A. Watry, *Ho! For Wonderland: Travelers' Accounts of Yellowstone, 1872-1914* (Albuquerque: University of New Mexico Press, 2009), pp. 124-155.

833. [Mrs. S.], "Wonders of Wonderland—The Famous Yellowstone—Five Days among Its Geysers, Its Peaks, Its Passes," *Newport* (RI) *Mercury*, October 6, 1888, p. 1.

834. [Mrs. S.], "Wonders of Wonderland," as cited.

835. Mrs. S., "Nature's Wonderland—The Great Wonders of the Nation's One Great Park Continued," *Newport* (RI) *Mercury*, October 13, 1888, p. 1.

836. As can be seen in chapter ten, stage-operator G.L. Henderson had been taking his tourists on this route since at least 1886, and now YNPTC was copying it.

837. Mrs. S., "Nature's Wonderland," as cited. The final part of this account was [Mrs.] S., "Westward Bound," *Newport Mercury*, December 8, 1888, p. 1. For Larry Mathews, see Lee H. Whittlesey, "'You Only Count One Here!': Larry Mathews and Democracy in Yellowstone, 1887-1904," *Yellowstone History Journal* 1#1 (2018): 3-27.

838. "Personal Points," *Bozeman Weekly Chronicle*, September 26, 1888, p. 3.

839. "Local Layout," *Livingston Enterprise*, October 18, 1888, p. 3.

840. "Personal Points" [Adam Deem moving to Livingston], *Livingston Enterprise*, October 20, 1888, p. 3; and X. [G.L. Henderson], "Park Branch Notes" [Horr has been granted a post office as soon as George Wakefield signs his name], *Livingston Enterprise*, December 22, 1888, p. 1. For more on this, see Lee H. Whittlesey, *Gateway to Yellowstone: The Raucous Town of Cinnabar on the Montana Frontier* (Helena: Two Dot Books, 2015), p. 109 and its endnotes.

841. For Wakefield's business trip, see "A Busy Man from Bozeman," *Butte Semi-weekly Miner*, February 6, 1889, p. 3. For his mining interests, see Geo. W. Wakefield, "Notice to Co-owners" [who were A.G. Hemphill and Frank Bellar], *Livingston Enterprise*, February 9, 1889, p. 2, col. 4. For his political connections involving barns, see "Carter's Latest Move," *Helena Independent*, March 30, 1889, p. 1. For his distillery interest, see "The Bozeman Distillery," *Helena Weekly Herald*, April 18, 1889, p. 8. For his YPA contract, see Gibson in McRae, "Inquiry," p. 93.

842. Testimony of George W. Wakefield in McRae, "Inquiry," p. 133, reproducing the original contract of May 3, 1889, between Wakefield and officials T.B. Casey (YPA) and T.F. Oakes (Northern Pacific Railroad). Rumors of the sale appeared as early as late March in the newspapers, but the official, confirming story did not appear until May 30. See "Local Layout" [rumors of sale], *Livingston Enterprise*, March 23, 1889, p. 3; "New Corporations," *St. Paul Daily Globe*, May 30,

1889, p. 4; "Local Layout" [Wakefield sells out to NPTC], *Livingston Enterprise*, June 8, 1889, p. 3; and "Local Layout" [Wakefield still manages "YPT company"], *Livingston Enterprise*, November 23, 1889, p. 3, col. 5. YPA official W.G. Pearce stated in his congressional testimony that he and E.C. Waters negotiated the sale of Wakefield's assets to YPA, without help from Gibson, and that the bulk of it occurred in February of 1889. Because this was many weeks before the newspapers got the story, one wonders whether Pearce simply misremembered the date. Pearce in McRae, "Inquiry," p. 119. There is some confusion surrounding it, but the signing of the 1889 leases appears to mark the moment that the name of the company officially went from YPATC to YNPTC. The looming necessary and costly repainting of the stagecoaches appears to have delayed it until sometime in the later 1890s. See McRae, "Inquiry," p. IV; Pearce in McCrae, p. 118; Wakefield in McCrae, p. 139; and Gibson in McCrae, p. 188. Haines has given the names and years as YNPTC, 1891-1898, and YPTC, 1898-1936, while noting that despite these name changes and reorganizations, these names "represent a continuous business operation." Haines, *Yellowstone Story*, II, pp. 133, 402n68.

843. "The Hand of the Prince," Helena *Daily Independent*, March 14, 1892, Morning, p. 5.

844. "Inventory of George W. Wakefield's Stock and Transportation Company...February 6, 1889," in McRae, "Inquiry," pp. 134-137.

845. G.L. Henderson, "Helena Letter," *Livingston Enterprise*, May 11, 1889, p. 6 stated that A.A. Deem was now running a hotel in Helena. "Personal Points," in the same issue, p. 3, stated that Deem's hotel was called the "Capital Hotel." See also "Personal Points" [Deem running Helena hotel], *Livingston Enterprise*, September 21, 1889, p. 5; and "Personal Points" [George Ash is superintendent of the "Wakefield Stage company"], *Livingston Enterprise*, May 4, 1889, p. 5. George Ash's elevation to Wakefield's immediate assistant gave him a foothold in the park and allowed him to eventually marry G.L. Henderson's divorced daughter, Jennie Henderson Dewing, on June 29, 1893. But he was in her life as early as April of 1887 in order for their son G.L.H. Ash to have been born on January 8, 1888 (this baby was named for his grandfather G.L. Henderson). George Ash had been in Bozeman as early as 1876, when he and E. Fridley drove and guided some of the earliest wagon trips to the park. Whittlesey, *Storytelling in Yellowstone*, pp. 199-200. With his wife Jennie, George Ash built and helped operate the present Mammoth General Store in 1895. He died in 1900, leaving a large hole in the Henderson family's operations. See Whittlesey, *"This Modern Saratoga of the Wilderness,"* pp. 221-222; and unabridged edition, pp. 183-193.

846. Gibson in McRae, "Inquiry," p. 82. See also G.L. Henderson, "Park Hotel Management," *Livingston Enterprise Supplement*, May 11, 1889, p. 1; and [Henderson], "Our Park Visit," *Livingston Enterprise*, July 23, 1887, p. 3.

847. R.S. Kayler, "A Trip to the Coast," *Railway Conductor 7*, March 1, 1890, p. 168.

848. Frazier A. Boutelle, *Report of the Superintendent of the Yellowstone National Park to the Secretary of the Interior, 1890* [period of July 1, 1889 through June 30, 1890] (Washington: GPO, 1890), p. 9.

849. Done [pseudonym], "Robb's Ramblings—Second Letter from Our 'Done,'" *Lima* (OH) *Daily Times*, August 1, 1889, p. 4. See also the other installment in the issue of July 27, 1889, p. 4, by "Robb" and entitled "Robb's Ramblings—An Interesting Letter from a Lima Traveler."

850. "The National Park—A Short Ramble Among Its Geysers, Fire Holes, and Canyons," *St. Paul Daily Globe*, July 21, 1889, p. 4.

851. Richard Grant in McRae, "Inquiry," p. 32; Payson Merrill in McRae, "Inquiry," p. 34; "Personal Points" [Hohenschuh will winter in Livingston], *Livingston Enterprise*, October 12, 1889, p. 3; and "Local Layout" [Hohenschuh promoted], *Livingston Enterprise*, October 4, 1890, p. 3.

852. For Beidler, see "Personal Points," *Livingston Enterprise*, June 15, 1889, p. 3; "Personal Points,

Livingston Enterprise, July 6, p. 3; "Local Layout" [fire takes the papers of Beidler's life], *Livingston Enterprise*, September 7, 1889, p. 3; "Personal Points," *Livingston Enterprise*, November 9, 1889, p. 3 [Beidler tells a tall tale to tenderfoot]; and Thompson, *Throw Down the Box!*, p. 86. Beidler worked in the park 1886-1889 as a stagecoach driver.

853. "Personal Points" [purchasing horses], *Livingston Enterprise*, August 24, 1889, p. 3; and "The Fourth in Livingston" [Wakefield's horse racing], *Livingston Enterprise*, July 6, 1889, p. 3.

854. "Personal Points" [two snippets: Wakefield returns from eastern trip; George Ash helps with new horses], *Livingston Enterprise*, May 10, 1890, p. 3; and "Local Layout" [Wakefield purchases still more horses], *Livingston Enterprise*, July 19, 1890, p. 3.

855. "The Editors Trip to See Yellowstone Park," *Daily Northwestern* (Oshkosh, WI), May 15, 1890, p. 4; "Combinations," *Centralia Enterprise and Tribune* (Centralia, WI), August 2, 1890, p. 21; "Brief Notes" [listing names of party], *Green Bay Press-Gazette* (Green Bay, WI), May 3, 1890, p. 3; "Chippewa Falls" [Mrs. George C. Ginty returns home], *The Weekly Leader* (Eau Claire, WI), August 11, 1890, p. 3; and F.B. Ginty, "Dear Uncle Samuel," *Wood County Reporter* (Grand Rapids [Wisconsin Rapids], WI), September 18, 1890, p. 8.

856. "Bogus Editors" quoted in *Chillicothe* (MO) *Constitution-Tribune*, August 27, 1890, p. 2; T., "The Boundless West," *Troy* (MO) *Free Press*, September 5, 1890, p. 1; and "Editorial Jottings," *Rolla* (MO) *New Era*, September 13, 1890, p. 3. For the bear story, see "Good Natured Bears—Bruin at His Best in the Yellowstone National Park," *St. Louis* (MO) *Republic*, September 7, 1890, section three, p. 17. For the "magnificent stage lines" quotations, see "The Yellowstone Park—A Kingdom Set Apart for the Recreation of a Nation," *Rolla* (MO) *New Era*, September 20, 1890, p. 3.

857. "Local Layout" [Michigan Press Association], *Livingston Enterprise*, July 26, 1890, p. 3; and "Wolverine Editors," *Salt Lake Herald*, August 5, 1890, p. 5. See also, "Michigan Editors in the City," *Chicago Tribune*, August 14, 1890, p. 3; and "Press Reception" [Michigan Press Association], *Crawford* (MI) *Avalanche*, July 24, 1890, p. 2.

858. Lilian Leland, *Traveling Alone: A Woman's Journey Around the World* (New York: John Polhemus, 1890), pp. 338-342. The opening of the Canyon Hotel plus the overcrowded Firehole and Upper Basin hotels and her mention of construction at Lower Geyser Basin all make it clear that her trip occurred in 1890.

859. "The New Geyser," *Aspen* (CO) *Weekly Times*, July 12, 1890, p. 1; and same headline in *Daily Yellowstone Journal* (Miles City, MT), July 12, 1890, p. 1. For E.C. Waters's negative personality, see Haines, *Yellowstone Story*, II, p. 47. For a recent study of Waters, see Mike Stark, *Wrecked in Yellowstone: Greed, Obsession, and the Untold Story of Yellowstone's Most Infamous Shipwreck* (Helena: Riverbend Publishing, 2016).

860. "Not a Stayer—The New Mammoth Geyser Showing Signs of Subsiding," *Los Angeles Herald*, July 10, 1890, p. 1; and "The New Crater Geyser—Volumes of Water Thrown Four Hundred Feet into the Air," *Evening Star* (Washington, DC), July 10, 1890, p. 2. See also, "The New Geyser," *Daily Yellowstone Journal* (Miles City, MT), July 12, 1890, p. 1, as quoted completely in Whittlesey, "Wonderland Nomenclature," 1988, Steamboat Geyser entry.

861. Carter H. Harrison, "Our Yellowstone Park—Carter Harrison Finds Good Scope for his Eloquence," *Chicago* (IL) *Sunday Tribune*, August 17, 1890, p. 25. This account—part two of his trip—was reproduced in full with many additions in Harrison's book *A Summer's Outing; and The Old Man's Story* (Chicago: Dibble Publishing Company, 1891). The quote, updated beyond the newspaper account, is from Harrison's book, p. 60. See also Harrison's part one of his trip, "Bigger than Niagara—The National Park, 'The Wonderland of the Globe'," *Chicago Sunday Tribune*, August 10, 1890, p. 7.

862. W.G. Pearce in McRae, "Inquiry," pp. 118-119; and Haines, *Yellowstone Story*, II, p. 120. The

stop-over had always been technically allowed; the tour agents said so, and so did the fine print on the tourists' coupons, but both Wakefield and YPA charged more for the privilege. Haines has explained that the practice "was discouraged by the transportation company, which did not like empty seats in its coaches. (They would allow a stopover if the entire coachload agreed to it; but how do you get eleven people to want the same 'extra' at the same time when it costs more?)" General Manager Pearce added: "It was reasonable that they should pay extra because the team with its driver was held waiting until those parties desired to move, and [thus] Mr. Wakefield and subsequently the Transportation Company always charged extra."

863. H.G.H., "A Land of Marvels—The Yellowstone National Park and Its Wonderful Scenery… Letters from a Naturalist—VI," *Detroit Free Press*, August 30, 1891, p. 8.

864. H.G.H., "A Land of Marvels," as cited.

865. Harrison, "Our Yellowstone Park," as cited.

866. Henry Estabrook, "Estabrook on His Travels," *Omaha* (NE) *World Herald*, September 27, 1891, p. 10.

867. Henderson, 1891, in McCrae, "Inquiry," pp. 289-290. See also "Rapid Transit in the Park," *Livingston Post*, March 10, 1900, in Ash Scrapbook, p. 20, YNP Archives; and Henderson, "The Two Wonderlands," *Livingston Enterprise*, December 3, 1898, p. 1.

868. "National Capitol—Senator Voorhees" [and Excelsior Geyser], *Idaho Statesman* (Boise, ID), July 22, 1890, p. 1; "In a Disturbed State—Excelsior Geyser in Yellowstone Park," *San Francisco Call*, July 22, 1890, p. 1; and "News of the Week" [Excelsior Geyser], *Idaho Semi-Weekly World* (Idaho City, ID), August 12, 1890, p. 2.

869. Harrison, *A Summer's Outing*, as cited, p. 39.

870. D [B.W. Driggs], "The Yellowstone Park," *Deseret Weekly News* (Salt Lake City, UT), August 23, 1890, p. 298. This can be seen at: http://books.google.com/books?id=lmHUAAAAMAA-J&dq=%22yellowstone%22%20%22hot%22&pg=PA273#v=onepage&q=%22yellow-stone%22%20%22hot%22&f=false via Google Books.

871. "The National Park," *Troy* (MO) *Free Press*, September 26, 1890, p. 2.

872. Charles Mantz, "Yellowstone Park—Observations Made by a Former Fredericktonian," *The News* (Frederick, MD), August 12, 1890, p. 3. For a history of this specific geyser, see Whittlesey, "Monarch of All These Mighty Wonders—Tourists and Yellowstone's Excelsior Geyser, 1881-1890," *Montana the Magazine of Western History* 40#2 (Spring, 1990), cover and pp. 2-15.

873. The *Helena* (MT) *Herald* and the *Anaconda* (MT) *Standard*, which seem to have been the first two Montana newspapers to pick up the story, agreed that the incident occurred on Thursday, July 24. See "Dropped Dead in the Park," *Helena Herald*, July 26, 1890, p. 1; and "The Great Northwest—A Tourist Drops Dead," *Anaconda Standard*, July 27, 1890, p. 3. Pelton's basic biography at Ancestry.com also agrees, giving his birthdate as August 3, 1824 and his death date as July 24, 1890. Meanwhile the Livingston papers were slow to pick the story up. See "Local Layout," *Livingston Enterprise*, August 2, 1890; and *Livingston Post*, July 31, 1890.

874. "Broke a Blood Vessel—Ex-Congressman Pelton Dies While Climbing a Mountain," *St. Paul* (MN) *Daily Globe*, July 27, 1890, p. 8; "Coast Items" [Guy Pelton], *Morning Call* (San Francisco, CA), July 29, 1890, p. 6; "Dropped Dead in the Park," *Helena Independent*, July 26, 1890, Morning, p. 1; and "Dropped Dead on an Outing," *Rock Island* (IL) *Daily Argus*, July 26, 1890, p. 2. See also "Obituary—Guy R. Pelton," *New-York Tribune*, July 28, 1890, p. 7. The ex-congressman's death got widespread publicity, running in many newspapers throughout the country, including the Washington, DC *Evening Star* (July 28, p. 7), Baltimore's *The Sun* (July 29, p. 3), the San Francisco *Examiner* (July 27, p. 2), the Minneapolis *Star Tribune* (July 26, p. 1), the

Indianapolis Journal (July 26, p. 2), the Bloomington (IL) *Daily Leader* (July 26, p. 1), the *Rock Island* (IL) *Argus* (July 26, p. 2), and the New York *World* (July 30, p. 1), to name only a few.

875. "Swindled in Yellowstone Park—Judge Lambert Tree Says Tourists are Treated Outrageously," *The Sun* (New York, NY), August 10, 1890, p. 7; same headline, same story in *The Times* (Philadelphia, PA), August 11, 1890, p. 2; and "Yellowstone Park Abuses—Judge Lambert Tree Says the Management Cheat[s] Tourists," *Evening Star* (Washington, DC), August 11, 1890, p. 6. The original newspaper to break the story was apparently the *Chicago Evening Post*, but digital-files of that paper have not been located.

876. "Swindled in Yellowstone Park," as cited.

877. "Yellowstone Park Scandals," *Chicago Herald*, August 11, 1890, p. 4. During George Wakefield's testimony to congress in 1892, a questioner read this paragraph to Wakefield and ended with "in obedience to the transportation company." Said Wakefield, "The transportation company never gave any such orders." A follow-up question asked, "Did you turn the man [driver] off that did it?" Wakefield answered, "Yes, sir; he was discharged." Wakefield in McCrae, "Inquiry," pp. 141-142.

878. "Fleeced by the Railroad People—Visitors to Yellowstone Park Inconvenienced—Eight People in One Room," *Chicago Tribune*, August 15, 1890, p. 1; and John G.H. Meyers quoted in McRae, "Inquiry," p. 30.

879. Meyers quoted in "Fleeced by the Railroad People," *Chicago Tribune*, as cited. The long quote is from Meyers in McRae, "Inquiry," pp. 30-31. The history of Firehole Hotel, including this incident and mountain lion sightings, has also been told in Lee H. Whittlesey, "Hotels on the Firehole River in Yellowstone, 1880-1891, and the Origins of Concessioner Policy in National Parks," as cited, pp. 22-25.

880. "Imposition on Tourists—It Flourishes in the Yellowstone National Park...The Government Should Act," *Chicago Daily Tribune*, August 21, 1890, p. 1; and "The Yellowstone Park Outrages," *Chicago Daily Tribune*, August 21, 1890, p. 4.

881. "Yellowstone Park—The Interior Department Exercised Over Charges of Mismanagement," *Baltimore* (MD) *Sun*, September 1, 1890, p. 1; and "Tourists Imposed On," *St. Paul Daily Globe*, September 1, 1890, p. 5.

882. "To Be Investigated—Complaints of Overcharges and Poor Service in the National Park," *New North-West* (Deer Lodge, MT), August 22, 1890, p. 2; "Disgruntled Tourists," *Livingston Enterprise*, August 23, 1890, p. 1; and "A Neighborly Exchange...A Special Agent May be Sent to the Park," *Helena Independent*, September 2, 1890, p. 1.

883. Secretary of Interior John N. Noble testifying to House of Representatives Committee on Public Lands, March 31, 1892, and quoting his letter to George Wakefield of August 13, 1890, in McRae, "Inquiry" as cited, p. 35. Wakefield admitted in his own testimony that he received but did not answer this letter. Wakefield in McCrae, p. 140.

884. "The National Capital...The Interior Department Will Carefully Examine Complaints from Yellowstone Park Tourists," *Helena Independent*, September 1, 1890, p. 1; and "Interior Exercised by Charges of Mismanagement," *Baltimore Sun*, September 1, 1890, p. 1.

885. Secretary of Interior John N. Noble to George W. Wakefield, no date [October, 1890], quoted in McRae, "Inquiry," p. 35; and Wakefield's testimony in McRae, "Inquiry," pp. 140-141.

886. The quote is from "A Montanian in Washington," *Anaconda* (MT) *Standard*, December 17, 1890, p. 2. The other citations are as follows: "Court House Cullings" [Livingston Land and Improvement Company], *Helena Independent*, August 31, 1890, p. 5; and "General News of the State" [lobbying for Cooke City], *Helena Independent*, December 24, 1890, p. 3. For his mining interests

at Cooke City, see Geo. W. Wakefield, "Notice to Co-owners" [A.G. Hemphill and Frank Bellar, who were Wakefield's mining partners at Cooke City], *Livingston Enterprise*, February 9, 1889, p. 2, col. 4.

887. "Two New Concerns" [incorporating YNPT Company] *St. Paul* (MN) *Globe*, January 21, 1891, p. 2; and "Local Layout" [incorporating YNPT Company], *Livingston Enterprise*, January 24, 1891, p. 3.

888. Congressman (and Chairman of the Committee) McRae wrote in his opening statement and summary of the history of YNPIC/YPA that this meeting took place on February 17, 1891. McRae, in "Inquiry," p. VII.

889. Wakefield in McCrae, "Inquiry," pp. 147-148. Also present in this meeting, probably as a witness for Secretary Noble, was Thomas Musick of the Interior Department, who later testified about it. Musick in McCrae, p. 230.

890. McCrae, his report, in "Inquiry," p. VIII; and McCrae quoting others, pp. 81, 147, 182.

891. "The Bozeman Hotel Leased," *Livingston Enterprise*, January 24, 1891, p. 1; and "Bozeman's Fine Hotel," *Helena Independent*, January 25, 1891, morning edition, p. 3.

892. "Bozeman's Fine Hotel—The Elegant New House Leased by Geo. Wakefield and John Callaghan—To Be Thrown Open Not Later than the First Day of March," *Helena Daily Independent*, January 25, 1891, p. 3; "The Pride of Bozeman," *Helena Independent*, March 3, 1891, p. 1; "A Handsome Monument—Bozeman's $100,000 Hotel to be Opened to the Public Tomorrow," *Butte Weekly Miner*, March 5, 1891, p. 6; and "A Pride to All Montana—Brilliant Opening of Bozeman's Beautiful New Hotel," *Anaconda Standard*, March 3, 1891, p. 1.

893. McRae, "Inquiry," p. I; and Charles Gibson in McRae, p. 188. YPA secretary/treasurer W.G. Pearce confirmed, apparently from memory, that both Wakefield's forfeiture and Huntley's new lease (the first time) were granted at about the same time, which was "about the first of April [1891]." Pearce in McRae, p. 122. Wakefield's mention of reading about Noble's new announcement of the forfeiture in a newspaper article appeared in McCrae, "Inquiry," p. 149. In his summary of the affair's history, Congressman McCrae stated that Secretary Noble "on the 30th of March [1891], made a lease to Mr. S.S Huntley for the transportation business only and without any obligation to build any [park] hotels, and provided in the lease itself that it should not commence [take effect] until the 1st of November following [1891], thereby giving him [seven months and in practicality] fourteen months, that is, until the 1st of June, 1892, to prepare to commence business under the lease." McCrae, his conclusionary report, in "Inquiry," p. IX.

894. McCrae, his report, in "Inquiry," pp. IX-X. There was more, as there always is. The lease required Huntley to post a $10,000 bond, which Noble later, arguably unjustly, did not require (p. 223).

895. "Bozeman the Beautiful" [purchasing additional horses], *Helena Independent*, May 11, 1891, p. 1; "General News of the State—Livingston" [Wakefield returns with three carloads of horses], Helena *Daily Independent*, May 15, 1891, Morning, p. 6; "Personal Points" [Wakefield returns with four carloads of horses, or 75 head], *Livingston Enterprise*, May 9, 1891, p. 3; and "Personal Points" [Looking for still more horses], *Livingston Enterprise*, July 4, 1891, p. 3.

896. [Charles W.] Bowron, "Through the Park—Beauties of the Yellowstone—Visit to Mammoth Hot Springs…," *Daily Northwestern* (Oshkosh, WI), July 25, 1891, p. 1; and "Personal Points" [a late season due to stormy weather], *Livingston Enterprise*, July 4, 1891, p. 3. Mr. Bowron's other chapters appeared in the editions of July 22, July 28, July 30, August 1, and August 4, with full identification of Charles W. Bowron in the edition of July 22 at "Short Notes," p. 4.

897. [Charles W.] Bowron, "By Way of Closing—Pointers from Yellowstone—A Few Answers to Numerous Questions—How to Go—The Cost and Prices, Curios and Souvenirs—A Petrified Story," *Daily Northwestern* (Oshkosh, WI), August 4, 1891, p. 1.

898. "The Editors Abroad—Citizens Receive the Nation's Newspaper Men with Open House—Successful Opening of Seventh National Editorial Convention—The Largest Aggregation of Editors in the World's History…," *St. Paul Globe*, July 15, 1891, p. 1; "Great Minds Commune—National Editorial Association in Convention Assembled at St. Paul Today," *Knoxville Republican* (Knoxville, TN), July 21, 1891, p. 3; and "St. Paul News—Editors…Take Their Departure—Yellowstone Park and Duluth are Their Points of Destination," *Star Tribune* (Minneapolis, MN) July 19, 1891, p. 3. Congressman Thomas McCrae's congressional investigation placed the number of journalists in this party at one hundred forty-eight. McCrae, "Inquiry," pp. XI, 97.

899. [James Mitchell], "Yellowstone Park—The Great National Pleasure Grounds of America—Wonderland of the World—The Land of the Great Geysers, Boiling Lakes and Springs, Grand Canyons, Majestic Falls, Snow-Capped Peaks, Bright Flowers, Etc.," *Arkansas Democrat* (Little Rock, AR), August 12, 1891, p. 6. Like the newspapers above, Mitchell said there were 154 attendees who went to Yellowstone from St. Paul.

900. E.B. Alrich, "Trip to Yellowstone Park," *The Public Record* (Cawker City, Kansas), August 13, 1891, p. 1.

901. T. Sambola Jones, Frank A. Arnold, and Joseph Leicht, "Appreciative Journalists," *Arkansas Democrat* (Little Rock, AR), August 15, 1891, p. 8. This resolution was also quoted in full in Congressman McCrae's congressional investigation, per "Inquiry," p. 97. The work of fiction was Ida M. Lane, "Miss Morrison's Stage Driver," *The Independent* (New York), vol. 42, number 2161 (May 1, 1890), p. 26.

902. "The Geological Excursion," *Livingston Enterprise*, September 12, 1891, p. 1. The ICG, composed of about sixty foreign geologists and twenty Americans, had just finished meeting at Washington, DC for several days and were now traveling in the West, with special attention being paid to Yellowstone. Some of the nation's most famous geologists were included, such as Arnold Hague, Walter Weed, S.F. Emmons, G.K. Gilbert, and C. Gilbert Wheeler. See "Congress of Geologists," *The Sun* (New York, NY), August 27, 1891, p. 7; "The Graphic System—Maj. Powell Explains it to the International Geological Congress," *Evening Star* (Washington, DC), August 31, 1891, p. 1; "Distinguished Visitors—Members of the International Congress of Geologists Looking at Montana Rocks—They Come from St. Paul on a Special Train of Seven Cars," *Helena Independent*, September 7, 1891, p. 5; "The Geological Congress," *Livingston Enterprise*, September 5, 1891, p. 2; and "Local Layout" [Walter Weed], *Livingston Enterprise*, September 5, 1891, p. 3.

903. Thomas McKenny Hughes and Mrs. Caroline Hughes, "Excerpts from the Hughes Diary while Attending an International Geological Congress in America in 1891," no date [1891], vertical files, YNP Library, pp. 6-7, 12.

904. Hughes and Hughes, "Excerpts," pp. 12, 14-15.

905. Hughes and Hughes, "Excerpts," pp. 15-18.

906. "Local Layout" [large excursion parties declining], *Livingston Enterprise*, August 8, 1891, p. 3; "Local Layout" [ticket agents arriving]; *Livingston Enterprise*, September 12, 1891, p. 3; and "Tickled the Crowd—The Northern Pacific Trip to Yellowstone Delighted the Ticket Agents…," *St. Paul Daily Globe*, September 21, 1891, p. 2.

907. "Arrived at the Park—A Splendid Run Brings the Ticket Agents to the Yellowstone," *St. Paul* (MN) *Daily Globe*, September 13, 1891, p. 8.

908. "Ticket Agents' Travels," *St. Paul Daily Globe*, September 14, 1891, p. 4.

909. Northern Pacific Railroad, "From Chicago to the Yellowstone," *The Station Agent*, Vol. 6 #32, October, 1891, p. 53.

910. "Local Layout" [closing transportation for the season], *Livingston Enterprise*, October 3, 1891, p. 3.

911. "Personal Points" [horses to winter quarters], *Livingston Enterprise*, October 17, 1891, p. 3; and "Personal Points" [Hunter's Hot Springs], *Livingston Enterprise*, November 21, 1891, p. 3.

912. "Bozeman," *Helena Daily Independent*, March 13, 1892, p. 7. However, "Bozeman Briefs," *Anaconda Standard*, March 10, 1892, p. 3, stated that the price was $15,000.

913. "Live Montana Towns" [Libbie's party], *Helena Daily Independent*, April 24, 1892, Morning, p. 6.

914. "The Hand of the Prince—Two Residents of Helena and a New Lease in the National Park—It is Charged that Secretary Noble is Serving the Interests of Russell B.—Sir Charles Gibson's Troubles with the Secretary of the Interior Concerning Leases," *Helena Daily Independent*, March 14, 1892, Morning, p. 5, and incorrectly attributed to the "Livingston Standard," instead of the *Anaconda Standard*.

915. McCrae's summary and personal opinions of the entire affair may be found in "Inquiry," pp. I-XV. For the rest of this paragraph, see "Gen. Noble's Body is to Lie in State," *St. Louis* (MO) *Star and Times*, March 24, 1912, p. 16; "Taft Mourns for Noble—President and Mrs. Benjamin Harrison Send Messages of Sympathy," *St. Louis* (MO) *Globe-Democrat*, March 24, 1912, p. 10; "General Noble's Burial Monday Afternoon," *St. Louis Post-Dispatch*, March 24, 1912, p. 16 (Beta Theta Pi adopts resolutions of regret on Noble's death); and "Plans Noble Memorial," *St. Louis Globe-Democrat*, March 30, 1912, p. 2, which said that the state of Oklahoma was planning a memorial to him at Guthrie and that Oklahoma Territory had been opened under his Secretaryship in 1889. Noble Avenue in Guthrie was named for him as was one of the local city parks. "Gen. Noble Seriously Ill," *St. Louis Globe-Democrat*, March 22, 1912, p. 2 stated that he served as Secretary of Interior 1889-1893. Oklahoma Territory was organized under his administration in 1889; Noble, Oklahoma was named for him; and he was sometimes called the "Father of Oklahoma" (even though he annoyed many Indians by opening the territory to settlement). See also "Gen. Noble Funeral Monday Afternoon," *St. Louis Globe-Democrat*, March 23, 1912, p. 1. For the NPS history involving Secretary Noble, see "The Department of Everything Else [Interior]—Nationwide Concerns," May 17, 2001, at https://www.nps.gov/parkhistory/online_books/utley-mackintosh/interior4.htm accessed November 24, 2020.

916. McCrae, summary of the history, in "Inquiry," pp. VIII-IX; and quoting others, in "Inquiry," pp. 43, 81, 183.

917. "Live Montana Towns" [Wakefield heading east], *Helena Daily Independent*, April 24, 1892, Morning, p. 6; and "Bozeman" [Wakefield returns to Bozeman], *Helena Daily Independent*, May 15, 1892, p. 6.

918. "Local Layout," *Livingston Enterprise*, April 9, 1892, p. 3, says the story of sale of his stock to Huntley is "wholly without foundation." A similar story was published in "Jottings About Town," *Helena Daily Independent*, April 11, 1892, Morning, p. 8.

919. "The Park Hotel Privileges," *Livingston Enterprise*, March 5, 1892, p. 1. Another hint of the congressional bill appeared in "Bozeman Affairs" [Wakefield], *Anaconda* (MT) *Standard*, March 24, 1892, p. 7.

920. McCrae, "Inquiry," pp. VI, 27.

921. McRae, "Inquiry," p. I. Huntley was an old stagecoach-operator in Montana.

922. Thomas McRae, "Inquiry into the Management and Control of the Yellowstone National Park," 52d Cong., 1st Sess., House Report 1956, SN-3051, July 20, 1892.

923. Gibson in McRae, "Inquiry," live testimony to Congress, May 10, 1892, p. 188.

924. John Noble in McCrae, "Inquiry," pp. 34-35.

925. For example, see N.P. Langford's letter praising George Wakefield, which appeared as "Our Na-

tional Park—Who is Responsible for Difficulties Experienced by Tourists," *St. Paul* (MN) *Daily Globe*, October 1, 1890, p. 2. See also the annual reports of the superintendents of Yellowstone, 1886-1891; many documents published in McRae, *Inquiry*; and "Noble's Hostility—The Secretary of the Interior's Attitude Toward the Yellowstone Association—His Action in the Premises to Be the Subject of Congressional Inquiry—Injustice Toward the Parties Who Have Made the Park Accessible to Tourists," *St. Paul* (MN) *Dispatch*, April 9, 1892.

926. G.L. Henderson in McCrae, "Inquiry," p. 206.

927. Wakefield in McCrae, "Inquiry," p. 150. Clearly Noble's formal notification of the two men occurred sometime between May 3 and May 10. On May 8, the *Helena Independent* announced in connection with the Bozeman Hotel that "the Wakefields have moved to their residence on Black street." See "Bozeman," *Helena Daily Independent*, May 8, 1892, Morning, p. 6.

928. With regard to the amount Silas Huntley and Harry Child paid for the transportation plant, W.G. Pearce, YPA's chief financial officer, stated: "When the matter came up a year ago, it was agreed by Messrs. Gibson, Casey, Oakes and myself to offer the property for $100,000 cash, rather than to be bothered by attempting to maintain our rights in court. Subsequently Mr. Oakes and Mr. Casey concluded to offer the outfit at $70,000, preferring to take that than to put up with further annoyance. The amount $70,000 was the valuation placed upon the property by Mr. Huntley. Yesterday the outfit was sold for $70,000, half cash, other half on credit. The purchaser assumed also our contracts for additional coaches, harness[es], horses, etc., required for season of 1892 amounting to between $10,000 and $15,000." Pearce in McRae, "Inquiry," pp. 124-125. George Wakefield stated with regard to the cost of the "transportation plant": "We were to be given $70,000[,] half of what the plant is actually worth. We were to be given $70,000 for that plant last November, as I understand it. Since that time[,] it has cost us about $2,500 to winter and keep the stock. Interest on that amount of money would amount to about $2,500 more, or very close to it. I wish to state that the value of the plant to the association was worth $120,000 to $130,000 in the shape it was in, and they realized out of it about $65,000." Wakefield in McCrae, "Inquiry," p. 176; see also McCrae's personal report on pp. X-XII.

929. "After a Sharp Fight—Helena Men Win the Contest Involving Transportation in the National Park—The Old Company Bought Out May 5 and Possession Taken the Next Day—S.S. Huntley Now Has the Contract with Uncle Sam for Ten Years—Operations Begin in June," *Helena Daily Independent*, May 22, 1892, p. 8.

930. Thomas Musick, Department of Interior, placing this telegram from "Lt. Sands" into evidence in Congress, in McCrae, p. 233. Lt. Sands's first name and middle initial are in McRae, "Inquiry," p. 200.

931. C.E. Gibson in McCrae, pp. 125-126. See also the testimony of T.B. Casey, Vice President of YPA and one of the directors of YNPTC, in McRae, "Inquiry," pp. 277-278.

932. C.E. Gibson in McCrae, p. 125. Considering that Noble had already decisively decided against Wakefield by this time, Charles Eldon Gibson's appearance in Washington in place of his father might not have mattered.

933. Charles Eldon Gibson in McCrae, p. 126. For a later taste of the "harbor in Texas" scandal, see "After Prince Russell—The Grand Jury of Aransas Harbor May Indict Him and Others—Charged with Fraud in the Disposal of Alleged Town Lots—Hundreds of Texans and Eastern People Induced to Invest on the Strength of a Name," *Helena* (MT) *Daily Independent*, September 28, 1891, Morning, p. 7.

934. McCrae, his report in "Inquiry," p. X.

935. C.E. Gibson in McCrae, "Inquiry," p. 126.

936. C.E. Gibson in McRae, "Inquiry," pp. 126-127. The provision he read to Noble was as follows: "And that it [YPA] will generally conduct its business so as to furnish good, proper, and sufficient hotel, livery, and stage transportation." He additionally stated in his brief given to Secretary Noble: "There is nothing in the lease that declares that the business shall be conducted by the association directly or that prohibits it from employing an agent." C.E. Gibson, Brief [in support of YPA and George Wakefield], March 23, 1891, in McCrae, "Inquiry," p. 129. The complete brief was published at pp. 129-132.

937. McCrae, his report in "Inquiry," pp. X, XII.

938. "Scoring Gen. Noble—Mr. Charles Gibson's Charges Against the Secretary of the Interior," *St. Louis Post-Dispatch* (St. Louis, MO), February 26, 1892, p. 1.

939. "At Bozeman," *Anaconda* (MT) *Standard*, June 5, 1892, p. 6; and "Bozeman," *Helena Independent*, August 7, 1892, Morning, p. 1.

940. "Yellowstone Park Privileges," *The Weekly Tribune* (Great Falls, MT), June 16, 1893, Morning, p. 8.

941. "Bozeman Life," *Anaconda Standard*, October 11, 1894, p. 8; and "In Livingston," *Anaconda Standard*, June 2, 1895, p. 10.

942. "Local Notes," *Billings Weekly Gazette*, January 5, 1897, p. 3; and "Bozeman Bits," *Daily Inter Mountain* (Butte, MT), September 23, 1899, p. 9.

943. "Traded a Hotel for a Ranch," *Anaconda Standard*, November 25, 1897, p. 14.

944. Bill and Doris Whithorn, *Photo History of Aldridge: Coal Camp that Died A-Bornin'* (Minneapolis: Acme Printing and Stationery, no date [1966]), p. 161.

945. "Livingston News," *Daily Inter Mountain* (Butte, MT), March 21, 1901, p. 5. Through this swap, Wakefield moved to Cinnabar, and the Amos Chadbourn family—original settlers at Cinnabar—moved to Shields Valley and established the small village of Chadbourn, Montana. The quote, "Like Banquo's ghost, it will not down," is from Shakespeare's "Macbeth," and it has been quoted and used by many subsequent writers since actors first performed the play in 1606.

946. "George W. Wakefield, Pioneer of Montana Dead—Operated First Stage Line in Park," *Livingston* (MT) *Enterprise*, June 5, 1917, p. 3. See also "Mrs. Margaret Wakefield Passed Away Last Night," *Butte* (MT) *Miner*, June 9, 1903, p. 3.

INDEX

ABOUT THE AUTHOR

Lee H. Whittlesey's forty-five-year studies in the history of the Yellowstone region have made him an expert on Yellowstone's vast literature and have resulted in numerous publications. He is the author, co-author, or editor of sixteen books and some sixty journal articles, including *"Off with the Crack of a Whip": Stagecoaching Through Yellowstone and the Origins of Tourism in the Interior of the American West*, volume one (2022, Riverbend Publishing) and *This Modern Saratoga of the Wilderness: A History of Mammoth Hot Springs* (2022, National Park Service).

In 2000, Whittlesey published *The Guide to Yellowstone Waterfalls and Their Discovery* (Westcliffe Publishers) in which he and two co-authors revealed to the world for the first time the existence of more than 300 previously unknown waterfalls in Yellowstone National Park. For this accomplishment, he was featured on ABC News, NBC News, the Discovery Channel, the Travel Channel, and *People* magazine.

In 2015, Whittlesey published a new edition of his book about Truman Everts entitled *Lost in the Yellowstone*, a new edition of his well-known book *Death in Yellowstone*, and his book *Gateway to Yellowstone: The Raucous Town of Cinnabar on the Montana Frontier* (Rowman and Littlefield with Two Dot Books).

In 2020, the two-volume *The History of Mammals in the Greater Yellowstone Ecosystem, 1796-1881: An Interdisciplinary Analysis of Thousands of Historical Observations* by Whittlesey and NPS Interpreter Sarah Bone was published by Kindle Direct Publishing of Seattle. This book entailed thirty years of research.

Whittlesey served as Archivist and then Park Historian for the National Park Service at Yellowstone National Park for twenty-seven years, and previously served in that park as Ranger Naturalist/Interpreter, Law Enforcement Ranger, and in numerous other positions. He has a master's degree in history from Montana State University and a law degree (Juris Doctor) from the University of Oklahoma. On May 19, 2001, because of his extensive writings and long contributions to Yellowstone National Park, Idaho State University conferred upon him an Honorary Doctorate of Science and Humane Letters. On May 3, 2014, Montana State University awarded him an honorary Ph.D. in history. From 2006 through 2011, he served as an adjunct professor of history at Montana State University.

Whittlesey has often appeared in television programs to talk about Yellowstone's history.

He appeared in Ken Burns's six-part special, *The National Parks: America's Best Idea,* on PBS, and the Arun Chaudhary film shot for President Obama's White House. He starred in the British Broadcasting Corporation's hour-long program entitled "Unnatural Histories—Yellowstone," and on Montana PBS's history of Yellowstone. He is also a frequent speaker at history conferences.

Whittlesey retired as Park Historian for the National Park Service at Yellowstone National Park in 2018. He now lives in the Livingston, Montana area, where he writes in retirement.

Other books by Whittlesey are: *Myth and History in the Creation of Yellowstone National Park* (with Paul Schullery, 2004, University of Nebraska Press); *A Yellowstone Album: Photographic Celebration of the First National Park* (1997, National Park Service); *Storytelling in Yellowstone: Horse and Buggy Tour Guides* (2007, University of New Mexico Press); *Yellowstone Place Names* (1988, 2006, Montana Historical Society); *Ho! for Wonderland: Travelers Accounts of Yellowstone, 1872-1914* (with Elizabeth Watry, 2009, University of New Mexico Press); *Images of America: Yellowstone National Park* (2008) and *Images of America: Fort Yellowstone* (both with fellow historian Elizabeth Watry, Arcadia Press); and the voluminous library-manuscript *Wonderland Nomenclature* (1988, Microfiche from Montana Historical Society).